The Game That Would Be King

For Sebastian and Violette

BRENDAN MURPHY

THE GAME THAT WOULD BE KING

THE UNCHARTED HISTORY OF SOCCER 800–1800 AD

Meyer & Meyer Sport

British Library Cataloguing in Publication Data
A catalogue record for this book is available from the British Library

The Game That Would Be King
Maidenhead: Meyer & Meyer Sport (UK) Ltd., 2026
ISBN 978-1-78255-285-7

Aachen, Auckland, Beirut, Cairo, Cape Town, Dubai, Hagendorf, Hong Kong, Indianapolis, Maidenhead, Manila, New Delhi, Singapore, Sydney, Tehran, Vienna

Member of the World Sport Publishers' Association (WSPA), www.w-s-p-a.org

Printed by Versa Press, www.versapress.com
Printed in the United States of America

ISBN 978-1-78255-285-7
Email: info@m-m-sports.com
www.thesportspublisher.com

Manufacturer under the GPSR
Meyer & Meyer Fachverlag und Buchhandel GmbH
Von-Coels-Str. 390
52080 Aachen, Germany
www.dersportverlag.de

CONTENTS

PREFACE

Hit it, catch it, throw it, bounce it, carry it, parry it. Kick it. Any combination can be used to create a ball game. All British and Irish ball sports are related, folding in, branching out. This book began as a history of football observed through the prism of British and Irish newspapers. The ambition was to trace its development from its origins to the formation of the Football Association (FA) in 1863. While researching, I unearthed a wealth of material from alternate sources, some of it unseen for centuries. To ignore it was unthinkable. The scope was broadened to include parliamentary and other calendar rolls, privy purse and private expenses, calendars of state papers, royal charters and manuscripts, livery company, burgh, and parochial records, university statutes, coroners' inquests, manorial and drama accounts, pamphlets and broadsides, and illustrated manuscripts. So great was the volume of additional riches that the timeline was truncated to 1800.

Another intention was to limit the book to British and Irish sports, but Europe and North America intruded to such a degree that they became an integral part of the tale. European ball games that impacted the evolution of homegrown sports also found a voice, principally the Dutch game of *kolven*, and the Icelandic game of *knattleikur*. References to lesser-known ball games cropped up in source material with intriguing regularity: trapball, stowball, stoolball, closh. The little written on them is insubstantial, yet they were once commonplace and well-loved. I believe their presence enriches the book. There are more popular ball games known only to the passionate—camping, *knappan*, Cornish hurling, and *soule*—that were hugely popular in their day and cannot be ignored. Some sports have doggedly weathered the centuries, like those cruise ship perennials quoits and shuffleboard. The inclusion of better-known sports—hockey, tennis, hurling, baseball, and bowling—is inevitable, and adds colour to football's journey. I have attempted a work of picaresque non-fiction: football and other games are *dramatis personae*.

There is little value in writing a sweeping history of ball games without the social, religious, and political context, and I have threaded this throughout. That large sections are devoted to Ireland is not partisan; the incendiary climate of the times led politicians to equate groups of Irishmen playing football or hurling with insurrection, a sentiment reflected in a wealth of newspaper references. Where possible, the book is written in the present tense to convey a sense of immediacy, to bring alive the men and women whose forgotten contributions are retold. We are so accustomed to sepia-tinted photographs of superannuated players that we forget they were once young and vibrant. Twelve of the fifteen who gathered at the Freemason's Tavern to establish the FA on 26 October 1863 were under twenty-five. The oldest was thirty-two. Four were still at school.[1] Those past lives are closer than we think. A deceased friend's grandfather knew Scottish polymath Thomas Carlyle. Another Renaissance man, Jean Philippe de Bela, best known for his twelve-volume *History of the Basques*, was still alive when Carlyle was an infant. Bela, in turn, was an infant when Samuel Pepys was alive, and Pepys father lived during the reign of Elizabeth I.

The text is peppered with newspaper articles, anecdotes, and stories that bring the centuries alive and contextualise ball games, placing them in the here and now, as it was then. The vast majority of anecdotes mention ball games; other items were chosen from the same newspaper a sporting reference appeared in, usually the same page. For brevity's sake, lengthy bibliographic titles have been shortened, e.g., *Gods arrovves* rather than *Gods arrovves, or, Two sermons, concerning the visitation of God by the pestilence Very profitable to be read at all times, but especially in the time of Gods visitation.* The original wording is retained in all available English quotes. Early references are usually law-related—fighting, accidents, murder, etc.—or contained within poems and literature, permitting no more than a partial-sighted view of the history of ball games.

Some historical works attribute ball games as football with no evidence, other than their inclusion in previous books. Nowhere is this more evident and detrimental than the widespread attribution of William Fitzstephen's c1180 mention of a ball game as the first reference

1 Mitchell A., *Found: the founders of the Football Association. Scottish Sport History.* https://www.scottishsporthistory.com/sports-history-news-and-blog/found-the-founders-of-the-football-association. Accessed 3 February 2024.

to football. A typical example is found in Andrew Lang's 1900 book *A History of Scotland.* He writes: "According to the author of the *Book of Pluscarden*, who resided much in France, the Scots were treacherously attacked while playing football during a truce."[2] Only two decades before, the English translation of the *Book of Pluscarden* describes the Scots as "playing at ball".[3] The 1489 original reads, "*Scotis ad palmam ludentibus*".[4] *Ad palmam ludentibus.* Palm play. In other words, they are playing the French game of *jeu de paume*, the precursor to modern tennis. "Ball" is not even mentioned. For this reason, all references were cross-checked with the earliest sources available or, better still, the original text. Those in Latin, Anglo-Norman, Middle French, Middle English, etc., were translated. Where an error was found in a modern reference or an earlier book provided more information, the latter was referenced.

Interpreting illustrated manuscripts proved problematic. It is a perpetuated error to include shepherds with crooks as an example of early stick and ball players. More common still, a shepherd with a crook and a round object in his hand. Usually, he is holding a loaf of bread. This was a commonly used religious motif, the good shepherd and the bread of life. If the bread is crossed, it is not a stitched leather ball, it symbolises the crucifixion. Reading the accompanying text often provides its Eucharistic context. Similarly, men with staffs or clubs without a ball are not at sport. Ambiguous images in manuscripts are best ignored. Shepherds had crooks, clubs were common weapons, and every circular object is not a ball. If a sphere is on the ground or mid-air—especially if characters are interacting with it, preferably adopting a sporting stance—and there are sticks, skittles, bats, etc., it is safe to assume it is a ball game.

I have arbitrarily divided Essex into north and south by a line running from Bishop's Stortford to Clacton-on-Sea. Camping was largely played in the north of Essex and football in the south, and I have used the line to loosely determine this. An inordinate amount of source reports of

---

2 Lang., A. *A History of Scotland.* 4 Vols. William Blackwood and Sons, Edinburgh, 1900. Vol. 1. p. 294.

3 Skene, F.J.H, *The Book of Pluscarden.* 2 Vols. William Paterson, Edinburgh, 1880. Vol. 1. p. 265.

4 Skene, F.J.H, *Liber Pluscardensis.* 2 Vols. William Paterson, Edinburgh, 1877. Vol. 1. p. 354.

"football games" are from East Anglia. Given the interchangeability of the terms and the popularity of camping until the end of the eighteenth century, I have tentatively considered ambiguous games in Suffolk, Norfolk, Cambridgeshire, and north Essex as camping. I acknowledge the risk of overestimating the number of camping matches using this approach.

This book is far from the last word on the history of ball games; current knowledge delivers more questions than answers. There is room for optimism. History constantly reveals itself as newspapers and other source material are added to online resources, and historians fossick through manuscripts. A stumbling block was the variety of spellings accrued across time. The stem for football is variously spelt fout, foote, ffoote, ffote, footte, fotte, futte, futt fut, fute, fote, fout, foute, foat, faut, and foot. They are succeeded by variations of ball: bal, balle, bale, baule, and bawlle. The two may be joined, hyphenated, or separate: football, foot-ball, foot ball. Alternate spellings also apply to cricket, camping, hockey, and tennis. The French game of *soule* posed a particular problem; most variations—*solle, soul, soulle, souller, solorie, soler, cheolare, cheoller, chole, choller, chouiller, choule, boulle de chalandas, and mellat*—were in French, often Middle French. Latin texts proved equally challenging.

I am indebted to the following databases for most of the references cited, and without whom this book would have never materialised: *British Newspaper Archive*, *Early English Books Online*, *Gale Primary Sources*, *ProQuest*, *Internet Archive*, *HathiTrust*, *Project Gutenberg*, *University of Michigan Library*, *Google Books*, *British History Online*, *TannerRichie Publishing* (MEMSO), *The Statistical Accounts of Scotland 1791–1845*, *Newspapers.com*, *The National Archives*, *Cricket Archive*, *HeinOnline*, *Harvard University Archives*, *America's Historical Newspapers* (Readex), and *Newspaper Archive*. I am particularly grateful to the *Dictionaries of the Scots Language* website. Indebtedness, too, to the owners of four independent websites, whose content was a source of great wealth and a conduit to otherwise inaccessible treasures: *Protoball*, *Scottish Sports History*, *Scottish Football Origins*, and *Electric Scotland*. Several books provided copious references, allowing original texts to be tracked down, none more so than David Block's *Baseball Before We*

Knew It: A Search for the Roots of the Game. Ariel Hessayon's chapter in *The Palgrave Handbook of Sport, Politics and Harm* and Toshiro Nakafusa's article *A study of historical sources and phrases referring to ball games in Medieval Britain* were invaluable.[5] Unpublished theses were similarly gratifying, particularly those by Gwen Rhiannon Prys Roberts (1932), Robert Malcolmson (1970), Emma Lile (2006), and Taylor Aucoin (2019). My thanks also go to Leah Shopkow for her advice on Lambert of Ardres, and Martyn Cornell for sourcing two impossible to find references.

Effusive praise must go to Meyer & Meyer Sport for accepting this book for publication. I extend especial gratitude to Meyer & Meyer Sport's international programme director, Liz Evans, for her guidance and faith, and for giving the silent souls within a voice. I owe a final debt of gratitude to those historians who have come before me, on the shoulders of whom I stand on tiptoes, peering around, craning my neck: Francis Peabody Magoun, Morris Marples, Gwen Rhiannon Prys Roberts, Eric Dunning, Kenneth Sheard, Robert W Malcolmson, and David Dymond.

5 Nakafusa, T., *A study of historical sources and phrases referring to ball games in Medieval Britain.* The Japan Journal of Sport History, 2018, 31: 19–35.

PROLOGUE
3500BC–678AD

In ancient Athens there is a festival game, *asklōiasmos*.[1] Contestants hop on oiled goatskins filled with wine, and the last to slip off is the winner. Another ball game is far more popular. *Episkyros* is played with two equal sides of twelve to fourteen players. A line is described with stone chippings along the centre of a pitch marked out with parallel lines.[2] The teams stand along their boundary line, and a ball is placed at the centre. On signal, they rush for the ball. The player who reaches it first tosses the ball over his opponents to get it towards their line. The opposition aim to intercept the ball and do likewise. To and fro goes the game until a player oversteps his boundary line and his team is defeated. It is unclear when *episkyros* developed; undisputed descriptions date to the first century AD, though it is likely that Plato refers to the game c369BC.[3] A third game, *phaininda*, is also played. Athenaeus famously quotes Antiphanes's description.[4,5]

> The player takes the ball elate,
> And gives it safely to his mate,
> Avoid the blows of th'other side,
> And shouts to see them hitting wide;
> List to the cries, "Hit here," "hit there,"
> "Too far," "Too high," "that is not fair,"
> See every man with ardour burns,
> To make good strokes and quick returns.[6]

---

1 Fantuzzi, M., Hunter, R., *Tradition and Innovation in Hellenistic Poetry*. Cambridge University Press, 2004. pp. 4–5.

2 Gardiner, E.N., *Athletics of the Ancient World*. Clarendon Press, Oxford, 1930. p. 235.

3 Cornford, F.M., *Plato's Theaetetus*. Bobbs-Merrill Company, Indianapolis, 1959. pp. 20–21 (146a).

4 Fl. c200AD.

5 C408–c334BC.

6 Yonge, C.D. (trans.). *The Deipnosophists*. 3 Vols. Henry G. Bohn, London, 1854. Vol. 3. p. 24.

It must have been a rough game, for Antiphanes adds, "Wretch that I am, my neck's so stiff." Athenaeus says that the philosopher Ctesibius[7] "was no bad player. And there were many friends of Antigonus the king who used to take off their coats and play ball with him."[8,9] The game involves feigning and intercepting. Different translations drastically alter the essence of the game. The stilted passage quoted is elsewhere translated as: "When he got the ball he delighted to give it to one player while dodging the other; he knocked it away from one and urged on another with noisy cries … 'Outside, a long pass, beyond him, over his head, a short pass.'"[10] The cries in a third translation include: "out of bounds", "right beside him", "on the ground", "too short", and worryingly, "pass it back in the scrimmage".[11] The term scrimmage (as scrummage) in the sporting sense is not heard of until 1848; a sobering example of the pitfalls of sports history and the need for restrained conclusions. The term appears in *Recollections of Rugby*. Only eighteen words in, C. H. Newmarch writes of his childhood at Rugby School and "the pleasures of a scrummage at football."[12] Newmarch is referring to the 1830s, when he was a pupil at Rugby.

A c510BC ball game, likely to be *phaininda*, is depicted on a marble relief at the base of a Greek funerary kouros statue.[13] Two sides of three players face each other. The players are positioned in forward, middle, and back rows. One of the rear players is about to throw the ball. His teammates dart forward, one readying to receive it. The opposition's defender is ordering the front player to move back, while their middle player also prepares to catch the ball. It is likely that each player represents several in a line. While little else is known of *phaininda*, the Roman game of *harpastum* is believed to have been essentially the same. It is important to differentiate ball sports involving teams, from other forms of ball games. Ball play in ancient Greece was a

---

7 285–222BC.

8 Either Antigonus I 382–301BC or Antigonus II 320–239BC.

9 Yonge, C.B. (trans.). *The Deipnosophists*. 3 Vols. Henry G. Bohn, London, 1854. Vol. 3. p. 24.

10 Gardiner, E.N., *Athletics of the Ancient World*. Clarendon Press, Oxford, 1930. p. 233.

11 Gulick, C.D. (trans.). *The Deipnosophists*. 7 Vols. William Heinemann, London, 1928. Vol. 1. p. 66.

12 Newmarch, C.H., *Recollections of Rugby*. Hamilton & Adams, London, 1848. pp. 1, 131.

13 Gardiner, E.N., *Athletics of the Ancient World*. Clarendon Press, Oxford, 1930. Plate 213.

ubiquitous pursuit. According to Athenaeus, Timocrates the Lacedaemon wrote a treatise on ball playing.[14,15,16] Aristotle recommended balls as suitable presents for children,[17,18,19] and Dionysius I of Syracuse enjoyed ball play, Sophocles too.[20,21,22,23] Simpler games were also played in gymnasia, such as bouncing a ball against a wall or the floor and striking it with the flat of the hand on the rebound. Plato mentions several men present, raising the prospect of an early version of fives.[24,25]

The first reference to a ball game in literature is played by women. In Homer's *Odyssey*, c800BC, Princess Nausikaä plays with her maids. "They then threw off their veils and turned to playing ball, and white-armed Nausikaä was their leader as they sang ... when the princess next tossed the ball ... she missed the handmaid, and sent it into a deep eddy."[26] Their cries of dismay wake the stranded, naked Odysseus, who mingles among them. In Apollonius's c300BC *Argonautica*, Zeus is given a ball in infancy: "I will give you Zeus's all-beauteous plaything ... a well-rounded ball ... All of gold are its zones, and round each double seams run in a circle; but the stiches are hidden, and a dark blue spiral overlays them all."[27] The remarkable description implies four or more segments. Better still, a few lines later: "This I will give you; and you, strike with your shaft and charm the daughter of Aeëtes with love for Jason." He is to woo her with his prowess in a stick and ball game. While there are earlier depictions of stick and ball games, it is the first written reference in history.

---

14 Active early fourth century.

15 Sparta was part of Lacedaemon.

16 No copy of the book is known to have survived.

17 O'Sullivan, L., *Playing Ball in Greek Antiquity.* Greece & Rome, 2012, 59:1, p. 20.

18 384–322BC.

19 The Euro 2020 trophy is based on an ancient Greek vase, though not one of the few that depict ball play.

20 C432–367BC.

21 Gardiner, E.N., *Athletics of the Ancient World.* Clarendon Press, Oxford, 1930. p. 230.

22 C496–406BC.

23 O'Sullivan, L., *Playing Ball in Greek Antiquity.* Greece & Rome, 2012, 59:1, p. 21.

24 Gardiner, E.N., *Athletics of the Ancient World.* Clarendon Press, Oxford, 1930. pp. 77, 84.

25 Fives: The ball is struck with the hand against a wall and again on the rebound.

26 Green, P. (trans.). *Homer: The Odyssey.* University of California Press, 2018. lns 100–101, 115–116.

27 O'Sullivan, L., *Playing Ball in Greek Antiquity.* Greece & Rome, 2012, 59:1, p. 21.

Greek author and Homerian expert Agallis[28] believes her fellow—albeit mythic—Corcyraean Nausikaä invented ball play.[29] Dicaearchus[30] attributes it to the Greek city state of Sicyon,[31] while Hippasus of Metapontum[32] credits Sparta with its invention.[33] Herodotus argues otherwise. *The Histories* tells of the reign of the mythic King Atys of Lydia, who ruled from c1220 to c1190BC.[34,35] During a famine, the citizens survive by eating one day and fasting the next. Fasting days are occupied by playing ball, dice, knucklebones, and other games, so "that they might not feel the want of food." Irrespective of source, organised ball play is likely to have originated as dances, incorporating tumbling and ball skills. Athenaeus mentions two men known for their skills "at this game", Demoteles[36] and Chaerephanes.[37,38]

The Macedonians who conquer Athens in 338BC share a similar regard for ball play; Alexander the Great, himself, plays.[39] The first recorded competitive player is Aristonicus. Around 330BC, "The Athenians made Aristonicus the Carystian, Alexander's ball-player, a citizen of the city on account of his skill, and they erected a statue to him."[40] While the skill for which he received the highest honour the city can bestow is probably diplomatic, the statue is likely to have depicted his ball skills. Sparta appears passionate about ball sports. Organised games are played by graduating cadets. The rules are unknown, though evidence suggests it is a variation of *episkyros*.[41,42] Pollux[43] describes it

28 Third century BC.

29 O'Sullivan, L., *Playing Ball in Greek Antiquity*. Greece & Rome, 2012, 59:1, p. 24.

30 C350–c285BC.

31 Yonge, C.D. (trans.). *The Deipnosophists*. 3 Vols. Henry G. Bohn, London, 1854. Vol. 3. p. 23.

32 Fl. c500BC.

33 O'Sullivan, L., *Playing Ball in Greek Antiquity*. Greece & Rome, 2012, 59:1, p. 24.

34 430BC.

35 In what is now southeast Turkey.

36 Fourth century BC.

37 Ruled Athens 452–451BC.

38 Yonge, C.D. (trans.). *The Deipnosophists*. 3 Vols. Henry G. Bohn, London, 1854. Vol. 3. p. 23.

39 O'Sullivan, L., *Playing Ball in Greek Antiquity*. Greece & Rome, 2012, 59:1, p. 22.

40 Ibid, p. 17.

41 Ibid, p. 26.

42 It is unclear which game came first; an offshoot does not accord with Hippasus's view of Sparta.

43 Fl. closing decades of 2nd century.

as *sphairomachia*—battle with a ball—and Plato recommends it played in full armour to train citizens to defend their state.[44,45] If a Spartan game for contemporary teenagers is anything to go by, the cadet game is brutal. Played without a ball, two companies of naked youths try to command an artificial island surrounded by ditches.[46] Players hit, kick, punch, and push their opponents into the water, in a manner not dissimilar to British mob (folk) football.[47,48] As late as 160AD, victories of young Spartans at an annual contest of an unspecified ball game are recorded; sides of fifteen or more, representing their local district, play a tournament game.[49] The origins of *episkyros*, *phaininda*, and the Spartan version, cannot be dated with certainty, but they are well established by the mid-fourth century BC.

The Romans conquer Athens in 146BC. They have their own competitive ball game, *harpastum*; according to Athenaeus, the Roman name for *phaininda*. The Romans play other games: sky-ball, where a player throws a ball up for others to catch; *trigon*, where players stand at the corners of a triangle and throw the ball to each other; and a piggy-back game, where the mounted must catch the ball.[50] The latter is similar, if not identical, to an ancient Egyptian game. *Harpastum* is a team sport that involves feinting (pretending to throw the ball to one player, then throwing it to another) and intercepting. A *follis*, the smallest and hardest of the four balls available, is used.[51,52]

Harpastum is Athenaeus's favourite game. He writes, "There was a great deal of exertion and labour in a game of ball, and it causes great straining of the neck and shoulder." Isidorus of Miletus[53] mentions "the circle of players standing by and waiting", while an amusing anecdote

---

44 O'Sullivan, L., *Playing Ball in Greek Antiquity*. Greece & Rome, 2012, 59:1, p. 26.

45 Plato. *Laws*. c357–347BC: see Plato *Leg* 796b.

46 Golden, M., *Sport and Society in Ancient Greece*. Cambridge University Press, 1998. p. 9.

47 Gardiner, E.N., *Athletics of the Ancient World*. Clarendon Press, Oxford, 1930. p. 231.

48 Here on in, mob football will be referred to as folk football.

49 Gardiner, E.N., *Athletics of the Ancient World*. Clarendon Press, Oxford, 1930. p. 231.

50 Ibid, pp. 230–231.

51 Balls from smallest upwards: *harpastum* (hard and stuffed with hair), *pila* (stuffed with feathers), *paganica* (stuffed with feathers), *follis* (appears to have been filled with air).

52 Gardiner, E.N., *Athletics of the Ancient World*. Clarendon Press, Oxford, 1930. p. 233.

53 Fl. c6th.

from Sidonius provides further detail.[54,55] It concerns an elderly man, a good player in his youth: "Now he was repeatedly pushed by the inside runner from his place in the standing circle, then again, being brought inside the ring, he failed alike to cut across, or to dodge the path of the ball on its course, as it flew close to his face or was flung over his head; and he would often bend low in a flying tackle and then scarcely manage to recover from his staggering swerve. So, he was the first to retire from the stress and strain of the game, puffing and blowing in a state of internal inflammation."[56]

Sidonius himself claimed to be the "leading champion of the ball."[57] He writes of an indoor game: "I found … opposing ball-players bending low amid the whirling evolutions of the *catastrophae*."[58,59] Ball players are known as *sphaeristerum* and play in purpose-built rooms within gymnasia called *sphairisteria.* There are even ball coaches (*spharistai*), though it is unclear whether they teach *harpastum*, *phaininda,* or both.[60] Whatever the game, it is a handling one. No Greek or Roman game allowed kicking of the ball. Galen's *On Exercise with a Small Ball* provides most insight into *harpastum*:[61]

"People face each other, vigorously attempting to prevent each other from taking the space between, this exercise is a very heavy, vigorous one, involving much use of the hold by the neck, and many wrestling holds … the loins and legs are also subject to great strain in this kind of activity; it requires great steadiness on one's feet. Advancing and leaping to the side, too, represent a considerable exercise for the legs … the act of coming forward exercises one set of nerves and muscles to a greater extent, the act of retreating another; and that of dodging to the side others still … anyone failing, accurately and quickly to perceive the trajectory

---

54 C430–c483AD.

55 Gardiner, E.N., *Athletics of the Ancient World.* Clarendon Press, Oxford, 1930. p. 233.

56 Anderson, W.B. (trans.). *Sidonius: Poems and Letters.* Harvard University Press, 1965. 2 Vols. Vol. 2. pp. 232–233.

57 Ibid, p. 231.

58 Ibid, p. 453.

59 *Catastrophae* from the Greek *katastrophē:* "an overturning; a sudden end," from *katastrephein*: "to overturn".

60 Gardiner, E.N., *Athletics of the Ancient World.* Clarendon Press, Oxford, 1930. p. 233.

61 C165–175AD.

of the ball must miss his catch. The mental faculties, moreover, are sharpened by the concern not to drop the ball and to prevent the opponent from seizing it … it has the power to give both of them [body and soul] the most important types of training—those which the rulers of the city would especially command their generals to undertake … attacking at the right time, seizing one's opportunity, appropriating the enemy's possessions either by force or by unexpected attack, and keeping guard over what has already been acquired … recovering what one has lost, or anticipating the enemies' policy."[62]

Galen is casting *harpastum* as sublimated warfare. In truth, it is an upper-class game, well removed from chariot racing, boxing, gladiatorial combat, pentathlon, and wild beast shows.[63] Players may choose posts involving less exertion: "One must then adopt a middle position, not moving from the median, and alternate between gentle advances and remaining in the same place." A player may take up a position where he exercises his arms in throwing, or one that requires a lot of running and quick, long throws, or another that "involves holds, throws, and catches, and yet is not swift."[64] Romans of all age can play. According to Pliny the Younger, retired consul Spurinna keeps up a strict health regime: "When he has covered seven miles, he goes on foot again for a mile … When the hour for the bath is announced … he walks naked in the sun. He then throws a ball forcefully for some time, since with this type of exercise too he wars on old age."[65,66] Spurinna is eighty.

~

The first reference to a ball used for *kicking* is earlier rather than later. *Four Classics of Huangdi*, c403–221BC, records a war between Huangdi and Chiyou tribes, c2697–2599BC.[67,68] The defeated Chiyou is killed and skinned. His hair is used as a flag, then stuffed in his stomach to make

---

62 Singer, P.N., *Galen: Selected Works*. Oxford University Press, 1997. pp. 300–302.

63 Mangan, J.A. (ed.)., *Militarism, Sport, Europe: War without Weapons*. Frank Cass, London, 2003. p. 48.

64 Singer, P.N., *Galen: Selected Works*. Oxford University Press, 1997. p. 303.

65 Walsh, P.G. (trans.). *Pliny the Younger Complete Letters*. Oxford University Press, 2006. p. 56.

66 Pliny the Younger c61–c112AD. Letters written 100–109.

67 The only known manuscript was written 205–195BC.

68 Carrozza, P., *A Critical Review of the Principal Studies on the Four Manuscripts Preceding the B Version of the Mawangdui Laozi*. BC Asian Review, 2002, 13, p. 50.

a ball for the soldiers to kick around.[69] The more skilful are rewarded. At some point, probably around the time the manuscript was written, Chinese balls were termed *Ju*. Prior to that, the jade or stone balls used were unsuitable for kicking.[70]

The ancient Chinese kicking game is called *Cuju* (from *Cu* kick, *Ju* ball). The term is first used by Si Maquian, c96–91BC, in reference to the time of Emperor Xuan, in 328BC, when the public are said to be happy playing instruments, engaging in cock or dog fighting, or playing *Cuju*.[71] He adds that expert *Cuju* players and swordsmen "mixed together".[72] The next reference is c81–70BC, when Huan Kuan records his wealthiest contemporaries fishing, cockfighting, playing *Cuju*, and walking their dogs.[73] Several other references from the first century BC indicate a period of popularity. In 8BC the reclusive court poet, Yang Xiong, writes that "making chess pieces by sawing wood, or cooking skin to make a *Ju* should follow certain rules. Similarly, a society should have its rules and laws as well."[74] Ball-making as an analogy for good government reflects its status, and pairing it with chess its ubiquity. The *Ju* ritual involves stuffing the cooked skin with hair or other fillers.[75] The emperor Gaozu "built a huge football pitch (*cujong*) in his palace ... nobles and wealthy citizens also had private pitches."[76] Gaozu is possibly the one advised by an exasperated councillor that *Cuju* is undignified for an emperor.

Later writings demonstrate that *Cuju* is no less popular in 70BC. *25 Articles about Cuju*, c54–92AD, a chapter within the *History of the Han Dynasty*, is the earliest known writing dedicated to sport. That the widely read text includes *Cuju* indicates its popularity. "The *Ju*",

69 Yang, L., *Chinese Ju and World Football*, Advances in Social Science, Education and Humanities Research, 2018, 120, p. 276.

70 Ibid, p. 276.

71 Ibid, p. 277.

72 Mingda, M., *Sima Qian and the Way of the Sword in Ancient China*. In: Chao, H., Jaquet, D., Kim, L. (eds.)., *Martial Culture and Historical Martial Arts in Europe and Asia*. Springer, Berlin, 2023. p. 60.

73 Yang, L., *Chinese Ju and World Football*, Advances in Social Science, Education and Humanities Research, 2018, 120, p. 277.

74 Ibid, p. 277.

75 Ibid, p. 277.

76 Riordan, J, Jones, R. (eds.)., *Sports and Physical Education in China*. Routledge, Abingdon, Oxon, 1999. p. 33.

it says, “is a solid, soft, and light ball made with animal skin or offal, and stuffed with hair or other objects.”[77] The chapter is incorporated into military manuals. *Cuju* itself had been used in training since at least 200BC, though it went by another name. At the turn of the millennium it is known as *taju bingshi*, “football game for the power of soldiers”.[78] During a campaign, c140–117BC, general Huo Qubing has an area dug out for his soldiers to play the game.[79] During the Tang Dynasty (618–907AD), the *Ju* evolves into an inflatable ball made of animal bladder encased in square strips of leather; the Chinese character for *Ju* contains the component for leather.[80] By the Song Dynasty (960–1279AD), a dozen leather pieces are used, turnover stitching is employed to hide thread ends, and a standard weight of fourteen *liang* is established.[81,82]

Details of how the game was played are rare before the eighth century, and are usually in relation to military exercises.[83] *Cuju*, as described from the Tang Dynasty onward, is a cross between dancing and keepie uppie. Most of the body, except the arms and hands, can be used to keep the ball in the air, though there are elaborate rules.[84] Choreographed movements have scintillating names: the black dragon wags his tail, vermillion phoenix shakes his head.[85] An issue with symbolic expressions is the difficulty in interpreting meaning in a modern context. “Ball” alone has over forty idioms, including “moon on a bank of clouds”, “great peace under heaven”, “six ingots of silver”, and “turtle’s back”.[86]

The game has a solo version and at least ten team games, each with multiple rules. Solo *Cuju* comprises choreographed juggling, using

---

77 Yang, L., *Chinese Ju and World Football*, Advances in Social Science, Education and Humanities Research, 2018, 120, p. 277.

78 Rowley, C., *The Shared Origins of Football, Rugby, and Soccer*. Rowman & Littlefield, Lanham, Maryland, 2015. p. 8.

79 Gardiner, E.N., *Athletics of the Ancient World*. Clarendon Press, Oxford, 1930. p. 15.

80 Yang, L., *Chinese Ju and World Football*, Advances in Social Science, Education and Humanities Research, 2018, 120, pp. 278, 276.

81 Ibid, p. 279.

82 Around 560 grams. FIFA specifies 410–450 grams.

83 Vogel, H.U., *Homo Ludens Sinensis: Kickball in China from the 7th to the 16th Centuries*. In: Lo, V. (ed.)., *Perfect Bodies, Sports, Medicine and Immortality*. British Museum, London, 2012. p. 42.

84 Ibid, p. 40.

85 Ibid, p. 40.

86 Ibid, p. 40.

different parts of the foot and ankle, across three cycles of eighteen, seven, and thirty-one kick patterns. Terms include "phoenix holding a pearl in its beak", "fattening the goose", and "the immortal crosses the bridge".[87] Team games involve either passing, for example, "the leather is worn out", and "sun and moon traverse the palace", or competitive goal games.[88] In one, two sides of six must kick the ball through a 35 cm diameter vertical ring at the top of two central posts, ten metres from the ground. Another version has a silk cord across the posts, over which the ball is kicked. No game is known to have employed two goals. Both games require much skill.[89] The ball must be continually juggled with various parts of the body to stop it hitting the ground, as well as passed between players.

Some team games have no goals. Players are arranged into pairs on a pitch divided into several areas. The aim is to get the ball onto the ground of another pair's area. Either opponent can prevent this, but only by controlling the ball with their ankle or the tip of their foot.[90] Manuals describe sixteen varieties of kicks, including shoulder kicks, breast kicks, "splayfoot" kicks, and an "embroidered-sash" kick. Each kick is divided into as many as eighteen subtypes, and patterns have names like "monk jumps into the well".[91] The exquisite precision required is exemplified in the description of "riding-the-horse upper instep kick": "The balls falls on the right ankle; turning backwards, the upper instep kick is used; over the head the ball passes to the next player, and one has to call: 'Pass!'".[92] Adherence to rules is paramount, particularly playing with fairness and respect toward other players. The game as a whole operates within a distinct religious and ethical framework. A version of the game is described in a moral poem by Li Yu:[93]

> A round ball and a square wall,
> The ball flying across like the moon,

87 Ibid, p. 40.

88 Ibid, p. 41.

89 Ibid, p. 41.

90 Ibid, p. 42.

91 Ibid, pp. 41–42.

92 Ibid, p. 42.

93 50–130AD.

While the teams stand opposed.
Captains are appointed and take their places,
No allowances are made for relationship,
According to unchanging regulations
There must be no partiality.
But there must be determination and coolness,
Without the slightest irritation at failure.
And if all this is necessary for football
How much more for the business of life.[94]

The poem implies a square playing area, a novel shape compared with the rectangular, oval, and diamond shapes of modern pitches.[95] There are fixed rules, and impartiality is emphasised, suggesting adjudicators. Tellingly, victory is paramount. "The winners were rewarded with flowers, fruit and wine, and even with silver bowls and brocades, while the captain of the losing team was flogged, and suffered other indignities."[96,97]

Judging from literary references, *Cuju* is particularly popular during the Han (206BC–220AD), Tang (618–907AD), and Song (960–1279AD) dynasties. Lines from famous poets of the Tang Dynasty include: "Cuju kicked out is usually above the bird", "no dust blows in kicking ball, since it rains and just clears up", "I have nothing to do the whole day, then suddenly hear the sound of ball-kicking across the street", and "playing Cuju for ten years makes me long for the far place."[98] Both military and public manuals are silent on female participation. They are reduced to spectators, delighting in the erotically charged movements of the players. A Tang dynasty poem reflects this:

His merit won he was feted at the Hall of Unicorn Virtue.
Quick as a monkey on the ballfield, with a falcon's grace,

---

94 Gardiner, E.N., *Athletics of the Ancient World.* Clarendon Press, Oxford, 1930. p. 16.

95 Wrestling, boxing, taekwondo, and jiu-jitsu are all played in a square arena.

96 Giles, H.A., *The Civilization of China.* Henry Holt and Company, New York, 1911. p. 155.

97 While unlikely, if the 1930 translation is faithful, Yu's poem contains the earliest mention of football and captains in history. The translation used from the 1970s onward uses *Cuju* rather than football, and mentions referees.

98 Sun, Q., Mao, L., Li, C., *Illustrated Book of Traditional Chinese Sport.* World Scientific Publishing, Singapore, 2024. p. 252.

Three thousand ladies titled their heads to watch him,
Trampling shiny earrings as they crowded for a view.[99]

Nevertheless, during the Tang Dynasty, Wang Jian writes, "My wife enjoys kicking ball in Hanshi Festival, she loves ball gambling with others."[100] Women are also depicted playing *Cuju* on a bronze mirror, a round fan, a tomb relief, and at least one painting.[101] Much later, Li Yu (1611–1680AD) writes:

Their sweat stained faces are like flowers under dew,
Their fair brows dusty from the toil
Remind one of willow leaves in the mist.
Hidden are their slender fingers in the sleeves,
While a pull at the red skirts shows their tiny feet.
The ball is kicked time and again,
The maids blushing but speechless.
They are watched with envy
by the gallant youths of Chang'an.[102]

As *Cuju* declines in popularity during the Yuan and Ming periods, the sport is taken up by acrobats within female-only *Cuju* societies, who play despite bound feet. A player's name has even survived, the first known female kicker of a ball, the acrobat *Cuju* player Peng Yunxiu.[103] Naturally, children played, at least from the twelfth century onwards, though probably since *Cuju* was invented. Like Shrovetide has its folk football, the annual Hanshi Festival features *Cuju*, and there are several references to "the conditions of organising the activity of showing ball".[104] During the Song period, urbanisation results in a

99 Vogel, H.U., *Homo Ludens Sinensis: Kickball in China from the 7th to the 16th Centuries*. In: Lo, V. (ed.)., *Perfect Bodies, Sports, Medicine and Immortality*. British Museum, London, 2012. p. 48.

100 Sun, Q., Mao, L., Li, C., *Illustrated Book of Traditional Chinese Sport*. World Scientific Publishing, Singapore, 2024. p. 252.

101 Vogel, H.U., *Homo Ludens Sinensis: Kickball in China from the 7th to the 16th Centuries*. In: Lo, V. (ed.)., *Perfect Bodies, Sports, Medicine and Immortality*. British Museum, London, 2012. p. 44.

102 Ibid, p. 44.

103 Ibid, p. 44.

104 Sun, Q., Mao, L., Li, C., *Illustrated Book of Traditional Chinese Sport*. World Scientific Publishing, Singapore, 2024. p. 252.

degree of egalitarianism. *Cuju* societies are established where people of all classes co-mingle, albeit within a hierarchical structure.[105] Teams travel to play in "leisure parks", and "famous gardens", and perform for noblemen and at the imperial palace. The names of three top male players have also been handed down: Meng Xian, Lu Bao, and Li Guangyan.[106]

Both Tang and Song emperors are known to have played. A contemporary painting captures Zhao Kuangyin, the first emperor of the Song Dynasty (960–1279AD), playing *Cuju* with his brother, as adoring ministers look on. Several performances are also recorded during the dynasty. *Cuju*'s popularity continues for another century with continuous poetry references to the end of the Yuan Dynasty (1279–1368AD); it is during this period that female players are first mentioned. *Cuju*'s social status declines during the Ming Dynasty (1368–1644AD). The game becomes associated with prostitutes, who play outside brothels to attract customers. The first Ming emperor bans brothels and *Cuju*, believing the sport diminishes, rather than augments, military training.[107,108] By the third emperor, the ban is probably lifted, as an illustration shows him watching court eunuchs play.[109] The game's decline is by no means precipitous; it is not until the middle period of the Qing Dynasty (1644–1911AD) that *Cuju* disappears from society. As late as 1841, a Dutchman provides an account of winter sports in the Chinese court: "The Emperor made his appearance on a sort of sledge, supported by the figures of four dragons. This machine was moved about by several mandarins … Whole troops of civil and military officers soon appeared, some on sledges, some on skates, and others playing at football on the ice; and he that kicked up the ball was rewarded by the Emperor."[110]

The Silk Road, a network of trades routes between east and west, opens in 130BC, operating until the Ottoman Empire closes it down in 1453. It is argued that the Silk Road introduces football to the west

105 Vogel, H.U., *Homo Ludens Sinensis: Kickball in China from the 7th to the 16th Centuries.* In: Lo, V. (ed.)., *Perfect Bodies, Sports, Medicine and Immortality.* British Museum, London, 2012. p. 6.

106 Ibid, pp. 5, 10.

107 Chao, G., *Chinese Traditional Theatre and Male Dan.* Routledge, Abingdon, Oxon, 2022. p. 24.

108 Jek, T.W. (ed.)., *Origins of Chinese Sports.* Asiapac Books, Singapore, 2008. p. 37.

109 Sun, Q., Mao, L., Li, C., *Illustrated Book of Traditional Chinese Sport.* World Scientific Publishing, Singapore, 2024. p. 251.

110 *Staffordshire Advertiser.* 2 January 1841. p. 4.

via Egypt, Greece, Rome, France, and England. Evidence is lacking; indeed, the reverse could be true.[111,112] *Kemari* (kick-ball), the Japanese version of *Cuju*, is first recorded in 664AD, despite Chinese explorers reaching Japan in 57AD.[113] Even then, *kemari* does not attain widespread popularity until the twelfth century. When the Japanese Soccer Association is founded in 1921, football is considered an alien game, clearly distinguishable from *kemari*; in other words, they are different games, with no clear familial relationship.[114] When the West is first exposed to *Cuju* is unknown, but there is no evidence it influenced any ball game played in Europe, including *harpastum*, which was probably introduced into Britain by the Romans no earlier than 43AD. *Cuju* bears little relation to early European ball games. Not only are there significant differences in "technical skills, sequences of movements, and the use of the body", but the sport has different social origins, political functions, and religious and moral aspects, that set it apart from early European football.[115]

None of Britain's early ball games exhibit any of the hallmarks of *Cuju*. The game's discipline is antithetical to the anarchic free-for-all of folk football. What *is* remarkable is that *phaininda* (408–334BC), *episkyros* (369BC), the Spartan cadet game (357–347BC), and *Cuju* (328BC), are first recorded within eighty years of one another.[116] While this predates the Silk Road by two centuries, it is possible that knowledge of one or other games was disseminated, to be taken up and fashioned according to cultural values. The Mesoamerican game of hipball is a much earlier sport than *phaininda*, *episkyros*, the cadet game, and *Cuju*, but the onset of its peak popularity in 400BC coincides with the appearance of all four. The mention of ball play in China c2697–2599BC and in Lydia c1220–1190BC are undoubtedly origin myths; both are recorded the century

111 Yang, L., *Chinese Ju and World Football*. Advances in Social Science, Education and Humanities Research, 2018, 120: 276–281.

112 Vogel, H.U., *Homo Ludens Sinensis: Kickball in China from the 7th to the 16th Centuries*. In: Lo, V. (ed.)., *Perfect Bodies, Sports, Medicine and Immortality*. British Museum, London, 2012. p. 48.

113 Guttmann, A., Thompson, L., *Japanese Sports: A History*. University of Hawai'i Press, 2001. p. 26.

114 Horne, J., Manzenreiter, W. (eds.)., *Japan, Korea and the 2002 World Cup*. Routledge, Abingdon, Oxon. p. 90.

115 Vogel, H.U., *Homo Ludens Sinensis: Kickball in China from the 7th to the 16th Centuries*. In: Lo, V. (ed.)., *Perfect Bodies, Sports, Medicine and Immortality*. British Museum, London, 2012. p. 40.

116 Assuming Antiphanes was twenty when he wrote of phaininda. If he was sixty, the difference is as narrow as forty years.

before the first contemporary reports of ball games, arguably at a time interest is quickening and nascent sports developing.[117]

Cuju, then, appears to have developed in the fourth century BC and is highly valued as an aspect of military training for centuries, implying a degree of rigour. It is popular both among the people and the upper classes and nobility, who ultimately rub shoulders in *Cuju* societies. The game is played before emperors in purpose-built pitches at the imperial court, reflecting its kudos. It can be played individually or as a team sport with two sides or several pairs. *Cuju* involves kicking and juggling elements; arguably, variations involve greater or lesser degrees of each. Competitive games have two types of goals and are played on square pitches, some small enough for private use, some large, probably within the range of those used for cricket, baseball, and the seven codes of football.

~

While Asian and European ball games *might* have ancient origins, there is no doubt about Central American games. Mesoamerica was a cultural region encompassing the upper half of Central America and most of Mexico. The region was home to the Maya, Olmec, Mixtec, Zapotec, Teotihuacán, and Aztec civilisations.[118] Many ball games were played—including a stickball game—though little is known of them. The pan-Mesoamerican game of hipball is an exception. The game was played in a court with a rubber ball, which could only be struck with the hips. There appears to have been both a ceremonial aspect and a utility in dampening conflict between important families and social groups.[119] The earliest known ball court dates from 1650BC.[120] It was found in the lowlands of southern Mexico, then home to the Olmec.[121] Over two thousand three hundred ball courts have been found across Mesoamerica, including those of the Aztecs, demonstrating hipball's importance to multiple

117 C475–300BC and 430BC respectively.

118 Approximate timespans of the civilizations: Olmec 1600BC–350BC; Maya 1000BC–1521AD (cities established from 750BC); Mixtec 1500BC–1523AD; Zapotec 750BC–1521AD; Teotihuacan 600BC–750AD; Aztec 1300–1521AD.

119 Beekman, C., *Recent Research in Mexican Archaeology*. Journal of Archaeological Research, 2010, 18:1, p. 62.

120 Blomster, J.P., Salazar Chávez., *Origins of the Mesoamerican ball game*. Science Advances, 2020, 6:11, p. 1. https://doi.org/10.1126/sciadv.aay6964. Accessed 15 December 2023.

121 1500–400BC.

civilisations across thousands of years.[122] Courts were often placed near temples and funerary shrines, suggesting ritualistic symbolism.[123] Shared features across all ballcourts include an alley enclosed by parallel walls or mounds.[124] The oldest is open at both ends. Its mounds are ten feet high, with a stepped bench, presumably for spectating. The earthen court is ninety yards long and three yards wide.[125] Over time, walls replaced mounds and courts were surfaced with stone.

Ceramic figurines from 1250BC onward depict players. Most wear thick padded belts to protect the hips, and loincloths, and round pendants or pectorals.[126] Rubber balls were solid, and the larger balls could cause significant injury, which is why many figurines wear headgear. While this is practical and nothing like the elaborate ceremonial headwear, there may have been a hierarchical element. It would also make sense for team players to wear similar headwear for identification. Others have different degrees of arm, leg, chest, torso, neck, and groin padding. The first three are presumably for a variant that allows multiple parts of the body to strike the ball; the latter three are probably protective but could serve a dual function, with groin padding for the bravest players. An interesting variation was found in a shaft tomb in West Mexico. The figurines wear no padded belt but have a single lower leg padded and hold staffs or bats, and some appear to be wearing mitts.[127] It is likely they represent stickball players. Another leg pad and cricket springs to mind. What is remarkable is that these figurines are the *earliest* evidence of Mesoamerican ball games, dating to 1700BC: three thousand seven hundred and twenty-five years ago.

Rubber balls have also been discovered. Fourteen from one shrine range from three to eleven inches in diameter. The earliest dates to

122 Ibid, p. 3. Accessed 15 December 2023.

123 Earley, C.C., *The Mesoamerican Ball game*. https://www.metmuseum.org/toah/hd/mball/hd_mball.htm. Accessed 1 February 2024.

124 Blomster, J.P., Salazar Chávez., *Origins of the Mesoamerican ball game*. Science Advances, 2020, 6:11, p. 1. https://doi.org/10.1126/sciadv.aay6964. Accessed 15 December 2023.

125 FA pitches vary from 100–130 × 50–100yds.

126 Blomster, J.P., Salazar Chávez., *Origins of the Mesoamerican ball game*. Science Advances, 2020, 6:11, p. 3. https://doi.org/10.1126/sciadv.aay6964. Accessed 15 December 2023.

127 Blomster, J.P., Salazar Chávez., *Origins of the Mesoamerican ball game*. Science Advances, 2020, 6:11, p. 3. https://doi.org/10.1126/sciadv.aay6964. Accessed 15 December 2023.

1600BC; the rest were left as offerings across hundreds of years.[128] By c550BC, ball courts are closed off at the ends; later still, the closure is done in such as a way as to give courts their characteristic "I" shape.[129] Vertical walls also give way to sloping sides. Maya and Aztec artefacts demonstrate "the ritual and political focus of the ball game, with symbolism that included the regeneration of life and the maintenance of cosmic order. The origin narratives of the Maya, as codified in the *Popol Vuh*, implicate the ball game as part of a contest between heroic mortals and underworld deities in the creation of the universe."[130] Surviving imagery indicates that frequent fruits of victory were captives and human sacrifice.[131] While ceremonial sacrifice at ritual games may be paramount, cities have multiple courts, so it is likely that hipball was played largely for fun. No doubt it was hugely popular in the streets and fields, and played in rudimentary dirt courts. Still, so much is conjecture, based on little knowledge.

The Maya city of Chichén Itzá, in the Mexican state of Yucatán, grew prominent c600AD. The city had at least thirteen ball courts, including the largest and best-preserved court in Mesoamerica, which measures 183 × 76 yards and retains two upright stone hoops built into the parallel walls.[132,133] Current opinion is divided over whether ball games were played in it or if it was a monument to the game. That it equates to twenty-three tennis courts, and the medium hipball court size was 36.5 × 10 yards, implies the latter.[134,135] The rules of the Maya game can only be guessed from wall and devotional paintings and the game fields themselves. What is likely is that teams have between two and six players, and there is a suggestion that a referee is used. The right hip, right elbow, or right knee is used to "kick off". The rubber ball—generally believed to weigh three to four kilograms—is passed between players but cannot

---

128 Ibid, p. 3. Accessed 15 December 2023.

129 Ibid, p. 4. Accessed 15 December 2023.

130 Ibid, p. 1. Accessed 15 December 2023.

131 Earley, C.C., *The Mesoamerican Ball game*. https://www.metmuseum.org/toah/hd/mball/hd_mball.htm. Accessed 1 February 2024.

132 Blümchen, G., *The Maya Ball Game*. Cardiology, 2009, 113, p. 232.

133 Scarborough, V.L., Wilcox, D.R. (eds.)., *The Mesoamerican Ballgame*. University of Arizona Press, Tucson, 1991. p. 148.

134 Ibid, p. 137.

135 Blümchen, G., *The Maya Ball Game*. Cardiology, 2009, 113, p. 232.

touch the ground, and hands cannot be used.[136] Passing the ball through the stone hoop requires outrageous skill or luck.

Maya vases depict a large rubber ball, usually painted black but sometimes red; the Maya word for blood also means rubber.[137] The conquistadors first encounter a Mesoamerican ball game on the islands of the Caribbean, watching the "sport at ball" in Hispaniola.[138,139] The indigenous civilisation, the Taíno, have their own version of the Aztec game *ullamaliztli.* Over a hundred possible ball courts have been unearthed across the islands, and the sport is named after them: *Batey.* Clearly, the islanders have contact with the mainland—Cancún is only one hundred and thirty-three miles from the eastern tip of Cuba.

Most is known about the *ullamaliztli* (hipball), as first-hand accounts are recorded by Spanish missionaries and conquistadors. Points are lost in several ways: forced or accidental fouls, not getting the ball across the central line, the ball dying down in your own half, the ball ending up in your end corners, and using the wrong part of your body.[140] A certain number of points are needed for victory, though on the rare occasion the ball goes through the hoop—the equivalent of a hole-in-one—that team immediately wins. Cortez takes twelve players to Spain in 1528, and several games of *ullamaliztli* are played at court. One is captured in a woodcut by German painter Christoph Weiditz (1498–1559), who is present.[141] Two players are pictured. One is passing to the other. Both appear to be using their buttocks, which are covered for protection. The backs of their hands are also covered, palms unseen, implying the ball may be struck with the hand. Their elbows, knees, and shoulders are red, suggesting other parts of the body are used. Other Mesoamerican tribes have several variations, for example the Zapotec have *quiquijaya* and *taladz*i, the Mixtex *yocotondi* and *yochihi* and the Purépecha *querehta* and *apantzeti.*

---

136 Ibid, p. 232.

137 Leyenaar, T.J.J., *Ulama, The Survival of the Mesoamerican Ball game.* Kiva, 1992, 58:2, pp. 117–118.

138 Ibid, p. 117.

139 Stevens, J. (trans.). *The General History of the Vast Continent and Islands of America*, by Antonio de Herrera Tordesillas, 1601. 6 Vols. s.n., London, 1740. Vol. 2. p. 98.

140 Jones, C., *The Rubber Ball Game.* Expedition Magazine, 1985, 27:2, pp. 45, 47.

141 University of Pennsylvania Libraries. 2004.003.00.0001. *Mexica men Playing Tlachtli.* https://openn.library.upenn.edu/Data/0026/2004_003_00_0001/data/web/5176_0000_web.jpg. Accessed 1 February 2024.

After the conquest of the Aztec, a process of Catholic conversion begins. Anything related to existing rituals is banned, including indigenous games. In exchange, the Spanish introduce their own game *pelota mano* (handball), adapted to incorporate the rubber balls that impress them more than the indigenous games themselves.[142] That the first rubber ball to reach Europe is taken by Columbus testifies to their fascination.[143] Other than the gaping hole left by the ceremonial function of *ullamaliztli*, the switch to *pelota mano* appears to have been relatively seamless and to have filled *ullamaliztli's* critical role in day-to-day society. A local variation, *pelota mixteca* is still played widely among the Oaxacan of Mexico.[144]

The Dominican friar Diego Durán's 1581 account of *ullamaliztli* is striking: "in one hour the ball did not stop bouncing from one end to the other, without a miss, using only their buttocks, never touching it with the hand, foot, calf, or arm … Both teams were so alert in keeping the ball bouncing that it was amazing … It was considered a foul to touch with the hand or any other part of the body except the parts I have mentioned [buttocks and knees] … aside from being esteemed by the sovereigns, they were given notable dignities, were made intimates of the royal house and court, and were honoured with special insignia."[145]

He goes on to describe the game as it was played in ball courts:

"Many a time have I seen this game played … But the most important was lacking, namely the enclosure where the contest took place … and the rings through which they cast and passed the hail … ball courts existed in all the illustrious, civilized, and powerful cities and towns … A regular competition existed between the two [types of communities]. [The ball courts] were enclosed with ornate and handsomely carved walls. The interior door was of stucco, finely polished and decorated with figures of the god and demons to whom the game was dedicated and whom the players held to be their patrons in that sport … They were … narrow

---

142 Berger, M.E., *From Ollamalizti to Pelota Mixteca and beyond.* Leiden University, Netherlands, 2016. p. 173. https://scholarlypublications.universiteitleiden.nl/access/item%3A2862281/view. Accessed 17 December 2023.

143 Leyenaar, T.J.J., *Ulama, The Survival of the Mesoamerican Ball game.* Kiva, 1992, 58:2, p. 117.

144 Berger, M.E., *From Ollamalizti to Pelota Mixteca and beyond.* Leiden University, Netherlands, 2016. p. 170. https://scholarlypublications.universiteitleiden.nl/access/item%3A2862281/view. Accessed 17 December 2023.

145 Jones, C., *The Rubber Ball Game.* Expedition Magazine, 1985, 27:2, p. 45.

in the middle and wide at the ends. The corners were built on purpose so that if the player's ball fell into one it was lost and was considered a find … In the square corners (which served as ends or goals) a great number of players stood on guard to see that the ball did not penetrate."

"The main players stood in the centre facing the ball, and so did the opponents since the game was carried out similarly to the way they fought in battle or in special contests. In the middle of the walls of this enclosure were fixed two stones facing one another, and each had a hole in the centre … One team put the ball through the hole of the stone on one side while the other side was used by the other team. The first to pass its ball through won the prize. These stones also served as a division, for between them, on the floor, was a black or green stripe. This was done with a certain herb and no other, which is a sign of pagan belief. The ball always had to be passed across this line to win the game, because if the ball, projected by the backsides or by the knee, went bouncing along the floor and passed the stripe the width of two fingers, no fault was committed; but if it did not pass, it was considered a foul play. The man who sent the ball through the stone ring was surrounded by all. They honoured him, sang songs of praise to him, and joined him in dancing. He was given a very special reward of feathers or mantles and breech-cloths, something highly prized. But what was most prized was the honour involved: that was his great wealth. For he was honoured as a man who had vanquished many and had won a battle."

There is even earlier source material: a narrative account describing life at the court of Montezuma II, in 1519:

"The King took much Delight in seeing the Sport … The Ball was made of the Gum of a Tree that grows in hot Countries, which having Holes made in it distils great white Drops, that soon harden, and being work'd and moulded together, turn as black as Pitch. The Balls tho' hard and heavy to the Hand, did bound and fly as well as our Footballs, there being no need to blow them, nor did they use Chaces but vy'd to drive the adverse Party, that is to hit the Wall, the others were to make good, or to strike it over. They struck it with any Part of the Body, as it hapned, or they could most conveniently; and sometimes he lost that touch'd it with any other Part but his Buttock, or Hip, which was look'd upon among them as the greatest Dexterity; and to this Effect that the Ball might rebound the better, they fastened a Piece of stiff Leather on their Buttocks. They must strike it every time it rebounded…

"On the Side Walls, they fix'd certain Stones like those of a Mill, with a Hole quite through the Middle, just as big as the Ball, and he that could strike it through there won the Game, and in Token of its being an extraordinary Success, which rarely hapned, he had thereby a Right to the Cloaks of all the Lookers on … On a lucky Day, at Midnight, they perform'd certain Ceremonies and Enchantments on the two lower Walls, and on the Midst of the Floor, singing certain Songs, or Ballads; after which a Priest of the great Temple … utter'd some Words [and] threw the Ball about the Tennis-court four Times, and then it was consecrated … *Motezuma* carried the *Spaniards* to this Sport, and was well pleas'd to see them play at it."[146]

An almost identical account in another book adds that players are penalised if they use anything other than their hips or buttocks; also that the ball must be kept in the air and not touch the walls.[147] The implication that balls cannot be struck on the rebound differs from the first account.[148] The chapter in the second book is translated as *The Tennis play in Mexico* and the ball court is referred to as a tennis court, though the author also adds the correct term, *Tlachco.* The previous chapter is intriguing. *The footeplayers that played before Mutezuma* describe Montezuma watching "players, who play with their féete, as we doe with oure handes. These have a cudgell like unto a pastlers rowler, whiche they tosse high and lowe, as it were a bal in the ayre, straunge to beholde. They use other playes to passe the tyme, in such an order, that it séemed marvellous to the lookers on. *Cortez* broughte into *Spayne* some of these players."[149,150] The "footeplayers" is almost certainly not a reference to football or

146 Stevens, J. (trans.). *The General History of the Vast Continent and Islands of America,* by Antonio de Herrera Tordesillas, 1601. 6 Vols. s.n., London, 1740. Vol. 2. pp. 340–342.

147 Nicholas, T. (trans.). *The Pleasant Historie of the Conquest of the Weast India, now called new Spayne,* by Francisco López de Gómara, 1552. Henry Bynneman, London, 1578. pp. 179–180.

148 Both books were written by authors who had not travelled to the Americas, using the first-hand accounts of those who had.

149 Nicholas, T. (trans.). *The Pleasant Historie of the Conquest of the Weast India, now called new Spayne,* by Francisco López de Gómara, 1552. Henry Bynneman, London, 1578. p. 178.

150 Cortez also exported nine-foot jugglers, little persons and albinos of both sexes, malformed individuals, jaguars, pelicans, and an armadillo.

stickball; there is no mention of a ball. The mention of cudgels tossed in the air implies juggling with the feet. The cudgels are short, "like unto a *pastlers rowler*", a pastry chef's rolling pin. Stickball and football *were* played in the Maya city of Teotihuacán, one thousand years before. The c450–650AD murals of the Tepantitla compound depict multiple ball games, including seven men with sticks and balls playing within a defined space.[151] A second mural is momentous. Known as the Paradise of Tlaloc, the vibrant mural is filled with dozens of characters singing and playing.[152] Some are playing with balls. Two separate figures are kicking balls. It is the earliest representation of football in history.

~

A few words on balls. The oldest Chinese balls are around three thousand years old. Found in the Yanghai cemetery in 2020, they are cricket-ball sized, made of leather, and filled with hair.[153] Mesoamerican rubber balls date back three thousand six hundred years. But they are not the oldest. A ball was discovered in a child's grave in Tarkhan, Egypt. The linen rags rolled into a ball and secured with string was probably a favourite toy, left by inconsolable parents for their child to play with in the afterlife. The tomb is four and a half thousand years old.[154] There are depictions of ball games in the tomb of Baqet III in Beni Hasan cemetery, in Egypt. Dating from four thousand years ago, they are the oldest in history. One painting shows two men throwing balls to one another while piggybacking on two other men. Another shows four women juggling balls, and a third a game of catch with two teams of three women.[155] Elsewhere in the cemetery, is the tomb of a local governor c1900BC. A wall painting portrays two men with sticks playing with a ball.[156] It is the first drawing of a stickball game in history.

---

151 Uriarte, M.T., *The Teotihuacan ball game and the beginning of time.* Ancient Mesoamerica, 2006, 17:1, p. 21.

152 Richard Balthazar. https://richardbalthazar.com/2020/07/05/tlalocan-the-paradise-of-tlaloc/. Accessed 1 February 2024.

153 Wertmann P., Chen, X., Li, X., Xu, D., Tarasov, P., Wagner, M. *New evidence for ball games in Eurasia from ca. 3000–year-old Yanghai tombs in the Turfan depression of Northwest China.* Journal of Archaeological Science: Reports, 2020, Vol 34, Article 102576, p. 1.

154 Ibid, p. 1.

155 Gardiner, N.E., *Athletics of the Ancient World.* The Clarendon Press, Oxford, 1930. p. 5.

156 Wertmann P., Chen, X., Li, X., Xu, D., Tarasov, P., Wagner, M. *New evidence for ball games in Eurasia from ca. 3000–year-old Yanghai tombs in the Turfan depression of Northwest China.* Journal of Archaeological Science: Reports, 2020, Vol 34, Article 102576, p. 1.

The earliest depiction of a ball game in Europe is from 540 to 520BC, fifteen hundred years later. By a remarkable coincidence it shows three figures—possibly two women and a child—sat on the shoulders of three men, eagerly waiting for a seventh figure to throw the ball.[157] A few decades later, another game is shown on a marble relief at the base of a Greek funerary kouros statue.[158] Four players watch from the sides as a pair in the centre use two-foot sticks, curved at the ends, to battle over a ball. Three of the other four players are also holding sticks. This is likely to be the obscure game of *keretizein* ("to play a game with a horn"), possibly named after the shape of the stick.[159] One must wait a century for anything remotely resembling a kicking game in Europe: a Greek marble relief of a youth balancing a ball on his thigh as a boy looks on.[160]

It may not appear so, but Europe dawdled in the depiction of any sport—if hunting can be called that. The Lascaux cave in France has over six hundred wall paintings, including a number of hunting scenes. The oldest, dating back seventeen thousand years, shows a bird-headed man charged by a bison.[161] On the Indonesian island of Sulawesi, there is a cave painting of human-like figures hunting a wild pig. The world's first story is an inconceivable fifty-one thousand years old.[162]

---

157 The British Museum. Museum number: 1837, 0609.65. https://www.britishmuseum.org/collection/object/G_1837–0609–65. Accessed 1 February 2024.

158 Gardiner, N.E., *Athletics of the Ancient World.* The Clarendon Press, Oxford, 1930. Plate 213.

159 Andreu-Cabrera, E., González, M.C., Ruiz, J.R., Chinchilla-Mira, J.J. *Play and childhood in ancient Greece.* Journal of Human Sport and Exercise, 2010, 5:3, p. 344.

160 The National Archaeological Museum, Athens. 873, Part of a marble grave stele, found in Piraeus. 400–375BC.https://www.namuseum.gr/en/collection/klasiki-periodos-2/. Accessed 1 February 2024.

161 Aubert, A., Lebe, R., Oktaviana, A.A., et al., *Earliest hunting scene in prehistoric art.* Nature, 2019, 576, p. 448. https://doi.org/10.1038/s41586–019–1806–y. Accessed 1 February 2024.

162 Oktaviana, A.A., Johannes-Boyau, R., Hakim, B., et al., *Narrative cave art in Indonesia by 51,200 years ago.* Nature, 2024, 631, p. 814. https://doi.org/10.1038/s41586–024–07541-7. Accessed 21 September 2024.

CHAPTER ONE
679–1099

It is 679, and English clerics need pulling into line. The earliest known injunction against games decrees, “that bishops or any of the ecclesiastical order who has professed a religious life shall not use weapons, nor have lyres, nor any symphonic music, nor permit any games, or games before the faith.”[1] Somewhere between 699 and 705, an unknown Lindisfarne monk writes a life of St Cuthbert, who lived from c637 to 687. An early passage reads: “When he was a boy of eight years … many youths were gathered together one day on a piece of level ground, and he too was found among them. They began thereupon to indulge in a variety of games and tricks; some of them stood naked, with their heads turned down unnaturally towards the ground, their legs stretched out and their feet lifted up and pointing skywards; and some did one thing and some another.”[2] Other than handstands, there is no indication of the games played. It is a flat surface, but balls go unmentioned.

In 721, the Venerable Bede completes both prose and verse versions of the *Life of Cuthbert*. He writes, “For Bishop Trumwine of blessed memory used to relate what had been told him by Cuthbert himself, how on a certain day, a large crowd of boys in a field were engaged in the usual contests and he himself was present: in accordance with the usual thoughtlessness of children at play, most of them were twisting their limbs into various unnatural contortions.”[3] What usual contests? Ball sports? Of note, Bede and Cuthbert were born and raised in the Saxon kingdom of Northumbria, an early adopter of ball games; indeed, Cuthbert is patron saint of Northumberland. It is only one hundred and sixty-seven years after the fall of the Roman Empire when Cuthbert reaches the age of eight. And Bede wrote his book, in 721, on Lindisfarne, where

1 Wilkins, D. (ed.)., *Concilia Magnae Britanniae et Hiberniae*. 4 Vols. R. Gosling, F. Gyles, T. Woodward, C. Davis, London, 1737. Vol. 1. p. 46.

2 Colgrave, B. (ed.)., *Two Lives of Saint Cuthbert; A Life by an Anonymous Monk of Lindisfarne and Bede’s Prose Life*. Anon., *Vita Sancti Cuthberti*. Greenwood Press Publishers, New York, 1969. p. 65.

3 Ibid, p. 157.

Cuthbert had been bishop. Seventy-two years later, the first Viking raid on the British Isles targets Lindisfarne.

A mid-twelfth century manuscript of Bede's book decides it is a ball game.[4] One illustration depicts Cuthbert at play. Seven figures are divided into two groups, one in green, the other peach. The peaches appear to be women. One figure has swung her hockey-like stick, and a green player opposite has caught the hand-sized ball. A peach stands between, head tilted, appearing to call out, possibly the score. Another peach dives acrobatically for another hand-sized ball, while the last peach appears to have a thigh strain and is attended to by a green. The final green breaks the fourth wall, beckoning to someone outside the panel.[5]

In an anonymous life of Cuthbert, c1300–1325, "he pleide at þe bal" with his friends, until he is talked out of such idle games by a young boy.[6] Cuthbert declares: "we ne schullen none more."[7] In Middle English *chullen* (or *schullen*) means to kick. In this version, the boys are playing football. If written before 1302, it is the second earliest *reference* to football in history.

The game in the Bede manuscript appears well established. The hockey-like stick is a crucial feature. Where did it come from? Stick and ball games are evident across multiple civilisations. The four-thousand-year-old tomb of the local governor in Beni Hasan cemetery contains the wall painting of two men with sticks and a ball.[8] In China's Yanghai cemetery, a leather ball was deposited in three tombs, and curved wooden sticks in ten others, c1000BC.[9] There is also a marble relief on a c510BC Greek tombstone of two players with curved sticks, battling over a ball, while four more look on, three of them with sticks.[10] Another Chinese cemetery has a tomb with six

4 University College, Oxford, MS 165, Bede, *Life of Cuthbert*, fol. 8.

5 A later version of Cuthbert's life, contained in a fourteenth century manuscript, says, "in his eigtethe zere, wit children he pleyde atte balle", but there is no mention of sticks.

6 Þ, pronounced 'th' as in *thick*, is an Old English character and is retained in quotes.

7 Horstmann, C. (ed.)., *The Early South-English Legendary, or Lives of Saints*. N. Trübner and Co., London, 1887. p. 359.

8 Wertmann P., Chen, X., Li, X., Xu, D., Tarasov, P., Wagner, M. *New evidence for ball games in Eurasia from ca. 3000–year-old Yanghai tombs in the Turfan depression of Northwest China*. Journal of Archaeological Science: Reports, 2020, Vol 34, Article 102576, p. 1.

9 Ibid, p. 1.

10 Gardiner, N.E., *Athletics of the Ancient World*. The Clarendon Press, Oxford, 1930. Plate 213.

pictorial bricks c25–220AD.[11] Each brick depicts a man on horseback holding a curved stick and chasing a ball. Finally, in the Maya city of Teotihuacán, murals dated c450–650AD depict several ball games, including a mural of seven men with sticks and balls playing within a defined space.[12]

In 747, at the Council of Clovesho, the Archbishop of Canterbury decrees that "three days before the Lord's ascension into heaven, they [people] should come with fasting … not mingled with vanities, as is the custom of many, or of the negligent, or of the unskilled, that is to say, with games and horse-racing, and great feasts."[13] Nine hundred years later, a future Archbishop of Canterbury has a bowling green at his palace in Lambeth.[14]

Ball games are not specifically referred to in mainland Britain until the tenth century. While the *Historia Brittonum* is believed to have been written c829, the earliest intact manuscript containing the relevant passage dates to c944.[15] The Arthurian story tells of a fourth-century search for the true king of Britain. "In consequence of this reply, the king sent messengers throughout Britain, in search of a child born without a father. After having inquired in all the provinces, they came to the field of Aelecti, in the district of Glevesing, where a party of boys were playing at ball."[16,17] The fatherless boy turns out to be a wizard. Glevesing, a minor kingdom between the Usk and Rhymney rivers in Monmouthshire, now falls within the county of Glamorgan in south Wales. The earliest reference to a British ball game is played by a wizard. Written as history, it is undoubtedly a story, but a story placed squarely in Wales.

---

11 Wertmann P., Chen, X., Li, X., Xu, D., Tarasov, P., Wagner, M. *New evidence for ball games in Eurasia from ca. 3000–year-old Yanghai tombs in the Turfan depression of Northwest China.* Journal of Archaeological Science, Reports 34, 2020, p. 4.

12 Uriarte, M.T., *The Teotihuacan ball game and the beginning of time.* Ancient Mesoamerica, 2006, 17:1, p. 21.

13 Wilkins, D. (ed.)., *Concilia Magnae Britanniae et Hiberniae.* 4 Vols. R. Gosling, F. Gyles, T. Woodward, C. Davis, London, 1737. Vol. 1. p. 97.

14 James, L. (ed.)., *The Household Accounts of William Laud, Archbishop of Canterbury, 1635–1642.* Boydell & Brewer, Martlesham, United Kingdom, 2019. p. xxi.

15 The Vatican Recession: Dumville, D.N., *The Textual History of the Welsh-Latin Historia Brittonum.* 3 Vols. Unpublished PhD thesis, University of Edinburgh, 1975. Vol. 1. pp. 8, 18.

16 Gunn, W. (trans)., *The Historia Brittonum, commonly attributed to Nennius.* John and Arthur Arch, London, 1819. p. 26.

17 Campum Aelecti. Believed to have been near the village of Maesaleg (in English Bassaleg), now a suburb of Newport.

An incomplete manuscript, c900, known as the Chartres recension, was discovered in 1890. Its text ends agonisingly close to the passage on ball games.[18,19] Whether this, or the lost c829 manuscript, included the passage on ball games may never be known.[20,21] Nonetheless, when the boy is questioned, he reveals that his father is a member of the Roman consular class.[22] The story is set before the fall of the Roman Empire, and *harpastum* was known to be an upper-class pursuit. Did the Roman game reach Wales? More likely, the author is describing a contemporary ball game.

All later interpretations of the story—including French and Dutch versions—mention a ball game. A Viking game is plausible. The first raid on Wales is in 852.[23] Hegemony over north Wales is achieved by the 870s, though unlike Dublin and York, the Vikings secure no foothold. Influence fizzles out c820, reignited by a second phase of raids on the north beginning c950.[24] There are suggestions but no proof of Viking settlements, certainly in south Wales, which is subject to occasional raids but little else. Such harrying is unlikely to endear cultural influence. Even if the earliest proven date (c944) rather than the date of the lost manuscript (c829) is used, the boys in Aelecti are likely to be playing a game devoid of Viking influence. Such a game may be Brittonic, predating invasions, or have been introduced by the Romans or by subsequent settlers—Angles, Saxons, Jutes: all three are implicated. Most likely it is a hybrid, recast by waves of invaders. Influence is heterogenous. Occupiers settle in different parts of the British Isles, impressing their culture differentially. The Roman Conquest sputters north of York, and outside of the cities their political influence is minor. Culture spreads farther. If they bring *harpastum*, it is bound to impact existing ball games, notwithstanding the

---

18 Faral, E., *La Legénde Arthurienne*. Librairie Ancienne Honoré Champion, Paris, 1929. p. 28.

19 The manuscript (Bibliothèque Municipale, Chartres, MS 98) was destroyed by allied bombing during World War II.

20 Higham. N.J., *King Arthur: The Making of the Legend*. Yale University Press, New Haven and London, 2018. p. 179.

21 In the absence of strong collateral information supporting its presence in a lost text, the oldest extant manuscript will be used for the dating of an event.

22 Mangan, J.A. (ed.)., *Militarism, Sport, Europe: War Without Weapons*. Frank Cass, London, 2003. p. 50.

23 Redknap, M., *The Vikings in Wales*. In: Brink, S., Price, N. (eds.)., *The Viking World*. Routledge, Abingdon, Oxon, 2011. p. 401.

24 Ibid, p. 402.

minimising effect of regional remoteness. Who knows how *harpastum* evolves down the centuries or how it benefits indigenous games. During the second half of the sixth century, one hundred years after the fall of the Roman Empire, the Gallo-Roman writer St Gregory of Tours mentions a team game involving running with a ball.[25] Tours is south of Paris, well away from the influence of any early version of *soule*, the ball game played in the north. The game is likely to be *harpastum*.

Romans may bring more than *harpastum* to Britain. Notwithstanding existing trade routes, when they thrust open the creaking gates of Albion, exotic culture pours in. From far and wide. The influence brought to bear on local games is unknowable. Angles, Saxons, and Jutes settle in discrete areas, enriching local culture. Any or all may bring a ball game, freshening and embellishing customary sports. It may explain the presence of geographically unique games, *knappan* in Wales, hurling in Ireland, Cornish hurling in the West Country, camping in East Anglia. The boys in Aelecti may be playing an early form of *knappan*. There is still the far-reaching influence of the Normans to consider. And who knows if Greeks visit pre-Roman Britain, bringing *episkyros* as they trade for copper, gold, and tin. Perhaps there are earlier visitors still, during the Bronze Age,[26] especially in the boom years of mining in southwest Ireland, north Wales, and Cornwall. Ireland, Wales, Cornwall. Hurling, *knappan*, hurling.

Other factors need weighing. When the Beaker people arrive c2400BC, neolithic Britons are gradually displaced. Within a few hundred years, only ten per cent of their gene pool remains.[27] By the time the Angles and Saxons begin to settle c440AD, Britain is a patchwork of Brittonic tribes. Kingdoms collapse before Anglo-Saxon might. Until recently, the Celts were considered a homogenous population of Britons pressed to the edges of the isles by the Anglo-Saxons. DNA studies suggest otherwise. Tribes of Britons do not give up their homelands and flee to the fringes to establish new kingdoms. Those kingdoms already exist. And they are the ones that survive. The Dumnonii, for example, had lived in what became Cornwall since pre-Roman times, long enough to have developed their

---

25 Mangan, J.A. (ed.)., *Militarism, Sport, Europe: War without Weapons*. Frank Cass, London, 2003. p. 49.

26 c2400–800BC.

27 Olalde, I., et al. *The Beaker phenomenon and the genomic transformation of northwest Europe.* Nature, 2018, 555: 190–196.

own idiosyncratic culture, including sports.[28] If tribes *had* fled, the DNA of those in Scotland, Wales, and Cornwall would be similar. They are distinct. In fact, modern day people in north and south Wales are more genetically distinct than the Scottish are to the English.[29] Likewise, people in Devon and Cornwall are no more similar than northern English and Scottish are. There is no distinct Celtic race. The term reflects a cultural identity, not a race of people. Ancient Brittonic kingdoms comprise genetically discrete tribes. Moreover, Britons in areas settled by invaders are not eradicated like the Beaker people, they are assimilated. Since remote kingdoms exist before the Anglo-Saxons arrive,[30] it is arguable that the distinctive ball games of Cornwall and Wales develop locally without external influence, or deviate from a common ancestor, with later variably penetrative Roman influence.

The Angles and Saxons spread westwards to Wales and northwards to present-day Northumberland, Cumberland, and the Scottish Borders. Together with Westmoreland, these northern lands are early adopters of kicking and carrying games.[31] All four regions are part of the Angle kingdom of Northumbria, which extends south to Manchester and Huddersfield. Another Angle kingdom is East Anglia, the future home of camping. The third is Mercia, bordered by Northumbria, Wales, East Anglia, and the Saxon kingdom of Wessex. The Angles establish kingdoms from the east. Acceptability and cultural influence wane as they move westwards. If they do bring their own game, it may explain the early adoption of ball games in the narrow upper half of Northumbria, incorporating Edinburgh, the Scottish Borders, Northumberland, Cumberland, and Westmoreland. As Northumbria expands south like a triangle, less cultural impact is felt in western areas (in what is now Lancashire and Cheshire); later, though by no means the latest, adopters of ball games.

It is the Britons in the kingdom of East Anglia who are most likely to be influenced by the incoming culture. The western border of East Anglia

---

28 Huscroft, R., *Making England, 796–1042*. Routledge, Abingdon, Oxon, 2019. p. 1.

29 Leslie, S., et al. *The Fine-Scale Genetic Structure of the British Population*. Nature, 2015, 519: 309–314.

30 Mid-fifth to early seventh century.

31 The respective terms are used throughout to imply a predominantly kicking or predominantly carrying game. Both would have included kicking and carrying elements; some stick and ball games may also have included them.

is farther east than the eastern border of other kingdoms. An attractive foothold, it will be home to nostalgic first loves and first settlements, the historic heart of the annexation. The Angles might bring a prototypical game to share, altering any indigenous game to such a degree that the game of camping is the closest approximation there is to an original Anglo-Saxon sport. No regional games are known to exist before the Saxon kingdoms of Wessex, Essex, Kent, and Sussex are formed. Nevertheless, Saxons may arrive with an admiration of ball games, but none they lay claim to, and they embrace a local sport that existed before uninterrupted historical records began. There is no proof that any of the Germanic tribes had a ball game, including Angles, Saxons, Jutes, Ostrogoths, Visigoths, Franks, or Vandals.

Only one southern town will become known as an early adopter of ball games, and the Angles, Saxons, or both may be the reason. Kingston upon Thames sits on the border between Angle Mercia and Saxon Wessex. An assembly of Saxons is held at Kingston in 838, probably at the royal estate. Surviving manuscripts describe Kingston as "Kyningestun *famosa illa* [sic: villa] *locum*": that famous village.[32] "All the bishops and nobles of the land are present."[33] The Archbishop of Canterbury officiates. New alliances are forged. The archbishop recognises King Ecgberht's eldest son, Aethelwulf, as heir. Significantly, he acknowledges Wessex hegemony over other Saxon kingdoms, pivoting away from the Angles. After pledging loyalty to Ecgberht, Wessex is named the supreme kingdom. Within earshot of Mercia. The same year, Cornish warriors join forces with Vikings but are slammed by Ecgberht before leaving their own kingdom. Other than a raid here, a plunder there, it is one of the few instances of Viking contact with the region, leaving little scope to influence local hurling.

In 886, the seven kingdoms are united by King Alfred (the Great) of Wessex, who becomes king of the Anglo-Saxons. In 900, his son Edward is crowned at Kingston upon Thames, as is Edward's son Athelstan in 925. Within two years, Athelstan overcomes the last Viking outpost—the Kingdom of York—to become the first King of England. Eadred is crowned

32 Lysons, D., *The Environs of London: being an historical account of the towns, villages, and hamlets, within twelve miles of that capital interspersed with biographical anecdotes*. 4 Vols. T. Cadell, The Strand, London, 1792. Vol. 1. p. 215.

33 Ibid, p. 215.

King of England at Kingston upon Thames in 946, so too Æthelred in 979. Æthelred comes to the throne as a child and becomes the longest-serving of the first twenty-nine kings, eclipsed by Henry VI. His ascent is bloody. Half-brother King Edward is murdered by those convinced Æthelred is the legitimate heir. The sixteen-year-old is killed in Corfe Castle, site of the second oldest *annual* Shrove Tuesday football game known.

Nobility from every corner of the realm converge on Kingston upon Thames for coronations, including Angle kingdoms that will later prize ball games. Is it at one of these that the town is meaningfully exposed to the game? Annual Shrovetide games have been recorded at Kingston upon Thames since the 1790s. By 1810, games are mentioned in neighbouring Hampton Wick and Twickenham, and the town is rivalling Derby as the epicentre of Shrovetide football. Kingstonians have a legend: "There is a popular tradition, handed down for the last four hundred years among the inhabitants of Kingston, that this game is commemorative of a defeat sustained by the Danes at the hands of the townsmen of Kingston during the celebration of their Shrovetide sports: and that the Captain of the Danish forces having been slain, and his head kicked about by the people in derision, the custom of kicking a Foot Ball on the anniversary of that day has been observed ever since."[34]

The legend's roots are tangled with truth. Aethelstan *is* crowned in Kingston, and he does oust the remaining Vikings in York. There is more. London is founded by the Romans and thrives until the Jutes, Angles, and Saxons make landfall in the fifth century. It blossoms again when mercantile Danes establish businesses in the ninth century. The town is girdled by dozens of hamlets and villages, later to be absorbed: Wemba Lea, Hemstede, Grenwic, Fullan hamme, Pechamme, Lambehithe, Totinge. To the southwest, adjacent to Todyngton, is the village of Kyningestun. Increasingly influential, London attracts the Viking's Great Heathen Army, which attacks it in 842 and 851, and sees out the winter there in 871/72. Sixteen years on, Alfred defeats them at the Battle of Edington. There is no evidence Vikings attack Kingston, though it is easy to see how attacks on London and the town's royal connections could be folded into legend.

---

34 Biden, W.D., *History and Antiquities of the Ancient and Royal Town of Kingston-upon-Thames*. William Lindsey, Kingston, 1852. pp. 58–59.

There is an even more fanciful origin for the Shrovetide game: "In the year 754 or 755 Kenulf, king of one of the petty Saxon tribes, allured by the beauty of a Maid to Merton, was treacherously slain there by Kynard. In revenge for his death the Kingston people armed and hastened to the spot, where they signally defeated the forces of the assassin and carried off his head in triumph."[35] In reality, Kenulf is King of the Mercians from 796 to 821, and dies in Wales. Far-fetched, too, that the town can overcome a Saxon tribe. When Alfred overcomes the Great Heathen Army of Vikings in 868, a treaty is drawn up. Half of England falls under Danish rule until 954. Danelaw territory extends from East Anglia to Whitby, sweeping west to Derby and south to London. The Danes continue to be an—albeit diminishing—power until driven out by William the Conqueror in 1069.[36] If the Danes bring their own ball game, local sport will be greatly modified across Danelaw, none more so than East Anglia, where the majority settle. But there is no evidence that Danish Vikings have a ball game to bring.

The effect of successive invasions varies in Scotland and Ireland. The Romans leave the Gaels of Ireland unmolested, and the Picts and Gaels of Scotland withstand them (while Cornwall is largely untouched).[37] Minimal, if any, direct influence on the development of local ball games might be reasonably inferred. Anglo-Saxons reach as far north as Edinburgh. If they bring a game, it will undoubtedly modify those to the south, including border games. The Saxons do no more than give Ireland a desultory once-over, insulating its indigenous sports. The Vikings are more pragmatic. After their raid on Lindisfarne,[38] they go on to settle in the northern and western fringes of Scotland and the isles of the Hebrides, Orkney, and Shetland. These Norsemen may have a ball game, but there is no evidence of dissemination. Only in Orkney is there an historic association with a game, but is it Norse in origin?

From 795, Norse Vikings plunder their way through large swathes of Ireland. The pillaging forces do not linger, neither are the locals

35 Ibid, p. 59.

36 In 911, William's forefather, Rollo, became the first Viking king of Normandy. The game of *soule* is played historically in the region.

37 Charles-Edwards, T.M., *Wales and the Britons, 350–1064*. Oxford University Press, Oxford, 2013. p. 31.

38 793AD.

well-disposed, suggesting minimal influence. It is more pronounced when they return in 914, colonising Ireland for the first time in its history.[39] The immediate sphere of political and cultural influence is limited to the newly formed coastal settlements of Dublin, Wexford, Waterford, and Cork, and the estuary town of Limerick. While the Norsemen remain for a century, the vast majority of the country is left to its own devices. Nevertheless, a Norse ball game would seed across the island, modifying local sports. In the absence of Roman and Anglo-Saxon influence, descriptions of Irish sports predating Viking settlement in 914—or, more powerfully still, before the first Viking raids of 795—will give as close an account as is possible to original Gaelic, and possibly Brittonic, games.

The *Corpus iuris Hibernici* is a collection of Irish legal tracts.[40] One, the *Book of Aicill*, is purportedly third century. It is far more likely to be seventh century, and the earliest known manuscript is twelfth century. This book on criminal law includes a ruling on playing unspecified ball games on the green of a fort: "the person is exempt who nobly strikes off the ball upon the green ... or playing a game upon it ... because every green is free."[41] There are additional laws about retrieving a ball from private property based on necessity, consent, and damage.[42] What that ball game is becomes clear in a later judgement on hurling injuries: "I deem the person exempt from liability who strikes the ball with his hurlet from the hurling hole to the place of the *grifid*, or from the place of the *grifid* to the place of the division, or from the hole in which it is, until it reaches the place in which it usually is." In other words, a hurler is not liable if he is playing by the rules and inadvertently injures another.[43]

Another tract, *Mellbretha* (*Sports Judgements*), deals with the legalities of twenty sports. The earliest extant manuscript is fourteenth century, but based on textual analysis, *Mellbretha* was written between 600 and 700. That it is partly in Old Irish—only used from 600 to 850—

39 Excluding the Gaels themselves, who settled in Ireland c4000 BC, overcoming the neolithic Irish, who had lived there since at least 31,000 BC.

40 Binchy, D.A. (ed.), *Corpus iuris Hibernici*. 7 vols. Dublin Institute for Advanced Studies, Dublin, 1978.

41 Anon., *Ancient Laws of Ireland*. 4 Vols. Vol. 3. pp. 255–256. TannerRitchie Publishing, Burlington, Ontario, Canada, 2017.

42 Ibid, p. 257.

43 Ibid, p. 555. The meaning of *grifid* is unknown. It does not appear in Old Irish dictionaries.

appears to confirm the date, a powerful argument against Viking impact on sports in the manuscript. Hurling is one game, others include wrestling, swimming, leaping, and horse riding.[44] A third seventh century law book, the *Senchus Már*, mentions correct attire.[45] The fourteenth century manuscript reads, "Satin and scarlet are for the son of the king of Erin, and silver on his scabbards, and brass rings upon his hurling sticks."[46] While the earliest copies of all three books date from the twelfth to the fourteenth centuries, linguistic and non-linguistic features confidently date all three texts to the seventh century, going so far as to pinpoint *Senchus Már* to 660–680;[47] credible support that hurling existed in seventh century Ireland, a century before the first Viking incursions. With Roman influence in Ireland minimal at best, hurling may have been played before the invasion of Britain in 43AD.[48]

Today, hurling is the national sport of Ireland. It is embedded in mythology. A game was said to have been played at the First Battle of Mag Tuired, in 1072BC: "Thereupon Ruad with twenty-seven of the sons of courageous Mil sped westwards to the end of Mag Nia to offer a hurling contest to the Tuatha De. An equal number came out to meet them. The match began. They dealt many a blow on legs and arms, till their bones were broken and bruised, and fell outstretched on the turf, and the match ended."[49] The Fir Bolg win the hurling, but the Tuatha Dé Danann win the battle. The c1160 *Book of Leinster* is a compilation of Irish verse and poems harvested from older manuscripts.[50] Much is believed to have been handed down from the oral tradition, an ancient method of passing down stories, once common in Ireland and Iceland.

44 Binchy, D.A. (ed.)., *Mellbretha.* Celtica, Vol. 8, 1968, pp. 144–154; Sayers, A. *Games, Sport, and Para-Military Exercise in Early Ireland.* Aethlon, 1992, 10:1, pp. 105–123.

45 Wadden, P., *The Pseudo-Historical Origins of the Senchas Már and Royal Legislation in Early Ireland.* Peritia, 2016, Vol. 27, p. 142.

46 Anon., *Ancient Laws of Ireland.* 6 Vols. TannerRitchie Publishing, Burlington, Ontario, Canada, 2017. Vol. 1. p. 147.

47 Breatnach, L., *The Early Irish Law Text Senchas Már and the Question of its Date.* E.C. Quiggin Memorial Lectures 13. Department of Anglo-Saxon, Norse and Celtic, University of Cambridge, 2011. p. 42.

48 Alternatively, hurling was created between the first and sixth centuries.

49 Trinity College, Dublin: MS. 1319, *Cath Muige Tuired Cunga*, fifteenth century, pp. 90a–99b (33). Fraser, J. (trans.). *The First Battle of Moytura.* Ériu, 1916, Vol. 8, pp. 1–63.

50 Trinity College, Dublin: MS. 1339, *The Book of Leinster*, c1160. L.L. fo. 62a–63a. Dunn, J. (trans.)., *The Ancient Irish Epic Tale Táin Bó Cúailnge*, David Nutt, London, 1914. pp. 47–48.

It contains the most complete version of *Táin Bó Cúailnge* (*The Cattle Raid of Cooley*), the epic tale of the Irish demi-god Cú Chulainn, including his childhood exploits:

"The boy [Cú Chulainn] fared forth and took his playthings with him. His little lath-shield he took, and his hurley of bronze and his ball of silver ... He would give the ball a stroke with the hurl-bat, so that he sent it a long distance from him. Then with a second throw he would cast his hurley so that it went a distance no shorter than the first throw ... Then he would catch up his hurl-bat and pick up the ball ... The little lad went on to the play-field into the midst of the [one hundred and fifty] boys, and he whipped the ball between his two legs away from them, nor did he suffer it to travel higher up than the top of his knee, nor did he let it lower down than his ankle, and he drove it and held it between his two legs and not one of the boys was able to get a prod nor a stroke nor a blow nor a shot at it, so that he carried it over the brink of the goal away from them."

The one hundred and fifty princes are incensed. "The urchin insults us," one cries, "Throw yourselves all on yon fellow, and his death shall come at my hands ... They cast their thrice fifty hurl-bats at the poll of the boy's head. He raises his single toy-staff and wards off the thrice fifty hurlies, so that they neither hurt him nor harm him, and he takes a load of them on his back. Then they throw their thrice fifty balls at the lad. He raises his upper arm and his forearm and the palms of his hands against them and parries the thrice fifty balls, and he catches them, each single ball in his bosom."[51]

The brink of the goal. History's first mention of a goal *to score in*. The second will not be for another four hundred years. And there is that hurley, or hurling stick. Another stick and ball game. *Camán*, the modern name for a hurley, derives from the Old Irish *cammán*, a shepherd's crook.[52] It is unknown when *The Cattle Raid of Cooley* was first transcribed, if or when it appeared in the oral tradition, and if the hurling story was always included.[53] The earliest version of *The*

51 Dunn, J. (ed.)., *The Ancient Irish Epic Tale of Táin Bó Cúalnge*. David Nutt, London, 1914. pp. 47–48.

52 S.Ó. Cadhla., *Modern and Folk Sport: Translating and Not Translating Traditions*. Béaloideas. 2015, 83, p. 63.

53 The earliest surviving manuscript (c1100) of *The Cattle Raid of Cooley* is missing the hurley text. The story is believed to have been handed down through oral storytelling, with linguistic features suggesting an eighth century origin. Nevertheless, the first definitive date with hurley included has been used—c1160.

Cattle Raid of Cooley is contained within *Lebor na hUidre* (*Book of the Dun Cow*).[54] Dated to before 1106, linguistic criteria date the story to well before.[55] To maintain fidelity, and in the absence of further evidence, the *Lebor na hUidre* manuscript is used for dating the ball game. The manuscript also contains a similar, shorter version of Cú Chulainn and the princes. Hurling balls and sticks are mentioned, but there is no goal.[56]

The *Lebor na hUidre* manuscript contains another gem: the earliest mention of driving a ball into a hole with a stick: "When they played Shoot-the Goal it was Cú Chulainn who filled the hole with his shots, and they were helpless against him. When it was their turn to shoot at the hole, all together, he turned them aside single-handed and not one ball got in … When they played the Stripping-Game he stripped them all stark naked. They couldn't even pluck the brooch from his cloak."[57] The seventh century *Book of Aicill* also references bats and holes, but the ball is struck *from* "the hurling hole to the place of the *grifid*." The version in the c1160 *Book of Leinster* lends greater consistency. There is clearly a variant where the object is to get the ball into a hole:

"Thrice fifty boys at one end of the green and a single boy at the other, and the single boy won the victory at the goal and at hurling from the thrice fifty boys. When it was at hole-play … and it was their turn to drive and his to keep guard, he would catch the thrice fifty balls just outside of the hole, and not one went by him into the hole. When it was their turn to keep guard and his to drive, he would send the thrice fifty balls into the hole without fail, and the boys were unable to ward them off."[58]

~

The English monk Ælfric Bata mentions a stick and ball game in his *Colloquies*, a textbook of communication skills, written in Canterbury,

54 The Royal Irish Academy, Dublin: MS 23, E 25: Cat. No. 1229. *Lebor na hUidre*. Before 1106. In: Kinsella T. (trans.), *The Táin: From the Irish Epic Táin Bó Cúailnge*, Oxford University Press, 1970.

55 While the story appears to be much older, work commenced on the *Lebor na hUidre* manuscript c1075–1100.

56 Kinsella, T., *The Táin: From the Irish Epic Táin Bó Cúailnge*, Oxford University Press, Oxford, 1970. pp. 74–76.

57 Ibid, p. 82.

58 Dunn, J. (trans.)., *The Ancient Epic Tale Táin Bó Cúalnge*. David Nutt, London, 1914. p. 55.

c1000.[59,60] Set in a monastic school, one scene shows the boys tiring of their studies.

> **Boy 1:** Master, may we play for a while!
> **Teacher:** Yes, you may, because it is a festival. I now give you permission to play until the evening signal.
> **Boy 2:** Now it's good for us to be alive! Let's all go together to play outdoors with our staffs and our ball or hoop.
> **Boy 3:** You, boy, lend me a staff, and I will give you back two staffs at once, if you wish.
> **Boy 4:** I have enough. And if you want to play hoop with me, I'll give you a whip so we can both play, taking turns. If you want to play with a ball, I'll lend you both my ball and my staff to play with.[61]

The earliest mention of ball sport in English history is a stick and ball game. It is clearly well established and popular; some boys have more than one staff. *Colloquies* was shocking in its day, scandalously portraying monastic sadism and paedophilia. When a boy confesses to stealing, the monk orders two boys to beat him with rods: "One boy should stand on the right side of his arse and the other on the left. Hit him on the arse and back by turns. Flog him well first, and I'll do it after."[62] There is no mercy. "Hit harder you fool! He's making fun of your blows. He doesn't feel them at all." When the boy cries that he is about to die, the monk snaps back, "You're not dead yet." Later, another boy moans, "I don't have breeches, except for the ones bloodied when I was recently beaten with rods."[63] When a monk asks a boy to "come here right away, kiss me, and put your hands around my neck and give me a kiss", the boy deftly declines.[64] It is not an isolated incident. The monks of Bata's

---

59 Stevenson, W.H. (ed.)., *Early Scholastic Colloquies*. The Clarendon Press, Oxford, 1929. p. 32.

60 Bata was a monk at Winchester. Winchester College was an early adopter of football and developed its own rules.

61 In the Latin original, staff is *baculus*, pl. *baculis*, and ball is *pila*.

62 Gwara, S., Porter. W.D. (eds.)., *Anglo-Saxon Conversations: The Colloquies of Ælfric Bata*. Boydell Press, Woodbridge, 1997. p. 167.

63 Dumitrescu, I.A., *Violence, Performance and Pedagogy in Ælfric Bata's Colloquies*. Exemplaria, 2011, 23:1, p. 72.

64 Ibid, p. 73.

monastery regularly order boys to accompany them alone to the toilet. Requests are complicit.

> "You, my little brother, come with me to the privy."
> "Sir, I don't dare to go with you without my master's permission."
> "You're lying, for sure!"
> "I'm not lying, believe me."
> "I'll ask him now. Brother, sir, is this boy allowed to go with me to my necessity?"
> "He may indeed, dearest friend."[65]

One boy trapped in a privy with a monk blesses his faculties: "Thank God I'm not blind or too drunk."[66] Ecclesiastical authorities make a carefully worded attempt to expunge rampant pederasty in monasteries in the *Regularis Concordia*, c972: "Neither brothers nor abbots should embrace youths or little boys or thoughtlessly kiss them."[67] Tacit becomes explicit: "A monk should not presume to lead away any of the boys or youth for a private indulgence, not even on the pretence of a spiritual matter … nor should the teacher himself have the liberty to go away with any single boy without a third nearby as a witness."[68] The rod and whip are ever close in Bata's satire. Written over a millennium ago, the prose remains relevant and fresh: "Beware, and be careful, and grab your books quickly, and read and sing before he comes here, lest he find us idle or kidding around when [he] comes. I'm warning you. There! He's standing behind the gate now, and he's listening to whether we're reading or singing anything. And look, he's here right now!"[69]

It is unclear when carrying games like folk football or predominantly kicking games first appear. One would expect carrying, kicking, or combined games to predate the use of a stick, and perhaps it was so prior to available records. While carrying and kicking were clearly combined—one dominating the other according to region—it is possible all three intersected. The later evolution of ball games appears to be

65 Ibid, p. 75.
66 Ibid, p. 76.
67 Ibid, p. 74.
68 Ibid, p. 75.
69 Ibid, p. 82.

from stick to carrying to kicking. Combined carrying and kicking games evolve into the seven codes of football, which allow varying degrees of handling and carrying. Handling-only games evolve into sports such as basketball, volleyball, handball, and water polo. Modern stick and ball varieties eclipse both. Major sports include baseball, hockey, cricket, tennis, snooker, ice hockey, and golf.

While the Normans poorly penetrate Scotland, they exert considerable influence there from c1113, especially in the Borders. As such, they are likely to shape Scottish games of the era. In Ireland, Viking suzerainty ends after the Battle of Clontarf in 1014. A hundred and fifty years of balmy independence follows. Then the Normans arrive. They spread quickly, exerting huge cultural influence. Do they bring a ball game?

CHAPTER TWO
1100–1299

The illustration in the mid-twelfth century manuscript has no haloed green Cuthbert. The Vikings have long ploughed off, the Normans cross-pollinated: the illustrator is unlikely to know anything about the ball sports of five hundred years before. The manuscript's game should be regarded as contemporary. The ball game in the tenth century *Historia Brittonum* differs from an early thirteenth century version of the story by French poet Robert de Boron.[1] The Welsh wizard boy is now the sorcerer Merlin.[2] When the king's men find him with a "great company of boys" he is *choulloient* with a *croche*. *Choulloient* is Old French for "they played at *soule*", *croche* is a shepherd's crook.[3] In 944, the wizard boy is playing an unspecified ball game; by c1200, Merlin is playing a stick and ball game. Like Cuthbert. In 1125, William of Malmesbury tells the story of Venus as a statue.[4] It is based on an older—possibly Romano-British—story, but no reference exists in his work. A recently married young senator calls his friends together to feast:

"When by moderate drinking they had excited hilarity, they went out into the field to promote digestion either by leaping, or hurling, or some other exercise. The master of the banquet, who was leader of the game, called for a ball to play with, and … placed the wedding ring on the outstretched finger of a brazen statue … but when almost all the others had attacked him alone, tired with the violence of the exercise, he left off playing first, and going to resume his ring, he saw the finger of the statue clenched fast in the palm."

---

1 Gaston B.P., Ulrich. J. (eds.)., *Merlin: Roman en Prose du XIIIe siècle*, by Robert de Boron. Librairie de Firmin, Didot et C., Paris, 1886. p. 43.

2 The wizard boy is first recast as Merlin by Geoffrey of Monmouth c 1136. Monmouth makes no mention of balls. Wright. N. (ed.)., *The Historia Regum Brittaniae of Geoffrey of Monmouth*. 4 Vols. D.S. Brewer, Cambridge, 1985. Vol. 1. p. 140. ln. 438.

3 Gillmeister, H., *Golf on the Rhine: On the Origins of Golf, with Sidelights on Polo*. The International Journal of the History of Sport, 2002, 19:1, p. 2.

4 Giles, J.A., *William of Malmesbury's Chronicles of the Kings of England*. Henry G. Bohn, London, 1847. p. 232.

The story tells us much. Assuming he is not referring to throwing things for fun, they are playing a ball game called hurling, played with multiple players. Sticks are unmentioned, and may not be used, as in Cornish hurling. The senator is the leader of the game, is singled out, and is first to quit the game. But translations can be misleading. In Latin it reads: "They go out into the field to lighten their full stomachs either by jumping, throwing, or by some other force. He himself … the standard bearer of the game, asked for the ball … he was the first to remove himself."[5] That is all that is said of the game. Yet another problem arises. The Latin text is edited from an earlier manuscript. But which one? Several survive. Was some of the ball game edited out? Perhaps the translation used the earliest manuscript. Perhaps not. William of Malmesbury is believed to have been born in Sherbourne, Dorset, where hurling is played. Did he deliberately change throwing to hurling? One can only dig so deep before hitting stone.

William Fitzstephen's c1180 biography of St Thomas Becket contains an encomium to twelfth century London, and is the richest surviving description of the city at that time.[6] A chapter covers sports, as written by John Stow in 1598, the earliest known translation from the original Latin: "In the holy days all sommer the youth are exercised in leaping, dancing, shooting, wrastling, casting the stone, and practising their shieldes: the maydens trippe it with their timbrelles [tambourine], and daunce as long as they can be."[7] It includes an early account of a modern ball game. For over two hundred years, sources have translated *ball game* as *football game*, to the point it has become received wisdom.[8] It is universally cited as the first reference to football in England, and is so baked in as to demand scrutiny. While the original Fitzstephen text is lost, five copies from the Middle Ages have survived. Four contain the section on games and pastimes. The fifth, c1380, omits the section but is worth mentioning. The copyist had a poor knowledge of Latin and, "simply copied what he thought he read in his original without regard to linguistic accuracy

---

5 Stubbs, W., *Willelmi Malmesbiriensis Monachi De Gestis Regum Anglorum.* 2 Vols. Eyre and Spottiswoode, London, 1887. Vol. 1. p. 256.

6 Jenkins, J., *St Thomas Becket and Medieval London.* History, 2020, 105:367, p. 655.

7 Stow, J., *A Survay of London.* John Wolfe, London, 1598. p. 69.

8 Stubbs, W., *Willelmi Malmesbiriensis Monachi De Gestis Regum Anglorum.* 2 Vols. Eyre and Spottiswoode, London, 1887. Vol. 1. p. 214.

… Of even greater significance, however, are the compiler's efforts to amend his text to reflect something of the fourteenth-century London with which he was familiar."[9] The scribe makes errors and modernises the manuscript. Nevertheless, he copies from the only manuscript of London origins, c1321–1325, the one most likely to be faithful to the original.

The Latin text of the London manuscript reads: "*Praeterea, quotannis, die quae dicitur 'Carnilevaria' ut a puerorum ludis incipiamus … Post Prandium exit in campos omnis juventus urbis ad ludum pilae celebrem. Singulorum studiorum scholares suam habent pilam.*"[10] "Moreover, every year on the day called Carnival to begin with the games of the children … After lunch the entire youth of the city goes to the fields for the famous game of ball. The scholars of each study have their own ball."

Ludum pilae celebrem means celebrated ball game, *suam habent pilam* they have their own ball. *Pilam* is ball. No mention of football. It continues: "*singulorum officiorum urbis exercitores suam singuli polam in manibus.*" "The followers of the various city guilds each have a pole in their hands." In the first passage, *polam* has arguably been mistranslated as *pilam*. *Polam* is pole. Even without the translation, the followers each carry a pole for the game, and each class—rather than each person—has their own ball. They are not playing football; they are playing a stick and ball game, probably against the scholars. It makes sense: there are repeated contemporary references to stick and ball games, but none to football. Besides, this is c1180. Football is not mentioned until 1302, the first Shrovetide football game in 1373, and an annual Shrovetide game in 1539. Even then, if the earliest manuscript is used to date Fitzstephen's game, it takes place in c1321. Perhaps the mistranslation is a deliberate attempt to change a stickball game to the now popular game of football.

Stow's 1598 printed translation is baffling. The Latin text he uses is essentially the same; he too uses *pilam* rather than *polam*.[11] His translation is abridged but includes, rather than omits, stick (as bastion):

9 Kleineke, H., *Carleton's book: William FitzStephen's 'Description of London' in a late fourteenth-century common-place book*. Historical Research, 2001, 74:183, p. 119.

10 *Liber Custumarum*. In: Riley, H.T., Monumenta Gildhallæ Londoniensis. 3 Vols. Longman, Green, Longman, and Roberts, London, 1860. Vol. 2. Part 1. p. 11.

11 Stow, J., *A Survay of London*. John Wolfe, London, 1598. p. 480.

"Every yeare also at Shrovetueseday … the schoole boyes do bring cockes of the game to their Mayster … after dinner, all the youthes goe into the fieldes, to play at the ball. The schollers of every schoole have their ball (or bastion) in their hands."[12,13] Apprentices are out, but stick (bastion) remains: the students carry one or the other. Stow also omits "celebrated" (*celebrem*). What is consistent is that Stow and the Latin text mention Shrove Tuesday (*Carnilevaria*). In other words, Fitzstephen is saying that Shrove Tuesday stick and ball games are an annual event. John Strype's 1720 expanded and updated version of Stow's *Survay of London* retains bastion but includes *polam* in the Latin text, presumably because he had gone to the original source and believed that Stow had erred in using *pilam*.[14]

A fault line appears in a 1767 book on the life of Henry II. An overview of Fitzstephen casually mentions that "Among their diversions in time of peace he mentions cock-fighting and foot-ball."[15] Cracks spread in a 1772 translation of Fitzstephen's book. Bastions are omitted, and a critical line translates *ludum pilae celebrem* as "the famous game of foot-ball."[16] Just like that. An 1813 book reinforces the notion. Quoting Strype's "Ball or Bastion in their hands", it adds that, "it should seem that Foot-ball is meant here."[17] The myth is masoned in William Thoms's 1842 edition of Stow. He includes Stow's Latin translation, and cross-references it with one of the four original manuscripts *Lansdowne 398/2*, written in the late fourteenth or early fifteenth century. Thoms fudges, including *pilam* and omitting bastion. A footnote acknowledges Strype's *polam*, adding that the Lansdowne manuscript substitutes *pilam/polam in manibus*, for the ambiguous *suam fere singuli*: "nearly everyone has their own". History crumbles as Thomas translates *lusum pilae celebrem* to "the well-

12 Ibid, p. 68.

13 Bastion from the Anglo-Norman baston (plural bastions) meaning stick or staff. Later editions change it to baston.

14 Strype, J., *A Survey of the Cities of London and Westminster.* 2 Vols. Churchill, A., Knapton, J., Knaplock, R., et al, London, 1720. Vol. 1. p. 247.

15 Lyttelton, G., *The History of the Life of King Henry the Second.* 5 Vols. W. Sandby and J. Dodsley, London, 1767. Vol. 2. p. 316.

16 Pegge, S., *Fitz-Stephen's Description of the City of London.* B. White, London, 1772. p. 46.

17 Ellis, H. (ed.), *Observations on Popular Antiquities*, by J. Brand. 3 Vols. Rivington, Wilkie and Robinson, John Walker., et al, 1813. Vol. 1. p. 62. First published in 1777, the previous two editions do not mention Strype's passage.

known game of foot-ball."[18] The error divides and multiplies. Hereon in, Fitzstephen is describing football.

Stow aside, all the texts describe the game as well-known, famous, or celebrated. The sport, the fixture, or both? That Fitzstephen subsequently adds that grandees attend the game suggests a celebrated fixture. Celebrated enough for Fitzstephen not to mention the ball game played. Coincidentally, the next reference to a ball game is in the second Bible Window of Canterbury Cathedral, where Thomas Becket was murdered in 1170. The stained-glass window, c1180–1220, has a panel called the Six Ages of Man. A boy is depicted holding a hooked stick and a cricket-sized ball. The figures are nobility, this boy is no shepherd. The age of youth defined by a stick and ball game suggests it is not only widespread, well-known, and popular, but that it is the predominant ball sport in England. The celebrated sport.

The stick game is delighted. Supreme. Sovereign. She tosses a ball from hand to hand, graces the world with her irresistible smile. Nine of the first ten references in Britain and Ireland to specify a sport refer to her. There might be a tenth. An English manuscript that may be as old as 1025 depicts a child with a woman and a man, presumably his parents.[19] The child has thrown two small balls in the air, and each adult has a ball. Another leaf is ambiguous. Abraham's sons Ishmael and Isaac stand outside a palace, tossing balls or possibly oranges in the air.[20] Isaac may be juggling, while Ishmael is holding a long stick, its end lost from view. Is it a stick and ball game? Either way, the first folio constitutes the oldest portrayal of ball play in modern European history.

In medieval Britain, folk football is a popular pursuit, often played on feast days. Quite when it began is unclear. It is a perplexing truth that the names early ball games went by are unknown. The forefather of the various codes of football was not called mob or folk football. It is widely held to have descended from *harpastum*. True, carrying the ball is the principal mode of conveyance, but while *harpastum* involves limited numbers playing within a circumscribed space, folk football involves two sides from neighbouring villages or opposite ends of a

18 Thoms, W.J., *The Survey of London, Written in the Year 1598, by John Stow*. Whittaker and Co., London, 1842. p. 214.

19 British Library: Cotton MS Claudius B IV, *Old English Hexateuch*, c1025–1099, fol. 102r.

20 Ibid, fol. 35v.

town, battling for dominance over long distances. Unlike *harpastum*, folk football has few rules. Local variations and kicking of the ball undoubtedly occur. The aim is to drive the ball by whatever means possible to a goal, usually a prominent landmark in the town or local countryside—a well, a gate, a church porch, a bridge—miles from their opponents' goal. Brute strength is the dominant driver, though speed has its advantages, perhaps teamwork too. There is little if any strategy. The game allows rivals to legitimately kick, punch, poke, bite, elbow, shove, and knee each other. It is more like the Spartan game, where youths vie for territorial supremacy.

It may be a version of the sport that causes a boy's death in the twelfth century, though there is no mention of kicking, carrying, sticks, or even a ball. The *Chronicon Montis Sereni* records that in 1137: "It happened in the game, which is called the children's game, in which he himself was participating, that a certain boy was trampled to death."[21] You need a mob game or similar to be trampled to death. If it is an early reference to a ball game, Britain cannot lay claim. The tragedy occurs in Germany. There are other early German references. Around 1050, pupils play unspecified ball games in a monastery school, while "Maidens fair, tossing the ball", signals the onset of spring for German songwriter Walther von der Vogelweide, c1200.[22,23] The German book *Dialogue on Miracles*, c1219–1223, relates the story of a boy who is given a magic stone by the Devil. The stone turns him into a genius, but he falls ill and dies. His soul is carried away by demons who hurl it down a valley, "as if they were playing ball."[24] In 1147, a French monastery is gifted seven *ballone*.[25] They are likely to be used for playing catch, a common pursuit in the cloisters of France. A theologian substantiates this c1160. During the Feast of Fools,

---

21 Gießauf, J., Iber, W.M., Knoll, H. (eds.)., *Fußball, Macht und Diktatur: Streiflichter auf den Stand der historischen Forschung*. StudienVerlag, Innsbruck, Austria, 2014. p. 65.

22 *Monastic Research Bulletin*, 2009, 15, p. 27. https://www.york.ac.uk/media/borthwick/documents/publications/MRB15.pdf. Accessed 2 February 2024.

23 Phillips, W.A., *Selected Poems of Walter von der Vogelweide the Minnesinger*. Smith, Elder, & Co., London, 1896. p. 56.

24 Von E Scott, H., Swinton Bland, C.C. (eds.)., *Caesarius, The Dialogue on Miracles*. Harcourt, Brace and Company, New York, 1929. Vol. 1. p. 40.

25 Endrei, W., Zolnay, L., *Fun and Games in Old Europe*. Ravasz, K., Gaster. B. (trans.). Corvina, Budapest, 1986. p. 100.

Bishops and Archbishops customarily play sports in the monasteries and "demean themselves so far as to play ball."[26]

~

It is the late fifth century, and the Romans are sniffling with nostalgia. Some Britons sense an opportunity, the pragmatic agonise over the power vacuum, others predict anarchy. Candidates swagger across Europe. Franks, Angles, Visigoths, Ostrogoths, Saxons, Jutes, Vandals. The population of southwest Britain is fortunate, well removed from advancing hordes, but it may not always be so. What to do? Where to go? Join the Picts in Scotland? Er, no. Ireland and its good-natured raiders? Er, no. Northwest France? Armorica sounds alluring. I'm packed, get the ball. By 570, there is a bishopric and Armorica is rebadged Britannia. Land of the Britons.[27] Cornish migrants settle in southwest Britannia, bringing their tongue with them.[28] Before they diverge in the eighth century, Breton and Cornish are the same language, philologically distinct from other Celtic languages.[29] The region is still called *Cornouaille*. Do the Cornish migrate with a ball game that branches into *soule*? Does *soule* then spread eastward to what will become Normandy and Picardy, where it is later played?

Lambert of Ardres is born c1140.[30] He enters the priesthood and becomes chaplain of the Picardy town of Ardres, thirty-four miles south of Dover.[31] From 1198 to 1206, he writes *The History of the Counts of Guines and the Lords of Ardres*. In one passage, Count Eustace of Guines (c1036–c1064) is told the story of Rainier of Boulogne, an utter tyrant whose rule leads to violent unrest.[32] According to the sole English translation of the original Latin: "... one man was beaten at

26 Longmuir, J., Donaldson, D. (eds.)., *An Etymological Dictionary of the Scottish Language* by John Jamieson. 5 Vols. Alex Gardner, Paisley, 1879. Vol. 1. Under, '*Abbott of Unressoun*'; Harris, M., *Sacred Folly: A New History of the Feast of Fools*. Cornell University Press, United States, 2011. p. 54.

27 Todd, M., *The South West to AD 1000*. Routledge, Abingdon, Oxon, 2014. p. 239.

28 Ibid, p. 240.

29 Ibid, p. 240.

30 Shopkow, L. *Lambert of Ardres, The History of the Counts of Guines and Lords of Ardres*. University of Pennsylvania Press, 2001. p. 2.

31 London is sixty-eight miles from Dover.

32 The identity of Rainer of Boulogne is unclear. The story is probably a literary device to engineer a dig at his contemporary Reynold of Boulgone (c1165–1227). Other possibilities include Count Ralph of Ternois and Arras (d892), Raganar from the *Annals of Saint Bertin* (c875), or the son of Ragnar Longneck (c929).

Boulogne … Another one was torn bodily from a church at Calais and cut limb from limb and castrated, and his genitals were kicked around by girls and women, as though they were playing a game of ball."[33] The original Latin text provided in an 1855 book does not mention kicking, rather the genitals are cut off and played with in the manner of a game of ball.[34,35] The book also provides an Old French version: "*à fachon de pelotte pour jouer a la palme.*"[36] In the fashion of palm ball play. Are his genitals kicked or palmed? The English translator emphasises that subtle linguistic changes over time can profoundly affect translation. It is doubtful the braying crowd of Calais want to throw fresh genitals at each other when they can kick them; then again, the delicate organs would not last a good kicking. Whichever "sport", the date must be ascribed to when the book was written, c1198–1206.

A later extract speaks of the local pasturelands before Ardres was built. At that time the area was called Arda. In Lambert's words: "*ubi rustici homines et incompositi ad bibendum vel ad cheolandum, vel etiam herkandum, propter agri pascui largam et latam planiciem convenire solebant.*"[37] This has been translated to, "where simple and rustic men used to gather to drink, loiter, or even carouse because of the broad and wide flatness of the pastureland."[38] The essence of the Old French text is that the rustics meet to get drunk.[39] The meaning of *herkandum* is unclear. The word is never used again. In 1970, Anne Lombard-Jourdan corrects it to *mercandum*: trade.[40] A 1762 edition of Charles Du Cange's seminal glossary of Middle and Low Latin translates herkandum so: *Herpandum, vel Harpandum, voce confecta*

---

33 Shopkow, L. *Lambert of Ardres, The History of the Counts of Guines and Lords of Ardres*. University of Pennsylvania Press, 2001. p. 69.

34 "raptis membratim discerpitur, et genitalibus abscisis ad modum ludi pilæ à puellulis et mulieribus ludificatur."

35 Godefroy de Menilglaise. (ed.)., *Chronique de Guines et D'Ardre, par Lambert, Curé D'Ardre*, Jules Renouard, Paris, 1855. p. 55.

36 Ibid, p. 54.

37 Ibid, pp. 228–229.

38 Shopkow, L. *Lambert of Ardres, The History of the Counts of Guines and Lords of Ardres*. University of Pennsylvania Press, 2001. p. 134.

39 Godefroy de Menilglaise. (ed.)., *Chronique de Guines et D'Ardre, par Lambert, Curé D'Ardre*, Jules Renouard, Paris, 1855. pp. 226–228.

40 Lombard-Jourdan, A. *Du problème de la continuité: Y a-t-il une protohistoire urbaine en France*. Annales Histoire, Sciences Sociale. 1970. 24:4, p. 1140.

ex Harpastum:[41] "*Herpandum,* or *Harpandum*, in the finished voice from *Harpastum.*" *Harpastum.* The Roman carrying game. It adds: "*quod loco citato vel maxime convenit*": "which is most suitable for the place cited." The broad and wide flatness of the pastureland: an ideal space for ball games.

There is more. The 1855 Latin–Old French edition of Lambert includes clarification notes. Having translated *cheolandum* as loiter in the text, it is referred to as meaning *cheolare*: "to play at choule, ball that is pushed with the foot, or ball that is blown up with the stick. In Brittany, soule ... The game of soule is very popular with Low-Bretons."[42] Anne Lombard-Jourdan defines *choleandum* as "*jouer à la soule"*.[43] Playing at *soule*. Using Lambert's *choleandum* as a reference point, the original Du Cange glossary of 1678 describes *cheolare* as, "to propel the bladder-ball with the foot, a game familiar to our villagers in Picardy."[44] So, by 1678 the game is played with the foot, at least in Picardy. A 1766 book by Du Cange complicates matters. Other terms are included, implying the game is still played with sticks: "C*houlla* or *choule* is a game where a wooden ball is propelled with a stick."[45] *Choule* is a Gallic word, suggesting Gaulish origins. *Crossare* is a curved stick used to propel a ball,[46] *clicha* a wooden ball,[47] and *chucu* a wooden or ivory ball.[48] Not the type you would kick. Du Cange adds that the old northern French dialect word *choulloient*—they played at *choule*—derives from *cheolandum.* In old Parisian French the word changes to *soulaient*—they played at *soule*. Perhaps they were drinking, loitering, and playing *harpastum* after all. Or *chouler à la crosse*. Or both.

---

41 Carpentier, P. (ed.), Du Fresne Du Cange. C, *Glossarium mediae et infimae Latinitatis.* 10 Vols. Fratrum de Tournes, Geneveni, 1678. 1762 edition. Vol. 3. p. 617.

42 Godefroy de Menilglaise. (ed.), *Chronique de Guines et D'Ardre, par Lambert, Curé D'Ardre*, Jules Renouard, Paris, 1855. p. 537.

43 Lombard-Jourdan, A. *Du problème de la continuité: Y a-t-il une protohistoire urbaine en France*. Annales Histoire, Sciences Sociale, 1970, 24:4, p. 1140.

44 Du Cange. C., *Glossarium ad Scriptores Mediae et Infimae Latinitatis.* 10 Vols. Ludovicum Billaine, Paris, 1678. Vol. 1. p. 962.

45 Carpentier. P. (ed.), Du Fresne Du Cange. C, *Glossarium Novum ad Scriptores Medii ÆVI.* 3 Vols. Le Breton, Saillant, Desaint, Paris, 1766. Vol. 1. p. 950.

46 Ibid, p. 1209.

47 Ibid, p. 994.

48 Ibid, p. 955.

To summarise, if Lambert is writing about pre-Ardres peasants playing choule and *harpastum*, the text translates to: "where rustics gathered to drink and play *choule*, or even *harpastum*, because of the broad and wide flatness of the pastureland." Robert de Boron mentions *choulloient* in his poem *Merlin,* not long after Lambert's book. It is unclear if the *soule* in Lambert's book is a stick or a kicking version, no mention is made of either. And the date? The passage relates to a time when the region is yet to be called Ardres. An abbey was founded in *Ardres* in 1027, and a family was allied to the Barons of *Ardres* in 1028, so it was before then.[49] It is unknown when *harpastum* was played until, but it is more likely to be the tenth or eleventh centuries than the late twelfth, when Lambert wrote his book. Did *harpastum* overlap with *soule*, or is it Lambert's whimsy? Without further evidence, the late twelfth century must be used as the timepoint the games are played, rendering *harpastum* fanciful.

Lambert is not the first to mention *soule*: a Latin manuscript from 1152 reads, "When the inhabitants of Fontanæ burgi … in the middle fields … had gathered for a certain game, commonly called o Houle."[50] The 1776 edition of Du Cange corrects *Houle* to *choulla*.[51] It is an intriguing passage. No mention is made of how it is played, only that it is well-known and requires a field to play in. And the town of fountains? Tucked away in northeast Normandy, twenty-six miles from the English Channel, lies the village of Fontaine-le-Bourg. If you close your eyes, you can see them playing from the belfry of the eleventh century church.

A third twelfth century reference is found in 1170: "*Une pelote urent, s-n furent zoleur*", "*soule* played with a ball".[52,53] Intriguingly, it is contained within a poem by an Anglo-Norman poet. After Bata and Malmesbury, it is only the third literary reference to a ball game in

49 Harbaville, L.J., *Mémorial historique et archéologique du département du Pas-de-Calais.* 2 Vols. Topino, Pas-de-Calais, 1842. Vol. 2. p. 48.

50 Carpentier, P., (ed.)., Du Fresne Du Cange. C, *Glossarium Mediæ et infirmæ latinitatis.* 10 Vols. L. Favre, Niort, France, 1885. Vol. 4. p. 254–255.

51 Carpentier, P., (ed.)., Du Fresne Du Cange. C, *Glossarium Manuale ad Scriptores Mediæ et infirmæ latinitatis.* 6 Vols. Le Breton, Saillant, Desaint, Paris, 1776. Vol. 4. p. 92.

52 Pope, M.K., Reid, T.B.W. (eds.)., *The Romance of Horn.* Thomas. 2 Vols. Anglo-Norman Society, 1955. Vol. 1. p. 162. ln. 4884.

53 *Soule* may or may not be referenced in one of the dozens of adaptations of Reynard the Fox, who first appears in Nivard of Ghent's *Ysengrimus*, in 1152.

English history.[54] Why does he specify that it is played with a ball? Is it a variant, played without a stick? Football. It would be the first reference in history, one hundred and thirty-two years before the second. No one knows if there was an early name for the stick game played in mainland Britain. All the evidence points to *soule* being a stick and ball game, possibly superseding a folk football game in popularity. It remains a stick game for several hundred years before it becomes a folk football game, in France anyway. The area around Ardres was already part of a vast territory called Normandy, ruled by Normans since 911. Normans are a mixture of Norsemen—who first arrived in 845—and local Franks and Gauls. Norse Vikings may have introduced ball games, but there is no evidence they had one. Was there a pre-Roman game in the area, which absorbed elements of *harpastum*, then further evolved over time? It has been suggested the Normans introduced England to the stick game of *soule* in 1066, but Ælfric Bata mentions a stick game c1000. Where do stick games in the British Isles originate? The Romans had no stick game. Was it introduced by the Angles, Saxons, or Jutes in the fifth century? Of the Vikings, only the Icelandic branch had a stick game. Was it them?

~

The thirteenth century awakens with Layamon's poem *Brut*. The section on King Arthur includes a great feast. When it is over, Arthur and all his knights, chieftains, earls, bishops, and barons leave town and head to the countryside, where they "spread over the fields" for a three-day sports festival. Events include riding, wrestling, leaping, archery, foot races, and sword fighting. Spectacular prizes are on offer for the winners of each event: gold, silver, land, castles. The nobility of the realm have gathered and "All the queens … and all the ladies, leaned over the walls, to behold the knights, and the folk play."[55] There is one more event. "*Sūme heo drivē balles, wide ȝeond þa feldes.*"[56,57] "Some they drove

54 This means that ten of the first twelve references to a designated sport in Britain and Ireland are stick and ball games.

55 Madden, F. (ed.)., *Layamon's Brut, Or Chronicle of Britain*. 2 Vols. Society of Antiquaries of London, 1847. Vol. 1. p. 616.

56 Ibid, p. 616.

57 Þ, pronounced 'th' as in *thick*, is an Old English character and is retained in quotes. ȝ pronounced "zh" as in *collision* is another Old English character and is also retained in quotes.

balls wide, across the fields."[58] This may refer to any number of balls sport, including stick and ball games. There is an argument for an early form of golf. Footballs can also be driven. This from one of Alexander Barclay's eclogues: "The sturdie plowmen, lusty, stronge and bolde, Overcommeth the wynter with dryvynge the fote ball, Forgettynge labour and many a grevous fall."[59] Irrespective of the game, Layamon's *Brut* is an historic sporting moment, for it contains the earliest mention of *ball* in the English language.

The only known manuscript of the Icelandic *Egil's Saga* dates to c1230 but refers to the years 850–1000. Egil has anger issues. Losing a ball game, he kills his opponent with an axe. Egil is six years old.[60] In the next scene, his father "goes berserk" during a ball game. He kills Egil's friend, then grabs ten-year-old Egil, who is saved by his old foster mother. She manages to dodge his father and jump from the cliff into the sea, but he throws a boulder that hits her between the shoulder blades, "and neither she nor the rock ever came to the surface again."[61] The game is believed to be *knattleikur* (ball game), a stick and ball game peculiar to Iceland. Facets of the game can be gleaned from several sagas. Sides are picked and players line up to face each other for man-to-man marking, bats (*knatttré*) are used to both strike and catch the ball (*knottr*), which is small and hard and can be both thrown and caught, they are playing within the confines of a field, where the ball can go out of play, and they are playing in winter.[62] Except for the throwing component, these are all are features of modern Irish hurling.

Knattleikur is popular. A recurrent theme in sagas is the presence of big crowds. At least seven sagas include a bat and ball game, though few use the term *knattleikur*. Several sagas mention a single bat, which an opposing player can take.[63] Did the Vikings invent *knattleikur* after

---

58 Layamon borrowed shamelessly from *Roman de Brut* c1155, by the Norman author Wace. *Roman de Brut* has no driven balls, though there is throwing of the stone. Weiss, J.E., *Wace's Roman de Brut: A History of the English*. University of Exeter Press, 1999. p. 264. ln. 10528.

59 Fairholt, F.W. (ed.)., *The Cytezen and Uplondyshman: An Eclogue By Alexander Barclay*. Richards, London, 1847. p. 5.

60 Pálsson, H., Edwards, P. (trans)., *Egil's Saga*. Penguin Books Ltd, Harmondsworth, Middlesex, 1973. pp. 93–94.

61 Ibid, p. 95.

62 Gunnell, T., *The Relationship between Icelandic "Knattleikur" and Early Irish Hurling*. Folklore of Ireland Society, 2010, 80, p. 54.

63 Gogosz, R., *Rules and Aspects: Study with the Special focus on Saga-Age Iceland*. Unpublished PhD thesis, University of Rzeszów, Rzeszów, Poland, 2016. p. 139.

they settled in Iceland in 874, then spread it abroad? Did the Irish adopt their game, or adapt their own? Several lines of evidence suggest that *knattleikur* has Irish origins. The first mention of hurling being played refers to the seventh century, in contrast with *knattleikur* in the ninth. Irish texts provide powerful evidence, with references in three seventh century books: *Senchus Már*, *Mellbretha,* and *Book of Aicill*. *Egil's Saga* is the earliest extant manuscript to mention *knattleikur* and covers the oldest saga. No textual analytics suggest a date earlier than the thirteenth century manuscript. Taking into account the oldest available manuscripts, *Egil's Saga* was written c1230, and *Lebor na hUidre* c1106.

No contemporary reports of a stick game survive from thirteenth century Iceland. If the game has died out by then, the dates in *Egil's Saga* may be accurate, passed down in an oral tradition stemming from the date of the story, though this still fixes the game to the ninth century at the earliest. If *knattleikur* was created by Icelandic Vikings, one would expect it to spread to mainland Scandinavia. There is no evidence mainland Vikings had a stick and ball game before or after Iceland is settled.[64] Mainland Vikings plunder Ireland before Iceland is settled. More compelling still is the evidence that large numbers of Viking settlers live in the Scottish Isles and Ireland before settling in Iceland, exposing them to hurling in its native environment. The final point is remarkable. DNA and other evidence demonstrate that around forty-three per cent of original settlers in Iceland were from Ireland and Scotland:[65,66,67]

It is known that Scottish and Irish people are transported to Iceland. A proportion of them are women married to Vikings and their offspring.

---

64 Gunnell, T., *The Relationship between Icelandic "Knattleikur" and Early Irish Hurling*. Folklore of Ireland Society, 2010, 80, p. 54.

65 Ebeneserdóttir, S.S., et al. *Ancient genomes from Iceland reveal the making of a human population*. Science (2018) 360: 1028–1032; Plomp, K.A., Gestsdóttir, K.D., Price., Collard. M. (2021) *The Composition of the Founding Population of Iceland: A New Perspective From 3D Analyses of Basicranial Shape*. Plos ONE 16(2): e0246059; Helgason et al. *Estimating Scandinavian and Gaelic Ancestry in the Male Settlers of Iceland*. American Journal of Human Genetics, 2000, 67:3, 697–717.

66 A non-DNA based study demonstrated that in the founding population of Iceland, individuals from southern Britain were present in larger numbers than the Irish and Scottish combined: Plomp, K.A., Gestsdóttir, K.D., Price., Collard. M. (2021) *The Composition of the Founding Population of Iceland: A New Perspective From 3D Analyses of Basicranial Shape*. Plos ONE 16(2): e0246059.

67 In a similar manner, the founding European population of Greenland were a mixture of Celts and Vikings.

Gaelic peoples have usually been cast as thralls, but many appear to move voluntarily, free settlers and relatives and friends of inter-married women.[68] A staggering sixty-six percent of founding female settlers are Gaels. Thirty per cent of males are Gaels, a significant minority. All told, around half the population are Gaels. The diaspora is reflected in today's European Icelandic population. Seventy-five per cent of the patrilineal ancestry is from Scandinavia, while sixty-two per cent of their matrilineal ancestry is from the British Isles, principally Scotland and Ireland.[69] It is inconceivable the Irish do not bring hurling with them. While thraldom thrives, and Gaelic men are more likely to be buried in unmarked graves, many have traditional Viking burials. There is sufficient cultural cachet to propagate hurling.

Taken together, there is strong evidence that any stick game played in Iceland is an early version of hurling. The closing argument is simple: which of the two genetically distinct Icelandic stock is more likely to have invented the stick and ball game *knattleikur*, those from a country with a stick and ball game, or those from a country without one? Similarly, which stock introduced the oral culture of storytelling to Iceland, those from a country with an oral tradition, or those from a country without one? Another custom that arose in the thirteenth century is Norse mythology, forged by Snorri Sturlson, the same poet who wrote *Egil's Saga*. Ireland's oral narrative tradition predates those seventh century texts, developing centuries before Iceland was inhabited.[70] Ireland's rich mythological orality was indisputably shipped to Iceland. Was an Hiberno–Norse mythology created, underpinning the emergence of Icelandic sagas and Norse mythology, handed down the generations to Sturlson via a culture of storytelling?[71,72] The argument stands. Which stock is more likely to have created the conditions for an emergent mythology, the Irish or the Vikings?

---

68 Karras, R.M., *Slavery and Society in Medieval Scandinavia*. Yale University Press, New Haven and London, 1988. p. 49.

69 Helgason, A., Sigurðardóttir, S., Gulcher, J. R., Ward, R., Stefánsson, K. *mtDNA and the origin of the Icelanders: Deciphering signals of recent population history*. American Journal of Human Genetics, 2000, 66:3, 999–1016; Helgason, A., et al. *Estimating Scandinavian and Gaelic Ancestry in the Male Settlers of Iceland*. American Journal of Human Genetics, 2000, 67:3, 697–717.

70 Nagy, J.F., *Orality in Medieval Irish Narrative: an Overview*. Oral Tradition, 1986, 1/2, p. 272.

71 Richter, M., *Medieval Ireland and Iceland—Worlds Apart?* In: *Saluting Ivan Gurevich*. Brill, Leiden, Netherlands, 2010. p. 163–164.

72 Humphrey, A.C., *Norse-Gaelic Contacts in a Viking World: Studies in the Literature and History of Norway, Iceland, Ireland, and the Isle of Man*. In: *Scandinavian Studies*, 2020, 92:2, pp. 250–253.

A smattering of English soldiers arrive in 1169, Strongbow by invite in 1170, and Henry II in 1171. Henry grants the citizens of Bristol the right to live in, and manage on his behalf, the city of Dublin.[73] Trade links between the two cities have existed since the eleventh century, but this is something darker, reward for their assistance in subjugating the city the year before, during the Norman Invasion of Ireland.[74] Vengeance is bequeathed. On Easter Monday 1209, a crowd of Anglo-Norman Dubliners venture two miles outside the city walls to spectate and play: "The Bristolines of this Cittie, and other English inhabitants of the same, had by ancient custome a sport which they called *hurleing of balls*, and which they exercised upon Festivall Dayes. These Bristolines challenged another partie of the Cittie to hurle with them."[75] The "Birrnes" and "Tooles" clans, pushed back to the Dublin hills and Wicklow Mountains, descend to slaughter them.[76] Around three hundred men, women, and children are murdered, on what is dubbed Black Monday.[77]

What game are they playing? That it is described as an ancient sport played by Englishmen implies it is not Irish hurling.[78] Nevertheless, the account is written by an Englishman, so perhaps the resident English have picked up the Irish game. Bristol is only ten miles from Wales, separated by the Bristol Channel. Could it be *knappan*? Unlikely, as it is not an English game, and horses would be surely mentioned. Cornish hurling? The border is only ninety miles from Bristol. Unlikely. Non-Bristolian English play too, though they may have learned the rules. Ælfric Bata has already mentioned a stick game in 1000, and the sport Fitzstephen witnesses, c1180, is a stick game. The Dublin game may be played with sticks, but it is possible that *hurleing of balls* (contracted to hurling), is a

73 It is the earliest known manuscript pertaining to Dublin.

74 Martin, F.X., *Allies and an Overlord, 1169–72*. In: Cosgrove, A. (ed.), *A New History of Ireland: Volume II, Medieval Ireland 1169–1534*. Oxford University Press, 2008. p. 98.

75 Harris, W. (ed.), *The History and Antiquities of Dublin, Collected from Authentic Records and the Manuscript Collections of Sir James Ware, Knt.* Manuscript, 1678. p. 60.

76 The O'Byrne and O'Toole clans. Ware, J., *The Antiquities and History of Ireland*. E. Dobson, and M. Gunne, Dublin. p. 41.

77 In *The History and Antiquities of Dublin* James Ware reports five hundred deaths, while in *The Antiquities and History of Ireland* he reports three hundred. Walter Harris, noted for his anti-Catholic views, is known to have doctored passages in *The History and Antiquities of Dublin*.

78 The account is written four hundred years after the event, by James Ware, who may have been unaware that there was also an Irish version of hurling, confirmed in *Book of the Dun Cow* dated to before 1106. The "Bristolines" settled in Dublin from 1171 onward.

contemporary name for folk football, perhaps *the* name. After all, Cornish hurling does not use sticks. It also makes sense if it *is* an English game.

After Fitzstephen, the Dublin game is the second oldest festival day match on record. Calling it an ancient custom is confusing. Bristolines have only been there thirty-eight years. By the thirteenth century, *hurlen* has several interrelated meanings: "to rush violently or quickly", "to come into collision with", "to knock or throw forcibly", and "to drag or pull forcibly". Quick, violent, knock, pull, colliding, throw, and drag. What better way to describe folk football. *Hurlen* is a Middle English word (derived from the Low German *hurrlen*: to throw, or to dash), dating it to c1150 at the earliest.

There is another possibility. The stick used in ball games is believed to have originated as a shepherd's crook. Another French term for a shepherd's staff is *houlette.* A *houlette* is not only to secure sheep. A French–Old French dictionary defines another use: "*avec laquelle le berger lance de la terre sur ses moutons pour les faire advancer*": "with which the shepherd throws earth on his sheep to make them move forward."[79] Hurling earth. In fact, *houlette* derives from the Old French *houler.* To throw. Houler, hurling. Perhaps the Bristolines *are* playing a stick and ball game, "throwing" the ball with their sticks. Does the word hurling in the Bristoline game derive from Old French rather than Low German, a Norman name change for the existing English stick and ball game? The Irish are already playing their own sport of hurling when the Anglo-Normans invade. It is worth noting that the Gaelic name for hurling is *iománaíocht.* Hurling is the English name for the Irish game. It is almost derogatory. *Iománaíocht* is derived from *iomáin,* "driving". They are driving the ball not hurling it. The Bristolines, then, are unlikely to be using sticks, the odds are that they are carrying the ball and hurling it, just as they do in Cornish hurling. Perhaps folk football was called hurling and only the Cornish retained the name.

~

The thirteenth century is a dangerous time. The medieval threshold for violence is low, and impulsivity is high. In 1222, "neere unto hospitall of Matilde" the men of London best those of the suburbs at wrestling.[80]

---

79 Van Daele, H., *Petit Dictionnaire de l'Ancien Français.* Librairie Garnier Frères, Paris, 1940. p. 241.

80 Stow, J., *The Annales of England.* George Bishop and Thomas Adams, London, 1605. pp. 269–270.

The Bailiff of Westminster "devising to be revenged" organises a return match a week later. Not long into the game, the men of the suburbs tool up and "foullie" wound the Londoners, who are "forced to runne into the Citie." The mayor cautions against retribution, suggesting they seek reparation from the Abbot of Westminster. But this is the thirteenth century, so they go to the suburbs and "pulled downe manie houses." When the Abbot rides to London to complain, the locals steal a dozen of his horses and "cruellie" beat his men. And when the panicked Abbot slips out "a backe doore of the house" and makes his escape "by a boate on the Thames", Londoners pelt him with stones in "greate abundance." The city of London considers itself a quasi-autonomous state. No one tries it on and gets away with it. Rejoice! Be jubilant! But when the cocky ringleader tells the "great army" summoned to the Tower of London he wishes he had gone further, he is summarily hanged. "Then the Justiciar" entering the city with the army, rounds up the culprits, "whole feet and hands he caused to be cut off." Dirty work done, the king's regent steps in, removing the mayor, and erecting "a great gibbet", swaying with symbolism. "After heavy threatnings", the citizens pay Henry III "many thousand marks", and everyone knows their place.

The exquisite French manuscript, which contains the poem *Lives of Edward the Confessor* is given to Henry in 1245. The paean to the English king who ruled from 1042–1066 is one of the first to compare fortune to a ball game:

> According to fortune and her riot,
> Which in war makes of people a ball,
> According to the custom of war,
> Now to lose, and now to conquer.[81]

Now to lose? The beatified king when he dies in 1066. His execrable father-in-law manages to put his own son Harold on the throne, flagrantly ignoring the wishes of Edward, who had wanted William II, Duke of Normandy, to inherit the crown. Later that year, Edward gets his wish. And now to conquer. The Calendar of Inquisitions from the reigns of

81 Luard, H.R. (ed.)., *Lives of Edward the Confessor*. Longman, Brown, Green, Longmans, and Roberts, London, 1858. p. 195.

Henry III (1216–1272) and Edward I (1272–1307) records multiple murders. Self-defence is frequently used as a plea. Hamon chases his brother with an iron-shod fork saying, "Flee, robber, or you shall die."[82] When they reach a twenty-five-foot ditch, Nicholas turns and stabs Hamon. Adam, "given to drink", stabs William with his sword,[83] while John, chased into a dead end, mortally clubs his assailant.[84] Two watchmen, derelict in their duty, are found at home by Roger and John, who are accosted by both men and their wives with sticks. Cornering Roger they "lay upon him, took him by the private parts and would have killed him" had he not killed one with his short knife. "Adam struck Alan with his sword slant-wise across the head, so he died at once", and Roger struck John "under the eye so that he died of the blow."[85] And when Reynold takes an arrow in the testicles, he gamely pursues the archer "with cry and horn, and killed him with his sword."[86]

All manner of weapons are used: bare fists, spiked axe, hatchet, spade, stick, bow, pitcher, poleaxe, stave, lance, scythe, reaping hook, shovel, and candlestick. There is terror too. When Beatrice murders a man in Newcastle, the sheriff's clerk threatens that "having drawn her teeth, he would carnally know her against her will."[87] Misadventures are common. A man kills his wife when his knife misses the cat chewing on his hung beef, and when Richard shoots at a kite, the arrow plunges into his brother's head.[88,89] A snowball takes out a man's eye, another has his ear bitten off by a horse, and Desiderata le Champneys is accidentally dispatched by a poisoned arrow.[90,91,92]

There are ball-related deaths. In 1268, a newly married couple in Yorkshire are asked by William Selisaule for a ball, "which is the custom

---

82 *Calendar of Inquisitions Miscellaneous*. 4 Vols. The Hereford Times Limited, 1916. Vol. 1. p. 637.

83 Ibid, p. 629.

84 Ibid, p. 631.

85 Ibid, p. 632.

86 Ibid, p. 320.

87 Ibid, p. 538.

88 Ibid, p. 564.

89 Ibid, p. 578.

90 Ibid, p. 80.

91 Ibid, p. 320.

92 Ibid, p. 570.

to give."[93] Having no ball, they give him a pair of gloves as a pledge they will provide one later. A little after, others approach them for a ball. They explain they have already given a pledge. "The men of Byrun would not believe them but still asked for the said ball; and so there arose a dispute, and the wedding party, being slightly drunk assaulted the men of Byrun with axes and bows and arrows, and wounded very many." When William rushes back to appease the dispute, one of the bridal party wounds him in the chest with an arrow. The man draws again. William lunges at him, swings his stick … and mortally strikes another man who gets between them. The custom of ball giving at weddings continues for centuries. Traditionally used for playing football, this may be one of the earliest references to the game, though it is equally likely to refer to a stickball game.

Accidents begin to enter records. In Strafford, in 1266, Walter de Wyndhul and Alan de Hertil collide running for the ball.[94] Alan falls on Walter's sheathed knife. With no apparent injury they play on, then go to the tavern. When Alan's arm swells up the next day, he bizarrely attributes it to the new ale they drank. Walter applies leeches but Alan succumbs five days later. Once again, no distinction is made between a carrying/kicking game and a stick game. In 1277, a ten-year-old dies in Lincoln.[95] Robert is playing at ball (*ad pilam*) with Geoffrey when both hit the ball with their sticks (*baculis*) at the same time. Geoffrey's stick and the ball hit Robert under the ear, and he dies three days later. The stick game is referred to only as *at ball*, in all likelihood an umbrella term for ball games, though notably it is not called hurling. A similar accident near Newcastle in 1280. When Henry and David race to the ball, David's sheathed sword hits Henry's stomach, with the full force of David against the hilt. Henry clings on for five days.[96] Another accident in 1280. John and his Fleet Street neighbours are shooting at a target with crossbows. John puts a ball in his crossbow. It ricochets off a pear tree and mortally strikes William on the side of the head.[97] Finally, in 1279,

93 Ibid, p. 121.

94 Ibid, p. 567.

95 Ibid, p. 592.

96 Ibid, p. 599.

97 Ibid, pp. 597–598.

a man swings at a ball with his staff, misses, and thwacks another man's head, killing him instantly.[98]

There is a fallacy that the first mention of football (second if you adhere to the Fitzstephen myth) is contained in an allegedly historic account of a boy killed by Jews in Lincoln, in 1255. In his account, the author, Matthew Paris, makes no mention of a ball game,[99] neither does Robert of Gloucester, an Anglo-Saxon chronicler of the late thirteenth century.[100] Blatantly antisemitic,[101] the event is repeated by Chaucer, c1395, Robert Fabyan in 1516, Richard Grafton in 1569, and Raphael Holinshead in 1577. There is no ball game. The first ballad to recount the tale, in the late thirteenth century, has no ball game.[102] It is not until the 1765 ballad by Thomas Percy that "they play at the ba",[103] and not until 1806 that Hugh "kick'd the ba' wi' his right foot, and catch'd it wi' his knee."[104]

Other accidental deaths are plentiful. In Oxfordshire, in 1261, a man falls below his cart wheels, a woman falls into a vat of molten lead, a boy is crushed by a water wheel, another boy drowns in a well, and a third is bitten by a pig.[105] Other games, other deaths. In 1289, following "a great wrestling", a fight breaks out among the fighters. William Smith is floored with swords and sticks. To prevent his death, Alice Witfax throws herself on him, landing on his drawn knife.[106] A similar story in 1300. Henry Bateman and William de Gamelingey are playing *penyperche* in a tavern, in Eton.[107] They fall out. Williams grabs Henry's throat;

---

98 Hessayon, A., *Beastly Furie, and Exstreme Violence*. In: Wagg, S., Pollock, A.M. (eds.)., *The Palgrave Book of Sport, Politics and Harm*. Springer Nature Switzerland, Cham, Switzerland, 2021. p. 29.

99 Hume, A., *Sir Hugh of Lincoln*. John Russell Smith, London, 1849. pp. 7–10.

100 Ibid, p. 10.

101 Stories of the ritual killing of a Christian child were repeated both in England and abroad. Speaking of a charge made in Poland in 1407, Abraham Hume (1814–1884) writes: "It is gratifying to know, however, that in nearly all the countries of Europe, the most intelligent and distinguished Christian people regarded the accusation as a slander, from a very early period." Ibid, p. 31.

102 Dahood, R., *The Anglo-Norman 'Hugo de Lincolnia'*. The Chaucer Review, 2014, 49:1, pp. 1–38.

103 Ibid, p. 34.

104 Jamieson, R., *Popular Ballads and Songs*. J. Ballantyne and Co., Edinburgh, 1806. p. 151.

105 Jobson, A.L., *The Oxfordshire eyre roll of 1261*. Unpublished PhD thesis, University of London, 2005. pp. 72–74, 76,

106 *Calendar of Inquisitions Miscellaneous*. 4 Vols. The Hereford Times Limited, Hereford, 1916. Vol. 1. p. 618.

107 Penyperche is undoubtedly penny prick. Players cast iron sticks at a mark, classically pennies on wooden sticks. In other words, the pennies perch.

Henry draws his knife. When Reynold comes to assist Henry, he is "dashed violently upon the unsheathed knife".[108] Antisocial behaviour in Oxford, in 1292. Two men play in the street with "a club and a great ball", before damaging textiles and assaulting the couple who own the shop.[109] Another reference to a stick and ball game.

Multiple murders involve a *balstaf.* The instrument's purpose remains unknown. Is it the staff used in stickball games? Ball-staff? There is a Balstaff Fen in Cambridgeshire, East Anglia, an early proponent of ball games. On 4 August 1301, when William Baaman beats two dogs belonging to Philip de Spynez with a stick, Philip's steward—clearly a dog-lover—retaliates. He "beat the said William on the arms and shoulders with a stick called a 'balstaf,' so that he languished until Monday and then died."[110] Six months later, Copin le Kyng is killed in the London ward of Candelwykstrate (Candlewickstreet). When a seller approaches bawling "Costard apples for sale", Copin and his friend try to take extra apples. They assault Thomas who comes to the "costers" defence, then abuse Thomas "as far as Fancherche". Thomas turns and strikes Copin on the left side of his head "with a staff called *Balstaf,* inflicting a wound an inch long and two inches deep," and an identical wound on the right side.[111] When Gilbert Beeston dies from a savage blow to the head, in 1321, the inquest believes that burglars used the balstaff found in his house.[112]

In 1322, John de Eddeworth is taking Walter de Selby to the Tower of London, when he bumps into John de Tygre, the man who murdered his brother, Osbert.[113] Soon after the Feast of the Circumcision (1 January), de Eddeworth and two companions track de Tygre to Sopers Lane. They chase him as far as Wodestrete, where de Tygre falls "over heap of dung". De Eddeworth inflicts mortal sword wounds. Two penetrate de Tygre's

---

108 *Calendar of Inquisitions Miscellaneous.* 4 Vols. The Hereford Times Limited, Hereford, 1916. Vol. 1. pp. 637–638.

109 Salter, H.E. (ed.), *Records of Mediæval Oxford.* The Oxford Chronicle Company, Ltd, 1912. p. 11.

110 *Calendar of Inquisitions Miscellaneous.* 4 Vols. The Hereford Times Limited, Hereford, 1916. Vol. 1. p. 507.

111 Sharpe, R.R. (ed.), *Calendar of Coroner's Rolls of the City of London, A.D. 1300–1378.* Richard Clay and Sons Limited, London, 1913. p. 14.

112 Gross, C. (ed)., *Select Cases from the Coroners' Rolls, A.D. 1265–1413.* 9 Vols. Bernard Quaritch, London, 1896. Vol. 9. p. 73.

113 Sharpe, R.R. (ed.), *Calendar of Coroner's Rolls of the City of London, A.D. 1300–1378.* Richard Clay and Sons Limited, London, 1913. pp. 44–45.

skull. A companion busies himself with his "Balstaf" on de Tygres "sides, back, arms and neck." Fifty-one years on, eight men assemble with swords and knives in Sopers Lane, "under colour [pretence] of playing with a football, in order to assault others, occasion disputes, and perpetuate other evil deeds."[114] The 1373 incident is on Shrove Tuesday, making it the earliest Shrove Tuesday football game known.[115] The month de Tygre expires, a dozen drunken Londoners are singing and shouting at midnight. When William de Grymesby reprimands them, they dare him to come out of his shop. Hmm. He tears out with a "Balstaf", runs after Reginold de Freestone "and smashed the whole of his head therewith."[116]

Balstaffs are drawn to heads. Some months later, Cristina le Shepherd and her husband Richard kill Lucy Faukes in their home in Aldgate. Cristina holds her down, while Richard crushes "the whole of her head" with his "Balstaf".[117] And when the cook of the Archdeacon of Winchester enters the house of Agnes Fulberd, charged with taking her to the Archdeacon, her husband and his friends drive him out The Good Samaritan who comes to his aid is chased into a cobbler's shop and dispatched "with a staff called 'balstaf' … so that the skull was broken into the brain."[118] In 1324, William Cok tries to stab a stranger, Simon le Walssh, on Wodestrete. Thank heavens for *balstaffs*. Cok's head is soon stoved in.[119] The year after, when Walter de Benigtone and seventeen others share four gallons of beer at a brewhouse there is a darker purpose. They intend to "carry off Emma, daughter of the late Robert Pourt." They have stones in their hoods, and carry "swords, knives, and other weapons", to ensure no one gets in their way. But they are hot-headed. And have no game plan. Provoked with minimal affront, they attack Emma's ward. The neighbours pile on, and Walter takes a *balstaf* to "the

---

114 Hessayon, A., *Beastly Furie, and Exstreme Violence*. In: Wagg, S., Pollock, A.M (eds.)., *The Palgrave Book of Sport, Politics and Harm*. Springer Nature Switzerland, Cham, Switzerland, 2021. pp. 38–39.

115 Aucoin, T., *When the Pancake Bell Rings*. Unpublished PhD thesis, University of Bristol, 2019. p. 109.

116 Sharpe, R.R. (ed.)., *Calendar of Coroner's Rolls of the City of London, A.D. 1300–1378*. Richard Clay and Sons Limited, London, 1913. p. 47.

117 Ibid, p. 48.

118 Ibid, p. 79.

119 Ibid, p. 99.

top of his head."[120] *The Tale of Beryn* (c1420), attributed tenuously to Geoffrey Chaucer, contains the lines:

> "He berith a balstaff," quod the toon, "& els a rakis end."
> "Thow faillist," quod the Miller, "þowe hast nat wel þy mynde;
> It is a spere, yf þow canst se, with a prik to fore."[121]

> "He bears a balstaff," said the toon, "or else a rake's end." "You fail," said the Miller, "you have not well your mind. It's a spear, if you can see, with a prick at the front."

There is confusion over what a *balstaff* is. It bears other names: "Of wooden instruments we find b*alstaff*, or *balghstaff*, otherwise known as *balkstaff*."[122] *Balgh* means rounded or a swelling, probably both in this case. It might be a stickball staff but is as likely to be a knobbed quarterstaff. In 1326, Walter de Hoddesdone takes a *Balghstaf* to the back of the head and sustains a knife wound to the forehead "four inches long and penetrating the brain."[123] Five days later, Agnes de Wycoumbe takes the *Balghstaf* from the man she is arguing with in Aldgate and strikes him on the back and sides. A butcher and a potter come to her aid, finishing him off with staves.[124] The next record is not until 1340, when carpenter William de Langebrigge is struck with a *balghstaf* and stabbed with a knife, "inflicting a mortal wound on his back four inches deep and one and a-half inches broad." Dissatisfied with their work, de Langbrigge is then "struck in all parts of his body with [four] 'balghstaffs'".[125] Combined knife and *balstaff* attacks appear efficient. Thirty-seven years on, skinner William de Wygemelle is disposed of with both a *balghstaff* and a three-edged knife.[126]

The Oxford delinquents are playing on the feast of St Gregory, one of the calendar's many holy days. In 1280, an unspecified Whitsuntide

---

120 Ibid, p. 115.

121 Furnivall, F.J., Stone, W.G. (eds.)., *The Tale of Beryn*. Asher & Co., Berlin, 1909. p. 6. lns 153–155.

122 Sharpe, R.R. (ed.)., *Calendar of Coroner's Rolls of the City of London, A.D. 1300–1378*. Richard Clay and Sons Limited, London, 1913. p. xxiii.

123 Ibid, p. 164.

124 Ibid, p. 162.

125 Ibid, p. 262.

126 Ibid, p. 192.

ball game is recorded at Ulgham, Northumberland.[127] The Strafford and Newcastle games take place on a Sunday. There is no more welcome day. For workers it is a day of leisure. Their games are tolerated. It is only from the sixteenth century onwards that the Church considers the Sabbath a day of devout observation and those flouting it fit for punishment. In 1220, the Bishop of Durham prohibits priests "or anyone else in the church" from advertising or taking part in scot-ales (*scotallorum*).[128] Scot-ales are not a reference to *hales*—the old Scottish name for football—but to *scotale*, the Anglo-Norman term for a drinking feast. Two years later, a provincial synod in Scotland forbids wrestling matches and other sports in churchyards.[129] That year, the Bishop of Salisbury adds: "We forbid dances or indecent and dishonourable games, which invite lasciviousness, to take place in cemeteries."[130] When the practices continue, heavyweights are brought in. In 1255, the Bishop of Durham issues a proclamation against games and scot-ales, ratified by Pope Alexander IV, Henry III, and the Archbishop of Canterbury. There is a curious addition: "Moreover, we forbid the lifting of rams on wheels, and the games in which it is contested to achieve the feat."[131] It appears that the raising of battering rams is a competitive show of strength. The Synod of Exeter, in 1287, adds combats, dances, and stage plays, ordering local clergy to police breaches.[132]

The anonymous *Ancrene Riwle*, c1225, is the go-to manual for female anchoresses. One chapter covers temptations. "Know then, dear sisters, there are two sorts … external and internal …" Inner temptations include "immoral indulgences, or the desire of them."[133] Suffering through sickness, the author advises, combats devilish temptations and avoids the agonies, "of hell world without end … all the woe of this world compared to the very least pain of hell is nothing but ball-play." Temptation will only increase

127 Aucoin, T., *When the Pancake Bell Rings*. Unpublished PhD thesis, University of Bristol, 2019. p. 306.

128 Wilkins, D. (ed.)., *Concilia Magnae Britanniae et Hiberniae*. 4 Vols. R. Gosling, F. Gyles, T. Woodward, C. Davis, London, 1737. Vol. 1. p. 574.

129 Johnson, W., *Byways in British Archaeology*. University Press, Cambridge, 1912. p. 196.

130 Wilkins, D. (ed.)., *Concilia Magnae Britanniae et Hiberniae*. 4 Vols. R. Gosling, F. Gyles, T. Woodward, C. Davis, London, 1737. Vol. 1. p. 600.

131 Ibid, p. 707.

132 Ibid, p. 196.

133 Morton, J. (ed.)., *Ancren Riwle*. J.B. Nichols and Sons, London, 1853. p. 181. TannerRitchie Publishing, Burlington, Ontario, Canada, 2021.

as the years go by, "In the first years it is nothing but ball-play."[134] The originals *bal pleowe* and *bal-pleouwe* are early examples of "ball play" in the English language, and of the multiple spellings that will tax historians.

A thirteenth century tale tells of a sultan who, fearing for his life, spends "iii. yeres in the castell of Cayre for fere of his men except a day y[t] he came downe to y[e] playn and came there to play at the foreball, his horse fyll vnder hym and brake his legge."[135] "Foreball" is ambiguous; it could be a misspelling when translated from the original French, e.g., foteball. It appears the game is played on horseback. Polo in its established form originated in China and Persia around the third century, and was the sport of the elite.[136] It is hypothesised to have been introduced to Persia by the Parthian dynasty (247BC–224AD).[137] A Persian text, dating to the early seventh century, records the deeds of the third century founder of the Sasanian dynasty, who bested the Parthian princes at polo.[138] It is unsurprising, then, if the sultan plays polo.

As for China, a cemetery has a tomb with six pictorial bricks c25AD–220AD.[139] Each brick depicts a man on horseback holding a curved stick and chasing a ball, pushing the date back to as early as the first century. The first mention in Chinese literature is not until 710, when a game is played before the emperor.[140] The second is in the tenth century, when a statesman sends a bullet-pointed memorandum to the emperor, upbraiding him on playing polo to excess. "When a sovereign plays a subject, there must be contention," he begins, "one will feel ashamed, the other exultant." Secondly, "to jump on a horse and swing a mallet, galloping here and there, with no distinction of rank, but only eager to be first and win, is destructive of all ceremony between sovereign and subject." Lastly, "to make light of the responsibilities of empire, and run

134 Ibid, p. 219.

135 Hayton, Frère., *Here begynneth a lytell cronycle*. Richard Pynson. London, c1520. Part 3, p. 29.

136 Parrish, C., *Origin, diffusion and development of polo: an East to West cultural flow.* Sport in Society, 2018, 21:8, p. 1159.

137 Chehabi, H.E., Guttann, A., *From Iran to All of Asia: The Origin and Diffusion of Polo.* The International Journal of the History of Sport, 2002, 19:2–3, p. 385.

138 Ibid, p. 385.

139 Wertmann P., Chen, X., Li, X., Xu, D., Tarasov, P., Wagner, M., *New evidence for ball games in Eurasia from ca. 3000–year-old Yanghai tombs in the Turfan depression of Northwest China.* Journal of Archaeological Science, Reports 34, 2020, p. 4.

140 Giles, H.A., *The Civilization of China*. Henry Holt and Company, New York, 1911. p. 155.

even the remotest risk of accident, is to disregard obligations to the state and to her Imperial Majesty the Empress."[141]

Around 1262, Adam de la Halle writes the first French comedy of manners, *Le Jeu de la Feuillée* (*The Play of the Leaf*). Written in Picard dialect, the play contains the line, "This no-good rake beats me, so that I am covered in bumps like a wooden cholette," one of the many spellings of the staff used for soule.[142] In 1283, he writes another play in dialect, *Le Jeu de Robin et de Marion* (*The Game of Robin and Marion*).[143] It includes the suggestive lines:

> Rob: God! that my stomach is tired,
> From the choule of the other time!
> Mar: Say, Robin, faith you owe me,
> Have you a choulé? God give it to you![144]

Depictions of sport in twelfth and thirteenth century art are enlightening. One example is in the Geneva cathedral of St Pierre, which has a capital sculpture of five naked youths.[145] One holds a ball. None hold a stick. The following century, a c1260–1275 book of hours shows two boys bowling to each other, while two men throwing balls appear in an Italian decretum c1270–1280.[146,147] A mid-thirteenth century Flemish manuscript on the history of science and philosophy contains a marginal[148] of four men with curved sticks. Two are fighting over a ball on the ground, another is at ease, and the fourth has swung his stick above his shoulder.[149] It is the earliest image of the Flemish stick and ball game *kolven*. The earliest written reference follows in 1261, in Jacob van Maerlant's poem of the

---

141 Ibid, p. 156.

142 Mernier, P. (trans.)., *The Play of Madness*, by Adam de La Halle. Series: Studies in the Humanities. Peter Lang Publishing, Inc., New York, 1997, Vol. 22, p. 45, lns 540–541.

143 Langlois, E. (ed.)., *Le Jeu de Robin et Marion*, by Adam Le Bossu. Fontemoing, A. Paris, 1896. p. 51.

144 In this context, choule is the game and choulé the ball.

145 The Index of Medieval Art. https://theindex.princeton.edu/s/view/ViewWorkOfArt.action?id=74BC2EB7-5CCB-4063-8F74-7B17D30D2B57. Accessed 30 July 2023.

146 Fitzwilliam Museum, Cambridge, England: MS 300, *Psalter-Book of Hours*, c1260–1275, fol. 174r.

147 The Index of Medieval Art. https://theindex.princeton.edu/s/view/ViewWorkOfArt.action?id=93AD6A06-FB64-4BD5-9732-61893F57340C. Accessed 30 July 2023.

148 Marginal (PL, Marginalia): an illustration or text in the margin of a manuscript.

149 Bibioltheek Brugge: MS. 251, *Speculum Doctrinale*, c1250, fol. 149r.

legend of King Arthur.[150] The Flemish manuscript also has an image of a man swinging at a ball with a thin straight bat.[151] The book only has a handful of pictures. That *kolven* is chosen reflects its importance in contemporary society. This is made clear in 1387. When sports associated with gambling are banned in the Dutch seaport of Brielle, *kolven* is still permitted beyond the city walls: "*den bal mitter colven te slaen buten der veste*."[152] "To play the ball with a club outside the town walls." The thirteenth century's last reference to ball games is in November 1292. The Privy Purse Expenses of Duke John of Brabant shows a payment of sixpence given *pro pila grossa*—for a big ball.[153,154,155]

Another fatality is the century's foremost sporting reference. In Bicester, Oxfordshire, in 1261, William Stirchup kicks the ball. Nine-year-old Stephen le Taylor chases it, trips, and falls on his scissors.[156] Like many others, it is not the wound that kills him. He dies of sepsis five days later. Stephen will never know his importance, but he provides the first mention of a *kicking* game in modern history, twelve hundred years after the Roman Conquest.

---

150 Van Maelant, J., van Veltham, L., *Merlijn, de tovenaar van koning*. 1261. Griffioen Grafiek, Hilversum, Netherlands, 2004. p. 29.

151 Bibioltheek Brugge: MS. 251, *Speculum Doctrinale*, c1250, fol. 222v.

152 Nijs, G., Nijs. S., *750 Years 'Mit ener Coluen.'* Golfika—The Magazine of the European Association of Golf Historians & Collectors. n.p.

153 Burtt, J.B. (ed.)., *The Camden Miscellany, Volume the Second*. Printed for the Camden Society, 1853. p. 1.

154 The Duchy of Brabant covered much of what is now Belgium, and North Brabant in the Netherlands.

155 In 1290, John married Margaret, daughter of Edward I of England. Attending the marriage, the duke lost £272 at chess—one hundred and twenty years' wages for a skilled tradesman.

156 Jobson, A.L., *The Oxfordshire eyre roll of 1261*. In: Wagg, S., Pollock, A. (eds.), *The Palgrave Book of Sport, Politics and Harm*, Springer Nature Switzerland, Cham, Switzerland, 2021. p. 27.

CHAPTER THREE
1300–1399

The fourteenth century is mean-spirited. From the get-go. The early years usher in the Little Ice Age. Extending to 1850, it is the coolest era since the Ice Age entered its interglacial period eleven thousand years before. In 1315, when stinging winters and wet summers have become a way of life, Europe is hit by the Great Famine. Millions perish. By the time food supplies recover, in 1322, the continent has slid into high unemployment, rising prices, widespread disease, and lawlessness. Chaos. What to do? Time for a joint Anglo-French crusade in the Holy Land; only Philip VI of France and Edward III fall out, triggering the Hundred Years War, which drags on for a hundred and sixteen years. In the winter of 1338/39, the River Liffey freezes over, allowing Dubliners to dance, run, play at ball, and light fires to roast herrings on.[1] Play continues to Ash Wednesday, no doubt with incidental Shrovetide ball games on ice. Make merry. Make merry. Make merry while you can. Within a decade, the Black Death decimates Europe. Tens of millions perish.[2,3]

Ball games are not without peril. In 1302/03 a Cornishman dies: "The hundred of Trygshire present a death from a kick received when playing at foot-ball" (*ad pila pedis*).[4,5] It is the first mention of a *football game* in history. In 1303, a student in Oxford is "playing at ball" when he is killed by an Irish Sheld Hall scholar, assisted by two other Irish clerks;[6] and in 1305, eight Oxford undergraduates, returning from an evening game in a local meadow, kick Edith de Denyses's door down, rifle through her

1 Gilbert, J.T., *Annals of Ireland.* 2 Vols. Longman and Co., London, 1884. Vol. 2. p. 381.

2 *The Black Death: The Plague, 1331–1770.* University of Iowa Library. http://hosted.lib.uiowa.edu/histmed/plague/. Accessed 31 December 2023.

3 Around forty per cent (possibly sixty per cent) of all Europeans; fifty per cent of Parisians.

4 Horwood, A.J. (ed.), *Year Books of the Reign of King Edward the First. Years XXX and XXXI.* Longman, Green, Longman, Roberts, and Green, London, 1863. p. xxxviii.

5 Shires were subdivided into hundreds for administrative and judicial purposes.

6 Somers, M.H., *Irish Scholars in the Universities at Paris and Oxford before 1500.* Unpublished PhD thesis, The University of New York, 1979. pp. 111–112; Salter, H.E. (ed.), *Records of Mediæval Oxford.* The Oxford Chronicle Company, Ltd, 1912. p. 11.

possessions, and threaten her.[7] All eight evade justice. Both incidents occur on holy days, when there is time and permission to play.[8] Two years later, mention is made of Oxford students returning through the East Gate "from their games in the open fields".[9] In Newcastle Lyons, Co. Dublin, in 1308, another sheathed dagger accident.[10] Seeing the approaching ball, two spectators run onto the field to kick it. A collision, a knife, a thigh.

More tragedies. In 1313/14, William and Adam are playing ball in the churchyard of St Nicholas's in Sturry, Kent. When the balls bounces, and Adam hits it, he fatally strikes William's daughter below her ear.[11] In the London ward of Candelwykstrete, a boy dies when he falls from an upper storey, retrieving a ball from a gutter.[12] In the same annual roll (1337), a woman with "falling sickness" (epilepsy) dies from a fall; a drunken sailor falls from a rope; a drunken naked man at the top of a flight of stairs "for the purpose of relieving nature" falls to his death; and a man descends an empty well to clean it, but is "overcome by the foul air and immediately died." Other games are associated with deaths. In Northamptonshire, in 1301, two brothers are casting the stone, when one is hit on the head.[13] There is another death in the county, in 1315: "there was a game called 'le wrastleng' at Isham, which attracted many people; a quarrel arose, and Thomas was shot with an arrow; he recovered from his wound, but died of a disease called 'le flux' [dysentery]."[14,15] It is the first documented case of the term "wrestling".

In 1320, eight Suffolk men are brought before the court leet for bloody fights (*traxit sanguinem*) during *campyng* games in Hollesley and forfeit a day's pay.[16] It is the first mention of camping in history.

---

7 Thorald Rogers, J.E. (ed.)., *Oxford City Documents, Financial and Judicial, 1268–1665*. Clarendon Press, Oxford, 1891. p. 177–178.

8 The Feast of the Annunciation and the Feast of St Bartholomew respectively.

9 Salter, H.E. (ed.)., *Records of Mediæval Oxford.* The Oxford Chronicle Company, Ltd, 1912. p. 11.

10 Griffith, M.C. (ed.)., *Calendar of the Justiciary rolls, or, Proceedings in the Court of the Justiciar of Ireland.* The Stationery Office, Dublin, 1905. p. 103.

11 Maitland, F.W., Harcourt, W.V., Bolland, W.C. (eds.)., *Year Books of Edward II. Vol. V. The Eyre of Kent, 6 & 7 Edward II. A.D. 1313–14.* Bernard Quaritch, London, 1910. p. lxxxvii.

12 Sharpe, R. R. (ed.)., *Calendar of Coroners Rolls of the City of London, 1300–1378*. London, 1913. p. 191.

13 Gross, C. (ed)., *Select Cases from the Coroners' Rolls, A.D. 1265–1413*. Bernard Quaritch, London, 1896. Vol. 9. p. 69.

14 Ibid, p. 62.

15 "Flux" is an Old English word.

16 Suffolk Review, 2012, 59, pp. 23–27. https://www.medievalists.net/2013/08/historian-uncovers-evidence-of-football-match-from-1320/. Accessed 13 October 2023.

The sport is still played in Hollesley five hundred years later.[17] That year, a chivalric romance *The Proces of Seuen Sages* contains the lines:

> "With that bal togider thai plaid
> That on hit hente, that other hit threw."[18]

"They played together with the ball. One caught it, [and] another threw it." There is evidence ball play is well tolerated. This from *King Alexander*, c1300: "Theo thridde him taughte to play at bal."[19] "The third taught him to play at ball." In 1332, William de Spalding, canon of Sculdham in neighbouring Norfolk is at ball (*ad pilam*).[20] When he kicks the ball with his foot (*cum pede*), his friend collides and falls on the canon's sheathed knife. The mortified canon successfully applies to Pope John XXII for dispensation. Like Suffolk, Norfolk is camping country, and the canon is probably playing it: the terms camping and football were used interchangeably.[21] Similarly, in mid-century King's Lynn, Norfolk, a boy has a fatal accident playing football, and a man is killed after a quarrel at football.[22,23]

Monasteries are the wealthiest landowners in England. Ten per cent of a peasant's crop is diverted for religious purposes as tithes.[24] Each abbot decides how to spend their revenue stream, what to give back in kind, and how actively to pursue defaulters. In 1320, the tenants of the Vale Royal

---

17 Moor, E., *Suffolk Words and Phrases*. J. Loder, London, 1823. p. 63.

18 Weber, H., *Metrical romances of the thirteenth, fourteenth, and fifteenth centuries*. 3 Vols. George Ramsay and Co., Edinburgh, 1810. *The Proces of Seuen Sages*. Vol. 3. p. 78.

19 Ibid, *Kyng Alisaunder*. p. 32. ln 660.

20 "Regesta 72: 1320–1321", in *Calendar of Papal Registers Relating To Great Britain and Ireland: Volume 2, 1305–1342*, ed. W H Bliss (London, 1895), pp. 212–217. *British History Online* http://www.british-history.ac.uk/cal-papal-registers/brit-ie/vol2/pp212–217. Accessed 5 January 2024.

21 An inordinate amount of source reports of "football games" are from East Anglia. Given the interchangeability of terms and the popularity of camping until the end of the eighteenth century, the author will tentatively consider games in Suffolk, Norfolk, Cambridgeshire, and north Essex as camping. From the nineteenth century onwards, given the steep decline in the popularity of camping, the author will treat games as football, despite the preponderance of newspaper reports from this region. There is a risk of overestimating the number of reported camping matches using this approach.

22 Owen, D. (ed.), *The Making of King's Lynn: A Documentary Survey*. Oxford, 1984. pp. 19, 428.

23 Hessayon, A., *Beastly Furie, and Exstreme Violence*. In: Wagg, S., Pollock, A. (eds.), *The Palgrave Book of Sport, Politics and Harm*. Springer Nature Switzerland, Cham, Switzerland, 2021. p. 38.

24 Dodds, B., *Tithes in the Late Middle Ages*. The Agricultural History Review, 2005, 53:2, p. 125.

Abbey in Cheshire become "disgusted with their landlords".[25] Acts of violence break out. In 1321, the abbot's servant John de Boddeworth is killed by the Brethren of Oldynton, who "afterwards cut off his head, and carried it away with them, and kicked that head with their feet like a ball and made their sport therewith."[26] A new abbot is installed the following year, but the bond tenants repeatedly challenge the abbot's authority, and the conflict drags on until he is murdered in 1339.

A more general clash centres around churchyards, with clergy increasingly intolerant of their use for impious pursuits. In 1303, Robert Manning of Brunne's devotional book *Handlying Synne* condemns carols and wrestling in churches and churchyards.[27] Durham Priory issues nine injunctions against its tenants from 1377 to 1384.[28] At the Synod of Ely, in 1364, Bishop Durham's 1255 proclamation to clerics is reiterated: "We also command that in every church it should be solemnly denounced, that no one should lift [battering] rams on wheels, or institute other games in which they compete for bravery. Compotations (scot-ales) are also prohibited."[29] Three years later, the Archbishop of York bans games on or in church property.[30]

~

Ball games are rowdy enough to earn civic bans. They also expend time and energy that could be better served honing skills to defend England or attack other countries. In the fourteenth century, Plantagenet kings ban the game six times: Edward II (1314), Edward III (1331, 1349, 1363, 1365), and Richard II (1389).[31] In April 1314, the Mayor of London on behalf of the king decrees: "And where there is great uproar in the City, through certain tumults arising from the striking of great footballs in

25 *Chester Chronicle.* 11 March 1825. p. 4.

26 "Pleas and evidences: Fos. 21–30", in *The Ledger Book of Vale Royal Abbey*, ed. John Brownbill (Manchester, 1914), pp. 37–62. *British History Online.* http://www.british-history.ac.uk/lancs-ches-record-soc/vol68/pp37–62. Accessed 5 January 2024.

27 Furnivall, F.J. (ed.)., *Robert of Brunne's 'Handlyng Synne,': A.D. 1303.* Kegan Paul, Trench, Trübner and Co., Ltd., London, 1901. lns 8987–8988.

28 Aucoin, T., *When the Pancake Bell Rings.* Unpublished PhD thesis, University of Bristol, 2019. p. 104.

29 Wilkins, D. (ed.)., *Concilia Magnae Britanniae et Hiberniae.* 4 Vols. R. Gosling, F. Gyles, T. Woodward, C. Davis, London, 1737. Vol. 1. p. 61.

30 *Ibid,* p. 68.

31 Dunning, E., Sheard. K., *Barbarians, Gentlemen, and Players.* Australian National University Press, 1979. p. 23.

the fields of the public, from which many evils perchance may arise, which may God forbid, we do command and do forbid, on the King's behalf, upon pain of imprisonment, that such game shall be practised from henceforth within the said City."[32] The original Norman French reads *grosses pelotes de pee*: big balls of [the] foot. It is the first mention of *footballs* in history. Clearly, football is widespread in the capital, rowdy enough to merit a ban of its own. Fencing is the only other sport mentioned: "no one shall keep within the City, or in the liberty thereof, a school for fencing." Football smiles. News is news. Hello world.

It has been suggested that the 1314 ban refers to playing in the streets and not in fields.[33] A transcriptive error *is* possible. Perhaps *en prees du poeple* should read *en press du poeple*, Anglo-Norman for "in the *crowds* of people". It makes sense. The ban is within the city, not in the open fields surrounding the city walls. Besides, playing in the busy streets of London would be a tiresome nuisance and far more likely to jeopardise the public. Irrespective of the text, the ban is likely to include churchyards. In 1385, the Bishop of London issues a letter threatening excommunication for a number of violations committed in the churches and churchyards of the parish of St Paul's, which ministers to the entire capital.[34,35] Old St Paul's Cathedral is particularly treasured. There is fear for the integrity of the "stained-glass windows and stone images … which adorn the fabric and culture of the whole church", from shooting at crows and doves, throwing stones at birds nesting in the crevices, playing ball outside and palm-ball within.[36] "Other dishonest" games carry on inside churches, as well as the buying and selling of merchandise. By 1409, men and boys are still playing inside Old St Paul's, dogs are "doing dirtiness", officials are playing ball in the close, and women are "slipping in in the evening twilight."[37]

---

32 Riley, H.T., *Munimenta Gildhallæ Londoniensis*. 3 Vols. Longman, Green, Longman, and Roberts, 1862. Vol. 3. pp. 440–441.

33 Hessayon, A., *Beastly Furie, and Exstreme Violence*. In: Wagg, S., Pollock, A.M (eds.)., *The Palgrave Book of Sport, Politics and Harm*. Springer Nature Switzerland, Cham, Switzerland, 2021. p. 30.

34 Carlin, M., Rosenthal, J.T., *Medieval London: Collected Papers of Caroline. M. Barron*. Medieval Institute Publications, Western Michigan University, Kalamazoo, 2017. p. 172.

35 Old St Paul's was completed in 1314, the year of the first football ban. It was destroyed in the Great Fire of London in 1666.

36 Wylie, J.H., *History of England under Henry IV. Vol. II. 1405–1406*. 1894. AMS Press Inc, New York, 1969. p. 184.

37 Ibid, p. 185.

Traders, principally Germans of the Hanseatic League, settle in London as early as the tenth century. By the fourteenth century, they have a guildhall and surrounding shops in the Steelyard area of London. The guildhall is off-limits to Englishmen for fear trading secrets will be exposed, and no ball play is allowed inside.[38] Edward III's 1331 proclamation specifically limits games near Westminster: "His Majesty the King prohibits on pain of imprisonment any child or other playing near the palace of Westminster during Parliament, at bars or at other games, or who lays hands on members or otherwise impedes them going about their business." The games are such a nuisance that the ban is repeated twelve times over the next two decades.[39]

By 1349, plague has ravaged England. Archers are desperately needed to maintain the English supremacy demonstrated at Crecy three years earlier. In Latin, *pilam pedivam* means football. The 1349 Latin text is unavailable, though the English translation is identical to the 1363 and 1365 bans, so the Latin is presumably the same. The 1363 text reads: "*Iactus Lapidam, Llignorum, et Ferri, et quidam pilam manualem, pedivam, et bacularum, et ad Canibucam et Gallorum Pugnam.*"[40] Literally, "the throwing of Stones,[41] Wood[42] and Iron[43], and in some ball, manual, foot, and staff, and with *Canibucam* and Cock-Fighting." *Pilam: manualem, pedivam, bacularum.* Handball, football, stickball.

The 1365 ban uses the same text as the 1363 ban, but when the copyist transcribes it, a single mistake is made. *Canibucam* is changed to *cambucam*, a bishop's hooked staff.[44] As a result, John Strype's widely-cited 1720

38 Ibid, p. 74.

39 Roberts, G.R.P., *Popular Recreation in the Middle Ages.* Unpublished MA thesis, McGill University, 1932. Appendix A. p. 1.

40 Ibid.

41 The sport has never been determined. In 1603 (*Description of Penbrokeshire*), George Owen mentions … "casting of the barre, sledge, stone, or hurling the Bowles, or Ball" as historical pursuits, as does Joseph Strutt: "the stone, the barre, or the plummet … the sledge hammer was also used for the same purpose" See, Hone, W. (ed.)., *The Sports and Pastimes of the People of England.* Strutt, J., 1801. Thomas Tegg, London, 1845. p. 75. Throwing of the stones, then is likely to have been akin to the putt, hammer, or discus. Alternatives are marbles, or a forbear of bowling cf. bocce or pétanque.

42 A reference to loggets. Pieces of wood are thrown at a stake and the nearest wins.

43 A reference to quoits. The players attempt to toss iron rings onto a wooden pin.

44 *Tracts Relating to Ireland.* 2 Vols. M.H Gill, University Press, Dublin, 1843. Vol. 2. p. 23; Roberts, G.R.P., *Popular Recreation in the Middle Ages.* Unpublished MA thesis, McGill University, 1932. p. 68.

translation of the 1365 ban reads: "hurling of Stones and Wood and Iron; Hand-Ball, Foot-Ball, Stick-Ball, and in Cambuck, and Cockfighting."[45]

Without considering that a stick game is already mentioned in the ban, historians incorrectly translate *cambucam* to *cambuck* and designate it as an early form of hockey, an assumption that continues to this day.[46] Strype, himself, places a query in the margin beside *cambuck*, clueless as to its meaning. Other than the 1365 ban, *cambuck* is only mentioned once more, incorrect propagation notwithstanding: a 1486 Latin-Dutch dictionary mentions two phrases: "*cambuca een kolf*"and "*In cambucare kolven*", which appear to mean a "kolf club" and "playing kolven with a club."[47] An identical ban, issued by the Archbishop of Dublin in 1365, uses *canibucam* twice.[48] Is it possible *canibucam* is itself a mistake? Adding an "s" converts it to *canisbucam*: dog bite. Does this mean dogfighting? Unlikely, as dogfighting only rose to prominence in the eighteenth century.[49]

An alternate suggestion is that *canibucam* is slang for bull-baiting.[50] The pursuit involves the baiting and killing of a bull by dogs. Perhaps this is where dog bites come in. It makes sense, as *canibucam* is listed separately from ball sports and paired with cockfighting, and unlike the ball games, no comma separates them. When the 1363 edict repeats the games, a semicolon provides further separation from ball games: "*pilam manualem, pedivam, vel bacularum; aut Canibucam et Gallorum Pugnam.*" If true, the 1349, 1363, and 1365 proclamations are banning the "hurling of Stones and Wood and Iron; Hand-Ball, Foot-Ball, Stick-ball; and Bull-Baiting and Cockfighting."

The theory has support. In 1788, Robert Henry translates the 1363 text. In place of cambuck he writes "bull-bating".[51] Follow-up bans by

---

45 Strype, J., *A Survey of the Cities of London and Westminster*. 2 Vols. s.n., London, 1720. Vol. 1. p. 251.

46 Roberts, G.R.P., *Popular Recreation in the Middle Ages*. Unpublished MA thesis, McGill University, 1932. p. 68.

47 Gheraert., *Vocabularis: Gemmula vocabulorum*. Gerard Leeu, Antwerp, 1486. n.p.

48 Rymer, T. (ed.)., *Fœdera Conventiones, Literæ, et Cujuscunque Generis Acta Publica*. 20 Vols. A. and J. Churchill, London, 1708. Vol. 4. p. 468.

49 Evans, R.D., Forsyth, C.J., *Entertainment to Outrage: A Social Historical View of Dogfighting*. International Review of Modern Sociology, 1997, 27:2, p. 61.

50 *Tracts Relating to Ireland*. 2 Vols. M.H Gill, University Press, Dublin, 1843. Vol. 2. p. 23.

51 Henry, R., The History of Great Britain. 6 Vols. P. Byrne, J. Jones, Dublin, 1789. Vol. 4. p. 515.

Richard II (1389), Henry IV (1410), Edward IV (1477), and Henry VII (1496, 1503) make no mention of cockfighting, bull-baiting, *canibucam*, or *cambuck*, despite the immense popularity of blood sports.[52] Perhaps previous bans demonstrate an imperviousness to sanctions, and they are quietly dropped. Authorities may be complicit; bloodthirsty citizens are ripe for war. By 1389, the guild of St Martin at Stamford yearly hunt a bull with dogs, while in fifteenth century Coventry and Worcester, bulls must be baited to death before a butcher can handle them.[53] Bullrings minimise risk to the public, and with the bull tied at the centre, there can only be one winner, reducing the likelihood of gambling. In 1410, Henry IV omits stick games from his edict, suggesting a diminishing interest.[54] Similarly, bans on throwing stones, loggets, and quoits[55] are ultimately superseded by prohibition of bowls and closh,[56] while handball gives way to tennis.

In Ireland, the mixing of Anglo-Normans with *les Irrois enemyes*—the Irish enemy—lends itself to hand-wringing. "Each generation of settlers was being steadily absorbed in the stronger vitality of the Irish."[57] Englishmen born in Ireland are known as "Irish dogs".[58] In 1366, the Statutes of Kilkenny are renewed, replacing those of 1310 and 1326. A settler is at risk of forfeiture, imprisonment, or death if they take an Irish wife, give their child an Irish name, speak Irish, trade with the Irish, play quoits or hurly, ride bareback, or grow "a beard above his mouth" without shaving at least fortnightly.[59] Specifically, they are banned from "horlings, with great sticks and [unreadable: a ball?] upon the ground, from which

52 England and Wales. Sovereign. *Actis made by Dyuers our most Noble Progenytours Knynges of this Realme Agaynst Unlaufull Games* [Proclamations. 1536]. London, 1536. https://www.proquest.com/books/actis-made-dyuers-our-most-noble-progenytours/docview/2240946247/se-2. Accessed 10 July 2023.

53 Roberts, G.R.P., *Popular Recreation in the Middle Ages*. Unpublished MA thesis, McGill University, 1932. p. 27.

54 Ibid, Appendix A. p. 3.

55 Players attempt to toss iron rings onto a wooden pin.

56 A Flemish forbear of croquet. A bowl (klos) is driven through a hoop, using a spade- or chisel-shaped instrument.

57 Wylie, J.H., *History of England under Henry IV. Vol. II. 1405–1406*. 1894. AMS Press Inc, New York, 1969. p. 143.

58 Hardiman, J. (ed.)., *A Statute of the Fortieth Year of King Edward III, enacted in a Parliament held in Kilkenny, A.D 1367*. Dublin University Press, 1843. p. 19.

59 Wylie, J.H., *History of England under Henry IV. Vol. II. 1405–1406*. 1894. AMS Press Inc, New York, 1969. pp. 143–145.

great evils and maims have arisen."[60,61] It is a toothless tiger. It speaks to the national ardour for hurling that the articles were "ne kept after the making of them eight days."[62] A poem that year by Gofraigh Fionn Ó Dálaigh advises soon-to-be leader Domhnall to lay down his hurling stick and pick up his sword.[63] In 1401, John Colton, the Archbishop of Armagh, prohibits "galbarey" from being played over Easter, as it results in mortal sins, beatings, "and even murders."[64] Galbarey is said to be a form of hurling popular in the north of Ireland,[65] but no other source can be found. The word may derive from *gall Breathnach*, Gaelic for "Briton foreigner", reflecting the influx of settlers. They may bring their own stick and ball game, preferring it to Irish hurling.

~

Illuminated manuscripts provide a rich source of material. The preponderance of ball games reflects popularity and cultural acceptance. Depictions of catch far outnumber specific games. The mid-twelfth century English illustration of St Cuthbert is an anomaly; most other portrayals of ball games are not seen for over a century and are almost exclusively French.[66] Similarly, while churches are a rare source of imagery, the west façade of Lyon Cathedral has a seven-hundred-year-old stone portal sculpture of two youths.[67] One has a ball, the other a club. Monkeys at ball are a recurring theme. A leaf in a c1325 book of hours shows two monkeys with a ball each and a man about to catch a third;[68] another shows three monkeys bowling stitched balls.[69] A similar scene is repeated in a psalter, which also has an image of two monkeys playing what appears to be an early version of trapball,

---

60 Hardiman, J. (ed.), *A Statute of the Fortieth Year of King Edward III, enacted in a Parliament held in Kilkenny, A.D 1367.* Dublin University Press, 1843. p. 22.

61 It is called horlings in the original Anglo-Norman.

62 Hurling, horling, hurley, hurly.

63 Rouse, P., *Sport and Ireland: A History.* Oxford University Press, 2015. p. 15.

64 Reeves, W. (ed.), *Acts of Archbishop Colton.* University Press, Dublin, 1850. p. xviii.

65 Wylie, J.H., *History of England under Henry IV. Vol. II. 1405–1406.* 1894. AMS Press Inc, New York, 1969. p. 160.

66 Unless otherwise stated, all illuminated manuscripts are French.

67 *The Index of Medieval Art.* https://theindex.princeton.edu/s/view/ViewWorkOfArt.action?id=0CCAAB3A-78D1-43CD-9990-BD09986D6D69. Accessed 30 July 2023.

68 *The Index of Medieval Art.* https://theindex.princeton.edu/s/view/ViewWorkOfArt.action?id=0CABFC75-E14C-4E5D-BC52-70EA5C4D99EF. Accessed 30 July 2023.

69 Trinity College Cambridge: MS B11.22, *Book of Hours (Use of Rome),* 13th–14th centuries, fol. 5v.

known to have been played in the fourteenth century.[70,71] A ball nestles in a Y-shaped stick. The stick is at an angle supported by a smaller stick, which if kicked sharply releases the ball. This can then be struck towards the second monkey, whose arms are held out, ready to catch it. A German manuscript also portrays two monkeys.[72] One is throwing a ball to the other, who is holding a narrow-handled stick, positioned ready to strike.

In one breviary a man cannot look more like a goalkeeper as he dives to his right for a golden ball.[73] Elsewhere, a book of hours has a man with cloven hooves swinging a clubbed stick at a ball;[74] an illustration in the *Romance of Alexander* has a nun with a ball beside a monk with a straight, narrow-handled stick;[75] a Flemish psalter clearly shows a boy about to strike a ball with a hooked staff, while a boy below readies to catch it;[76] and an English *Book of Genesis* depicts an unwitting Isaac playing ball with a curved stick, while Abraham shields his eyes as he gazes adoringly at God.[77] In bowling images, a man hits a ball with a stick to bowl over skittles;[78] a boy bowls at a six-inch t-shaped stick;[79] another bowls at a six-inch stick with a ball already beside it as another boy claps and a third directs him;[80] and a man stands in front of another man's head capped with a skittle-shaped hat, behind two football-sized bowls.[81] An unusual image shows a man with a bat, and a cowl covering his face. A man guides him to hit a large ball, and a third is in the process of bowling.[82]

---

70 Bodleian Library, Oxford: MS Douce 6, *Psalter*, c1320–1330, fol. 34r.

71 Ibid, fol. 96v.

72 Walters Art Museum, Baltimore: MS W148, *Douce-Walters Homilary*, c1300–1349, fol. 281v.

73 Morgan Library, New York: MS M.373, *Breviary*, c1325, fol. 225v.

74 Morgan Library, New York: MS 754, *Hours of Saint-Omer*, c1320–1330, fol. 40v.

75 Bodleian Library, Oxford: MS Bodleian 264, *Romance of Alexander,* c1338–1344, fols. 21v, 22r, 63r.

76 Bodleian Library, Oxford: MS Douce 6, *Psalter*, c1320–1330, fol. 148r.

77 The Index of Medieval Art. https://theindex.princeton.edu/s/view/ViewWorkOfArt.action?id=9BFE68BC-737E-4AC2–A234–E1B7B6286343. Accessed 30 July 2023.

78 British Library, London: MS Roy. 2. B. VII, *Psalter of Queen Mary*, c1310–1320, fol. 167r.

79 Barber Institute of Fine Arts, Birmingham, England: MS 90946, *Metz Hours*, c1345–1350, fol. 51r.

80 Médiathèque Jacques Chirac, Troyes, France: MS 193426, *Vie de Sainte Marguerite*, c1300, fol. 171r.

81 Morgan Library, New York: MS M.754, *Hours of Saint-Omer*, c1320–1330, fol. 19v.

82 Bodleian Library, Oxford: MS Douce 6, *Psalter*, c1320–1330, fol. 82v.

A book of hours, c1300–1310, has two illustrations of players hitting balls with their palms, a game called *jeu de paume* ("palm-play"), the forefather of tennis.[83] *Jeu de paume* is fashionable in French society. The 1292 Rolls of Paris record the unknown profession of *paumier*, possibly a manufacturer of balls or courts.[84] In 1316, Louis X le Hutin (the Quarrelsome) overheats during a game of *jeu de paume*, in the forest of Vincennes.[85] Retiring to a grotto he cools too quickly, catches a fever, and dies. A c1347–1350 instruction manual for kings and princes depicts *jeu de paume*: a boy is about to strike a cricket-sized ball with his hand. In another illustration, a boy is about to bowl underarm.[86] Charles V includes *jeu de paume* (and *soule*) in his April 1369 edict: it must remain the preserve of the upper classes. *Soule* is the peasant game, but the king seeks to deny them both.[87] They cannot be so easily expunged. In 1397, the Provost of Paris bans playing at the palm, dice, cards, ball, and bowls, except on festival days.[88]

The first recorded manslaughter associated with *jeu de paume* takes place in 1382.[89] "Gasgone and his brother Yuan fell out toguyder, playeng at tennes, and Gasgone gave hym a blowe."[90] When Yuan complains, their father's reaction is unhinged. He accuses Gasgone of conspiring to poison him. From then on, he mistrusts Gasgone, ultimately stabbing him in the neck. In 1399, Charles VI watches *jeu de paume* from the barred windows of his château while convalescing from an acute psychotic episode.[91] Another royal tragedy befalls Charles VIII of France. On 8 April 1498, he takes his wife "to see the tennis plaiers in the trenches of the castle … and they two entered into a gallerie … the King as he entered, knocked his browe against the doore … afterward he beheld a

83 Walters Art Museum, Baltimore: MS W.88, *Book of Hours* c1300–1310, fols. 59v, 70r.

84 Géraud, H., *Paris Sous Philippe-le-Bel*. Crapelet, Paris, 1837. p. 529.

85 Marshall, J., *The Annals of Tennis*. Horace Cox, London, 1878. p. 3.

86 Morgan Library, New York: MS M.456, *Avis aus roys*, c1347–1350, fol. 68v.

87 Luce, S, *La France pendant la guerre de cents ans*. Hachette, Paris, 1890. p. 106.

88 Lacroix, P. (ed.)., *Le Moyen Age et la Renaissance*. 2 Vols. M.A. Rivaud, Paris, 1849. Vol. 2. n.p.

89 Bourchier, J. (trans.). *Sir John Froissart's chronicles*. 2 Vols. J. McCreery, London, 1812. Vol. 2. p. 74.

90 Bourchier's translation is from 1523.

91 Marshall, J., *The Annals of Tennis*. Horace Cox, London, 1878. p. 3.

great … tennice playing, talking familiarly with all men … [until] he fell backward and lost his speech." He dies nine hours later.[92]

The game secures the murder of King James I of Scotland. After James's two older brothers die, the eleven-year-old is to be sent to France for safekeeping. The plan is thwarted when he is captured by pirates and sent to England. His father dies fifteen days later, and he becomes king in absentia. For eighteen years. When Henry VI releases him, in 1424, he returns to Scotland paranoid of those who governed during his captivity. His arbitrary slaughter of relatives and perceived adversaries is self-fulfilling. A conspiracy crystallises in 1437. He is in lodgings in a convent in Perth when they come for him.[93] Cornered, James pulls up the floorboards and hides "amongis thordure of the privay that was all of hard stone and none wyndow ne issue thereupon, save a litill square hole …"[94] Any hopes of escaping through the sewer's hole were dashed three days earlier: "whane he played there at the pawme the ballis that he plaid withe oft ranne yn at that fowle hole." James has the hole sealed with stone. The privy seal. Louis X, Charles X, James I. Kings should steer clear of *jeu de paume.*

Another page from the c1300–1310 book of hours portrays a man with a large paddle-shaped bat about to hit a football-sized ball thrown by another.[95] The coal-shovel shaped paddle is held in one hand, down rather than aloft, as if he intends to sweep the ball up The mystery game is repeated later. This time the man holds the paddle aloft, gripped in both hands, ready to strike the ball with a backhand.[96] Are they playing an early form of tennis? That it is not the classic stick game is evident in a later leaf depicting two men with thin sticks, curved at the ends.[97] The sticks are crossed as they battle for the merest shadow of a ball.

---

92 Danett, T. (trans.). *The historie of Philip de Commines, knight, Lord of Argenton.* Ar. Hatfield, London, 1601. p. 342.

93 Oram, R. (ed.)., *The Kings and Queens of Scotland.* The History Press, Cheltenham, England, 2001. pp. 118–122.

94 Elphinstone, W., Stevenson, J., *The Life and Death of King James the First of Scotland.* Edinburgh Printing Club, 1837. p. 56.

95 Walters Art Museum, Baltimore: MS W.88, *Book of Hours,* c1300–1310. fol. 25r.

96 Ibid, fol. 193.

97 Ibid, fol. 40v.

Another French manuscript, c1300–1340, has two marginalia of interest.[98] The first depicts a man and woman with straight narrow bats, one wider at the end. The woman is about to throw then strike the mid-sized ball she is holding. The man adopts a posture similar to a baseball hitter, ready to swing at the ball. The second mirrors the c1300–1310 book of hours. Two men with long curved sticks compete for a cricket-sized ball. Both have modern, almost golf-like, grips on their sticks. A manuscript c1338–1344 includes two sporting illustrations.[99] The first depicts a nun about to throw a cricket-sized ball to a monk holding a straight narrow-handled bat aloft. Two nuns and two monks line up opposite, hands raised. The middle monk and the nun's hands are clearly separated, as if waiting to catch the ball. The other illustration shows a game of lawn bowls between two men. One is adopting a classic stance as he releases his ball, while a woman is running or dancing at the centre of the green.

The French manuscript has other curiosities: a man bends over and defecates next to a horrified woman, a hen walks on stilts, giant rabbits shoot men with crossbows, a bare-cheeked man leans over and passes wind, and monkeys get drunk. A further manuscript, c1375–1400, shows a man holding a tapered bat and a football-sized ball. A second man prepares to catch the ball, arms readied.[100] The following leaf has a family tree of "William Bastard", otherwise known as William the Conqueror. An incongruous doodle beside the tree portrays a dragon biting into a disc held by a man with a knobbed club. Historian beware. It could be a ball game, but it is probably a man with a shield fighting a dragon. Elsewhere, mice hang a cat, and a fox with a crutch consults a monkey physician. The manuscript is of particular interest, as it is one of the few in Anglo-Norman.

Among the seven hundred illustrations of the incomparable *Hours of Jeanne d'Evreux,* c1324–1328, one grisaille shows a man blowing up a football-sized ball, using a pipe similar to the copper tubes used centuries later.[101] It could be argued it is a depiction of the medieval musical instrument the bladder pipe, but the design is wrong. While the ball may be

---

98 British Library: MS Royal 10 E IV, *Decretals of Gregory IX*, c1300–1340, fols. 98v, 94v, 95r.

99 Bodleian Library, Oxford: MS Bodleian 264, *Romance of Alexander*, c1338–1344, fols. 22r, 63r.

100 Royal Library: Royal MS 14 BV, *Genealogical Chronicle of the English Kings*, c1375–1400, fol. 4r.

101 The Metropolitan Museum of Art, New York: MS 54.1.2, *The Hours of Jeanne d'Evreux, Queen of France,* c1324–1328, fol. 47r.

for throwing, games of the period invariably use small balls. The illustration might be an early portrayal of a football. In Gloucester Cathedral one panel of a stained-glass window, c1350, depicts a man gripping a hooked stick with both hands.[102] The stick is raised, his body adjusted, as if he is about to strike the ball coming towards him at ankle height. The cathedral also has two carved misericords from the same period. One shows two boys with five balls and three dice, the other two boys with a medium-sized ball. One boy in the first carving appears to have just thrown dice, but his leg is cocked as if ready to strike a ball, suggesting football; the other appears to be bouncing balls, suggesting *jeu de paume*.[103] The balls vary in size from small to medium. The second pair similarly palm the ball, but there is ambiguity, and it is possible they may be trying to kick it.[104] Gloucester's Benedictine abbey of St Peter's hosts Parliament in 1378. The monks are glad to see the back of the Londoners: "Their monastery had been made into a kind of fair; wrestlers and ball-players had tramped the greensward and set butts about their trim new cloisters."[105]

A number of cited illustrations are incorrect. For example, an illuminated manuscript, c1300–1325, contains a full-sized picture of a monk holding a bat with a man's face at the club end and a large ball.[106] The image is contained in a history of the Bible, and all the other images are biblical. Moreover, illustrations for ball games are invariably small. Caution is needed. A similar image, c1250, has an image of a man holding a bat and what appears to be a ball but is a loaf of bread scored with a cross, representing the Host. Both accompany the same psalm and carry the word *incipiens*: the fool. They are early depictions of jesters, and their clubs represent a jester's sceptre. A c1300 illustration accompanying the same psalm is midway between the two: the man holds up a loaf of bread, but his club has a man's head.[107]

~

Literature finds use of football. *Octavian* is a French romance, c1229–1244. It is written in Picardian dialect, an area known to play *soule*. It is

102 Clavner, N., *The Great East Window of Gloucester Cathedral and its Heraldic Glass*. Journal of the British Archaeological Association, 2018, 171:1, p. 105, fig. 4C.

103 Fig. 32.8 https://www.misericords.co.uk/gloucester.html. Accessed 23 July 2023.

104 Ibid, fig. 33.13

105 Wylie, J.H., *History of England under Henry IV. Vol. III. 1407–1410*. Longmans, Green, and Co., London, 1896. p. 121.

106 Bodleian Library, Oxford: MS Douce 211, *Biblio Historiale*, c1400–1425, fol. 258v.

107 Robert de Boron's Welsh Merlin (early 1200s) uses a shepherd's crook.

unclear if the original references *soule*, but a Middle English translation, c1350, mentions football: "And some he swilke a boxe lent That the heved fro the body went, Als it were a foteballe."[108] "And some he gave such a blow, that the head went flying from the body like a football." It is the first known mention of a *football* in the *English* language. In the Latin version of the poem, three presents are given to a child, a ball, a whipping top, and a golden crab.[109] A second Middle English translation, c1350, has a scene where a knave tries to seduce a woman. He slyly throws his head into her bosom (barm) asking her to play with his nether regions, praying she will give in to temptation:

> He drewe that heede, with lowryng chere,
> Into the lady barm:
> And seyde: 'Pley thè with that ball!
> I prey, God yeue thè evell will fall.[110]

The Proverbs of Hending (before 1325), uses a stickball analogy to offer sound advice to women.

> Þe maide þat ʒevit hirsilf alle
> Oþir to fre man, oþir to þralle
> Ar ringe be ſet an honde,
> And pleiit with þe croke and wiþ þe balle,
> And mekit gret þat erst was smalle,
> Þe wedding got to sconde.
> 'ʒeve þi cunte to cunnig,
> And crave affetir wedding.'
> Quod Hendyng.

> "The maid who gives herself entirely to either a free man or a serf before a ring is set on [her] hand, and plays with the crook and with the ball, and makes big what once was small, ruins

108 Hudson, H., *Four Middle English Romances*. Medieval Institute Publications, Kalamazoo, Michigan, 2006. p. 92. lns 1385–1387.

109 Weber, H.W., *Metrical Romances of the Thirteenth, Fourteenth, and Fifteenth Centuries*. 3 Vols. George Ramsay and Company, Edinburgh, 1810. Vol. 3. p. 299.

110 Ibid, p. 166.

the wedding. 'Give your cunt to cunning and desire a wedding.' Quoth Hending."[111]

In 1373, eight are charged with assembling with swords and knives, "under colour [pretence] of playing with a football, in order to assault others, occasion disputes, and perpetuate other evil deeds against the peace in Sopers Lane, Cheap and Cordwainer Street."[112] The incident is on Shrove Tuesday, making it the earliest Shrove Tuesday football game known, one of only a handful of pre-Reformation games on record.[113] Six of the eight are tailors, the other two skinners.[114] Perhaps four skinners got away, and it was a six-a-side. Is it coincidence they are in the Cordwainer ward? Cordwainers are shoemakers. They make footballs. Skinners are in the hide trade. Allied trades (especially tanners) believe they should be the ones to make footballs. Have the skinners turned up to provoke the cordwainers into a fight or to challenge the tailors? The latter is likelier: London tailors have significant links to football down the centuries.

The tailors and skinners bear a later grudge. Both Worshipful Companies receive their Royal Charter in 1327. By 1484, they squabble over who marches ahead of who in annual civic processions to such a degree the Solomonic lord mayor resolves that they take it in turns. They are also required to invite the other company for dinner on alternate years. In 1515, an order of precedence of Livery Companies is established under Henry VIII. Both are ranked sixth and seventh, switching annually.[115] Perhaps their dispute is already established in 1373, when they meet in the ward of the cordwainers. Maybe they receive their charters on the same day. The Worshipful Company of Goldsmiths receive their charter in 1327 and sit fifth. Pity the Girdlers. They are granted a charter in March 1327, but only manage twenty-third.

---

111 Dutton, M.L., *Chaucer's Cunning: An Incarnational Pun and an Omission in the Middle English Dictionary*. The Chaucer Review, 2018, 53:1, p. 40.

112 Hessayon, A., *Beastly Furie, and Exstreme Violence*. In: Wagg, S., Pollock, A.M (eds.)., *The Palgrave Book of Sport, Politics and Harm*. Springer Nature Switzerland, Cham, Switzerland, 2021. pp. 38–39.

113 Aucoin, T., *When the Pancake Bell Rings*. Unpublished PhD thesis, University of Bristol, 2019. p. 109.

114 Otherwise known as pelters, they skinned, prepared, and sold animal hides and furs.

115 Often wrongly cited as the origin of the term at sixes and sevens. Chaucer uses the term in 1374.

At least the skinners and tailors can glance behind at the cordwainers, a distant twenty-seventh. And the unfortunate butchers, founded as early as 975AD, end up twenty-fourth.

Ball games prove troublesome in county Durham. In 1380, during the Shrove Tuesday game in Wolviston, a player is "hit on the shin and gravely injured while playing football" (*ludabat ad pilam pedalem*).[116,117] The game is notable for another reason: it is the second oldest Shrovetide game on record. The same year, 20s fines are handed out when a fight erupts at a Durham ball game between Wearmouth and Southwick.[118,119] Two Christmas games are also recorded in Durham: in Southwick in 1382, and Aycliffe in 1383.[120] Both are unspecified "ball games", that could be combination, carrying, sticking, or kicking. Either way, ball games are widely popular, their violence and vice an endemic problem that could merge with peasant grievances and threaten the realm. Then again, they serve a function as refined warfare. Southwick sanctions festive games but issues shilling fines for ad hoc games in the graveyard after Mass.[121] Aycliffe orders "all the tenants of the township that none shall play at ball."[122] The Durham village of East Merrington does not pussyfoot. In 1382, it threatens 40s fines for "ball-play".[123,124]

Statutes prove toothless and are regularly re-enacted. In 1389, Richard II issues a nationwide edict. A later translation is regularly quoted: "suche servauntes and laborers shall have bowes and arowes, and use the same the sondayes and hollydayes, and leave all playenge at tenyce or football, and other games called coytes, dyce, castynge of

116 Aucoin, T., *When the Pancake Bell Rings*. Unpublished PhD thesis, University of Bristol, 2019. p. 104.

117 Durham Cathedral Archive, GB-0033–DCD-Regr-1, Register 1, fol. ii. 95r. https://iiif.durham.ac.uk/index.html?manifest=t1mjd472w442&canvas=t1tr781wg294. https://n2t.durham.ac.uk/ark:/32150/s1pz50gw11v.xml. Accessed 24 October 2023.

118 Coulton, G.G., *The Medieval Village*. The University Press, Cambridge, 1925. p. 94.

119 A draconian fine; around two months' wages for a skilled tradesman. It was probably shared between the culprits.

120 Aucoin, T., *When the Pancake Bell Rings*. Unpublished PhD thesis, University of Bristol, 2019. pp. 306–307.

121 Coulton, G.G., *The Medieval Village*. The University Press, Cambridge, 1925. p. 93.

122 Ibid, p. 93.

123 Ibid, p. 93.

124 The cost of a horse, or three cows.

the stone, kayles,[125] and other such importune games."[126] The original Anglo-Norman reads, "les jeues as pelotes; siõn a meyn come a piee."[127] The earliest translation does not mention tennis: "the pleyes at the ball, nother hand nor foote." Handball and football. The first known reference to tennis is a decade later in John Gower's *In Praise of Peace*.[128] The first recorded fine for handball is in Essex in 1393/94, when John Bygelot and John atte Woode are "amerced 1d for continually playing at handball" (*ad pilam cum* manu).[129] Thomas Illeyghe is charged 12d for the same offence, in 1419/20.[130]

~

A c1316 French poem mentions an obscure game, *jeu de bonde*. Rarely found in history, it has been classified as a variant of *jeu de paume*, though an argument can be made for *soule*. The passage in question reads:

> *Tant qu'il avint qu'aprés la messe,*
> *Un jour en esté trois ou quatre*
> *Fuilz de borjois, pour eulz esbatre...*
> *Le gieu de bonde commencierent.*
> *L'un fiert l'estuef, l'autre rachace,*
> *Chascun pour fair bonne chace.*
> *Assés jouerent longuement.*[131]

In Old French, *bonde* means bounce or peasant, while *bondir* is to rush off briskly or with gusto.[132] *Chace* is a bouncing strategy used in *jeu de paume*, but also means chase. To confuse things further, if Middle French

---

125 An early version of skittles, using a stick rather than a bowl.

126 Luders, A., et al. (eds.)., *The Statutes of the Realm.* 11 Vols. Reprinted from 1816 edition by Dawsons, London, 1963. Vol. 2. pp. 354–355.

127 Ibid, p. 57.

128 Macauley, G.C. (ed.)., *The Complete Works of John Gower.* 4 Vols. Clarendon Press, Oxford, 1901. Vol. 3. p. 490. lns 295–296.

129 *Essex Archives Online.* https://www.essexarchivesonline.co.uk/ViewCatalogue.aspx?ID=326128. Accessed 25 October 2023.

130 *Essex Archives Online.* https://www.essexarchivesonline.co.uk/result_details.aspx?ThisRecordsOffSet=3&id=326164. Accessed 25 October 2023.

131 Roques, M. (ed.)., *Le Roman de Comte D'Anjou.* Jehan Maillart, c1316. Paris, 1931. p. 53, lns 1708–1715.

132 Kelham, R. (ed.)., *A Dictionary of the Norman or Old French Language.* Edward Brooke, London, 1779. p. 31; Van Daele, H., *Petit Dictionnaire de l'Ancien Français.* Librairie Garnier Frères, Paris, 1940. p. 58.

(1330–1500) has crept in, *bonde* can mean a bung to plug a barrel, and *bondir* to leap.[133,134] *Estuef* is a ball. If peasant and chase are used, the passage reads: "It happened that after the mass one day in summer, three or four sons of the town went out to amuse themselves … the game of peasants began. One sped with the ball, the others chased. Each chased well and they played for a long time." While this clearly implies a carrying game, using the alternative meanings of *bonde* and *chace* suggests *jeu de paume.*[135] But *jeu de paume* is historically played indoors. *Longue paume* is the outdoor version but does not involve running with the ball. And how can they bounce the ball while chasing the man *with* the ball? Of note, the sole reference to a location for *jeu de bonde* is in 1395, in Lisieux, Normandy.[136] *Soule* country. The poem describes an ad hoc rustic game requiring only three or four players, the equivalent of a kickaround. *Le gieu de bonde.* The game of peasants.

The passage contains rare material to support the theory that medieval ball games have their roots in warfare, in this case via chivalric tournaments. In the 'passage of arms', one group of knights defends a narrow passage from an equal number.[137] The passage is often the gate to a castle or town. The parallel with a person or team defending their territory is clear, whether it is a hoop, a wicket, or one half of a badminton court. Attacks on the passage are called *chasser* and counter-attacks *rechasser.* Both appear in the passage as *chace* and *rachace.* A later example is found in Edmund Spenser's *The Faerie Queen* (1590). Two knights chasing a messenger are themselves pursued by King Arthur: "So ran they all, as they had bene at bace, They being chased that did others chase."[138] There is evidence *chace* and *rachace* are associated with other medieval ball games.[139] The same applies to the terms "within" and "without". In Malory's 1485 *Le Morte D'Arthur,* Sir Galahad competes at a tourney:

---

133 *Dictionnaire du Moyen Français (1330–1500).* http://zeus.atilf.fr/dmf/. Accessed 29 April 2023.

134 Bung is interesting. It will later become a theory for the origin of the term "hockey".

135 Roques translates *bonde* to bouncing: (Roques, M. (ed.)., *Le Roman de Comte D'Anjou.* Jehan Maillart, c1316. Paris, 1931. p. 279); as does Gillmeister: Gillmeister, H., *Tennis, A Cultural History.* Leicester University Press, London and Washington, 1997. p. 39.

136 Gay, V., *Glossaire archéologique du Moyen Age et de la Renaissance.* 2 Vols. Librairie de la Société Bibliographique, Paris, 1887. Vol. 1. p. 174.

137 Gillmeister, H., *Medieval Sport: Modern Methods of Research—Recent Results and Perspectives.* The International Journal of the History of Sport, 1988, 5:1, p. 53.

138 Spenser, E., *The Faerie Queen.* Thomas Y. Crowell & Company, New York, 1903. p. 416.

139 Gillmeister, H., *Medieval Sport: Modern Methods of Research—Recent Results and Perspectives.* The International Journal of the History of Sport, 1988, 5:1, p. 55.

"Thus thurgh his grete hardynesse he bete abak alle the knyghtes without, And thenne they within cam oute and chaced hem alle aboute."[140]

These tournament terms are mentioned in several books of the late 1200s, the time when ball sports begin to appear in texts.[141] The chivalric use of *chaser* and *rechasser* provides further support that *jeu de bonde* is a kicking/carrying game. In a passage in *The Awntyrs* [Adventures] *off Arthur*, c1450–1475, a ghost foretells "Arthur's death, Gawain's death, and the disintegration of the fellowship, all through treason."[142] Once varnished with heroism and laughter, the Round Table is desolate. A lone child stirs the dust of the empty hall: "In riche Arthures halle, The barne playes at the balle."[143] In *The Turke and Sir Gawain*, the Turk takes the knight to the castle of the "King of the Isle of Man". The king's "hideous rout of giants strong and stout and uglie to look uppon", are so big "thou shalt see a tenisse ball that never knight in Arthurs hall is able to give it a lout."[144] Once there, the king challenges them: "Goe feitch me forth my tennisse ball, for play will I and see."[145] Sir Gawain and the Turk take on seventeen giants with a ball of brass "made for the giants hand; there was noe man in all England were able to carry it." All the giants are dying "to have struck out Sir Gawaines braine", but there can only be one winner.

Jousting is a dangerous, unregulated sport. Neither is it safe for the public. At each venue, knights and their entourage treat the locals despicably, demanding to be hosted and fed, stealing what they like. Henry I (r.1100–1135) and Henry II (r.1154–1189) ban jousting tournaments, as do several popes, who believe imperilled bodies imperil souls.[146,147] As the twelfth century winds to an end, Richard I

---

140 Sommer, H.O. (ed.)., *The Noble and Joyous Book Entytled Le Morte D'Arthur* by Thomas Malory. David Nutt, London, 1889. p. 689.

141 Gillmeister, H., *Medieval Sport: Modern Methods of Research–Recent Results and Perspectives.* The International Journal of the History of Sport, 1988, 5:1, p. 57.

142 Hahn, T. (ed.)., *Sir Gawain: Eleven Romances and Tales.* Medieval Institute Publications, Kalamazoo, Michigan, 1995. https://d.lib.rochester.edu/teams/text/hahn-sir-gawain-awntyrs-off-arthur. Accessed 29 September 2024.

143 Ibid, lns 309–310.

144 Ibid, *The Turke and Sir Gawain*. lns 131–133, 140–142.

145 Ibid, lns 73–74.

146 In 1130, 1139, 1148, and 1179. The papal ban was repealed by the Avignon pope John XXII in 1316. The repeal was not recognized by Rome.

147 McKenzie, C.R.L., *Sport, The Crown & The Common Law.* Unpublished PhD thesis, Bond University School of Law, 2001. p. 28.

establishes the first sporting regulatory authority in history. His 1194 *Proclamation on Tournaments* legitimises jousting, "So that our peace shall not be broken, the power of our judiciary shall not be threatened, and loss shall not fall on our royal forests."[148] Knights now require a licence, and must purchase passes for tournaments, which are restricted to five jousting venues.

If medieval warfare provides inspiration for the development of ball games, two transformative events are critical in the establishment of team sports. The associative nature of guilds in medieval Europe brings workers together in a "club" setting. "Guilds played a significant, sometimes dominant, role in urban society, taking responsibility for the lives of their members from child apprenticeship through working life into retirement, death, and burial."[149] Guilds bestow kinship and command loyalty. Similarly, the industrialisation of Britain pours labour into cities and men into factories, establishing communality and an interface for sociability.

Estuef, Middle French for ball, is of uncertain etymology, though it suggests an egg, and various spellings include *estouef* (lit. an egg), *esteuf*, and *estueaf*.[150] The word makes its first appearance in the thirteenth century, when balls are invariably oval, unable to maintain their shape after a few rough games.[151] The French poem *The Pilgrimage of Human Life*, c1330–1332, mentions an *estuef* and a playing stick. The author is a Cistercian monk at Chaalis Abbey, forty-one miles south of the Normandy border: "*Un estuef me faut pour jouer, Et une crocë a souler*."[152] "I need a ball to play, and a crook for *souler*." In 1369 Froissart spells it *estoef*, and in 1420 it is *estouef*.[153,154] Nevertheless,

148 Ibid, p. 29.

149 Szymanski, S., *A Theory of the Evolution of Modern Sport*. Journal of Sport History, 2008, 35:1, p. 25.

150 *ATILF (Analyse et Traitement Informatique de la Langue Française)*. https://lecteur-few.atilf.fr/lire/170/249. Accessed 6 January 2024.

151 Brosman, P.W., *The Frankonian Element in Old French*. Peter Lang Inc., Lausanne, Switzerland. p. 164.

152 Stürzinger, J.J. (ed.), *Le Pelerinage de la Vie Humaine*. Guillaume de Deguileville. Nichols & Sons, 25 Parliament Street, London, 1893. p. 370. lns 11835–11836.

153 Froissart, J., *Oeuvres de Froissart*. 3 Vols. Aug. Scheler, Brussels, Belgium, 1870. Vol. 1. p. 93. ln. 228.

154 Carpentier, P. (ed.), Du Fresne Du Cange. C, *Glossarium mediae et infimae Latinitatis*. Firmin Didot fratres, Paris, 1678. 1840 edition. 10 Vols. Vol. 2. p. 338.

it is likely that *estuef* comes from the Germanic tribe of Franks. *Stôt* is ball in Old Franconian, and spellings include *estoet* and *estuet*.[155] At its height, the Frankish empire covers what is now Belgium, France (except Brittany), and western and southern Germany. It is ruled by the Merovignian dynasty, c457–751, following the fall of the Roman Empire. Their successors, the Carolingians, rule until 987, before the Franks give way to the Capetians, who rule France until 1792. With such vast cultural influence, the Frankish would imprint their language upon the Latin of the day. *Stôt* is likely to have been used until Old French emerged from Vulgar Latin, within decades of the fall of the Franks. From there it would have evolved into *estuef.*

Controversy in 1323, when the elders of the city of Ambian take *l'estuef* from people playing on church land on the day of Lent.[156] Ash Wednesday. The day after Shrove Tuesday. The city is Amiens, in Picardy. The Ambians are a Belgian tribe from Northern Gaul. The Gauls dominate much of Europe from c400–300BC, until usurped by the Romans. It is a long bow to suggest that *soule* has Gaulish roots; it is far likelier it spread eastwards from Brittany. In 1348, an official document from Paris, presumably a coroner's roll, says that "the said deceased went … to play with others at *soule* in severe frost."[157] Paris. *Soule* is radiant. She is on the up.

In 1355, twelve miles east of Amiens, Hugh of Le Hamel in Picardy is arrested while she is playing at *soule*.[158,159] Notwithstanding a transcription error, it is the earliest record of a *woman* playing a ball game in modern history. Two years later, in a statement of what appears to be legal evidence, "the petitioners and several other people of the country were going to frolic at a game called choule."[160] Six years later, "several of the inhabitants of the town of Chaillevello … were playing

155 *ATILF (Analyse et Traitement Informatique de la Langue Française)*. https://lecteur-few.atilf.fr/lire/170/249. Accessed 6 January 2024.

156 Carpentier, P. (ed.)., Du Fresne Du Cange. C, *Glossarium mediae et infimae Latinitatis*. 10 Vols. Firmin Didot fratres, Paris, 1678. 1840 edition. Vol. 2. p. 325.

157 Ibid, 1846 edition. Vol. 6. p. 292.

158 Ibid, 1840 edition. Vol. 2. p. 338.

159 While Hugh is a male name, the Latin text uses the female *eam arrestasset*, not the male *eum arrestasset*.

160 Carpentier, P. (ed.)., Du Fresne Du Cange. C, *Glossarium mediae et infimae Latinitatis*. 10 Vols. Firmin Didot fratres, Paris, 1678. 1840 edition. Vol. 2. p. 338.

with each other "*ad soulam crossare*" [*soule* with a stick], and then the reaper came up … telling the aforesaid *soulants* [players] or *Crossants* that some carters … were leading their carts through the fields."[161] "*Soule* in the usual way is played outside the town" of Neufchâtel, Normandy, in 1369. The game appears to get out of hand, as someone asks them to calm down or stop. Whatever happens next, the matter is serious enough to make the State Calendar Rolls.[162] In the usual way. Stick instead of the emerging kick? Thirteen years later, "The drunkenness in the usual manner took place outside the town [Neufchâtel] … certain players, while getting drunk, bloodied a priest's face."[163] A letter from 1374 attests to the game's longevity: "In Chauny, in Vermandois, we were accustomed to it for so long that there is no memory to the contrary."[164]

In 1387, it is recorded that men of Lyons-la-Fôret and the county of Vexin Normand "are accustomed to a fight and assemble on the day of Lent to *Souler* and play Solle against each other in front of the Abbey of Our Lady of Mortemer."[165,166] That New Year's Day, the youth of La Chelles in Picardy, northwest France, play *Chouler à la crosse—soule* with a stick.[167,168] Earlier that year, "as they were playing a certain game called Choler de la crosse … the ball of the said game was sent by one of the company high into the air."[169] Another for the Rolls. Perhaps it makes a deadly descent. *Soule* is played in Paris, in front of the chapel of St Eustache in 1393, while in 1397, ten children are recorded playing *soule*, and Narbonne University prohibits "*ad pilam vel ad crossiam vel ad ludos*

161 Ibid, Vol. 2. p. 668.

162 Ibid, 1846 edition. Vol. 6. p. 321.

163 Luce, S., *La France pendant la guerre de cents ans*. Hachette, Paris, 1890. p. 112.

164 Gougaud, L., *La soûle en Bretagne et les jeux similaires du Cornwall et du Pays de Galles*. Annales de Bretagne. 1911. 27:4, p. 573.

165 Carpentier, P. (ed.)., Du Fresne Du Cange. C, *Glossarium mediae et infimae Latinitatis.* 10 Vols. Firmin Didot fratres, Paris, 1678. 1846 edition. Vol. 6. p. 321.

166 Vexin Normand and the bordering village of Lyons-La-Forêt lie in what is now Normandy. The Vexin were a Gaulish tribe. The county fell into Norman hands after several raids by Rollo in the ninth century.

167 From which lacrosse takes its name: the game is a variant of existing games played by Native Americans.

168 Carpentier, P. (ed.)., Du Fresne Du Cange. C, *Glossarium mediae et infimae Latinitatis.* 10 Vols. Firmin Didot fratres, Paris, 1678. 1840 edition. Vol. 2. p. 668.

169 Ibid, 1840 edition. Vol. 1. p. 715.

insultuosus"—ball games with sticks and other insulting games.[170,171,172] *Soule* basks *sous le soleil.* Narbonne. The south of France. Four hundred miles from Paris. *Soule* has to pinch herself. A new century dawns. What glories will it bring? She is far too popular for the authorities to halt. A shadow blots the sun. *Soule* smiles generously but declines the servant's wine. She has a game in the cloisters at three.

The spy whispers. "*Arbalestiers.*" Philip V cocks his ear. "*Archiers.*" Philip nods. He needs crossbowmen. He needs archers. In 1254, Louis IX seeks only to ban dice and chess, but the beatified Philip is popular and shrewd, a skilled negotiator.[173] His 1319 ban forbids games that do not serve the defence of France, including "*soularum villarumque ludos et his similes*" — "*soule* and village games and the like."[174] *Soule*'s association with villages is clear. Philip establishes local militia to keep the peace. Many of the men that had played *soule* will stop others, imperious in their uniforms. There is no mention of kicking in the Latin original, though a 1901 translation brackets the game as *soules* (*ballon a pied*)."[175] *Ballon a pied*: football.

Translations can be deceptive. When does *soule* morph from stick to kick? According to recorded history, the kicking game emerges later, an offshoot that comes to dominate. This does not rule out the possibility that *soule* originates as a kicking game. And why the same name? Surely a new one should be coined for the kicking game. Perhaps not. Hurling encompasses stick and carrying versions, possibly a kicking–carrying game too. Charles V follows Philip's prompt, in 1369, banning *soule* without mention of a kicking game.[176] Authorities in Brussels issue a

---

170 Jusserand, J.J., *Les Sports et jeux d'exercice dans l'ancienne France.* Plon-Nourrit et Cie, Paris, 1901. p. 270.

171 Godefroy, F., *Dictionnaire de l'ancienne langue française et de tous ses dialects.* 10 Vols. Paris, 1885. Vol. 5. p. 58.

172 Rashdall, H., *The Universities of Europe in the Middle Ages.* Henry Frowde, London, 1895. p. 670.

173 Michel, G. (ed.)., *Les Edicts et Ordonnances des Rois de France.* 4 Vols. Antoine Fontanon, Paris, 1611. Vol. 1. p. 672.

174 Jusserand, J.J., *Les Sports et jeux d'exercice dans l'ancienne France.* Plon-Nourrit et Cie, Paris, 1901. p. 24.

175 Ibid, p. 24.

176 In 1319, *jeux de palets, quilles, soule* (*ballon a pied*), etc.; in 1369, *tous jeus de dez, de tables, de paume, de quilles, de palet, de soule, de billes*, etc. In 1319, *soule* is specified as *ballon a pied*, or football, but not in 1367. 1319: Jusserand, J.J., *Les Sports et jeux d'exercice dans l'ancienne France.* Plon-Nourrit et Cie, Paris, 1901. p. 24. 1367; Carpentier, P. (ed.)., Du Fresne Du Cange. C., *Glossarium mediae et infimae Latinitatis.* 6 Vols. Firmin Didot fratres, Paris, 1678. 1733 edition. Vol. 2. p. 283.

similar edict in 1360. A stick game is explicit: "*wie met colven tsolt es om twintich scellinge oft op hare overste cleet.*"[177] *Colven* is stick and *tsolt* means "plays the *soule* game". In other words: "The playing of *soule* with a stick is banned, and anyone playing will be fined twenty shillings or lose their overcoat." *Kolven* soon eclipses *soule* as the name for the Flemish stick game.

Religious games are tolerated in France. As early as 1160, in French cathedrals at Christmas, "it is customary for archbishops and bishops to play with their subordinates in the cathedral close and to even indulge in a ball game."[178] By the late fourteenth century, in Auxerre Cathedral, a dance called *pelota* (ball game) is observed every Easter: "the dean and as many as 'a hundred' canons would gather at a paved stone labyrinth ... the newest member of the chapter carried a large leather ball."[179,180] In 1412, the cathedral chapter orders that the ball should be "smaller than usual, but too large to be grasped in one man's hand, requiring two hands to stop it."[181] A later description says that the ball is passed from the dancing dean in the middle to each dancing person in the circle around him.[182] In 1471, a fresh canon, convinced the practice is banned, refuses to provide a new ball.[183] Auxerre's "governors, magistrates, and citizens" are up in arms until he concedes. An 1826 paper mentions the ceremony's discontinuation in 1538.[184] It also reports "a curious battle" in Buckingham. A young man with no power below his knees, compensates with upper body strength. When he quarrels with "an acknowledged good boxer", they agree to a duel of fists. The youth, fighting from a sitting position, "gave his antagonist a complete drubbing ... and 'finished him in style,' to the great satisfaction of many spectators."[185] There is a

177 Gillmeister, H., *Golf on the Rhine: On the Origins of Golf, with Sidelights on Polo*. The International Journal of the History of Sport, 2002, 19:1, p. 2.

178 Harris, M., *Sacred Folly: A New History of the Feast of Fools*. Cornell University Press, United States, 2011. p. 54.

179 Ibid, p. 56.

180 Auxerre FC launched the careers of Laurent Blanc, Eric Cantona, Djibril Cissé, and Stéphane Guivarc'h.

181 Harris, M., *Sacred Folly: A New History of the Feast of Fools*. Cornell University Press, United States, 2011. p. 56.

182 Ibid, p. 56.

183 Ibid, p. 59.

184 *Star*. 12 December 1826. p. 3.

185 Ibid.

reference to church games as late as 1624, in Thomas Middleton's play *A Game at Chess*:

> I'll make him the balloon-ball of the churches
> And both the sides shall toss him; he looks like one,
> A thing swelled up and mingled with drink and urine,
> And will bound well from one side to another![186]

"A very satirical thing [that] gives very great enjoyment," raves the Florentine Ambassador. "Merriment, hubbub, and applause," says the Spanish ambassador.[187] He is being sarcastic. The play is a satire on Anglo-Spanish politics, unfolding as a chess game. The pieces include James I of England, Philip IV of Spain, and Charles, heir to the English throne. Most bile is directed at the Black Knight, the former Spanish Ambassador, and villain of the piece; most biting comedy at the Fat Bishop, the corpulent, morally corrupt Primate of Dalmatia and all Croatia (who dies a month after the premiere). In the ballon-ball verse, the Black Knight is talking about the Fat Bishop. It gets worse. The bishop's sleaze is later lampooned with stomach-churning luridness: "Forbear, or I shall melt in the place I stand, and let forth a fat bishop in sad syrup."[188] The characters are so barely concealed that the production causes outrage. Who else but the Ambassador has an anal fistula, so mockingly skewered by Middleton. The play is pulled nine days later.

By the fourteenth century football is a simile. Chaucer's *Canterbury Tales* begins with *The Knight's Tale*. The knight describes a battle, visceral and intense, skewered chests, helmets hewed, jetting blood, crushed bones. Many knights are unhorsed: "Ther stomblen steedes stronge, and doun gooth al; He rolleth under foot as dooth a bal."[189] "Their strong steeds stumble now, and down goes all. One rolls beneath their feet as doth a ball." Thomas Walsingham's c1394 *St Albans Chronicle* pulls no

---

186 Howard-Hill, T.H. (ed.)., *A Game at Chess*. Manchester University Press, 1993. Act 2, Sc 2, lns 73–76.

187 Streete, A., *Polemical Laughter in Thomas Middleton's A Game at Chess (1624)*. English Literary Renaissance, 2020, 50:2, p. 296.

188 Ibid, p. 328.

189 MacCracken, H.N. (ed.)., *The College Chaucer*. Yale University Press, New Haven, 1913. *The Knights Tale*. p. 76. lns 2613–2614.

punches. His opus includes thirty-three couplets lashing the Flemish. It concludes:

> And therefore, ye fflemmynges, that flemmynges ben named,
> To compare with englisshmen, ye aught to be ashamed!
> Ye be nothing elles worth, but gret wordes to camp;
> Sette ye stiff, & beth in pees, God give you quadenramp![190]

"And therefore, you Flemings, that Flemings be named, to compare with Englishmen you should be ashamed! You're worth nothing more than big words to kick, sit still and bathe in piss, God give you bad luck!" Walsingham has more to say in *Historia Anglicana.* In 1379, when the Scottish harry the plague-riddled north of England, they attack those "brought to their knees by disease and pestilence" like "inhuman brutes." When they kill the uninfected and behead them: "they were not afraid to strike and rebound with their feet, in the manner of those who play with the ball."[191] The concluding words of one version berate the youth of today who, "enjoy protracted vigils beyond midnight, and sleep until noon, playing football, and gambling with horrible oaths."[192]

Bartholomew the Englishman is living in Paris when his encyclopaedia *De proprietatibus rerum* (On the Properties of Things) is completed, c1240. It is such a bestseller one hundred manuscripts still survive. When it is finally translated into English, in 1398, it includes the phrase "in pleiinges of balles and of stertinges", "in the act of playing ball and cavorting."[193] English is grappling with its own terminology for ball games. In the 1370s, John Wycliffe rails against Catholic clergy who use Christian men as "shulde chulle a foot-balle."[194,195] In Middle English *chulle* means kick, from *chullen*: to kick. No coincidence it sounds remarkably like *choule*. The equivalent verb in Old English is *spornettan*,

---

190 Robbins, R.H., *A Middle English diatribe against Philip of Burgundy.* Neophilologus, 1955, 39, p. 142.

191 Riley, H.T. (ed.)., *Thomae Walsingham, quondam monachi S. Albani, Historia Anglicana.* 2 Vols. Longman, Green, Longman, Roberts, and Green, London, 1863. Vol. 1. pp. 409–410.

192 Ibid, 1864 edition. Vol. 2. p. 406.

193 Lewis, R.E. (ed.)., *Middle English Dictionary.* University of Michigan Press, 1990. Part S.14. p. 686.

194 As should kick a football.

195 Arnold, T. (ed.)., *Selected English works of John Wyclif.* Clarendon Press, Oxford, 1871. p. 280.

from which the kicking sense of "to spurn" derives.[196,197] *Chullen* derives from the Old Norman word *chouler*: to kick a ball, and from the Medieval Latin *cheollāre*, which equates to Du Cange's *cheolare*: to propel a ball with the foot. The term is also used c1340–1349, when Richard Rolle writes: "And chulles hym as men don a balle þat is casten fro hande to hande."[198] "And kicks him like men do a ball that is thrown from hand to hand."

In 1678, Charles Du Cange writes that *cheolare* is a game familiar to the villagers in Picardy; but the word is medieval, just as *chullen* is Old French. The implication is that *choule* (or any of its variations) refers to the kicking game, and any early references with no mention of a stick could refer to it. This includes Lambert's *cheolandum*, c1198–1206. If so, it is football's first reference, and makes the village of Ardres the site of the world's oldest football pitch. History may reference far more kicking games than is commonly accepted. It also means that *chulle* arrived with the Normans. Why the name did not attach itself to the English game is unknown. Kick, derived from the German *kiken*, eclipsed *chulle* and *spornettan*.[199] Similarly, Anglo-Saxon *fõt* is favoured over Latin *pedalis* and Anglo-French *pé*, just as *bal* is preferred to the Latin *pila*. Ball. A word so old its lineage is rooted in Proto-Indo-European, a language believed to have originated six and a half thousand years ago. Balls have been around forever. Ball is an easy pick. Did an English love of frankness prompt the names of ball games of the hands and feet, or did the burgeoning confidence of a nation that had moulded its own inimitable language encourage it to go its own way? Either way. Handball. Football.

---

196 Wright, J., Wright, E.M., *Old English Grammar.* Henry Frowde, Oxford University Press, London. 1908. No. 657. p. 313.

197 "That like a football you do spurn me thus?" Cunningham, H., *The Works of William Shakespeare. A Comedy of Errors.* Methuen and Co., London, 1907. Act 1, Sc 2, lns 82–85.

198 Horstman, C. (ed.), *Yorkshire Writers: Richard Rolle of Hampole and his Followers.* 2 Vols. Swan Sonnenschein & Co., London, 1896. Vol. 2. p. 67.

199 Stratmann, F.H., Bradley, H., *A Middle English Dictionary, Containing Words Used by English Writers from the Twelfth to the Fifteenth Century.* Lowe and Brydone Ltd., Thetford, Norfolk, 1891. p. 376.

CHAPTER FOUR
1400–1499 I

Seven kings warm the throne across the embattled century. The Hundred Years' War dominates the first fifty years, the Wars of the Roses the second. The bitter wrangling of the divided House of Plantagenet likewise cleaves the century: three kings from Lancaster, three from York. The Plantagenets are dethroned, and the Middle Ages consigned to history by the spectacular arrival of the Tudors in 1485. Neither house loves football. Across the century, the game receives fifteen proclamatory bans. This bloody century must have its archers. Seven are nationwide, eight municipal: Halifax, London, and Leicester twice, Northallerton and Walsall.[1,2] The Halifax fine rises from 1s in 1450, to 1s 4d in 1454, no doubt inflated by recidivism.[3] In Leicester, "Unlawful gamons … that is to sey at dyce, cardyng, haserdyng, tenes, bowlys, pykkyng with arowes, coytyng with hors-shon, penypryk, foteball, ne cheker in the myre", draw fines of 6d, and for the owners of the gardens or places where they are practised, 4d.[4,5] At least there are jobs to be had. The 1450–1452 accounts of the Corporation of Lydd, in Kent, include, "for a cry made for keeping the wacche and the warde on the sea-shore 1d. For another cry to cease ball [pilam] playing, and to take to bows 1d."[6] Tennis is

1 Dunning, E., Sheard, K., *Barbarians, Gentlemen and Players. A Sociological Study of the Development of Rugby Football.* Australian National University Press, Canberra, 1979. p. 30.

2 Hessayon, A., *Beastly Furie, and Exstreme Violence.* In: Wagg, S., Pollock, A.M (eds.)., *The Palgrave Book of Sport, Politics and Harm.* Springer Nature Switzerland, Cham, Switzerland, 2021. pp. 31–32.

3 Marples, M., *A History of Football.* Secker and Warburg, London, 1954. p. 30.

4 *The Scottish Law Review and Sherif Court Reports.* 79 Vols. William Hodge and Co., Glasgow, 1901. *The Scottish Law Review and Sherif Court Reports.* Vol. 17. p. 272.

5 *Haserdyng* (hazard) is a dice game; *pykking with arrows* is believed to have involved throwing arrows at a target; *penypryk* is penny prick: participants throw iron sticks at a mark, classically pennies on wooden sticks; *coytyng with hors-shon* is quoits with horseshoes; and *ne checker in the myre* is probably *dun in the mire*: "An old Christmas game … in which the horse in the mire is represented by a heavy log, and the players compete to lift and carry it off." Drabble, M., Stringer, J., Hard. (eds.)., The Concise Oxford Companion to English Literature. Oxford University Presse, 2007. https://www.oxfordreference.com/display/10.1093/acref/9780199214921.001.0001/acref-9780199214921-e-1880?rskey=8Mi6go&result=1. Accessed 11 October 2024.

6 *Report of the Royal Commission on Historical Manuscripts.* 16 reports. Eyre and Spottiswoode, London, 1877. Vol. 6. Pt. 1. p. 520.

becoming a nuisance. By 1457, the cry is "that no man shulde playe at the tenys."[7]

A 1409 decree prohibits the Hocktide tradition of "hokkyng": couples married in the preceding year are "captured", and then released once they provide money to buy footballs; maddening but harmless.[8] The indenture includes the word foteballe.[9,10,11] Hocking is difficult to put down. Between 1406 and 1442, it is banned fourteen times.[12] Henry IV renews his ban on football and other sports in London, in 1410;[13] anyone "that doth contrary … shall have imprisonment by Six Days."[14] In 1477, Edward IV outlaws many games, including "dise, coyte, foteball … closshe, keyles, halfbowle, handyn and handowte, and quekeborde."[15,16] Latin and English versions of the proclamation call football *pilam pedal* and fotebal, and tennis *tenis* and *tenys*.[17] Football and other games are sanctioned over the twelve days of Christmas, the last five are not; played around taverns and considered games of chance, they are believed to be

7 *Fifth Report of the Royal Commission on Historical Manuscripts*. Eyre & Spottiswoode, London, 1876. Report. 1. p. 521.

8 Hocktide was the second Monday and Tuesday after Easter.

9 "Memorials: 1409" in *Memorials of London and London Life in the 13th, 14th and 15th Centuries*, ed. H T Riley (London, 1868), pp. 570–576. *British History Online*. http://www.british-history.ac.uk/no-series/memorials-london-life/pp570–576 Accessed 26 August 2023.

10 A common variation was for men to tie up women on the Monday, and vice versa on the Tuesday. A similar, widespread, year-long tradition was to wait outside churches and ask newly-weds for money for a football.

11 Bishop Carpenter banned the practice in Worcester in 1450.

12 Roberts, G.R.P., *Popular Recreation in the Middle Ages*. Unpublished MA thesis, McGill University, 1932. p. 41.

13 England and Wales. Sovereign. *Actis made by Dyuers our most Noble Progenytours Knynges of this Realme Agaynst Unlaufull Games* [Proclamations. 1536]. London, 1536. https://www.proquest.com/books/actis-made-dyuers-our-most-noble-progenytours/docview/2240946247/se-2. Accessed 10 July 2023.

14 Luders, A., Tomlins, T.E., France, J., Taunton, W.E., Raithby, J. (eds.)., *The Statutes of the Realm*. 11 Vols. London, 1810–1828. Vol. 2. p. 163.

15 Given-Wilson, C. (ed.)., *The Parliament Rolls of Medieval England*. The National Archives. Boydell and Brewer, 2005. http://www.sd-editions.com.ap1.proxy.openathens.net/AnaServer?PROME+0+start.anv. Accessed 4 June 2023.

16 Closshe: a Flemish forbear of croquet. A bowl (klos) is driven through a hoop, using a spade- or chisel-shaped instrument. Keyles, more commonly kayles: an early version of skittles, using a stick rather than a bowl. Half-bowle: a solid half ball is used to knock down skittles. Handyn and handowte: unknown, but believed to be a stick and ball game. See: Bostwick, A.E., Champlin, J.D. *Young Folk's Cyclopedia of Games and Sports*. New York, 1890. p. 224. Quekeborde: similar to shovelboard.

17 'Folios 141–151: Feb 1478–9', in *Calendar of Letter-Books of the City of London: L, Edward IV-Henry VII*. Edited by Reginald R Sharpe (London, 1912), *British History Online*, accessed October 11, 2024, https://www.british-history.ac.uk/london-letter-books/voll/pp162-170.

gateways to robberies, murder, and other "heinous Felonies."[18] Persons permitting such games on their property face a staggering three years imprisonment, those playing two years; both incur an additional ten pound fine.[19,20]

Middle English is usurping Latin. The 1440 *Promptorium Parvulorum Sive Clericorum* (*A Storehouse for Young Scholars*) translates *piludius* as a "*pleyare at the balle*", and *pililudo* as "*pleyyn at the balle*",[21] while a 1483 English–Latin wordbook translates *pila pedalis* as *fute balle*.[22] A Parisian book of hours, c1400, is rich in sporting images.[23] There are two men bowling, and two boys with spinning tops. One image has two men with griffin legs. One is holding a ball; the other is pointing to the text: "Rest from pleasure and let me not forget my ignorance." In a similar image a griffin-man is set to bowl while another points to his right. A fifth image has a man about to hit a bouncing cricket-sized ball with a curved stick. A man holding a curved stick stands opposite. The adjacent leaf shows two men with rectangular paddle sticks, playing with an early shuttlecock—a rounded stick with feathers at the end. The game is battledore, an early version of badminton played by the lower classes, though there is evidence it was played at the English royal court in the twelfth century. The image is the first known depiction of early badminton.

One illustration depicts trapball.[24] A man with a paddle-shaped bat is standing before a waist-high stick, bifurcated two-thirds up. A crook-shaped stick pivots in the cleft, and a ball rests in the crook. The rules of the game are simple. When the stick is struck, the batsman hits the rising ball as far as he can. Another scene has two men playing ball

---

18 McKenzie, C.R.L., *Sport, The Crown & The Common Law*. Unpublished PhD thesis, Bond University School of Law, 2001. p. 42.

19 Luders, A., Tomlins, T.E., France, J., Taunton, W.E., Raithby, J. (eds.)., *The Statutes of the Realm*. 11 Vols. London, 1810–1828. Vol. 2. pp. 478–479.

20 A year's wages for a skilled tradesman in 1477. £8800 in 2024.

21 Mayhew, A.L., (ed.)., *Promptorium Parvulorum*. Galfridus Anglicus. Kegan Paul, Trench, Trübner and Co., Ltd., London, 1908. pp. 351, 357. A transcription of Winchester Cathedral's 1485 manuscript.

22 Herrtage, S. J. H. (ed.)., *Catholicon Anglicum: an English-Latin Wordbook, Dated 1483*. N. Trübner & Co., London, 1882. p. 404.

23 Bodleian Library, Oxford: MS Douce 62, *Book of Hours*, c1400–1410, fols. 96r, 72v, 143r, 117r, 101v, 102r.

24 Ibid, fol. 122r.

with upturned brooms.[25] While the ball is scored, they are unlikely to be jesters or sacramental shepherds, as they have makeshift sticks, the ball is cricket-sized, and there is no mention of Psalm 52. A ninth folio shows what may be closh, an early form of croquet. A half-kneeling man appears to be using a wooden block to hit a ball through a small arch on the ground. A man stands opposite, holding a faintly-outlined narrow-handled straight bat. Behind him is another ball and a pointed object with a wide base.[26] Another illustration shows six of these objects lined up. An angry-looking man with a long stick intends to knock them over, seemingly not in the spirit of the game.[27] Images elsewhere confirm them as skittles.[28,29] The manuscript is illustrated by a Frenchman, so all games depicted are played in France and recognisable enough to garland a religious work. There is earthiness too. One leaf depicts a monkey spreading his buttocks, daring a bowman to aim true.[30] Other sports are included, hunting and fishing, jousting and water-quintain, there are even butterfly catchers; but there is no football. *Soule* is referenced in other French manuscripts: an adolescent with a curved stick, a griffin man with curved stick and ball.[31,32] All these illuminated stickball games across the fourteenth and fifteenth centuries. *Soule* kicks off the square toed boots favoured by peasant players, slips into her silk poulaines, and reclines on the window seat. She taps her staff idly against them, luxuriating in her popularity.

The most remarkable images are found on three leaves of a French book of hours. The first leaf has eleven players with sticks, gathered into three groups in a picturesque setting.[33] Four sticks are curved, the others straight, ending in rectangular blocks. Five sticks are inserted

25 Ibid, fol. 136v.

26 Ibid, fol. 47v.

27 Ibid, fol. 65v.

28 E.g., Morgan Library, New York: MS M.763, *Der Renner*, c1475–1499, fol. 133v.

29 A similar picture depicts a half-kneeling man with a stick and small ball opposite six skittles. See, Bibliothèque Cantonle et Universitaire, Lausanne, U 964, end of the thirteenth century, fol. 364r.

30 Bodleian Library, Oxford: MS Douce 62, *Book of Hours*, c1400—410, fol. 49v.

31 Bibliothèque Nationale de France, Paris, MS. Fr. 22532, *Livre des proprietés des choses de Bathélemy l'Anglais,* c1401–1500, n.p. Image 169: https://gallica.bnf.fr/ark:/12148/btv1b90592858/f169.item.zoom. Accessed 29 April 2023.

32 *The Index of Medieval Art*. https://theindex.princeton.edu/s/view/ViewWorkOfArt.action?id=D71270E1-F91A-491B-8125–0D749436649F. Accessed 30 July 2023.

33 Musée Condé, Chantilly: MS 0076, 1362, *Heures d'Adélaïde de Savoie*, c1460–1465, fol. 002v.

midway into the blocks at right angles, like croquet mallets, two are inserted into one end, creating a straight stick. Two groups play on grass in the foreground. Within each group, a player is attempting to putt a cricket-sized ball at a two-foot tapered narrow pole planted in the ground. Two men in the background employ a golf-sized ball with their mallet-like sticks. Two others idle with curved sticks. Without doubt, the image depicts an early form of golf. The second leaf is fascinating.[34] In the foreground, six men play five others at *soule* on grass. They all have curved sticks except one player who has a mallet-like stick. Surprisingly, the brown ball is football-sized and possibly cased in leather. A four-a-side battledore game plays out in the centre of the page. The players have square thin-handled paddle-bats, one of which has launched a dart-like shuttlecock. A third leaf also depicts early golf.[35] All three men hold rectangular block sticks. One is hoping to knock his cricket-sized ball against a thin pole on a grass mound. His stick resembles a modern putter. Another ball at the bottom of the mound has attracted a dog's attention. Further up the page, four players are rudely interrupted by the appearance of a celestial host, ushering in God. Elsewhere, boys throw snowballs, and a boy leaps over a rope held by two friends.[36,37] A Flemish book of hours, c1540, contains the first known illustration of established golf.[38] Three men hold sticks resembling irons. They appear to have wooden shafts and metal heads. One is nudging his golf ball into the hole; another is putting from four yards out.

No known manuscript contains an illustration of football. The ambiguous misericords of Gloucester Cathedral may carry the earliest depictions. A c1450 misericord at All Souls College, Oxford, possibly has another: a man has his legs splayed, with what looks like a deflated football at one foot.[39] Wrestling and jousting aside, misericords infrequently carry carvings of sport. There are two in Barcelona Cathedral, which

---

34 Ibid, fol. 011v.

35 Ibid, fol. 029.

36 Ibid, fol. 012v.

37 Ibid, fol. 009.

38 British Library, London: MS 24098, *Book of Hours, Use of Rome (The 'Golf Book')*, c1540, fol. 27.

39 Hessayon, A., *Beastly Furie, and Exstreme Violence*. In: Wagg, S., Pollock, A.M (eds.)., *The Palgrave Book of Sport, Politics and Harm*. Springer Nature Switzerland, Cham, Switzerland, 2021. p. 62.

was constructed between 1298 and 1448. The first shows a large figure playing a portable organ. A figure peeks out from under the organist's skirt and hits a ball with a club.[40] The second depicts a man with a curved stick in his hands and a ball between his feet, a rare early representation of a stickball game in Spain.[41] Another exception is a 1552 misericord in Champeaux, France, featuring two boys playing battledore with paddles identical to table tennis rackets.[42]

In 1410, the Bishop of Lincoln bans ball play, grazing animals, blasphemous talk, and archery from the graveyard of the cathedral.[43] The prior of Bicester Priory, Oxfordshire, is not so inclined. The 1425 accounts include a gift from the prior of fourpence each "to sundry persons playing at football on the feast of St Katherine, Virgin and Martyr."[44,45] It is in Bicester, in 1261, that little Stephen le Taylor fell on his scissors, inadvertently bestowing the world with the first mention of a *kicking* game in modern history.[46] The accounts list gifts given to those who assist the priory on feast days: servants who clean the fishpond near the mill receive 6d apiece, a harper 8d, a minstrel 12d, and a Carmelite preacher 3s 4d.[47] The players provide a spectacle worthy of a gift, and the inference is that they were asked to play.

Wye College, Kent, is established to educate secular priests and schoolchildren in 1447/48. Its founding statutes includes a ban on dice, ball games, or participation "in the games called Somergamys", particularly with the intention of making money.[48] It is the first known interdiction against "summer games", which incorporate summer festivities like May Day, and

---

40 SH-09. https://www.misericords.co.uk/barcelona_des.html. Accessed 10 August 2023.

41 Block, C.E., *Corpus of Medieval Misericords Iberia*. Harvey Miller Publishers, Turnhout, Belgium, 2009. p. 22.

42 *The Index of Medieval Art.* https://ima.princeton.edu/digital-image-collections/view/21032. Accessed 30 July 2023.

43 Archer, M., *The Register of Bishop Philip Repingdon*. 3 Vols. Lincoln Record Society, 1963. Vol. 1. p. 182.

44 £14 in 2024.

45 Dunkin, J., *The History and Antiquities of Bicester, a Market Town in Oxfordshire*. Richard and Arthur Taylor, Shoe-Lane, Bicester, 1816. p. 246.

46 Jobson, A.L., *The Oxfordshire eyre roll of 1261*. In: Wagg, S., Pollock, A. (eds.), *The Palgrave Book of Sport, Politics and Harm*, Springer Nature Switzerland, Cham, Switzerland, 2021. p. 27.

47 Ibid, p. 246.

48 Gibson, J.M., *Records of Early English Drama. Kent: Diocese of Canterbury*. University of Toronto Press Incorporated, 2002. pp. 911–912.

"idle and frivolous but not necessarily indecent plays."[49] Indecorous enough for the Church. Monk Robert de Brunne lumps it with dancing and carols as immoral practices: "Daunces, karols, somour games, Of many swych come many shames."[50] A collection of festival sermons includes a conundrum. Where do you bury those who "dye sodeynly as in playingis of balles and stirtyngis [leaping]." No last rites, no churchyard. Unless. Give the corpse a right old scrubbing, says the priest, and it cleanses the soul too.[51]

The clergy themselves are not averse to offending God. In 1453, the Synod of Cashel specifies that priests must avoid games of chance, abstain from violence and theft, and not grow beards or nourish their hair.[52] The Archbishop of Canterbury is eager to sweep clerical offences under the carpet. In 1462, a callow Edward IV, new to the throne and easily influenced by him, prohibits all "judges or officers to try or punish any archbishop, bishop, or other clergyman for treason, ravishing women, or any other crime."[53] In 1466, the provincial council in York, feels the need to remind priests this is not a carte blanche. It declares that priests should be busy with their books, and avoid shops, shows, "cells of suspected women", and "noxious or prohibited games."[54] "Wrestling, archery, or games which may provide the cause or occasion of sin, dissension, hatred, or strife", are inserted in 1518.[55] Perhaps football is a different matter. In 1439, during the Anglo-French peace convention in Calais, a football match is organised in honour of the Bishop of Vicq, in Catalonia. The only named player is the Archbishop of Rheims, who sustained such a "shinner", he is unable to attend a conference the following day.[56]

~

49 Wenzel, S., *'Somer Game' and Sermon References to a Corpus Christi Play.* Modern Philology, 1989, 86:3, p. 276.

50 Furnivall, F.J. (ed.), *Robert of Brunne's "Handlyng Synne,": A.D. 1303.* Kegan Paul, Trench, Trübner and Co., Limited, London, 1901. lns 4681–4682.

51 Weatherly, E.H. (ed.), *Speculum Sacerdotale.* Oxford University Press, 1936. p. 231.

52 Wilkins, D. (ed.), *Concilia Magnae Britanniae et Hiberniae.* 4 Vols. R. Gosling, F. Gyles, T. Woodward, C. Davis, London, 1737. Vol. 3. p 567.

53 Tomlins, F.G., *A History of England.* 3 Vols. John Williamson and Co., London, 1839. Vol. 1. p. 525.

54 Wilkins, D. (ed.), *Concilia Magnae Britanniae et Hiberniae.* 4 Vols. R. Gosling, F. Gyles, T. Woodward, C. Davis, London, 1737. Vol. 3. p. 605.

55 Ibid, p. 667.

56 Hook, F.W., *The Lives of the Archbishops of Canterbury.* 12 Vols. Richard Bentley, London, 1867. Vol. 5. pp. 232–233.

In 1390, John Gower writes in *Mirour de l'Omme* of preventing a good return at *jeu de paume*.[57] He adds that a ball is a child's greatest treasure.[58] Nine years later, in *In Praise of Peace*, he provides the earliest known reference to tennis.

> Of the Tenetz to winne or lese a chace,
> Mai no lif wie er that bal be ronne.[59]

"Whether the chase is won or lost at tennis cannot be known until the ball is run" is a metaphor for life: success cannot be guaranteed with victory now, it is contingent on future events.[60] Tennis pares her broken nails. She has scraped into fourteenth century, borne on a metaphor. Victory now, but what of her future? She turns her hands, considers her palms. Hers is an English name, probably taken from the Anglo-Norman *tenez*: To hold. To hold what? A racket? Is this when rackets appear and a name required for this new game? Spellings abound: *tenetz* (Gower, 1399), *tenys* and *tynes* (Lydgate, c1415), *tenyes* (1418), *tenyys pley,* and *chase* (*Promptorium Parvulorum,* 1440),[61] *teneys pleyare* and *teneys* (1441), *tenyce* (Tiptoft, 1481) *tennys* (1493), *tenisse* and *tennisse* (*The Turke and Sir Gawain*, c1500), *tenyse* (1528), and *tennise* (1599),[62] not to mention *tenise*, *tenies*, *tenes*, *tennes*, and *teneis*.

Her first fifteenth century reference appears in 1415, when John Lydgate celebrates the protracted siege of Harfleur, the prelude to Agincourt:

"A tonne of tenys ballys I shall hym sende, For to pleye him with all … Swyche tenys bally I schal hym sende As schall tere the roof all of his all … For they shall play with harflete A game at tynes [tennis] … myne pleyers that y have hedyr brought. Their ballys beth of stonys round [the players I have brought here have round stone balls] … Tenys seyde the grete gonne, How felawes we go to game."[63]

---

57 Macaulay, G.C., *The Complete Works of John Gower.* 4 Vols. Henry Frowde, University of Oxford, 1899. Vol. 1. p. 90. lns 7741–7744.

58 Ibid, ln 1458.

59 Ibid, lns 295–296.

60 Ibid, p. 554.

61 Mayhew, A.L., (ed.)., *Promptorium Parvulorum.* Galfridus Anglicus. Kegan Paul, Trench, Trübner and Co., Ltd., London, 1908. pp. 76, 476.

62 Ibid, p. 717.

63 Nicolas, N.H., Tyrrell, E., Brushfield, T.N. (eds.)., *A Chronicle of London from 1089 to 1483.* Longman, Rees, Orme, Brown and Green, 1827. pp. 216–217, 220–221.

Three years later, the Worshipful Company of Grocers are sick of non-fellows playing tennis in their hall: "They schalle not suffre no man to playe at Þe tenyes withinne the sayd place, Excepte thoo that ben Fremen Shoppeholderys of Þe sayd Feleshepe."[64] Like countless rulings against sport, it fails to stand the test of time, and is restated in 1443.[65] A John Audelay poem in praise of the infant Henry VI, in 1426, and another Audelay poem, in 1439, are the only other references before she emerges triumphant, the *enfant terrible* of ball games.[66]

It begins with the 1440 *Promptorium Parvulorum*: "Chase: of tenyys, pley or oder lyke".[67] While she is banned in Westminster in 1441, five years later the Privy Council mentions specified places "to pleye at Þe teneys balle."[68] In 1448, a fallout between the townspeople and clergy of Exeter includes the closure of the cloisters to the public. The bishop has a point: "Ungoodly ruled peple, most custumabely yong peple … have exercised unlawfull games, such as the toppe, queke, penny-prykke, and most atte tenys, by the which the walles of the saide Cloistre have be defowled and the glas wyndowes all to brost [broken]."[69,70] They duly comply. Sort of. Three years later, in a rambling edict, the bishop issues a warning to those playing tennis in the churchyard of the Church of the Blessed Mary of Ottery. The pious are troubled by "laughter, shouting, immoderate mirth, indecent and indiscreet dances, indecent mockeries, and harmful plays proper to the market-place or the stage … some persons … do not fear … to play, or rather to mock, at a ball game commonly called tennis [tenys] in the churchyard."[71]

---

64 Lewis, R.E. (ed.)., *Middle English Dictionary*. 13 Vols. University of Michigan Press, 1993. Vol. 11. p. 219.

65 Kingdon, J.A. (ed.)., *Facsimile of First Volume of Ms. Archives of the Worshipful Company of Grocers of the City of London, A.D. 1345–1463*. 2 Vols. Richard Clay and Sons, London, 1886. Vol. 2. p. 124.

66 Halliwell, J.O. (ed.)., *The Poems of John Audelay: A Specimen of the Shropshire Dialect in the Fifteenth Century*. 14 Vols. T. Richards, 1844. Vol. 14. p. viii.

67 Mayhew, A.L., (ed.)., *Promptorium Parvulorum*. Galfridus Anglicus. Kegan Paul, Trench, Trübner and Co., Ltd., London, 1908. pp. 76, 476.

68 Lewis, R.E. (ed.)., *Middle English Dictionary*. 13 Vols. University of Michigan Press, 1993. Vol. 11. p. 219.

69 Moore, S.A., *Letters and papers of John Shillingford, mayor of Exeter 1447–1450*. J.B. Nichols and Sons, Parliament Street, London, 1871. p. 101.

70 Penny prick: players cast iron sticks at a mark, classically pennies on wooden sticks. Toppe may be spinning tops, while queke is likely to be quekeborde, a game similar to shovelboard.

71 Wasson, J.M. (ed.)., *Devon*. University of Toronto Press, 1986. pp. 328–329.

Sport is testing the patience of the mayor of Walsall. In 1450, he threatens citizens with jail if they play "at eny unlawefull games, except in Cristemas, as dyce, tables, cardes, cloch, tenes, foteball …"[72] Norwich's meandering edict of 1424—that banned "pleye atte tenyes, ne coyting, ne dises, ne non other disonest pleyes, upon peyn of prisonment"—is given a crisp makeover at the end of Henry VII's reign: "arresten alle maner of nyghtwalkers, baratoors [brawlers], and mysdoers, comune tenyse pleyers, and hasardowris [dice players], bowlers, valiant [able-bodied] and mighty beggers."[73]

In one of Wakefield's Towneley Plays, c1450, the three shepherds have one object each to present to the Infant Jesus. The third shepherd says: "I bring the bot a ball: Have and play the withall, And go to the tenys."[74] "I bring thee but a ball, play with it, and go to the tennis." Precious and fragrant, and fit for a god. In the late 1450s, a man is paid a penny for crying out that "no man shulde playe at the tenys; another is paid 2d in 1462 "for two cryis, one for tenys pleyers, another for the waycche." Double standards, then, the following year when Syr Wylyam Warner is paid 4s 1d "for money leyd owht be hym for pleyying at the tennys", and in 1464 when a servant pays the 3s 4d "that my mastyr lost at tenys to Syre Robart Chamberley."[75]

In March 1458, the first of a series of entries appears in the Register of Accounts of the Ironmongers' Company, when a payment is made by "the seyd Wardeyns for ballis."[76] From the 1460s to the early 1470s, the company sells an average of four thousand tennis balls a year, and from 1474–1477, six thousand.[77] Why ironmongers are in the tennis business is unknown. Between 1470 and 1530, the company's tennis ball sales wax and wane

---

72 Willmore, F.W., *A History of Walsall and Its Neighbourhood.* W. Henry Robinson, Walsall, 1887. p. 166.

73 Blomefield, F., *An Essay Towards a Topographical History of the County of Norfolk.* 3 Vols. W Bulmer and Co., London, 1806. Vol. 3. pp. 139, 188.

74 Cawley, A.C., *The Wakefield Pageants in the Towneley Cycle.* The Manchester University Press, England, 1958. p. 62. lns 733–736.

75 Turner, T.H. (ed.), *Manners and Household Expenses of England in the Thirteenth and Fifteenth Centuries.* Shakespeare Press, London, 1841. pp. 221, 252.

76 Marshall, J., *The Annals of Tennis.* Horace Cox, London, 1878. p. 58.

77 Kathman, D., *"The Madnes of Tenys" and the Commercialisation of Pastimes in Early Tudor London.* In: Bishop, T., Bloom, G., Lin, E. (eds.), *Games and Theatre in Shakespeare's England.* Amsterdam University Press, 2021. p. 74.

as London authorities intermittently curb the sport.[78] Bans on tennis and other sports are passed in 1473, 1476, 1477, and 1479. The latter specifies a six–day incarceration for those engaging in "the madnes of Tenys playing [,] playing at Cailles Closh ffoteball disyng and cardyng."[79] The madness of tennis playing. Her coolest headline yet. Sales plunge from 1477–1479, rally in 1482, peak from 1509–1517, are unrecorded between 1517 and 1523, then steady nicely until 1530.[80] Nineteen thousand are sold from 1515–1516. Profit margins are impacted by the price of balls, from a peak of 20d per gross from 1466–1477 to 12d from 1503 onwards.[81] The cause is undoubtedly European imports flooding the market. During the reign of Edward IV (1442–1483), the "Artificers" and "Handcrafty men and women" petition parliament. They have been "gretely empoveryshed and grevously hurt and hyndred … by the grete multitude of Chaffares [trade] and wares perteyning to their craftes and occupations" from overseas competitors, and "praye the Kyng" ban the importation of certain goods, "that is to sey, eny Wollen Bonettes, Tenys Balles …"[82]

Edward listens. Tennis balls and woollen bonnets are among the myriad items barred from importation in 1463. Others include bodkins, galoshes, curtain rings, and stirrups.[83] France retaliates. In 1480, Louis XI declares that only French *jeu de paume* ball-makers' wares can be bought.[84] The 1467 Ordinances of Worcester state that "no man pley at tenys or pame (palm ball) w^t^yn the yeld [guild] halle … uppon peyne" of an eleven pence fine.[85,86] Tennis is considered the English name for *jeu de paume*, the French palm and ball game played without a racket; here it is listed separately, implying a different game, at least in England. Pame is lengthened in 1471, when "men might a wageor make, And with

78 Ibid, p. 70.

79 Ibid, p. 72.

80 Ibid, pp. 75, 77, 81.

81 Ibid, pp. 75, 81.

82 Marshall, J., *The Annals of Tennis*. Horace Cox, London, 1878. p. 59.

83 Accounts 1–23. In: *The Pinners' and Wiresellers' Book, 1462–1511*, ed. Barbara Megson (London, 2009), pp. 1–20. *British History Online* http://www.british-history.ac.uk/london-record-soc/vol44/pp1-20. Accessed 22 October 2023.

84 Roberts, G.R.P., *Popular Recreation in the Middle Ages*. Unpublished MA thesis, McGill University, 1932. p. 77.

85 Smith, J.T. (ed.), *English Gilds: The Original Ordinances of More Than One Hundred Early English Gilds*. Oxford University Press, 1870. pp. 372, 387.

86 A day's wages for a skilled tradesman.

ther bowys a ffeld have it tried, Or at the Paame ther, ther pleasure for to take."[87] *Pame* is also used in 1475, in a translation of one of the first feminist writers, Christine de Pisan: "It is right well done that his body be put in exercise of som maner of labour and travayll, as in playing at the pame or at the baas or othir like pleyes."[88] *Baas* is probably prisoner's bars or prison base, a tag game with two teams and multiple variations. The commonest version is a single-base, two-team tag game. A player is put on the base of the opposing side and teammates try to rescue him from "prison" without being tagged.[89] Prison bars is mentioned in the parliamentary roll of March 1332. It is clearly associated with mischief: "Our lord the king forbids on pain of imprisonment that any child or other person should play at bars or at other games, or remove people's hoods, lay hands on them in any part of the palace of Westminster during the Parliament which is summoned there, or cause any trouble." Though only a tag game with neither bat nor ball, it is the earliest mention of a *base game* in history; an ancient relative several times removed from baseball, it is the first in its bloodline. Base royalty.

By-laws are introduced in the borough of Pershore, Worcestershire, toward the end of the fifteenth century. Playing tennis, football, or dice carries a shilling fine, while mastiffs must be kept indoors overnight.[90] Similarly, tennis, ball games, cards, and *kailes*, are banned in Sherborne, Dorset, in 1462, with a hefty fine of 6s 8d for transgressors.[91,92] The vicar of Baston, Lincolnshire, is unconcerned. In 1473, he is accused of wasting time, playing with laymen at a game called *le tenys*.[93]

In 1495, Henry VII bans "disying, carding, tenys, pleiying bowls, clossh, or any other unlawfull game" outwith "the twelve days of

---

87 Gairdner, J. (ed.), *The Paston Letters, A.D. 1422—1509.* 6 Vols. Chatto and Windus, London, 1904. Vol. 6. p. 69.

88 Bornstein, D. (ed.), *The Middle English Translation of Christine de Pisan's Livre du Corps de Policie.* Winter, Heidelberg. 1977. p. 47.

89 For other variations see: Hone, W. (ed.), *The Sports and Pastimes of the People of England,* by Joseph Strutt, 1801. Thomas Tegg, London, 1845. pp. 78–80.

90 "The borough of Pershore." In *A History of the County of Worcester: Volume 4,* ed. William Page and J W Willis-Bund (London, 1924), pp. 151–155. *British History Online* http://www.british-history.ac.uk/vch/worcs/vol4/pp151-155. Accessed 22 October 2023.

91 Brailsford, D., *British Sport: A Social History.* The Lutterworth Press, Cambridge, 1997. p. 15.

92 A fortnight's wages for a skilled tradesman.

93 Owen, D.M., *Episcopal Visitation Books.* In: Munby, L.M. (ed.), *Short Guides to Records.* The Historical Association, 1972. p. 15.

Christmas".[94] Football goes unmentioned, so does palm-ball. "Tenys playng, bowelys, and closse" still displease him in 1504.[95] Each time, he bans *tenys* not palm-ball.[96] Tennis gives Henry her mutinous smile. Kings come and go; she is here to stay. Henry looks sheepish. She *is* the latest thing. Is he too old at thirty-seven? Gods blood, no! Between 1494 and 1498, royal payments are made for the hiring of a court, balls purchased, and for his "losse at tenes."[97] His privy purse expense of £4 "to a Spaynyard the tenes pleyer" is preceded by 10s "to one that joculed the King", possibly a jester.[98] A few weeks later, he pays 1s "for balls at the paume play", and £1 7s 8d "for the Kinges losse at tenes", and there are tennis debts to Hugh Denes, Jack Haute, Charles Somerset, and "the new pleyer."[99] Henry plays at indoor tennis courts at Sheen, Windsor, Woodstock, Wycombe, and Westminster. And when Philip of Burgundy, King of Castile, visits Windsor in 1506, he is entertained with exhibition tennis between various knights. After a while, Philip rises from his cloth of gold cushion and plays two games "with the racket".[100] Perhaps this is why custom rules relax. The 1493 Custom Rolls of the Port of Exeter record the importation of "tennys balls".[101] The June rolls add that the *Flower of Calais* docked, "laden with 2 pipes and 1 hogshead of Tenys balles, 3 lasts and 3 barrels."[102,103]

A chase is a marker laid on the court to indicate where a second bounce has occurred, part of the complex rules of *jeu de paume*.[104] Chase and bounce. How these terms intersect with the possible interpretations

94 Given-Wilson, C. (ed.)., *The Parliament Rolls of Medieval England.* The National Archives. http://www.sd-editions.com.ap1.proxy.openathens.net/AnaServer?PROME+0+start.anv+id=EDWARDIV. Accessed 22 October 2023.

95 Ibid.

96 *The Statutes of the Realm.* 9 Vols. Dawsons of Pall Mall, London, 1963. Vol. 2. pp. 568, 657.

97 Marshall, J., *The Annals of Tennis*. Horace Cox, London, 1878. pp. 60–61.

98 Bentley, S., *Excerpta Historica*. Richard Bentley, London, 1833. p. 98.

99 Ibid, pp. 98, 101, 113.

100 Marshall, J., *The Annals of Tennis*. Horace Cox, London, 1878. p. 62.

101 *Customs Rolls of the Port of Exeter.* 150 Vols. In: *Report and Transactions of the Devonshire Association*. W. Brendon and Son, Ltd., Printers, Plymouth, 1912. Vol. 44, p. 533.

102 Ibid, p. 541.

103 Hogshead: a cask with a capacity of 222 litres. Pipes were long, narrow containers. A last could refer to the weight or volume of a load. The ship carried three lasts of tar.

104 *Hazard and chase*: https://www.royaltenniscourt.com/the-game/service-and-chases. Accessed 11 July 2023.

of *chace* in *jeu de bonde* as "chase" the ball or "bounce" the ball is unknown. *Jeu de bonde*—the game of bounce—is probably an ancestral relative of tennis but might be an early reference to *soule*.[105,106] One of only two mentions is in the c1316 French poem *Le Roman de Comte D'Anjou*.[107] *Longue paume* is likelier than *soule* as chases are mentioned, and *bonde* in the poem is translated to bounce: "It happened that after the mass one day in summer, three or four sons of the town went out to amuse themselves. One sped with the ball, the others chased. Each chased well and they played for a long time." It is notable that the book is published the same year Louis X dies following a game of *jeu de paume* in the forest of Vincennes.[108] Louis is probably playing *longue paume*; the term appears with regularity from 1573.[109] Whatever game *jeu de bonde* is, the passage is momentous in the annals of sport. It is the first *description* of a ball game in modern history.

"Of tenyys, pley or oder lyke." Other like. Such as *jeu de paume*. In 1415, Henry V is eager to seize France. In Shakespeare's play, the young king is goaded into action by a gift from the Dauphin. "What treasure, Uncle?" he asks. "Tennis balles, my Liege." Henry flips:

> When we have matcht our Rackets to these Balles,
> We will in France (by Gods grace) play a set,
> Shall strike his fathers Crowne into the hazard.
> Tell him, he hath made a match with such a Wrangler,
> That all the Courts of France will be disturb'd
> With Chaces.[110]

Shakespeare squeezes in set, match, courts, rackets, balls, strike, hazard, and chases. The tennis of the day, "royal tennis", is akin to *jeu de paume* with rackets. Played in an indoor court, three of the walls have a sloping

---

105 Gillmeister, H., *Tennis, A Cultural History*. Leicester University Press, London and Washington, 1997. p. 39.

106 See earlier for the argument in favour of *soule*.

107 Roques, M. (ed.)., *Le Roman de Comte D'Anjou*. Jehan Maillart, c1316. Paris, 1931. p. 53, lns 1708–1715.

108 Marshall, J., *The Annals of Tennis*. Horace Cox, London, 1878. p. 3.

109 De Baif, J.A., *Evres en Rime de Jan Antoine de Baif Secretaire de la Chambre du Roy*. s.n., Paris, 1573. n.p.

110 Shakespeare, W., *The Life of Henry the Fifth: reprinted from the first folio, 1623*. Act 1, Sc 2, lns 265–270.

roof to play off. The net is higher, and the ball is harder and hit with a pear-shaped racket. The end of the court opposite to where the ball is served is the hazard. Tennis is a popular metaphor. In *The White Devil*, Lodovico remarks:

> T' have poison'd his prayer-book …
> Or th' handle of his racket,—O, that, that!
> That while he had been bandying at tennis,
> He might have sworn himself to hell, and strook
> His soul into the hazard![111]

Another character Flamineo is no better. When asked who someone is, he replies:

"A new up-start: one that swears like a falconer, and will lie in the duke's ear day by day like a maker of almanacs; and yet I knew him since he came to th'court smell worse of sweat than an under-tennis-court-keeper."[112] Earlier, the Duke of Brachiano is ready to "Racket away five hundred crowns at tennis."[113,114] Betting on a sum worth twenty horses appears imprudent, but in 1598, the 3rd Earl of Southampton loses eighteen hundred crowns at tennis in Paris.[115,116] Sixty-eight horse

Ever the poacher, Shakespeare's tennis ball story was used by John Audelay in a poem praising Henry's only child, the young Henry VI, c1426: "And send him ballis him with to play. Then was he wyse in wers withalle, And taȝt Franchemen to plai at the ball. With tenes hold he ferd ham halle.[117] Henry V's father is also linked to tennis. The 1388 domestic records of the future Henry IV include a loss of 26s 8d playing handball (*ad pilam manuelam*) with two of the Duke of York's men.[118,119]

---

111 Webster, J., *The White Devil.* 1612. sig. GV. Act 5, Sc 1, lns 69, 71–74.

112 Ibid, Act 5, Sc 1, lns 146–150.

113 Ibid, Act 2, Sc 1, ln 182.

114 Eight and a half years' wages for a skilled tradesman.

115 Over thirty years wages for a skilled tradesman.

116 Harrison, G.B., *The Elizabethan Journals.* University of Michigan Press, 1955. p. 319.

117 Halliwell, J.O. (ed.), *A Specimen of the Shropshire Dialect in the Fifteenth Century.* 14 Vols. T. Richards, 1844. Vol. 14. p. viii.

118 Wylie, J.H., *History of England under Henry IV. Vol. III. 1407–1410.* Longmans, Green, and Co., London, 1896. p. 326.

119 Three month's wages for a skilled tradesman.

Charles, Duke of Orléans, is only twenty when he is captured at the real Battle of Agincourt in 1415. Held captive for twenty-four years, he develops his poetry skills. By 1339, he is approaching forty-five, the age then associated with the onset of old age and a decisive moment in contemporary tennis.[120] He uses the game (*jeu au paume* in the original) as an allegory of ageing to devastating effect:

> I have been playing tennis with Ageing
> For so long that I have now reached
> Forty-five; we are playing
> For a proper stake, not for nothing.
> I feel myself strong and capable enough
> To stay in the game until this point,
> And I fear nothing except Anxiety.
>
> For Anxiety discourages me so
> From playing and goes about stopping
> All the shots I make to gain advantage.
> He is too good at retrieving them,
> For fortune helps him out.
> But I have Hope on my side,
> And I fear nothing except Anxiety.
>
> Old Age is furious with distress
> That the game is taking so long,
> And she says in her spiteful way
> That she will from now on
> Mark the chaces to hurt me.
> But I don't care; I defy her.
> And I fear nothing except Anxiety.[121]

Henry V's month-long siege of Harfleur ends a month before Agincourt. It has been described as "a watershed moment in the history of warfare

120 Putter, A., *Personifications of Old Age in Medieval Poetry: Charles d'Orléans and William Langland.* The Review of English Studies, 2012, 63:260, pp. 396–397.

121 Ibid.

… the first time an English army had made extensive use of gunpowder weapons." John Lydgate celebrates it within months: "My gonnys shall lyn upon this grene, For they shall play with harflete A game at tynes as y wene[122] … Tenys seyde the grete gonne, How felawes go we to game … Fyftene before seyd London … XXX^{ti} is myn seyd Messagere … The kynges doughter, seyde … Fyve and forty that is no nay."[123] The numbers are said to represent the weight of each cannonball but are likelier to be a tennis metaphor: the shots of the nicknamed cannons are called out as tennis points: "No nay"—"nothing", may be an alternate phrase for game over. Fifteen. Thirty. Forty-five. Game over.

Tennis scores are said to have been recorded on two clockfaces, with each quarter marking a score. Forty-five was used instead of forty, perhaps the five was dropped as a casual contraction. Sixty was included to mean "game", in the sense of game won. European clocks were invented in the early fourteenth century, became widespread in the fifteenth, and began to display minutes in the late seventeenth. It is conceivable, then, that the system was invented for the elite few who had access to clocks in the fourteenth century. The last decade is likeliest as there are no known references to the scoring system before this. It would mean that the earlier version of *jeu de paume* had a different scoring system. Written in 1435, *Le Jeu de la Paulme Moralisé* is a Flemish book that provides a moral interpretation of how the scoring system arose.[124] That an author is theorising on its origins in 1435 suggests that the system is much older than c1390.[125] Another theory concerns *longue paume*, the outdoor version of *jeu de paume*. Believed to predate the short version, the game's first serve is made forty-five feet from the rope, and players advance fifteen feet for each subsequent serve until they reach the rope: forty-five, thirty, fifteen, game.[126] In modern *longue paume*, gaining ground remains central, but while there are a series of parallel lines, none create a fifteen-foot zone.

122 Nicolas, N.H., Tyrrell, E., Brushfield, T.N. (eds.)., *A Chronicle of London from 1089 to 1483*. Longman, Rees, Orme, Brown and Green, 1827. p. 220.

123 Ibid, pp. 220–221.

124 Schepens, L.; *Le Livre du jeu de la paulme moralisé*. Revue blege de Philologie et d'Histoire, 1962, 40:3, pp. 804–814.

125 Thédié, J., *Quinze–Trente–Quarante–Jeu: La fin de six cents ans de mystère*. La Jaune et la Rouge, Août/Septembre, 2001, pp. 36–37.

126 Ibid, p. 37.

An extra layer of complexity arises from the description of a ball game, in 1677, played by the Miami Nation in North America. It is a cross-country game, yet French fur trader Nicholas Perrot describes it as similar to *longue paume*.[127] All other descriptions describe or imply that *longue paume* is played within a fixed outdoor court, presumably longer than a royal [indoor] tennis court where *jeu de paume* is exclusively played. Henry VIII plays outdoor *longue paume*; one cannot see him capering cross-country, irrespective of his vitality.[128] More confusing still, the French King Louis X dies following a game of *jeu de paume* in the forest of Vincennes in 1316.[129] The assumption is that the chronicler has confused the two terms; that or there *was* a cross country version of *longue paume*, at least in the fourteenth century. Perhaps *jeu de bonde* is the earlier name for the cross-country version of *longue paume*. The term *longue paume* only appears with regularity from the late sixteenth century.[130] Perrot muddies the waters further when he adds that Miami players use curved sticks.

If the clock face theory is true, the 0 of the 60 represents zero points. When a point was scored the hand moved from 0 to 15. Since 0 resembled an egg, it is believed that the French used *l'ouef* as slang for no points, and that in England this became love. No one knows why 60 was dropped. Ironically, Lydgate is forty-five when Charles, Duke of Orléans, is captured in 1415. Another tennis reference in Lydgate's play demonstrates Shakespeare's penchant for homage: the Dauphin has his ambassadors send, "A tonne of tenys ballys I shall hym sende, for to pleye him with all."[131] Henry flies into a rage: "Swyche tenys bally I schal hym sende as schall tere the roof all of his all."[132] "Such tennis balls I will send him, as shall tear down the high roof of his hall." He cannot let it go. At Harfleur, playing on his army's virility, Henry bellows: "Myne pleyers

127 Perrot, N., *Mémoire sur les moeurs, coustumes et relligion des sauvages de l'Amérique septentrionale*. A. Franck, Leipzig & Paris, 1864. pp. 43–45.

128 De Miraument, P., *Le Prevost de L'Hostel, et Grand Prevost de France*. Pierre Chevalier, Paris, 1615, p. 362.

129 Marshall, J., *The Annals of Tennis*. Horace Cox, London, 1878. p. 3.

130 De Baif, J.A., *Evres en Rime de Ian Anotine de Baif Secretaire de la Chambre du Roy*. s.n., Paris, 1573. n.p.

131 Nicolas, N.H., Tyrrell, E., Brushfield, T.N., *A Chronicle of London from 1089 to 1483*. Longman, Rees, Orme, Brown and Green, 1827. p. 220.

132 Ibid, p. 217.

that y have hedyr brought, their ballys beth of stonys round."[133] "The players I have brought here have round stone balls." Lydgate also talks of the "tenys off eternal wo",[134] and warns of falsehood that "turneth as a bal."[135] An anonymous panegyric to Agincourt, c1425–1475, treads now familiar ground:

"And sume what in scorne and dispite [the Dauphin] sentehym [Henry V] a touneffulle of teneys Balles that he shulde playe hym and for alle his lords … And anoon he [Henry V] lette make Tenes-Balles for the dolfyn in alle the haste they he myght … and there he [Henry V] playede at the Tenys with his harde Gonne stones that were shot into the towne."[136]

Truth is blander than fiction. During his swansong, the contemporary chronicler Thomas Otterbourne registers the episode occurring in 1414: "In Lent, when the king was at Kenilworth, Charles, the … Dauphin sent balls to the Parisians for the boys to play with. To whom the king of the English wrote, saying that he would soon send balls to the Londoners, with which he would surprise and terrify their houses."[137] Hardly heroic. Henry V's response is brattish and tasteless, and chillingly contemptuous of his subjects. It is the Dauphin who conducts himself in princely fashion, sending balls to his citizens at Lent; at Shrovetide, no less: clearly, the French also celebrate Lent with ball games. The following year, English propaganda goes into full spin. The exchange is rewritten and passes into Agincourt lore.

In 1427, twenty-five-year-old Margot de Hainot travels to Paris for three weeks as part of the Duke of Burgundy's retinue. She takes the capital by storm: "[*Elle*] *laquelle jouait mieux à la paume qu'oncques homme eut vu, et avec ce jouait devant main derrière main très puissamment, très malicieusement, très habilement, comme pouvait faire un homme, et peu venait d'hommes à qui elle ne gagnât, si ce n'était les plus puissants joueurs*."[138] "[She] played jeu de paume better than any man had seen, playing hand after hand, very powerfully, very mischievously,

133 Ibid, p. 220.

134 Furnivall, F.J., *The Pilgrimage of the Life of Man*. Kegan Paul, Trench, Trübner and Co., Ltd., London, 1899–1904. p. 128. ln. 4869.

135 Bergen, H. (ed.)., *Lydgate's Troy Book, A.D. 1412–20*. s.n., s.l., 1906. pp. 56, 725.

136 Macdonald, R.J., *Mediæval Artillery in a Former Expeditionary Force Overseas*. Journal of the Society for Army Historical Research, 1922, 1:3, p. 113.

137 Hearn, T. (ed.)., *Duo Rerum Anglicarum*. 2 Vols. s.n., Oxford, 1732. Vol. 1. pp. 274–275

138 Stanajic Petrovic, N., *L'Enseignement du Tennis en France Origines, Histoire Évolutions et Perspectives*. Publish Room Factory, France, 2023. n.p.

as skilfully as any man, and only the most powerful players could beat her." She returns to Burgundy "star de l'esetuf"—star of the ball. She is the world's first tennis superstar.

Jeu de paume probably crossed with the Normans, evolving into, or rebranded as, tennis. The difference between the games of handball (*pila manualis*) and palm-ball (*pila palmaria*) is unclear. The former implies a catching and throwing game, the latter striking with an open hand. In 1389, Richard II outlaws handball and other games, with no mention of palm-ball; ditto Henry IV in 1410 (both written in Anglo-Norman).[139] The two games are never recorded in the same breath. Are they synonyms? After all, *jeu de paume* was also called *jeu de meyn* and *pelotes a meyn* on occasion.[140] The Latin *pila manualis* is used in England from at least 1486, appearing in Dame Juliana Berners' *Boke of Saint Albans*.[141] *Pila palmaria* is mentioned by Erasmus, as late as 1522. Despite seven years in England, he is probably referring to *jeu de paume*.[142] From the fifteenth century onward, the terms handball and tennis are used concurrently but similarly never appear in the same document, suggesting synonymity. The mid-century book *The Wars of Alexander the Great* references handball: "The herne-payn [skull], the hand-balle, the hat made of twygges."[143] *Bowlis* and *ball playe* are also mentioned.[144] It is believed that rackets were introduced in the 1380s, based on a reference in Chaucer's *Troilus and Criseyde Cressida*: "But kanstow playen raket, to and fro, Nettle in, dokke out, now this, now that, Pandare?".[145,146] Given the fifty year wait for the next reference, this is doubtful, and the alternate meaning of inconstant or changeable is likelier. Besides, the text is taken from the earliest manuscript to contain the passage, written in the mid-fifteenth century. Another possibility is

---

139 Raithby, J. (ed.)., *The Statutes of the Realm*. 9 Vols. Dawsons of Pall Mall, London, 1963. Vol. 2. pp. 57, 163.

140 Roberts, G.R.P., *Popular Recreation in the Middle Ages*. Unpublished MA thesis, McGill University, 1932. p. 75.

141 Baldes, W. (ed.)., *Boke of Saint Albans*. Elliott Stock, Paternoster Row, London, 1901. n.p.

142 Erasmus, D., *Familiarum Colloquiorum*. John. Frobenius, Basle, Switzerland, 1522. n.p.

143 Skeat, W.W. (ed.)., *The Wars of Alexander*. N. Trübner & Co., London, 1886. p. 107. ln. 1895.

144 Ibid, p. 196. ln 1929.

145 Bell, R. (ed.)., *The Poetical Works of Geoffrey Chaucer*. 4 Vols. George Bell and Sons. Vol. 3. p. 196.

146 The second line refers to the use of dock leaves for nettle stings. The author has inverted the proverb, 'dock in, nettle out'.

a 1439 John Audelay poem. He translates an original French passage as: "King Fraactes … sent hym thre dees forgid square of gold, to pleye racket as a child chaungable."[147] "King Fraactes sent him three gold dice to play racket with, for he was as changeable as a child." While this uses "play racket" as changeable again, there may be a double meaning: in the French original, the character plays *iouer en maniere*:[148] "hand game". By 1450, a corporation of racket manufacturers is established in Paris.[149]

~

In 1409, the Corporation of London issues a bond to six tapestry makers and two others.[150] Civil behaviour to the "mistery of Cordwainers" is demanded, with assurances they will not collect money for *pila pedali* (footballs), "cok sylver", or thrashing fowl "in the streets and lanes of the city."[151] Cock threshing involves throwing weighted sticks at a tethered cock until it dies. Cock silver is the entrance fee for those wishing to take part. The penalty for breaching the order is an exorbitant £20, an indication of their vexatiousness.[152] Making footballs is the preserve of cordwainers (shoemakers); surely it would be simpler to ask for a ball? The six tapicers appear in court a fortnight before Shrovetide, implying the ball was meant for a Shrove Tuesday game. Is the holiday game forbidden or just the means of procuring a ball? Probably the tapicers' conduct. Unruly pursuits characterise Shrovetide more than any other festive day, and football and threshing cocks are sanctioned at marriage celebrations. Cock threshing, throwing, and fighting persist for at least half a millennium: cock threshing is mentioned in 1352, while cockfighting is ineffectually prohibited by Cromwell in 1658, revived by Charles II, and only put down in public places in 1860.[153] There are

---

147 Bergen, H. (ed.)., *Lydgate's Fall of Princes*. 4 Vols. The Carnegie Institute of Washington, 1923. Vol. 2. p. 661. Pt 5, lns 2700–2701.

148 Whiting, K.E. (ed.)., *The Poems of John Audelay. Early English Text Society. Extra Series*. 1931, 184: 244.

149 Heimermann, B., *L'Internationale du Tennis*. Editions Ramsay, Paris, 1982. p. 198.

150 "Roll A 40: 1408–09", in *Calendar of the Plea and Memoranda Rolls of the City of London: Volume 3, 1381–1412*, ed. A H Thomas (London, 1932), pp. 289–301. *British History Online* http://www.british-history.ac.uk/plea-memoranda-rolls/vol3/pp289–301. Accessed 4 August 2023.

151 Moral repugnance of animal cruelty remained low for centuries. Legislative bans existed in some form from the fourteenth century onward but only targeted working-class "sports" and were poorly implemented.

152 Three years' wages for a skilled tradesman.

153 Roberts, G., *Lofthouse and its Neighbourhood*. 2 Vols. s.n., Leeds, 1885. Vol. 2. p. 32.

dedicated cockpit houses, and it is even played in a Yorkshire church during Easter 1661.

Dublin's Corpus Christi civic pageantry is an annual Shrovetide custom that begins in earnest in 1466.[154] From 1469, men married during the previous twelve months must bear a ball in a Shrove Tuesday procession, and pay for the privilege.[155] Bearing wedding balls is first recorded in Dublin in 1455 but is independent of Shrove Tuesday until 1469.[156] The procession does not culminate in a Shrovetide game, but a similar, later custom, in Chester does.[157] Some Dubliners do not want to be a part of it. The canny marry on Shrove Tuesday; the practice is curbed in 1572–73, when the authorities finally catch on.[158] A 1594 assembly roll legislates for those seeking to avoid their duty by slipping out of the city. Any who depart fifteen days or less before "Shrovetuesday" are fined.[159] As late as 1596 a tanner is fined for not bearing a ball on "Shroftuysdaye", and the ceremony is known to continue until 1621.[160,161] A "standing" ball is twice specified, though not in the sense of a standing custom. Perhaps the ball is mounted on a heavy pole, and the long walk through Dublin intolerable; as part of the Chester Shrove Tuesday football game, the saddlers present a painted wooden ball on a spear to the drapers. Expense may be a factor. The tanner is ordered to march with his company, in all likelihood the tanner's guild. Must they all be kitted out in festive finery at his expense? The practice is finally abolished for those with a modest income, in 1600.[162] Little wonder: the fine equates to a hundred days' wages for a skilled tradesman.

---

154 It is first noted in 1462.

155 Fletcher, A.J., *The Civic Pageantry of Corpus Christi in Fifteenth and Sixteenth Century Dublin.* Irish Economic and Social History, 1996, Vol. 23, p. 74.

156 Gilbert, J.T., Mulholland, R., Weldrick, J.F. (eds.)., *Calendar of Ancient Records of Dublin.* 19 Vols. Joseph Dollard, London, 1889. Vol. 1. p. 289.

157 There are no records of the Chester game before 1533.

158 Fletcher, A.J., *Drama, Performance, and Polity in Pre-Cromwellian Ireland.* University of Toronto Press, 2000. p. 384.

159 Gilbert, J.T., Mulholland, R., Weldrick, J.F. (eds.)., *Calendar of Ancient Records of Dublin.* 19 Vols. Joseph Dollard, London, 1889. Vol. 2. p. 277.

160 Ibid, p. 294.

161 Aucoin, T., *When the Pancake Bell Rings.* Unpublished PhD thesis, University of Bristol, 2019. p. 118.

162 Gilbert, J.T., Mulholland, R., Weldrick, J.F. (eds.)., *Calendar of Ancient Records of Dublin.* 19 Vols. Joseph Dollard, London, 1889. Vol. 2. p. 339.

In 1681, a dictionary describes ball-money: "It is a custom in some parts of England, when a Maid is married in a Parish, her associates require Ball-money of the Bride, towards the support of their future Ball-playing, and for reparation of the loss of one of their Play-fellows."[163] The link between footballs, Shrovetide, capturing the recently wed, parading recently married men, ball-money, and guilds demanding footballs from craftsmen on the Shrove Tuesday after their wedding, suggests fertility ancestry. There are also temporal links. Shrovetide usually falls in February, not only the height of the football season, but also the last month of the peak four-month wedding cycle, which accounts for fifty per cent of marriages.[164] Little wonder Shrove Tuesday is a day of abandon, with cavorting and merrymaking, feasting and football, music and dancing, its unbridled ribaldry fending off the austerity of Lent.

Playing in churchyards continues to be censured. This by John Mirk, c1405: "Bal and bares and suche play, Out of chyrchezorde put a-way."[165,166] In the marginalia of a c1450 copy of the book, someone includes: "Danseyng, cotteyng, bollyng, tenessying, hand ball, fott ball, stoil ball & all manner other games out cherchyard."[167,168] Assuming it is not the shadowy Gloucestershire game of stowball, it is considered the first known mention of stoolball.[169] While uncommon, the spelling "cherchyard" is mentioned as early as 1433, adding weight to the stoolball date.[170] Then again, references may stem from 1439 and 1447: at the Easter Monday festival in Ripon, Yorkshire, *le Pykestolle* was played both years.[171] A penny was paid for bread and beer for the events. Pykestolle is Middle English for pitchstool; surely an early form of stoolball. Stoolball has blue blood. It is baseball's oldest *direct* ancestor, though it does not

---

163 Blount, T., *Glossographia*. Tho. Newcomb, London, 1681. p. 73.

164 Aucoin, T., *When the Pancake Bell Rings*. Unpublished PhD thesis, University of Bristol, 2019. p. 140.

165 Casting of the barre was an early form of shot put. It was a favourite pastime of Henry VIII.

166 Peacock, E. (ed.), *Instructions for Parish Priests*. Kegan Paul, Trench, Trübner & Co., Ltd., London, 1902. p. 11. lns 336–337.

167 Ibid, p. 11; Bodleian Library, Oxford; MS Douce 103, *Instructions for Parish Priests*, fifteenth century, fol. 126r.

168 Cotteyng, quoits; bollyng, bowling.

169 There is a caveat: it is unclear when the margin text was added.

170 Cutts, E.L., *Scenes and Characters of the Middle Ages*. Virtue and Co., London, 1872. p. 104.

171 Baskervill, C.R., *Dramatic Aspects of Medieval Folk Festivals in England*. Studies in Philology, 1920, 17:1, pp. 41–42.

use bats or bases (two stools) until the eighteenth century. The next reference to stoolball does not appear until 1564.[172] While predominantly a women's sport, the long-held belief it was originally played by milk maids using milking stools is speculative.

Francis Willughby provides the first known rules in his ground-breaking sports book of 1672: "The plaiers being aequally divided according to their strength and nimbleness" turn over a stool, so its seat faces the field. The players of one side stand at the stoole. One of them "posts the ball towards the other side, who stand as farre of from the stoole, as they thinke hee can post. If any of them catch the ball hee must post it back againe towards the stoole. If any of that side catch it they post it back againe, & so backwards and forwards as long as they keepe it up … instead of a stoole they sometimes use a great stone."[173]

The obsolete term "post" means to toss a ball up with one hand and hit it with the other. Willoughby's description leaves a lot of gaps. What happens if either side fails to catch the ball or the stool is hit, under what circumstances do they change sides, is there a scoring system? Only when bats and a second stool are introduced does it begin to resemble cricket. A bat is first mentioned in a 1733 poem, and two stools in Johnson's 1755 dictionary.[174,175] By that time, cricket is an established sport. A bat and two stools are absent from other contemporary descriptions.

Only six other sixteenth century references to stoolball are known of. Two more have been exhumed. On 7 November 1586, Robert Fisher of Romford is charged with "plaieinge at stoole bawle in service tyme, and gave crewell words to the churchwardens for demandinge xxiid. of him for his absence."[176] Fisher and his potty mouth are in luck; his only penalty is an outstanding shilling fine. The second reference is in 1623, when three youths in Maldon are indicted for playing stoolball during Sunday service.[177] Both offences are in Essex, the site of the

172 Clark, A. (ed.)., *The Shirburn Ballades, 1585–1616*. Clarendon Press, Oxford, 1907. p. 48.

173 Beharry, S., *The Prehistories of Baseball*. McFarland & Company, Jefferson, North Carolina, 2016. p. 182.

174 Ibid, p. 182.

175 Block, D., *Baseball Before We Knew It: A Search for the Roots of the Game*. University of Nebraska Press, Lincoln, Nebraska, 2005. p. 112.

176 Hale, W.H., *A Series of Precedents and Proceedings in Criminal Causes, Extending from the Year 1475–1640*. Francis & John Rivington, London, 1847. pp. 188–189.

177 Clark, A. (ed.)., *The Shirburn Ballades, 1585–1616*. Clarendon Press, Oxford, 1907. p. 48.

earliest recorded game, in 1564, when a complaint is "made against the constables that they had suffered 'stole-ball' to be played on Sundays."[178] The episode is recurrently misattributed as occurring in Malden in Surrey, rather than Maldon, Essex. Another match plays out in Maldon in 1583. Edward Anderkyn and four others are caught playing stool-ball on a Sunday.[179] Essex is clearly an important hub: these games comprise four of the five earliest known. The fifth is an outlier. In 1614, a game takes place between the villages of Pottersbury and Yardley Gobion, in Northamptonshire, one hundred and twenty-three miles away.[180] Maldon is not only steeped in stoolball history. Stoolball must stand aside and make way for the young pretender, for another sport is recorded there in 1562, possibly the earliest known in history. In 1562, John Porter and his servant play "an unlawful game called 'clycett'."[181] Cricket?

178 Ibid.

179 Ibid.

180 Ibid, p. 84.

181 Benham, W.G., *Essex Borough Arms and the Traditional Arms of Essex and the Arms of Chelmsford Diocese*. Benham and Company, Colchester. 1916. pp. 22–23.

CHAPTER FIVE
1400–1499 II

Clerics are apt to stray. In 1391, the Archbishop of Canterbury—so fierce he yells an abbot into a heart attack—orders priests not to frequent shops, spectacles, or other dishonourable places, or noxious and illicit games.[1] By 1466, it is necessary to add that clerics avoid the cells of suspect women."[2] In 1448, vicars will be penalised a week's wages if they play ball on the grounds of Salisbury Cathedral, specifically beneath the common hall.[3] Presumably, windows have been broken. The public are debarred from churchyard sports. In 1472, a shilling fine is imposed for football or handball in the churchyard of Wyghton, Yorkshire.[4] The records also note that a wandering actor had sex with a woman in the churchyard.[5] The same year, the church in Salton, Yorkshire, introduces a tuppenny forfeit for football, handball, and wrestling below the cemetery.[6] Twenty-five miles away, in Salton, the ante is unduly upped in 1519: "*ludi inhonesti prout pililudus pedalis & manualis, viz. tutts & handball ac penyston. Desistant sub pena excom.*" "Stop playing dishonest ball games with the hands and feet, namely, tutts and handball and penyston, or face excommunication."[7] The 1859 book containing the quote describes tutts as "a game at ball; the name is probably a local one." It is probably a reference to tut-ball, a base and ball game similar to stoolball.[8] If true, it is the earliest

1 Wilkins, D. (ed.), *Concilia Magnae Britanniae et Hiberniae*. 4 Vols. R. Gosling, F. Gyles, T. Woodward, C. Davis, London, 1737. Vol. 3, p. 214. Tabernas (shops) rather than tavernas (taverns) is consistently used in several edicts.

2 Ibid, p. 605.

3 Wordsworth, C., Macleane, D. (eds.), *Statutes and Customs of the Cathedral Church of Salisbury*. William Clowes and Sons Limited, London, 1915. p. 322.

4 Raine, J. (ed.), *The Fabric Rolls of York Minster*. Publications of the Surtees Society. Durham, 1859. Vol. 35. p. 257.

5 *Fornicatur cum.*

6 Raine, J. (ed.), *The Fabric Rolls of York Minster*. Publications of the Surtees Society. Durham, 1859. Vol. 35. p. 255.

7 Ibid, p. 270.

8 Block, D., *Baseball Before We Knew It: A Search for the Roots of the Game*. University of Nebraska Press, Lincoln, Nebraska, 2005. pp. 135–138.

known reference to a *ball and base* game in history. Of note, a book of Sheffield dialect refers to tut-ball as being a synonym for pize-ball, also known as cuck-ball.[9] Pize-ball is a six-a-side game with three or four markers, usually stones known as tuts fixed in a field. A player hits the ball with their hand and runs around the markers. If they are pized (hit) with the ball, they are burned (out), and the next player is in. Tuts, then, are bases. There is no evidence that pize-ball and tut-ball are played with bats. The 1519 order, for instance, bans hand and foot games with no mention of bats. The second oldest reference to the sport, in 1575, sums up the rules in a sentence: "And throwen his ball although I toucht no tutte."[10] Two of the rare references to tutts (as tutte) appear in the county of Devon, hundreds of miles from Yorkshire. The first provides no particulars, the date is opaque—but no later than 1650—and it is mentioned alongside globes (possibly golf) and skystgrote.[11] A groat is a coin, so perhaps skystgrote is a coin tossing game. The second from 1777/8 reads: "A Sort of Stool Ball much practised about the Easter Holidays, particularly at Exeter."[12]

The 1859 book defines Penyston as "a game at ball so called, probably taking its name from the village of Peniston." It is delightful to think that Penistone—which in the 1840s becomes one of several pioneering football villages nestled in a pocket of Yorkshire—creates an eponymous game played seventy miles away. The truth is drabber. Penny cast is a similar game to quoits. Flat round stones are aimed at a target. Previously called penny-stane, it has regional spellings, including pennystonne and pennistone.[13] It is referenced in the epic *The Actes and Life of the most Victorious Conqueror, Robert Bruce King of Scotland (c1375), the first book to be written in the Scots language, rather than Scottish Gaelic:* "In-till ane place, the way Wes nocht a penny-stane cast of breid."[14] "[the

9 Addy, S.O. (ed.), *A Glossary of Words Used in the Neighbourhood of Sheffield*. Trübner & Co., London, 1888. p. 176.

10 Block, D., *Baseball Before We Knew It: A Search for the Roots of the Game*. University of Nebraska Press, Lincoln, Nebraska, 2005. p. 136.

11 Wasson, J.M., *Records of Early English Drama: Devon*. University of Toronto Press, 1986. p. lviv.

12 Block, D., *Baseball Before We Knew It: A Search for the Roots of the Game*. University of Nebraska Press, Lincoln, Nebraska, 2005. p. 137.

13 *Dictionaries of the Scots Language*. https://www.dsl.ac.uk/entry/dost/penny_stane. Accessed 10 February 2024.

14 *Mackenzie, W.M. (ed.), The Actes and Life of the most Victorious Conqueror, Robert Bruce King of Scotland. Book 16, by John Barbour. Adam and Charles Black, London, 1909. p. 288.*

way got narrower] until the route was no wider than the throw of a penny-stone sized piece of bread." The game is mainly referenced in Scotland. An 1828 edition of Johnson's *A Dictionary of the English Language* includes a glossary of Scottish words and phrases. Penny-stane: "A stone used as a quoit for playing with; also the game itself"; while "penny-stane cast" is "A distance not greater than a man may throw a quoit."[15]

Literature continues to reference football. The anonymous *Laud Troy Book* covers Thebes and the Trojan War, treading the same ground as *The Knight's Tale*:

> Gret was the assaut that thei be-gonne,
> Every man on other ronne;
> Hedes reled aboute over-al
> As men playe at the fote-bal.[16]

"They began a great assault, every man chasing another, heads rolled about all over, as men play at footballs."

In 1411, Thomas Hoccleve writes of a debauchee:

> In pride and lecherie was alle my thought;
> No more I hade sette verraily ne rought
> A wife or maide or another to defoule,
> Than to shete or pleye at the balle or boule.[17]

"All I thought of was pride and lechery. I thought no more of thirsting after a wife or maide or another to deflower, than to shoot or play at ball or bowls." Hoccleve could be unkind. A short roundel inverts the desired appearance of fifteenth century women:

> Hir mowth is nothyng scant, with lippes gray;
> Hir chin unnethe may be seen at al;

15 Johnson, S., *A Dictionary of the English Language*. W. Strahan, London, 1755. n.p.

16 Wülfing, J.A., *The Laud Troy Book. A Romance of about 1400.* 2 Vols. Kegan Paul, Trench, Trübner & Co., Ltd., London, 1902. Vol. 2. p. 373. lns 12670–12672.

17 Wright, T. (ed.), *De Regimine Principum. A Poem by Thomas Occleve*. J.B. Nichols, London, 1860. p. 24.

Hir comly body shape as a foot ball;
And she syngith ful lyk a papejay.[18]

"Her mouth is large with grey lips, her chin is almost non-existent, she is shaped like a football, and sings like a parrot." And this from John Lydgate:

This fair floure of womanheed,
Hath two pappys also smalle,
Bolsteryd out of length and breed,
Lyche a large campynge ball.[19,20]

"This fair flower of womanhood has two small breasts, which pushed together resemble a large camping ball." Others are comical. *Mankind* was the most controversial morality play of its day; any seriousness offset by the high jinks of four disreputable characters, cajoling Mankind into a life of vice. Scene two ends with the five of them heading off for a game of football: "What how, ostler, hostler! Lende ws a foot-ball! Whoppe, whow! a-now, a-now, a-now, a-now!"[21] Lydgate makes a soberer contribution in 1426. His translation of a French poem contains the earliest description of how camping is played:

Pleye at the cloos, among, I shal,
And somwhyle Rennyn at the bal
Wyth a Staff mad lyk an hook;
And I wyl han a kampyng crook.[22]

18 Tremaine, W.R., *A Critical Edition: Poems by Thomas Hoccleve*. Unpublished MA thesis, The University of British Columbia, 1968. p. 123. *Praise of His Lady*, lns 9–12.

19 Halliwell, J.O. (ed.), *Minor Poems of Dan John Lydgate*. C. Richards, London, 1840. p. 200. *When She Hath on Hire Hood of Grene*.

20 Camping balls were cricket-ball sized for cross-country games, larger and air filled for close games. Lydgate (c1370–c1451) was from the camping county of Suffolk.

21 Furnivall, F.J., Pollard, A.W. (eds.), *The Macro Plays*. Humphrey Milford, Oxford University Press, 1904. p. 27; Anon., *Mankind*. Sc 2, lns 725–726.

22 Furnivall, F.J. (ed.). *The Pilgrimage of the Life of Man*. Kegan Paul, Trench, Trübner & Co., Ltd., London, 1899. p. 306. lns 11,181–184.

"I'll play at the close with the others, and run at the ball with a staff made like a hook, I will have a camping crook." Written a century after the first mention of camping, the game uses a hook-shaped stick. The poem is a translation of a French poem, written in 1332. Lydgate changes the sport to suit an English audience: the original is *crocë a souler, soule* with a crook.[23] He also mentions bowls, kayles, chess, and cards. Kayles, an early version of skittles (nine-pins), is first mentioned under the reign of Edward II (1284–1327): "Ther-fore has ure mayster, ofte horled [hurled] mi kayles."[24] "Therefore has your master often hurled my kayles." The implication is that the balls were thrown, rather than rolled, at the skittles. Remarkably, bowling balls of the day have bias, like those used in lawn bowling. Bias is achieved by shaping one side to produce a non-circular ball, which provides turn. Greater shaping provides more turn. In his book of 1463, German cardinal Nicholas of Cusa draws parallels between a new bowling game and man's lopsided soul set into motion by God. His cousin the Duke of Bavaria asks him about "this fun and new game." Di Cuse explains that the ball, rendered slightly concave on one side "by the art of the lathe operator", is "suited to a movement that is not perfectly straight and that is also not perfectly circular … the bowling ball can be fashioned in an infinite number of ways, in accordance with differing relationships between its surfaces … the same line is never again described … because it is always hurled differently … the bowling-ball's motion sometimes ceases suddenly, when the ball lands on its own flat surface."[25]

~

In 1421, Thomas Stowne of Copford, Essex, is assaulted by Richard Stogg with *quodam campyngrock*: some camping crook.[26] Unsurprisingly, Copford is close to the Suffolk border. The fifteenth century is a rich source for camping. In 1440, the first English–Latin dictionary, the *Promptorium Parvulorum,* is published. Written by a Norfolk friar, it contains only twelve thousand words. Camping is of sufficient cultural value—at least

23 Stürzinger, J.J. (ed.)., *Le Pèlerinage De Vie Humaine*, by Guilluame de Deguileville. Nichols & Sons, London, 1893. ln. 11,836.

24 Wright, T., Halliwell-Phillipps, J.O. (eds.)., *Reilquiæ Antiquæ. Scraps from Ancient Manuscripts.* 2 Vols. John Russell Smith, London, 1845. Vol. 1. p. 292.

25 Hopkins, J., *Nicholas of Cusa: Metaphysical Speculations. Volume 2, De Ludo Globi (The Bowling Game).* Arthur J. Banning Press, Minneapolis, 2000. pp. 1182–1184.

26 Hessayon, A., *Beastly Furie, and Exstreme Violence.* In: Wagg, S., Pollock, A.M (eds.)., *The Palgrave Book of Sport, Politics and Harm.* Springer Nature Switzerland, Cham, Switzerland, 2021. p. 38.

to an East Anglian monk—to make the cut. He refers to *campynge* as *pedipiludium* or the game of football,[27,28] *camper* as a *pleyar at the fotte balle*, *campyon* as *athleta* (athlete) or *pugyl* (boxer), and *kampyn* as *pedipilo* (to play at football).[29] A seventeenth century appendix adds: "*Campynge,* the game of football. This ancient game deserves the more attention from us because, if it was not peculiar to the East Angles and East Saxons, it has probably been always a particular favourite with them. Ray (1627–1705) says that in his time, it prevailed mostly in Norfolk, Suffolk, and Essex."[30]

The *Middle English Compendium* offers further definitions: *campen* and *camping*: to play a kind of field game, *camping bal*: a ball used for this sport; *crok*: a curved stick used for this sport, *pightel*: a field used for this sport.[31] There are two versions of camping, then, one that predominantly or exclusively strikes the ball with a foot, and the other with a stick. The plethora of stick and ball images in art suggests that camping begins as a stick game, with football emerging from it in the fourteenth or fifteenth century.

Campian means to fight. An appropriate name for this war of a game.[32] In *A Concise Dictionary of Middle English*, *camp* is *a* contest, and *campen* is *to* contest.[33] It adds, that *campen* it associated with *kapp*, an Old Norse word meaning contest or courage. Warrior is *kempe* or *cempe* in Anglo-Saxon, and *kempa* in Old Norse. Thomas Browne (1605–1682) includes *kamp* in a list of words "of common use in Norfolk or peculiar to the East Angle Counties", together with feft, fangast, paxwax, and thokish.[34,35,36] Camping's philological roots strongly suggest Anglo-

27 Pedipiludium: sport with the foot.

28 Mayhew, A.L., (ed.)., *Promptorium Parvulorum*. Galfridus Anglicus. Kegan Paul, Trench, Trübner and Co., Ltd., London, 1908. p. 70.

29 Ibid, pp. 70, 252, 636.

30 Naturalist John Ray (1627–1705) was born in Essex, close to the Suffolk, border. He studied at Cambridge.

31 *Middle English Compendium*. https://quod.lib.umich.edu/m/middle-english-dictionary/dictionary/MED6611. Accessed 22 October 2023.

32 Dymond, D., *A Lost Social Institution: The Camping Close*. In: *Rural History*, 1990, 1:2, pp. 165.

33 Mayhew, A.L., Skeat. W.W., *A Concise History of Middle English from A.D. 1150–1580*. Henry Frowde, Oxford University Press, 1888. p. 38.

34 Browne, T., *Certain Miscellany Tracts*. s.n., London, 1684. p. 146.

35 Thomas Browne was a physician and author who settled in Norwich in 1637.

36 Feft: to present (a person) with something; fangast: a marriageable maid; paxwax: the thick neck ligament supporting the back of the skull of quadrupeds; thokish: slothful.

Saxon or Viking ancestry, introduced by settlers in East Anglia, that or the invaders lent their name to an existing game. If camping *was* a local game, how did it survive the might of Saxon culture; nowhere was it more dominant than in East Anglia. Conversely, like the Vikings there is no evidence that Germanic tribes had their own ball game. The likeliest explanation is that it was a fearsome homegrown sport that caught on with the Saxons.

According to Bede, when European tribes invaded in the fifth and sixth centuries, Saxons settled in what is now Essex, Sussex, and Middlesex, Jutes in Kent, and Angles in East Anglia.[37] Angles are clearly implicated if the first evidence of the game arises after they settle but before the Vikings arrive. While Bede's book, written a century before the Viking's first mainland raid, makes no mention of camping, he also covers the Roman occupation and makes no mention of *harpastum*, or any other ball game for that matter. There is no known mention of camping until those court leet documents of 1320—five hundred years after the first Viking invasion.

Two decades after William the Conqueror is crowned, the *Domesday Book* records all land and landholdings across vast swathes of England. Written in Latin, it calls the village of Shudy Camps in Cambridgeshire *Campus*. Shudy Camps has a c1200 church, implying it is established enough to attract major finance. By the fourteenth century, it is known as Little Camps. Castle Camps, in the same county, was called *Canpas* (Canvas) in the *Domesday Book*, at that time a Saxon manor and village. Given the two subsequent references in the book to *Campas*, this may be a misspelling. The book also records Campsey in Suffolk, Campsall in Yorkshire, and Campton in Bedfordshire.[38] It is worth adding that Ælfric Campe held Dedham Manor in north Essex in 1066. An Ælfric Campe is also mentioned within the Cambridgeshire folio of the Domesday book. While the context is unclear, it is likely that these places were named after them.

In 1173, there is a battle between Henry II and French and Flemish mercenaries led by the Earl of Leicester, close to the village of Fornham

37 Sellar, A.M., *Bede's Ecclesiastical History of England*. George Bell and Sons, London, 1970. p. 30.

38 Powell-Smith, A., Palmer, J.J.N., Open Domesday. https://opendomesday.org/place/?indexChar=C. Accessed 22 October 2023.

St Genevieve, in Suffolk. In 1560, *Le Camping Close* is itemised in the holdings of the late Sir Thomas Kytson. The field, which may well have been the battleground, was previously owned by the Benedictine Abbey of St Edmund, built c1020.[39] Though the prefix *le*, implies an Anglo-Norman term, it is probably Middle English given that *campen* means to fight or contend.[40,] *Le campingplace* is recorded in Fulbourn, in 1540, and *le Camping Close*, in Orwell, in 1600, both in Cambridgeshire. Given that Cambridgeshire and Suffolk are camping counties, all three are arguably camping closes.

A dearth of early references suggests that camping became a popular pursuit in the second half of the fifteenth century. In 1452, a *campynglonde* is mentioned in Stanton, Norfolk, the first concrete evidence of a dedicated camping field.[41] There are several more fifteenth century references, including a camping *pightle* in 1466, and a camping close in 1476.[42,43,44] In 1474, Dr John Botwright, Doctor of Divinity and Master of Corpus Christi College, Cambridge, bequeaths a triangular piece of land to the parish of Swaffham, Norfolk, for sport.[45,46] Shortly after he is buried in the church, the adjacent field is named the Camping Land. In 1484, Sibton Abbey, Suffolk, refers to a piece of land it owns called Campyng Place.[47] That year, the abbey pays William Trusse 2s 8d "for firming the two-acre enclosure known as the *Campyngclos*."[48,49] Three years later it is referred to as *Campyng' clos*.[50] Similarly, the 1498

39 Thomson, R. M., *The Archives of the Abbey of Bury St Edmunds*. Boydell Press, Woodbridge, Suffolk, 1980. p. 1.

40 Gage, J., *The History and Antiquities of Hengrave, in Suffolk*. J. Carpenter, London, 1822. pp. 10–11.

41 Dymond, D., *A Lost Social Institution: The Camping Close*. In: *Rural History*, 1990, 1:2, pp. 165–192.

42 Pightel/pightle is Norfolk dialect for a small field or enclosure, the odd-shaped piece left after subdividing land into rectangular fields.

43 Cullum, J., *The history and antiquities of Hawsted*. J. Nichols, London, 1784. p. 113.

44 As late as 1796, a camping-pightle existed in Weston, Suffolk: Ketton-Cremer, R.W., *Camping – A Forgotten, Norfolk Game*. Norfolk and Norwich Archaeology Society, 1931. p. 91.

45 Dymond, D., *A Lost Social Institution: The Camping Close*. In: *Rural History*, 1990, 1:2, p. 167.

46 Botwright was born in Swaffham and became its rector. A free school was built on the land c1725.

47 Denney, A.H. (ed.)., *Sibton Abbey Estates. Selected Documents 1325–1509*. W.S. Cowell Limited, Ipswich, 1960. p. 90.

48 Ibid, p. 108.

49 £113 in 2024.

50 Brown, P. (ed.)., *Sibton Abbey Cartularies and Charters*. Part 4. The Boydell Press, Woodbridge, Suffolk, 1988. p. 70.

accounts of the Priory of Felixstowe, Suffolk, record a payment of 4s 2d to five men for five days work in *le Campyngclos*.[51,52]

The Paston Letters—correspondence between the Paston family from 1422–1509—impart unparalleled insights into daily life during Wars of the Roses and the reign of Henry VII. The family are named after the titular Norfolk village, twenty miles north of Norwich, at the time the second largest city in England. In January 1463, Margaret informs her husband that: "Men of the [unreadable text] shuld make redy her [their] bald batts and her clot schon."[53] Bald batts are believed to be bats for ball games, while clot schon are shoes shod with thin plates of iron. It may be strongly inferred that a camping game is to be played, and the players wear specialised boots. If so, it is the earliest reference to sports shoes in history.

Most camping closes are flat and lie adjacent to the parish church or churchyard, or form part of the village nucleus.[54] Suffolk has by far the most camping closes; the majority in Cambridgeshire and Essex lie close to the Suffolk border; Norfolk's are dotted throughout the county.[55] The hundred of Blackbourne, Suffolk, alone has eleven camping closes across its thirty-three parishes.[56,57] In 1458, four men of Tillingham, in the camping area of east Essex, admit to playing ball during divine service.[58] They get away with a reprimand from the dean. Over three hundred years later, the town hosts an eleven-a-side football game against Dengie.[59]

~

In the late fifteenth to early sixteenth centuries, a dispute is recorded concerning the rights of villagers to play sports on Litcham Common, Norfolk. Sire Thomas Bolewere has witnessed, "Schettynges

51 Five days' wages for a skilled tradesman.

52 Dugdale, W. (ed.), *Monasticon Anglicanum*. 7 Vols. James Bohn, London, 1846. Vol. 4. p. 564.

53 Gairdner, J. (ed.), *The Paston Letters, A.D. 1422—1509*. 6 Vols. Chatto and Windus, London, 1904. Vol. 4. p. 67.

54 Dymond, D., *A Lost Social Institution: The Camping Close*. In: *Rural History*, 1990, 1:2, p. 166.

55 It is likely that many camping closes are yet to be discovered, which could alter the mapping considerably.

56 Dymond, D., *A Lost Social Institution: The Camping Close*. In: *Rural History*, 1990, 1:2, pp. 170.

57 A hundred was the subdivision of a shire for administrative purposes.

58 Hair, P. (ed.), *Before the Bawdy Court*. Paul Elek, London, 1972. p. 38.

59 *Chelmsford Chronicle*. 22 June 1787. p. 1.

wrestelynges puttynges of the ston". Other witnesses add, "rennyng at the fotebal for kakes" and "renning for the spere."[60] "Archery, wrestling, putting of the stone … running at the football for cakes, running for the spear." A c1470 poem extolling the virtues of a carefree life, reveals that ball skills are a winning asset:

> In every place he is loved over alle
> Among maydens grete and smale
> In daunsyng, in pyping, and rennyng at the balle,
> In every place wher-so he go.
> They leten lighte by [think little of] housebonde-men,
> Whan they at the balle renne;
> They casten her love to yonge men
> In every place wher-so they go.[61]

Accidents can be spurious. In 1424, to establish his right as heir at a post-mortem, a man produces several witnesses to confirm the day he was born in 1403.[62] One, "John Hendyman, 54 years and more, was at Selmeston that day playing football with his fellows and broke his left shin." It is a dramatic Wednesday for the Sussex villagers: a new priest celebrates his first mass, a young man is buried, a child is baptised, a man dies, another's servant is captured by French forces, a villager visiting a friend in Eastbourne arrives to find that he has "hanged himself from a tie-beam." Long memories too. Suspicious, then, that another 54-year-old Sussex villager breaks his shin at football under identical circumstances in Chidham the following year.[63] Credibility breaks when it turns out that the exact same incidents that occurred in Selmeston passed the day the heir was born. One testimony is from the same man.

It turns out to be a well-worn deceit, used since at least 1420, when proof of age of the knight Henry de Plesyngton is required. A string

60 King, P.M. (ed.)., *The Routledge Research Companion to Early Drama and Performance*. Routledge, Abingdon, Oxon, 2017. p. 175.

61 Stevick, R. D., *One Hundred Middle English Lyrics*. The Bobbs-Merrill Company, Inc., Indianapolis, United States, 1964. *A, a, a, a, Yet I love where-so I go*. p. 141.

62 King's College London, 2014. Mapping the Medieval Countryside. https://inquisitionspostmortem.ac.uk/view/inquisition/22–531/. Accessed 9 August 2023.

63 Ibid, https://inquisitionspostmortem.ac.uk/view/inquisition/22–665/. Accessed 9 August 2023.

of witnesses with impeccable memories come forward, including John Upton, who was playing football at the Old Bull Pyt in Stamford, Lincolnshire, the day he was born.[64] A birth in Thorpe-le-Soken, north Essex, is supported by another broken shin at football, and a broken leg elsewhere.[65] The village is close to the Suffolk border, and will host Essex v Suffolk in 1761, and again in 1791. Both are advertised as football, but the terms in camping country are interchangeable.[66] The same year, a shin fracture during a football match, a broken arm, and hangings occur on the same day in Layer Marney and Woodham Walter, both in Essex.[67,68] Similarly, a man's right to his dead father's estate in Little Laver, Essex, rests on a broken shin at football, and a man hanging from a tie-beam.[69] The same shin injury and suicide—with added fractured arm—happens in Wilcote, Oxfordshire, in 1403.[70] A man breaks his shin after a collision at football, at Odell, Bedfordshire, in 1410; another breaks his shin, and two break their arms, one a luckless prisoner, who slips his shackles and vaults the churchyard wall.[71] The same tricks are employed for a birth in Dry Drayton, Cambridgeshire, in 1417,[72] incorporating events lifted from a proof of age claim in Sproughton, Suffolk, in 1441.[73] It is given away by the tired storyline of the broken shin. If an embellished 1417 game went ahead, it is only the third Shrovetide match known. Seven of the eleven cases take place between 1423 and 1425. The locations are interesting; four in Essex and one in Suffolk, both camping counties. Half are from contiguous counties, suggesting word of mouth.

In 1424, John Combe is beaten over the head and shoulders "playing at ball with great clubs" at Quidhampton, Wiltshire.[74] The assault is so savage "he could neither hear nor see." Normandy-born Osmund, the

64 Ibid, https://inquisitionspostmortem.ac.uk/view/inquisition/21-216/. Accessed 9 August 2023.

65 Ibid, https://inquisitionspostmortem.ac.uk/view/inquisition/22–361/. Accessed 9 August 2023.

66 Dymond, D., *A Lost Social Institution: The Camping Close*. In: *Rural History*, 1990, 1:2, pp. 179.

67 King's College London, 2014. Mapping the Medieval Countryside. https://inquisitionspostmortem.ac.uk/view/inquisition/22–364/. Accessed 9 August 2023.

68 Ibid, https://inquisitionspostmortem.ac.uk/view/inquisition/22–189/. Accessed 9 August 2023.

69 Ibid, https://inquisitionspostmortem.ac.uk/view/inquisition/22–360/. Accessed 9 August 2023.

70 Ibid, https://inquisitionspostmortem.ac.uk/view/inquisition/22–528/. Accessed 9 August 2023.

71 Ibid, https://inquisitionspostmortem.ac.uk/view/inquisition/24–272/. Accessed 9 August 2023.

72 Ibid, https://inquisitionspostmortem.ac.uk/view/inquisition/25–351/. Accessed 9 August 2023.

73 Ibid, https://inquisitionspostmortem.ac.uk/view/inquisition/25–528/. Accessed 9 August 2023.

74 *The Wiltshire Archaeological and Natural History Magazine*. C. H. Woodward, Devizes, 1901–1902. Vol. 32. p. 235.

second Bishop of Old Sarum (Salisbury), who died in 1099, sees fit to intervene. Appearing in a vision, he instructs John to make a wax model of his injured head and shoulders and offer it at the Bishop's tomb.[75,76] John recovers, as does a girl struck on the head with a quoit, who makes the same offering. Intriguingly, there is a Camp Down less than two miles from Quidhampton. A 1936 book listing Members of Parliament from 1439 to 1509 is peppered with offences. It calls the Quidhampton game cricket when it is clearly not. [77] Each case records the profession of the plaintiff: mercer, draper, butcher, shipowner. The entry suggests that the injured man is local MP John Combe, whose profession is given as cricketer.[78] While the implication is astounding—there are professional stick and ball players in fifteenth century England—no other records exist to substantiate it.

Misadventure comes to light in 1426. A friar in County Galway admits to playing a game, "in which players held a long thin blunt-pointed stick, which they threw one after the other." The friar strikes a layman on the temple. The friar pleads dispensation on the grounds that the layman went about "eating and drinking" for six months before dropping dead.[79] The Bishop of Shap Abbey, Cumberland—a county with a rich footballing heritage— pronounces judgment on a feud between Thomas Salkend and Thomas Curwen, in 1473. One of the "dyverce varyances of querells" includes a football game in which the latter's tenant is "sore hurt atte the foteball" by the former's servant.[80] In 1480, footballers are indicted for "riotously claiming land as a common playing ground, and chanting threats."[81] Nothing other than flagrant murder can be recorded at a Shrove Tuesday football match

---

75 Ibid.

76 Osmund was beatified thirty-one years later. He is the patron saint of paralysis and mental illness.

77 Wedgwood, J.C., *History of Parliament (1439–1509).* His Majesty's Stationery Office, London, 1936. p. 210.

78 Ibid, p. 209.

79 "Lateran Regesta 261: 1425–1426" in *Calendar of Papal Registers Relating To Great Britain and Ireland: Volume 7, 1417–1431*, ed. J A Twemlow (London, 1906), pp. 452–458. *British HistoryOnline*http://www.british-history.ac.uk/cal-papal-registers/brit-ie/vol7/pp452–458.Accessed 11 June 2023.

80 Ragg, F.W., *Two Documents relating to Shap Abbey.* Transactions of the Cumberland & Westmorland Antiquarian & Archeological Society 9, 1909, Series 2, Vol 9, p. 280.

81 Baker, J., *The Oxford History of the Laws of England.* 12 Vols. Oxford University Press, 2003. Vol. 6. p. 273.

in Pontefract, Yorkshire, in 1477. Robert Pilkington stabs Leonard Metcalf in the heart for accidentally kicking the ball at him. Cattle theft and setting fire to a chapel are added to the charges. Pilkington is sentenced to be hung but escapes the gallows by pleading the Benefit of Clergy.[82] Originally established to ensure clergy could avoid secular law and only be tried in ecclesiastical courts, it has been extended to lay persons who can read from the Bible. The usual text is the first sentence of the fifty-first Psalm, dubbed the "neck verse". In another case, a man who can read three words of the Bible but not string any together avoids the death penalty.[83] Another who is unable to read but can spell is likewise spared.[84] Others read well but are hanged.[85] One verse leads to another:

> If a clerk had been taken
> For stealing of bacon,
> For burglary, murder, or rape,
> If he could but rehearse
> (Well prompt) his neck-verse
> He never could fail to escape.[86]

A 1799 *Staffordshire Advertiser* sheds light on fifteenth century amusements: "For the Great: horsemanship, tilts, and tournaments. Common people: boxing, wrestling, leaping, running, quoits, &c. Foot-ball was a great favourite; and hand-ball by persons of great rank, on horseback, as well as on foot, for great sums."[87] Sometime between 1424 and 1437, David Rait, confessor to James I of Scotland, lists typical pastimes for children as ball games, chess, kayles [ninepins], catch, and "ryne at baris". Running at bars, the Scottish term for prison bars, is also mentioned in the Scottish poem, Ratis Raving:[88] "Ryne at baris, and at

82 Hessayon, A., *Beastly Furie, and Exstreme Violence*. In: Wagg, S., Pollock, A.M (eds.)., *The Palgrave Book of Sport, Politics and Harm*. Springer Nature Switzerland, Cham, Switzerland, 2021. p. 40.

83 Bacon, N.F., *Benefit of Clergy–A Legal Anomaly*. Kentucky Law Journal, 1927, 15:2, p. 96.

84 Ibid, p. 97.

85 Ibid, p. 97.

86 Ibid, p. 97.

87 *Staffordshire Advertiser*. 23 February 1799.

88 Rawson Lumby, J. (ed.)., *Ratis Raving and other Moral and Religious Pieces*. Trübner & Co., London, 1870. p. 126.

the ball, And at the caich play with all."[89] Written around 1499, *Chrysts-Kirk of the Grene* tells of a mass brawl at a country fair, during which: "Fresh men cam in and hail'd the dulis, And dang them down in dailis."[90] "And fresh men came in and hailed the dool, and knocked them down in numbers."[91] A hail can mean scoring a goal, or the cry given when a goal is scored; the dulis (dool) is the predetermined 'goal' in Scottish folk football—a tree, a hole, a point in a river.

In 1442, John Oll' becomes Prior of Coldingham, in the Scottish Borders. In 1446, he stands before the Ecclesiastical court at Durham Cathedral. "Serpentlike tongues" are hissing that he comes from a line of serfs, not freemen, an "obnoxious" allegation, he protests, driven by "the devouring flame of jealousy and foul malice."[92] He produces the sworn testimonies of thirteen men to prove the Oll's were freemen "since time out of mind." An elderly man recalls one day seeing "around sixty of that surname playing football … who were named among the best valetti [yeomen] of the barony and as free men."[93] The slanderer loses, but mud sticks. Oll' resigns four months later.[94] There is a twist. A year on, he is promoted to the position of Proctor of Durham Cathedral's Priory.[95] By the following year he has risen to subprior.[96] No one of servile birth can attain these lofty positions. An eye on the prize all along, Oll' established his freeman credentials to progress his career.

Oll' should be more than satisfied. He has hauled himself up from commoner to bursar to steward to prior to proctor to subprior. But there is another twist. Oll' had tried to clear his name before a new prior was appointed to Durham, but the case was delayed and a prior appointed an agonising three weeks before his case was heard.[97] He had been after the Durham crown. Hopes dashed, he does it the hard way. Within days of

---

89 Ibid, p. 61.

90 Rogers, C. (ed.), *The Poetical Remains of King James the First of Scotland*. s.n., Edinburgh, 1873. p. 95.

91 Ramsay, A., *The Ever Green*. Robert Forrester, Glasgow, 1875. p. 14.

92 Durham University Archives. Durham Cathedral Archive: Register IV. fol. 34r–36v. https://reed.dur.ac.uk/xtf/view?docId=ark/32150_s15999n339g.xml. Accessed 12 August 2023.

93 Ibid, fol. 34r-36v.

94 Ibid, fol. 39v.

95 Ibid, fol. 25r-v.

96 Ibid, fol. 66r.

97 Ibid, fol. 28v-29r.

his subpriorship, he is positioning himself as natural heir.[98] The Prior of Durham cannot be blind to his schemes; nor that four months later, Oll' presents himself before James II of Scotland, soliciting protection.[99] In 1444, he had even petitioned Pope Eugene IV directly for the privilege of a portable altar.[100] No, the prior is no fool. In 1450, he appoints him as the Prior of Finchale, a holiday retreat for the monks of Durham.[101] Oll' is heard of no more.

Soule spans *le quinzième siècle*. In 1400, "it is a customary amusement [in Artois, a province of northern France, east of Picardy] for the groom to give a ball for *soule* and throw it up for the guests to play *soule*, and they courteously frolic", a tradition usually recorded in England and Scotland.[102] If the precursor to soule was introduced by the Cornish when they migrated in the fifth and sixth centuries, then the wedding tradition may have accompanied it. This would mean the Cornish had an existing ball game at least four hundred years before the first known mention of ball games in England c1000AD. In 1402, someone is playing and watching *soule* in a garden in Puchevillers, Picardy.[103] It even spreads to the French capital. In 1407, people play *soule* on the frozen Seine.[104] *Soule* is sufficiently widespread to attract regional synonyms. In 1420, one "Jean Cailliel asked the petitioner if he would like to be amused by what they call Soloire, and for them to have fun and play Soler."[105] The same year, the game is referred to as *chole*, and the stuffed ball is *carried*.[106]

Celtic Britannia has evolved into the independent duchy of Brittany.[107] Charles V's 1369 ban on *soule* is inconsequential. They

---

98 Ibid, fol. 66v-67v.

99 Dobson, R.B. (ed.)., *Durham Priory 1400–1450*. Cambridge University Press, 1973. p. 326.

100 *History of the Berwickshire Naturalists' Club*. 1904. Vol. 18. p. 126.

101 Raine, J. (ed.)., *The Charters of Endowment, Inventories, and Account Rolls of the Priory of Finchale*. J.B. Nichols, London, 1837. p. xxviii.

102 Carpentier, P. (ed.)., Du Fresne Du Cange. C, *Glossarium mediae et infimae Latinitatis*. 10 Vols. Firmin Didot fratres, Paris, 1678. 1846 edition. Vol. 6. p. 321.

103 Ibid, 1840 edition. Vol. 2. p. 338.

104 Cousinot, G., Cousinot de Montreuil, G., Vallet de Viriville, A., *Chronique de la Pucelle, ou, Chronique de Cousinot*. Paris, 1859. p. 378.

105 Carpentier, P. (ed.)., Du Fresne Du Cange. C, *Glossarium mediae et infimae Latinitatis*. 10 Vols. Firmin Didot fratres, Paris, 1678. 1846 edition. Vol. 6. p. 285.

106 Ibid, 1840 edition. 10 Vols. Vol. 2. p. 338.

107 They unite in 1532.

finally impose their own in 1440: “Some parishes … have been engaged on holidays … in a detrimental and dangerous game, played with a big, powerful ball, a game colloquially known as mellat.”[108] Offenders will be excommunicated and fined one hundred sols, “of whatever rank or condition they belong”,[109] a clear dig at the upper echelons, who remain subordinate to the church. Breton *soule* is named after the ball used, a *mell*,[110] while *mellata* is Breton for “hit with a mallet”, implying a stick game.[111] In 1450, *soulle* or *boulle de chalandas* is customarily played on Christmas Day between the married and unmarried of Coriac, in Auvergne, central France.[112,113] “The said Soulle or Boulle” is taken “from one place to another to gain the prize.” Around this time, Picardians take on neighbouring Artois, “at a place where two hundred or more people from the local villages assembled.”[114] Like England, local matches pit married against unmarried, another custom that may link to fertility. Drinking and *soule* are inseparable, largely because games take place on holidays—Christmas and Candelmas, New Year’s Day and Shrove Tuesday.[115]

In one passage in Arnoul Gréban’s 1453 religious drama *Le Mystère de la Passion*, Lucifer says, “Hold on my little dragons, my young school disciples, play a little solle instead of languishing in manure.”[116] Gréban hails from the town of Le Mans, twenty-five miles south of Normandy. Despite the ban, two lords in Brittany are granted the right to play *soule*: the Lord of Tronscorff, in 1456, and the Lord of Cancouët, in 1493.[117]

108 Gougaud, L., *La Soule en Bretagne et les jeux similaires du Cornwall et du Pays de Galles*. Annales de Bretagne, 1911, 27:4, pp. 576–577.

109 Six days’ pay for a skilled tradesman.

110 Gougaud, L., *La Soule en Bretagne et les jeux similaires du Cornwall et du Pays de Galles*. Annales de Bretagne, 1911, 27:4, p. 577.

111 Breton dictionary online: https://displeger.bzh/en/verb/mellata. Accessed 28 April 2023. *Mell-droad* is football in Breton, c.f., Cornish *pel droos*.

112 Carpentier, P. (ed.)., Du Fresne Du Cange. C, *Glossarium mediae et infimae Latinitatis.* 10 Vols. Firmin Didot fratres, Paris, 1678. 1846 edition. Vol. 6. p. 321.

113 Chalandas is another name for Christmas. In: Reichel, K-H., *Grand dictionnaire général auvergnat-français*. Éditions Créer, 2005. p. 160.

114 Luce, S., *La France pendant la guerre de cents ans*. Hachette, Paris, 1890. p. 113.

115 Ibid, p. 113

116 Paris, G. Raynaud, G. (eds.)., 1473 *Le Mystère de la Passion d’Arnould Greban.* F. Vieweg, Paris, 1878. p. 289. lns 22112–22114.

117 Gougaud, L., *La Soule en Bretagne et les jeux similaires du Cornwall et du Pays de Galles*. Annales de Bretagne, 1911, 27:4, p. 577.

In 1481, *soule* returns as *chaule*,[118,119] while in 1493, a statute describes *soule* as "a game in use among the Gallo-Flanders, in which they do not propel a ball with their feet, but use a wooden ball called a *Soule* or *Soulette* and try to push it as far as they can with a club."[120] The implication is that the kicking game has become commoner than the stick game. What is most compelling is that the game is played in French Flanders, to the east of Artois. In other words, the game is played along the entire northern seaboard. An 1889 glossary of Anglo-Norman describes *soule* as a game played with a wooden ball and a stick.[121] It goes on: "it is still in use in some parts of Normandy and was once very fashionable in this province. As it had become the occasion of struggles in which players often suffered serious injuries, it was prohibited by a decree of Normandy's parliament on 27 January 1494." *Soule* shrugs. She has survived glacial winters and will survive hundreds more. Statutes cannot kill her.

~

By the fifteenth century, football has become a cultural phenomenon. Three events bear witness to its growing popularity. The most interesting is an entry in the accounts of the London Brewers' Company for the years 1421–1423: "The names of Crafftes and Fraternites þat [that] deden hyren owre halle … with þe sommes of monye þat þey dede payen … of þe ffootballe pleyers be ij tymes … xx d."[122] "The names of crafts and fraternities that did hire our hall … with the sums of money that they did pay … of the football players be 2 times … 20 pence."[123] Of the football players. It is the earliest example of a *football team* in history, arguably a club attached to the guild. The Brewers' Hall contains either a "chapel of the great chamber" or is decorated with sconces and prayer texts, so it is implausible the players hire it to

118 Other terms include, *choler, choler de la crosse, choulla, cheolare, crossar, crossare, sole, soula,* and *solle.*

119 Carpentier, P. (ed.)., Du Fresne Du Cange. C, *Glossarium mediae et infimae Latinitatis.* 10 Vols. Firmin Didot fratres, Paris, 1678. 1840 edition. Vol. 2. p. 338.

120 Ibid, Vol. 2. p. 325.

121 Moisy, H., *Glossaire Comparatif Anglo-Normand.* Caen, 1889. p. 185.

122 Magoun, F.P., *Football in Medieval England and in Middle-English Literature.* The American Historical Review, 1929, 35:1, p. 40.

123 Four days' pay for a skilled tradesman.

play in.[124,125] More likely, they hold annual meetings, which indicates a society or club. The Brewers' Company is a second-tier guild; renting the hall generates revenue. Banquets are common with larks, swans, plovers, eels, woodcock, conies, and plentiful beer.[126,127] From 1421 to 1423, the hall is hired to seventeen different craft guilds, as well as the Fraternity of the Cross, The Brotherhood of the Trinity, and the Penny Brotherhood.[128,129] The football players are the only non-brotherhood, fraternity, or guild mentioned, so they must be considered respectable. That they are welcomed back reinforces the notion. The casual mention of *footballe pleyers* hints at a common, longstanding organisation. Perhaps they are part of the Brewers' Company, obviating the need for an appellation.

A football match between three hundred tailors will take place on Kennington Common in 1729, three hundred years after the *ffootballe pleyers* are mentioned.[130] Founded before 1300, the tailors' guild builds its own hall in 1347. The halls of the brewers and tailors are only two miles from the common. It is not implausible that ball games are played there by different craft guilds from the fourteenth and fifteenth centuries onward. Indeed, Shrovetide ball games are recorded in multiple cities over time, including Corfe Castle, London, Perth, Carlisle, Duns, Chester, Glasgow, Dublin, and Jedburgh. All nine of these are organised by craft guilds or city corporations.[131]

In 1476, William Caxton sets up the first printing press in England. Ten years later, Dame Juliana Berner's *Boke of Saint Albans* is published, containing treatises on hawking, hunting, coat-armour,

124 Metcalfe, C., *William Porlond Clerk to the Craft and Fraternity of Brewers of London, 1418–1440*. Transactions of the London and Middlesex Archaeological Society, 2013, Vol. 63, p. 270.

125 The existing Brewers' Hall in Aldermanbury Square, Barbican, is on or adjacent to the site of the original hall.

126 Unwin, G., *The Gilds and Companies of London*. Methuen & Co., London, 1908. pp. 194–195.

127 The Brewers' Company often fell afoul of the mayor, Richard (Dick) Whittington, who once fined them for artificially raising the price of beer in London taverns. Ibid, p. 233.

128 Ibid, p. 181.

129 Guilds included the Girdlers, Dyers, Armourers, Glaziers, Galochemakers, and Haberdashers.

130 The closest league or non-league football club to the Brewers' Hall (as the crow flies) is Arsenal FC (2.62 miles Emirates Stadium, 2.67 miles Highbury Stadium) followed by Millwall FC (2.74 miles The Den, 3.17 miles The Old Den). The Gymnastic Society, the earliest named club to play football, played at Kennington Common in the 1780s (2.27 miles away).

131 Aucoin, T., *When the Pancake Bell Rings*. Unpublished PhD thesis, University of Bristol, 2019. p. 138.

fishing, and *blasing* of arms. When explaining the use of balls in coats of arms, she is at pains to distinguish the word for ball: "this terme pila is take for a certan rounde istrumet to play with, the wich istrumet servys other while to the hande and then it is calde i laytn pila manualis as here. And other while it is an instrument for the foote and then it is calde in latyn pila pedalis, a fote bal."[132] A crude illustration shows three circles against a white background. A roundel (circle) is the earliest known emblem to appear on a coat of arms, c1200–1215. The German for roundel is *kugel*: historically a wooden bowling ball, (a *kugelbahn* was a bowling green). While the vast majority of emblematic roundels do not represent balls used in games, the *Boke of Saint Albans* sanctions such usage, and their inclusion suggests they have already been used for that purpose. In 1496, Caxton publishes *Hic Incipit Paruus Catho* which contains a warning:

> Whan fortune hath yeven the felicit
> And set the on high than be war of a fal
> Than sueth ofte suche sharp adversite
> Fals fortune tourneth as doth a bal.[133]

"When fortune has made you happy and you're on a high, beware of a fall. So often sharp adversity follows, and false fortune turns like a ball." A similar warning in an early fifteenth century translation of Petrarch's *De Remdiis*:

> Wele and woo pleyen at Þe balle.
> neÞur of hem kan holde longe Þe balle stille,
> but hedur and Þedur it (goÞ) contynuely.[134]

"Wealth and woe play at ball. Neither of them can hold the ball still for long, but hither and thither it (goes) continuously."

---

132 Baldes, W. (ed.)., *Boke of Saint Albans*. Elliott Stock, Paternoster Row, London, 1901. n.p.

133 Cato, Marcus. Porcius., *Hic Incipit Paruus Catho*. William Caxton, London, 1476. s.n., Early English Books Online Text Creation Partnership, 2011. https://quod.lib.umich.edu/e/eebo/A18231.0001.001/1:2.1?rgn=div2;view=fulltext. Accessed 18 August 2023.

134 Diekstra, F.N.M. (ed.)., *A Dialogue Between Reason and Adversity. A Late Middle Age Version of Petrarch's De* Remediis. Van Gorcum and Co., Assen, Netherlands, 1968. p. 32.

Around 1480, a rhyme is doing the rounds:

> I saw iij hedles playen at a ball,
> An hanlas man served hem all;
> Whyll iij mouthles men lay and low,
> Iij legles a-way hem drow.[135, 136]

"I saw three headless playing at ball, a handless man served them all, while three mouthless men lay down to shout, three legless men threw them out." None of the men are able to do what is required: the headless to play football, the handless to serve, the mouthless to shout, and the legless to throw them out. The verse mimics a mid-century proverb ending: "Iij heddelyse men playd at ball, I heddelyse man servit them all."[137]

A few years later there is news of a miracle, one of almost five hundred facilitated by the intercession of the dead Henry VI. In Caunton, Nottinghamshire, William Bartram comes across neighbours off for a game of football. He joins them "out of good fellowship". During the game he is kicked "in a very tender organ", which almost splits in two. Unsurprisingly, he develops chronic excruciating pain, but when he dreams of the old king, lo! his health is restored.[138] The second-hand description of the Caunton game as told by the friar tasked with compiling the miracles is engrossing: "the game … is what some people call football … youths of the peasant class propel a large ball, not throwing it in the air but rolling it along the ground, and not even striking and turning it with their hands, but using their feet. A game … altogether detestable and … of all the games the most barbaric, low and vile, and one that seldom ends without some injury, mishap or other mischief to the players."[139] He goes on: "The boundaries had been marked and the game had started; and, when they were striving manfully, kicking in opposite directions, and our hero had thrown himself in the midst of the fray, one of his fellows

135 Orme, N., *The Culture of Children in Medieval England*. Past & Present, August 1995, 148, p. 79.

136 Variations on this rhyme were in use as recently as the 1960s.

137 Meech, S.B., *A Collection of Proverbs in Rawlinson MS D 328*. Modern Philology, 1940, 38:2, p. 125.

138 Hanham, A., *Henry VI and his Miracles*. p. 646. *Richard III Society*. https://richardiii.net/wp-content/uploads/2021/08/12–148–Henry-VI-and-his-Miracles.pdf. Accessed 18 August 2023.

139 Ibid, pp. 648–649.

… kicked him by misadventure."[140] A *football pitch* with boundaries, kicking the ball along the ground, playing to opposite ends. Football fastens his blue doublet slashed with lilac silk, smooths his vermilion hose. He slips on his coat, scarlet velvet, edged in sable. He pivots to the mirror with a serene air, graces himself with a satisfied smile.

Henry also bestows miracles on those struck blind, disfigured by plague, struck by lightning, trapped in a well, buried alive, and stuck in a cess-pit.[141] His sanctification is encouraged by his nephew Henry VII. As first to rule after the Plantagenets, he is eager to legitimise Tudor claims to the throne. Henry VI is an ineffectual king, the antithesis of his father, Henry V. He is pious, kind to the poor, hates violence, and suffers a depressive episode of such severity it leaves him mute for seventeen months. Under his rule England loses the Hundred Years' War, begrudgingly relinquishing the third of France it owns. The calamity ignites the thirty-year Wars of the Roses. Nevertheless, football thrives during his forty-year reign: football is never banned, and the first football club appears. Importantly, in 1440, he founds Eton College, that future hotbed of ball games, as the "Kynge's College of our Ladye of Eton besyde Windesore."[142] Three years later, he purchases *Le Werde*, a ten-acre plot of land north of the college.[143] For generations after it is known as the Playing Fields.[144] Two other fields, the Upper and Lower Shooting-Fields, are secured in 1563/64—presumably for archery practice—connected to the Playing Fields by Sheep's Bridge.[145] Surprisingly little is heard of the playing fields in the early days of Eton, and no mention of play there until 1666, when Pepys records in his diary: "Thence to the porter's, in the absence of the butler, and did drink of the College beer, which is very good; and went into the back fields to see the scholars play."[146]

140 Magoun, F.P., *Football in Medieval England and in Middle-English Literature*. The American Historical Review, 1929, 35:1, p. 43.

141 Hanham, A., *Henry VI and his Miracles*. pp. 642–643. *Richard III Society*. https://richardiii.net/wp-content/uploads/2021/08/12-148-Henry-VI-and-his-Miracles.pdf. Accessed 18 August 2023.

142 Wightman Wood, W., *Sketches of Eton*. Seeley, Jackson, and Halliday, London, 1874. p. 1.

143 Hornby, J.J., *Walks round about Eton and Eton buildings*. R. Ingalton Drake, Eton, 1895. p. 56.

144 Cust, L., *A History of Eton College*. Duckworth & Co., London, 1899. p. 235.

145 Ibid, pp. 235–236.

146 Wheatley, H.B. (ed.)., *The Diary of Samuel Pepys M.A. F.R.S.* George Bell & Sons, London, 1893. n.p.

In Scotland, Jameses I–IV all issue bans, covering 1424–1491. The first reads: "[the] king forbiddes that na man play at the fut ball under the payne of iiijd."[147,148] It is the first mention of *football in Scotland.* James II follows in 1457, ordering archery practice for all males over twelve, at the expense of football and golf: "…wapinschawingis be haldin be the lordis ande baronys spirituale and tempale four tymis in the yeir. And at the fut ball ande the golf be utterly cryt doune and not usyt."[149] "Weapon shows to be held by the lords and barons spiritual and temporal four times a year; and football and golf to be utterly cried down and not used." Another milestone: the earliest reference to *golf* in Scottish history. The need to ban it infers widespread popularity. By 1471, it is considered that "futbal and golf be abusit in tym cumyng", when there is need of marksmanship.[150] Twenty years later, the Scottish parliament adds: "in na place of the realme there be usit fute-ball, golfe, or uther sik [such] unprofitabill sportis."[151]

James III dies in battle before Johannes de Irlandia has completed *The Measure of Wisdom.* He dedicates it to James IV instead. The theological treatise confirms the prevailing view: "the young noblis … suld tak thai play … in the hand bow … and nocht in bowlis, fut bal, or sic playis."[152] In April 1497, 2s is "giffen to Jame Dog to by fut ballis to the King", while five months later, the king spends 12d on "half ane dosane" unspecified balls.[153] Dog buys plenty for the king: hawks, armour, silver bridles, bowstrings. James is still only twenty-four, and his "fondness for games, glee and merriment of every kind" extends to bowls, football, and "the cache" [fives].[154] He plays bowls in April 1487, and in June and December 1501, probably in alleys, for in 1497, "lang [long] bowlis"—bowls played on a green, is specifically recorded.[155] In May 1496, he plays *cach* one

147 Fourpence.

148 *The Acts of the Parliament of Scotland.* 11 Vols. Printed by Command of his Majesty George the Third, 1814. Vol. 2. p. 5.

149 Ibid, p. 48.

150 Ibid, p. 100.

151 *Encyclopaedia Britannica.* 29 Vols. Cambridge University Press. 1910–1911. 11th Edition. Vol. 12. p. 219.

152 *Dictionaries of the Scottish Language.* https://www.dsl.ac.uk/entry/dost/futeball. Accessed 5 August 2023.

153 Dickson, T. (ed.), *Accounts of the Lord High Treasurer of Scotland, 1473–1498.* 13 Vols. H.M. General Register House, Edinburgh, 1877. Vol. 1. pp. 330, 358.

154 Taylor, D., *The Pictorial History of Scotland.* 2 Vols. Virtue & Co., London, 1852. Vol. 2. p. 551.

155 Dickson, T. (ed.), *Accounts of the Lord High Treasurer of Scotland, 1473–1498.* 13 Vols. H.M. General Register House, Edinburgh, 1877. Vol. 1. p. 332.

day and *kilis* (ninepins) the next.[156,157] His accounts continually refer to him playing golf and football, and there are frequent payments for balls for *cache* and for money lost at the game.[158]

The 1457 act banning golf—restated in 1471 and 1491—does not stop James from buying what are widely held to be golf clubs in 1502. On 21 September his accounts record: "Item, the xxj day of September, to the bowar of Sanct. Johnestoun for clubbes, xiiijs."[159] An identical payment is made in December 1504, to the man, "quhilk brocht [which brought] clubbes to the King in Melros."[160] That February, James and the Earl of Bothwell play golf for what appears to be a wager of three French crowns.[161] It is the first known match in history. Judging by the royal accounts, James comes out the worse. At the time, clubs cost a shilling, and the feather-stuffed leather golf balls four shillings the dozen.[162] Notably, the February accounts also record a payment of nine shillings "for golf clubbes and balles to the King that he playit with."[163]

It is reasonable to conclude that the unspecified clubs are not for golf. In the preface to the 1900 volume, the editor confirms this. Clubs "were used for beating the cover with when putting up the quarry to the hawks", and were regular purchases.[164] Hunting aside, golf has another rival. In December 1501, James IV plays 'bylis' (bowls) with "Jhone Andersone, that wantis feit and handis."[165] Andersone receives 14s. It is unclear if he is missing both hands and feet and, if so, how he beat the king; the result is not recorded. When James plays the Lord of Murray the following June, he pays

156 Ibid, Vol. 1. p. 275.

157 Taylor, D., *The Pictorial History of Scotland.* 2 Vols. Virtue & Co., London, 1852. Vol. 2. pp. 551–552.

158 Ibid, Vol. 2. p. 552.

159 Dickson, T. (ed.)., *Accounts of the Lord High Treasurer of Scotland, 1473–1498.* 13 Vols. H.M. General Register House, Edinburgh, 1877. Vol. 2. p. 341.

160 Balfour Paul, J., *Accounts of the Lord High Treasurer of Scotland.* 13 Vols. H.M. General Register House, Edinburgh, 1900. Vol. 2. p. 470.

161 Balfour Paul, J., *Accounts of the Lord High Treasurer of Scotland.* 13 Vols. H.M. General Register House, Edinburgh, 1900. Vol. 2. p. 418.

162 Hutchinson, H.G., *Golf.* Spottiswoode and Co., London, 1892. p. 14.

163 Balfour Paul, J., *Accounts of the Lord High Treasurer of Scotland.* 13 Vols. H.M. General Register House, Edinburgh, 1900. Vol. 2. p. 418.

164 Balfour Paul, J., *Accounts of the Lord High Treasurer of Scotland.* 13 Vols. H.M. General Register House, Edinburgh, 1900. Vol. 2. p. c.

165 Ibid, p. 117.

out 14s for "quhilk he tynt ... at the bylis." "Which he lost ... at the bowls."[166] James keeps his court at Stirling Castle. Sometime between 1538 and 1543, a football gets stuck in the rafters of the Queen's Chamber. It will remain undisturbed for four hundred and fifty years and is the world's oldest known football. In 2012, a replica was made using a pig's bladder "collected from an abattoir at some confusion and for a nominal fee the morning of the slaughter."[167] The ball is subjected to the seven tests used by FIFA to determine if a ball is fit for use.[168] The football is small, the size of a futsal ball, and one-third the weight of a modern football. Bull's bladders were also used in footballs and would produce a larger ball. The replica was durable when the bladder retained moisture, not so when dry, implying that footballs were stored in a damp environment in the sixteenth century. The ball was found to be bouncy, not good for long kicks, and better suited to a small pitch; certainly not a ball for folk football.[169]

The origin of one of the Border feuds that dominate the sixteenth and seventeenth centuries occurs in the mid-1400s, when Nicol, a son of the 2nd Lord Maxwell, is killed by the Laird of Cockpool at football.[170] Football will frame the feuds for centuries. A Scottish allegorical poem, *King Hart*, provides one of the last references of the fifteenth century. The titular king (symbolising Soul) writing his will, reflects on his youth and how *Delivernes* (Agility) propelled him to play "at ball and boull". He bequeaths *Delivernes* his injuries:

> This brokin schyn, that swellis and will nocht swage,
> Be heir to him; he brak it at the ball:
> And say to him that it sal be his wage;
> This breissit arme be heir to him at all.[171]

---

166 Balfour Paul, J., *Accounts of the Lord High Treasurer of Scotland.* 13 Vols. H.M. General Register House, Edinburgh, 1900. Vol. 2. p. 152.

167 Hanson, H., Harland, A., *The 16th Century Football: 450 years old sports technology assessed by modern standards*. Procedia Engineering, 2012, 34: 373.

168 Ibid, p. 374.

169 Ibid, p. 378.

170 Sir William Fraser. *The Annandale family book of the Johnstones, Earls and Marquises of Annandale*. 2 Vols. s.n., Edinburgh, 1894. Vol. 1. p. clx.

171 Small. J., *The Poetical Works of Gavin Douglas, Bishop of Dunkeld.* 4 Vols. William Paterson, Edinburgh, 1874. Vol. 1. p. 119.

"This broken shin, that swells and won't heal, that I broke at football, I give to him, it shall be his wage; he can have this torn arm too." Another admonishment appears in the same manuscript, courtesy of an unknown author:

> Brissit brawnis, and brokin bains,
> Stiff discorde and wastie wanis,
> Crukit in eld, syn halt withall,
> Thir are the bewteis of the fut-ball.[172]

"Torn muscles and broken bones, arguments and poverty at home, crooked in old age then lame, these are the beauties of the football game." The beauties of football. If only they knew.

---

172 Ibid, pp. 153–154.

CHAPTER SIX
1500–1599 I

Someone is bored. The prelims of a 1504 copy of Terence's *Comedies* are covered with doodles. Among the squiggles and scribbles, a nonsense sentence includes the words: "for to plaie [illegible word] Paul at the foot ball."[1] Another Roman poet is to thank for the earliest mention of the Welsh game of *knappan*, in 1558. Thomas Phaer in his interpretation of Virgil's *Æneid* mentions *knappan* as still played in Wales, implying it has been around for a while.[2] That Phaer was raised in Norwich is worthy of note. His take on the *Æneid* changes boys spinning tops to a football game: "as whan by strength of slyng is cast a whirlyng ball, Whom boyes for their disport, in cloyster wide, or vacant halles … It thrown with force, before them falls … From youth to youth that rolles, their corage kindlith more by knoxe [knocks]."[3] In other words, the game is an excuse for a brawl. While Virgil's *Eclogues* are silent on ball games, an eclogue from the early sixteenth century treats football sympathetically. Two shepherds discuss the relative merits of town and village life:

> They have great pleasure supposynge well to dyne,
> When men ben busyed, in kyllyng of fat swyne.
> They get the bladder and blowe it grete and thyn,
> With many beanes or peasen bounde within,
> It ratleth, soundeth, and shyneth clere and fayre,
> Whyle it is throwen and cast up in the ayre,
> Echeone contendeth and hath a grete delyte,
> With fote and with hande the bladder for to smyte.
> Yf it fall to grounde they lyfte it up againe,
> This wyse to labour they count it for no payne,

---

1 Terentii, P., *Aphri Comicorum Elegantissimi Comedie.* s.n., 1504. n.p. https://www.google.com.au/books/edition/P_Terentii_Aphri_comico_elegātissimi_co/dJhvsPWqtLUC?hl=en&gbpv=1. Accessed 4 June 2023.

2 Brammall, S., *The English Aeneid, Translations of Virgil, 1555–1646.* Edinburgh University Press, 2015. p. 27.

3 Phaer, T., *The whole .xii. bookes of the Æneidos of Virgill.* Wyllyam How, London, 1573. n.p.

Rennynge and leapynge they dryve away the colde.
The sturdie plowmen, lusty, stronge and bolde,
Overcommeth the wynter with dryvynge the fote ball,
Forgettynge labour and many a grevous fall.[4]

The poem is a reworking of Mantuan's sixth eclogue. The 1498 original provides captivating details of Italian boys at ball:

They tosse it up, and catch it at rebounds:
Now with their feet they kick it; by and by
Their armes imbrace it: if aloft it fly,
With stretchtout Fists they meet it, and again
Repell it: if it fall, they run amain
And mount it up, so toyling at their play.[5]

Boys in worn-out jackets squeal in delight as the pig is killed. Into the bladder go the beans, and into the air goes the bladder. They kick it, catch it, fist it away; and when it lands, they run at full pelt and up it goes again. The boys are aping their masters, posturing as they play street *calcio. Calcio*'s swagger is unstudied. His is a stately game, reserved for princes and noblemen; a Florentine more luminous than the House of Medici, capering about piazzas, bouncing off loggias. Around 1410, he emerges from the evening shadows of the Piazza Santo Spirito, shimmering in the heat haze, dazzling in the slanted rays, affording a tantalising glimpse.[6] He will not grace history for another sixty years. In 1470, out he springs. *La palla al calcio* (*The calcio ball*) recounts a fifteen-a-side game.[7] Nobles and craftsmen, stripped to their doublets, play side by side, "strong as bulls and light of foot".[8] Craftsmen are named: the Giant, Champ, Hotskin, Hedgehog, Freckles, Black Peter, Heifer, Sunshine,

4 Fairholt, F.W. (ed.)., *The Cytezen and Uplondyshman: An Eclogue By Alexander Barclay*. Richards, London, 1847. pp. 4–5.

5 Harvey, T. (trans.)., *The Bucolicks of Baptist Mantuan in Ten Eclogues*. Humphrey Moseley, London, 1656. p. 52.

6 Magoun, F.P., *Il Gioco del Calcio Fiorentino*. Italica, 1942, 19:1, pp. 5–6.

7 Terry-Fritsch, A., *Somaesthetic Experience and the Viewer in Medicean Florence*. Amsterdam University Press, 2020. pp. 224–225.

8 Wood, K., *Balls on wall, feet on streets: Subversive Play in Grand Ducal Florence*. Renaissance Studies, 2017, 32:3, p. 373.

The Nut, Lefty, and Stinger.[9] Honour and lasting glory are at stake. The rectangular pitch is enclosed by fans, and trumpeters signal kick-off. A rough and ready game ensues. Players are hit, thumped, and knocked over. "Some rush in and some limp off, there's chest-butting and flying blows. There's tackling high and tackling low, they play the man to knock him out, and shout and swear and threaten war."[10]

Music and fireworks honour the victors who strut around the piazza with their adoring fans. This is far from the polished *calcio* of the future. It is more akin to English folk football or *soule*. The roots of the game are likely to stem from the peasant classes, rough and egalitarian under the Republic, until appropriated and sanitised by the de Medicis. *Calcio* can lay claim to one of the earliest games on ice. In January 1491, a three-day match is played on the frozen Arno; the river permits further play in 1511.[11,12] The de Medicis lay claim to the sport before the century is out. When Piero the Unfortunate succeeds Lorenzo de Medici in 1492, he is so obsessed with *calcio* that his courtiers scour Italy for players.[13] Piero is passionate about sport, gathering around him the stars of boxing, *pallone*, *calcio*, and wrestling.[14,15]

In February 1530, a match plays out during Charles V's siege of Florence in full view of the enemy. Brazenly positioned trumpeters are met with a cannon shot that sails over their heads.[16] Biting their thumbs at the enemy lifts spirit but fails to halt the progression of starvation and plague. When the siege is raised in August, one-third of the population has perished. The exiled de' Medicis slide back into power. Another *calcio* game six years later celebrates the astute marriage of Alessandro

---

9 Ibid, p. 225.

10 Ibid, p. 226.

11 Magoun, F.P., *Il Gioco del Calcio Fiorentino*. Italica, 1942, 19:1, p. 6.

12 Zollinger, M., *Calcio Fiorentino Revisited: A Biographical Puzzle Finally Solved*. The International Journal of the History of Sport, 2000, 17:4, p. 82.

13 Brown, A., *Piero di Lorenzo de' Medici and the Crisis of Renaissance Italy*. Cambridge University Press, 2020. p. 121.

14 Napier, H.E., *Florentine History: From the Earliest Authentic Records to the Accession of Ferdinand the Third, Grand Duke of Tuscany*. 6 Vols. Edward Moxon, London, 1847. Vol. 3. p. 491.

15 *Pallone* was a game played with a large ball filled with air. The ball was struck with a *bracciale*, a wooden sleeve studded with blunted wooden spikes worn over the forearm.

16 Trollope, T.A., *A history of the Commonwealth of Florence, from the earliest independence of the Commune to the Fall of the Republic in 1531*. 4 Vols. Chapman and Hall, London, 1865. Vol. 4. p. 527.

de' Medici to Charles V's daughter.[17,18] The depleted citizens keep their feelings to themselves. A liveried match accompanies Lucrezia de' Medici's wedding in 1558. One team wear yellow satin, the other white. Three days later, players who missed out hold their own match, showily upstaging the first with white and red silver tinsel outfits.[19] The account mentions the three *calcio* positions for the first time: rushers (forwards), interferers, and strikers. Rushers form three groups of five, who begin play on the halfway line. Behind them are five interferers, then four forward strikers. Three back strikers occupy the rear line.[20]

A 1569 match honours the visit of Archduke Karl of Austria, and an exhibition match is played in Lyon for King Henry III of France in 1575.[21] Matches mark the marriages of the Duke of Mantua in 1584, and Virginia de' Medici the following year.[22] An immense crowd of forty thousand attend the six-a-side match of 1585. The teams wear gold and silver livery, and are distinguished by green and yellow berets. A comedy *calcio* follows. The last known game of the century is a fifteen-a-side in 1589. One team wears pink silk, the other turquoise, both "abundantly trimmed with gold".[23] Satin and tinsel hardly suggest a rough game. The liveried showpieces of the Piazza Sante Croce are restrained, but less anodyne versions hark back to the days of the Republic. The first handbook of *calcio* is written by Giovanni de' Bardi in 1580.[24] He describes three types: *calcio diviso* are scratch games (sides made up of players from different teams), *calcio di disfide* are challenge games, and *calcio a livrea* are liveried festival matches. A standard team has twenty-seven players, and games are largely played for two hours in the evening from January to March.[25]

---

17 Alessandro is assassinated seven months later.

18 Magoun, F.P., *Il Gioco del Calcio Fiorentino.* Italica, 1942, 19:1, p. 8.

19 Ibid, p. 9.

20 Zollinger, M., *Calcio Fiorentino Revisited: A Biographical Puzzle Finally Solved.* The International Journal of the History of Sport, 2000, 17:4, p. 82.

21 Magoun, F.P., *Il Gioco del Calcio Fiorentino.* Italica, 1942, 19:1, p. 10.

22 Ibid, p. 11.

23 Ibid, p. 11.

24 De' Bardi, G., *Discorso Sopra Il Giuoco Del Calcio Fiorentino.* Nella Stamperia de'Giunti, Firenze, 1580.

25 Ibid, p. 4; Terry-Fritsch, A., *Somaesthetic Experience and the Viewer in Medicean Florence.* Amsterdam University Press, 2020. pp. 236, 238.

The fundamentals are familiar. Two teams on a rectangular pitch attempt to get the ball over the goal line of the other within a certain time. Highest score wins. The ball can be kicked or punched over the line to score a goal (*cacchia*).[26] Players can kick, dribble, and tackle, but they can also catch and punch the ball, and shake, grab, and push to reach the ball. Fault-points are given for throwing or striking the ball with an open hand, or for sending the ball into touch.[27] *Calcio* is ubiquitous. Anyone with a ball from any class in any number can play, wherever there is space. In 1559, a *calcio* ditty captures the youths of Florence playing in a meadow:

> Al Prato, al calcio, su giovani assai,
> Hor che le palle balzan più che mai!
> Non è giuoco più ricco o bel di questo.[28]

"At the Prato, at calcio, are many young people, now the ball leaps higher than ever! There is no game richer or more beautiful." Antonio Scaino's seminal book on sport is published in 1555.[29] His focus is on tennis, though other games are covered, including an account of *calcio* as played in Venice and Padua. The tennis court is the world, he writes. Individuals play out their destiny, framed by rules and angles but in charge of their shots, movement, and power.[30] In 1608, during his extended trip in Europe in a single pair of shoes, Englishman Thomas Coryat chronicles a ball game in Venice:

"Here every Sunday and Holy-day in the evening the young men of the citie doe exercise themselves at a certaine play that they call Baloone [*Pallone*], which is thus: Sixe or seven yong men or thereabout weare certaine round things upon their armes, made of

26 Terry-Fritsch, A., *Somaesthetic Experience and the Viewer in Medicean Florence*. Amsterdam University Press, 2020. p. 218.

27 It is unclear if fault-points were aggregated into the score (like tries and conversions in rugby), or counted separately (like rouges and byes) to be used in the event of a tie.

28 Il Lasca. (ed.)., *Tutti i Trionfi, Carri, Mascherate ò canti Carnascialeschi andate per Firenze*. 1559. s., s.l. p. 349.

29 Scaino, A., *Trattato del giuoco della palla*, 1555. Gabriele Giolito de' Ferrari, et Fratelli, Venice, 1555. n.p.

30 Beretta, M., *Training Tennis Players through Natural Philosophy: From Scaino's Trattato to Garsault's. Art du paumier*. Nuncius, 2013, p. 28.

timber, which are full of sharpe pointed knobs cut out of the same matter ... having put this round instrument upon one of their armes, they tosse up and downe a great ball, as great as our football in England: sometimes they will tosse the ball with this instrument, as high as a common Church, and about one hundred paces at the least from them ... I have seene at the least a thousand or fifteene hundred people there."[31]

As is customary, Coryat's book is prefaced with mock panegyrics, from the likes of John Donne and Inigo Jones. Many prick his self-importance, some savagely. Mercifully, Ben Jonson shields him with an affectionate sketch.[32] One of John Sanford's kinder lines reads: "Thou Chesse-board pawne, who on one paire of shoes Hast trode the foot-ball of this worlds Centre."[33]

~

"Item, received for the campyng sporte: 18s. 3d."[34,35] So say the 1501/02 accounts of the "parishe of Seynt Andrewe's, in Heybregge."[36] Many camping fields adjoin churches that own the land, and the payment is probably annual rent. Heybridge is in north Essex, fifteen miles from the Suffolk border. The outgoings include an "Item paide to Willyam Alexander, for nayle and spyke ageynst the campyng—1s. 4d.", possibly for a wooden fence.[37] Other outgoings are for the repair of the "grete bell-claper", for a "bell-roppe", and "payde to a plomer [plumber] for mendynge of the church lede—4d."

A satirical poem about John Jaybird by John Skelton, tutor to Henry VIII, reads:

---

31 Coryat, T., *Coryat's Crudities*. 2 Vols. Robert MacLehose & Company, Ltd., Glasgow, 1905. Vol. 1. p. 385.

32 Sugandhi, A., *A Portrait of Thomas Coryat: Extracted from the Panegyric Verses and the Introduction to his Crudities*. Bulletin of the Department of Historical, Cultural and Social Studies, Kyoto University, 2102, Vol. 9. p. 54.

33 Coryat, T., *Coryat's Crudities*. 2 Vols. Robert MacLehose & Company, Ltd., Glasgow, 1905. Vol. 1. p. 117.

34 Seventeen days' wages for a skilled tradesman.

35 The financial year ran from 29 September (the first day of Michealmas) until 28 September. The system is still used in the United States (ending 30 September).

36 Nicols, J., *Illustrations of Antient times in England, in the Fifteenth, Sixteenth, and Seventeenth Centuries*. J. Nichols, London, 1797. p. 161.

37 Ibid, p. 162.

For this knavate,
By the holy Rode,
Dyd never man good:
I pray you all,
And prey shall,
At this trentall[38]
On knees to fall
To the fote ball.[39,40]

Both Skelton and Jayberd are from Diss in Norfolk, dyed-in-the-wool camping land. Jayberd is not popular. This is Skelton earlier in the poem:

Double-hearted and double-tongued,
Worn out by old age, suspected of all, loved by none.
He is buried amonge the wedes.
God forgeve hym his mysdedes!
… Now here he lies stark dead,
Never a toth in his heed.
Adeiu, Jayberd, adue."[41]

Perhaps Skelton has influence. In the inventory of 1523–1525, royal cordwainer, Cornelius Johnson, makes a pair of hand-stitched leather football shoes for Henry VIII.[42,43] While his 4s boots are the first recorded, football boots must already be in use.[44] Ball-making is a profession now. A sixteenth century Anglo-Italian dictionary defines *palloniero* as "a footeball maker", while number ninety-seven of *A Thousand Notable Things* pioneers a life jacket.[45] To start, "take two peeces of good Neates

---

38 A set of thirty requiem masses.

39 The poem is one of five by Skelton set to music by Vaughan Williams in 1936. *Five Tudor Portraits* premiered, fittingly, in Norwich, in a concert conducted by the composer.

40 Brownlow, F.W. (ed.), *Epitaph on John Jayberd of Diss, Sixth Eclogue*. In: *John Skelton 1463–1529, The Collected Poems*. 3 Vols. The Cedar Hill Press, Holyoke, Massachusetts, 2016. Vol. 3. Part. 3. p. 16.

41 Ibid, p. 14.

42 Hayward, M., *Dress at the Court of King Henry VIII*. Routledge, Abingdon, Oxon, 2017. pp. 113, 332.

43 Ibid, p. 114. The inventory includes three pairs of velvet knee-length boots, fifteen pairs of Spanish leather knee-length boots, six pairs of winter boots, and thirty-six pairs of velvet shoes.

44 Six days' work for a skilled tradesman.

45 Florio, G. (ed.), *A Worlde of Wordes, or, Most Copious and Exact Dictionarie of Italian and English*. Arnold Hatfield, London, 1598. p. 254.

[ox] lether well tand and drest, such as footeballes be made of … and of such a length as wyll make a sufficient girdle."[46] A pipe is used to blow up the tightly-stitched pieces, and three inflated ox bladders encased in leather, "lyke unto a foote ball", are stiched into the girdle, one to fit snug against the lower back, and one for each flank. The author attributes the invention to Niccolò Machiavelli, "in his excellent *Booke of the Arte of Warres*", of 1521. In 1526, Essex writer Nicholas Breton writes a book of prose, portraying months of the year, hours of the clock, and Holy Days. This from January: "the Squirrell now surveyeth the Nut and the Maple, and the Hedgehogge rowles up himselfe like a football.[47] And from March: "the Foot-ball now tryeth the legges of strength, and merry matches continue good fellowship." It is the first mention of a *football match* in history.

At the start of *Utopia*, Thomas More's Portuguese protagonist laments of England: "… stewes, wynetavernse, ale houses, & tiplinge houses, with so manye noughtie, lewde, and unlawful games, as dyce, cardes, tables, tennis, boules, coytes; do not all these sende the haunters of them streyghte a stealynge, when theyr money is gone?"[48] All these sports are gambled on. In 1532, three years before he is beheaded, More snipes about the reformist William Tyndale "For so he maye translate the worlde in to a foteball yf he joyne therwyth certeyne cyrcumstaunces, and saye this rownde rollynge foteball that men walke uppon and shippes sayle uppon."[49] And in the Tower, soon to be executed, he says of Anne Boleyn: "These dances of hers will prove such dances, that she will spurne our heads off like foote bals; but it will not be lōg ere her head will dance the like dance."[50] While More reflects on football, John Calvin, co-architect of the Protestant Reformation, plays Sabbath football in Geneva. Erasmus—that giant of the Renaissance—is neutral. In 1509, he mentions a man who boasts "to make a mache with any man

46 Lupton, T., *A Thousand Notable Things of Sundry Sortes*. John Charlewood, London, 1579. pp. 301–302.

47 Breton, N., *Fantasticks serving for a perpetuall prognostication*. Miles Flesher, London, 1526. n.p.

48 Ellis, F.S. (ed.)., *Utopia*, by Thomas More, 1516. Kelmscott Press, London, 1893. pp. 44–45.

49 Hessayon, A., *Beastly Furie, and Exstreme Violence*. In: Wagg, S., Pollock, A.M. (eds.)., *The Palgrave Book of Sport, Politics and Harm*. Springer Nature Switzerland, Cham, Switzerland, 2021. p. 67. and London, 1973, p

50 More, C., *The Life and Death of S^r. Thomas Moore*. n.p., 1642. p. 301.

at footeball."[51,52] Erasmus spends the next five years at Queen's College, Cambridge, where football will be forever popular.

In July 1507, two perpetual vicars in the Diocese of Bath and Wells are upbraided for playing hand-ball (*ad pilam manualem*) when they should have been at matins. If they fail to attend matins, first mass, and vespers for the next fifteen days, they will lose their habits for three weeks.[53] On the same day, two "vicars non-perpetual", fight in the house of a suspected woman … at 10 of the night", while two clerks are ordered to be back, "within the church when the bell rings for curfew", and not "frequent the house of a suspected woman." At a synod in 1518, the Archbishop of Dublin imposes a 40d fine on clerics for playing football, and another 40d for "the repair of the church where such games are practised."[54,55] In 1519, the curate of St Mary's church in Hawridge, Berkshire, is defrocked for "*ludit ad pilam pedalam in camisia sua*"—playing football in his shirt, while in 1529 a convocation of provincial prelates reminds clerics not to play dice or "other forbidden games", and not to frequent taverns.[56,57] Defrocked for football in a shirt sounds punitive; perhaps it was all he wore.

In January 1540, the Shrovetide football game between saddlers and shoemakers is banned in Chester. The annual Tuesday game customarily commences when a member of the guild of drapers throws up the ball from the cross "on the Roodee outside Watergate."[58] The player who seizes the ball runs as fast as he can, hoping to reach the courthouse and win the ball.[59] Other players can do "anything they thought of to wrest the ball from the handler." In 1609, Chester antiquarian David Rogers

51 Chaloner, T. (trans.)., *The Praise of Folly*, by Desiderius Erasmus. s.n., s.l., 1549. n.p.

52 Match a man, not a football match in the modern sense.

53 Bird, W.H.B., Baildon, W.P. (eds.)., *Calendar of the manuscripts of the Dean and Chapter of Wells. Volume II.* 2 Vols. H.M. Stationery Office, 1907. p. 205.

54 A week's wages for a skilled tradesman. £110 in 2024.

55 O'Flanagan, J.R., *The Lives of the Keepers of the Great Seal of Ireland.* 2 Vols. Longmans, Green, and Co, London, 1870. Vol. 2. p. 154.

56 Cunnington, P., Mansfield, A., *English costume for sports and outdoor recreation from the sixteenth to the nineteenth centuries*. Adam and Charles Black, London, 1969. p. 48.

57 Wilkins, D. (ed.)., *Concilia Magnae Britanniae et Hiberniae*. 4 Vols. R. Gosling, F. Gyles, T. Woodward, C. Davis, London, 1737. Vol. 3. p. 660.

58 Baldwin, E., Clopper, L.M., Mills, D. (eds.)., *Cheshire including Chester.* University of Toronto Press Incorporated, 2007. pp. lxviii, 327.

59 Ibid, p. 327. One manuscript says that the football could be taken, "to any of the 3 howses either of the mayor or either of the Sheriffes … to wine the same ball."

writes of the 1539 game that appears to have led to the ban. It is folk football at is roughest. Rogers prefaces with context: "these customes are of as greate force beinge truly anchant as any Record or deed of specialtie which and proved by the custom belongeinge to the crowne."[60] He goes on: "muche harme was donne some in the great throunge fallinge into a transe, some havinge theire bodies brused and crushed, some theire armes, heades and legges broken, and some otherwise mayemed, or in perrill of theire liffe."

The 1540 edict states that "the said occupacions of shoumacres Which Alwayez tyme out of memory of mannz Remembraunc have gevun and delyverid yerlye upon teuesday, Commonly caulyd shroft teuesday … unto the drapars … one bale of Lether Caulyd a fout baule of the value of iij s. iiij d. or Above to pley at from thens to the Comon haule of the Said Citie."[61,62,63] The custom is that the guild of shoemakers gives the ball to the guild of drapers, before the mayor. Similarly, the guild of saddlers presents a painted wooden ball on a spear to the drapers before the mayor. Those men married in the previous year gift a ball of silk or velvet.[64] Following the ban, football is replaced with foot races, horse races, and archery competitions, and the annual mayoral gifts a silver bell from the saddlers, and six silver arrows from the shoemakers.[65] The bell becomes a prize for the horserace, the arrows for the newly established foot-race. Failing to observe the new ceremony will result in a £10 fine.[66,67]

The 1539 match is the earliest known *annual* Shrove Tuesday fixture in history. The 1565 *Vale-Royall of England* erroneously places the last game in 1533: "The offering of Ball and foot-Balls were put down, and the silver bell offered to the Maior on Shrovetuesday."[68] While the fixture's

---

60 Ibid, p. 328.

61 Baldwin, E., Clopper, L.M., Mills, D. (eds.)., *Cheshire including Chester*. University of Toronto Press Incorporated, 2007. pp. 75–76.

62 A week's wages for a skilled tradesman.

63 Specially decorated balls are a long-standing and ongoing feature of Shrovetide football.

64 Aucoin, T., *When the Pancake Bell Rings*. Unpublished PhD thesis, University of Bristol, 2019. p. 93.

65 Baldwin, E., Clopper, L.M., Mills, D. (eds.)., *Cheshire including Chester*. University of Toronto Press Incorporated, 2007. p. 87.

66 Ibid, p. 329.

67 Ten cows or fourteen months' wages for a skilled tradesman.

68 Smith, W., Webb., *The Vale-Royall of England or, The County Palatine of Chester*. Daniel King, London, 1656. p. 194. All other evidence points to 1539. Henry Gee was mayor in 1534 and again in 1540, from which the confusion may have arisen.

provenance is unknown due to its absence in available records, "tyme out of memory of mannz Remembraunc" and "beinge truly anchant" suggest an extended pedigree. If each generation is born every twenty years, and at least some great-grandfathers and mothers in Chester survive to eighty, that would date the games to at least 1459. There is an incidental entry in 1548. John Orton invites a group of people "to goe to the grene to the meypoll ther and they wold pleye att the Ball."[69] On the way, he makes a sly innuendo about an absent woman, to the effect that judging by her clothes she made more money "lyeing" under Mr Egerton than his sister did mowing.

Rogers's breviary casts a dazzling light upon Tudor Chester. Like many historical annals, daily life is recorded in meticulous detail, and it says something about football that so few references are found. Hidden among Chester's sports and ceremonies, pageants and festivities, church inventories and guild affairs, play-cycles and fairs, are angels on stilts, elephants, dragons, unicorns, feathered devils, and dromedaries. Expenses are legion: for marmalat and mynstrells, moris dansares and musitioners, hoopes of wheat and bushells of malt, whysteles and bottelles, gonnpother and crabefysshes. Griff Yuan's wife is paid for washing the curtains, and Thomas Poole's son receives a gift for not getting the role of God. Money is spent on cakes for rehearsals, drinks after rehearsals, bacon for the players' breakfasts, and midsummer drinks at Mr Moumfort's tavern. Money is due for three old cheeses and three pounds of prunes, giants and gold buttons, malmsey and sec, hogsheads of wine and pottells [half-gallon containers] of ale, hour glasses and candlesticks, taffeta and tinsel, buskins and hose, spangles and spurs, and the gilding of God's face.[70]

Over in Dublin, "The establishment of disbursements made out of the Cittie Treasury in the time of King Henry the Eight", include 3s 4d per annum to the mayor for "bringing in the balls at Shrovetide." Richard Darby receives 13s 4d for the same task.[71] The document's title

69 Baldwin, E., Clopper, L.M., Mills, D. (eds.), *Cheshire including Chester*. University of Toronto Press Incorporated, 2007. pp. 27–29.

70 See: Baldwin, E., Clopper, L.M., Mills, D. (eds.), *Cheshire including Chester*. University of Toronto Press Incorporated, 2007.

71 Harris, W. (ed.), *The History and Antiquities of Dublin, Collected from Authentic Records and the Manuscript Collections of Sir James Ware, Knt. By Robert Ware, Son of that Learned Antiquary*. Manuscript, 1678. p. 91.

is misleading: many awardees are paid long after Henry is dead. This makes the dating of the annual Dublin Shrovetide game problematic. Henry dies in 1547. Does the Dublin game predate the first recorded annual Corfe Castle game of 1551, or the earliest of them all, the Chester game of 1539? Either way, the Dublin games are highly regarded: only twenty-five items make the list, two of which are the Shrovetide balls. The difference in payments—3s 4d and 13s 4d—suggests a significant passage of time.

~

Like all medieval kings, Henry VIII must protect the "gyft of God" that is his realm.

Archery yes, football no. The year Henry is crowned, Willielmus Welton is arraigned for playing football (*pilam pedalem*) and other illicit amusements.[72] When Henry renews his father's ban, in 1527, football is added to the list: "[none] shall play at the tenys, caylles, foteball, &c. But to have bowes and arrows, and use them on holy days."[73,74] Christmastime and feast days are spared. A 1528 proclamation targets another diversion: "The newfanglenes and wanton pleasure that men have in using crossbows and handguns" deters archery practice.[75] Handguns. Longbows are obsolescent. Pistols penetrate thicker steel. They kill more people. The first known gun-related death in England is near Hull, in 1519, when a woman runs in front of a French bookbinder at target practice.[76] Gunpowder weapons lead to the demise of archery but remain in short supply until the 1540s.[77] An unforeseen advantage of firearms is that they require no strength: "bullets owed nothing to the muscle power that tensed a bow-stave or wound the string of a crossbow into its notch."[78] Artillery greatly reduces the need for hand-to-hand combat, resulting in a decline in wrestling as an integral aspect of military training. Riding also becomes less of a necessity, as cavalry gives way to infantry.

---

72 Peacock, A. (ed.), *Instructions for Parish Priests by John Myrc*. Trübner & Co., London, 1868. p. 75.

73 *The Boke of Justices of Peas*. Robert Redman, 1527. n.p.

74 Caylles or kayles: an early version of skittles (nine-pins), using a stick rather than a bowl.

75 Gunn, S., *Archery Practice in Early Tudor England*. Past and Present, 2010, 209:1, p. 53.

76 Ibid, p. 75.

77 Ibid, p. 76.

78 Colón Semenza, G.M., *Sports, Politics, and Literature in the English Renaissance*. University of Delaware Press, 2003. p. 41.

The downturn in the "trayning up of men in the knowledge of martiall and warrelike affaires and exercises" confers more time for leisure sports but is likely to leave the population sedentary.[79] There is a levelling up too. War is no longer a finishing school for knights; social and class differences are dissolved. A peasant may shoot a king.[80]

Divining the inevitable, "the bowyers, fletchers, stringers, and arrowhead-makers of this your realm", petition Henry in 1541.[81] Parliament enacts The Unlawful Games Act for the debarring "of divers and many unlawful Games and Plays, occupied and practised within this Realm, to the great Hurt and Lett [hindrance] of Shooting and Archery."[82] It commands every man below sixty to own a bow and arrow, driving up sales stratospherically. To ensure no pursuit is overlooked, the ban includes, "many and sundry new and crafty Games and Plays" devised by "divers and many subtil inventative and crafty Persons." Absurdly, it bans "any other new unlawful game hereafter to be invented."[83] Named sports include tennis, bowls, quoits, closh, loggets, and shove-groat.[84] Football goes unmentioned, neither does the act forbid sports at Christmas. That year, 4d fines are issued for the puzzling offences of allowing "tenys pley" in a house and keeping a "football called Tenis pley".[85]

Sports are only one of a raft of illegal activities of the era. Others include selling beef from mad cows (*vacca furiosa*), harbouring vagabonds pretending to have knowledge of physiognomy and palmistry, eavesdropping, practising surgery without a licence, and having unduly long dinner breaks.[86] It is not only Henry. In 1549, in the ducal state of Florence, Cosimo de' Medici hears of youths gathering in the streets

---

79 Ibid, p. 53.

80 Colón Semenza, G.M., *Sport, War, and Contest in Shakespeare's Henry V.* Renaissance Quarterly, 2001, 54:4, p. 1262.

81 Pickering, D., *The Statutes at Large from the Magna Charta to the End of the Eleventh Parliament of Great Britain.* Joseph Bentham, Cambridge, 1763. Volume 5. p. 79.

82 Ibid, p. 80.

83 Ibid, p. 84.

84 Pickering, D., *The Statutes at Large from the Magna Charta to the End of the Eleventh Parliament of Great Britain.* 29 Vols. Joseph Bentham, Cambridge, 1763. Vol. 5. pp. 80–81.

85 Loder-Symonds, F.C., Wodehouse, E.R., *The Manuscripts of Rye and Hereford Corporations.* Eyre and Spottiswoode, London, 1892. p. 314.

86 Baker, J., *The Oxford History of the Laws of England.* 12 Vols. Oxford University Press, Oxford, 2003. Vol. 6. pp. 272–273.

to play pall-mall across several months. Others play at *pome* in Piazzo San Marco to the accompaniment of trumpets and fireworks.[87] Cosimo responds, prohibiting "game-playing in the streets or squares … cards, dice, bats, balls."[88] Pome is a seven-a-side wrestling game similar to prison bars. Both sides "defend against capture and attempt to capture players from the other side."[89]

Writers weave a hazardous path, supporting pastimes the capricious king currently approves of, criticising those unlikely to find favour. This from Thomas Elyot in his 1531 treatise on statesmanship: "Foote balle is nothynge but beastely fury, and extreme violence, wherof procedeth hurte, and consequently rancour and malice do remayn with them that be wounded. Wherfore it is to be put in perpetuall sylence."[90] He throws in a caution about tennis: "Tenese, seldome used, and for a little space, is a good exercise for yonge men, but it is more violent than shoting, by reason that two men do play."[91] Three years later, he softens. *The Castell of Helth* divides healthy exercises into groups. Those "compound of violent exercise and swifte" include "daunsynge of galyardes", "throwynge of the balle, and rounnynge after it", and "footeballe play".[92,93] He includes ball games in a Latin thesaurus: "Thou arte good at the harpe, good at tennice", together with a phrase: "To receive or take the ball handesomly and diligently, and to caste or strike it agayne … cunningly."[94] Jean De Meung agrees that "the tenise court, foote ball, and the wrastling, Is for young mens health a verie good thing", though the original French lists *paume* (*jeu de paume*), *la balle*, and *lice* (jousting).[95,96] Humanist Juan Luis Vives also advocates the javelin, running, and playing ball, as they "combine honour with pleasure … the aim of such games is to promote

87 Wood, K., *Balls on wall, feet on streets: Subversive Play in Grand Ducal Florence.* Renaissance Studies, 2017, 32:3, pp. 374–375.

88 Ibid, 376.

89 Ibid, 375.

90 Elyot, T., *The Boke Named the Governour.* Thomas Berthelet, London, 1537. p. 93.

91 Ibid, p. 92.

92 A galyarde was a popular lively dance in triple time, with complicated steps and turns.

93 Elyot, T., *The Castell of Helth.* 2 Vols. Thomas Berthelet, London, 1541. Vol. 2. p. 50.

94 Cooper, T., Estienne, H., Elyot, T., *Thesavrvs Lingvæ Romanæ & Britannicæ.* Henry Wykes, London, 1564. n.p.

95 De Meun, J., *The Dodecahedron of Fortune.* John Pindley, London, 1613. p. 127.

96 De Meun, J., *Le Plaisant ieu du Dodechohedron de Fortune.* Jean Huguetan, Lyon, 1581. p. 127.

the growth of the body, not to make boys wild and ferocious."[97] Sport is recommended for schoolboys in 1550:

> To shote, to bowle, or cast the barre,
> To play tenise, or tosse the ball,
> Or to rene base, like men of war,
> Shal hurt thy study nought at al.[98]

Others worry that sport will lead to the demise of reading:

> Bokes be not set by: there tymes is past, I gesse;
> The dyse and cardes, in drynkynge wyne and ale,
> Tables, cayles, and balles, they be now sette a sale,
> Men lete theyr chyldren use all such harlotry,
> That byenge [buying] of bokes they utterly deny.[99]

Richard Whitford treads the well-worn path of Sabbatarianism: "in no wyse they use suche vanytees as … berebayting & bulbaytyng, foteball, tenesplayeng, bowlyng, nor these unlawful games of cardynge, dycynge, closshynge, with suche other unthryfty pastymes, or rather losetymes."[100] In 1526, labouring under the centuries-old misapprehension that it will enrich the drilling of archery, Cardinal Wolsey enacts further futile legislation against games and pastimes. Every assizes, sessions, tourns, and leets in the land must enforce the orders, those failing to do so will be at the king's "high displeasure" and "extremely punished."[101] Not much happens. In 1528, impatient at the lack of progress, Wolsey authorises the removal and burning of "tables, dice, cards, bowls, closhes, tennis balls and all other things pertaining to the said unlawful games."[102] It is no surprise that "the people murmured against the cardinal, saying he

---

97 Watson. F. (trans.)., *Vives: on Education*. University Press, Cambridge, 1913. p. 121.

98 Cowper, J.M. (ed.)., *The Selected Works of Robert Crowley*. N. Trübner & Co., London, 1872. p. 73.

99 Neville, W., The castell of pleasure. Henry Pepwell, London, 1518. n.p.

100 Whitford, R., *A werke for housholders or for them ye haue the gydynge or gouernaunce of any company*. Wynkyn de Worde, London, 1530. n.p.

101 Heinze, R.W., *The Proclamations of the Tudor Kings*. Cambridge University Press, 1976. p. 91.

102 Ibid, p. 93.

grudged at every man's pleasure saving his own": from 1526–1529, he has a royal (indoor) tennis court installed at Hampton Court, the first in England.[103] Ironically, Wolsey falls irretrievably foul of Henry in 1529, and is removed from the palace. Anne Boleyn is watching a game of tennis at the court when she is arrested in 1536.[104] Once Wolsey is gone, Henry, rather than trying fruitlessly to ban games, begins to issue royal licenses for tennis courts, bowling alleys, and gambling houses.[105]

When Henry is not banning games, he is playing them: archery, hunting, hawking, fishing, bowls, tennis, cards, dice, backgammon, and shovelboard. In 1521, the twenty-nine-year-old king is described by the Venetian ambassador as "extremely fond of tennis, at which game it is the prettiest thing in the world to see him play, his fair skin glowing through a shirt of the finest texture."[106] In addition to football shoes, Henry has tennis slippers and drawers made, and blue velvet "tenys cotes" to wear when he rests.[107] In 1523, Henry partners the Holy Roman Emperor at doubles "tennice" against the Princess of Orange and the Earl of Devonshire, and then the Marquess of "Brandenborow" and Lord Edmonde. "They departed even handes on bothe sydes after XI games fully played."[108] In 1525, the ambassador adds that Henry plays tennis "most dexterously".[109] And when his right foot balloons after a tennis injury, the French guests at his masked ball make sure to match his black slippers, lest he be recognised.[110] Blue velvet coats. Tennis is soignée, her fashion all the rage. In Shakespeare's *Henry IV, Part II*, Henry V

---

103 Real (or Royal) tennis was played indoors. Lawn tennis is first recorded in 1591, apparently for the diversion of Elizabeth I. In: Weir, A., *Henry VIII: King and Court.* Vintage Books, London, 2010. p. 520.

104 Weir, A., *The Lady in the Tower.* Vintage Books, London, 2010. p. 166.

105 Kathman, D., *"The Madnes of Tenys" and the Commercialisation of Pastimes in Early Tudor London.* In: Bishop, T., Bloom, G., Lin, E. (eds.)., *Games and Theatre in Shakespeare's England.* Amsterdam University Press, 2021. p. 83.

106 "Preface to the First Edition", in *Letters and Papers, Foreign and Domestic, Henry VIII, Volume 1, 1509–1514,* (London, 1920) pp. vii–lxxiv. British History Online https://www.british-history.ac.uk/letters-papers-hen8/vol1/vii-lxxiv. Accessed 29 February 2024.

107 Law, E., *A Short History of Hampton Court.* George Bell and Sons, London, 1897. p. 62.

108 Hall, E., *The Union of the two noble and illustre famelies of Lancastre & Yorke.* Richard Grafton, London. 1547. n.p. The chronicler is unlikely to have known the rules of royal tennis if he believed a match could be drawn after eleven games.

109 Brewer, J.S. (ed.)., "Introduction, Section 4", in *Letters and Papers, Foreign and Domestic, Henry VIII, Volume 4, 1524–1530.* London, 1875, pp. clxxv-ccxxv. *British History Online* http://www.british-history.ac.uk/letters-papers-hen8/vol4/clxxv-ccxxv. Accessed 3 June 2023.

110 Ibid.

needles Edward Poins: "What a disgrace it is for me to remember … how many pairs of silk stockings thou hast; viz. these, and those that were thy peach-coloured ones? Or to bear the inventory of thy shirts … the tennis court-keeper knows better than I."[111] And this from Thomas Dekker, in 1607: "He courts ladies … and sometimes venters so farre upon the vertue of his pomander, that he dares tell 'hem how many [holland] shirts he has sweat at tennis."[112] In 1609, Dekker describes the "Tennis-court" as a place where "young gallants 'published' their clothes"; Ben Jonson adds, in their "tennis-court socks, or slippers sol'd with wool."[113]

In 1529, record is made of the demolition of Westminster tenements, "where is now builded the new garden, the tennis plays, and cockfight"; while an invoice is paid to Anthony Ansley "for tennis balls six times, at Calais and Greenwich" in 1532.[114,115] Ansley is "keper of the king's tennes playe" and Henry's most frequent tennis partner. When Ansley is paid in 1529, the accounts record other professions in the king's pay, including astronomer, tinsel merchant, ostrich feather maker, and "cook for the King's mouth".[116] Henry's mouth demands a French chef, Pero Doulx. Richard Fowler must have mixed feeling about working in a palace. He is paid 2d a day "for keping and scowring the urin pottes of lede at Grenewiche." By 1543, Thomas Johns "a page to the chamber" is made master of all the King's tennis plays within the palace of Westminster and elsewhere in England."[117] He holds the position for forty-one years.

---

111 Irving, H., *The Complete Works of William Shakespeare*. P.F. Collier and Son Company, New York, 1901. p. 504.

112 Marshall, J., *The Annals of Tennis*. Horace Cox, London, 1878. p. 72.

113 Ibid.

114 "Henry VIII: June 1536, 16–30", in *Letters and Papers, Foreign and Domestic, Henry VIII, Volume 10, January–June 1536*, ed. James Gairdner (London, 1887), pp. 504–530. *British History Online* http://www.british-history.ac.uk/letters-papers-hen8/vol10/pp504–530. Accessed 3 June 2023.

115 "Henry VIII: Privy Purse Expences" in *Letters and Papers, Foreign and Domestic, Henry VIII, Volume 5, 1531–1532*, ed. James Gairdner (London, 1880), pp. 747–762. *British History Online* http://www.british-history.ac.uk/letters-papers-hen8/vol5/pp747–762. Accessed 24 October 2023.

116 "Henry VIII: Treasurer of the Chamber's Accounts", in *Letters and Papers, Foreign and Domestic, Henry VIII, Volume 5, 1531–1532*, ed. James Gairdner (London, 1880), pp. 303–326. *British History Online* http://www.british-history.ac.uk/letters-papers-hen8/vol5/pp303–326. Accessed 3 June 2023.

117 "Henry VIII: December 1543, 21–31", in *Letters and Papers, Foreign and Domestic, Henry VIII, Volume 18 Part 2, August-December 1543*, ed. James Gairdner and R H Brodie (London, 1902), pp. 271–282. *British History Online* http://www.british-history.ac.uk/letters-papers-hen8/vol18/no2/pp271-282. Accessed 3 June 2023.

In 1536, a list of creditors to Sir Francis Weston deceased includes "a poor woman that Hannesley of the tennis play had married for balls I cannot tell how much."[118] A backstory will emerge concerning Weston, who has no nose for intrigue.

Henry VIII knows how to throw a party. On 3 October 1518, the *Treaty of London* is signed, promising peace across Western Europe. Henry hosts the French. The banqueting hall is "decorated with huge vases of gold and silver".[119] After supper, guests are served "countless dishes of confections and other delicacies. Large bowls filled with ducats and dice were then placed upon the table for such as liked to gamble." Henry's mother, Elizabeth of York, is not averse to dice and cards. Her privy purse expenses reveal an outgoing of 8s 4d in October 1502, "to my Lady Gilford for money by hure delivered to the Quene's grace at Ewelme playing at dice."[120] In December, there is a payment of £2 10s "to the Quenes grace upon the Feest of Saint Stephen for hure disporte at Cardes this Christmas."[121,122]

Henry lays wagers on dog races, hunting, and shooting, and gives gratuities to diverse entertainments, including a performing dog, a man who outraces his dog, and a man who can ride two horses at once. He loses huge sums. £163 at tennis and dice one day in Boulogne,[123] £3,243 across three years.[124] In January 1532 he loses fifteen games of tennis at 40s each.[125] Two losses are recorded the following day; arguably, his temper puts paid to further games. To be fair, victories go unrecorded, as the privy purse expenses record expenditure only. An unorthodox expense is recorded in October 1532: £45 to the Cardinal of Lorraine for beating

---

118 Gairdner, J. (ed.)., *Letters and Papers, Foreign and Domestic of the Reign of Henry VIII.* 22 Vols. TannerRichie Publishing, Burlington, Ontario, Canada, 2005. Vol. 10. p. 358.

119 Brown, R. *Calendar of state papers and manuscripts, relating to English affairs, existing in the Archives and collections of Venice, and in other libraries of Northern Italy.* Longmans, Green, Reader, and Dyer, 1867. p. 463.

120 Harris Nicholas, N., *Privy purse expenses of Elizabeth of York: wardrobe accounts of Edward the Fourth.* William Pickering, Chancery Lane, London, 1830. p. 52.

121 Ibid, p. 84.

122 Enough to buy two horses.

123 Forty horses

124 Nine hundred horses.

125 "Henry VIII: Privy Purse Expences", in *Letters and Papers, Foreign and Domestic, Henry VIII, Volume 5, 1531–1532*, ed. James Gairdner (London, 1880), pp. 747–762. *British History Online* http://www.british-history.ac.uk/letters-papers-hen8/vol5/pp747–762. Accessed 24 October 2023.

Henry at tennis. It is not Henry's day. That evening, he loses £111 at dice to the cardinal and Lords Norfolk and Suffolk.[126] Twelve years later, after playing tennis, the cardinal "drank a cup of drink and suddenly died."[127] He is not the only one. In 1535, the Duke of Brandenburg plays tennis after a banquet in his honour, in Valencia. "He caught a fever in overheating himself, and died in three days."[128]

Henry allows others to bet on his games. One courtier scoops £45. Ironically, George Boleyn wins his bet on a tennis game between Henry and Francis Weston. The money soon circles back to Henry. A doubles game is recorded on 16 December 1531: "paied to one that s'ved [served] on the king's side at Tennes at hampton-courte." In the early months of 1532, Henry loses at shovelboard on five separate occasions. Twelve losses at bowls are recorded over a three-year period, including one at the hands of Anne Boleyn, six months before their marriage. That June, Robert Lee is paid "for the making of the Bowlyng Aley" at Eltham Palace.[129] Three years after Henry's death, there is unmaking: "my Lord Mayor, with both the sheriffs, rode to the bowlinge allyes and play-houses at Pawles wharf and by Aldgate, and there finding divers simple persons and vagabondes playing at tables and bowles … [did] brake theyr playing tables in peeces."[130] Henry's daughter Mary also plays bowls. In April 1540, she is recorded as losing a game on a wager of paying for breakfast.[131] Mary is more spirited than her fabled piety suggests: "She loved jewels and fine clothes, gambled compulsively, and continued to develop her musical talents … [but] it was her zeal for

---

126 Thirty horses. Thirteen years' wages for a skilled tradesman.

127 Gairdner, J., Brodie, R.H. (eds.)., "Henry VIII: February 1545, 16–20", in *Letters and Papers, Foreign and Domestic, Henry VIII, Volume 20 Part 1, January-July 1545.* London, 1905, *British History Online* http://www.british-history.ac.uk/letters-papers-hen8/vol20/no1/pp90–101. Accessed 3 June 2023.

128 "Henry VIII: July 1525, 1–13" in *Letters and Papers, Foreign and Domestic, Henry VIII, Volume 4, 1524–1530*, ed. J S Brewer (London, 1875), pp. 655–673. *British History Online* http://www.british-history.ac.uk/letters-papers-hen8/vol4/pp655–673. Accessed 3 June 2023.

129 Harris Nicholas, N., *The Privy Purse Expenses of King Henry VIII from November MDXXIX, to December MDXXXII.* William Pickering, London, 1827, pp. xx, xxxiii-xxxiv, 20, 36–37, 134, 180, 183, 186, 188, 189, 193, 195, 206, 209–212, 216, 218, 220, 229, 268, 278, 283, 368.

130 Hamilton, W.D. (ed.). *A Chronicle of England During the Reigns of the Tudors, from A.D. 1485 to 1559.* Charles Wriothesley, c1508–1562. Two vols. J.B. Nichols and Sons, London, 1875, Vol 2. p. 43.

131 Madden, F. (ed.)., *Privy Purse Expenses of the Princess Mary, daughter of King Henry the Eighth, afterwards Queen Mary.* William Pickering, London, 1831. p. 88.

dancing which aroused their particular ire."[132] Such is her passion, the young King Edward writes to her "to attend no longer to foreign dances and merriments."

In 1529, eighteen-year-old Francis Weston is Henry VIII's favourite page. He plays tennis and bowls and gambles with the king. In short, he is "daintily nourished under the King's wing."[133] That December, he is given a Christmas bonus and two fine pairs of hose. At Easter 1530, he is given a bonus and beats Henry at four games of "Tennes". When he marries that May, Henry gives him £6 13s 4d, and wishes him "better fortune than he himself had found in marriage."[134,135,136] Clothes are gifted, a bonnet, shirts, plentiful hose. He receives bonuses at Easter and Christmas and just because. In January 1532, he wins a tidy sum by beating Henry "at tenes". He bests him at bowls in July, dice in August, cards in October, cards (thrice), dice, and backgammon in November, cards and dice in December.[137] His purse bulges.

Basking in Henry's favour rarely ends well. On 4 May 1536, Weston is sent to the Tower of London, accused of high treason and criminal familiarity with the queen. He is not alone. William Brereton, Henry Norris, Richard Page, and court musician Mark Smeton are similarly charged. Anne's brother George is accused of high treason and incest. Diplomat, courtier, and poet Thomas Wyatt joins them in the tower on a charge of treason. Less than a fortnight later, Weston is beheaded. Two days before Anne. Only Page and Wyatt survive. Wyatt witnesses the deaths of Weston et al from his cell. *Circa regna tonat*, he says of the purge. It thunders around the crown.[138]

Anyone challenging the authority of the king should measure themselves up. Henry Gold, a parson in Middlesex, makes a complaint

---

132 Colón Semenza, G.M., *Sports, Politics, and Literature in the English Renaissance.* University of Delaware Press, 2003. p. 50.

133 Weir, A., *The Lady in the Tower: The Fall of Anne Boleyn.* Vintage Books, London, 2010. p. 129.

134 Ibid, p. 130.

135 "Henry VIII: Privy Purse Expences" in *Letters and Papers, Foreign and Domestic, Henry VIII, Volume 5, 1531–1532*, ed. James Gairdner (London, 1880), pp. 747–762. *British History Online* http://www.british-history.ac.uk/letters-papers-hen8/vol5/pp747–762. Accessed 24 October 2023.

136 A year's wages for a skilled tradesman.

137 Harris Nicholas, N., *The Privy Purse Expenses of King Henry VIII from November MDXXIX, to December MDXXXII.* William Pickering, Chancery Lane, London, 1827, pp. 11, 17–18, 23, 37–38, 46, 78, 86, 96, 98, 186, 229, 248, 265, 271, 272, 275, 277, 278.

138 Betteridge, T., Freeman T.S (eds.) *Henry VIII and History.* Taylor and Francis, Abingdon, 2016. p. 1.

"ayenst his parisshons for ther tithes." He accuses them of short-changing him, adding that they "use unlawful games, as bowls, football, dice and cards, and that they have committed riots."[139] He goes further: they are plotting to kill me. Someone is. Gold cannot see the fool in the mirror. He overreaches when he hitches his wagon to servant-cum-prophetess Elizabeth Barton. The "Holy Maid of Kent" is nationally lauded, convincing enough to secure successful meetings with Cardinal Wolsey, Thomas More, and Henry VIII.[140,141] But a king may yea today and nay tomorrow. His mood sours when her politically motivated revelations oppose his exacting negotiations to divorce Catherine. He will die if he marries Anne Boleyn, she reveals, and he will go to Hell. Thomas Cranmer and Thomas Cromwell go for the jugular.[142] She is interrogated. She recants. She is executed. Gold and four other clerics who widely disseminate her visions are "attainted of high treason" and hanged beside her.[143,144]

Never speak ill of the king. Reason with your tongue. In 1535, George Taylor stands accused of saying, "The King is but a knave and liveth in avowtry [adultery], and is an heretic and liveth not after the laws of God," adding, "I set not by the King's crown, and, if I had it here, I would play at football with it."[145] It is suggested to Thomas Cromwell that Taylor be "hanged, drawn and quartered, and his quarters set up in Buckingham, Aylesbury, Wycombe and Stony Stretford." Two months later, a drunken Richard Tydder is caught breaking into "his master's hall". When the King's Watchmen arrive, he also says that the knave lives in *avowtry*,

139 "Henry VIII: April 1534, 16–20", in *Letters and Papers, Foreign and Domestic, Henry VIII, Volume 7, 1534*, ed. James Gairdner (London, 1883), pp. 199–210. *British History Online* http://www.british-history.ac.uk/letters-papers-hen8/vol7/pp199–210. Accessed 22 August 2023.

140 In 1519, Wolsey had warned off priests from "generally dishonest games": Wilkins, D. (ed.)., *Concilia Magnae Britanniae et Hiberniae*. 4 Vols. R. Gosling, F. Gyles, T. Woodward, C. Davis, London, 1737. Vol. 3. p. 687.

141 Gertz, G, Toscano, P., *The Lost Network of Elizabeth Barton*. Reformation, 2021, 26:1, p. 124.

142 Ibid, pp. 126–127.

143 "Henry VIII: January 1534, 11–15", in *Letters and Papers, Foreign and Domestic, Henry VIII, Volume 7, 1534*, ed. James Gairdner (London, 1883), pp. 16–30. *British History Online* http://www.british-history.ac.uk/letters-papers-hen8/vol7/pp16–30. Accessed 22 August 2023.

144 Gold acted as Barton's interpreter to the pope's ambassador.

145 "Henry VIII: February 1535, 21–28", in *Letters and Papers, Foreign and Domestic, Henry VIII, Volume 8, January-July 1535*, ed. James Gairdner (London, 1885), pp. 98–124. *British History Online* http://www.british-history.ac.uk/letters-papers-hen8/vol8/pp98–124. Accessed 22 August 2023.

whose head he would like to see "run upon the ground like a football." The Sergeant-at-Law writes to Thomas Cromwell: "The breaking of the house that time at night to the intent to rob is burgularie and felony, for which he ought to die; but he is a clerk, and can speak Latin, and write very well."[146] It is unknown if Tydder's Latin keeps his blood from clotting.

Even kings congeal. 1546 slams behind Henry. He is in the void, harried by baying ghosts. Poles, Howards, Boleyns. Wolsey, Cromwell, More. He plummets into the blackest sea, clings to driftwood, washes up in the new year. January will not have him. Only ghosts. His favourite dogs sum up his reign: Cut and Ball. Two months later, Henry II is crowned King of France. He considers *soule* to be one of the "finest exercises" and is known to play during his reign. This from the poet Pierre de Ronsard: "We played divided into two troops, each wearing a different livery just like today, so that adversaries and friends could easily recognise each other in the fray."[147] The king's troops wear white livery, the others red. They are probably playing the carrying version of *soule*, for the historian Pierre de Brantôme writes, "If he wasn't playing tennis, he was playing carrying ball, or at ball, or pall mall."[148] In a French book of 1615 Henry is recorded playing outdoor *longue paume* and indoor *jeu de paume*.[149]

Henry II comes to a sporting end. In a jousting match to celebrate the conclusion of the Italian Wars, he rides off before his visor is fastened. His opponent's hollow lance strikes him squarely in the face. Several splinters penetrate his right orbit, resulting in a fatal brain abscess.[150] Henry VIII has his own jousting accidents. Foreshadowing Henry II, in 1524 he fails to lower his visor and Charles Brandon's lance smashes into

---

146 "Henry VIII: May 1535, 11–20", in *Letters and Papers, Foreign and Domestic, Henry VIII, Volume 8, January–July 1535*, ed. James Gairdner (London, 1885), pp. 262–277. *British History Online* http://www.british-history.ac.uk/letters-papers-hen8/vol8/pp262-277. Accessed 22 August 2023.

147 Binet, C., *Discourse on the Life of Pierre de Ronsard, Gentleman Vendomois, Prince of French Poets*. Paris, 1586. Vol. 4. p. 8. In: L'Agora. http://agora.qc.ca/documents/Football--Le_sport_et_les_jeux_dexercice_dans_lancienne_France__La_*soule*_par_Jean-Jules_Jusserand. Accessed 22 August 2023.

148 De Brantôme, P., *Oeuvres du seigneur de Brantôme*. 14 Vols. London, 1779. Vol. 3. pp. 277–278. In: L'Agora. http://agora.qc.ca/documents/Football--Le_sport_et_les_jeux_dexercice_dans_lancienne_France__La_*soule*_par_Jean-Jules_Jusserand. Accessed 22 August 2023.

149 De Miraument, P., *Le Prevost de L'Hostel, et Grand Prevost de France*. Pierre Chevalier, Paris, 1615, p. 362.

150 Zanello, M., Charlier, P., Corns., Devaux, B., Berche, P., Pallud, J., *The Death of Henry II, King of France (1519–1559). From myth to medical and historical fact*. Acta Neurochir, 2015, 157: 145–149.

his forehead. Henry laughs it off. Twelve years later, the now forty-five-year-old king is unseated by his opponent's lance. His armoured horse falls on his legs. The resulting injuries contribute to the constant pain and ulcers that blight the rest of his life. He does not joust again.

Soule remains popular. Further bans are required. In 1507, in Amiens, Picardy's *soule* town since at least 1323 *choule* is banned on Saints Days, punishable by sixty Parisian sols.[151,152] The Normandy diarist Gilles de Gouberville mentions *soule* multiple times. On Friday 15 January 1551, he records that he played *soule* all day in a five hundred a-side game.[153] One thousand playing Friday *soule* in winter. It is a fierce carrying game. One man is thrown backwards and knocked out. He is thought to be dead and cannot be roused for hours. Two days later, the twenty-nine-year-old de Gouberville cannot make it to church, "I was so tired from *soule* … I couldn't help myself."[154] On Sunday 14 January 1552, his team play a ball game against Cherbourg. The match is drawn, and the ball is cut in half, a piece for each team.[155] That Boxing Day, "After dinner, I threw the ball at *soule* until dusk."[156]

On Sunday 14 January 1554, de Gouberville sends letters to his cousin and to Captain du Teil, asking for reinforcements for *soule* the next day. Plenty are recruited, and the game starts after mass. Robert Potet throws up the ball, and "the game was debated" all afternoon. The ball is taken "as far as Bretteville", where Gratian Cabart seizes the ball and wins the game.[157] Supper follows and "four pots of very good cider". This is *soule* played for many hours over long distances, French folk football. De Gouberville's diaries also reveal that *soule* is played over Christmas, and he records a game on Shrove Sunday 1554: "After Vespers, married

---

151 Loudcher., J-F., *Of the game of Folk-football in France (16th to 19th century).* p. 3. https://www.researchgate.net/publication/289999487_Of_the_game_of_Folk-football_in_France_16th_to_19th_century_The_impossible_sportivisation_of_a_traditional_physical_practice#fullTextFileContent. Accessed 6 January 2024.

152 Five days' wages for a skilled tradesman.

153 Gougaud, L., *La soûle en Bretagne et les jeux similaires du Cornwall et du Pays de Galles.* Annales de Bretagne, 1911, 27:4, p. 575.

154 *Journal de Gilles de Gouberville pour les années 1549, 1550, 1551, 1552.* Société des Antiquaires de Normandie, Caen, 1895. p. 227.

155 Ibid, p. 308.

156 Ibid, p. 304.

157 Tollemer, A. (ed.)., *Journal manuscrit d'un sire de Gouberville.* Journal de Valognes. 17 February 1870–20 March 1872. G. Valognes, 1872. pp. 169–170.

men played unmarried until nightfall."[158] *Soule* is brutal. On Christmas Eve 1555, "Cantepye, running against me, pushed me so hard with his fist on my right nipple, that I couldn't speak, and with great difficulty I was brought back here. I passed out on the way and lost my sight for nearly half an hour, by which I was forced to take to bed."[159] He spends Christmas Day in bed with "strong, great pain" in his chest. He remains bedbound till the twenty-eighth. On another occasion he tears his breeches "from the knee to the middle of the thigh."[160]

There are other entries: He goes to the strike in Cherbourg in 1554[161] and sees people playing *soule*;[162] he watches a priest playing *soule* all day; "vespers said", he plays with friends and servants by the church until night-time; in 1557, married men of the parish play unmarried.[163] Elsewhere, a custom on "King's Day" is recorded in Rochefort-en-Terre, Brittany, in 1554. Men married since the previous King's Day must give the local Lord of Rochefort a *soule* ball.[164] With one foot planted firmly against the wall of the church, each man must attempt to throw the ball over the large communal oven ("*le four a ban*"), presumably located in the town square.[165] Failure to do so results in a fine.

~

Edward VI inherits his father's war against Scotland and France. In 1550, his country near-bankrupt, he ends hostilities with Scotland, and returns Boulogne to the French. He receives 400,000 gold crowns in exchange for the town and ports.[166] Gaspard de Coligny, acting as diplomat, is invited to London, where he is fêted.[167] He dines with the twelve-year-

158 Jusserand, J.J., *Les Sports et jeux d'exercice dans l'ancienne France*. Plon-Nourrit, Paris, 1901. p. 288.

159 Ibid, p. 273.

160 Ibid, p. 273.

161 The Cherbourg strike was one of the earliest in French history. The first recorded was the printers' strike, in Lyon in 1539.

162 Moisy, H., *Glossaire Comparatif Anglo-Normand*. Caen, 1889. p. 186.

163 Jusserand, J.J., *Les Sports et jeux d'exercice dans l'ancienne France*. Plon-Nourrit, Paris, 1901. p. 288.

164 Gougaud, L., *La soûle en Bretagne et les jeux similaires du Cornwall et du Pays de Galles*. Annales de Bretagne, 1911, 27:4, p. 579.

165 Ruelle de Four à Ban lies directly in front of the church; its midpoint is 40 metres (132 feet) away.

166 £750B in 2024.

167 Whitehead, A.W., *Gaspard de Coligny, Admiral of France*. Methuen & Co., London, 1904. pp. 40–41.

old king, receives presents of gold and gilded plate, and is entertained with bull and bear-baiting. Later, he and his brother command opposing sides at football. Clearly, the French are familiar with football; toadying ministers would not arrange an unknown game that might displease de Coligny. Edward cannot be averse to the game: every detail of the carefully choregraphed summit would need royal approval. As for football, it is another evolutionary milestone: the first reference to a player *captaining* his team.

July 1553 entertains three monarchs, if Lady Jane Grey is counted. The sickly Edward dies on the sixth. After a three-day interregnum, Lady Jane Grey's disputed nine days unfold. She is unseated on the nineteenth, and Mary is enthroned. The teenager in the tower is a thorn in Mary's side. What would her father do? Wait for the furore to settle, conduct a show trial, use any means to avoid clemency. Thomas Wyatt's rebellion drops into her lap. Mary nods, Mary signs. Lady Jane Grey is executed. Wyatt's father survived the father, Thomas does not survive the daughter.

The Company of Freeman Marblers at Purbeck play annually at Corfe Castle, Dorset.[168] A document dated 3 March 1551, declares that any marbler married the year before Shrove Tuesday must pay a shilling. The man last married must also donate a ball.[169] The Shrovetide game marks the initiation of apprentices. In 1661, a document stipulates that the marblers must provide a ball and a pound of pepper, paid to the Lord of the Manor, in order to preserve an ancient right of way from Corfe Castle to Ower Quay, along which the ball is kicked on Shrove Tuesdays.[170] On Shrove Tuesdays in Harding, Flintshire, in Wales, "it was the custom … for the lord of the manor by his bailiff to provide a foot-ball and throw it down in a field near the church (called thence Foot-ball field), in which field … the young and old met, all to play football."[171]

---

168 Marshall, F. (ed.)., *The Rugby Union Game*. Cassell and Co., London, 1892. p. 4.

169 Magoun, F.P., *History of Football from the Beginnings to 1871*. Kolner Anglistische Arbeiten, 1938, Vols. 31–33, pp. 104–105.

170 While Chester lays claim to the first annual Shrovetide game, in 1539, a document may be unearthed to supplant it.

171 Myers, T., *Time's Telescope for 1826*. Sherwood, Gilbert, and Piper, London, 1826. p. 38. The period is not specified.

By 1558, Elizabeth warms the throne. In 1576, fourteen men from Ruyslippe and Woxbridge are charged with assembling unlawfully "with unknown malefactors to the number of one hundred ... and played a certain unlawful game, called foote-ball ... there was amongst them a great affray, likely to result in homicides and serious accidents."[172,173] When Cambridge students play locals in a Shrove Tuesday fixture in Chesterton, in 1579, "the sayd townsmen of Chesterton had layd divers staves secretely in the church porch of Chesterton, and in playing did pike quarrells agenst the schollers, and did bringe owte there staves, wherewith they did so beat the Schollers that diveres hed there heads broken; divers being otherwise greatly beaten, wear driven to runne through the river; divers did crye to Parise the constable to keep the queen's pease, who then, being a player at the foote bale with the rest, did turne to the schollers, willing them to keep the queenes pease, and turning himself to the townsmen of Chesterton, willed them to beat the Schollers downe."[174]

At the inquiry at the Dolphin Inn, Cambridge, a witness reveals that it was well-executed: "when they were hotte in playe, sodonlye one cryed, Staves!"[175] Another adds: "And longe Johan, servant to Mr Brakyn, did folowe one Edward Wylton, scholler of Clarehall, with a javelin ... [to] runne the said Wylton thorough, for so the said Johan, said he would doe."[176] The encounter is adjacent to the church, the traditional East Anglian location for camping fields. Indeed, an 1840 Tithe Map for Chesterton shows a four-acre field called Camping Close. Camping is the principal sport at the time (as late as 1899, an elderly Norfolk man had seen plenty of camping games but "I never seed a game o' football in my life"), so it is credible the 'foote-ball' game is a camping match.[177] Similarly, on a February Sunday in 1599, ten men of White Notley, north Essex, indulge in "the fotebal, whereon grew bludshedd contrary to her

---

172 Coulton, G.G., *The Medieval Village*. The University Press, Cambridge, 1925. p. 481.

173 Ruislip and Uxbridge.

174 Heywood, J., Wright, T. (ed.)., *Cambridge University Transactions*. 2 Vols. Henry G. Bohn, London, 1854. Vol. 1. p. 305.

175 Ibid, p. 305.

176 Ibid, p. 306.

177 Dutt, W.A., *The Last Camping Match*. The Badminton Magazine, 1899, 9:48, p. 92.

Maties peace."[178] The Dolphin Inn inquiry bans football and bear-baiting in Chesterton, "provoking protests from the Chesterton constables."[179] Perhaps more than one constable is involved in affray. On 5 March 1583, football culminates in something more serious:

"Coroner's inquisition—post-mortem taken at Sowthemyms, Co. Midd., in view of the body of Roger Ludforde, yoman there lying dead: With verdict of jurors that Nicholas Martyn and Richard Turvey, both late of Southmyms, yomen, were on the 3rd instant between 3 and 4 p.m. playing with other persons at foote-ball in the field called Evanes Feild at Southmyms, when the said Roger Ludforde and a certain Simon Maltus of the said parish yomen came to the ground, and that Roger Ludforde cried out, 'Cast hym over the hedge,' indicating that he meant Nicholas Martyn, who replied, 'Come thowe and do yt'; That thereupon Roger Ludforde ran toward the ball with the intention of kicking it, whereupon Nicholas Marten 'cum cubito dextri brachii sui' [with his right forearm] and Richard Turvey 'cum cubito sinistri brachii sui' struck Roger Ludforde on the fore-part of the body under the breast, giving him a mortal blow and concussion, of which he died within a quarter of an hour; and that Nicholas and Richard in this manner feloniously slew the said."[180]

Football is dangerous for passers-by. Playing in London produces "divers dangerous disorders … overthrowing smalle children, aged and impotent poore personnes, and women great with childe."[181] In December 1576, London's Court of Aldermen order "that there be no more footbeall playe or other dysorderly exercise used w^th^in the Royall exchaunge at any time", adding, "no more footeball playe be heareafter used" anywhere within the City.[182] A decade later, London households

178 *Essex Archives Online*. https://www.essexarchivesonline.co.uk/result_details.aspx?ThisRecordsOffSet=1&id=233967. Accessed 25 October 2023,

179 'The city of Cambridge: Town and gown', in A History of the County of Cambridge and the Isle of Ely: Volume 3, the City and University of Cambridge, (London, 1959) pp. 76–86. British History Online https://www.british-history.ac.uk/vch/cambs/vol3/pp76–86. Accessed 29 February 2024.

180 "Middlesex Sessions Rolls: 1583", in *Middlesex County Records: Volume 1, 1550–1603*, (London, 1886) pp. 135–145. British History Online https://www.british-history.ac.uk/middx-county-records/vol1/pp135–145. Accessed 29 February 2024.

181 Griffiths, P., *Youth and Authority: Formative Experiences in England 1560–1640*. Oxford University Press, 1996. p. 139.

182 Ingram, W., *The Business of Playing*. Cornell University Press, Ithaca, New York, 1992. p. 196.

are instructed to "take order with all their servants and prentizes".[183] A 1593 review concludes that edicts have failed "to inhibite the outragious playe at football", pedestrians having to steer a course through "divers great ryotts".[184] By 1599, it is played "in everie part" of London, such that people "can harldlie pass through the streets".[185] This does not stop London's haberdashers from cashing in. One shop, c1580, sells, "Dials, Tables, Cards, Balls, Puppets, Ink-horns, Tooth-picks." It is the earliest evidence of a shop *selling balls*.[186]

While the football season appears to run from February until May, February is the month for three-quarters of all accidents and injuries, probably because of the frozen ground. John Pyrry trips over another player's legs in a February game and smashes his chest and stomach on the ground. He runs off to a hedge, vomits, then dies.[187] John Tyler also trips, falls, and perishes.[188] And when Giles Hill darts after the ball that John Waylett has thrown towards the goal, he falls and dies of his injuries the following day.[189] In February 1508, Thomas Bryan falls on his own knife while playing football in Yeovilton, Somerset.[190] The following February, sixty gather for a "whurlyng" match in Tregorden, Cornwall. John Coulynge is running with the ball when Nicholas Jaane throws him to the ground. Coulyng breaks his leg and dies within the month.[191]

At a game in in Great Shelford, Cambridgeshire, on 8 February 1523, William Hay obstructs William Merten so forcefully that Hay dies as a result of his fall.[192] They are probably camping, as a close is recorded in Little Shelford in 1775.[193] Twelve days later, in Allerston, north Yorkshire,

---

183 Griffiths, P., *Youth and Authority: Formative Experiences in England 1560–1640.* Oxford University Press, 1996. p. 139

184 Ibid, p. 139.

185 Ibid, p. 139.

186 Seymour, R., *A Survey of the Cities of London, and Westminster, Borough of Southwark, and Parts Adjacent.* 2 Vols. J. Read, London, 1734. Vol. 2. p. 353.

187 Von Mallinckrodt, R., Schattner, A., *Sports and Physical Exercise in Early Modern Culture.* Routledge, Abingdon, Oxon, 2016. p. 55.

188 Ibid, p. 55.

189 Ibid, p. 55.

190 Hessayon, A., *Beastly Furie, and Exstreme Violence.* In: Wagg, S., Pollock, A.M (eds.)., *The Palgrave Book of Sport, Politics and Harm.* Springer Nature Switzerland, Cham, Switzerland, 2021. p. 49.

191 Ibid, pp. 49–50.

192 Ibid, p. 50.

193 Wale, J.H., *My Grandfather's Pocket-book.* Chapman and Hall Limited, London, 1883. p. 176.

John Langbern and Roger Bridkirk collide running for the ball. Roger falls on top of John, crushing him to death.[194] In February 1582, during a football game (*pilam pedestrem*) in Gosfield, north Essex, John Pye is "guarding the goal". Richard Elye has the ball. He barrels violently into "the weak man", and Pye collapses with fatal injuries.[195] Poor Pye. Guarding the goal for all his life was worth. Still, his death brings immortality. Guarding the goal: the inquest makes the first reference to a *goalkeeper* in history. The same assize files record multiple trials for witchcraft, including Alice Hunt for fatally bewitching six cows. Other arraignments include the theft of a "frostye" coloured steer, a woman remanded for pregnancy, and a man guilty of stealing a doublet, a pair of hose, a bow, ten arrows, and a tawny coloured hat.

Death smiles mirthlessly. Thomas Blyth wipes his beaded brow, pardoned for accidentally killing another player with a "peny knife … at foot ball, in 1515."[196] At an inquisition at Hatfield Broad Oak, Essex, in March 1567, sixteen men swear that during a game of "footeball" on Branton Meade, Thomas Paviott and Henry Ynggolde collide chasing the ball. Ynggolde, over-exerted, cannot rise, and dies hours later.[197] Eleven are fined for playing the game. In April 1582, during a football game in the village of West Ham, south Essex, Thomas Turner "dashed" John Warde of East Ham "to the ground, so that he died instantly."[198] Turner is acquitted. The same year, Edward Bell blames an argument during a "foote ball play … about the beginning of Lent" for an assault on James Hapten in Writtell, south Essex. Hapten counters it arose because Bell spoke in defence of John Paine, recently executed for treason.[199] Lent commences on Ash Wednesday, so there is a high chance it is a Shrovetide game.

---

194 Hessayon, A., *Beastly Furie, and Exstreme Violence*. In: Wagg, S., Pollock, A.M (eds.)., *The Palgrave Book of Sport, Politics and Harm*. Springer Nature Switzerland, Cham, Switzerland, 2021. p. 50.

195 *Essex Archives Online*. https://www.essexarchivesonline.co.uk/result_details.aspx?ThisRecordsOffSet=44&id=338223. Accessed 25 October 2023.

196 "Henry VIII: July 1515, 3–15", in *Letters and Papers, Foreign and Domestic, Henry VIII, Volume 2, 1515–1518,* (London, 1864) pp. 174–190. British History Online https://www.british-history.ac.uk/letters-papers-hen8/vol2/pp174–190. Accessed 1 March 2024.

197 *Essex Archives Online* https://www.essexarchivesonline.co.uk/result_details.aspx?ThisRecordsOffSet=3&id=332305. Accessed 25 October 2023.

198 *Essex Archives Online*. https://www.essexarchivesonline.co.uk/result_details.aspx?ThisRecordsOffSet=43&id=588371 Accessed 10 August 2023.

199 Dasent, J.R. (ed.)., *Acts of the Privy Council of England*. 46 Vols. Eyre and Spottiswoode, London, 1896. Vol. 13. pp. 417–418.

An inquest is held into the demise of Issac Fuller during a football (*pilem pedalem*) match at the camping close in Bocking, north Essex, in 1583. "The said Fuller with ill intent came between the said Avdesley [sic] and the others and began to play, saying, 'we are making work for the surgeon.' After which he violently pushed the said Addesley so that they fell to the ground, by which fall the said Fuller who was feeble and weak was shattered and died [five days later]."[200] Finally, the death of Humfry Witcom of Gloucester is recorded in 1593: "servant to Wido Nevette whoe died with a blowe one the heade at football."[201]

Other games kill. In Brechin, in 1509, John Thowless has his sentence reduced "for the slaughter of Alexander Meill ... by the stroke of a 'golf-club.'"[202] Clubbed to death: the first golf-related murder in Scotland. John Hasapote and William Kynge are larking around with some children, playing at catch, in Wheatley, Oxfordshire, in 1526. When Hasapote falls on the ball, Kynge falls on him, accidentally freeing his dagger from its sheath and piercing Hasapote's heart.[203] Bell-ringing is a popular sport well into the nineteenth century. In the late 1500s, a man is caught up in the rope and his head dashed on the paving.[204] Two others meet a similar fate. In 1573, a man is hit on the head by a small but heavy bell, while in 1570 a man is hit by a broken section of bell clapper, crushing his head, and catapulting half his brain out.[205] Another accidental death, in 1591. During a wrestling match in Moulsham, Essex, "Thomas Hewy, yeoman", seizes "William Egham, gentleman", around the waist. As they fall, Hewy's head lands under Egham's body.[206] Deaths are reported at pitching the bar (dagger misfortune) and throwing the

---

200 *Essex Archives Online*. https://www.essexarchivesonline.co.uk/result_details.aspx?ThisRecordsOffSet=1&id=203890. Accessed 25 October 2023.

201 *Baptisms, marriages and burials 1558–1707*. National Archives Online: https://discovery.nationalarchives.gov.uk/details/r/0fa5b006–f18e-482b-b559–d94b0cd68ea8. Accessed 26 October 2023.

202 Pitcairn, R., *Criminal Trials in Scotland*. 2 Vols. William Tait, Edinburgh, 1833. Vol. 1. Pt. 1. p. 108.

203 Hessayon, A., *Beastly Furie, and Exstreme Violence*. In: Wagg, S., Pollock, A.M (eds.)., *The Palgrave Book of Sport, Politics and Harm*. Springer Nature Switzerland, Cham, Switzerland, 2021. P. 51.

204 Von Mallinckrodt, R., Schattner, A., *Sports and Physical Exercise in Early Modern Culture*. Routledge, Abingdon, Oxon, 2016. p. 57.

205 Ibid, p. 57.

206 Knafla, L.A., *'John at Love Killed Her': The Assizes and Criminal Law in Early Modern England*. The University of Toronto Law Journal, 1985, 35:3, pp. 317–318.

sledge (bystander misfortune).[207] Killings recorded in the same assizes include John Winchester's murder of John Bristol by forcing a sheathed knife down his throat, and the separate poisonings of Eleanor Swyft's husband, son, and another man. She uses ratsbane, the preferred poison of the day. Winchester is hanged, Swyft is found not guilty.[208] More gruesomely, George Tilley stabs a carpenter in the groin, Robert Olliffe murders Elizabeth Payne with a scythe, Thomas Shepherd fractures his mother's skull with a pikestaff, and Alice Thedam kills her twelve-year-old stepdaughter with a hatchet and hides her corpse under a plum tree, then in a field of oats, and then a pond. She is found not guilty.[209] Even the season of goodwill has its horrors. John Sanway breaks his neck performing a "Cristmas playe" in 1552, and in 1563, John Hypper fatally crushes his testicles "playinge Christenmas games" on Boxing Day.[210]

At the December 1561 Essex Sessions, two "brycklayers" and two tapsters are charged with playing "ffooteball" on Passion Sunday.[211] A tapster, a chandler, and an ostler are also charged with mumming in the Christmas "hollydaies".[212] Two months later, thirteen are charged with playing football in Good Easter, south Essex, and receive a 12d fine.[213] The following Easter, mention is made of a Sabbath game between the south Essex parishes of Stondon, and Kelvedon, followed by an all-night card session; while Richard Jeffrey of Asheldham, south Essex, assembles a "company together" for football on Easter Monday 1592, "in evening service time."[214,215] Is Hugh Bailye a good liar? In 1598, in Great Baddow, south Essex, during "the tyme of evening praier he was in the

---

207 Ibid, p. 318.

208 Ibid, p. 310.

209 Ibid. pp. 313, 316.

210 Von Mallinckrodt, R., Schattner, A., *Sports and Physical Exercise in Early Modern Culture*. Routledge, Abingdon, Oxon, 2016. p. 54.

211 *Essex Archives Online*. https://www.essexarchivesonline.co.uk/ViewCatalogue.aspx?ID=255908. Accessed 10 August 2023.

212 Engaging in door-to-door revelry masked and disguised for money. It included mimed action, and mumchance—a game played with (often weighted) dice. Only 'mom, mom, mom,' could be said by the mummers.

213 *Essex Archives Online*. https://www.essexarchivesonline.co.uk/ViewCatalogue.aspx?ID=255908. Accessed 10 August 2023.

214 Ibid.

215 Haigh, C., *The Plain Man's Pathways to Heaven: Kinds of Christianity in Post-Reformation England, 1570–1640*. Oxford University Press, 2007. p. 84.

churchyard with a foote ball under his arme." His explanation is that the "youths of this parishe being at play with the youths of other parishes, there was so much noyse amongst them, that the minister could not be heard to the prophaning of the Saboth daie … he went owt & took the ball from the youths and was coming into the church …"[216] He is sent away with a warning.

Sacrilegious outrages stack up. In his visitation articles 1572–1574, the Bishop of Rochester demands that Sunday football is stopped.[217] In Durham, in 1579, John Boukell spends a week in jail and is fined a shilling for playing "on Soundaye at football in tyme of service."[218] That March, John Boyce of Stoke, in one of the more unorthodox similes, is prosecuted for "lykening the Trinitie to a foote ball playe."[219] Nine men of West Markham, Nottinghamshire, are cited "for playinge at foot ball in the church yard" in January 1584. Six are fined, while another, cited for fighting in the churchyard, has since "bled" (died).[220] Four years later, there is more mischief in Nottinghamshire. William Bolton is ordered to pay 10s to the poor box "for ringing the belles unorderly to the disturbance of the parish and for playing at the foteball" in the churchyard.[221] That year, a youth in Amberley, Sussex, is in trouble for Sabbath football, fighting, and laughing in church.[222] Thomas Tucke of Harston, Cambridgeshire, "was at the foteball in the tyme of eveninge prayer on sondaye last", in 1590. His defence is "that he was then in the Campinge Close but did not playe."[223] John Pitscottie and friends are similarly reprimanded for football play in Muirton, Perthshire, on the Sunday before Shrove Tuesday.[224] Ringleaders often take the hit. In 1592,

216 Hale, W.H., *A Series of Precedents and Proceedings in Criminal Causes, Extending from the Year 1475–1640.* Francis & John Rivington, London, 1847. p. 218.

217 Marples, M., *A History of Football.* Secker and Warburg, London, 1954. p. 54.

218 *The Publications of the Surtees Society.* George Andrews, Durham, 1850. Vol. 22. p. 119.

219 Hale, W.H., *A Series of Precedents and Proceedings in Criminal Causes, Extending from the Year 1475–1640.* Francis & John Rivington, London, 1847. p. 173.

220 Nottinghamshire History. http://www.nottshistory.org.uk/articles/tts/tts1926/actbooks2.htm. Accessed 10 February 2024.

221 *Transactions of the Thoroton Society of Nottinghamshire.* Thoroton Society, 1927. Vols. 30–32, p. 29.

222 *DEPOSITION BOOK.* National Archives Online. https://discovery.nationalarchives.gov.uk/details/r/fcba383f-e1c6–4530–89d2–c154bc4e4a57. Accessed 26 October 2023.

223 Munby, L.M. (ed.), *Short Guides to Records.* Own, D.M., *Episcopal Visitation Books.* Historical Association, 1972. p. 185.

224 Chambers, R., *Domestic Annals of Scotland, from the Reformation to the Revolution.* W. & R. Chambers, Edinburgh, 1859. p. 331.

Richard Jeffercy "had procured company together and plaied at foote-ball", fittingly in Hackwell. The south Essex man is fined fourpence. Likewise, a man in Bawtry, South Yorkshire, is caught playing Sunday stoolball and trying to rope others in.[225,226]

Anne Hynde of Hartbury, Gloucestershire, answers to no man. In 1592, she is charged with dancing on a Holy Thursday and throwing stones at the "glass windows of the church", on a Sunday, no less. When upbraided, she tells the vicar to "go home to his wench behind the door."[227] Elsewhere in Gloucestershire, six play tennis in Hardwicke during evening service, and five play bowls in Oddington.[228] Twelve are arraigned for Sabbath football in Wilmington, Kent, in 1594, and ten for playing football at Stowey, Somerset, during evening prayers, in 1598.[229] The following year, two are fined for *le footeball* in the churchyard of St Werburge's, Chester.[230] In the same sessions, a man is charged for selling ale and keeping *le shofleboord* tables at his house, and a tanner is charged with not repairing his hedge "to the annoyance of his neighbour". There are worse transgressions. In 1566, five are apprehended for playing football in York Minster. Only two are punished: Christopher Dobson, who took the ball in, and Oswald Atkinson, who struck the ball. Both are "laide over the stocke and have six yerts with a byrchen rod" on their "buttocke[s]".[231] Then there is sport of a different kind. When Richard Dunstead of Peverel, Essex, skips afternoon service, he is found with the sawyer's wife, in her kitchen, "with his points untrussed and his hosen in his hand and his buttons unbuttoned."[232]

Tennis ruffles her hair with deliberate negligence. Gangly, they say. She prefers lissom. Blossoming. Her fame grows with her. Football has no issue. Cousin, hand, racket. Licences are required to keep the courts, which are cropping up everywhere. One is granted

---

225 Marples, M., *A History of Football*. Secker and Warburg, London, 1954. p. 54.

226 Adams, Q.T., *Laudianism in the North: The Impact of Laudianism in the Archdeaconery of Nottingham*. Unpublished PhD thesis, University of Houston, 2021. p. 236.

227 Ibid, p. 84.

228 Ibid, p. 84.

229 Ibid, p. 84.

230 *ff.1-124 Henry Hardware, Mayor. f.1. Cover (parchment). Labelled "1600. 42 QE"*. National Archives Online: https://discovery.nationalarchives.gov.uk/details/r/56ff93ee-e111-42f2–bb4f-852669fee585. Accessed 26 October 2023.

231 Hair, P. (ed.), *Before the Bawdy Court*. Paul Elek, London, 1972. p. 173.

232 Haigh, C., *The Plain Man's Pathways to Heaven: Kinds of Christianity in Post-Reformation England, 1570–1640*. Oxford University Press, 2007. p. 86.

to Christopher Whytchecott, in 1561, for a "tennys playe" for "divers strangers, ambassadors and other nobles and gentlemen"; another to Edward Arnold, for all honest persons, "no vagabondes, apprentices, and servauntes."[233,234] Two years later, Thomas Singleton is granted the title of keeper of "the Tennys Playe" at Ludlow Castle for life.[235] And when Richard Prowze gets his licence for a tennis court and a garden with bowling alleys, "others of the inferior sort" are judged unclubbable.[236] A tennis court even opens up in the "late monastery of Blacke Freers", long since gutted in the dissolution.[237] Leasing sites as sports venues has precedence: footballers hire the hall of the Brewers' Guild in 1421–1423, and in 1500, St Thomas's Hospital Southwark is hiring out space that can be used as "a tenysplay & cloishbane, with all maner edifices, gardeyns, & grounds."[238] The Flemish game of cloish (closh) is a forbear of croquet. A bowl (klos) is driven through a hoop, using a spade-shaped club. It is clearly popular, as a cloishbane—the alley on which it is played—is advertised rather than the bowling alley it can no doubt double as.

Tennis rackets are referenced by two Scottish poets, William Dunbar, c1507, and David Lindsay in 1530. In Dunbar: "Sa mony rakkettis, fa mony ketche-pillaris. Sic ballis, sic nackettis, and sic tutivillaris." "So many rackets, so many catch players. What a lot of balls, and naquets, and rogues."[239,240] *Naquets* were boys who marked out chases in *jeu de paume*. Lindsay's reads: "Sum gart hym raiffell at the rakcat; Sum harld hym to the hurly hakcat."[241,242,243] "Some made him revel at the racket, some dragged him to the hurly-hacket."

---

233 *Calendar of the Patent Rolls preserved in the Public Record: Elizabeth [I].* 5 Vols. His Majesty's Stationery Office, London, 1948. Vol. 2. 1560–1563. p. 218.

234 Ibid, p. 97.

235 Ibid, 1960. Vol. 3. 1563–1566. p. 84.

236 Ibid, p. 328.

237 Ibid, 1939. Vol. 1. 1558–1560. p. 414.

238 Murray, J.A.H. (ed.)., *A New English Dictionary on Historical Principles.* 10 Vols. Clarendon Press, Oxford, 1893. Vol. 2. C. p. 520.

239 Laing, D. (ed.)., *The Poems of William Dunbar.* 3 Vols. Laing and Forbes, Edinburgh, 1834. Vol. 2. p. 26. lns 66–67.

240 Naquets and ketche-pillaris. In: Jamieson, J., *An Etymological Dictionary of the Scottish Language.* 2 Vols. The University Press, Edinburgh, 1808. Vol. 1. n.p.

241 Hamer, D. (ed.)., *Heir beginnis the complaint of Schir David Lindesay.* In: *The Works of Sir David Lindsay of the Mount.* Scottish Text Society, Edinburgh, 1931. p. 45.

242 Taylor, D., *The Pictorial History of Scotland.* 2 Vols. Virtue & Co., London, 1852. Vol. 2. p. 434.

243 Hurly-hacket: A childhood game of sliding down a steep bank.

Lord Berners's 1523 translation of Froissart's fourteenth century *Chronicles* mentions "playeng at tennes", but the original references *jeu de paume.*[244] In France, Charles IX plays *jeu de paume* under the watchful eye of his faithful commander Gaspard de Coligny, the man had "captained" the football team in England, in 1550.[245] The date is 22 August 1572, notable because an attempt is made on de Coligny's life later that day. Coligny survives only to be assassinated two days later by order of the king. It is part of a wider plot to snuff out Huguenot influence by killing its most prominent leaders. The day becomes known as the St Bartholomew's Day Massacre. Three thousand are slaughtered in Paris, seven thousand across the fifteen provincial towns.[246]

In 1570, a papal bull *Regnans in Excelsis* is issued, excommunicating Queen Elizabeth. A Latin verse taunting the Pope is rapidly "Englyshed" and volleyed back.[247]

> Now when at length the pleasant time of Shrovetide comes in place,
> And cruell fasting dayes at hande approch with solemne grace:
> Then olde and yong are both as mad, as ghestes of *Bacchus* feast,
> And foure dayes long they tipple square, and féede and never reast.
> Downe goes the Hogges in every place, and puddings every wheare
> Do swarme: the Dice are shakte and tost, and Cardes apace they teare …
> … And hereto ioyne they foolish playes, and doltish dogrell rimes,
> And what beside they can invent, belonging to the times.
> To play they go, to casting of the stone, to runne, or shoote,
> To tosse the light and windie ball, aloft with hande or foote.[248]

244 Berners, J.B. (trans.)., The chronicles of Froissart. MacMillan and Co. London, 1800. p. 332; Marshall, J., *The Annals of Tennis*. Horace Cox, London, 1878. p. 20.

245 Meylan, A., *Vie de Gaspard de Coligny, Amiral de France*. Ch. Meyrueis, Paris, 1862. p. 322.

246 Jouanna, A., Bergin, J., *The Saint Bartholomew's Day Massacre: The Mysteries of a Crime of State*. Manchester University Press, 2013. p. 3.

247 Naogeorgus, T., *Agriculturae sacrae libri quinque*. n.p., Basel, Switzerland, 1550.

248 Googe, B., *The Popish Kingdome, or reigne of Antichrist, written in Latine verse by Thomas Naogeorgus, and englyshed by Barnabe Googe*. London, 1570. p. 58.

It is a good account of contemporary Shrovetide festivities. They know how to party. They drink and feast and sport and gamble with bacchanalian brio. For four days. The See of Canterbury grows intolerant of clergy planting both feet on earthly soil. On 1 December 1574, the Bishop of Wells issues the Archbishop's decree, "that if any vicars shall frequent the city, and there play unlawful games, such as hand-ball and the like, he shall be suspended and shall forfeit his allowances for one week for the first offence, for a fortnight for the second offence, for a month for the third offence, and after that may be expelled for a further offence; because scandal has been incurred by the church through their frequenting such unlawful games."[249] Twenty-two years later, a seemingly supernatural event rocks Wells Cathedral. During a sermon, "there entered in at the West Windowe of the church a darke and unproportionable thing of the bignes of a football, and went along the wall on the pulpit side, & sodainely it seemed to breake, but with no lesse sound and terrour, than if an hundred double canons had been discharged at once, and therewithal came a most violent storm and tempest of lightening and thunder, as if the church had been full of fire … this tempest bought with it the most terrible stench … as it ceased it brake down some stone worke and melted the … irons of the clocke."[250]

The phenomenon of ball lightning remains unexplained. Gervase of Canterbury describes an event above the Thames, in 1195: "A sort of fiery globe threw itself down into the river; with a spinning motion it dropped time and again."[251] In 1556, future Member of Parliament Nicholas Walshe of Little Sodbury, Gloucestershire, inherits his father's estate after "a fiery sulphureous globe passing from one window to another," rolled "in at the parlour door at Dinner time." One sibling dies on the spot, the other six and their father within two months.[252] In 1628, a football match is arranged in Bedfordshire between Chidlington and Luton. A man rings the church bell to assemble the players. "Suddainly

249 Baildon, W.P. (ed.)., *Calendar of the Manuscripts of the Dean and Chapter of Wells*. 2 Vols. Hereford Times Limited, Hereford, 1914. Vol. 2. pp. 294–295.

250 Stow, J., *The Annales or Generall Chronicle of England*. Thomas Adams, London, 1615. p. 782.

251 Gasper, G.E.M., Tanner, B., *A Marvellous Sign and a Fiery Globe: A Medieval English Report of Ball Lightning*. Weather, 2022, 77:7, p. 232–233.

252 Stenhoff, M., *Ball Lightning: An Unsolved Problem in Atmospheric Physics*. Springer US, New York, 1999. p. 73.

it thundering was seene a blacke ball come rumbling down a hill neare by, which tooke its course directly into the Church, there it flew into the Belfree, and first slew him that tolled the bell, then it flustered about the Church, and hurted divers of them, and at last bursting; left a filthy stinke like that of brimstone."[253]

The fireball that tears through the Church of St Pancras in Widecombe-in-the-Moor, Devon, in 1638, has echoes of Wells Cathedral. When a thunderstorm develops during Divine Service, "extraordinarie lightening came into the Church so flaming, that the whole Church was presently filled with fire and smoke, the smell whereof was very loathsome, much like unto the scent of brimstone, some said they saw at first a great fiery ball come in at the window and passe thorough the Church."[254] Many are fatally burned; one woman has her "flesh torne about her back almost to the very bones." One man dies when his head is "smitten against the wall", another has "his skull rent into three peeces, and his braines throwne upon the ground whole, and the haire of his head, through the violence of the blow at first given him, did sticke fast unto the pillar or wall of the Church, and in the place a deepe bruise into the wall as if it were shot against with a Cannon bullet." The bowling alley beside the churchyard is "turned up into pits and heapes." The anonymous pamphlet describing the event prefaces the account with Psalm 46:8: "Come behold the works of the Lord, what desolations hee hath made in the earth." All for the greater good.

253 Atwell, G., *An apology, or, Defence of the divine art of natural astrologie*. n.p., London, 1660. p. 19; Burton, H., *A Divine Tragedie lately acted*. J.F. Stam, Amsterdam, 1636. n.p.

254 Anon., *A true relation of those sad and lamentable accidents, which happened in and about the parish church of Withycombe*. R. Harford, London, 1638. pp. 6–12.

CHAPTER SEVEN
1500–1599 II

The fierce passion football arouses is spoken of in 1582.[1] A minister engages a youth in Socratic dialogue. When asked of his intentions, the youth does not hold back: "I meane first to heare divine service, then after dinner I will have a cast at dauncing, that done, I wil have one bout at footbal, then perchaunce I shalbe somewhat whote, and then I meane to tosse the potte, till perhaps I shall be thrise out, that is, I shall have both my money out of my purse, my witte out of my head, and all the drinke out of the potte. Then perhaps if I do reserve any money unspent, I will see what melody a payre of bones will make, if I can get any company." The minister is horrified. "Dauncing, dicing, drunkennes, footeball play" (and fornication) on the Sabbath is enough "worke for the Divell, his damme, his eldest sonne, and one of his houshold servants." The minister's scriptural fervour so wears the youth down, that the fresh convert exclaims: "May I run up and down upon the face of the earth, as did Cain, for often times have I in heart murdred my brother at football."

In 1305, the chancellor of Oxford University bans a Michaelmas jousting tournament near the city because it will disrupt students, who are itching to attend.[2] Chess and musical instruments are forbidden at Queen's College in 1340, but it takes until 1386 for New College to prohibit ball games.[3] William of Wykeham establishes New College in 1379. Three years later, he establishes Winchester College as a feeder school. Founding statutes are established in 1398. Rowdiness is singled out. Because of "incautious and unregulated games … the chapel, cloister, or hall could frequently be damaged or even deformed in the walls, stables, pictures, and glass windows … [we] strictly prohibit the throwing of

---

1 Fetherston, C., *A Dialogue agaynst light, lewde, and lascivious dauncing*. Thomas Dawson, London, 1582. n.p.

2 Eleanor Chance, Christina Colvin, Janet Cooper, C J Day, T G Hassall, Mary Jessup and Nesta Selwyn, '*Social and Cultural Activities*', in *A History of the County of Oxford: Volume 4, the City of Oxford*, ed. Alan Crossley and C R Elrington (London, 1979), pp. 425–441. *British History Online* http://www.british-history.ac.uk/vch/oxon/vol4/pp425–441. Accessed 11 November 2023.

3 *Statutes of the Colleges of Oxford*. 3 Vols. J.H. Parker, Oxford, 1853. Vol. 1. *Statutes of New College, Oxford*. p. 49.

stones and balls … and, in addition, dances, wrestling matches … at any time ever."[4] Indoors, they strictly prohibit "wrestling matches, dances, revelry, leaping, singing, clamours, tumult and excessive noise, spillings of water, beer, and other liquids."

Westminster School is founded a dozen years earlier. Both are early adopters of a kicking game. Other colleges follow suit, though none mention football. Laws are enshrined in the original statutes of Oxford colleges: All Souls bans ball games in 1438,[5] Magdalen (no keeping of dogs, ferrets, birds of prey, or songbirds, no hurling balls, sticks, or stones, no dice, and no cards) in 1459;[6] Corpus Christi (similar, though ball play is permitted in the garden, "for the sole purpose of exercising body and mind") in 1517;[7] Brasenose (who minimise wriggle room, forbidding *any* animal, and any noxious, dishonest, or illegal game) in 1521;[8] and Christ Church (wooden balls mentioned with dice and cards are probably for a gambling game) in 1527. St John's College bans football outright in 1555, as well as prohibiting the "disorderly" growth of hair and beards.[9,10] It is the earliest mention of football at Oxford or Cambridge. Not all comply. In August 1594, seventeen Trinity students and eighteen of St John's are fined 5s each for playing football.[11,12] It gives an idea of the numbers playing, though others may slink away. King's College, Cambridge's proscription extends to wolves, bears, stags, and monkeys.[13] Students everywhere can be wayward. The 1541 Statutes of the University of Paris ban students from ball games, theatres, and *hujusmodi turpia loca*—other wicked places.[14]

---

4 *Founder's Statutes of Winchester College*. Records of Early English Drama Online. https://ereed.library.utoronto.ca/records/hamps-ridp244980624/. Accessed 21 October 2023.

5 *Statutes of the Colleges of Oxford*. 3 Vols. J.H. Parker, Oxford, 1853. Vol. 1. *Statutes of All Souls College, Oxford*. p. 45.

6 Ibid, Vol. 2. *Statutes of Magdalen College, Oxford*. p. 43.

7 Ibid, Vol. 2. *Statutes of Corpus Christi College, Oxford*. p. 68.

8 Ibid, Vol. 2. *Statutes of Brasenose College, Oxford*. p. 27.

9 Ibid, Vol. 3. *Statutes of Christ Church College, Oxford*. p. 66.

10 Ibid, Vol. 3. *Statutes of St John's College, Oxford*. p. 65.

11 Five days' wages for a skilled tradesman.

12 *1594 [Exhibita] coram Dre Duport, Procan:', 1586–95*, GBR/0265/UA/VCCt.III 4. Cambridge University Library. https://archivesearch.lib.cam.ac.uk/repositories/2/archival_objects/55055. Accessed May 27, 2023.

13 Cobban, A.B., *English University Life in the Middle Ages*. UCL Press Limited, 1999. p. 204.

14 Murray, D., *Memories of the Old College of Glasgow*. Jackson, Wylie & Co., 1927. p. 480.

In 1557, the university chancellor, Reginald Pole, limits football at Cambridge: "No one shall use dice or painted cards, or play at football, except at those seasons when it is permitted by the statutes of the colleges."[15] By 1574, the university forbids students to "resort or go to any play or game either kept at Gog-Magog Hills or elsewhere within five miles of Cambridge", or face a fine of 6s 8d, 20s[16] if play is after 8 p.m.[17] Ironically, in 1530, the mayor of Oxford accuses the vice chancellor of returning confiscated dice, cards, tables, and bowls to students. The vice chancellor snaps back at the corporation's maintenance of illegal tennis courts to bring in extra rent.[18]

Oxford attitudes soften over the coming decades. In 1575, the then vice chancellor bans bear, bull, or horse-baiting, bowling alleys, or dancing schools on university grounds, but only without his permission, and a university doctor rents a bowling alley in Oxford.[19] In Cambridge in 1580, legislation restricts football to within colleges, though ball games are forbidden against walls. The law is explicit: "no scholar to do it except within their Colleges and allowing no strangers to join in. Penalty—the rod in the common schools for those underage, others 5s. The little green between Trinity College and the river is allowed."[20]

These are not empty threats. In 1584, a batch of students are punished for playing football and meeting in the fields to fight.[21] Millesent, Smyth, and Spring of St John's College, and Wright of Clare Hall are imprisoned, while Westfield of Clare Hall, Ramsonne of Trinity College, and Emerson of Trinity College are "to be beaten in the schools." Thirteen are fined 5s. Moore is fined 20s and suspended from his degree, and Rookes must "declaim in the schools on the subject of obedience." Wright has his 5s fine remitted, as he "was committed to the Tolbooth and beaten by his tutor."

15 Heywood, J. (ed.), *Collection of Statutes for the University and the Colleges*. William Clowes & Sons, Charing Cross, London, 1840. p. 243.

16 A month's wages for a skilled tradesman.

17 Marples, M., *A History of Football*. Secker and Warburg, London, 1954. p. 72.

18 Eleanor Chance, Christina Colvin, Janet Cooper, C J Day, T G Hassall, Mary Jessup and Nesta Selwyn, *Social and Cultural Activities*, in *A History of the County of Oxford: Volume 4, the City of Oxford*, ed. Alan Crossley and C R Elrington (London, 1979), pp. 425–441. *British History Online* http://www.british-history.ac.uk/vch/oxon/vol4/pp425–441. Accessed 11 November 2023.

19 Ibid.

20 *Buckle Book, 1577–1588*, GBR/0265/UA/Collect.Admin.6A. Cambridge University Library. https://archivesearch.lib.cam.ac.uk/repositories/2/archival_objects/8597. Accessed May 27, 2023.

21 Ibid. Accessed 27 May 2023.

Within the month, the vice chancellor issues a new decree: "that no scholler should play at foteball before michaelmas come twelmonth; yf any scholler of what degree so ever did playe in eny colledge for the first tyme he should pay 5s, for the ijd time 10s and for the third he should be banished; And if any should playe in the streates of the towne, or in the fieldes or in any other place within fyve myles of the towne of Cambridge for the first tyme he should be banished."[22] Strong stuff.

In the face of insurmountable resistance, the statute is watered down in 1595: "the hurtfull and unschollerlike exercise of Footeball and meetings tendinge to that ende doe from henceforth utterly cease (except within places severall to ye Colledges, and that for them only that be of ye same Colledge) without noiye or outcry."[23] In 1584, Oxford University's more troublesome staff are openly playing football "to the great disorder of the University."[24] A ban ensues: "no minister or deacon shall go into the fields to play at foot-ball, or beare any weapon to make any fraye or maintain any quarrel."[25] Transgressors are banished and reported to the Bishop.[26] The chancellor has reason to be cautious. In 1595, an affray breaks out in the High Street during a Shrovetide football game.[27]

Cambridge's Vice-Chancellor's Court covers other transgressions.[28] Scholars are not to "gadd up and downe" the streets under pain of imprisonment. Some undergraduates go "a mommyng with visures", some are caught bowling, others scrap with butchers' servants. A scholar of Pembroke Hall is imprisoned for three days then "beaten in the public schools for proposing scandalous, inept and opprobrious questions at an exercise and for secretly entering and throwing stones during plays at Corpus Christi College." The university court also holds jurisdiction

---

22 Ibid. Accessed 27 May 2023.

23 Clark, J.W., *Football in the Sixteenth and Seventeenth Centuries*. Cambridge Review, 1908, p. 307

24 Madan, F., Butler, A.J., Allfrey, E.W., *Brasenose College Quatercentenary Monographs*. 2 Vols. Clarendon Press, Oxford, 1909. Vol. 2. Pt. 1. pp. 35–36.

25 Wordsworth, C., *Social Life at the Universities on the Eighteenth Century*. Deighton, Bell, and Co., Cambridge, 1874. p. 179.

26 Rashdall, H., *The Universities of Europe in the Middle Ages*. Henry Frowde, London, 1895. p. 670.

27 Eleanor Chance, Christina Colvin, Janet Cooper, C J Day, T G Hassall, Mary Jessup and Nesta Selwyn, *Social and Cultural Activities*, in *A History of the County of Oxford: Volume 4, the City of Oxford*, ed. Alan Crossley and C R Elrington (London, 1979), pp. 425–441. *British History Online* http://www.british-history.ac.uk/vch/oxon/vol4/pp425-441. Accessed 11 November 2023.

28 Buckle Book, 1577–1588, GBR/0265/UA/Collect.Admin.6A. Cambridge University Library. https://archivesearch.lib.cam.ac.uk/repositories/2/archival_objects/8597. Accessed May 27, 2023.

over the citizens of Cambridge for "lesser" crimes.[29] The records from 1577 to 1588 are filled with assignations, defamations, the "drawing of blood", and the selling of spoiled, damaged, or underweight goods. Men are imprisoned, fined, or beaten if they cannot pay. One man asked if he regrets saying "lewd and unseemly words", repeats them and is returned to the Tolbooth. A singing master is banished "for lewd and filthy behaviour" towards six of his female scholars, Edward Bucke, Joan Pickdon, and Joan Bentley are found in one bed, and Oliver Homes takes into his house, "idle rogish women verie suspiciouslie."

These are not good times for women. The wife of the cook of Clare Hall is "adjudged to the cockyng-stoole" for "scolding and slaundering her neighbours." In this instance, she is probably tied to the cocking stool outside her house, to the riotous relish of her neighbours. Summation and sentencing is delivered blithely. Lylles Hume is charged with "whooredom scholdyng and fighting", and must stand in the bull-ring with a paper on her back; Elizabeth Jeffraye is to be "drawen throwe the ryver" as a "bolsterer of ill women"; Margaret Webbe is "to be carried to the bryge and there to be drawen over the water at a botes tayle [stern]"; Alice Harryson is to be whipped the length of the market and then banished; and Margaret Duxberye to be committed until Saturday, to stand two hours in the bull-ring, to be carted through the streets, and then banished "for whoredom." Chancellery concern is saved for the fixing of wine prices: "muscatel 8d a quart, malmsey 7d, sack 6d, red claret and white 4d."

Schools may be more forgiving of football. William Horman becomes a pupil at Winchester College in 1468. After a period as headmaster at Eton, he returns in 1495. He publishes a textbook *Vulgaria*, in 1519, providing pupils with sentences to translate to improve their grasp of Latin including, "we wyll playe with a ball full of wynde" and "he hyt me in the yie [eye] with a tenys balle."[30] Ball games are probably played at Winchester College. A kicking–carrying game is the likeliest Horman is referring to, given the ball in stick games is harder. Horman adds a delightful sentence: "Yrchyns or hedge hoggis full of sharpe prykyllis whan they know that they be hunted make them rounde lyke a balle."[31]

29 Ibid. Accessed 27 October 2023.

30 Lyte, H.C.M., *A history of Eton College (1440–1910)*. Macmillan, London, 1911. p. 107.

31 Herrtage, S. J. H. (ed.), *Catholicon Anglicum: an English-Latin Wordbook, Dated 1483*. N. Trübner & Co., London, 1882. p. 404.

"Urchins or hedgehogs, full of sharp prickles, curl up like a ball when hunted."

~

Richard Mulcaster speaks to the widespread popularity of football in 1581. Of note is his call for referees, reduced physical contact, and smaller sides of comparable capability:

"Footeball play … could not possibly have growne to this greatnes … if it had not had great helpes, both to health and strength … though as it is now commonly used, with thronging of a rude multitude, with bursting of shinnes, and breaking of legges, it be neither civil, neither worthy the name of any traine to health. Wherin any man may evidently see the use of the trayning maister. For if one stand by, which can judge of the play, and is judge over the parties, and hath authoritie to commaunde in the place … Some smaller number with such overlooking, sorted into sides and standings, not meeting with their bodies so boisterously to trie their strength: nor shouldring or shuffing one another so barbarously … Footeball strengtheneth and brawneth the whole body … it is good for the bowels and to drive downe the stone and gravell from both the bladder and kidneies."[32]

Mulcaster is a progressive, none more so than when he advocates sport and exercise for girls: "those persons, which are to be instructed in this … I take to be children of both sortes, male and female, young boyes and young maidens."[33] It may be no coincidence that Mulcaster is the first headmaster at the Merchant Taylor's School, in London, in 1561. The school is founded by the "Worshipfull Companie of the Merchaunt Tailers", itself founded in 1323. It is the tailors who scrap with tanners under pretence of playing football on Shrove Tuesday 1373, the first known Shrovetide football game in history (an Ash Wednesday *soule* game is recorded in 1323).[34] Mulcaster promotes football as of educational benefit; indeed, he is so forward-thinking that many of his arguments "were not heard again until the nineteenth century."[35] In many ways, the

32 Mulcaster, R., *Positions Wherein Those Primitive Circumstances Be Examined.* Thomas Vautrollier, London, 1581. pp. 104–105.

33 Ibid, p. 132.

34 Carpentier, P. (ed.)., Du Fresne Du Cange. C, *Glossarium mediae et infimae Latinitatis.* 10 Vols. Firmin Didot fratres, Paris, 1678. 1840 edition. Vol. 2. p. 325.

35 Marples, M., *A History of Football.* Secker and Warburg, London, 1954. p. 69.

ethos of the school *is* Mulcaster: he remains headmaster for a quarter of a century.

Thomas Cogan also believes in the health benefits of football. Of sports, "some are swift … some are strong or violent … some are vehement as dancing, leaping, football play."[36] Christopher Langton is another proponent, advocating "haukynge, huntynge, daunsyng, running, leaping, tennes, and footeball" as good exercise.[37] And while John Caius disapproves of the violence in camping—"rather a laming of legges, than an exercise"—he approves of the game, "if the hurt may be avoyded."[38] Thomas Tusser, who is born in Essex and spends much time in Norfolk and Suffolk, is more interested in the welfare of the camping close:

> In medow or pasture (to growe the more fine)
> let campers be camping in any of thine:
> Which if ye doe suffer when lowe is the spring,
> you gaine to yourself a commodious thing.[39]

His *December's Abstract* similarly ends: "Get campers a ball, To campe there withall!"[40] Philip Sidney mirrors the format of Alexander Barclay's 1514 eclogue for the first mention of *women's* football:[41] "A tyme there is for all, my mother often sayes, When she, with skirts tuckt very hy, with girles at football playes."[42] Thomas Churchyard writes of holiday games:

> At Whytsontyed, at Paece and Yuell:
> He gave his housholde leave to play,

36 Cogan, T., *The Haven of Health*. Thomas Orwin, London, 1589. p. 2.

37 Langton, C., *An introduction into phisycke with a universal dyet*. Edward Whyt, London, c1545. n.p.

38 Caius, J., *A boke or counseill against the disease commonly called the sweate*. Richard Grafton, London, 1552. p. 29.

39 Payne, W., Herrtage, S.J., *Five Hundred Pointes of Good Husbandrie*. Trübner & Co., London, 1878. p. 64.

40 Ibid, p. 60.

41 Sidney attended Shrewsbury School, the town where football was banned in 1594. It is not inconceivable that Sidney played football. The school was an early adopter of football and instrumental in the world's first football rules—the Cambridge Rules.

42 Grosart, A.B. (ed.)., *The Complete Poems of Sir Philip Sidney*. 3 Vols. 1580. Chatto and Windus, London, 1897. Vol. 1. p. 208.

And than at stoelball all the day
Ye might have founde the mery gyrls,[43,44]

He also writes of football: "About the ball, the finest fellowes flocke, They winne the goale, that hath the greatest skill."[45] David Lindsay, the man who baptises Charles I, also has affection for the game. His 1540 play contains the lines:

Thocht I preich not, I can play at the caiche.
I wait thair is nocht ane amang ʒow all,
Mair ferilie can play at the fut ball;
And, for the carts, the tabils, and the dyse,
Above all persouns I may beir the pryse.[46]

"Though I preach not, I can play at the catch [fives]. I bet none of you are better at football [than me]. As for cards, backgammon, and dice, above everyone I will win the prize." Lindsay speaks of different balls in a later passage: "Sir scho hes sworne that scho sall sla me, Or ellis byte baith my balloks fra me." "She's sworn to kill me, or bite my bollocks off."[47] In a c1550 poem, he writes:

He wan the pryse above them all,
Baith at the Buttis and the Futeball
Till everie solace he was abill,
At cartis, and dyce, at Ches, and fabill [sic].[48]

"He beat everyone at archery and football. He could play every game: cards, dice, chess, backgammon (tabill)." In the 1591 translation of the Italian poem *Orlando Furioso*, Charlemagne's eponymous knight "tost

43 Churchyard, T., *The firste parte of Churchyardes chippes contayning twelve severall labours*. Thomas Marshe, London, 1575. *A Fayned Fancye betweene the Spider and the Gowte*. lns 114–117.

44 At Whitsuntide, Easter, and Yule.

45 Chalmers, G., *Churchyard's Chips Concerning Scotland*. Longman, Hurst, Rees, Orme, and Brown, London, 1817. p. 182.

46 Lindsay, L., *Ane Satyre of the thrie Estaits*. Robert Charteris, Edinburgh, 1602. p. 116.

47 Ibid, p. 145.

48 Lindsay. L., *The historie of ane nobil and wailzeand squyer, William Meldrum*. Henry Charteris, Edinburgh, 1593. np.

him like a football up on hye, whence he fell down and brake his neck."[49] Charlemagne and Orlando reappear in 1600, in the anonymous Jacobean play *Charlemagne*.[50] Football steals a scene with a one-line walk on: "I am the verye foot-balle of the starres." At the end of Robert Greene's pastoral romance *Menaphon*, two characters declare their love while teasing one another. After Carmela mercilessly ribs her shepherd lover, Doron, comparing his face to kitchen grease, his eyes to worms, his lined face to furrows in the soil, and his pale face to her mother's cow, she says:

> Ah leave my toe and kisse my lippes my love,
> My lies and thine, for I have given it thee:
> Within thy cap tis thou shalt weare my glove,
> At foote ball sport thou shalt my champion be.[51]

The ribald allusion to her glove is clear. It is his for the taking. With lots of skilful ball play. Doron returns the jibes, likening her eyes to cherry juice, her lips to "two fair cucumbers", and her teeth to the "tusks of the fattest swine." In 1590, Greene writes: "Is it griefe of bodie or of minde that keeps thée on holidaies from frisking it at the footeball."[52] Greene is better known for his pamphlet *A Groats-worth of Witte*, written shortly before his early death in 1592. One passage lambasts an unnamed, upcoming playwright. "An upstart crow, beautified in our feathers", he writes, a thinly-veiled accusation of plagiarism.[53] The upstart's plays are bombastic, he adds, and he is appropriating Christopher Marlowe's style. In short, he is "the only Shake-scene in the country." Shakespeare is devasted. He has recently switched from acting to writing and is struggling; the plague has shut down theatres, and he needs money badly. "His Tiger's heart wrapped in a Player's hide", Greene snipes, before offloading bile on another three playwrights. One is Thomas Nashe, another football metaphorist. Greene attends Norwich Grammar School,

---

49 Harington, J. (trans.)., *Ludovico Ariosto's Orlando Furioso*. 1516. Clarendon Press, Oxford, 1972. p. 331.

50 Schoell, F.L. (ed.)., *Charlemagne (The Distracted Emperor)*. Princeton University Press, 1920. p. 38.

51 Dyce. A., *The Dramatic and Poetical Works of Robert Greene & George Peele*. Routledge, Warne, and Routledge, 1861. p. 291.

52 Greene, R., *Greene's Never Too Late*. Thomas Orwin, London, 1590. n.p.

53 Harrison, G.B. (ed.)., *A Groats-Worth of Witte*. The Bodley Head Ltd., London, 1923. p. 45.

in Norfolk, and Nashe is born in Suffolk, both camping counties. They also attend Cambridge University, suggesting early exposure to football. Apparent friends, Nashe writes the introduction to *Menaphon*, in which he makes sly digs at Greene:

"idiote art-masters, that intrude themselves to our eares as the alcumists of eloquence, who … think to outbrave better pens with the swelling bumbast of a bragging blanke verse … position Poets … that swarme like Crowes to a dead carcas, but flie like Swallows in the VVinter, from any continuate subiect of witte. The efficient whereof, I imagine to issue, from the upstart discipline, of our reformatorie Churchmen, who account wit vanitie, and poetrie impietie."[54]

Upstart. Crow. By 1593, the plague shows no signs of subsiding. A prescient book warns, "of all vehement and immoderate exercise, which doth provoke sweate, as is tennis, dancing, leaping, running, footeball, hurling, and such like: because they doe ouermuch heate the body, and open the pores of respiration, whereby the enfected ayre hath the more scope to enter our bodyes."[55] It is no surprise that hurling is included. The author is from Devon. A contemporary writer finds wretchedness in the twenty-three pleasures of life. He ranks them in precedence of gratification before "describing in a perfect mirror, the miseries of man." Beauty; riches; honour; love; horses, hawks, and dogs; music; dancing, leaping; wrestling; climbing; fencing; tennis; shooting; bowling, etc. Divinity crawls across the line. Football does not make the list. Gambling is the torment of tennis and bowling: "Tennis is a costly game, Which cost considered, soone will driue away, The déere delight that growes by Tennis play … To bowling Allies, that both day and night, If light would serve they would not be away, But wast their wealth upon that foolish play."[56]

A planning application is submitted in the 1570s for the construction of bowling alleys on the consecrated ground of the former Blackfriars Abbey. A 'not in my back yard' petition objects to the "swernge Noyse

---

54 Smith, G.G., *Elizabethan Critical Essays*. 2 Vols. Oxford University Press, London, 1904. Vol. 1. pp. 308, 316.

55 Kellwaye, S., *A defensative against the plague contayning two partes or treatises*. John Windet, London, 1593. p. 13.

56 Munday, A., *The paine of pleasure, describing in a perfect mirror, the miseries of man*. s.n., London, 1583. n.p.

and Cryinges" to the "annoyaunce and disturbance of all the Neighboures."[57] Three alleys are built. Residents moan fruitlessly of the "Prentyces watermen and other sortes of servantes as also of others being for the most part very poore men, where they … consume their money to their undoing usinge suche detestable swearing with such noyse and cryinge and sometimes with fraying [fighting]."[58] It is not always so. In 1580, when permission is sought to construct a roofed alley "for the recreation of honest Citisens to bowle in fowle wether", the Lord Mayor of London lambasts bowling as attracting "all sortes indifferently even the worst and meanest."[59]

Bowling empties his jug and signals for more ale. He rubs his paunch and belches. Broad appeal, that's what he has, from the crown all the way down. From eight to eighty. Bowling giggles at his own repartee. His bladder makes itself known. He rises unsteadily, thinks better of it, slumps back down. What did that young dramatist call him? They had spoken of his variety and of his lineage—greens and alleys, and portraits in thirteenth century books of hours—before he had drunk the greenhorn under the table. That was it. It was the last word he had muttered before passing out. Falstaff.

Some deaths defy the plague. Marlowe and Greene's deaths are shrouded in mystery, but while the *enfant terrible*'s demise is suitably Bondian, Greene's is murkier. The writer, Gabriel Harvey, an enemy of Nashe's, put it down to "not of the plague, nor of the pox, as a gentleman said, but of a surfeit of pickle herring and Rhenish wine."[60] Is the herring pickled or red? At the time, "Pickle herring" is the name of a clown, akin to Punch or Scaramouche.[61] Riddle me this. Where is my corpse, where is my death, cold is the scent, hot is the breath. A theory posits that Greene dies on the same day as Shakespeare. Because he *is* Shakespeare.[62] Seven months after Greene's death, Shakespeare publishes his first work, the

---

57 Ibid, p. 56.

58 Highley, C., *Blackfriars in Early Modern London: Theater, Church, and Neighborhood.* Oxford University Press, 2022. p. 98.

59 Davies, C., *Bowling Alleys and Playhouses in London, 1560–90.* Early Theatre, 2019, 22.2, pp. 53–54.

60 Hopkins Hughes, S., *Robert Greene, King of the Paper Stage.* p. 32. https://politicworm.files.wordpress.com/2010/04/hughes-king-of-the-paper-stage.pdf. Accessed 4 June 2023.

61 Ibid, p. 33.

62 Ibid, pp. 1–62.

poem *Venus and Adonis*. Less than two months later Marlowe is stabbed to death. The stage is set.

In October 1598, Father Thomas Wright is in prison. He writes to his ally the Earl of Essex, "I am made the object of revenge and the football of suspicions." Once released, he distances himself from Essex's machinations. Wright has already tempted the noose, converting Shakespeare's rival Ben Jonson to Catholicism when they meet in prison. Jonson has killed a man in a duel, but escapes death by reciting the neck verse. The year before, he is jailed on a charge of "leude and mutynous behaviour" for the play *The Isle of Dogs*, which he co-wrote with Nashe. Nashe lies low. In Norfolk. In 1596, he had published a book attacking Gabriel Harvey. The prologue contains the line: "one that stands, as it were, at the line in a tennis-court, and takes everie ball at the volley."[63] Around 1600, Nashe disappears. Forever. Does he do a Greene? Is he in on the joke? Great Yarmouth thrives on its centuries-old trade in herrings. The full title of Nashe's last book, full-caps and all, is *Nashes Lenten Stuffe, Containing, The Description and first Procreation and Increase of the towne of Great Yarmouth in Norffolke: With a new Play never played before, of the praise of the RED HERRING.*[64]

Rabelais's *Gargantua and Pantagruel* references ball games: "the Knuckles, the Neck, the Breast, the Liver, the Spleen, the Tripes, the Kidneys, the Bladder, wherewith they make Foot-balls."[65] In the original it is "*la vessie dont on joue à la balle*", the bladder we play ball with.[66]

---

63 Nashe, T., *Have with You to Saffron-Walden*. John Danter, London, 1596. p. 21.

64 Greene in 1592, Marlowe in 1593, Nashe around 1601: Mysterious deaths litter the theatrical world in the 1590s. Lord Strange, patron to Shakespeare, Marlowe, and Spenser is widely believed to have been poisoned in 1594, aged thirty-five. Thomas Kyd, famous in his day for *The Spanish Tragedy*, is arrested in 1593 on charges of "anti-Alien libel". Kyd blames his old roommate Marlowe, who dies in an apparent pub brawl in Deptford two weeks later, fortuitously witnessed by a top government spy. Kyd dies four months after Strange, also thirty-five. The cause of his death is unknown, though it is believed to have been hastened by torture during his imprisonment. Finally, in 1589, Thomas Watson, a playwright believed to have co-authored *Arden of Faversham* with Shakespeare, intervenes in an argument between Marlowe and a landlord's son, which has descended into a duel. Watson kills the man in self-defence and is jailed for five months in Newgate Prison. Au fait with the cast of Marlowe's death, he apparently dies of the plague in 1592, aged thirty-six. Alternative theories are to be found in: Johnson, I., *Renaissance Man: The World of Thomas Watson*. New Generation Publishing Ltd., 2021.

65 Motteux, P.A. (trans.), *Pantagruel's voyage to the oracle of the bottle being the fourth and fifth books of the works of Francis Rabelais*. Richard Baldwin, London, 1694. Le Quart Livre. p. 29.

66 Clouzot, H. (ed.), *Gargantua et Pantagruel*. 5 Vols. Bibliothèque Larousse, Paris., 1913. Vol. 1. p. 136.

Rabelais is probably referencing *soule*. More importantly, of Gargantua's vast abbey, "Between the other two towers were the courts for tennis and football."[67] In the original football is *de gross balle*.[68] Whatever the game, it is compact, played on a court, and sufficiently common to be referenced by an author from western France. Rabelais contrasts this with the better-known freer game: "unto the meadows where they played at the ball (*à la balle*), the long-tennis (*à la paume*), and at the pile trigon."[69,70,71] He adds the innuendo-laden motto of the students of Orléans: "Un éteuf en la braguette, En la main une raquette."[72] A ball in your codpiece, a racket in your hand.

The French Renaissance poet Amadis Jamyn writes a sonnet on a ball game, *Pour un Jeu de Balle Forée*.[73,74] While translated as *A Game at Football*, the sport is not mentioned in the original, only *la Balle force*, the forced ball. Undoubtedly, this is *soule*, the kicking–carrying version now dominating the name, the French football of its time. The original also describes the ball as round. Perhaps this was always the intent, but early balls sag and end up egg-shaped.

> When I behold a football to and fro
> Urged by a throng of players equally,
> Who run pell-mell, and thrust and push and throw,
> Each party bent alike on victory;
> Methinks, I see resembled in the show,
> This round earth poised in the vacant sky,
> Where all are fain to lay each other low,
> Striving by might and main for mastery.

---

67 Urquhart, T. (trans.)., *The Life of Gargantua and the Heroic Deeds of Pantagruel*. 5 Vols. George Routledge and Sons, London, 1883. Vols. 1. p. 173.

68 Clouzot, H. (ed.)., *Gargantua et Pantagruel*. 5 Vols. Bibliothèque Larousse, Paris., 1913. Vol. 1. p. 139.

69 Ibid, Vol. 1. p. 74.

70 Three players play at ball in a triangle, probably throwing it to one another.

71 Urquhart, T. (trans.)., *The Life of Gargantua and the Heroic Deeds of Pantagruel*. 5 Vols. George Routledge and Sons, London, 1883. Vols. 1 & 2. p. 74.

72 Ibid, Vols. 1 & 2. p. 206.

73 Willem, L. (ed.)., *Ouvres Poétiques de Amadis Jamyn*. s.n., Paris, 1878. p. 51.

74 The sonnet is composed in the French style, which post-dates the Italian, but pre-dates the Shakespearian; in this case, it takes the form: abba abba ccd ede.

The ball is filled with wind: and even so
It is for wind most times that mortals war;
Death the sole prize they all are struggling for:
And all the world is but an ebb and flow;
And all we learn, when as the game is o'er,
That life is but a dream, and nothing more.[75]

In 1558, a Frenchman enthuses about football in London: "The persons engaged in trade or handicraft gain more in this place in a week than those in Germany or Spain do in a month. For you may see the hat-makers and joiners, and other artisans, commonly playing at ball for a crown piece, which is hardly to be seen in any other place, and more particularly so on a working day."[76] In 1576, George Gascoigne returns the compliment. Writing that the English adopt foreign customs then change them for the worse, he includes the line that, "of a Spanish codpeece, we make an English football."[77]

Tennis is decidedly *en vogue*. In the financial year 1559/60, £1,699 worth of tennis balls are imported into England, on a par with white herrings, feathers, and salted eels, and outstripping maces, marmalade, and matches.[78,79] In 1580, it is reported that the brother of the King of France, "has been sick, from excessive playing at tennis, but finished his physic on Saturday last and intends to … repose himself at the Abbey of Bourgueil."[80] Sport may, conversely, be a salve to spiritual ailments. A 1580 book presents the churchly benefits of exercise: "When we plaie at tennis, we refresh our wearied spirits and memories, by the which meanes we are better able to study, and to get knowledge, whereby our

75 Waddington, S.W. (ed.)., *The Sonnets of Europe. Early French Poets.* Walter Scott, London, 1888. p. 143.

76 *The Parterre of Fiction, Poetry, History, and General Literature.* 4 Vols. Effingham Wilson, London, 1835. Vol. 2. 14 February 1835. p. 108.

77 Gascoigne, G. *A Delicate Diet for Daintiemouthde Droonkardes.* s.n., London, 1576. n.p.

78 Appendix III: Value of imports, 1559/60 and 1565/6, in *The Port and Trade of Early Elizabethan London: Documents*, ed. Brian Dietz (London, 1972), pp. 152–155. *British History Online* http://www.british-history.ac.uk/london-record-soc/vol8/pp152–155. Accessed 29 October 2023.

79 £500,000 in 2024.

80 Addenda: Miscellaneous 1580, in *Calendar of State Papers Foreign: Elizabeth, Volume 17, January-June 1583 and Addenda*, ed. Arthur John Butler and Sophie Crawford Lomas (London, 1913), pp. 532–571. *British History Online* http://www.british-history.ac.uk/cal-state-papers/foreign/vol17/pp532–571. Accessed 29 October 2023.

faith is strengthened."[81] While football and tennis should be balanced with hard work, the author endorses "anie manlie kinde of exercise, for they stirre up a certeine livelinesse in a man."

In 1564, the Thames freezes over. Between London Bridge and Westminster, John Stow writes: "ye same newyers even, beynge sondaye, people playde at ye footte ball on ye thams by great nombars … dyvars Gentyllmen & othars, set up pryckes on ye Thams, and shott at ye same … as boldy and thankis be gyvyn to god a[s] saffly, as it had bene on ye drye lande … costardmongars playnge at ye dysse for apples; & ye people went on ye thams in greatar nombars then in eny streat in london."[82] Winter is all very well for English football, but according to Francies Sabie, French lovers characteristically play tennis in summer: "At this time the top, the tennis ball was a pastine: At this time no smal delight he toke in a foteball."[83] This is confirmed by Sir Robert Dallington, in 1604, who writes that the French play "in the heat of the summer, and height of the day, when others were scarce able to stirre out of dores."[84] Of courts, he adds: "yee cannot finde that little *Burgade*, or town in France, that hath not one or more of them. Here are, as you see, three score in *Orleans*, and I know not how many hundreds there be in *Paris*." And on players: "ye would think they were born with rackets in their hands, even children themselves manage them so well, and some of their women also." So popular is *jeu de paume* that a devoted and well-patronised guild—*Communauté des Maitres Paumiers-Raquetiers, Faiseurs d'Eteufs, Pelotes et Balles*—is founded in 1610. Following a three-year apprenticeship, a master has the privilege of making rackets and balls, and running courts.[85]

In 1566, Thomas Drant's *Second Satire* mentions tennis and football in the same breath:

---

81 Byrd, S., *A friendlie communication or dialogue between Paul and Damas*. s.n., London, 1580. p. 61v.

82 Furnivall, F.J. (ed.)., *Political, Religious, and Love Poems from the Archbishop of Canterbury's Lambeth Ms. No. 306, and Other Sources*. N. Trübner and Co., London, 1866. pp. xiv–xv.

83 Sabies, F., *Pan's Pipe, Three Pastoral Eglogues, in English Hexameter: Eglogue Second*. 1595. The University of Chicago Press, Chicago, 1910. p. 451. lns 39–40.

84 Beretta, M., *Training Tennis Players through Natural Philosophy: From Scaino's Trattato to Garsault's Art du paumier*. Nuncius, 2013, 28:1, p. 34.

85 Tadié, A., *The Seductions of Modern Tennis: From Social Practice to Literary Discourse*. Sport in History, 35:2, p. 291.

> Or when thou doest at footeball playe,
> Or tennice for pastyme:
> Whylste love of game dothe ease thy toyle,
> And helpe awaye the tyme."[86]

A 1591 Spanish–English dictionary translates tennis phrases, including: "to play at tennice", "a tenniscourt", "to marke the chase", "I have the advantage", "I have won the sette", and "my shirt is wringing wet."[87] That year, Queen Elizabeth is treated to a tennis game when she visits Elvetham Hall.[88] While tennis is a long-held favourite, football has not gone unnoticed by the well connected. Queen Elizabeth and Robert Dudley are Lord Willoughby de Eresby's godparents. Henry VIII considers Willoughby's grandmother for his seventh wife, if he can annul his marriage to her best friend Catherine Parr, but he dies within the year. A 1629 letter from writer James Howell, private secretary to Lord Sunderland, relates that, "many years ago, my Lord Willoughby, and he, with so many of their servants play'd a match at football against such a number of Countrymen, where my Lord of Sunderland being busy about the ball, got a bruise in the breast; which put him in a swoon for the present but did not trouble him till three Months after."[89,90,91]

Robert Dudley, 1st Earl of Leicester, has been friends with Queen Elizabeth since they were eight. He longs to marry her, but when his wife is found at the foot of the stairs with a broken neck, Elizabeth distances herself from the scandal.[92] It does nothing to quench their intense friendship, and Dudley continues to court her. Many believe him overfamiliar, not without cause. In March 1565, the queen is watching Dudley and the Duke of Norfolk at tennis. "My L. Rob. being verie hotte

86 Drant, T., *A Medicinable Morall, That is, The Two Bookes of Horace His Satyres*, Thomas Marshe, London, 1566. n.p.

87 Stepney, W., *The Spanish Schoole-master*. Scolar Press, Menston, England, 1971. p. 245.

88 Boyle, H.H., *Elizabeth's Entertainment at Elvetham: War Policy in Pageantry*. Studies in Philology, 1971, 68:2, p. 159.

89 Jacobs, J. (ed.)., *Epistolae Ho-Elianae: the familiar letters of James Howell*. 2 Vols. David Nutt, London, 1892. Vol. 1. p. 283.

90 The ailing Lord Sunderland died six months later.

91 Howell repeated the story in a letter from his prison cell in Fleet Prison in January 1646. The notorious prison was destroyed during the Great Fire of London. Howell, long-since released, died two months after the fire.

92 Richardson, A., *The Lover of Queen Elizabeth*. T. Werner Laurie, London, 1970. p. 58.

and swetinge, tooke the Q. napken owte of her hande and wyped his face, wch the Duke seinge saide that he was to saucie and swhore y^{t} wolde laye his racket upon his face. Hereupon rose a great troble and the Q. offended sore wth the Duke."[93] *Tengo la camiseta empapada.* My shirt is wringing wet.[94] That Christmas, Dudley proposes only for the young queen to spurn him. A decade later, he invites Elizabeth to Kenilworth Castle. It may be his last chance to woo her.[95] He receives her in style. There is lavish entertainment and a firework display heard twenty miles away. One Sunday, Dudley arranges for a newly wedded country couple and their party to joust before the queen. They are ill-dressed, and the groom is "lame of a leg that in his yooth was broken at football."[96]

Courtiers and courts do not mix. In 1579, Sir Philip Sidney and the Earl of Oxford are embroiled in the principal intrigue of the day, the queen's possible marriage to a Catholic. Factions are fluid, accusations fly. At forty-five, the twenty-three-year-old Duke of Anjou is Elizabeth's last serious contender. Should she? Oxford assents, Sidney demurs. Sidney is playing before visiting French commissioners, when the Earl of Oxford "abruptly came into the Tennis-Court" and asks him, ever-angrier, to leave. Sidney will "not be driven out by any scourge of fury", whereupon Oxford calls him a puppy, louder still when an incensed Sidney demands he repeat it. "Puppies are gotten by Dogs," Sidney returns, "and Children by men." Both poets stand, "like a dumb shew in a Tragedy", trying to process the traded insults.[97] Sidney finally storms off, Oxford plays tennis, and the French lap it up. The proposed duel never comes off. Sidney uses tennis to metaphorical excellence in *The Countesse of Pembrokes Arcadia.* When the tide of battle shifts suddenly: "Then Fortune (as if shee had made chases inow of the one side of that bloody Teniscourt) went of the other side the line … they loosing the ground, as fast as before they had woon it, onely leaving them to keepe it, who had lost themselves in keeping it."[98]

---

93 Strutt, J., *Sports and Pastimes.* Methuen and Co., London, 1801. p. 86.

94 Stepney, W., *The Spanish Schoole-master.* R. Field, London, 1591. p. 245.

95 Furninvall, F.J. (ed.), *Robert Laneham's letter describing a part of the entertainment unto Queen Elizabeth at the castle of Kenilworth in 1575.* Chatto and Windus, London, 1907. p. 22.

96 Elizabeth's three-week stay cost Dudley £19,000, £6M in 2024. The *Langham Letter*, ascribed to Robert Langham, describes her stay; it provides rich insights into Tudor life.

97 Nelson, A.H., *Monstrous Adversary: The Life of Edward de Vere, 17th Earl of Oxford.* Liverpool University Press, 2003. p. 195–196.

98 Sidney, P., *The Countesse of Pembrokes Arcadia.* John Windet, London, 1593. p. 132.

In January 1598, the 3rd Earl of Southampton is bested by Lord Willoughby during an argument. Determined on revenge, he bides his time, and "finding him between the tennis court wall and the garden, struck him." Willoughby retaliates, wrenching out some of the earl's famed auburn locks.[99] It is later that year that the earl loses eighteen crowns at tennis. The court occasions another of the earl's arguments, this time with the Earl of Montgomery, in 1610: "They fell out at tennis, where the rackets flew about their ears, but the matter was compounded by the King, without further bloodshed."[100] Violence on the court had extreme consequences three generations before. In June 1541, Sir Edmund Knevet strikes Master Cleere of Norfolk within the Tennis Court of the King's House. His punishment is draconian: loss of his right hand, his land, and his goods. Only a pardon by Henry saves his hand.[101]

Southampton is incendiary. In February 1597, he challenges the Earl of Northumberland to a duel, after he is accused, wrongly it seems, of speaking "offensive words of him". The terms are opaque. Southampton names the time and place but claims to have hurt his left arm playing the Italian game of *ballon*, so he cannot see it through. He is surely crimson when Northumberland replies that he knows he is right-handed but is happy to wait until his arm is better. Luckily for Southampton he is exonerated.[102] Three months later, Henry Noel, a favourite courtier of the queen, dies from a fever brought on by overheating during a match of *ballon*.[103]

The most famous tennis clash of all takes place in 1606, only this time Italians are playing the English game. Whether an actual match took place ending in a swordfight, or whether the court was chosen as a suitable site for a duel is unknown, eyewitness testimonies differ. In one version, they had argued over a game they had played for a bet of 10 scudi, and began "hitting each other with their rackets."[104] A

99 Ibid, p. 250.

100 Chalmers, W.H.G., *An apology for the believers in the Shakespeare-Papers*. Printed for Thomas Egerton, London, 1797. p. 153.

101 Marshall, J., *The Annals of Tennis*. Horace Cox, London, 1878. p. 68.

102 Folger Shakespeare Library. https://folgerpedia.folger.edu/mediawiki/media/images_pedia_folgerpedia_mw/archive/2/28/20170609171922!ECDbD_1597.pdf. p. 3. Accessed 10 March 2024.

103 Ibid, p. 5. Accessed 10 March 2024.

104 Hibbard, H., *Caravaggio*. Thames and Hudson, London, 1988. pp. 206, 368.

prearranged duel appears likeliest. In Rome, on 29 May, "the painter Michelangelo Caravaggio wounded and killed Ranuccio da Terni Tomassoni with a sword-thrust through the thigh."[105] Sustaining a head wound, Caravaggio flees to Naples. Caravaggio is the unparallelled genius of naturalism, but he is notoriously vindictive, violent, and unpleasant. He appears in police records for diverse crimes: assaulting a man over a prostitute, smearing excrement on his ex-landlady's door, then singing obscene songs outside her window to the accompaniment of a guitar, defacing another woman's house front, carrying his sword and dagger in public, then telling the policeman to "stick it up your arse", and throwing a plate of artichokes at a waiter. On one occasion, he is found with wounds to his ear and throat, he claims are self-inflicted.[106] Racket, weapon, brush. Ecce homo. Tennis's voice rings clear as a bell:

> Without, without here smothe I am,
> yet full of heare within:
> Rounde like a Boule: though feete I want,
> to runne I doe not lin.
> Although fine feathers light I lacke,
> yet mounte I doe alofte:
> And looke when I am striken, then
> my strength repaire I ofte.[107]

In 1584/85, a German nobleman travels through England and Scotland. He visits "the queen's palace … *Weittholl.* In front of it we first saw the tilt-yard, besides a ball-house, where they play at featherballs. There is also a long-stretched building, in which they play with wooden balls … this is called the boule house. Upstairs the gentlemen play, the common people below."[108,109] In other words, there is an alley for servants and soldiers. The facilities at Whitehall Palace are added by Henry VIII, including the Chief Close Tennis

---

105 Graham-Dixon, A., *Caravaggio: A Life Sacred and Profane*. Penguin Books, 2011. p. 313.

106 Moss, M., *Caravaggio: Painter on the Run*. Creston Books, Berkeley, California, 2016. pp. 356–357.

107 Kendall, T., *Flovvers Of Epigrammes*. John Kingston, London, 1577. *A Tennice Ball*. n.p.

108 Von Bülow, G., *Journey through England and Scotland Made by Lupold von Wedel in the Years 1584 and 1585*. Transactions of the Royal Historical Society, 1895, 9:234.

109 Featherballs: another name for early badminton; also called shuttlecock and battledore.

Court, a cockpit, bowling alleys and green, and a tiltyard for jousting and bear-baiting.[110]

William Cecil is the great survivor of Tudor politics. The twinkle-toed sidestepper of factions. Secretary of State, Lord Treasurer, he has Elizabeth's ear. He forces her hand on Mary Stuart's head, rescues England from the Armada, and dies negotiating peace with the Spanish. Succession is smooth. In 1582, Cecil hands his nineteen-year-old son, Robert, a letter listing ten dos and don'ts of a masterful life. The fifth precept recommends rich patrons: "Alwaies keepe some great man to thy friend … compliment him often, present him with many, yet small gifts." If the opportunity arises buy him something extravagant, he says, "as may bee dailly in sight, for otherwise thou shalt live like a hop without a pole, live in obscurity, and be made a footeball for every insulting companion to spurne [kick] at."[111] If you are a hoop, you need a stick to whirl you centre stage. And avoid enlisting, he adds, "for souldiers in peace, are like to chimnies in Somer." Eight years later, Robert is acting Secretary of State.

~

Scottish nobles have a fondness for football and golf. In 1527, the Lord of Panmure "tuk pleswr in playine at the fut bale, and for that caws the mwr [moor] of Bathil wos appointed, and dwrine [during] his days it was not castine [dug up], bot only reserwit for that game; lykwayes he exerciset the gowf, and oftymes past to Barry lynkes, quhan [when] the wadsie [wager] vos for drink."[112] Gowf is Scots dialect for golf. Describing his days at school in Montrose, Scottish reformer James Melville refers to a golf club as a glub for gowff.[113] In 1538, an Aberdonian man is in trouble for gambling during a game of goiff; and in Aberdeen, in 1545, Bessie Senyor is in trouble over thirty-three goif bawis (balls).[114]

---

110 "The Tennis Courts, etc.", in *Survey of London: Volume 14, St Margaret, Westminster, Part III: Whitehall II*, ed. Montagu H Cox, G Topham Forrest (London, 1931), *British History Online* https://www.british-history.ac.uk/survey-london/vol14/pt3/pp37-45. Accessed 19 October 2024.

111 Cecil, W., *The counsell of a father to his sonne, in ten seuerall precepts left as a legacy at his death*. Josepth Hunt, London, 1611. n.p.

112 Stuart, J. (ed.), Registrum de Panmure. 2 Vols. n.p., Edinburgh, 1874. Vol. 1. p. xxxii.

113 Mure, A., *Scottish Pageant 1513–1625*. Oliver and Boyd, Edinburgh, 1948. p. 59.

114 Jamieson, J., *Dr. Jamieson's Scottish Dictionary and Supplement*. 4 Vols. William Tait, Edinburgh, 1841. Vol. 3. p. 498.

Mary Queen of Scots's relationship with her husband, Lord Darnley, understandably sours when he and his henchmen drag her Italian private secretary from the dining table to the presence chamber, there to brutally murder him. Fifty-six frenzied knife wounds attest to Darnley's hatred.[115] What fortune, then, when Darnley is found strangled in his garden and his lodgings blown to smithereens within the year. Now Mary can marry the dreamy Earl of Bothwell. Two months later, spies observe her "one day, richt oppinlie at the feildis with the palmall and goif, and on the nycht planelie abusing hir body with Bothwell", who had been secreted in a concealed chamber below hers, accessed by a hidden passage.[116,117] It does not end well. In July 1567, only three months after her round of golf, Mary is forced to abdicate in favour of her two-year-old son, James. Mary is not done. In May 1568, she escapes her confinement in Lochleven Castle and flees to England. Elizabeth is having none of it.

In June 1568, an imprisoned Mary is permitted to walk "on the playing green" outside Carlisle Castle: "about 20 of her retinue played at footeball before hyr the space of two howers, very stronglye, nymbylly, and skilfullye, without any fowle playe offered, the smalness of theyr balls occasyoning theyr fayr playe."[118] Hugh Fraser, the 5th Lord Lovat, encourages football, putting the stone, and throwing the bar.[119] In 1573, the 7th lord, in his late twenties, "frequently tristed with the nobles and gentry, diverting themselves with … football … The chappell yard at Invernes was their gameing place. If it was football, be sure he had the first and last hale over the roap."[120] The Scottish version of football has a compact version, then, with small numbers on each side.[121] Hails or hales is the Scottish name for the game, while hail or hale refers to the

115 Weir, A., Mary Queen of Scots And The Murder of Lord Darnley. Vintage Books, London, 2008. p. 107.

116 "One day right openly at the fields with the pall mall and golf and on the night plainly abusing her body with Bothwell."

117 *Calendar of State Papers relating to Scotland and Mary Queen of Scots*. Vol. 2. (1563–1569). p. 558. https://sources-tannerritchie-com.ap1.proxy.openathens.net/browser.php?ipid=439238. Accessed 25 November 2024.

118 Jefferson, S. (ed.)., *The history and antiquities of Carlisle*. Whittaker and Co., London, 1838. p. 37.

119 Mackay, W. (ed.)., *Chronicles of the Frasers*. James Fraser. University Press, Edinburgh, 1905. p. xxxix

120 Ibid, p. 165.

121 Unlike Cornish hurling and camping, the Scottish hales is too similar to English variations of folk football to be considered a distinct entity.

goal itself and to scoring a goal, perhaps cried out when one is "roped". The Lovat reference to *hale* is the first in history. Here, it is scored by the ball passing over rather than under the rope as it is in rugby. When Lord Lovat trains his young clansmen in soldiery, he includes swimming, football, wrestling, and dancing, "fit for polishing and refining youth, and to keep them from effeminacy, baseness, loitering, and idleness."[122] He dies four years later, aged twenty-eight.

There is little literature on hails. In Robert MacGregor's 1881 book *Pastimes and Players*, he writes of shinty: "on many a clear, frosty, moonlight night do the country lads contend for the honour of 'hailing' (goals are always hails in Scotland at our game) the ball, and wonderful is the skill which the crack players display, as they 'birl' (or 'dribble,' as football players call it) the ball along-running it on past all obstacles and attacks, and keeping it well within reach of their club-head until they have passed all their opponents, and the hails lies before them within reach of the good player's *first* long shot."[123] Why first is italicised is unclear. Published in 1911, *A Scots Dialect Dictionary* of words from the seventeenth century onwards contains multiple definitions of hail: to drive a ball to the goal; the cry raised when the ball is so driven; the act of driving the ball; the goal at shinty, football, etc.; a game resembling hockey played at the Edinburgh Academy; and the place for playing off the ball.[124]

In 1927, David Murray, talking of his schooldays at Glasgow College, says that "the term 'goal' was unknown in Scotland. When either the foot-ball or the hand-ball had been kicked or gowfed by one side to the end of their opponents' ground the ball was said to be 'hailed', and the winning side had a 'hail'."[125] Excepting that one sport drives the ball with the foot and the other with a stick, Murray says the rules of the two games are practically the same, with the same number of players.[126]

---

122 Mackay, W. (ed.), *Chronicles of the Frasers*. James Fraser, University Press, Edinburgh, 1905. p. 171.

123 MacGregor, R., *Pastimes and Players*. Chatto and Windus, London, 1881. p. 75.

124 Warrack, A. (ed.), *A Scots Dialect Dictionary*. W. & R. Chambers, Edinburgh, 1911.

125 Handball in Scotland went by the names *gouff-the-ba* (hit the ball) and *han-an-hail* (hand-goal). In the early 1800s, the best handball player at St Andrews School "struck a ball with great force … and hit the Principal on the face." Murray, D. *Memories of the Old College of Glasgow*, Jackson, Wylie & Co., 1927. p. 427.

126 Ibid, p. 445.

He quotes an old boy of Edinburgh High School, writing of football in 1824:

> I hear it bounding on the yards again,
> Now comes the rush, the shouting, and the strain,
> The shin's disaster, and the answering wail.
> Blest he who caught the ball from all the train,
> Led off the van, pursued its muddy trail,
> And, victor, drove the bladder thundering to the Hale.[127]

The dialect dictionary contains other interesting finds: *kick-bonnety*, a boy's cap is used as a football until the owner can seize another's cap, which then becomes the football; *burley-whush*, "an obsolete game of ball", *kypie*, "a game played with a bat and a soft ball"; *dool-tree*, "a tree that marks the goal in playing ball"; *douse*, "to strike a ball out of play"; *kick ba*, "the game of football"; *kirk-the-gussie* (or *cashhornie*), "one set of players try to get a large ball into a hole using clubs, while the others try to drive it away"; a *knappin'-hole*, "the hole out of which two shinty players try to drive the ball in opposite directions"; *knirr, knurr, knout, nag, nag'n, noot, peg, chow, shinny ball,* and *doe,* "a wooden shinty ball"; *scuff,* "a bat for hand-ball, a battledoor"; *trip-trout,* "a game of shuttlecock in which a ball is used instead of a cork and feathers"; *sotter*, "in shinty, the first whack at the ball"; *stot-ba'*, "a game of ball"; *house-ba*, "a girls' game of ball"; and *bess*, "a boys' school-game with bat and ball, base-ball". There are other base game names: *ball-baises*, "a game of ball"; *ba'baises*, "same as ball-baises"; *bars*, "a schoolboys' game, prisoner's base"; and *rounders*, "the game of prisoner's base" (as is *prisoners'-relief*). *Ball-baises* is probably baseball. It might be the little-mentioned game *ball bias*, first recorded in 1844, but that game appears to have been limited to Kent. Of uncertain pedigree, *ball bias* is believed to be a base, bat, and ball game.[128] The book provides no origin date for *bess* or *ball-baises*. An 1818 dictionary contains the earliest known reference to *ba'baises*: "the name of a particular game at ball."[129]

---

127 Ibid, pp. 444–445.

128 Block, D., *Pastime Lost: The Humble, Original, and Now Completely Forgotten Game of English Baseball.* University of Nebraska Press, 2019. pp. 197–198.

129 Pickens, E., *A Dictionary of the Scottish Language.* James Sawers, Edinburgh, 1818. p. 7.

In May 1583, animosity erupts between Earl Marischal and the 5th Earl of Bothwell "upon a stroke given at foot-ball on Bothwell's leg by the master, after that the master had received a sore fall from Bothwell."[130] Their plan for a duel is thwarted when James VI intervenes, and "with some difficulty reconciled the parties." The fifth earl inherits his title from his maternal uncle, who had married Mary. He may have picked up football as a student at St Andrews University, or the Scottish Borders town of Kelso, where he is lay abbot.[131,132] He swaps his position for one at Coldingham Abbey, where John Oll' launched his bid for glory. James's gesture lacks foresight. Bothwell argues with everyone, the lord chancellor,[133] the Earls of Arran and Home,[134,135] even the prior of Coldingham.[136] In 1589, he plots with the Earl of Huntly[137]—whose father died in 1576, soon after kicking a football. Bothwell is imprisoned, released, imprisoned, released.

By 1591, he stands accused of, "being involved in the use of wax images, poison and other means to kill King James. The poison is allegedly made from flesh off the forehead of a newly calved foal and the skin of an adder. Also accused of being part of incantations and triangle-making to raise spirits to help him destroy the king."[138] Bothwell blames his enemies for damning him, including John Carmichael, whose subsequent murder is planned by the Armstrong clan at a football match in 1600. When Bothwell escapes prison, he is sentenced to outlawry. He rises twice against the king. In 1592, hotly pursued, he and other

---

130 *Calendar of State Papers relating to Scotland and Mary Queen of Scots*. Vol. 6. (1581–1583). p. 475. https://sources-tannerritchie-com.ap1.proxy.openathens.net/browser.php?ipid=442618. Accessed 29 October 2024.

131 Macpherson, R.G., *Francis Stewart Fifth Earl Bothwell, c.1563–1612: Lordship and politics in Jacobean Scotland.* Unpublished PhD thesis, University of Edinburgh, 1998. p. 124.

132 Ibid, p. 4.

133 Ibid, p. 203.

134 Ibid, p. 192.

135 Ibid, p. 148.

136 *Calendar of State Papers relating to Scotland and Mary Queen of Scots*. Vol. 9. (1586–1588). p. 18. TannerRichie Publishing. https://sources-tannerritchie-com.ap1.proxy.openathens.net/browser.php?ipid=444511. Accessed 29 October 2023.

137 Macpherson, R.G., *Francis Stewart Fifth Earl Bothwell, c.1563–1612: Lordship and politics in Jacobean Scotland.* Unpublished PhD thesis, University of Edinburgh, 1998. p. 172.

138 Goodare, J., Martin, L., Miller, J., Yeoman, L., *The Survey of Scottish Witchcraft, 1563–1736*. https://witches.hca.ed.ac.uk/index.cfm/case/C/EGD/124. Accessed 18 November 2023.

"declarit tratouris … was oppinly on Esk playand at the futt ball."[139] Exiled abroad, rumours swirl for the next decade, resurfacing in his final years when he is "past doing any harm, though he want not malice."[140] After spending most of 1611 "under the surgeon's knife", he dies in abject poverty.

In 1763, Allan Ramsay publishes the twelfth edition of *The Tea Table Miscellany.* It includes his ballad *The Bonny Earl Of Murray*, which recounts the murder of the Earl of Moray by the 6th Earl of Huntly in 1592. Huntly is thorough. He sets fire to the Earl of Moray's castle, then stabs him to death. The balled eulogises the slain earl:

> He was a braw [brave] gallant,
> And he play'd at the ba' [ball],
> And the bonny Earl of *Murray*,
> Was the flower among them a [all].[141]

The clergy of Scotland are not averse to football either. John Spottiswood, future Archbishop of Glasgow and St Andrews and Lord Chancellor of Scotland, is a noted player in his youth, as is his successor in Glasgow, James Law. Spottiswood marries David Lindsay's daughter. Lindsay had twice mentioned football in his Scottish poems, and just as he had baptised Charles I, so Spottiswood crowns him. In 1585, Spottiswood and Law, then young ministers at Calder and Kirkliston, respectively, are upbraided by the local synod for Sabbath football.[142] When they are not deposed, the thwarted minister for Prestonpans leads them away, calling them "my pretty football men."[143] He rebukes them before "his brethren", adding, "let me tell you what reward ye shall get for your lenity. These two men shall trample on your necks, and on the necks of the ministers of Scotland." His words come back to haunt the lenient. Spottiswood

---

139 Bain, J. (ed.)., *Calendar of Letters and Papers Relating to the Affairs of the Borders of England and Scotland. Vol. 1. A.D. 1560–1594.* H.M. General Register House, Edinburgh, 1894. p. 415.

140 Macpherson, R.G., *Francis Stewart Fifth Earl Bothwell, c.1563–1612: Lordship and politics in Jacobean Scotland.* Unpublished PhD thesis, University of Edinburgh, 1998. p. 425.

141 Ramsay, A., *The tea-table miscellany: a collection of choice songs, Scots and English.* 4 Vols. A. Donaldson and J. Reid, Edinburgh, 1763. Vol. 1. p. 357.

142 Livingston, J., *Memorable Characteristics and Remarkable Passages of Divine Providence.* William Duncan, Glasgow, 1754. pp. 3–4.

143 Ibid, p. 4.

presides over the 1610 assembly that abolishes the supremacy of the Church of Scotland over James I.

Football is as unsafe as ever. On the morning of 20 October 1576, George Gordon, 5th Earl of Huntly, goes hunting, bagging three hares and a fox. Returning to Strathbogie Castle, "he cryed for ane futeball, that he mycht play eftirnoune, and reprovit one Jhone Hamilton verie bitterlie because the ball was not reddie."[144] "He cried for a football, that he might play that afternoon and reproved one Jhone Hamilton very bitterly because the ball wasn't ready." He gives Hamilton half a mark to buy one.[145] He plays with friends that afternoon. When, "he had stricken the second strocke with his owin fute at the ball, he fell on the grene!" He is helped up but staggers and falls on his face. Taken to his room, frothing at the mouth, he begins to vomit black blood and dies within hours. Soon after, strange events are reported. Jhone and three other men collapse. They wake chilled and terrified, mirroring the earl's last hours. Later, the earl's brother, Patrick, hears "a grit noyse and din" from the earl's chamber. Patrick and Jhone enter the chamber, but Jhone is petrified and runs out. When the noise repeats, Patrick joins him. Later, it is heard a third time.[146] George Gordon. *First football ghost.*

The 5th Earl of Caithness is dubbed "Wicked Earl George". In February 1584, he murders David and Ingram Sinclair, on the day Ingram's daughter is to be wed. The brothers had been the principal gaolers of the Earl's father, and were responsible for his death in 1576. David is playing golf when the Earl rides up, draws his sword, and runs him through. "On doing so, he galloped over to Wester, and calling aside Ingram, who was at the time amusing himself with some friends at football, he drew out a pistol and shot him dead on the spot. He then coolly turned his horse's head towards Girnigoe, and rode off with as little concern as if he had merely killed a brace of moor fowl."[147]

In 1592, the Thane of Cawdor is murdered with a blunderbuss. The chief conspirator is interrogated under threat of "the boot". Not wanting

144 Pitcairn, R. (ed.), *Memorials of Transcriptions in Scotland, A.D. 1569–1573*, by Richard Bannatyne. Edinburgh Printing Company, 1836. p. 333.

145 £10 in 2024.

146 Pitcairn, R. (ed.), *Memorials of Transcriptions in Scotland, A.D. 1569–1573. By Richard Bannatyne.* Edinburgh Printing Company, 1836. pp. 334–337.

147 Saint-Clair, R.W., *The Saint-Clairs of the Isles*. H. Brett, Auckland, New Zealand, 1898. p. 196.

the bones of his lower legs crushed, he confesses. He admits meeting a co-conspirator in Dunoon after the fact, close to where Archibald Campbell, the future 7th Earl of Argyll, is "playing at the foot ball with Achinbreak and uthers [other] scholaris."[148,149,150] The assassination is part of a wider conspiracy that includes the murder of the "bonny" Earl of Moray (who had "play'd at the ba'") three days after the thane's. Fourteen years later, in Shakespeare's play, Macbeth becomes Thane of Cawdor, and then King of Scotland. Macduff murders him in a swordfight.

More blood is spilt. In May 1599, William Ridley of Willimontswyk is informed that six of the Armstrongs are crossing the border to play football in the West March, followed by "a drinkyng hard at Bewcastle house."[151] Perfect. Having had friends "murdered downe bye the sayd Scotes men", he can avenge them on English soil. Forty ride to Cumberland where six of the Armstrongs of Whythaugh and six men of Bewcastle are to play football. The match goes ahead. As Ridley's men lay in wait, they are ambushed by two hundred Armstrongs, who have spies of their own. Ridley's throat is cut. Thirty are taken prisoner to prevent reprisals, others are injured. Many are "sore hurt, especially John Whytfeild whose bowells came out, but are sowed up agayne, and is thought shall hardly escape, but as yet liveth."[152]

In an 1802 anthology of Border ballads, Walter Scott mentions Border skirmishes: Around 1585, the Scottish and English, "notwithstanding their mutual hostility … met frequently at parties of the chace and football; and it required many and strict regulations, on both sides, to prevent them from forming intermarriages, and from cultivating too close a degree of intimacy."[153] A decade later, Sir Robert Carey, Warden of the West Marches in Scotland, hears from his spies that, "a great match

148 His descendant, the 9th Duke of Argyll was the first patron of Rangers FC (founded 1872), in 1874. Three of the four founding members of the club were from the village of Rhu in Argyllshire.

149 Sir Dugald Campbell of Auchinbreak, 1576–1641. Archibald and Dugald, then 14–15, presumably schooled in Dunoon, and were playing with other pupils.

150 MacPhail, J.R.N. (ed.)., *Highland Papers*. T. and A. Constable, Edinburgh, 1914. p. 184.

151 Marples, M., *A History of Football*. Secker and Warburg, London, 1954. p. 61

152 Bain, J., *The Border Papers*. 2 Vols. H.M. General Register House, Edinburgh, 1896. Vol. 2. pp. 604–605.

153 Scott, W. (ed.)., *Minstrelsy of the Scottish Border*. 3 Vols. James Ballantyne, Edinburgh, 1802. Vol. 1. p. xlxxiv.

made at foote-ball" is to be held at Kelso that day.[154] The "chiefe riders" of the Scottish Borders are attending, implying the game is a ruse to facilitate an incursion across the border. In his memoirs, Carey uses a football analogy to convey that he had the upper hand: "I had the ball at my foote."[155] Carey holds a record. Upon hearing of the death of Queen Elizabeth, he gallops four hundred miles from London to Edinburgh in sixty hours, including changes of horses and pausing to sleep.[156]

In 1497, St Andrew's University bans football under pain of excommunication.[157] At some point the university relents and allows Shrovetide games. Both of its colleges are customarily presented with three 8d footballs to share on *Carnisprivii* (Shrove Tuesday). In February 1537, students are enraged when the Dean's ball, taken without permission, is confiscated. The day's football proves so ill-tempered, the university ends the tradition.[158] The Shrovetide game predates the Chester game by two years. Since it is referred to as a customary game, the implication is that it has been played for some time. The university, then, has a justifiable claim as hosting the oldest annual Shrove Tuesday game known.

Four days before *Fastern's E'en* (Shrove Tuesday) 1546, the hammersmiths of Perth order apprentices and servants, unless asked, not to join the football their masters are playing "under penalty of a pound of wax" for the altar of the church—a common fine of the day.[159] The same year, admission to the city's tailors' craft is contingent on providing a football for *Fastern's E'en*[160] Sometimes football is just a nuisance. In November 1549, twelve men from Banff, Aberdeenshire, are sentenced to eight days labour erecting a new tollbooth for "braking down of the sklattis of the kyrk, and glassin vindokis of the samyn be inordinatt

154 Scott, W., *The Poetical Works of Sir Walter Scott*. Baudry's European Library, Paris, 1838. p. 68.

155 Scott, W. (ed.)., *Minstrelsy of the Scottish Border.* 3 Vols. James Ballantyne, Edinburgh, 1802. Vol. 1. p. cxlviii.

156 Mandell, R.D., *Sport: A Cultural History*. Columbia University Press, New York, 1984. p. 140.

157 *St Andrew's University Publications*, 1964, Issue 56, p. cxxxii.

158 *Scottish History Society Publications*. Series 3. Acta Facularis Artium Universitatis Sanctiandree, 1413–1588. https://digital.nls.uk/scottish-history-society-publications/browse/archive/126826971?mode=transcription. Accessed 3 November 2023.

159 Magoun, F.P., *History of Football from the Beginnings to 1871*. Kolner Anglistische Arbeiten, 1938, Vols. 31–33. p. 89.

160 Mill, A.J., *Mediaeval Plays in Scotland*. William Blackwood & Sons, London, 1927. p. 11.

playing with hand ball and fuit ball upone the kyrk and kyrkyard."[161] "Breaking down the rooftiles of the church, and glass windows of the same by inordinate playing with handball and football upon the church and churchyard."

In December 1570, the bailies counsel of Peebles order there be, "na playing at the fute ball on the Hie Gait … under the pane of … viijs and cutting of the ball."[162] The town of Kirkcudbright, in Dumfries and Galloway, bans "futeball, cache [fives], kyllis [cayles] and uther games", in 1597, while in December 1598, George Kay, "confessit playing football under the night", dancing, and mumming, and is sentenced to two Sundays "bairfut and bairleggit."[163,164] Curiously, two weeks before, the same Elgin kirk sessions forbids all games to be played in the churchyards of the parish, "except the passing tyme at the futball."[165] Similarly, the following Christmas, a variety of festivities—"futballing through the toun, snaw balling, singing of carrellis or uther prophane sangis [songs]"—are forbidden, especially in the "Kirk or Kirk zaird [yard] thairoff (except futball)."[166] Townsfolk have a right to be confused. On the first Christmas Day of the new century, Pringill, Boynd, and Cuming have a kickabout in the churchyard and end up at the sessions.[167] Even so, Patrik Andersone can hardly use this as an excuse when he is found playing football in Robert Sutherland's yard, in 1604.[168]

Between 1574 and 1579, the Burgh of Glasgow's inventory records four annual payments to Johne Andro. "Sax futtballis" are bought each time, at a cost of 2s each.[169] In 1574, payment is made a week after

---

161 Cramond, W. (ed.), *The Annals of Banff.* New Spalding Club, Aberdeen, 1891. p. 26.

162 *Charters and Documents Relating to the Burgh of Peebles, A.D. 1168–1710.* Turnbull and Spears, Edinburgh, 1872. p. 324. https://electricscotland.com/history/peebles/chartersofpeebles.pdf. Accessed 3 November 2023.

163 Johnstone, M.B., Armet, C.M. (eds.), *Kirkudbright Town Council Records, 1596–1604.* Oliver & Boyd, Edinburgh and London, 1939. p. 402. TannerRitchie Publishing, Burlington, Ontario, Canada, 2010.

164 Cramond, W. (ed.), *The Records of Elgin, 1584–1779.* Reprinted from Elgin Courant & Courier, 1897. p. 55.

165 Ibid, p. 54.

166 Ibid, p. 63.

167 Ibid, p. 74.

168 Ibid, p. 127.

169 *"Extracts from the accounts: 1573–85".* In: *Extracts From the Records of the Burgh of Glasgow Vol. 1, 1573–1642*, ed. J D Marwick (Edinburgh, 1914), pp. 447–473. *British History Online* http://www.british-history.ac.uk/glasgow-burgh-records/vol1/pp447–473. Accessed 26 August 2023.

Shrove Tuesday; three days after in 1576; two days before in 1577; three weeks before in 1578; and five days after in 1579. 1575 is the outlier, two months before Shrove Tuesday. Clearly, there is an annual match, supported by the city's officials. By 1590, another shoemaker, John Neill, has the contract "furneissing yeirlie during his lyftyme vpoune Fastreinisevin of sex guid [good] and sufficient fut ballis, or ellis tuentie schillingis as the price thairof."[170] Andro was paid 2s a ball, Neill is raking in 3s 4d. In 1609, he is given "xxvis. viid, upon the xviii day of Feb. … for fute ballis to the town at Fastrenis evin conforme to the ald use."[171] Balls now cost 4s 4d. Neill is paid on the 28 February. Shrove Tuesday. Elsewhere in the inventory, statutes for selling bears, a thief banished and marked, a clock-keeper appointed, an appearance before a secret council, lepers expelled, a surgeon punished for slandering, an attack by pirates, and a thief pardoned and appointed executioner.

~

Mary is queen in 1555 when football is banned in London, and a general ban of "all unlawfull games, the gamers, and receptours [hosts]" is issued in Liverpool.[172] Under Elizabeth, further prohibitions are enforced: London in 1572 and 1581, Shrewsbury in 1594, Coventry in 1595. There appears to be wriggle room. Shrewsbury only bans football within the city walls. Similarly, the shoemaker's guild of Carlisle has an entry, c1595. "It is … agreed upon by the fellowship of this gyld that no journeyman or apprentice shall make any foot balle to sell or play withal without consent and knowledge of his or their maisters, and that they shall not play at football within the liberties of this cittie."[173] A 1527 ban of sports in Galway spares football. Hurling is not: "at no tyme the use ne ocupye the horlinge of the litill balle with hockie stickes or staves, nor

---

170 *"Extracts from the records: 1590"*. In: *Extracts From the Records of the Burgh of Glasgow Vol. 1, 1573–1642*, ed. J D Marwick (Edinburgh, 1914), pp. 149–156. *British History Online* http://www.british-history.ac.uk/glasgow-burgh-records/vol1/pp149–156. Accessed 26 August 2023.

171 *"Extracts from the accounts: 1607–41"*, in *Extracts From the Records of the Burgh of Glasgow Vol. 1, 1573–1642*, ed. J D Marwick (Edinburgh, 1914), pp. 473–484. *British History Online* http://www.british-history.ac.uk/glasgow-burgh-records/vol1/pp473–484. Accessed 26 August 2023.

172 Twemlow, J.A., *Liverpool town books, 1550–1862. Volume 1, 1550–1571.* The University Press, Liverpool, 1918. p. 51.

173 Ferguson, R.S., Nanson, W. (eds.)., *Some Municipal Records of Carlisle.* C. Thurnam & Sons, Carlisle, 1887. p. 180.

use no hande ball to playe without the walles, but onely the great foote balle, on payn of the paynis above lymittid."[174]

Other contemporary bans in Galway include Irishmen "bragging or boasting on the town", exclusion of "idle men and women", and "Disobedience to the Mayor" punishable by a fine and incarceration in the "lowest prison." Consideration is given to "Parleys in the town with Irishmen." Intriguingly, a c1548 English poem *Phylogamus* mentions "a Hurle Batte" without context.[175] It is never mentioned in England again. The attributed author, Luke Shepherd, is from north Essex where camping is played; arguably, he is referring to a camping crook. The Scottish poet Richard Maitland displays a curmudgeonly attitude to football.

> Quhen ȝoung men cummis fra the gren,
> Playand at the futbal had bein,
> with brokin spauld,
> I thank my God, I want my ein,
> And am so auld.[176]

"When young men return from football on the green with broken shoulder[s], I thank God I have poor eyesight, and I'm too old [to play]."

Ironically, Thomas Naogeorgus's posthumous treatise *The popish kingdome, or reigne of Antichrist*, which unsparingly disparages hundreds of Catholic mores, bequeaths them to posterity.[177] Those depraved Catholics. Some of their more outlandish customs have not stood the test of time: shutting up spirits in crystals as charms, hiding in caves during storms, and eating radishes to ward off malaria. Stranger still, their children go door-knocking at Christmas for fruits and pennies, and clothe stuffed Guys and toss them in blankets on festival days. They

174 *Historical Manuscripts Commission. Tenth Report, Appendix Part V. The Manuscripts of the Marquis of Ormonde, the Earl of Fingall, the Corporations of Waterford, Galway etc.* p. 402. TannerRitchie Publishing, Burlington, Ontario, Canada, 2008.

175 Germann, F., *Luke Shepherd, ein Satirendichter der englischen Reformationszeit.* T. Lapart, Augsberg, 1911. pp. 101–104.

176 Magoun, F.P., *Scottish Popular Football, 1424–1815.* The American Historical Review, 1931, 37:1, p. 4.

177 Naogeorgus, T., *The popish kingdome, or reigne of Antichrist.* Henrie Denham, London, 1570.

give presents on New Year's Day, throw snowballs, hide a penny in cakes on Twelfth Night, and shamelessly celebrate Shrovetide. And they dance. During "Holydayes", "when their dinner once is done, and that they well have fed, To play they go, to casting of the stone, to runne, or shoote, To tosse the light and windie ball, aloft with hande or foote: Some others trie their skill in gonnes, some wrestle all the day, And some to schooles of fence do go, to gaze upon the play."[178]

Known in his day as a "narrow-sould" Puritan, Philip Stubbes saw "evil in innocence, sin in mirth, the devil in dancing, and hell in Shakespere's art."[179] In his 1583 *Anatomie of Abuses* he rails against the pleasures of the day. Little is spared: "ye wild Moris … holes in their eares whereat they hangs ringes … tennisse … minstrelles … bowles … playes … looking glasses … ruffs [that] goe flip-flap in the winde." Do not dance: "Every leap or skip is a leap toward hel."[180] That "devilish pastime" football gets a pasting:

"A bloody and murthering practise, then a felowly sporte. For: dooth not every one lye in waight for his adversarie, seeking to overthrowe him and picke him on his nose, though it be uppon hard stones, in ditch or dale, in valley or hil, or what place soever it be, hee careth not, so he have him down. And that he can serve ye most of this fashion, he is counted the only felow, and who but he? So that by this meanes, sometimes their necks are broken, sometimes their backs, sometimes their legs, sometimes their armes, sometime one parts thrust out of joynt, sometime an other, sometime the noses gush out with blood, their eyes start out, and sometimes hurt in one place, sometimes in another.

"But whosoever escapeth away the best, goeth not scotfree, but is either sore wounded, craised, and bruseed, so as he dyeth of it, or els scapeth and no mervaile [marvel], for they have the sleights to meet one betwixt two, to dash him against the hart with their elbowes, to hit him under the short ribbes with their griped fists, and with their knees to catch him upon the hip, and to pick him on his neck, with a hundred such murthering devices: and hereof groweth envie, malice, rancour, choler, hatred, displeasure, enmitie and what not els: and sometimes fighting,

178 Ibid, p. 58.

179 Furnivall, F.J. (ed.), *Phillip Stubbes's Anatomy of Abuses in England in Shakespeare's Youth, A.D. 1583.* 2 Volumes in 3. N. Trübner & Co., London, 1882. p. 36.

180 Stubbes, P., *The Anatomie of Abuses*. Richard Jones, London, 1583. n.p.

brawlling, contention, quarrel picking, murther, homicide and great effusion of blood, as experience dayly teacheth."[181]

Thomas Nashe, Elizabethan satirist and frenemy of Robert Greene, annihilates Stubbes in *The Anatomie of Absurditie*: "I … hasten to other mens furie, who make the Presse the dunghill, whether they carry all the muck of their mellancholicke imaginations, pretending forsooth to anatomize abuses, and stubbe up sin by the rootes … I account such men never the holier, because they place such praise in painting foorth other mens imperfections."[182] As the century dwindles, Puritan convert and Oxford academic John Rainolds writes a treatise on the unlawfulness of acting. He debates with a defender of "common stage players", who writes: "No lesse in a manner, then if one beholding a great number of Scholers playing in winter time at football, should say the *Universities judgment doeth approove it*."[183] John Hayward fears for the coming century. This from his book on the overthrow of Richard II by Henry IV: "if this boldnesse not be beaten downe, our authority will fall into contempt and scorn, and be made a common foote-ball, for every base citizen to spurne at."[184] Hayward should not have dedicated the book to the Earl of Essex. Elizabeth's advisers sniff treachery. Does the book allude to her dethronement? Francis Bacon scours the book and says no, but Hayward is sent to the Tower anyway, there to quake until the queen's death.[185]

Queens may also yea and nay. A long-time favourite of the queen, Essex is so dazzled by his reflection, he cannot see what others do. Blunted acumen and ungovernable ambition. Death stalks him. When he overrides Elizabeth's policy in Ireland, he is put under house arrest, where "he plays now and then at tennis, and walks upon his leads [flat roofs] and garden."[186] On his release, he sinks his teeth into the hand

181 Ibid.

182 Nashe, T., *The Anatomie of Absurditie*. I. Charlewood, London, 1589. n. p.

183 Rainolds, J. *Th'overthrow of stage plays*. Richard Schilders, Middelburg, 1599. p. 152.

184 Hayward, J., *The First Part of the Life and raigne of King Henrie IIII*. John Wolfe, London, 1599. p. 34.

185 The First part of the life and raigne of King Henrie the IIII. https/www.rct.uk/collection/1023307/the-first-part-of-the-life-and-raigne-of-king-henrie-the-iiii-extending-to-the. Accessed 11 June 2023.

186 Brennan, M.G., *Robert Sidney and the Earl of Essex: A Dangerous Friendship Viewed Through the Eyes of Roland Whyte*. Sidney Journal, 2014, 32:1, pp. 25, 34.

that fed him, and is executed for treason. Exeter's son Robert and James I's son Henry are "near to each other in years, but nearer in affection." Henry dies aged eighteen, but not before their friendship is tested on the tennis court: "after a set or two, a dispute arose connected with the game." Henry calls Robert the son of a traitor. Furious, Robert strikes him on the head with his racket, "so shrewdly that he drew blood."[187] Humphrey Gifford's riddle merits the sixteenth century's last hurrah.

> What am I that wanting, both hands feete and head,
> Of all them that see me, being deemed for dead.
> Of breath have great store, and move too and fro,
> Now up, and now downe, now hye, and now low?
> Alas what hard fortune doth to mee befall:
> That guiltlesse am spited of great and of small.
> They strike me, and push mee, South, West, North and East:
> Yet doe I no harme to most, neither least.
> When as my breath fayling, I can doe no more,
> They then give mee over, and never before.[188,189]

187 Cust, E., *Lives of the Warriors of the Civil Wars of France and England*. John Murray, London, 1867. p. 272.

188 Gifford, G., *A Posie Of Gilloflowers, Eche Differing From Other In Colour and Odour, Yet All Sweete*. John Perin, London, 1580. pp. 75v–76.

189 Answer: "A football made of a bladder."

CHAPTER EIGHT
1600–1699 I

It was said of Queen Elizabeth that she sent her eagles to Spain but reserved her vultures for Ireland. In 1597, the corpse of the Governor of Carrickfergus is decapitated, and his head sent to Tyrone, where it is "made a football of by the rude gallowglass of the army."[1,2] This apparent act of impromptu barbarism is, in fact, retaliation for the killing of Gaelic chieftain Sir James MacDonnell's elder brother, whose head had been spiked at Dublin Castle.[3,4] In 1600, hatred towards the occupiers explodes. The mayor and townsmen seize the Constable of Limerick Castle, "cut off his head … and played at football with it."[5] Three years later, convinced Irish musicians are seditionaries, Elizabeth issues a proclamation to, "Hang all harpers where found and burn the instruments."[6,7] Other anarchic pursuits include "running at a Ball, with a Hurlett; and coyting of stones." In fact, the most dangerous of a long list are deemed to be, "sword dauncers, the Hurlett [,] Coits, and bagpipers."[8]

English paranoia is self-inflicted. From the 1550s onward, land is systematically grabbed and given to British settlers. Opposition is

---

1 Of Hebridean/west Scottish-Norse descent, Gallowglass (Gaelic: *gallóglach*, 'foreign warrior') were Irish mercenaries with a reputation for ruthlessness. In: Soodalter, Ron. *Scourge of the Gallowglass*. Military History, 2016, 33:2, pp. 64–71.

2 Hessayon, A., *Beastly Furie, and Exstreme Violence*. In: Wagg, S., Pollock, A.M (eds.)., *The Palgrave Book of Sport, Politics and Harm*. Springer Nature Switzerland, Cham, Switzerland, 2021. p. 19.

3 Pinkerton, W., *The "Overthrow" of Sir John Chichester at Carrickfergus, in 1597*. Ulster Journal of Archaeology, 1857, Vol. 5, p. 194.

4 Tudor poet Edmund Spenser saw a woman in Limerick raise her foster-son's head, "whilst he was quartered … and sucked up all the blood … saying that the earth was not worthy to drinke it." She poured the blood over "her face and breast, and tore her haire, crying out and shrieking most terribly." In: Spenser, E., *A View of the State of Ireland*. John Morrisson, Dublin, 1809. p. 104.

5 Atkinson, E.G., (ed.)., *Calendar of State Papers Relating to Ireland of the Reign of Elizabeth 1600, March-October*. Mackie and Co., Ltd., London, 1903. p. ii. TannerRitchie Publishing, Burlington, Ontario, Canada, 2006.

6 Williams, S., *Focus: Irish Traditional Music*. Routledge, Abingdon, Oxon, 2010. p. 53.

7 As a result, only two harps remain from this era. One, the Brian Boru harp is depicted on the Irish Coat of Arms, the old Irish pound, and all Irish euro coins. It is most well-known as the Guinness motif.

8 Fletcher, A.J., *Drama and the Performing Arts in Pre-Cromwellian Ireland*. D.S. Brewer, Cambridge, 2001. pp. 187–188.

brutally put down. After the Chief of the Maguire Clan and Lord of Fermanagh speaks up, "divers men, women and children" are killed in repeated raids, other woman taken ransom, and twelve thousand cows driven away.[9] When Maguire is finally given "faithful oaths" by the English, they betray him, behead his nephew, and hurl "it from place to place as a football."[10] The clan rises unsuccessfully. Maguire is killed in action and the vast majority of Fermanagh is taken by the Crown and given to settlers. In *The White Devil*, Francisco de' Medici threatens to play *calcio* with the head of his dead sister's husband: "Like the wild Irish, I'll ner think thee dead, Till I can play at football with thy head."[11]

A similar phrase is used in *The Captive-Captain*: "It had steel'd them with that wilde Irish ancient resolution, Never to hold themselves secure from their Foe, till they might play at foot-ball with his head."[12] A sixteenth century Gallowglass grave slab, in Inishowen, Donegal, demonstrates that warriors played other ball games. A curved stick and sliotar (ball) are masoned into the slab.[13] The stick may be for hurley or shinty; the Scottish game was widely played in the north of Ireland. A contemporary hurley, c1467–1531, was discovered in Derries, Co. Offaly, the oldest known.[14] In 1620, the Scottish politician Sir Robert Gordon sums up the mood as he confers shrewd counsel: "Eshew the footeball as a dangerous and unprofitable exercise. Use you diligence to take away the reliques of the Irishe barbaritie which as yet remains in your countrey, to wit, the Irishe langage, and the habit."[15] This does not stop the 6th Laird of Braidstane, Hugh Montgomery, from opening a school in Newtown, Co. Down, the same year, complete with "a green for recreation at goff, football, and archery."[16]

---

9 Trimble, W.C., *History of Enniskillen*. 2 Vols. William Trimble, Enniskillen, 1919. Vol. 1. p. 73.

10 Ibid, p. 74.

11 Webster, J., *The White Devil*. 1612. sig. GV. Act 4, Sc 1, lns 36–37.

12 Braithwait, R., *The Captive-Captain: Or, the Restrain'd Cavalier*. J. Grismond, London, 1665. p. 108.

13 Doyle, C., *Hair Hurling Balls: Review, Research, and Scientific Investigations*. Folk Life: Journal of Ethnological Studies, 2016, 54:1, p. 18.

14 Ibid, p. 15.

15 Fraser, W., *The Sutherland Book*. 3 Vols. William Fraser, Edinburgh, 1892. Vol. 2. p. 359.

16 Hill, G. (ed.)., *The Montgomery Manuscripts: 1603–1706*. James Cleeland, Thomas Dargan, Belfast, 1869. p. 126.

Ball games in Cork are ill-received, and ultimately banned in 1631: "a very barbarous and uncivil kind of sport upon Easter Tuesdays, May days, Whitson Tuesday, *viz.*, tossing of great balls, and hurling in the open streets with the small ball, great mischief have oftentimes happened, as the death of men, and many wounded and maimed in these sports, and many quarrels have followed, which were like to break into a general tumult within the city."[17] In Cloyne, Co. Cork, the prohibition of ball play, church ales, and banquets are embodied in the formulaic visitation articles imposed on churches.[18]

By 1649, country games are no longer immune, considered by paranoid Cromwellians as covert gatherings where hordes of malcontents fan the flames. An edict in Clonmel, Co. Tipperary, in 1640, aims "to prevent several abuses frequently committed at the footebale."[19] Anyone playing "after the portreiffe [bailiff] by sound of a horne shall signall for breaking of sd play, shalbe committed and punished as a breaker of the peace and a violator of the Lawes of the Kingdome."[20] It is the first mention in history of an instrument signalling the end of a ball game, anticipating the whistle by two hundred and thirty eight years. Intolerance continues under Charles II. In 1680, fears of a French incursion to liberate Irish Catholics, "the conquest of it would not be like a *Goal* at foot-ball, in an instant, but a work of time."[21] The author adds, chillingly, "a *Famine* hath ever put a period to all invasions or rebellions there."

It is Thomas Nashe who footballs the old century into history. In *Lenten Stuff*, he creates the verb "to football", meaning to knock: "They footebald their heades togither."[22,23] Owin Felltham alters the verb to mean kicked about: "to see how well-meaning simplicitie is foot-ball'd." [24,25] In another edition, he compares too little or too much spirit to walking

17 Kelly, J., *Sport in Ireland, 1600–1840*. Four Courts Press, Dublin, 2014. pp. 239–240.

18 Fletcher, A.J., *Drama and the Performing Arts in Pre-Cromwellian Ireland*. D.S. Brewer, Cambridge, 2001. p. 434.

19 Sheehan W., Cronin, M. (eds.)., *Riotous Assemblies: Rebels, Riots and Revolts in Ireland*. Mercier Press, Cork, 2011. pp. 43–44.

20 McGrath, B. (ed.)., *The Minute Book of the Corporation of Clonmel, 1608–1649*. Irish Manuscripts Commission, 2006. pp. 271–272.

21 Fitzgerald, D., *A Narrative of the Irish Popish Plot*. s.n., London, 1680. p. 27.

22 Nashe, T., *Lenten Stuff*. s.n., London, 1599. p. 46.

23 The book is set in Great Yarmouth, in the camping county of Norfolk.

24 Like Nashe, Felltham was a native of Suffolk.

25 Felltham, O. *Resolves: Divine, Morall, Politicall*. George Purslowe, London, 1623 p. 274.

with a high step or flat-footed: "As I care not for being powder, or the cap of the company; so I would not be earth, or the fool's foot-ball."[26] Even camp is en-verbed. In Thomas Drant's translation of Horace's *Ars Poetica*, mischievous teenagers are wont to kick their drunken elders:[27]

> Leste even younge folke selinge you drinke
> more then for you is méete,
> Do make of you mere mockinge stockes,
> and campe you with theire féete.[28]

"Lest youngsters sell you more alcohol than you can handle, then make you a laughingstock and kick you with their feet." Another passage reflects the skill in camping:

> He dare not turney, nor yet tilte which never knew the play:
> The stoole ball, top, or camping ball if suche one should assaye
> As hath no mannour skill therin, Amongste a mightye croude,
> Theye all would scréeke unto the skye and laughe at hym aloude.

Essentially, 'He wouldn't joust if he didn't know how, so why try to play stoolball, top, or camping?' The year before, Drant references other sports:

> Or when thou doest at footebal playe,
> Or tennice for pastyme,
> Whylste love of game dothe ease thy toyle,
> And helpe awaye the tyme.[29]

Samuel Rowlands provides an invaluable description of the sports of the day:

> Man, I dare challenge thee to throw the sledge,
> To jumpe, or leape over ditch or hedge,

---

26 Felltham, O. *Resolves: Divine, Moral, Political.* Whittaker & Co., London, 1840. p. 163.

27 Drant attended Cambridge University.

28 Drant, T., *Horace His arte of Poetrie, pistles, and Satyrs Englished.* Thomas Marshe, London, 1567. n.p.

29 Drant, T., *A Medicinable Morall.* s.n., London, 1566. n.p.

To wrasile, play at stooleball, or to runne,
To pitch the barre, or to shoote off a gunne,
To play at loggets, nine holes, or ten pinnes,
To trie it out at foot-ball by the shinnes;
At Ticktacke,[30] Irish, Noddie, Maw, and Ruffe.[31]
At hot-cockles,[32] leape-frogge, or blindman-buffe.
To drinke halfe pots, or deale at the whole canne:
To play at base, or pen and Ynk-horne sir Jhan:
To daunce the Morris, play at barly-breake:[33]
At all exploytes a man can thinke or speake:
At shove-groate, venter-poynt, or crosse and pile.[34]
At beshrow him that's last at yonder stile;
At leaping ore a Midsommer bon-fier,
Or at the drawing Dun out of the myer.[35,36]

In the *Knave of Clubbs*, he adds: "Then downe the staires the villain should be tost, Like to a footeball in a winters frost."[37,38] Rowland's 1600 phrase "to play at base" references prison base. Another follows, in 1609, in Ferdinando Pulton's comprehensive overview of criminal law. With respect to assemblies, multiple games are sanctioned, as their intent is not to "breake or disturbe the Peace: "Bowles … Tennis, Quoits, Cailes … Base, Footeball, Stoolcball, Handball, or such like

30 Similar to backgammon.

31 Irish, Noddie, and Maw and Ruffe were Elizabethan card games. "Irish" was colloquial for the Irish card game of Five-cards; now called Twenty-five, it remains popular in Ireland.

32 A blindfolded person must recognise friends by the slap they receive on their hand; the slaps make the hand "hot". The French version was called "la main chaud [hot hand]". A sixteenth century Flemish tapestry depicts shepherds and shepherdesses playing hot cockles. In this version, one participant hides his face in another's lap with one hand behind his back. Victoria and Albert Museum, London: 204143, c1500–1515. https://theindex.princeton.edu/s/view/ViewWorkOfArt.action?id=EF669937–2CE4–407F-B69E-A383DF2163D1. Accessed 9 August 2023.

33 A couple in a field try to capture other couples who may split up (breake) when about to be caught.

34 Shove-groat (shove-ha'penny) is a coin nudging game, the other two are coin-tossing games.

35 Dun out of the mire: Players compete to lift a heavy log and carry it off.

36 Rowlands, S., *Satire IV, Humors* ordinarie. In: *The Letting of Humours in the Head-Vaine*. s.n., London, 1600. n.p.

37 Rowlands, S., *The Knave of Clubbes*. W. Ferebrand, London, 1609. n.p.

38 Humphrey King writes similarly, "My swolne-sicke heart, with death is tost, Like to a foote-ball in a frost." See: *An Halfe-penny-worth of Wit, in a Penny-worth of Paper*. Edw. Blount, London, 1613. p. 35.

disports be also lawfull."[39] The very mention implies that base is not only for children. The treatise emphasises that, play as you like, break-out brawls are considered to be Riots. That football is known to be played solely to the feet, at least sometimes, is supported by a 1607 simile: "as a football is tossed to and fro on the plaine ground."[40]

While Shakespeare is no longer considered to have penned the 1600 play *Sir John Old-castle*, the eponymous hero is undoubtedly Sir John Falstaff of *Henry IV Part I* and *II*, written between 1596 and 1598, and the *Merry Wives of Windsor*, c1597. Preparing to join Henry V's army and put down a rebellion in the depths of winter, a thinly clothed brewer's servant Dick exclaims: "Master I hope we be no babes, for our manhood, our bucklers, and our towne footeballs can beare witnesse: and this lite parrell we have shall off, and weel fight naked afore we run away."[41] Later, a disguised Henry wanders his camp. Coming across Dick he says, "Al friends at footebal, fellowes al in field. Harry, and Dicke, and George, bring us a drumme, Give us square dice, weele keepe this court of guard." In 1988, a two-page manuscript of an unknown play was found in a 1586 copy of Homer's *Odyssey*. Dated to 1586–1600, the anonymous text consists of 29–32 lines of blank verse.[42] It is of great interest, as it is an analogue of a scene in Shakespeare's *Henry IV Part I, Act II*, published in 1598. In other words, Shakespeare may have plagiarised it. Two of the lines missing from *Henry IV* read: "if thou dost chopp of this head of mine to make a bottle or footeball of."[43]

In July 1596, Elizabeth is recovering from an illness. David Foulis writes to James VI of Scotland: "I praise God the ball is yet aloft."[44] Several football references pad out her remaining years. In 1601, John Gyttyns petitions for discharge from imprisonment, having been committed "for playing at the foot balle upon Shroftusdaie, and for

39 Pulton, F., *De pace Regis et Regni*. Adam Islip, London, 1609. p. 25v.

40 Ward, W., *Gods arrows*. Henry Ballard, London, 1607. p. 10v.

41 Anon., *The first part of the true and honorable historie, of the life of Sir John Old-castle, the good Lord Cobham*. V.S., London, 1600. n.p.

42 The Schøyen Collection: MS 1627, *Shakespeare Henry IV Part I*, c1586–1600, fol. 1v.

43 Phoenix, A., *Francis Bacon and the So-Called Dering Manuscript of Henry IV*. 2022. p. 84. https://sirbacon.org/downloads/aphoenix/HENRY%20IV%20–%20ORIGINAL%20SHAKESPEARE%20MANUSCRIPT%20IDENTIFIED.pdf. Accessed 5 September 2023.

44 *Report of the Royal Commission on Historical Manuscripts*. Eyre and Spottiswoode, London, 1877. Vol. 6. Pt. 1. p. 668.

throwing the balle from hime whene the serigent Hardinge demaunded the same."[45] A 1602 play reinforces the notion of a violent game: "Ile go to footeball and breake my shinnes."[46] The same year, while out riding, Robert ap Morgan jostles a postboy off his horse. The boy's leg is badly broken. When examined, ap Morgan is asked, tongue-in-cheek, if he has ever been a football player.[47]

In a similar vein, John Manningham records in his diary: *Hoste to his wife,* "Thou carest not for me, thou scornest and spurnest me, but yet, like those which play at footeball, spurne that which they runne after."[48,49] Another entry that year references the precursor to badminton: "The play at shuttlecocke is become soe muche in request at Court, that the making of shuttlecockes is almost growne a trade in London."[50] In the same entry, he writes that when Lady Effingham was playing at shuttlecock the Christmas past, she "upon a suddein felt hir selfe somewhatt." She retires to her chamber and has "a child without a midwife, shee never suspecting shee had bin with child." Shuttlecock must be popular: it appears in at least seven contemporary plays.[51] As well as mentioning tip-cat, hot cockles, and battledore, *Women Beware Women* has the following passage:

> Ward. Can you play at shuttlecock, forsooth?
> Isabella. Ay, and at stool-ball too, sir; I have great luck at it.
> Ward. Why, can you catch a ball well?
> Isabella. I have catched two in my lap at one game.
> Ward. What, have you, woman? I must have you learn.
> To play at trap too, then yar'e full and whole.[52]

---

45 Macray, W.D., Round, J.H., Jeaffreson, J.C. (eds.)., *The Manuscripts of Shrewsbury and Coventry corporations*. Eyre and Spottiswoode, London, 1899. p. 62.

46 Cooke, J., *A Pleasant Conceited Comedie.* Mathew Lawe, London, 1602. n.p.

47 "*Cecil Papers: January 1602, 16–31*", in *Calendar of the Cecil Papers in Hatfield House: Volume 12, 1602–1603*, ed. R A Roberts (London: His Majesty's Stationery Office, 1910), 22–43. *British History Online*, accessed February 16, 2024, http://www.british-history.ac.uk/cal-cecil-papers/vol12/pp22–43.

48 "Spurne": in this context, "kick".

49 Bruce, J. (ed.)., *Diary of John Manningham*. 1602–1603. J.B. Nichols and Sons, London, 1868. p. 74.

50 Ibid, p. 132.

51 Baird, C., *Stakes and Hazards: Games and Gaming in Early Modern Drama*. Unpublished PhD thesis, University of Reading, 2019. pp. 235–238.

52 Carroll, W.C. (ed.)., *Women Beware Women*, by Thomas Middleton. Bloomsbury, London, 2008. Act 2, Sc 3, lns 85–91.

Queen Elizabeth survives eight popes and four kings of France. Around Christmas 1602, she descends into "a settled and unremovable melancholie." Her godson finds her "in moste pitiable state", consumed with "choler and greife." When he reads poetry to cheer her, she tells him: "When thou dost feele creeping tyme at thye gate, these fooleries will please thee lesse."[53] By March 1603, she is described as "infinitely discontented", by night sitting "with sheddinge of tears to bewayle Essex", the favourite she executed for treason.[54] An infection takes hold, racking her throat. She sits for days, "mostly awake and not speaking at all … her melancholy humour … too deep rooted in her heart."[55] She dies on the twenty-fourth. John Manningham writes, "This morning about 3 at clocke hir Majestie departed this lyfe, mildly like a lambe, easily like a ripe apple from the tree."[56]

~

Elizabeth's younger rival, Mary Stuart, had died three decades before. She ascended the Scottish throne the week she was born. It takes her son, James VI, four hundred days longer. But he goes one better. He succeeds Elizabeth. In 1604, the year after his coronation, on a tour of his new kingdom, King James I visits Bishop Cannings, Wiltshire, where the minister provides "entertayment … with carters singing, with whipps in their hands; and afterwards, a footeball play. This parish would have challenged all England for musique, ringing, and footeball play."[57] James is not a fan. This from his 1599 *Basilikōn Doron*: "From this Court I debarre all rough and violent exercises, as the foot-ball, meeter for laming than making able the users thereof."[58] Nonetheless, James is passionately devoted to sports and encourages Sabbath pursuits, even football. Richard Bancroft, Archbishop of Canterbury from 1604 to 1610, is later described as "a Man of rough Temper, a stout Football-player."[59] James, on the other hand, is a lacklustre sportsman. His preference for hunting

53 Looms, C., *The Death of Elizabeth I*. Palgrave Macmillan, New York, 2010. p. 9.

54 Ibid, p. 9.

55 Ibid, p. 20.

56 Ibid, p. 29.

57 Clarke, A. (ed.), *Aubrey's 'Brief Lives.'* Clarendon Press Oxford, 1898. pp. 251–252.

58 James I, *Basilikōn Doron*. Reprinted by Wertheimer Lea &Co., London, 1887. *The Third Booke*, p. 143.

59 Coke, R., *A detection of the court and state of England during the last four reigns and the inter-regnum consisting of private memoirs, &c.* s.n., London, 1697. p. 57.

does not prevent unflattering falls, and "if he found he was excelled by anyone, he either sulkily abandoned the exercise altogether or revealed his chagrin."[60] James does not forget his countrymen, banning the import of golf balls from Holland, in 1618.[61] This maintains the price; in 1627, the Marquis of Montrose's accounts show a 10s payment for two golf balls. Directly above is a 16s outgoing for "balls in the tinnes court."[62]

In 1604, with plague ravaging the country, Nicholas Bownd takes to his pulpit in Norton, Suffolk, for the first of twenty-one "godly and fruitfull sermons … full of instruction and comfort." There is a unifying message. Praying will help. A lot. Five months of his sententious tirades, diminish then numb his parishioners. During week seven, he fixes his wrath on Sabbath pastimes, not because they spread plague, but because they are pastimes: "The Lords Sabbaths have bin most grievously polluted, by keeping of Faires on them, and by Interludes [short plays], Bearebaitings, Bulbaitings, and by other disorders of football and such like." He moves through the gears. "Oh how many thousand adulteries and fornications … are still committed … if there were no sinne among us but this, it were sufficient to provoke this great plague, and it may justly raigne in the bodies of a great many unto death, and in others in noysom and painfull ulcers and sores."[63] Pray. A lot.

No churchgoer is safe. Four years earlier, a Welsh cleric restricts himself to seven sermons. The last, "against fleshly lustes; and against certaine mischievous May-games, which are the fruit thereof", he fulminates against "that pestilent play at football upon the Lordes day." He provides a satisfying example: "a spectacle sufficient to terrifie all, whose heartes are not hardened in sinne … your neighbour being (as you know) at play this fortnight, with running against another man, brake his legg so lamentably that … the sight thereof made some of the beholders ready to faint. This wound could by no meanes bee cured … it brought him to his end … to the great discomfort and undoing of his poore wife and six Children … behold here the fruit of good fellowship (as

60 Davies, G., *The character of James I*. Huntington Library Quarterly, 194, 5:1, p. 47.

61 Cunningham, W., *Presidential Address*. Transactions of the Royal Historical Society, 1911, Vol. 5, p. 18.

62 Napier, M., *Memorials of Montrose and His Times*. 2 Vols. n.p. Edinburgh, 1848. Vol. 1. p. 178.

63 Bownd, N., *Medicines for the plague that is, godly and fruitfull sermons*. Adam Islip, London, 1604. pp. 81–82.

they call it) where their meetings are oftentimes mingled with their owne blood."[64] More follows. The idolatry of maypoles, "books of lustful love", and "wanton fornicatours". The rector has it all figured out. The same year, Sir William Jordan of Chitterne and Whitley, in Wiltshire, is granted arms. The crest is a football with the motto *Percussa Resurgo*: Strike me, I rise.[65] In other words, kick me, I bounce back. A fitting maxim for the unsteady ascent of football. An idiom in Thomas Dekker's play *Match Mee in London* indicates the physicality in football:

> John. You and I should both meet at one Ball,
> I being the stronger, yet you give the fall.
> Val. A kind of foot-ball slight, my Lord.[66]

In Dekker's allegorical play *The Whore of Babylon,* a character comes across "a number of men in gowns" (lawyers) in the street: "I asked one of them if they were going to foot-ball; yes said he, doe you not see those country fellowes, we are against them; and who do you thinke shall winne, said I, oh said he, the gownes, the gownes."[67] In *Blurt Master Constable*, Dekker writes of war: "I have seene more mens head up and downe like foote-balles at a breake-fast, after the hungry Cannons had pikt them, than there are Maiden-heads in Venice."[68] One of the most remarkable period quotes is in John Davies's fourth sonnet:

> For, Winds of Spight their highest sailes doe teare,
> Who make themselves nought else but subtill Windes,
> For, though a Foote-ball mounts oft by the same,
> Yet it is spurn'd [kicked] and made the People's game.[69]

Football. The people's game. Hands are still used. In *When You See Me, You Know Me*, Samuel Rowley's chronicle of Henry VIII, Will tells his

64 Roberts, H., *The day of hearing*. Joseph Barnes, Oxford, 1600. n.p.

65 *The Coat of Arms*. The Heraldry Society, Third Series, 2015, 11:1, 229, p. 35.

66 Dekker, T., *A Tragi-comedy: called, Match mee in London*. B. Alsop and T. Fawcet, London, 1631. p. 57. Act. 1.

67 Dekker, T., *The whore of Babylon*. Nathaniel Butter, London, 1607. n.p.

68 Dekker, T., *Blurt master-constable*. Edward Allde, London, 1602. n.p.

69 Davies, J., *The Holy Roode, or Christs Crosse*. Nathaniel Butter, London, 1609. n.p.

cousin Patch to creep up behind the king's chair and "cryboh" to scare him. Patch is wary. "But will hee not be angry?" "No" lies Will, "Hele lafe and be as merry as a mag-pie … all the house shall see him hugge thee in his armes, and dandle thee up and downe with hand and foot an thou wert a footeball."[70] Easily hoodwinked, poor Patch creeps up on Henry. "Boe! Boe!" "Mother of God!" cries Henry, "Out asse and tumble at my feete." Patch will not be dandled tonight. He will be kicked like a football instead: "For thus," barks Henry, "ile spurne thee uppe and downe the house."

The custom of married men playing unmarried is still in vogue. This from the play *Sir Giles Goosecappe*. "Why madam," says the eponymous hero, "we have a great match at foot-ball towards, married man against batchellers, & the married man be al my friends, so I wood faine marrie to take the married mens parts in truth." "The best reason for marriage that ever I heard, Sir Gyles," quips Hyppolita.[71] By the end of the play, the foolish knight is paired with Penelope and can rightly say, "Thanke you good my Lord as much as tho you had given me twentie shillings in truth, now I may take the married mens parts at footeball."[72] Football. His final word in the play. On the subject of wedlock, a 1615 book gives advice on the "canker that especially undermineth and fretteth the marriage bed." The answer is hiding in plain sight: "Lust, that boyling damned putrefaction of the bloud, that raging, ruling, headstrong sinne of this age … you fore-mentioned evils, you foote-ball players."[73]

Football remains popular in Scotland. In 1607, the minister at Aberlour "gave the parishioners a hail at football to induce them to assemble for worship."[74] The same year, the Earl of Dunbar writes to the Earl of Salisbury: "Your letter … I received lying on a couch, plagued in my left foot and my right hand, so as I am neither fit for football nor tennis, nor aught else that is good."[75] Nor aught else that is

70 Farmer, J.S. (ed.), *When you see me, you know me*, by Samuel Rowley. Tudor Facsimile Texts, England, 1913. p. 55.

71 Chapman, G. (attrib.), *Sir Giles Goosecappe, Knight*. John Windet, London, 1606. n.p.

72 Ibid.

73 Niccholes, *A., A Discourse, Of Marriage and Wiving*. s.n., London, 1615. pp. 19, 22–23.

74 Hew, S., *Fasti Ecclesiæ Scoticanæ*. 8 Vols. Oliver and Boyd, Edinburgh, 1926. Vol. 4. p. 334.

75 'Cecil Papers: September 1607, 16–30" in *Calendar of the Cecil Papers in Hatfield House: Volume 19, 1607*, ed. M S Giuseppi and D McN. Lockie (London, 1965), pp. 247–264. *British History Online* http://www.british-history.ac.uk/cal-cecil-papers/vol19/pp247-264. Accessed 24 August 2023.

good. That November, "About Martinmass began an extream frost; the river Ouze was wholly frozen up … Many sports were practised upon the ice, as shooting at eleven score … bowling, playing at football, cudgels, &c. And a horse-race was run from the tower at S. Mary Gate End along and under the great arch of the bridge to the Crain at Skeldergate postern."[76]

Football is still young and unruly. Cities tire. Manchester issues a ban in 1608: "… theire hath beene heretofore greate disorder in our towne of Manchest^{r} … glasse windows broken yearlye and spoyled by a companye of lewde and disordered p'sons usinge that unlawfull exercise of playing wth the ffootebale in ye streets … breakinge many mens windowes … and other great inormyties … no maner of persons hereaft^{r} shall playe or use the ffooteballe."[77] The next year, apprentices ignore the 12d fine and play "giddye yaddye or catts pallett and ffoote ball."[78,79] There was a similar ban in 1579, but only "Gede Gadye, or the Catt's Pallett" were banned for anyone over seven.[80] Transgressors spent two hours in the dungeon, and their parents or masters were fined 4d. It clearly does nothing and is re-enacted in 1583. Playing "Gidiegadie or the Cat's pallet, and Typing or hurling the Ball", in the churchyards or streets of Manchester, now incurs a 6d fine or two hours in the "Doungeon" for their parents.[81,82] It is interesting to see hurling mentioned and not football. As well as its use for the Cornish and Irish games, hurling (and hurl ball) may be synonymous with the kicking–carrying game. The 1608 ban is unheard above the clamour for the ball. More affirmative action is needed. From 1610, the city appoints "officers for ye ffooteball";[83]

76 Andrews, W., *Famous Frosts and Frost fairs in Great Britain*. George Redway, London, 1877. p. 10.

77 Earwaker, J.P. (ed.), *The Court leet records of the manor of Manchester, from the year 1552 to the year 1686, and from the year 1731 to the year 1846*. 12 Vols. Henry Blacklock and Co., Manchester, 1885. Vol. 2. pp. 239–240.

78 Dunlop, O.J., Denman, R.D., *English Apprenticeship and Child Labour: A History*. T.F. Unwin, London, 1912. p. 189.

79 Giddy gaddy, and cat's pallet are variations of tipcat. See: George, D.F. (ed.), *Lancashire: Records of Early English Drama*. University of Toronto Press, Buffalo, 1991. p. 322.

80 *Remains Historical and Literary Connected with the Palatine Counties of Lancaster and Chester*. The Chetham Society, Manchester, 1864. Vol. 63. p. 148.

81 Typing may refer to trapball.

82 Harland, H. (ed.), *A Volume of Court Leet Records of the Manor of Manchester in the Sixteenth Century*. s.n., 1864. Vol. 63, p. 156

83 Dunlop, O.J., Denman, R.D., *English Apprenticeship and Child Labour: A History*. T.F. Unwin, London, 1912. p. 189.

two are needed in 1615, three in 1617, for a population of seven thousand or so.[84]

Sheffield issues a ban in 1609: "no mans sonnes, servants, or apprentices, shall at any tyme hereafter play at certen games called the football, the trippe, the hornobillandes,[85] or bads."[86] Further north, the fine for playing in Kendal is 12d per person and 3s 4d for every broken window.[87,88] Guilds introduce bans of their own. In 1603, the Merchant Adventurers of Newcastle decree, "that no brother or sister to permit their apprentices to 'daunce dice carde mum or use any musick eyther by night or daye in the streetes.'"[89] As early as 1554, Newcastle passes an "acte for the apparel of apryntyses."[90] Sober clothing is expected. Velvet, lace, or embroidery can land you back at the start of your apprenticeship. By the Cromwellian era, the guild weighs in against the "extravagant" attire of apprentices, fussing over the design of shoestrings. Superfluity results in imprisonment.[91] The week before the Christmas of 1618, the Kirk session in Elgin, Scotland, bans "auld reitis and ceremonies expressly forbidden during the tyme callit Yooll … gwysing [mumming], dancing, singing carallis, play at the fut ball throch the toun … nather wemen to be cled in mens apparrell nor men in womens apparrell, casting of snaw ballis, hurling with stoollis on the streitis."[92] Hurling with stools on the streets is probably stoolball, though references to the game are scarce and largely confined to southeast England. The misdemeanours of Elgin citizens are recorded: two women throw snowballs on the Sabbath in 1601, Robert Kay plays "at the football throw the toun" in 1627, others play sabbath football in 1630 and 1653.[93]

84 Earwaker, J.P. (ed.), *The Court leet records of the manor of Manchester, from the year 1552 to the year 1686, and from the year 1731 to the year 1846.* 12 Vols. Henry Blacklock, Manchester, 1885. Vol. 2. pp. 305, 321.

85 A variant of shinty played in Sheffield.

86 Leader, J.D. (ed.), *The Records of the Burghery of Sheffield, Commonly Called the Town Trust.* Elliot Stock, London, 1897. p. 314.

87 Ibid, p. 190.

88 12d: A day's wages for a skilled tradesman.

89 Dunlop, O.J., Denman, R.D., *English Apprenticeship and Child Labour: A History.* T.F. Unwin, London, 1912. p. 189.

90 Ibid, p. 190.

91 Ibid, p. 190.

92 Cramond, W. (ed.), *The Records of Elgin: 1234–1800.* 2 Vols. Milne and Hutchison, Aberdeen, 1908. Vol. 2. p. 158.

93 Ibid, pp. 88, 198, 215, 282.

Football continues its association with antisocial behaviour. In 1609, a group of men are charged with assaulting the keeper, destroying fences, and hunting deer at the Earl of Salisbury's park in Canterbury, "under colour of playing at football or other such unlawful game or exercise."[94] Six years later, Edward Wharton of Edgware, Middlesex, is apprehended for telling the constable at Little Stanmore "that he would not come to the Musters, and diswadinge others asking them if they woulde goe see a footeball playe."[95] In 1600, Robert Booth and others are up for playing "campball" at Cawston, Norfolk, while in 1614 Anthony Parre stands accused of, "disorderly camping, profaning the churchyard at Calthorp in Norfolk, dirtying the clothes of women and maids there, and hurling the football at the head of Thomas Webster."[96,97,98] Sometime later, parishioners in Great Shelford, Cambridgeshire, are engaged in sabbath football against Little Shelford.[99] They are probably at camping, as a camping close is recorded in Little Shelford in 1775.[100] In 1609, twelve men from Thirsk, in Yorkshire, are charged with Sabbath football.[101] This may be reasonable execution of the law, but it is stretching it to indict two men for watching football in Bedfordshire; similarly a man in Guisborough, Yorkshire, who is guilty of "making a banquett for football players on the Sabaoth."[102]

Youths in London can be insolent. Servants and apprentices throw punches at constables and stones at the dog-killer. They discharge guns in the streets, throw turnips and snowballs at passers-by, and fireworks into passing carriages. Some pull down the Oxford gallows.[103] In 1621,

---

94 Manning, R.B., *Poachers and Keepers: A Social and Cultural History of Unlawful Hunting in England 1485–1640*. Oxford University Press, 1993. p. 189.

95 'Sessions, 1615: 1 and 2 August', in *County of Middlesex. Calendar To the Sessions Records: New Series, Volume 2, 1614–15*, ed. William Le Hardy (London, 1936), *British History Online* https://www.british-history.ac.uk/middx-sessions/vol2/pp344-350. Accessed 19 October 2024.

96 Dymond, D., *A Lost Social Institution: The Camping Close*. Rural History, 1990, 1:2, pp. 171–172.

97 Ibid, p. 172.

98 In 1839, another Thomas Webster displayed his painting *Football* at the Royal Academy Exhibition. It now hangs in the National Football Museum in Manchester.

99 Hessayon, A., *Gold Tried in the Fire*. Routledge, Abingdon, Oxon, 2016. p. 78.

100 Wale, J.H., *My Grandfather's Pocket-book*. Chapman & Hall Ltd., London, 1883. p. 176.

101 Marples, M., *A History of Football*. Secker & Warburg, London, 1954. p. 55.

102 Ibid, p. 55.

103 Griffiths, P., *Youth and Authority: Formative Experiences in England 1560–1640*. Oxford University Press, 1996. pp. 123, 128.

London's Common Council issues orders, "for my Lord Maior's day." Unruly children, servants, and apprentices are to allow ambassadors and noble persons to pass unhindered, and "should neither throw nor shoote anything at them … nor should use in the Exchange nor in any streete or lane … any uncivill sports as trapp, squibbes, football or the like."[104] Five years later, a Finsbury farmer protests that he "susteined much losse and damage" by "football play, trapp and catt, and other annoyances."[105]

Misadventures continue. In Groton, Suffolk, in 1604, "one Sewell was so bruysed through a fall which he had in Camping that he died thereof."[106] Five years earlier, another Sewell, from Great Dunmow, on the Essex-Suffolk border is fined 12s for playing football, assault, affray, and libel.[107,108] Similarly, in 1615, in Navestock, south Essex, (a village with a camping close),[109] Henry Millicent is killed during a game by a butcher's elbow.[110] In 1619, Sir Roger Townsend begins construction on the family seat of Raynham Hall, Norfolk, to the design of Inigo Jones. Consecrated stone is used from Coxford Abbey, which was dissolved in the Henrician Reformation and later passed to Townsend. Starting with the steeple, the first stone removed breaks a man's leg. "They proceeded in the Work, and overthrowing the Steeple, it fell upon a House by, and breaking it down, slew in it one Mr *Seller* that lay lame in it of a broken Leg gotten at Foot-ball, others having saved themselves by Fright and Flight."[111] It is not all bad news. In 1625, a thirteen-year-old student at St John's College, Cambridge, runs out of the college's tennis court to retrieve a ball. He falls in the Cam and is fished out "swolne and black", but makes a full recovery.[112]

The gouging of England by the Black Death creates social turmoil for decades. The blurring of class allows Norfolk peasant Clement

---

104 Ibid, p. 127.

105 Ibid, p. 138.

106 Dymond, D., *A Lost Social Institution: The Camping Close*. Rural History, 1990, 1:2, p. 181.

107 Krehbiel, D., *Heddwch! Heddwch! Sport and Cultural Identity in Early Modern Wales*. Unpublished MA thesis, University of North Carolina, 2006. pp. 41–42.

108 Eleven days' wages for a skilled tradesman.

109 Dymond, D., *A Lost Social Institution: The Camping Close*. Rural History, 1990, 1:2, p. 181.

110 *Essex Archives Online*. https://www.essexarchivesonline.co.uk/result_details.aspx?ThisRecordsOffSet=3&id=343299. Accessed 25 October 2023.

111 Spelman, H., *The History and Fate of Sacrilege*. John Hartley, London, 1698. p. 268.

112 Heywood, J., Wright, T. (ed.)., *Cambridge University Transactions*. 2 Vols. Henry G. Bohn, London, 1854. Vol. 2. pp. 329–330.

Paston to marry into a family connected enough to send his son to law school.[113] It takes the Pastons just one generation to rise from peasants to gentry. Within years the first Paston Letter (correspondence between the Paston family, providing a fascinating glimpse into the day-to-day lives of everyday people, from 1422–1509) is written. A collection of lesser-known Paston Letters date from the seventeenth century. By 1626, William Paston is a knight, and Katherine a lady. In February, she conveys sad news to her son, a student at Cambridge: "thy cosine Gawdy is a widow … he died of a consumption: his mother towld me onc that he gott that surfitt with tvoo violent playing at tenis. I thinke I towld the of it onc before, desiring that thow sholdest beware of the too great and continuall exercise of it." She adds, with maternal prerogative: "If thou lovest my liffe lett me intreat thee to be very Carfull of thy self for over heating thy blud."[114]

Later letters chart their ongoing ascent. In 1671, another William marries Charlotte Howard, the illegitimate daughter of Charles II and the Viscountess Shannon. Eight years later, his father becomes the 1st Earl of Yarmouth. In April 1671, William writes to his mother from France: "I doe not mean to be idle, but I will ply my French mightily and will learn tenis and lim[n]ing if there be such a master."[115] William is certainly idle when he returns. He shares his father's proclivity for financial bungling, doubling down on the debts he inherits. On Christmas Day 1732, having survived all male heirs, William dies, and the Paston family, who turned ghosts into the living, turn to ghosts.[116]

In 1605, Henry Peacham publishes a book on drawing and limning. He defends arts, "wrought with the hand …I see no reason why nature should be so much wronged … no more disgrace to a Lord to draw a fair picture, then to cut his Hawks meat, or play at footeball with his men."[117] Achilles, he adds, cooked for his guests, and Homer was a shipwright.

---

113 Weir, G., *Spelling, Punctuation and Material Culture in the Later Paston Letters*. Unpublished PhD thesis, University of Glasgow, 2018. n.p. https://theses.gla.ac.uk/30912/. Accessed 12 October 2024.

114 *This is Paston*. https://www.thisispaston.co.uk/index.php. Accessed 12 October 2024.

115 Ibid.

116 Weir, G., *Spelling, Punctuation and Material Culture in the Later Paston Letters*. Unpublished PhD thesis, University of Glasgow, 2018. n.p. https://theses.gla.ac.uk/30912/. Accessed 12 October 2024.

117 Peacham, H., *The Art of Drawing with the Pen, and Limming in Water Colours*. Richard Braddock, London, 1606. p. 3.

A few years later, Peacham publishes a book of emblems. These books comprise pictures containing a heraldic device with a title above and a poem beneath. *Divitiae* (Riches) has the following poem:

> The country Swaines, at footeball heere are seene,
> Which each gapes after, for to get a blow,
> The while some one, away runnes with it cleane,
> It meetes another, at the goale below
> Who never stirrd, one catcheth heere a fall,
> And there one's maimd, who never saw the ball.
> This worldly wealth, is tossed too and fro,
> At which like Brutes, each strives with might and maine,
> To get a kick, by others overthrow,
> Heere ones fetch't up, and there another slaine,
> With eager hast, and then it doth affront
> Some stander by, who never thought upon't.[118]

The poem mentions a goal and kicking the ball. The illustration shows a three-a-side football game. A player kicks the ball up, and the other five battle for it, arms aloft. So, the ball is carried as well as kicked. The ball has the markings of a heraldic orb.[119] Football is making subtle hints. In 1613, eight years after Samuel Rowley, Shakespeare publishes *All Is True*, his own version of Henry VIII. During the first act of a performance at the Globe Theatre, a spark from a fake cannon takes hold in the thatched roof, "consuming within less than an hour the whole House to the very grounds."[120] The audience escapes unhurt, though they have "but two narrow doors to get out … one man had his breeches set on fire … a provident wit put it out with bottle[d] ale."

The Globe is rebuilt, but its soul has fled. When it reopens in 1614, Shakespeare is nowhere to be seen. Gossips say the fire destroyed his health. And his muse. It transpires he has quit the cut and thrust of the capital for the tranquil life of a country squire. But not even genius can un-kiss words: tragedian and tragedy are inseparable. An inferno sweeps

118 Peacham., H., *Minerva Britanna*. W. Dight, London, 1612. p. 81.

119 The football on William Jordan's (*Percussa Resurgo*) heraldic crest has the same design.

120 Lee, S., *A Life of William Shakespeare*. Lee, Smith, Elder and Co., London, 1899. pp. 448–449.

through Stratford-Upon-Avon, destroying fifty-four houses.[121] For Shakespeare, "the fire that's closest kept burns most of all." His income as a leaseholder is threatened by field enclosures, and his freehold interests and pastureland may follow. The suffocating disputes hound Shakespeare to his grave. Life carries on in Stratford. The following year, two aldermen approach the workers and try to stop their enclosure work. When both are thrown to the ground, the architect of the scheme laughs at them "and said they were very good footeball players."[122] Two decades later, in the Fens of East Anglia, the tables are turned on enclosures, and football stands centre stage. Shakespeare has his say on football. In *A Comedy of Errors*, one of the twin servants dislikes the way he is treated by his brother's mistress who has confused the two:

> Am I so round with you as you with me,
> That like a football you do spurn me thus?
> You spurn me hence, and he will spurn me hither.
> If I last in this service, you must case me in leather.[123]

Another servant is the target in *King Lear*. Furious at his daughter's retainer, Lear strikes him. When the servant complains he does not like being hit, the Earl of Kent trips him and jibes, "Nor tripped neither, you base Football plaier."[124] Shakespeare's plays are sprinkled with children's games, boards games, and sporting references.[125] Bowls and tennis receive far more attention than football. Bowls is most popular, appearing in *Love's Labour's Lost*, *King Richard II*, *The Tempest*, *Coriolanus*, *Cymbeline*, *The Winter's Tale*, and most famously, *Hamlet*: "To sleep, perchance to dream—ay, there's the rub."[126] Tennis appears in *King Henry IV Part II*, *Pericles*, *King Henry V*, *Much Ado About Nothing*,

---

121 Ibid, pp. 466–467.

122 Bearman, R., *William Combe's Attempt to Enclose Open Fields at Welcombe, Stratford-upon-Avon, 1614–1619*. Midland History, 2021, 46:1, p. 44.

123 Cunningham, H., *The Works of William Shakespeare. A Comedy of Errors*. Methuen and Co., London, 1907. Act 1, Sc 2, lns 82–85.

124 *Mr. William Shakespeares Comedies, Histories, & Tragedies*. Isaac Jaggard, and Ed. Blount, London, 1623. Act 1, Sc 4, ln. 50.

125 See: Thiselton-Dyer, T.F., *Folk-lore of Shakespeare*. Harper & Brothers, New York, 1884.

126 The rub of the green. *Hamlet* has another bowling reference: "And bowl the round knave down the hill of heaven." Act 2, Sc 2, ln. 487.

King Henry VIII, *The Two Noble Kinsmen,* and *Hamlet*. Elsewhere, troll-my-dames in *The Winter's Tale*,[127] tick-tack in *Measure For Measure*, foot races in *The Taming of the Shrew*, nine men's morris in *A Midsummer Night's Dream*,[128] quintain in *As You Like It*, shovelboard in *The Merry Wives of Windsor*,[129] blindman's bluff in *Hamlet*, leap-frog in *Henry V*, bo-peep and handy-dandy in *King Lear*, "dun is in the mire"[130] in *Romeo and Juliet*, push-pin and hide-and-seek in *Love's Labour's Lost*, tray-trip, cherry-pit, and parish-top[131] in *Twelfth Night*, and filliping up the toad, quoits, see-saw, shove-groat, and span-counter[132] in *King Henry IV Part II*. There is chess in *The Tempest* and *King John*, tables in *Love's Labour's Lost* and *The Two Noble Kinsmen*, prison base in *The Two Gentlemen of Verona* and *Cymbeline*, wrestling in *As You Like It* and *Troilus and Cressida*, snowball fights in *Merry Wives of Windsor* and *Pericles*, stoolball and barley-break in *The Two Noble Kinsmen*, and flap-dragon in *Love's Labour's Lost*, *A Winter's Tale*, and *King Henry IV Part II*. Other pastimes mentioned or alluded to include bear-baiting, bull-baiting, cockfighting, bat-fowling, falconry, coursing, hawking, hunting, angling, archery, jousting, quintain, horse racing, fencing, dice, and cards.[133]

Umpire appears five times in the sense of an impartial arbitrator of competing sorrows.[134] Its first known use in sport is in 1706.[135] In the anthology of poems *Passionate Pilgrim* Shakespeare succinctly summarises life: "Youth is full of sport, Age's breath is short."[136,137] The mention of prison base in *The Two Gentlemen of Verona*, first published

127 A form of bagatelle.

128 Tick-tack and nines men morris are board games.

129 Backgammon.

130 Players compete to lift a heavy log and carry it off.

131 A large wooden spinning top kept in parishes, allowing exercise for peasants to keep them warm in winter.

132 A version of marbles.

133 The card games primero, noddy, bone-ace, laugh and lay down, and outvied are named; and the dice games hazard, tray-trip, and novum.

134 Originally *numpire* from *nonpir* "odd man", via *noumpere*. Oumpere appeared in the last quarter of the fourteenth century; *noumpere* disappeared by the end of the fifteenth. In: Transactions of the American Philological Association, 1891, Vol. 12, p. 272.

135 Similarly, boxing someone's ear is mentioned eight times, a century before the name is adopted by the sport.

136 Irving, H., *The Complete Works of William Shakespeare*. P.F. Collier and Son Company, New York, n.d., p. 1274.

137 All twenty poems in *Passionate Pilgrim* were originally ascribed to Shakespeare. Only five have since been authenticated, including the one the excerpt is taken from.

in 1598 but believed to have been written earlier, is only the fourth mention of a base game in history. Shakespeare gives us insight into games of the day and their popularity. Football gets as many mentions as chess and snowball fights. While sticking and kicking games are mentioned and a carrying game is not, football would have incorporated carrying, certainly folk football. Of note, when Hamlet and Horatio are in the graveyard, Hamlet bemoans the bones, asking in anguish if they were only good for loggets. A minute later, he is holding Yorick's skull. In the next (final) scene, before all hell breaks loose, Hamlet tells Horatio how he discovered the king's plot against him. "Ho!" he laments, "such bugs and goblins in my life." A few years later, the poet John Davis writes of hobgoblins: "Here, boisterous Bugbeares do at foot-ball play, With a still-tost and tumbled groning Ghost."[138]

There is bite in Shakespeare's *Antony and Cleopatra*. While Mark Antony gets to reference the children's game muss, the cheating game fast and loose, and allude to the card game trump, Cleopatra has the better of it. Awaiting news of her lover, Cleopatra is restless. She turns to address her friend:

> Cleo. Let it alone; let's to billiards: come, Charmian.
> Char. My arm is sore; best play with Mardian.
> Cleo. As well a woman with an eunuch play'd
> As with a woman. Come, you'll play with me, sir?
> Mar. As well as I can, madam.[139]

A minute later, a messenger arrives with news that Mark Antony has married Octavia. Cleopatra is incandescent. Infuriated by the bumbling messenger, she knocks him to the floor, hits him, then threatens to kick his eyes around like footballs:

> Hence, Horrible villain! or I'll spurn thine eyes
> Like balls before me; I'll unhair thy head:
> Stage direction: *She hales him up and down.*[140,141]

---

138 Davies, J., *Humours heav'n on earth with the civile warres of death*. Adam Islip, London, 1609. st. 176.

139 Shakespeare, W., *Antony and Cleopatra*. Folio 1, 1623. Act II, Sc 5, lns 1029–1033.

140 Ibid, 1105–1107.

141 Spurn in this context means to kick, and hales to drag (it is not a reference to Scottish football).

Cleopatra saves her best for last:

> Thou shalt be whipp'd with wire, and stew'd in brine,
> Smarting in ling'ring pickle.[142]

Ten of Shakespeare plays mention monsters, which remain an incredible if not implausible possibility. Excitement, then, when one is seen in St Leonard's forest, in Sussex. Three eyewitnesses describe a nine-foot scaly red and black "dragon": "It is of countenance very proud, and at the sight or hearing of men and Cattell, will raise his necke upright, and seeme to listen and looke about with great arrogancy: There are likewise on either side of it discovered two great bunches, so big as a large foote-ball, and (as some thinke) will in time grow to wings. … He will cast his venome about foure rodde[143] from him, as by woefull experience it was proved on the bodie of a man and woman comming that way, who afterward was found dead, being poyson'd and very much swelld, but not preyd upon."[144]

The gods are capricious. And spiteful. Spain's greatest writer, Miguel de Cervantes, dies within twenty-four hours of Shakespeare. In 1687, his unparalleled work of genius, *Don Quixote*, is debased into an English version, made "according to the Humour of our Modern Language." Basilio and Quiteria are replaced by childhood sweethearts, Basil and Maudlin. Both are broken-hearted when her father chooses a wealthy farmer's son, Martin, as her husband. The wedding is to be lavish, with "all the Fidlers and Minstrels I' the Countrey … Fellows to daunce upon the Ropes … juggling tricks … Jack-puddings and Merry-Andrews … Dauncing, Jumping, Hot-cockles, moulding of Cockle bread, Stool ball and Cudgel Playing." Basil is crushed. Martin is wealthier, but Basil is superior in all other respects: "he is by much the handsomer of the Two, and as active as a *Norfolk* Tumbler: For he will pitch a Bar the length of *Cheapside*; will kick ye a Camping-ball over Salisbury Spire."[145,146,147]

---

142 Shakespeare, W., *Antony and Cleopatra*. Folio 1, 1623. Act 2, Sc 5, lns 1108–1109.

143 Approximately fifty feet.

144 Anon., *True and wonderful, A discourse relating to a strange monstrous serpent or dragon, lately discovered.* John Trundle, London, 1614. n.p.

145 J.P., *The History of the most Renowned Don Quixote of La Mancha: And his Trusty Squire Sancho Pancha*. Tho. Hodgkin, London, 1687. p. 380.

146 Jack-puddings and Merry-Andrews were buffoons or jesters.

147 In the original, Basilio is described as a "gran jugador de pelota", a great ball player.

Among other adventures of the indefatigable knight, characters are footballed, bones are tennis-balled, and the Ladies of the Palace are bewitched with beards, which are described as "troublesome Stool-ball-stuffing."

~

A 1614 monograph mentions the prohibition of such sporting dives as dicing houses, tennis courts, and bowling alleys. Balls and rackets are also referenced.[148] Gambling is endemic in bowling alleys. In 1628, John Earle writes: "A Bowle Alley is the place where there are three things throwne away beside Bowls. To wit, time, money, and curses … the best sport in it is the Gamesters, and he enjoyes it that looks on and bets not."[149] The most poignant sporting metaphor is reserved for the bowling den. A veteran reflects on his youth when, "stuft with enuie and ambition", he joins the army:

"They usde me very curteously and gentleman-like awhile, like an old cunning Bowler to fetch in a yong kettling [inexperienced] Gamster, who will suffer him to win one Six-penny game at the first, and then lurch him in Sixe pounds afterward: and so they plaide wish [sic] me, still training me … into farre déeper and deadlier Battayles, where like villainous cheating Bowlers, they lurcht me of two of my best Limbes, *viz.* My right Arme, and right Legge, that so of a man of war, I became in shew a monster of warre."[150]

The same book describes the unrelenting misery of peasants:

"We plodded home to our Ploughs, carrying these heavy newes to our wives, … of our oppressions to come, by the burthen of uncharitable Fines … what a sad Christmas we al kept in the Countrie, without either Carrols, Wassel Bowles, dauncing of Sellengers round in Mooneshine nights about May-Poles, Shoeing the Mare, Hoodman blind, Hot-cockles, or any of our old Christmas Gambols."[151,152]

Dice makes history in 1622, when it becomes the first game mentioned in a newspaper. London's *Weekly* News reports that after hanging twenty-two French sailors, seventy of the guilty Dutch are made to roll dice to

---

148 Anon., *A Publication of His Ma'ties Edict*. Robert Barker, London, 1613. pp. 117–118.

149 Arber, E. (ed.)., *Micro-Cosmographie*. s.n., London, 1868. p. 61.

150 Middleton, T., *Father Hubburd's Tales: or The Ant and the Nightingale*. T.C., London, 1604. n.p.

151 Ibid.

152 Sellinger's Round was an immensely popular tune with an accompanying round dance.

see which twenty-two will swing in revenge.[153] The paper also carries news that two famous pirates—Captains Sampson and Ward—and many of their crew "are lately dead of plague." Elsewhere, pirates capture a galleon transporting artillery and a Spanish carrack carrying chests of gold and silver coins. Contemporary papers are packed with international politics and endless wars. And editors know their readers relish salacious witch trials. After a trip abroad, King James VI of Scotland becomes fascinated with witchcraft, sparking an epidemic of trials. Bizarrely, he is involved in interrogations. He even writes a book on the subject, *Daemonologie*.[154]

When James becomes king of England, he is too preoccupied with Catholic conspirators to worry about witches, though a trial crosses his path in 1605. Its origins lie in a 1598 football match in Oxfordshire. After his son gets into a fight with the Gregory brothers, Brian Gunter, the village's richest citizen, draws his dagger. He fatally strikes both brothers on the head with the pommel.[155] He goes unprosecuted, and a simmering blood feud ensues. In 1604, Gunter concocts a story that his daughter, Anne, has been demonically possessed by witches and gets her to name Elizabeth Gregory as one. It does not help Elizabeth's cause that she is widely regarded as "a notorious scolding body, & a vile curser and blasphemer."[156] Gunter has connections. His son-in-law is Regius Professor of Divinity at Oxford University, which ensures a high-profile trial with a cast of university witnesses for the prosecution. But Anne does a poor impersonation of possession at the trial, and Gunter gets pushy with the judges.[157] Elizabeth is acquitted.

Gunter doubles down. He secures a meeting with James I during the king's visit to the university, hopeful the champion of witchfinders will step in. But James is as interested in unveiling frauds as he is in rooting out the malefic.[158] And James smells a rat. At their fourth meeting,

153 *Weekly News*. 18 October 1622. n.p.

154 James R^{x}., *Daemonologie*, Robert Walde-graue, London, 1597.

155 Sharpe, J., *The Bewitching of Anne Gunter: A Horrible and True Story of Deception, Witchcraft, Murder, and the King of England*. Routledge, Abingdon, Oxon, 2000. p. 17.

156 Ibid, p. 48.

157 Ibid, pp. 133–135.

158 Ibid, p. 178.

tempted by the dangling of a potential suitor, wowed by the king and his dazzling court, and exhausted by her ceaseless theatrics, Anne confesses to the deception.[159] Never a dull moment for James. Three weeks later, he is knee-deep in the Gunpowder Plot.

Witchcraft sells papers, but sport only makes the news if it concerns nobility or litigation. Contemporary books and journals are key sources. Robert Burton's *The Anatomy of Melancholy* is the first textbook of psychiatry in the western world. Surely, this is a man who has suffered. Melancholy is "a perpetual anguish of the soul[160] … the Quintessence of adversity … no torture of body like unto it, no strappados, hot-irons … all other diseases whatsoever, are but flea-bitings to … this ocean of misery."[161] Burton advocates outdoor pursuits to maintain psychological health, including those "which are the common recreations of the countryfolkes." Football is included, hurling too, as well as wrestling, running, leaping, pitching bars, keelpins, tronks, and wasters.[162,163] A contemporary book of emblems reflects Burton's sense of futility:

> When we observe the *Ball*, how to and fro
> The *Gamesters* force it; we may ponder thus:
> That whil'st we live we shall be play'd with so,
> And that the *World* will make her *Game* of us.
> *Adversities*, one while our hearts constraine
> To stoope, and knock the Pavements of *Despaire*:
> *Hope*, like a Whirle-wind mounts us up againe,
> Till oft it lose us in the empty ayre.[164]

---

159 Ibid, p. 185.

160 Burton, R., *The Anatomy of Melancholy*. John Litchfield and James Short, Oxford, 1621. p. 46.

161 Ibid, p. 274.

162 Ibid, p. 342.

163 Keel pins is similar to kayles, an early form of skittles, using wooden sticks rather than bowls. A set of keelpins dug up from peat on Tronmacannie Moor, Galloway, consists of an eighteen-inch oak ball and seven thirteen-inch conical wooden pins with a circular top. In: Girvan, R. (ed.)., *Ratis Raving and Other Early Scots Poems on Morals*. William Blackwood & Sons Ltd., Edinburgh, 1939. p. 120. The game of tronks is difficult to determine. The Middle Dutch word *tronc* means tree trunk, prison, dungeon, or stocks. It may, therefore, be a version of throwing tree trunks, akin to tossing the caber. It could also mean "dun in the mire." Wasters were wooden swords.

164 Wither, G., *A Collection of Emblemes, Ancient and Moderne*. A.M., London, 1635. p. 16.

The proposed act to keep "holy the Sabbaoth Day", forgets to ban football in 1614.[165] Thank heavens Mr Glanvyle is at the House of Commons sitting to ensure its inclusion, and Mr Fanshaw for protesting that the penalty for breaches is "but a mockery". James heeds his mercantile subjects, and limits football in London: "Whereas greate disorders and tumults doe often arise and happen within the streetes and lanes neere adjoyninge to ye Cittye of London by playinge at the foote-ball: It is now Ordered that henceforthe all Constables doe from tyme to tyme represse and restrayne all manner of Footeball-playe in the lanes and streetes adjoyninge to the Cittye of London."[166] Still, James loves sports. This is no ban. He is asking for occasional restraint.

In 1611, Puritan propaganda is published as a beneficent dialogue between the author and successive pedlars. A character asks what happens if someone rings the church bells, "to call from plough to pancakes, and from thence to breake-bones, I meane to foote-ball, where some have had their necks broke."[167] Pancakes. A Shrovetide football reference, for sure. Within seven years the influential Puritan movement has eliminated Sunday amusements. King James retaliates. *The Book of Sports* lists what can be enjoyed on Sundays:[168] dancing (too carnal for Puritans), May games (too pagan), festivals (too depraved), morris dancing (too satanic) are in, bear-baiting and bowling are out. Football (too violent) slips in under the sanctioned "other games" section. The text outsmarts the Puritans. James argues that a lack of sport will lead to "filthy tipplings and drunkenness, and breed a number of idle and discontented speeches in their Ale-houses."[169] James is too canny to take sport from his subjects on their only day off. He has his hands full with Catholics and Puritans and needs unwavering support. Lose the people, lose the throne. Besides,

---

165 "House of Commons Journal Volume 1: 07 May 1614", in *Journal of the House of Commons: Volume 1, 1547–1629*, (London: His Majesty's Stationery Office, 1802), 476. *British History Online*, accessed February 16, 2024, http://www.british-history.ac.uk/commons-jrnl/vol1/p476.

166 "Middlesex Sessions Rolls: 1615", in *Middlesex County Records: Volume 2, 1603–25*, ed. John Cordy Jeaffreson (London: Middlesex County Record Society, 1887), 107–119. *British History Online*, accessed February 16, 2024, http://www.british-history.ac.uk/middx-county-records/vol2/pp107-119.

167 Spicer, J., *The sale of salt. Or The seasoning of soules*. Nicholas Okes, London, 1611. p. 408.

168 *The King's Majesties Declaration to His Subjects, Concerning Lawfull Sports to bee Used.* Bonham Norton and John Bill, London, 1618.

169 Marples, M., *A History of Football*. Secker and Warburg, London, 1954. p. 56.

one day he might have need of a nation of folk footballers unafraid of a good fight.

The declaration invokes a paradoxical response in Richard Conder of Croydon-cum-Clopton, in Cambridgeshire. "When I was a young man, I was greatly addicted to foot-ball playing; and as the custom was in our parish, and many others, the young men, as soon as church was over, took a foot-ball and went out to play. Our minister often remonstrated against our breaking the sabbath, which however had little effect, only my conscience checked me at times." When his minister is forced to read out *The Book of Sports* from the pulpit, Condor is "seized with a chill and horror not to be described …iniquity is established by a law, and sinners are hardened in their sinful ways … And from that time I never had the least inclination to take a foot-ball in hand."[170]

Sabbath culprits are plentiful in Nottinghamshire. Thomas Urrie, of Weston, admits to watching "foote bale playinge at Eveninge prayer uppon a Sundaye" in 1605.[171] Ten others are indicted for the same offence. In Nottingham, in 1608, thirty-five men are charged with "prophaninge the Sabaoth by theire beinge at the footebale in tyme of divine service."[172] Eleven admit only that "theie were in the meadowes lookinge uppon the footebale players upon Maye daye last past", four others "that theie were mett cominge from the footebale play." In 1609, eleven of Newark admit "that uppon Candlemas daye laste paste, theie and everye of them dyd playe at footebale & that theie weere not at divine service the same daye."[173] The following year, Hendry Cockit and John Child are charged with Sabbath "football" in the churchyard of Rolleston.[174]

In 1613, six "inhabitants" of Warsop, Nottinghamshire, admit to "playinge at footebale in the church and churchyard",[175] while in July 1620, John Cob of Cottam strikes Leonard Keaworthe while at "footeballe in the Churche yard upon Fastinge tuesdaie laste paste", with

---

170 Conder, E.R., *Josiah Conder. A Memoir.* John Snow, London, 1857. p. 3.

171 *Transactions of the Thoroton Society of Nottinghamshire.* Thoroton Society, 1927. Vols. 30–32, p. 42.

172 Ibid, p. 43.

173 Nottinghamshire History. http://www.nottshistory.org.uk/articles/tts/tts1926/actbooks2.htm. Accessed 12 May 2023.

174 Holy Trinity, Rolleston. http://www.rollestonchurch.org.uk/churchwarden.html. Accessed 25 August 2023.

175 *Transactions of the Thoroton Society of Nottinghamshire.* Thoroton Society, 1927. Vols. 30–32, p. 43.

three others.[176] Another Shrove Tuesday game for the inventory. Finally, when several men stand accused of playing football in the churchyard, they claim they stood by "while others did playe and some tymes as the ball came towards them they did strike it." Two of them are charged "for playing at Foote ball and fighting in the Church Yarde."[177] Perhaps Thomas Tonge and his friends would have escaped censure for "ringing on the Sabbaoth, for playing at Footeball in the Church Yarde" in Retford, Nottinghamshire, in 1634, had they not then used the bell ropes "to draw a plough after the manner of beasts about the Towne and church-yard."[178] They escape with a fine. Other Sabbath miscreants are punished for bear-baiting, shovelboard, nine holes, backgammon, "castinge" a bowl in a "quarrellinge" manner, attending a play, morris dancing, fishing, ferreting, catching larks, and playing bagpipes.[179]

Morris dancing's anarchic ribaldry ensures its popularity. While its supposed pagan origins are a myth (the first reference is from 1458) its indecency appals the clergy. Morris skips about the nettled Church, an ever-present at festivals. Around 1573, the Archbishop of York instructs ministers not to "suffer anye lords of misrule or sowmerr Lordes or Ladyes or anye disguised persons or others in christmasse or at may games or any minstrels morrie dauncers or others at Ryshebearings or at any other tymes to come unreverentlye into anye churche or chappell or churchyeard and there daunce or playe and unseemly partes with scoffes, jeastes or rybualde talke."[180,181] In 1585, "Church Ales, May games, morish dances, and other vaine pastimes upon the Sabath Dayes" are considered a "sacrifice to the Devil with Drunkeness and Dancing and other ungodly wantonnes."[182,183] As late as 1655, Puritans consider

176 Nottinghamshire History. http://www.nottshistory.org.uk/articles/tts/tts1926/actbooks2.htm. Accessed 12 May 2023.

177 *Transactions of the Thoroton Society of Nottinghamshire*. Thoroton Society, 1927. Vols. 30–32, p. 144.

178 Ibid, p. 144.

179 Nottinghamshire History. http://www.nottshistory.org.uk/articles/tts/tts1926/actbooks2.htm. Accessed 12 May 2023.

180 Johnston, A.F, Rogerson, M. (eds.), *Records of Early English Drama. York: I, Introduction, The Records*. 3 Vols. University of Toronto, Buffalo, 1979. Vol. 1. p. 358.

181 The Lord of Misrule was a villager picked to preside over the Feast of Fools. "Lordes and Ladyes" were the children picked to be the king and queen of their village during summer games.

182 Forrest, J., *The History of Morris Dancing, 1438–1750*. University of Toronto Press, Buffalo, 1999. p. 4.

183 Church ales were similar to modern church fêtes. In addition to food and entertainment, large amounts of alcohol were consumed, usually provided by the church at reduced rates to fund overheads and repairs.

maypoles and morris dancing as "heathenish and unlawfull Customs."[184] Morris dancing has another trick up his gathered sleeves: he knows when to rein in the sauciness; payments to morris dancers pepper the accounts of monarchs and nobles.

Locals are charged with playing camp-ball in the churchyard of Wetheringsett, in Suffolk, in 1611.[185] The following year, James Wilson is brought before Middlesex sessions, for gathering on a Sabbath "very many unknown persons in a certain place called Eely Field [Holborn], and did play with them a certain unlawful game called football."[186] At the April sessions, Agnes Godfrey is accused of killing three men by "practising certain devilish arts, called witchcraft."[187] She is acquitted of all three charges. Pity William Miller. He should not have stolen that cow. The Middlesex sessions casually record his final moments: "He asked for the book, read it and was burnt."[188] It could be worse. A banished seminary priest found in England is casually sentenced to "be hanged, dismembered, disbowelled, beheaded, quartered &c."[189,190]

The Water Poet, John Taylor, thinks highly of footballers. Discussing worthy fellows who alone may board the "fellow-ship": "she will be man'd and laden with none but with fellowes, she caries none but Foot-ball players, and Watermen."[191] Elsewhere in his collected works can be found: "fortune … hath play'd at Foot-ball with great Monarchies"; "like a foot-ball crams the vaulty skies"; and "to bandy balls of blasphemy."[192,193,194] One man is fortune's tennis ball; another is tossed "like time's Footeball."[195,196]

---

184 Ibid, p. 4.

185 Dymond, D., *A Lost Social Institution: The Camping Close*. In: *Rural History*, 1990, 1:2, p. 171.

186 "Middlesex Sessions Rolls: 1612", in *Middlesex County Records: Volume 2, 1603–25*, ed. John Cordy Jeaffreson (London: Middlesex County Record Society, 1887), 78–84. *British History Online*, accessed February 11, 2024, http://www.british-history.ac.uk/middx-county-records/vol2/pp78–84.

187 Ibid.

188 Ibid.

189 Ibid.

190 The sentenced are hung until nearly dead. This allows them to suffer the agonies of having their genitalia cut off and disembowelment.

191 Taylor, J., *All the VVorkes of Iohn Taylor, The Water Poet*. John Beale, Elizabeth Alde, Bernard Alsop, and Thomas Fawcet, London, 1630. *A Navy of Land Ships*. p. 86.

192 Ibid, *The Travels of Twelve-pence*. p. 73.

193 Ibid, *Laugh and Be Fat*. p. 73.

194 Ibid, *A Satyre*. p. 261. A play on bandy, the stick and ball game.

195 Ibid, *The Begger*. p. 101.

196 Ibid, *Farewell to the Tower-bottles*. p. 125.

In Taylor's *Sir Gregory Nonsence*, "They whorl'd the football of conspiring fate, and brake the shinnes of smugfac'd Mulciber",[197] while in his Sonnet 5: "Thou fortunes foot-ball, whom she us'd to toss, From wrong to wrong, from wo to wo againe."[198] Published in 1614, the anonymous *Philosopher's Banquet* includes the lines: "In every peddling Village, Borough, Towne, Ale plaid at foot-ball, and tript all down."[199]

Football is in its ascendancy. Hogging the news. By the late sixteenth century it has become the "biggest participation and spectator sport on Sundays."[200] Even so, some sports grab column space. In 1614, an organised stoolball match plays out between the villages of Pottersbury and Yardley Gobion, in Northamptonshire, one of the first organised games recorded in any sport.[201] Sabbath games are scurrilous enough for footnotes: cudgel players "whooping and hallo'ing" in the churchyard during service, twenty-two at bowls, William Brett trimming his bowling green.[202] Bowls merits a few sentences in a book on hunting, hawking, and angling: "the chusing of the Bowle is the greatest cunning; your flat Bowles being the best for close Allies [alleys], your round byazed Bowles for open Grounds of advantage,[203] and your round bowles like a Ball, for greene-swarthes that are plaine and level."[204]

Some prefer different Sabbath pursuits. Nicholas Crisp does not hold back when he is admonished for "playing with his pigs under a wall": "Shit on the church. What care I for the church?"[205] Sunday lust proves too much for others. Roger Walker "in carnal copulation with Dorothy the wife of Robert Shephard at divers times on Fridays and Sundays in prayer time"; Edward Wheatley and Robert Child's wife, the churchwarden having seen him come out of her back door; John Pippen

---

197 Ibid, *Sir Gregory Nonsence*. p. 4.

198 Ibid, *Sonnet 5*. p. 338.

199 Anon., *Philosopher's Banquet*. Nicholas Vavafour, London, 1633. p. 26.

200 Haigh, C., *The Plain Man's Pathways to Heaven: Kinds of Christianity in Post-Reformation England, 1570–1640*. Oxford University Press, 2007. p. 93.

201 Ibid, p. 84.

202 Ibid, p. 85.

203 The working classes were limited to uneven parks, whose bumps could be used to a player's advantage. This led to crown green bowling

204 Markham, G., *Country Contentments: Or, The Husbandmans Recreations*. Nicholas Okes, London, 1631. p. 58.

205 Haigh, C., *The Plain Man's Pathways to Heaven: Kinds of Christianity in Post-Reformation England, 1570–1640*. Oxford University Press, 2007. p. 85.

and Margaret Bacon in a ditch.[206] Others transgress in church: cracking nuts throughout the service, sticking a feather in a woman's hair, putting "lice upon the backs of one another." When Henry Enewe is reproved for talking during service, "he bade a turd for them."[207] Hopefully not for Richard Wright, who falls asleep during service, "and let out a very loud and beastly fart which caused laughter in the people." A sleeping man in Mucking, Essex, is no better, "letting go his water in great abundance, to the annoyance of those sat with him."[208]

Sabbath football hogs records and fills coffers; fines are fixed at 2s in Hexham, Northumberland.[209] In 1602, eleven are arraigned for playing in Lyndon, and nine for playing in North Luffenham, both in Rutland.[210] North Luffenham records other sins. In 1604, James Digby blows his horn in the churchyard during service, and in 1618 Richard Cooper swears at the churchwardens and says he would rather be excommunicated for three years than listen to the rector, adding that he does not care if he has to do penance every day.[211] A 1603 Northamptonshire match between Warmington and Clapton leads to the prosecution of eighteen spectators, and Francis Stradling is in trouble for selling ale at a football match between Slindon and Madehurst, Sussex, two more examples of organised fixtures.[212] Other Sunday matches play out in Amherst, Sussex, in 1630, and in Burnham, Essex, in 1638.[213] In 1632, a travelling reverend is in despair when Sabbath morris dancers, quaffers of ale, and football players tell him "wee know not that wee do ill."[214] The following year, John Honnicome and five others are arraigned in Worcestershire "concerning the usage of the unlawful game of footeball contrary to the Statutes of the land."[215] Statute or no, a character in a play that year remarks: "Your Lordship may make one at Football, Tis all the sport now

206 Ibid, p. 86.

207 Ibid, p. 87.

208 Ibid, pp. 87–90.

209 Marples, M., *A History of Football*. Secker & Warburg, London, 1954. p. 59.

210 Ibid, p. 93.

211 Ibid, pp. 189, 161.

212 Ibid, p. 93.

213 Ibid, p. 93.

214 Rogers, D., *A practicall catechisme*. John Norton, London, 1632. p. 41.

215 *Recognizance before John Charlett*. The National Archives: https://discovery.nationalarchives.gov.uk/details/r/e527e325-5e25-4317-aa1c-fb753c7408f1. Accessed 19 May 2023.

a dayes." The subsequent exchange reflects the prevailing bawdiness of the stage:

> *Dondolo.*
> Doe not women play too?
> *Grutti.*
> They are too light, quickly downe.
> *Morello.*
> Oyes, they are the best Gamesters of all,
> For though they often lye on the ground,
> Not one amongst a hundred will fall,
> But under her coates the Ball will [be] found.[216]

An ironmonger in Hemel Hempstead, "a man of a scandalous life" is fined and jailed for a number of offences, including "playing at 'Stoole' ball with the curate and others on a holiday."[217] On occasion, the Church gets to bless itself with smug satisfaction: "On Jan. 25. 1634. being the Lords day, in the time of the last great Frost 14. younge men presuming to play at football upon the yce on the river Trent, neere to Ganisborow, comming alltogether in a scuffle, the yce suddainly brake, and they were all drowned."[218] Another example of "Gods judgements upon Sabbath breakers" is given at Wicks in east Essex: "upon Whitsunday last in the afternoon two fellows meeting at football, the one killed the other."[219] Similarly, at Tidworth, Wiltshire, a Sabbath player breaks his leg, "which presently gangreenizing, he forthwith died thereof."[220]

In 1638, the Archdeacon of Suffolk issues a circular to his parishes: "Have any playes, feast, banquets, suppers, church ales, drinking, temporal courts, or leets, lay juries, exercise of dancing, stoole-ball, football, or the like, or any other profane usage been suffered to be kept

---

216 Shirley, J., *The bird in a cage*. B. Alsop. And T. Fawcet, London, 1633. n.p. Act 4, Sc 1

217 *Fifth Report of the Royal Commission on Historical Manuscripts*. Eyre & Spottiswoode, London, 1876. Part 1. p. 27.

218 Burton, H., *A Divine Tragedie lately acted*. J.F. Stam, Amsterdam, 1636. n.p.

219 Ibid.

220 Meriton, G., *Immorality, Debauchery, and Profaneness*. John Harris and Andrew Bell, London, 1698. p. 92.

in your Church, Chappell, or Churchyard?"[221] The same year, "footeball and stool ball" are played in the churchyard in March, Cambridgeshire, despite the Bishop of Ely frowning on "Chappell-yard … stoole-ball and foot-ball."[222,223] Dancing and fairs in churchyards are common practise in Wales, while the church in Barford-on-Avon in Wiltshire still bears marks made by fives players.[224] One exasperated vicar is buried where parishioners play ball, determined to end it from below and beyond.[225] Northamptonshire parishioners speak up, questioning the illegality of "ringing a peal or two, dancing, playing at football, barley-break … [on] Sunday after evening prayer."[226] In 1608, the vicar of Alton Pancras, Wiltshire, has the Church fuming, reprimanded for repairing to Cheselbourne "to football upon the sabbothe day", and "carried many parishioners with him."[227] Wiltshire churchwardens lean toward their parishioners. Those of Kingston Deverill refuse to prosecute Sabbath players, nor the tithingman of Fisherton Anger, a regular Sunday bowl player.[228] A Shrewton churchwarden allows his son to play trapball during divine service, another in Ludgershall is found with midsummer revellers on a Sunday, and one in Newton Toney misses service to attend a football match.[229]

In his 1612 book, *The Grammar Schoole*, John Brinsley mentions a stick and ball game. "The Schollers may be kept ever in their places, and hard to their labours, without that running out to Campo (as they terme it) at schoole times, and the manifold disorders thereof; as watching and striving for the clubbe."[230] Campo probably refers

221 Andrews, W. (ed.)., *Antiquities and Curiosities of the Church.* William Andrews and Co., London, 1897. p. 216.

222 Palmer, W. M., *Episcopal Visitation Returns for Cambridgeshire.* Cambridge, 1930. p. 52.

223 *Bishop Matthew Wren's Visitation Articles.* Records of Early English Drama Online. https://ereed.library.utoronto.ca/records/cambs-ridp292111096/. Accessed 21 October 2023.

224 Andrews, W. (ed.)., *Antiquities and Curiosities of the Church.* William Andrews and Co., London, 1897. p. 218.

225 Ibid, p 217.

226 Cressy, D., *Charles I and the People of England.* Oxford University Press, 2015. p. 271.

227 Bettey, J. H., *Rural Life in Wessex, 1500–1900.* Moonraker Press, 1987. p. 97; Haigh, C., *The Plain Man's Pathways to Heaven: Kinds of Christianity in Post-Reformation England, 1570–1640.* Oxford University Press, 2007. p. 93.

228 Underdown, D., *Revel, Riot, and Rebellion.* Oxford University Press, 1987. p. 94.

229 Ibid, p. 94.

230 Campagnac, E.T. (ed.)., *Ludus Literarius; or, The Grammar Schoole.* Constable & Co. Ltd., London, 1917. p. 299.

to the field the boys play in. That Brinsley taught in Leicestershire, suggests the prevailing dominance of stick and ball games in pockets of seventeenth century England.

~

John Chamberlain, a London gentleman who lives off his inheritance, writes to his friend, the future Secretary of State, Dudley Carleton, in 1600: "You may do well, if you have any idle time, to play the goode fellow and come and see our matches at football, for that and bowling wilbe our best intertainment."[231,232] Twelve years later, Carleton reports the death of the Scottish traitor Bothwell to James VI, by then King James I of England. The men of Kincaple, Fifeshire, are said to play football on Trinity Sunday that year.[233] The local game appears to be a regular Christmas feature. In 1618, it is named in the regional session minutes, ordering "that the superstitious observance of old rites and ceremonies expressly forbidden during the season called Yule be completely shunned and eschued."[234]

In 1600, Sir John Carmichael, the Scottish West March Warden, hosts a parley with Sandeis Ringan of the Armstrongs, a notorious family of outlaws. Carmichael's hopes of curbing the family's skulduggery are torpedoed when some of his men pour egg yolks into Ringan's scabbard. When Ringan draws his sword, he is incandescent and swears revenge.[235] That June, the Armstrongs attend "a grand foot-ball meeting, where the crime was concerted … The game of foot-ball, in particular … which continues to be a favourite Border sport, was the means of collecting together large bodies of moss-troopers, previous to any military exploit … when Sir Robert Carey was warden of the east marches … a great match at foot-ball at Kelso … was sufficient to excite his vigilance and his apprehension."[236] Two days later, Carmichael is ambushed by seventeen of the Armstrongs and slain with pistols and hackbuts. Ringan's son and a man known as "the Pecket" are arrested, tried, and sentenced.

231 Chamberlain is asking him to visit him in Knebworth, Hertfordshire, not London.

232 Williams, S. (ed.), *Letters Written by John Chamberlain*. J.B. Nichols and Sons, London, 1861. p. 70.

233 Magoun, F.P., *History of Football from the Beginnings to 1871*. Kölner anglistische arbeiten, 1938, Vols. 31–33. p. 91.

234 Ibid, p. 92.

235 Anderson, W., *The Scottish Nation*. A. Fullarton & Co., Edinburgh, 1860. p. 591.

236 Scott, W., *The Poetical Works of Sir Walter Scott*. Baudry's European Library, Paris, 1838. p. 50.

Their right hands are cut off before they are hanged and their corpses gibbeted.[237] While Border hostilities are fierce, feuds between Scottish and English officers are forbearing. Lord Scott of Buccleuch on one side and Emanuel Scrope on the other meet with their riders to discuss "their feats of robbery and fire-raising, and their duels, much as men might discuss a football match."[238]

In 1601, "pistolettis and hacquebuttis" are fired after a fallout during a "fute-ball" match between men of the master of Elphingstoun's estate in East Lothian and the locals.[239] More hackbuts and pistols, in 1610. Sir James Douglas of Drumlanrig Castle, Dumfries, files a complaint that William Kirkpatrick and others, "all armed with certain weapons and with hagbuts and pistolets [under the] pretext of the playing of a wood fute ball" arrive at the "Ball-grene" of the lands of Campbell, near the gate of the place of Drumlanrig and in a "bragging manner" make "provocatioun."[240] A wooden football needs gutsy players. Another altercation in 1624, this time in Ulladail, Fifeshire. Thomas Rose's recent bullying of Angus McRonald culminates in him brandishing his sword at a Sabbath church meeting and threatening to make a football of McDonald's head.[241] One of the Scottish noblemen charged with preventing raids on England is Sir Robert Kerr. In 1632, he writes to the Earl of Lothian about major renovations he is making to his house in Ancram, in the Scottish Borders. He mentions plans for "an utter [outer] green for football."[242] He adds that it would be used for his "heir to run at ring and glove, and play at football and these exercises which young men must have a place for, it being walld beyond the burne by the wayside that goeth up from the watter."[243] The green is extensive, large enough for a

237 Ibid, p. 153.

238 Lang, A., *History of Scotland from the Roman Occupation.* 4 Vols. Blackwood and Sons, Edinburgh and London. Vol. 2. 1546–1624. p. 522. TannerRitchie Publishing, Burlington, Ontario, Canada, 2014.

239 Masson, D. (ed.)., *The register of the Privy Council of Scotland.* 14 Vols. H.M. General Register House, Edinburgh, 1884. Vol. 6. 1599–1604. p. 262.

240 Magoun, F.P., *Scottish Popular Football, 1424–1815.* The American Historical Review, 1931, 37:1, p. 6.

241 Masson, D. (ed.)., *The register of the Privy Council of Scotland.* 14 Vols. H.M. General Register House, Edinburgh, 1896. Vol. 13. p. 456.

242 Laing, D. (ed.)., *Correspondence of Sir Robert Kerr, First Earl of Ancram and his son William, Third Earl of Lothian.* 2 Vols. R. & R. Clark, Edinburgh, 1875. Vol. 1. p. 67.

243 Ibid, p. 58.

horse rider to tilt at the ring. In 1620, John Gurdon is put to the horn (a public blast to denounce a rebel) for "ryding up and doun the ball grene of Kellie a long space" carrying hackbuts.[244]

In 1658, future judge Sir David Hume is studying at Edinburgh University. A college pitch had been approved by the town council as early as 1591, to be used by students on sanctioned days.[245] In an annual custom the university disapproves of, second-year students throw a football into the classroom of first-year students, and a match ensues.[246] Hume pledges an oath to play the banned match the following day.[247] Entreated not to go, Hume plays anyway. When he is sentenced to be whipped in his classroom for his misdeed, he refuses to consent. Hume is expelled (only to be readmitted after the intercession of a man of rank).

Sometime between 1672 and 1673, another Edinburgh University student Archibald Flint makes sketches of five sports: tennis, shooting, archery, table billiards, and football.[248] Francis Willughby provides the first clear drawing of a football pitch, in 1672, but it is Flint who first depicts men *playing* at football. Two goalposts, roughly ten feet in height (including supporting tripods) stand thirty feet apart in a field. Three crossbars span the posts, the lowest at the midway point. Two men in broad-brimmed hats are playing with a modern football-sized ball. The goals are fascinating. The tripods provide stability and transportability. Three theories have been posited for the crossbars, which appear too narrow to let a ball through.[249] Protecting breakables behind the goals, like windows, seems far-fetched if the goals are moveable. If the spaces between the crossbars *can* accommodate a ball, different points may be scored by kicking through the lower, wider space. If that were the case, one would expect the spaces to be of different sizes, creating three scoring values, but the upper two appear to be the same height and barely able to let a ball through. Moreover, if this was their function, one would expect

244 Masson, D. (ed.), *The register of the Privy Council of Scotland. 1619–1622.* 14 Vols. H.M. General Register House, Edinburgh, 1895. Vol. 12. p. 188.

245 Finlayson, C.P., *Illustration of Games by a Seventeenth Century Edinburgh Student.* The Scottish Historical Review, 1958, 37:123, p. 6.

246 Ibid, p. 6.

247 Hume, D., *Domestic Details by Sir David Hume of Crossrig.* T.G. Stevenson, Edinburgh, 1843. p. 6.

248 Finlayson, C.P., *Illustration of Games by a Seventeenth Century Edinburgh Student.* The Scottish Historical Review, 1958, 37:123, p. 3.

249 Ibid, pp. 7–8.

Flint to make it clear. On the other hand, the tripods appear detachable. If they were removed, the three spaces would be of equal height, suggesting the ball must be able to pass through them; this makes scoring possible but much more difficult.

In 1591, the college pitch is described as being "benorth the gallowis."[250] By Flint's time it is called Gallowgreen. Contemporary gallows consist of a horizontal beam supported by two vertical posts. Some have three levels like the Halifax gibbet and the generous Montfaucon gibbet, which accommodates forty-five. It is possible that the goal is a ghoulish representation of the local gallows, commissioned by indecorous students. Hangings continue at Gallow Green until 1865. The last to be "launched into eternity" is Dr Edward Pritchard, undone by an anonymous letter after poisoning his wife and mother-in-law with antimony.[251]

Football at Scottish schools and universities should not be underestimated; a rich history reflects football's popularity in Scotland, certainly around Edinburgh and south to the Borders. The city of Edinburgh is an early exemplar and is to be a key influencer in the development of the game. In the Latin version of James VI of Scotland and I of England's *Works*, football is termed *pila Scotica quae pede propellitur*: a Scottish ball propelled by the foot.[252] David Wedderburn, Master at Aberdeen Grammar School, publishes a Latin vocabulary in 1636. A few clues to how the game is played are revealed in the exercises: "Come! Choose sides", "pick your first man", "toss up the ball that we may begin the game", "you, keep the hail [be the goalkeeper]", "snatch the ball from that fellow if you can", "throw yourself against that man", "kick the ball", "this is the first hail", "some of the other side are getting behind us", "he is a good ball-man", and the perennial, "you aren't doing anything."[253]

Glasgow College seems to have taken football on later. There is evidence pupils at Glasgow Grammar School play in the late 1670s: the

250 Ibid, p. 6.

251 Cullen, W., *Some Reflections on the Case of Dr Pritchard.* Proceedings of the Royal College of Physicians of Edinburgh, 1998, 28, pp. 188–189.

252 Murray, D., *Memories of the Old College of Glasgow.* Jackson, Wylie, and Co., Glasgow, 1927. p. 425.

253 Magoun, F.P., *History of Football from the Beginnings to 1871.* Kölner anglistische arbeiten, 1938, Vols. 31–33, p. 94.

school's best scholar each year must pay for a football.[254] In 1686, students at Glasgow College engage in riotous behaviour on *Fasterns E'en*, which may have been attendant to a Shrove Tuesday football game. Payment of £17 8s is made for "what skaith [damage] the Collegians did to The town of Rutherglen at Fasterns-even."[255] A student at the end of the eighteenth century writes that it was "at a time when lectures and lecturers engaged far less of our attention than the delights of the foot-ball."[256] Old-style football, which falls under the umbrella of "hails", continues to be played there until the introduction of rugby and association football in 1870.[257] Even in 1857, "it was a rough and tumble game in which the contending sides swept across the low green … and back again like the hordes of Attila."[258] There were "regular games between two picked sides … the ball was kept going from nine o'clock until about three. All played in their ordinary clothes and some in their gowns. Tall silk hats were in fashion and used by most students … men at that time skated and played cricket in silk hats … The same thing went on at St Andrews … the gardener, George M'Vean, was an obliging man and kept the college football."[259,260]

In 1633, Scottish traveller William Lithgow pens an obsequious poem to the king. He complains that the youth of today have "growne effeminat, weare *Woemens* loks", adding:

> That Peace, and Idlenes, have spoyld my Youth.
> With *Cards* and *Drunkennesse,* lashivious *Lust:*
> And all *Prophanenes,* swearing and distrust:
> That now their Bodyes, are not half so strong.[261]

---

254 Fraser, W., *The Annandale family book of the Johnstones, Earls and Marquises of Annandale*. s.n., Edinburgh, 1894. p. 253.

255 Three weeks' wages for a skilled tradesman.

256 Murray, D., *Memories of the Old College of Glasgow*. Jackson, Wylie and Co., Glasgow, 1927. p. 442.

257 Ibid, p. 443.

258 Ibid, p. 443.

259 Ibid, pp. 445, 420.

260 There is a print of St Andrews students playing football in gowns, c1849, in Charles Rogers's *History of St Andrews, With a Full Account of the Recent Improvements in the City*. Adam & Charles Black, Edinburgh, 1849. Facing p. 117.

261 Lithgow, W., *Scotlands Welcome to Her Native Sonne and Soveraigne Lord, King Charles*. John Wreittoun, Edinburgh, 1633. n.p.

He knows the cause. It is not only "that base stinking weed" tobacco:

> For Manly excercise, is shreudly [wickedly] gone,
> Foot-ball and Wrestling throwing of the Stone:
> Jumping and breathing, practises of Strength,
> Which taught them to endure, hard things at length.[262]

Lithgow's life is punctuated by two horrific episodes. In his youth, when caught with the Laird of Bonnington's daughter (assuredly *in flagrante delicto*), "four blood-shedding wolves" cut off his ears.[263] Much worse is to follow. In Spain, in 1620, Lugless Willie (as he becomes dubbed) is mistaken for a spy and thrown into an Inquisition dungeon.[264] Hung by his shoulders, and his legs secured in a "three-planked rack", his kneecaps are crushed, and his hamstrings ruptured. Then they set to work on his arms, "cutting the crown, sinews, and flesh to the bare bones", and breaking his fingers. When he screams, they hit him in the face with cudgels. Still, he refuses to confess. He is then laid on a rack "to receive my main torments." Cords are tied over his calves, thighs, and upper arms, and attached to levers on both sides. The levers are turned twenty-one times at each of the six points, crushing his bones. Between every seven turns, he is interrogated. When his stubbornness persists, he is given water to drink, two pots, which he "gladly received, such was the scorching drought of my tormenting pain." When another pot is produced, he realises he is undergoing water torture. And when he clenches his teeth, they force them open with "iron cadges". When the ordeal is over, he is thrown in a cell for three weeks, and threatened daily with torture unless he confesses. He lies there broken, barely able to move, his wretched body covered in lice, "which lay crawling in clumps, within, without, and about my body; yea hanging in clusters about my beard, my lips, my nostrils and my eyebrows, almost inclosing my sight." Irrefutable proof why he thinks the youth of his day are weak. Lithgow can be forgiven ten thousand fawning poems.

---

262 Ibid.

263 Reid, T., *Notes on the life of William Lithgow, Traveller*. Proceedings of the Society of Antiquaries of Scotland, 1911, 45, p. 410.

264 Scott, G.R., *The History of Torture Throughout the Ages*. Luxor Press, London, 1886, pp. 172–176.

CHAPTER NINE
1600–1699 II

A 1600 book *A Pleasant Discourse of Six Gallant Marchants of Devonshire* begins with a poem extolling the virtues of Devon, among which:

> Great matches they make,
> And would undertake,
> With any that came,
> For all kinde of game,
> Shooting, and foote-ball,
> Wrestling with all,
> A hundreth pound a fall,
> To any that call.[1]

The fictional story of the gallant merchants follows. When the king visits Exeter after the Cornish Rebellion of 1497, a challenge goes out to all-comers in Devon and Cornwall to enrol in a three-day tournament. There are to be thirteen-a-side games each of wrestling, hurling, and football. Hurling is on the second day, "Where betwéene them, much valour and agilitie of bodie was shewed, as leaping, vauting, running and wrestling, wherein they excelled." Football follows on the third:

"The King to do them grace and encourage them to their play, caused a Noble man of his traine to cast up their Ball, which came no sooner on the ground, but was taken at advantage: then began the strength and nimblenesse of men to be tried, with lifting, throwing, and casting one the other, some with violence, others with fine slights, generally commended, continuing their sport without victory on either side, along time, untill by unhappie chance, one of Williams company, a proper man, and a Gentleman borne, was with a fall from a loftie mans armes, unfortunately slaine."

---

1 Roberts, H., *Haigh for Devonshire. A Pleasant Discourse of Six Gallant Marchants of Devonshire.* Thomas Creede, London, 1600. n.p.

A View of Devonshire has similar praise. Devonians surmount many others "in their ancient exercises ... of foot-ball, hurling and wrestling", which they play on "holy-days" and festivals.[2] In 1610, William Camden writes of standing stones near St Neot's in Cornwall, "seven or eight are pitched upright of equall distance asunder. The neighbour Inhabitants terme them Hurlers, as being by a devout and godly error perswaded, they had beene men sometimes transformed into Stones, for profaning the Lords Day, with hurling the ball."[3] Two years later, Michael Drayton praises Cornish hurling to the country[4] in his epic, *Poly-Olbion*. It speaks to the violence of the game:

> Or when the Ball to throw,
> And drive it to the Gole, in squadrons forth they goe:
> And to avoid the troupes (their forces that fore-lay),
> Through dikes and rivers make, in this robustious play;
> By which, the toiles of warre most livelie are exprest.[5]

His account of wrestling is equally impressive:

> With collars be they yokt, to prove the arme at length,
> Like Bulls set head-to-head, with meere delyver strength:
> Or by the girdles graspt, they practise with the hip,
> The forward, backward, falx, the mare, the turne, the trip,
> When stript into their shirts, each other they invade,
> Within a spacious ring, by the beholders made.[6]

He also includes "Barly-breake, and Prison-base". So does Henry Chettle in *The Tragedy of Hoffman*: 'I'le run a little course at base, or barely-breake,

---

2 Oliver, G., Bowes, P. (eds.)., *A View of Devonshire in 1630*, by Thomas Westcote, William Roberts, Exeter, 1845. pp. 42, 54.

3 Holland, P. (trans.)., Camden, W. (ed.)., *Britain: Or A Chorographicall Description of the Most Flourishing Kingdomes, England, Scotland, and Ireland*, by William Dugdale. George Bishop and Johan Norton, London, 1610. p. 192.

4 As opposed to hurling to goals. Both are described next.

5 Drayton, M., *Poly-Olbion: A Chorographical description of Great Britain*. Humphrey Lownes, London, 1612. p. 7.

6 Ibid, p. 6.

or some such toye to catch the fellow, and come back againe."[7] Devon-born, William Browne is no doubt thinking of hurling when he writes:

> And in a match at Foot-ball lately try'd
> (Having scarce twenty Satyres on thy side)
> Held'st play: and though assailed, kept'st thy stand
> Gainst all the best-try'd Ruffians in the land.[8]

Scarce twenty on thy side implies a cross-country game. Around 1640, King Charles I is told of a miracle in Cornwall. In 1624, twelve-year-old John Trelille, "playing at football after the manner of that country [hurling], snatching up the ball ran away with it, whereupon a girle in anger strook him with a sticke on the back bone, and so bruised or brake it, that for 16 years after he was forced to go creeping on the ground."[9] A dream urges him to bathe in a local holy well and pray in the adjacent chapel. He does this for three Thursdays in a row and is completely cured. Four years later, he enlists in Charles I's army and is killed within months at the Siege of Lyme Regis.

Cornish hurling, Welsh *knappan*, and East Anglian camping are still played in the seventeenth century. The earliest recorded *location* for Cornish hurling is at St Columb Major, in 1594.[10] A decade earlier, John Norden mentions hurling in his account of Cornwall:

"The Cornish-men, as they are stronge, hardye, and nimble, so are their exercises violent, two especially, Wrastling and Hurling. … The firste is acted in two sortes … the seconde likewise two ways, as Hurling to goales, and Hurling to the Countrye. The manner mighte be declared, but the use is not of necessitye."[11] Not of necessity. Richard Carew thinks otherwise. His first-hand account of an Elizabethan ball game is seminal. Hurling to goals is played in eastern Cornwall:

---

7 Farmer, J.S. (ed.)., *The Tragedy of Hoffman*, Henry Chettle, 1631. Tudor Facsimile Texts, England, 1913. n.p.

8 Browne, W., *Thirsis and Alexis*, in *The Shepheards Pipe*. Nicholas Okes, London, 1614. n.p.

9 Bacci, P.G. (attrib.)., *The Holy life of Philip Nerius, founder of the Congregation of the Oratory*. s.n., Paris, 1659. pp. 423–424.

10 Jewers, A.J. (ed.)., *The Registers of the Parish of St. Columb Major, Cornwall from the Year 1539 to 1780*. Hamilton, Adams, & Co., London, 1881. p. 146.

11 Norden, J., *Speculi Britanniæ pars: a topographical and historical description of Cornwall*. William Pearson, London, 1584. p. 29.

"There are 15, 20, or 30, players more or lesse, chosen out on each side, who strip themselves into their slightest apparell, and then joyne hands in ranke one against another. Out of these ranks they match themselves by payres, one embracing another, & so passe away: every of which couple, are specially to watch one another during the play. After this, they pitch two bushes in the ground, some eight or ten foote asunder; and directly against them, ten or twelve score off, other twayne in like distance, which they terme their Goales. One of these is appoynted by lots, to the one side, and the other to his adverse party. There is assigned for their gard, a couple of their best stopping Hurlers; the residue draw into the midst betweene both goales, where some indifferent person throweth up a ball, the which whosoever can catch, and cary through his adversaries goale, hath wonne the game. But therein consisteth one of Hercules his labours: for he that is once possessed of the ball, hath his contrary mate waiting at inches, and assaying to lay hold upon him. The other thrusteth him in the breast, with his closed fist, to keepe him off, which they call Butting, and place in weldoing the same, no small poynt of manhood.

"If hee escape the first, another taketh him in hand, and so a third, neyther is hee left, untill … hee eyther touch the ground with some part of his bodie, in wrastling, or cry, Hold; which is the word of yeelding. Then must he cast the ball (named Dealing) to some one of his fellowes, who catching the same in his hand, maketh away withall as before; and if his hap or agility bee so good, as to shake off or outrunne his counter-wayters, at the goale, hee findeth one or two fresh men, readie to receive and keepe him off. It is therefore a very disadvantageable match, or extraordinary accident, that leeseth many goales: howbeit, that side carryeth away best reputation, which giveth most falles in the hurling, keepeth the ball longest, and presseth his contrary neerest to their owne goale. Sometimes one chosen person on eche party dealeth the ball.

"The Hurlers are bound to the observation of many lawes, as, that they must hurle man to man, and not two set upon one man at once: that the Hurler against the ball, must not but, nor hand-fast under girdle: that hee who hath the ball, must but onely in the others brest: that he must deale no Fore-ball, viz. he may not throw it to any of his mates, standing neerer the goale, then himselfe. Lastly, in dealing the ball, if any of the other part can catch it flying between, or e're the other have it fast, he thereby winneth the same to his side, which straightway of defendant becommeth assailant, as the other, of assailant falls to be defendant. The least breach of these lawes, the Hurlers take for a just cause of going together by the eares, but with their fists onely; neither doth any among them seek revenge for such wrongs or hurts, but at the like play againe. These hurling matches are mostly used at weddings, where commonly the ghests undertake to encounter all commers."[12]

It is the earliest detailed account of a ball sport in modern history, a priceless description of a game with well-developed complex rules, rules that sound remarkably modern, a carrying game, similar to rugby, though with no kicking. Wonderful details pepper the text: picking sides, goals, goal sizes, goalkeepers, pitch length, drawing for ends, starting from the centre spot, man marking, tackling, pressing, passing, prohibition of forward passing, tactical marking, how to score goals. The game prizes possession, pressing, and tackling. All this in 1602, and doubtless long before. Carew's description of hurling to the country provides another spectacular glimpse into ancestral football and strengthens the notion of a Brittonic ancestor. Played in the west of Cornwall:

"Some two or more Gentlemen doe commonly make this match, appointing that on such a holyday, they will bring to such an indifferent place, two, three, or more parishes of the East or South quarter, to hurle against so many other, of the West or North. Their goales are either those Gentlemens houses, or some townes or villages, three or foure miles asunder, of which either side maketh choice after the neernesse to their dwellings. When they meet, there is neyther comparing of numbers, nor matching of men: but a silver ball is cast up, and that company, which can catch, and cary it by force, or sleight, to their place assigned, gaineth the ball and victory. Whosoever getteth seizure of this ball, findeth himselfe generally pursued by the adverse party; neither will they leave, till (without all respects) he be layd flat on Gods dear earth: which fall once received, disableth him from any longer detayning the ball: hee therefore throwet the same … to some one of his fellowes, fardest before him, who maketh away withall in like maner. Such as see where the ball is played, give notice thereof to their mates, crying, Ware East, Ware West, &c. as the same is carried.

12 Carew, R., *The Survey of Cornwall*. 2 Vols. S.S., London, 1602. Vol. 1. pp. 73^{v}–74.

"The Hurlers take their next way over hilles, dales, hedges, ditches; yea, and thorow bushes, briers, mires, plashes and rivers whatsoever; so as you shall sometimes see 20. or 30. lie tugging together in the water, scrambling and scratching for the ball. A play (verily) both rude & rough, and yet such, as is not destitute of policies, in some sort resembling the feats of warre: for you shall have companies layd out before, on the one side, to encounter them that come with the ball, and of the other party to succor them, in maner of a fore-ward. Againe, other troups lye hovering on the sides, like wings, to helpe or stop their escape: and where the ball it selfe goeth, it resembleth the joyning of the two mayne battels: the slowest footed who come lagge, supply the showe of a rere-ward: yea, there are horsemen placed also on either party (as it were in ambush) and ready to ride away with the ball, if they can catch it at advantage.

"But they may not so steale the palme: for gallop any one of them never so fast, yet he shall be surely met at some hedge corner, crosse-lane, bridge, or deep water, which (by casting the Countrie) they know he must needs touch at: and if his good fortune gard him not the better, hee is like to pay the price of his theft, with his owne and his horses overthrowe to the ground. Sometimes, the whole company runneth with the ball, seven or eight miles out of the direct way, which they should keepe. Sometimes a foote-man getting it by stealth, the better to scape unespied, will carry the same quite backwards, and so, at last, get to the goale by a windlace: which once knowne to be wonne, all that side flocke thither with great jolity: and if the same bee a Gentlemans house, they give him the ball for a Trophee, and the drinking out of his Beere to boote … when the hurling is ended, you shall see them retyring home, as from a pitched battaile, with bloody pates, bones broken, and out of joynt, and such bruses as serve to shorten their daies; yet al is good play, & never Attourney nor Crowner troubled for the matter."[13]

Ferocious folk football. With horses. Is it the descendant of a Celtic war game? The battle-hardened training rookies? They are a fighting people. Circa 700AD, Cornwall exists as *Cornubia*, later that century *Cornwalas*, "Britons of the horn of Britain".[14] Approximately twenty years later, they defeat an unnamed enemy—probably Saxons—at the

13 Ibid, Vol. 1. pp. 74v–75v.

14 Charles-Edwards, T.M., *Wales and the Britons, 350–1064*. Oxford University Press, 2013. p. 22.

Battle of Hehil.[15] The source contains a Welsh phrase, *A gware pelre â phen Saeson*: to play at hurling with Saxon heads.[16] Cornwall continues to do battle with West Saxons throughout the eighth century. In 815, the Saxon king, Ecgberht lays waste to Cornwall. Only a decade later, the Cornish are fighting the men of Devon. In 838, they form an alliance with Danish Vikings and attack the West Saxons, though they are easily put down.[17] They are subject to Viking aggression themselves, at Padstow, in 981.[18] As late as 1497, they remain bellicose, rebelling twice against Henry VII. It is no surprise, then, that in 1568, they are described as "the stoutest of all British nations" and "the most valiant in warlike affairs."[19]

It is notable that Wexford, which is steeped in hurling history, is the nearest Irish county to Cornwall, and only fifty miles from Wales. Perhaps hurling was transmitted this way, and the Cornish game developed unique features. A game is held between the hurlers of Wexford and Cornwall in the first half of the eighteenth century. It is unclear which rules are used, or whether it is an early example of compromise rules.[20] Wexford beat the home side. The people of southern Wexford spoke a unique dialect called *Yola*, believed to have evolved from Middle English introduced during the Norman invasion.[21] Wexford is their landing point, in 1169. Welsh Normans, French, and Flemish settle in the area, and *Yola* contains elements of each language.[22] Testament to hurling's importance to the community, the only complete *Yola* ballad to survive, c1688, tells the story of a hurling match between neighbouring parishes. Behind for most of the game, Tommy's side have a chance on goal:

---

15 Williams Ab Ithel, J. (ed.)., *Annales Cambriae.* Longman, Brown, Greenman and Longmans, London, 1860. p. 9.

16 Ibid, p. 120.

17 Charles-Edwards, T.M., *Wales and the Britons, 350–1064*. Oxford University Press, 2013. pp. 430–431.

18 Padel, O.J., *Slavery in Saxon Cornwall.* Hughes Hall, Cambridge, 2009. p. 6.

19 Borlase, W., *The Natural History of Cornwall.* W. Jackson, Oxford, 1758. p. 304.

20 Doyle, E., *The 'Yellow Bellies' and the Hurling Men of Cornwall.* History Ireland, 2003, 11:1, p. 8.

21 *Yola* was spoken in two baronies. It died out in one in the mid-eighteenth century, and in the other in the mid-nineteenth century. This example is taken from the Lord's Prayer: "*Oure vaader fho yaarth ing heaveene, ee hallowet bee t'naame.*" In: Guilfoyle, E., *Languages in Contact; Aspects of the Hiberno English Verb Phrase*. Unpublished MA thesis, McGill University, 1983. pp. 4–5. The last native *Yola* speaker died in 1998. There is a movement to revive the language.

22 The people of the Fingal area, in the north of Co. Dublin, had a related dialect, *Fingallian*. Now extinct, they were the only Anglo-Norman dialects in Ireland. Two *Fingallian* texts remain, one of which—the *Purgatorium Hibernicum*, c1670—also mentions hurling (as *camán*).

"Yesterday, we had a goal just in our hand … Tommy, who, by misluck was placed to drive in … Many a brave stroke by Tommy was made; the goal-keeper trembling … the ball-clubs they rattled … Tommy was open and so was the goal … our hearts came to our mouth … Up came the ball, and a tap or a shove would serve; but … venom too hard, he sunk his bat-club, and broke the handle in a pismire-hill [anthill]. The ball o'ershot the goal … like a fool in a mill, he looked in amazement … mischief fetch the man, betwixt you and Tommy and the pismire-hill."[23]

A contemporary match is described in a poem *Iomáin na Bóinne* (*The Boyne Football Match*) by Seamus Dall MacCuarta (c1650–1732/33). It is a twelve-a-side, fixed-rules game between the Meath villages of Slane and Duleek, one of many events at a sports festival that day. Several players are named, and "it was a joy to be … watching the boys."[24] Little details of the game are given, but there is skill in the game, goalkeepers are used, the twelve "hit their shoulders together"—possibly at kick-off or during a scrum, and a bugle signals the end of the game. Slane thrash Duleek and the partisan poet declaims them capable of beating any team.[25,26] More detail is given in 1698, when John Dunton takes in a game during his travels. It is a better-developed, tamer affair than the Cornish game:

"One exercise they use much is theire hurleing … they strike with a stick call'd commaan about three foote and an halfe long in the handle. At the lower end it is crooked and about three inches broad, and on this broad part you may sometimes see one of the gamesters carry the ball tossing it for 40 or 50 yards in spight of all the adverse players; and when he is like to lose it, he generally gives it a great stroak to drive it towards the goals. Sometimes if he miss his blow at the ball, he knocks one of his opposers down, at which noe resentment is to be shewn. They seldome come off without broken heads or shins in which the[y] glories verie much … they pick out ten, twelve, or twenty players of a side, and the

---

23 Barnes, W. (ed.)., Poole, J., *A Glossary, With Some pieces of Verse of the Old Dialect of the English Colony in the Baronies of Forth and Bargy, County of Wexford, Ireland.* J. Russell Smith, London, 1867. pp. 84–91.

24 *Historical Irish Corpus 1600–1926.* http://corpas.ria.ie/index.php?fsg_function=3&fsg_id=5446. Accessed 3 November 2024.

25 Ibid.

26 Meath Gaelic Athletic Association. https://meath.gaa.ie/clubs/slane/. Accessed 3 November 2024.

prize is generally a barell or two of ale, which is brought into the field and drank off by the victors on the spott, tho the vanquisht are not with out a share of it too. This commonly is some verie large plaine, the barer of grass the better, and the goales are 200 or 300 yards one from the other; and which ever party drives the ball beyond the others goale wins the day … their kindred and mistresses are frequently spectators … two or three bagg pipes attend the conquerors at the barrell's head and then play them out of the field. Att some of these meetings two thousand have been present together. They doe not play often at football, only in a small territory called Fingall near Dublin the people use it much, and trip, and shoulder verie handsomely."[27]

~

The Welsh game of *Knappan* is first described in 1603. George Owen's extensive first-hand account describes five annual fixtures in Pembrokeshire. These "standing *knappans*" comprise: "The first at the Berry Sandes betweene the parishes of Nevarne [Nevern] and Newport upon shroft tewsdaie yearely. The second at Pontgynon Eastermondaie, between the parishes of Melney [Meline] and Eglofferow [Eglwyswrw], the third on Lower Esterdaye at Pwll dy in Penbedow between the parishes of Penrith and Penbedow, the fourth and fift was wont to be at St Meygans in Kernes, between Kernes men of the partie and Emlyn men, and the men of Cardiganshire … the first upon Ascentiondaie the other upon Corpus Christi daie."[28] The last two are pitched battles with up to two thousand on foot plus mounted players. Smaller ad hoc matches take place on Holy Days and Sundays, with hundreds involved. There is a carnival atmosphere: "victualers with meate drinke and wine of all sortes, also merchantes, mercers and pedlers would provide stalls and boothes. Greate multitudes of people watch the game, others come to be seene (you know what kinde I meane)."[29]

Unlike Carew (hurling) and Moor (camping), Owen has played "oftentymes … which signes and seales [proof] I carrye in my heade,

---

27 Carpenter. A. (ed.)., *Teague Land, Or, A Merry Ramble to the Wild Irish*, by John Dunton. Four Courts Press, Dublin, 2003. pp. 91–92.

28 Owen, G., *The Description of Pembrokeshire*. Early nineteenth century transcript of the 1603 manuscript. images. 286–287. Casgliad y Werin Cymru: https://www.peoplescollection.wales/items/9156#?xywh=-588%2C-100%2C2230%2C1999. Accessed 15 May 2023.

29 Ibid, p. 287.

handes, and other partes of my bodye."[30] His testimony is indubitable. As well as passing mention of games in 1587 and 1588, Owen describes a standing *knappan*. There are no fixed numbers; whoever turns up plays. Barefooted players, wearing only a "light paier of breeches" contend "for glorie and renowne." Long hair and beards are ill-advised, for they are used as leverage. At two, the ball is thrown "bolt upright." Players try to get the *knappan*—a wooden ball boiled in tallow "for to make it slipperye", and of a size "soe as a man maye hold it in his hande, and noe more"—to their *gole* two or three miles away. Once again, the ball would have been painful to kick; indeed, there is no evidence *knappan* had a kicking element: "It is a strange sight to see a thowsand or fifteene hundred naked men concurre together in a cluster in following the knappan … scoutes or fore runners keep ahead of play to catch a ball thrown by a lustie hurler."

The ball is often played out to the swiftest runner, who seeks clear ground and hares away followed by "six hundred good footemen." If he encounters a scout, or is about to be overtaken, he hurls it forward, hoping a teammate will reach it first. Across country they fly, "negotiating hedge, ditch, pale, or wall, hill, dale, bushes, Rivers or Rocke." If they are not horsed, only the fittest spectators can follow the action. This can be their downfall. Any too close get pulled into the game and served "a Bastonado or two, if he be on horse … half a dozen cuffes if he be on foote." An interesting tactic occurs when sides are clearly uneven. Two men from the smaller side face one another. One grasps the ball to his stomach, the other grabs his teammate about the middle: "And then cometh more of the same side, and lay gripes on and rounde aboute them both, so that you shall see a hundred or vi score thus clustred together, as bees."[31] The other side use any means to get to the *knappan*. If the pair with the ball grow weary, play stops for fifteen minutes. The game restarts with the same manoeuvre. It is a skilful game, says Owen. Still, horsemen carry "monstrouse cudgells, of iii foote and half longe … if he [the runner] hold the knappan yt it is lawful for the assaylante to beate him with the cudgel." Footmen use stones in their fists, and horsemen find the strongest cudgel "soe huge as it were able to strike down an ox

30 Ibid, p. 299.

31 Ibid, p. 294.

or horse; he will alsoe assalt any for privatt grudge … sparing neither heade, face, nor anye parte of the bodie … gamesters return home from this playe with broken heads, blackfaces, brused bodies, and lame legges, yet laugheinge."[32]

Owen's happy gamesters is probably a romantic notion, few welcome serious injury or brutal payback. Indeed, he cites violence and defiance of "the Anciente custom of the play" for *knappan* being "banished and allmost forsaken." With rules of engagement, the game is "a most warlicke exercise" instilling tactics and discipline; without them, floundering armies run amok. Previously, footmen could only use "bare fistes", nor could horsemen ride among the barefooted footmen; those that did were legitimately pelted with stones. Cudgels were drawn through a ring to moderate thickness, and were made of hazel "soe as the same might harme, but not mightelye hurte." Crucially, only the man with the *knappan* could be struck, and only then after he had been warned three times to pass it on. Now "Privatt grudges are revendged … so that sometymes you shall see, fyve or vi hundred naked men beatinge in a clustere together, as fast as the fiste can goe … so that you shall see two brothers theron beateinge the other, the man the masiter, and frinde against frinde …"[33]

If folk football is sublimated warfare, this is all out war. The most fascinating aspect of the game is the presence of scrums: "And then cometh more of the same side, and lay gripes on and rounde aboute them both, so that you shall see a hundred or vi score thus clustered together, as bees." Little wonder the strategy is first heard of in Wales. The surprise is that it is in use in 1588. The next reference is in 1720, during a football match in Ireland.

Wales is one of the last outposts of Brittonic kingdoms, their territories compressed as fifth-century Anglo-Saxons spread westward. Britons are confined to Wales, Cornwall, Ireland; others seek refuge in Brittany. It is possible that *knappan*, like Cornish hurling, is a descendant of an ancient Brittonic game. While it may have been influenced or even been introduced by the Romans, it bears little more than a passing resemblance to *harpastum*. There is no evidence *knappan* was played in north Wales.

32 Ibid, pp. 288–293.

33 Ibid, p. 292.

Even in the south it appears to have been confined to Pembrokeshire and Cardiganshire in southwest Wales, well away from Romans, Angles, and Saxons. Ireland and Wales are less than fifty miles apart at their nearest point. That point is in Pembrokeshire. Nevertheless, a 1632 Welsh–Latin dictionary translates *pêl* (ball) into *pila,* while *pêl droid* (the game of football) becomes *harpastum.*[34,35] In 1582, Davids Owen and Howell, "and unnamed others" are charged with illegal "assemblies, assaults and forcible entries upon meadows, woods, and pasture", after a game of knappan near the village of Llandebie, in Carmarthenshire.[36] Clearly, the game had got away from them.[37] At a 1591 case in Pembrokeshire and another in Carmarthenshire in 1604, the game is considered a riot.[38]

The Normans are a different proposition. From 1068, they try to achieve suzerainty over Wales. The northern princes successfully repel them. The south folds. The Normans take Cardiganshire, in west Wales, though a century-long cycle of occupation and ejection follows. The unsettled Normans have little time to influence Cardiganshire culture; neither are locals likely to accept Norman customs; nonetheless, any new ball game might shape the existing sport. The tenacious northern princes repeatedly retake territory, and full subjugation of Wales is only achieved in 1283. By the late eighth century, a ball game is reported in Glamorganshire, south Wales, in *Historia Brittonum*; nevertheless, the earliest manuscript is tenth century, and must be used to date the game. It is possible that the ancient game was widespread in south Wales, if not throughout the country, though there is no evidence and no explanation as to why it died out. Why *knappan* and Cornish hurling have mounted players when folk football, camping, and Irish hurling do not is unknown. Was it an imported addition?

Pembrokeshire has a different experience with the Normans. The county is usurped in 1093, and falls under the control of Marcher barons who rule Welsh territories for the Crown. The Normans settle in south Pembrokeshire and maintain a strong presence, despite constant

34 Davies, J., *Antiquæ Britannicæ, Nunc vulgò dictæ Cambro-Britannicæ*. R. Young, London, 1632. n.p.

35 *Pêl droid* is actually a football, and *pêl-droid* the game of football.

36 The county bordering Pembrokeshire to the east, and Cardiganshire to the south.

37 Krehbiel, D., *Heddwch! Heddwch! Sport and Cultural Identity in Early Modern Wales*. Unpublished MA thesis, University of North Carolina, 2006. p. 40.

38 Ibid.

insurrections. The area is dubbed "Little England Beyond Wales". North Pembrokeshire is also ruled by a baron, but local mores are maintained. Peace is abstract. Welsh–English relations along the Pembrokeshire border are "marked by the most unrelenting hostility and uncompromising distrust … intercultural contacts were kept at a minimum in the interests of peace."[39] Hardly conducive to cultural exchange. Even so, in comparison with Cardiganshire, one would expect Norman customs to have a wider reach and existing games to be modified accordingly. With no clear evidence *knappan* is played in south Wales prior to the Norman Conquest, is it coincidental the Normans only gain a foothold in the south, the only piece of the country known to later play *knappan*? Pembrokeshire is said to have taken "little part in the development of distinctive Cambro-Norman institutions", but did it contribute one of the most unique?[40]

Whatever impact the Normans have in south Wales, the irony is that they come from Normandy, where *soule* is played. The Normans do not invade alone; they are accompanied by French, Angevin, and Breton adventurers. The Bretons also play *soule*; arguably *soule* originated there, created by successive migrations of Britons fleeing Anglo-Saxon settlers. The invading forces, then, may be importing a game similar to the one already played. In an 1872 paper, Edward Lowry Barnwell writes: "The game of *soule*, formerly played in Brittany, was identical with this [*knappan*], except that horsemen did not join in the game … The identity of this Welsh game of *cnapan* and the Breton *soule* is remarkable, for there are apparently no traces of it on other parts of France or in England. Nor is there any evidence that it was in existence in the northern counties of Wales. It had grown out of use in Wales in the time of Elizabeth … some few, and the *cnapan* amongst them, may be genuine relics of Celtic times and manners."[41]

Little is mentioned of *soule* in the seventeenth century. In Picardy, in 1668, the ball is thrown up midway between the villages: "each [side] kicks it violently and the strongest who bring it closest to theirs [village]

---

39 Nelson, L.H., *The Normans in South Wales, 1070–1171.* University of Texas Press, Austin, 1966. p. 83.

40 Ibid, pp. 83–84.

41 Barnwell E.L., *On Some Ancient Welsh Customs and Furniture.* Archaeologia Cambrensis, 1872, 3:12, pp. 337–338.

win the victory and the prize."[42] The author is speaking in the present tense; by then *soule* is a kicking game, at least in Picardy. The game's name has regional variations: *choule* in Picardy, *melat* in Brittany, in others *cheole, chaule, sole, soul.*[43] Like folk football, it is played on holy days between rival villages.[44] The description of camping is not until 1823, when Edward Moor provides a first-hand account of an East Anglian camping game:

"Goals were pitched at the distance of 150 or 200 yards from each other—these were generally formed of the thrown off clothes of the competitors. Each party has two goals, ten or fifteen yards apart. The parties, ten or fifteen on a side, stand in line, facing their own goals and each other, at about 10 yards distance, midway between the goals, and nearest that of their adversaries. An indifferent spectator, agreed on by the parties, throws up a ball, of the size of a common cricket ball, midway between the confronted players, and makes his escape. It is the object of the players to seize and convey the ball between their own goals.

"The rush is therefore very great; as is sometimes the shock of the first onset, to catch the falling ball—he who first can catch or seize it speeds therefore home pursued by his opponents (thro' whom he has to make his way) aided by the jostlings and various assistances of his own *sidesmen*. If caught and held, or in imminent danger of being caught, he *throws* the ball—but must in no case *give* it—to a less beleagured friend, who, if it be not arrested in its course or be jostled away by the eager and watchful adversaries, catches it; and he hastens homeward, in like manner pursued, annoyed, and aided—winning the notch[45] (or *snotch*) if he contrive to *carry*—not *throw*—it between his goals. But this, in a well-matched game, is no easy achievement, and often requires much time, many doublings, detours, and exertions.

"I should have noticed that if the holder of the ball be caught with the ball in his possession, he loses a *snotch*, if, therefore, he be hard pressed,

---

42 Du Fresne C. (ed.)., *Histoire de S. Louys IX. Du nom roy de France, ecrite par Jean sire de Joinville senéchal de Champagne*. Sebastien Mabre-Cramoisy, Paris, 1668. p. 188.

43 Grenier, P.M., *Introduction a L'Histoire Générale de la Province de Picardie*. M.M. Dufour et J. Garnier, Amiens, 1856. p. 112.

44 Ibid, pp. 112–113.

45 A notch was also the term used for cricket runs, recorded by making notches in a stick. In his glossary Moor states: "Snotch A notch. 'To cut a snotch in't.' Also, I think a knot."

he *throws* it to a convenient friend, more free and in breath than himself. At the loss (or gain) of a *snotch*, a recommence takes place, arranging which gives the parties time to take breath. Seven or nine notches are the game—and these it will sometimes take two or three hours to win … It is very animating to see twenty or thirty youths, stripped to the skin … amid the shouting and roaring of half the population of the contiguous villages … Sometimes a large football was used—and the game was then called 'kicking camp'—and if played in heavy shoes, 'savage camp.'"[46]

A further distinction is made between "rough-play" and "civil-play".[47] Rough-play allows boxing in addition to the wrestling and kicking of civil-play. Another variation covers long distances with unlimited players, "but the twelve-a-side camp was the more popular variety of the game, and no doubt gave more satisfaction to the *connoisseurs* than these pitched battles or 'fighting camps'."[48]

The descriptions of camping and Cornish hurling to goals include features common to many ball sports. Contrasting the two, it is hard to estimate the length of the hurling pitch. If "ten or twelve score" refers to feet, the pitch is sixty-five to eighty yards long (a standard football pitch is one hundred to one hundred and thirty yards); if yards it is two hundred to two hundred and forty yards long, consistent with camping—one hundred and fifty to two hundred yards. Hurling goals are four times smaller—eight to ten feet compared with thirty to forty-five feet. Hurling has fifteen to thirty players, camping ten to fifteen, implying a more physical, compact game, regardless of pitch size. Either way, they share the same method of scoring. Moor and Carew's accounts are first-hand, lending considerable validity. The parallels are intriguing (Cornish hurling in italics):

1. "An indifferent spectator … throws up the ball."
   some indifferent person throweth up a ball.
2. "… catches it; and he hastens homeward, in like manner pursued, annoyed, and aided—winning the notch (or snotch) if he contrive to carry—not throw—it between his goals."

---

46 Moor, E., *Suffolk Words and Phrases*. J. Loder, London, 1823. pp. 64–65.

47 Forby, R., *The Vocabulary of East Anglia*. 2 Vols. J.B. Nichols and Son, London, 1830. Vol. 1. p. 51.

48 Ketton-Cremer, R.W., *Camping—A Forgotten Norfolk Game*. Norfolk and Norwich Archaeology Society, 1931. p. 89.

... the which whosoever can catch, and cary through his adversaries goale, hath wonne the game.

3. "… he who first can catch or seize it speeds therefore home pursued by his opponents (thro' whom he has to make his way)."

   ... one of his fellowes, who catching the same in his hand, maketh away withall as before; and if his hap or agility bee so good, as to shake off or outrunne his counter-wayters, at the goale.

4. "If caught and held, or in imminent danger of being caught, he throws the ball—but must in no case give it—to a less beleagured friend, who … catches it; and he hastens homeward."

   ... hee eyther touch the ground with some part of his bodie, in wrastling, or cry, Hold; which is the word of yeelding. Then must he cast the ball (named Dealing) to some one of his fellowes, who catching the same in his hand, maketh away withall as before.

Another shared rule not mentioned by Moor is that "two men will not be allowed to engage one only." Another possible similarity between Cornish hurling and camping is ball size. Carew mentions a cricket-ball-sized silver ball for "hurling to the country." If hurling to goals uses the same one then, according to Moor's description, it is the same size used in camping, as well as in *knappan* and Irish hurling. In 1534, the churchwardens of Cratfield, Suffolk, give Wyll But 4d "for a ball to camp with", and in 1600, a *goal* at camping is mentioned by dramatist John Day:[49,50] "My name? I am not asham'd of my name: I am one Tom Strowd of Harling; I'll play a gole at Camp-ball, or wrassel a fall of the hip, or the hin turn with ere a Courtnoll of ye all, for 20 quarters of Malt, and match me height for height."[51,52] Francis Willughby's manuscript on a wide

49 Holland, W., *Cratfield Parish Papers*. Jarrold & Sons, London, 1895. p. 51.

50 Day, J., *The blind-beggar of Bednal-green with the merry humour of Tom Strowd the Norfolk yeoman*. R. Pollard and Tho. Dring, London, 1659. n.p. Act V.

51 Ibid.

52 Camp-ball, alternate name for camping. Hin turn, inturn: obsolete wrestling expression, "the act of putting a leg between the thighs of an opponent and lifting him up." A courtnoll was a contemptuous name for a courtier.

variety of games is unfinished when he dies in 1672. His description of football is spellbinding:

"They blow a strong bladder and tie the neck of it as fast as they can, and then put it into the skin of a buls cod and sow it fast in.[53] They play in a longe streete, or a close that has a gate at either end. The gates are called Gaols, as **A B**, **C D**.[54] The ball is thrown up in the middle between the gaols, as about **O**, the plaiers beeing æqually divided according to their strength and nimblenesse. **A** plaiers must kick the ball towards **C D** gaol, **C** plaiers towards **A B** gaol, and they that can strike the ball thorough their enemies gaol first win. They usually leave some of their best plaiers to gard the gaol while the rest follow the ball. They often breake one anothers shins when two meete and strike both togather against the ball, & therefore there is a law that they must not strike higher then the ball.

"Tripping Up of Heels is when one followes one of his enemies & to prevent him from striking the ball strikes that foot as hee runs, that is from the ground, which catching against the other foote makes him fall. All the slight is to hit that foot that is mooving and just taken from the ground, & then a little touch makes him fall. Suppose **þ** foot [is] fixed, **ß** [foot is] mooving from **n** to **m**. If it bee strooke on the outside before it comes to **R**, just against the fixed foote, it falls crosse behind the fixed foot at **L** and makes him fall. The harder the ball is blowne, the better it flys. They use to put quicksilver into it sometimes to keep it from lying still. The plaiers must at first stand all at their gaols, the ball lying just in the middle betweene them, & they that can run best get the first kick."[55]

The description includes picking sides, goals and goal sizes, goalkeepers, starting positions, throwing off from the centre spot, the first to the ball winning the first kick, how to score goals, a high tackle law, that the game is won by one goal, and tactics—tripping up, and leaving some of the best players to guard the goal. Pitch size is implied: the length of a long street or a football close. He even includes the first drawing of a football pitch. Warwickshire-born and Cambridge-educated, Willughby is only thirty-six when he dies, unaware he is the

53 Middle English *cod*: multiple meanings. In this context, probably scrotum.

54 He inserts a hand-drawn image. **A–B** is one goal, **C–D** the other. **O** is the centre spot.

55 Cram, D., Forgeng, J.L., Johnston, D. (eds.), *The Book of Games of Francis Willughby (1635–1672). A Seventeenth-century Treatise on Sports, Games and Pastimes*. Routledge, Abingdon, Oxon, 2016. p. 168.

first person in history to provide a detailed description of the game. His book also contains descriptions of stowball, stoolball, bandy ball, billiards, "shittle cock", quoits, bowls, "barly breakes", and prison bars, and an extensive account of royal tennis. Tennis balls aside, balls are described as "shreds of cloth rapped hard about a bullet, and then sowed about with overcast titch [stitch]. But the great balls for rebounding and tossing have no bullets in them."[56]

Camping, football, and Cornish hurling share field and to the country varieties. *Soule* probably made the switch from field to country by discarding its stick, whereas Irish hurling and bandy are likely to be field games *because* they kept theirs. *Knappan* is the outlier, solely to the country. Perhaps it is the horses. Football, *soule*, hales (the Scottish equivalent of football), and camping all existed alongside a stick version. English bandy (hockey) and Scottish shinty survive, *soule* and camping's stickball versions perished.

Field games share baked-in features: starting from the centre, fixed sides, goals, positional play, tackling, and passing. Pitch length and goal size are variable but fall within a discrete range. To the country games—Cornish hurling, camping, (folk) football, *soule*, and *knappan*—are less sophisticated, operating within basic parameters: rival factions convey a ball to a specified landmark in their own district, essentially by any means. To the country can only be played on feast days and holidays, when large groups are can be organised, limiting the establishment of robust rules. Field versions can be played formally on Sundays, and informally at any time, with any number of players: hundreds of thousands of games will be played across the year, allowing rules to be tried and tested, accepted or rejected, maturing across centuries. Which grew out of which is unknowable and largely inconsequential. Each channels a fundamental aspect of medieval warfare: the siege (field) and the battlefield (to the country).

A return to origins. When do these sports first develop, and are they offshoots of an original game? Irish hurling is mentioned in three seventh century books (confirmed via textual analytics, though the earliest manuscript is twelfth century); a Welsh ball game in the ninth century *Historia Brittonum* (the oldest manuscript is c944); an English stick

56 Ibid, p. 176.

and ball game in *Colloquies*, c1000; and *soule* in 1152. Confirmatory evidence of camping, football (including hales), *knappan*, and Cornish hurling come later. Pre-seventh-century history is silent. If the games are offshoots of an indigenous Brittonic sport, one expects them to develop idiosyncrasies over time while retaining some of the original DNA; also, that games bearing the most similarity are geographically close and/or furthest from outside influence. Kicking versions of football in the east, north, and south, and camping are examples of geographical connection; while the western sports of *knappan*, and Cornish hurling exemplify remote games. Stick games are a different matter. Their distribution is unknown prior to the fourteenth century, but from then on they are far-reaching, extending across Ireland, Scotland, England, Flanders, the Netherlands, and the entire northern seaboard of what is now France.

Soule's origin is obscure. Was it exported from Cornwall to Brittany in the sixth century, or from Normandy to England in the eleventh? Irrespective of Bata's mention of a stickball game c1000, the former is likelier. There is no evidence that a stickball game was regularly played in France, other than along the north coast. It is far-fetched to believe that ball games were popular throughout France before the fourteenth century, only to fall from favour. Early ball games head south across the English Channel. *Soule* lands in Brittany, and is propagated along the northwest coast to Normandy, Picardy, and Artois. The Cornish migrate to Brittany from the mid-sixth to the seventh century. This is when they are likely to introduce their customs to Brittany, including the tradition of supplying a ball at weddings. In other words, ball games are already played in Cornwall. This accords with the *Historia Brittonum* and those seventh-century Irish books. It is only one hundred and fifty years after the Romans depart, and one hundred years after the Anglo-Saxons arrive. Is the Cornish game introduced by one of them, or is it evidence of a Brittonic game, one of many played in pre-Roman Britain—it is unlikely that Cornwall alone was indulging.

Roman influence is doubtful. They leave Cornwall largely untouched.[57] Besides, Roman writers are silent on ball games in Britain; there is certainly no mention of *harpastum*. If introduced by Angles,

57 Charles-Edwards, T.M., *Wales and the Britons, 350–1064*. Oxford University Press, Oxford, 2013. p. 31.

how does it get to Cornwall? They never invade. Saxons do. The Cornish defeat what is probably a Saxon army, c720.[58] Conflict follows across the eighth century, and by 815, the Saxons have laid waste to Cornwall. But by that time, the Cornish have been settled in Brittany for at least two hundred years. The Vikings are immaterial. Angles, Saxons, and Vikings may have introduced ball games of their own, or influenced existing ones—camping is a prime example—but indirect evidence argues that ball games in Britain and Ireland were indigenous, and have been played since at least the sixth century.

~

There are dozens of examples of East Anglian fields dedicated to camping, which carry that prefix: Piece, Pightle, Green, Ground, Croft, Close, Meadow, Hill, Field, Place, Land, and Yard.[59,60,61] This is in sharp contrast to other counties. By the end of the fourteenth century, the Hertfordshire town of Hitchin has a Pitcher Pightle, Nine Corners, Morris Dell, Reel Place, and Clicketts, Closh, and Cock Closes.[62] A Foteballe Close is not established in Hitchin until Elizabethan times. This does not mean that football is not played earlier; the streets of Hitchin may be the preferred terrain,[63] and the introduction of a dedicated field an attempt to curb the practice.

Tom Strowd hails from the village of Harling, in Norfolk. Day, himself, is born in Norfolk, so would be familiar with the sport. He also attends Cambridge, where football is played.[64] It is not known if he played there, or at camping earlier. What is known, is that he did not cover himself in glory. He is sent down from Cambridge for stealing a book. Six years later, he is arrested for killing a fellow dramatist. The Camping Close of North Elmham, Norfolk, is mentioned throughout the

58 Williams Ab Ithel, J. (ed.)., *Annales Cambriae.* Longman, Brown, Greenman and Longmans, London, 1860. p. 9.

59 Dymond, D., *A Lost Social Institution: The Camping Close.* Rural History, 1990, 1:2, pp. 165–192.

60 Cricket was played on the Camping Land of Needham Market in 1814, and a balloon ascended from there in 1848. In 2025, Needham Market FC are managed by Kevin Horlock, who scored 44 goals for Manchester City and played 32 times for Northern Ireland.

61 There are at least four Essex villages with both a Great and Little Camp. On a similar note, there is a Hurling Field in St Buryan, Cornwall.

62 Hine, R.L., *The History of Hitchin.* George Allen & Unwin Ltd., London, 1929. p. 241.

63 Ibid, p. 244.

64 Since at least 1579, when the Chesterton affray took place.

churchwardens' accounts from 1539 to 1577;[65] close to the church, the two-acre field belongs to it. It was previously owned by the Le Taverner family from at least 1467, and at that time it was spelt Cäpyng close. By 1542, it is Campyng closse, Capÿge Closse in 1556. Several payments are made with respect to the camping close. In 1542, Wyllm lussher is paid 2s "for ye Campyng closse ferme." In 1543, 4s goes to "Wyllm lussher for londe fferme … & ye Campynclosse"; 15s to "Wyllm Rudd for ye wodd ye grew in Campyngclosse dytche"; and 12d to "Wyllm Smythe for ye hedgying of the ynward pte of ye Campyng Close dytche." Smythe is paid 20d the following year for "felling of thornes & hedgyng of ye Est syde of the Campyng Closse", while Thomas Lussher receives payments for firming of the camping close until 1556.

Most camping games have small sides, limited by the size of the close, generally between one and four acres. Commonly, twelve-a-side play for thirty minutes, and the side with most goals wins. There are goalkeepers and sidesmen but no other fixed positions. An alternate game, like the one described by Moor, lasts up to three hours, and is won by the side with most *snotches*, usually seven or nine. A *snotch* is not a goal. It is scored by catching an opponent in possession. A cross-country version—most likely between competing villages—allows for much larger numbers. There are other variations. Richard Chase (1715–1785), rector of St John's in Ilketshall, Suffolk, played in the camping ground to the west of the church. In the game he played, a cricket-sized ball was driven through a narrow goal.[66]

Essex also has fields prefixed by *camping*. The majority lie on the Suffolk border (twenty on one or other side), though there are outliers: one is in the south of the county, and another in the east.[67,68] Other than where Saxon land abuts Angle territory, the Saxon counties invariably use *football* for the game, and the prefix *football*. There are records of transfer of ownership of fields called *Football Close*. In 1568, Edward Hammond is granted the ownership of the two-acre *football close* in Buckland, Kent; a 1607 document describes Colmworth Rectory, Bedfordshire,

65 Legge, A.G., *Ancient Churchwardens' Account of the Parish of North Elmham*, from A.D. 1539 to A.D. 1537. Agas H. Goose, Norwich, 1891.

66 *Notes and Queries*, 1892, Series 8, Vol. 2. pp. 137–138.

67 Dymond, D., *A Lost Social Institution: The Camping Close*. Rural History, 1990, 1:2, p. 168.

68 The annual Shrovetide game in Dorking, Surrey, was often referred to as camping.

as bound by *footeball close* to the north;[69] in 1627, a *football close* in Chigwell, Essex, is granted to John Pennington for 100 marks; and in 1657, another is passed to Robert Bernard in Wyboston, Bedfordshire.[70,71] Piddington, Oxfordshire, has a *futbal plaine* in 1598,[72] and Garton, Yorkshire, a *Football-garth* in 1628,[73] while Edward Somes bequeaths his son *Football Field* in Stock, Essex, in 1668. Other variations include *Football Grene* (Hornsea, Yorkshire, 1689), *Football Ing* (Barraford, Lancashire, 1708), *Football Butts* (Toddenham, Gloucestershire, 1715), *Football Marsh* (Creedy Bridge, Essex, 1777), *Great and Little Football Field* (Nazeing, Essex), *Lower and Upper Football Field* (Churchill, Oxfordshire), *Football Ground* (Hailey and North Newington, both in Oxfordshire), *Football Yard* (Binbrook Saint Mary, Lincolnshire, 1714), and *Foot-ball Shutt* (Chelmorton, Derbyshire).[74,75]

Where there is war there is sport. This from the Anglo-Spanish War of 1625–1630: "some of our Men were unfortunately and unmanly surprised, and before they knew their owne danger, had there their Throates cutte; Some having their Braines beaten out with the stockes of Muskets; others, their Noses slic'd off; whilst some Heads were spurned up & downe the Streets like Footeballs, and some Eares worne in scorne in *Spanish* Hattes."[76] Where there is sport there is war. During a Sabbath match at Great Bedwyn, Wiltshire, the crowd becomes abusive. A fight

---

69 Bedfordshire Archives: https://bedsarchives.bedford.gov.uk/CommunityHistories/Colmworth/ColmworthRectories.aspx. Accessed 6 September 2023.

70 Two years and three months' wages for a skilled tradesman.

71 A Football Close exists in South Luffenham, Lincolnshire, in 1810, and in Baldock, Hertfordshire, in 1817.

72 "Parishes: Piddington," in *A History of the County of Oxford: Volume 5, Bullingdon Hundred*, ed. Mary D Lobel (London: Victoria County History, 1957), 249–258. *British History Online*, accessed February 16, 2024, http://www.british-history.ac.uk/vch/oxon/vol5/pp249–258.

73 Football Garths are also recorded in the Yorkshire villages of Sledmarre (1650), Kirkleatham (1668), Aberford (1675), Bainton (1682), Barwick-in-Elmet (1684), South Frodingham (1723), and Calverley (1792). A 1728 marriage settlement in Elmswell, Yorkshire, comes with Football Garth, Three Nooked Piece, and Spellow Close. Football Closes are found in the Yorkshire villages of Barlow and Yeadon, and in Crich, Derbyshire. Garth probably derives from the Old English word *gærstūn*, a grass enclosure, from the Old Norse *garðr*, an enclosure.

74 There was a farm called Campins, close to Steeple Bumpstead. The east Essex village had a Camping Close, which still goes by that name.

75 For details on Scottish ball greens visit Richard McBrearty's webpage: https://scottishfootballorigins.org/2021/03/31/the-ba-green-scotlands-ancient-playing-field/.

76 Peecke, R., *Three to one being, an English-Spanish combat, performed by a westerne gentleman*. Augustine Mathewes, London, 1626. n.p.

breaks out between players and spectators, resulting in fines for twelve players and fourteen "beholders."[77] Elsewhere, hooligans are named. John Hawkins is described as "a football player, a boxer, and a looker-on", while Agnes Halbert "was at the football playing, and the occasion of the boxing by her foul words and quarrelling."[78] Finally, in 1635, the citizens of Cropthorne, Worcestershire, are bound over "concerning the usage of the unlawful game of foot-ball."[79]

Matches can end in murder or misadventure. The 1600 parish register of Coggeshall, Essex, records that "Peter Marcant was slain in Campinge on Sunday."[80] In 1608, during a football game in Waterford Marsh, Hertfordshire, Thomas Sticklinge thrusts his knee into John Turner's body with such force, that Turner dies from his injury.[81] In 1612, during a game of "trape ball" in Easebourne, Sussex, John Hollys throws the ball to Ralph Hollys. The ball strikes Ralph's head, and he dies instantly.[82] In 1614, in Wadhurst, Sussex. Richard Longley, playing football with a stone in his hand, hits George Hosmer on the nose. Hosmer dies the next day.[83] Holding a stone sounds peculiar, but the game was sometimes played with one in each hand to ensure a purely kicking game. That year, a labourer John Pirrye breaks his leg at football in Walton, north Essex, having played it "for the space of 5 weeks or thereabouts on a Sunday."[84]

It goes on. In Aston, Derbyshire, in 1624, "A great multitude and assembly of people being gathered together a lamentable accident hapned … at a meeting at football play … where a man was slayne and more mischeefe might perchance have followed."[85] A match between

---

77 Haigh, C., *The Plain Man's Pathways to Heaven: Kinds of Christianity in Post-Reformation England, 1570–1640.* Oxford University Press, 2007. p. 93.

78 Ibid, p. 94.

79 *Report on Manuscripts in Various Collections.* 7 Vols. His Majesty's Stationery Office, London, 1901–1914. Vols. 1–2. p. 283.

80 Dymond, D., *The game of camping in eastern England.* The Local Historian, 2021, 51:1. p. 2.

81 Knafla, L.A., *"John at Love Killed Her": The Assizes and Criminal Law in Early Modern England.* The University of Toronto Law Journal, 1985, 35:3, p. 317.

82 Ibid, p. 317.

83 Ibid, p. 317.

84 *Essex Archives Online.* https://www.essexarchivesonline.co.uk/result_details.aspx?ThisRecordsOffSet=1&id=239220. Accessed 25 October 2023.

85 *Report on the Manuscripts of the Late Reginald Rawdon Hastings.* 8 Vols. Her Majesty's Stationery Office, London, 1947. Vol. 4. p. 206.

Long Whatton, Derbyshire, and Barton, Nottinghamshire, the following day is banned, "fearing the like evill accident or worse might ensure."[86] Another fatality, in January 1628, evidenced by George Broughton's release on bail for the murder of Henry Cleave at football.[87] Sometimes it is passers-by at fault. William Farmer stands before the Court of Chivalry[88] charged with calling Walter Kirckham a "base and skurvie fellowe" before "various persons of gentle blood" in Uppingham.[89] While the outcome is unknown, Farmer's defence is damning. Kirckham, seeing "youths att football passing through the street spurned att the ball and therewith fell to the grounde, having bene immediately before att the taverne; and Mr Farmer's younger brother, being about 16 yeres of age, and one of the youths playinge att football, came to Mr Kirkham and endeavoured to helpe him up, in requitall whereof Mr Kirkham presently stroke downe Mr Farmer's brother twice with his staff in his hande, and drewe his sworde on him and beate him."[90]

On 1 March 1633, Thomas Crosfield, speaking of Oxford, records in his diary that the usual Shrovetide customs are "frittering",[91] throwing at cocks, and "playing at stooleball in ye Citty by woemen & football by men."[92] Around this time, James Ware describes the feast day of St James in Dublin, "there is a great mart … the chiefest commodities … were Kilkenny-balls, frizzes, ales and cakes … the best fringed mantles and ruggs for bedding."[93] Kilkenny-balls are believed to be sliotars, the leather-covered cork balls used in hurling and shinty. The fair was described in 1610, as a "Great mart or fair,

86 Ibid, p. 206.

87 "Charles I - volume 91: January 19–31, 1628," in *Calendar of State Papers Domestic: Charles I, 1627–28*, ed. John Bruce (London: Her Majesty's Stationery Office, 1858), 521–539. *British History Online*, accessed February 16, 2024, http://www.british-history.ac.uk/cal-state-papers/domestic/chas1/1627–8/pp521-539.

88 The Court of Chivalry still deals with matters of genealogy and heraldry. The case was referred to the court on the basis of "denial of gentility".

89 JC Thring, headmaster at Uppingham School, was a central figure in the establishment of the rules of the Football Association, in 1863.

90 "356 Kirckham v Farmer," in *The Court of Chivalry 1634–1640*, ed. Richard Cust and Andrew Hopper, *British History Online*, accessed February 16, 2024, http://www.british-history.ac.uk/no-series/court-of-chivalry/356–kirckham-farmer.

91 Making pancakes.

92 Boas, F.S. (ed.)., *The Diary of Thomas Crosfield.* Selected and edited from the MS. in the Queen's College Library for the Royal Society of Literature. Humphrey Milford, London, 1935. p. 63.

93 Harris, W. (ed.)., *The History and Antiquities of Dublin*, by Robert Ware. Manuscript, 1678. p. 126.

ale only."[94] It was held on James Street, which ended in St James's Gate, the western doorway to the walled city, the site of the Guinness brewery since 1759.

Records from Carlisle, Cumberland, allude to a Shrovetide football game in 1611. In February, a *foat ball* is purchased for 8d.[95,96] In previous years, the records only mention the purchase of "playgames upon Shrovetewesdaie" (1603 and 1605), relating to events variously named silverplay, silver games, or playsilver.[97] These were probably horse races or cockfighting with silver prizes.[98] Certainly, in 1618 "a silver cup gilded" is established "for manteyning of A horse race for the Cytties use."[99] Over a century earlier, in 1491, an "Item of the playe silver" is recorded in the accounts of St Michael's Church in Bishop's Stortford, in Hertfordshire.[100] In 1612, Anthony Curwen writes of Carlisle's former racecourse, the Swifts: "all the grounds was one contynuse grounds and when I was a scholler at Karliell no hinderance to the footballe play nor to the essayes of running of naggs, men and women leaping and dauncing &c. upon every Shrove Tuesday."[101] Curwen has a son in 1621 and dies in 1638. The annual football he refers to will have been played c1590–1610. An English–French dictionary from 1611, suggests how the football purchased in Carlisle might perform: "*Baloter.* To bound or bounce high from the ground, like a football."[102]

The Carlisle records document that on Shrove Tuesday 1614, a 6d payment is made for "a foote bawlle upon the sandes" (price 6d) and a shilling prize for the "Boy that wonn the foote Boll."[103] In 1615, 6d is spent

---

94 Clarke, H.B., Simms, A., Gillespie, R., *Irish Historic Towns Atlas, Dublin, Part 1, to 1610.* 19 Dawson Street, Dublin, Royal Irish Academy, 2002. p. 27. https://s3–eu-west-1.amazonaws.com/assets.ria.ie/ihta/ihta-digital/viking-towns/dublin-part-i-1610/IHTA_11_Dublin+Part+1_Text.pdf Accessed 26 April 2023.

95 Half a day's wages for a skilled tradesman.

96 Douglas, A., Greenfield. P. (eds.)., *Records of Early English Drama: Cumberland, Westmorland, Gloucestershire.* University of Toronto Press, 1986. p. 25.

97 Ibid, pp. 65, 67, 25, 52.

98 Ibid, p. 52.

99 Ibid, pp. 91–92.

100 Glasscock, J.L., *The Records of St Michael's Parish Church, Bishop's Stortford.* Elliot Stock, London, 1882. p. 27.

101 Douglas, A., Greenfield. P. (eds.)., *Records of Early English Drama: Cumberland, Westmorland, Gloucestershire.* University of Toronto Press, 1986. p. 158.

102 Cotgrave, R. (ed.)., *A Dictionarie of the French and English Tongues.* Adam Islip, London, 1611. n.p.

103 Douglas, A., Greenfield. P. (eds.)., *Records of Early English Drama: Cumberland, Westmorland, Gloucestershire.* University of Toronto Press, 1986. p. 76.

on a "ffooteball for yonge men upon Shraffetwesdaye", but only 4d for a foat ball in 1617. A ffote ball is bought in 1619, and another the following financial year, sandwiched between outlays for Carlisle's Shrove Tuesday games and for pipers on Shrove Tuesday evening. The next financial year, the cost of a football has risen to 8d, falling to 6d in 1627, for "a foott balle on shrough Tuesday." In 1628, records are kept of the purchase of two "foott balles", and again in 1635 and the following two financial years (spelt footballs, ffoote balles, and foott balles respectively). In 1656, the mayor sends "a football to the sands." From 1661, football is a Shrove Tuesday feature until the eighteenth century. The popular game later moves to Easter, continuing well into the nineteenth century. In 1688, a merchant tailor in London funds the maintenance of the school in Asby, in neighbouring Westmorland, built on his land.[104] When he dies, his legacy includes the purchase of a football for the scholars each year, a coming together of the footballing county of Westmorland and the footballing tailors of London.

Christopher Jonson, future headmaster of Winchester College, enters as a pupil in 1549. During his schooling he is believed to have written a Latin poem, that includes the sports Wykehamists play.[105,106] A definitive argument attributes the poem to another pupil, Robert Mathew, c1647.[107] The long-held belief is that the passage describes quoits, handball, and a bat and ball game, possibly an early version of cricket. The passage translates to:

> We must go to the yoke of the lofty green mountains.
> Let the gang advance together, let them retreat together,
> And so, until the top of the mountain is touched, let us go.
> This low mountain straddles the valley like a girdle,
> This goal is not to be crossed with the feet, nor dare,
> Lest you have trembling fevers, lie down on the ground.
> Here, however, you learn to throw the discus well,
> Whether the ball delights the palm or through the breezes,
> You often get hit by the stick when bouncing the ball.

---

104 Scott, D., *Bygone Cumberland and Westmorland.* William Andrews & Co., London, 1899. p. 243.

105 Pupils of the school, named after founder William Wykeham.

106 Kirby, T.F., *Annals of Winchester College.* Henry Frowde, London, 1892. p. 422.

107 Cook A.K., *About Winchester College.* Macmillan and Co., London, 1917. pp. 4–10.

An earlier passage reveals where they play: "If only the light is present on Tuesday or Thursday, thanks to Catherine we saw the mountain tops." St Catherine's Hill is a three hundred and twenty feet-high hill on the edge of Winchester, a mile and half from the college. An Iron Age rampart, called the Trench, encircles the summit. The entire hill was bought by Old Wykehamists and donated to the college in 1930. Collegers played there until 1868 and have always called it "Hills" (hence Mathew's plurality).[108]

In terms of the games played there, throwing the discus appears self-evident, though it may be code for a different pitching game like casting the stone, or quoits—where players toss iron rings onto a wooden pin. Handball and a stick and ball game are clear. Yoke may refer to the size of the playing area. A yoke is the amount of land a pair of oxen can plough in a day—approximately an acre, or two-thirds the size of a standard football pitch, a sizeable area to play on.[109] The summit size is nineteen acres; perhaps the playing area is ringfenced. They go up and return as a group. The fifth and sixth lines are enigmatic. What does goal mean? Reaching the field, most likely. Arguably, the Trench is the line that must not be crossed, and if you lie down, you roll down … or face the fury of the summit's icy blasts. The hill is four hundred feet above sea level, so it is probably freezing during winter games.

The seventh line is a demarcation, introducing us to the sports played. Cricket is unlikely: cricket balls are not the bounciest. A stickball game is likelier: a clash of sticks as players try to get the ball. Drawing a fanciful bow, Mathew is using another definition of yoke, the arch of spears victorious Romans made their vanquished opponents march under. Perhaps it *is* a goal, then, an arched one, one you are not allowed to run through, and if you lay down by it, you will get trampled or struck by the ball. After all, a stick and ball game needs goals. While the poem proves Winchester plays a stickball game in 1647, the poem fails to reveal a direct lineage to Winchester College Football. The school's football rules, colloquially known as Winkies, are standardised by 1825 but remain unwritten until

---

108 Football until 1860, cricket until 1866. In: Wordsworth. C., *Annals of my Early Life, 1806–1846.* Longmans, Green and Co., London, 1891. p. 356.

109 A virgate is the annual equivalent; cf. bovate/oxgang and carucate.

1863.[110] Whatever the various sports played, the boys can barely wait till the afternoon, for Mathew adds, "As bees swarm in summer … after lunch we flew to the green mountains." Mathew's schooldays are sandwiched by college tragedies. Sometime before 1637, a scholar dies of a sword wound while performing a tragedy. A sorrowful friend writes:

> Deare heart that was so serious in ye rest,
> Of all his lyfe, he could not play in Jest,
> O too too true Tragaedian twas thy task,
> To practize to be murderd & to maske!
> A Deadman on ye stage…[111]

The year Mathew leaves for Oxford University, one of the masters, William Ayliff, resigns his post. Ayliff later marries a rich widow. Her wealth is based on a jointure—a portion of her deceased husband's estate to support her until her death. When she dies in her prime, the jointure goes with her. Bereaved and reduced, Ayliff defenestrates himself.[112] Poems remain an important source of football references. This from a 1623 poem by Edmund Waller:[113]

> With painted oars the youths begin to sweep
> Neptune's smooth face, and cleave the yielding deep,
> Which soon becomes the seat of sudden war
> Between the wind and tide that fiercely jar.
> As when a sort of lusty shepherds try
> Their force at football, care of victory
> Makes them salute so rudely breast to breast
> That their encounter seems too rough for jest,
> They ply their feet, and still the restless ball,
> Toss'd to and fro, is urged by them all:

110 James Pyke (Winchester student 1858–1865), a captain of football at Winchester, first committed the rules to paper. In: Wainewright, J.B. (ed.)., *Winchester College 1836–1906: A Register*. P. and G. Wells, Winchester, 1907. p. 158.

111 Anon., *On ye Death of Longland slaine in acting a Tragedy*. c1615–1637. https://ereed.library.utoronto.ca/collections/hamps/traditions/. Accessed 16 May 2023.

112 Cook A.K., *About Winchester College*. Macmillan and Co., London, 1917. p. 71.

113 Waller championed Charles I's cause. When he plotted to rouse Royalist sympathy in London, he escaped the gallows only because he was distantly related to Oliver Cromwell.

> So fares the doubtful barge 'twixt tide and winds,
> And like effect of their contention finds.[114]

In 1653, Izaak Walton's *The Compleat Angler* is published. He includes a poem by his friend Sir Henry Wotton. Wotton is a diplomat and poet, with two football connections: he is educated at Winchester and becomes Provost of Eton College. His poem includes the erotically ambiguous lines:

> Joan takes her neat-rubb'd pail, and now
> She trips to milk the sand-red cow,
> Where, for some sturdy foot-ball swain,
> Joan strokes a syllabub or twain.[115]

Spurned football swains can vent their spleen on a rival: "If he fall in love, hee'le be sure to single her out at the next Wake to dance with, and layes such blowes on her lips you may heare the smacke afarre off. If shee reject him, he growes melancholy, and insteed of sighes whistles out his breath; and if hee have a Rivall, challenges him at footeball."[116] Some games are played for prizes: "the morrow after they would play a match at footeball with them in the morning, for an angell a man."[117,118]

North of the border, Scotland still prohibits Sabbath sports. In Logie-Buchan, Aberdeenshire, in the early 1600s, "the Presbytery took vigorous measures for suppressing tulzying,[119] football, and even holding markets at churches, on the Lord's Day!"[120] In Aberdeen, in 1607, youths are charged with "Sabboathes … drinking, playing at futte-ball, dancing, and passing fra paroche to paroche";[121] in 1610, James Mill

---

114 Waller, E., *Of the Danger His Majesty (being Prince) Escaped in the Road at St Andero.* In: Gilfillan, G. (ed.)., *Poetical Works of Edmund Waller and Sir John Denham.* William P. Nimmo, Edinburgh, 1857. pp. 2–3.

115 Wotton, H., *On a Bank, as I Sate A Fishing: A Description of the Spring.* In: Le Gallienne, R., *The Compleat Angler*, by Walton, I., Cotton, C. The Bodley Head, London & New York, 1897. p. 59.

116 Saltonstall, W., *Picturæ loquentes. Or Pictures drawne forth in characters With a poeme of a maid.* Tho. Cotes, London, 1631. n.p.

117 Anon., *The Pinder of Wakefield.* G.P., London, 1632. p. 6.

118 Angel coins were in circulation from 1465–1642. A week's wages for a skilled tradesman.

119 Wrestling.

120 Sinclair, J., *The Statistical Account of Scotland, 1791–99.* William Creech, Edinburgh, 1845. Vol. 13. p. 812.

121 Magoun, F.P., *Scottish Popular Football, 1424–1815.* The American Historical Review, 1931, 37:1, p. 6.

is "playing at the gowf in tyme of preaching;[122] and in 1611, the Synod of Fife bans "menstrelling and futeball on the Sabbaoth in the feildis", of Strathbrock.[123] Nevertheless, the first Sunday of May in Dalserf, Lanarkshire, is celebrated with maypole dancing, the firing of guns, and football.[124]

As in England, laws bend to the will of the people. During a Scottish trial, in 1611, it is noted that "acts ... made against players at the golf and foot ball, and against merchants sailing in winter, are ineffectual, because they were never received in use or custom."[125] In 1620, several men in Abernethy swear to refrain from Sabbath football,[126] while in April 1630, David Lindsay is rebuked for "playing at the futtball and caitch" in Litil Balcurvie; John Wilkie is "also guiltie of the lyk fault."[127] That May, the Laird of Balmowto has to interevene when Mr Scrimgeor complains about his parishioners playing Sabbath "futball upon the groond" of Balmowto.[128] Two months later, "Purse, McWaty, [and] Fumester" are fined 6s 8d for "futeball on the Sabboth nicht" in Elgin.[129]

Over the next few years, multiple Elgin citizens are upbraided for fornication. Sarah Anderson being *trelaps* (sinned three times) must "sit nyne Sabbaths upon the place of publick repentance." James Powtie also takes the stool for "his sinn of fornication." Janet Dunkesone and Betty Buntine are both *quadrilapse* [four lapses]. Betty refuses the stool and Janet runs away, leaving her child in the churchyard. Margaret Mean's *quinquies lapsa* [five lapses] outdoes them all. When James Laying and Margaret Gray brazen it out for lack of evidence, they are grudgingly discharged but will pay, "if ever they salbe found together heirafter."

122 Mylne, R. S., *The Master Masons to the Crown of Scotland and Their Works*. Scott & Ferguson and Burness and Company, Edinburgh, 1893. p. 88.

123 Baxter, C., *The Synod of Fife*. 1611–1687. T. Constable, Edinburgh, 1837. p. 21.

124 Chambers, R., *Domestic Annals of Scotland, from the Reformation to the Revolution*. W. & R. Chambers, Edinburgh and London, 1859. pp. 401–402.

125 *The Officers of State against Robert Cowtie and Others*. Hein Online. https://heinonline.org/HOL/Page?men_tab=srchresults&handle=hein.stair/dcsestd0009&id=537&size=2&collection=stair&terms=foot%20ball&termtype=phrase&set_as_cursor=0. Accessed 24 February 2024.

126 Magoun, F.P., *Scottish Popular Football, 1424–1815*. The American Historical Review, 1931, 37:1, p. 7.

127 Stevenson, W. (ed.)., *The Presbyterie Booke of Kirkcaldie*. James Burt, Kirkcaldy, Scotland, 1900. p. 7.

128 Ibid, p. 9.

129 Ree, S. (ed.)., *The Records of Elgin 1234–1800*. 2 Vols. Printed for the Spalding Club, Aberdeen, 1908. Vol. 2. p. 215.

Alexander Lowrie and Janet Page prefer to be daring, caught *in flagrante delicto* in two parishes. Agnes Buntine is quadrilapse "with four several men", Symon Adamson and Janet Laying trelapse in fornication, and end up in sackcloth, and fornicator Alexander Robertson simply refuses to obey the kirk.[130]

In Banff, Aberdeenshire, two footballs are given annually in lieu of rent in 1629,[131] while unsanctioned football in the town's streets results in 40s fines in 1682.[132,133] The game is used to get rid of the minister of the small parish of Glassford, Lanarkshire, in 1638. When he advocates reform, the authorities call him "a profaner of the Sabbath, provoking and countenancing his parishioners at dancing and playing at the football on the day."[134,135] He is swiftly removed. When parishioners of Rayne and Culsalmond, Aberdeenshire, are found guilty, the register's entry carries the tone of gossipy old ladies: "scandalous behaviour in convening themselves upon the Lord's day to a public footballing."[136]

In 1642, the Kelso Records report, "the abuse of the Lord's Day by playing at football, catch, nyneholls, new boulls, and other gameing, after sermones, whereby God is offended."[137] The sinners are fined 20s each.[138] Four months later, parishioners are admonished for "abuseing of the kirk at footeball on Fastern's Even … It is ordained", it adds with impotent irritation, "that they shall not trouble the kirk with their footeball at that tyme, or any tyme."[139] Parochial reports of sorcery are plentiful in Kelso: Thomas Randall uses two stones, which he employs "with some charmlike words"; Robert Hoggart slanders Margaret McCall, stating

130 Stevenson, W. (ed.)., *The Presbyterie Booke of Kirkcaldie.* James Burt, Kirkcaldy, Scotland, 1900. pp. 21, 10, 26, 61, 42, 62, 66, 159, 393.

131 Magoun, F.P., *Scottish Popular Football, 1424–1815.* The American Historical Review, 1931, 37:1, p. 7.

132 Ibid, p. 7.

133 Twenty-two days' wages for a skilled tradesman.

134 Magoun, F.P., *History of Football from the Beginnings to 1871.* Kölner anglistische arbeiten, 1938, Vols. 31–33. p. 94.

135 Steward, L.A.M., *Rethinking the Scottish Revolution: Covenanted Scotland, 1637–1651.* Oxford University Press, 2016. p. 115.

136 Magoun, F.P., *History of Football from the Beginnings to 1871.* Kölner anglistische arbeiten, 1938, Vols. 31–33. p. 94.

137 *History of the Berwickshire Naturalist Club.* Henry Hunter Blair, Alnwick, Scotland, 1868. p. 333.

138 A fortnight's wages for a skilled tradesman..

139 *History of the Berwickshire Naturalist Club.* Henry Hunter Blair, Alnwick, Scotland, 1868. p. 333.

that he saw her appear in the likeness of a cat; an Englishman in Lothian … "pretends to judicial astrologie"; and a married couple "complean of John Brown, weaver, ther, for calling him a warwoof, and her a witch."[140]

In 1682, four armed Highlanders strong-arm their way into a cottage in Toddellhills, Aberdeenshire. They are hostile to the landowner and want all the tenants off his land. They tell his terror-struck tenants they want "to geat James Buchanes head to pleay at the football", before moving on to the next cottage. Now drunk, they threaten to seize Buchane, "stob him and ding aff his head and pleay at the football with it."[141] In the 1690s, Scotland is plagued with famine. John Sinclair writes that in Fordyce, Aberdeenshire, "The thing most remarkable was that for several years before the famine, adultery and fornication had been extremely frequent, to which the famine put an entire and speedy stop." He adds, "shortly after the Reformation, Popery … seems to have left the parish entirely, but the superstitions as to wells, spells, charms remained much longer … The east and west side of the parish continued their competition at the foot-ball after divine service."[142]

Shrove Tuesday football ends in a court case in Duns, Scotland, in 1686. John Bayne accuses two players of assaulting him while he is spectating. The defendants' lawyer lays out their case: "Ther being an ancient custome throughout all this kingdom to play at football upon Fasterneven, wher the maried men ordinarly play against the unmaried … William Edgar and John Watson, who were married men, having accidentallie encountered the said John Bayne, who wes ane unmaried man, the said John Bayne was dunge over in the shufell, who did thereupon spit upon the saids … faces, quherpon ther insewed ane small scuffell amongst them with their naked fists."[143]

The prosecution produces a wealth of witnesses with damning testimonies, including a doctor, a teacher, and a student of divinity. Edgar, Watson, and a third man beat the spectating Bayne, "upon his

140 Ibid, pp. 335–336.

141 Paton, H., (ed.), *The register of the Privy Council of Scotland.* 14 Vols. H.M. General Register House, Edinburgh, 1930. Third series. Vol. 13. pp. 183, 185.

142 Sinclair, J., *The Statistical Account of Scotland, 1791–99.* William Creech, Edinburgh, 1792. Vol. 3. p. 63.

143 Paton, H., (ed.), *The register of the Privy Council of Scotland.* 14 Vols. H.M. General Register House, Edinburgh, 1930. Third series. Vol. 12. pp. 146–150.

face … with their fists and battones … to the great effusione of his blood … calling him a treator to the town." As elsewhere, Shrovetide games stand outside the law, irrespective of the violence, reflecting an inalienable right of ritual. "If ther happened any differences, tumults or ryots to fall out therat, the samine [same] was never taken notice of aither by the sherife or bailzie [deputy]."[144] This particular case reaches the Privy Council as it is deemed "too obviously a digression from the main enterprise."[145] Their inalienable right is well-exercised; most Shrovetide games in the town end in brawls; another is recorded in 1724.[146]

The Borders town of Kelso attracts controversy when the schoolmaster runs afoul of the governing Presbytery in 1698. "He has," they say, "prostituted his Authority over his Scholars to contempt by playing at Foot-ball and games with them." The schoolmaster replies "that the people of Mers and Tiviotdale are too much addicted to that violent Sport; and the youth follow their example." Pupils of the two districts had already challenged one another and he oversaw the game to ensure fair play. "When the Ball came to his Foot," he adds, "I touch'd it. A most heinous Crime indeed."[147] In the 1690s, a Scottish ballad is published in a broadside. The humorous elegy of piper Habbie Simpson includes the lines: "and fiercely at Foot-ball he ran; At every Game the gree [prize] he wan."[148]

Women in Scotland play football. In August 1628, the Registers of the Presbytery of Lanark, record that, "Mr Jo^{n} Lindesay, minister at Carstares, having regratit the break of the sabbothe by the insolent behaviour of men and women in foot baling, dancing, and Barla Breks."[149] Two years before, the minister had branded six men "profaners of the Sabbath" for "fetching hame a maypole, and dancing about the same, upon pasch [Easter] sonday."[150] In 1642, he is at it again, "through occasion of a

144 Ibid, p. 89.

145 Ibid, pp. 23–24.

146 *Report on Manuscripts in Various Collections.* 7 Vols. His Majesty's Stationery Office, London, 1901–1914. Vols. 5–6. pp. 43–45.

147 Kirkwoord, J., *Mr. Kirkwood's Please Before the Kirk, And Civil Judicatures of Scotland.* D.E., London, 1698. pp. 62–63.

148 Sempill, R., *The life and death of the piper of Kilbarchan.* Scotland, n.p., c1690–1699. n.p.

149 Robertson, J. (ed.), *Ecclesiastical Records: Selections from the Registers of the Presbytery of Lanark.* s.n., Edinburgh, 1839. p. 6.

150 Ibid, p. 22.

tumultuous brithell [wedding], and promiscuous dancing at Carstars, there must have fallen out … great mischiefe and blood."[151,152] The kirk sessions of Lammingtoune, Lanarkshire, mention Shrovetide football and women in 1656: "The sessione considering ane super-titous and abominable custom yt hes continued still in this paroche, That men and women uses promiscuously to play at the foot-ball upon Fasting's Even; and also considering what evill and sadde consequences hes followed yt upon, viz. uncleannesse, drunkenness and fighting."[153] Permitting women to play football does not reflect a softening of contemporary Scottish misogyny. The same month, after a three-decade interlude, witch-hunts resume. Over the next two years, three hundred and thirty women are tried.[154]

~

When Dissenters separate from the Church of England, they flee the country to avoid persecution. On 20 September 1620, the Mayflower departs Plymouth with one hundred and two passengers. When they arrive on 21 November 1620, there are one hundred and three: Oceanus Hopkins and Peregrine White are born en route, William Butten dies. John Howland is washed overboard but survives.[155] In a nod to French ball games, one passenger is called George Soule. The Roanoke Colony had settled in 1584, but all one hundred and twenty of them disappear. The first enduring colony is established in Jamestown, Virginia, in 1607. Two years later, artisan Polish workers, imported to the colony, are recorded as initiating, "a ball game played with a bat … Most often we played this game on Sundays. We rolled rags to make the balls." [156] Is this the earliest reference to colonial sport in North America? Are Sadowski, Mata, Mientus, Stoika, Zrenica, and Stafanski disregarded heroes? No.

151 Ibid, p. 29.

152 Brithell: bridal.

153 Sinclair, J., *The Statistical Account of Scotland, 1791–99.* William Creech, Edinburgh, 1845. Vol. 6. p. 823.

154 Between 1590 and 1662, five witch-hunts took place, collectively lasting seven years. Around four thousand five hundred Scottish women were tried for witchcraft. Over sixty per cent were condemned to death. In March 2022, Nicola Sturgeon, the First Minister of Scotland, officially apologised for the persecution.

155 Bradford, W., *History of Plymouth Plantation 1620–1647.* 2 Vols. Houghton Mifflin Company, Boston, Massachusetts, 1912. Vol. 1. p. 151.

156 Block, D., *Baseball Before We Knew It: A Search for the Roots of the Game.* University of Nebraska Press, Lincoln, Nebraska, 2005. p. 101.

The purported diary that the information comes from has been rejected as a legitimate source.[157]

The second settlement is the Plymouth Colony of New England, founded in 1620 by the passengers of the Mayflower. The majority of them are from East Anglia, a third dyed-in-the-wool Puritans.[158] On Christmas Day 1621, the governor asks the settlers to work. Most refuse as "it wente against their consciences to work on ye day." The more Puritanical, who see the day as a Popish festival, dutifully comply. When they return at noon the governor finds the objectors, "in ye street at play, openly; some pitching the barr, and some at stoole-ball, and shuch like sport."[159] It is the first reference to colonial ball games in North America.

Clerics drift. In 1624, the Virginia assembly decrees that, "Mynisters shall not give themselves to excess in drinking or yette spend their tyme idelie by day or by night, playing at dice, cards or any unlawful game."[160] Cards and dice. A "great dishonour of God" the Massachusetts legislature calls them in 1670.[161] Two years later, the Connecticut Blue Laws add other infamies. No woman shall kiss her child on the Sabbath, neither can anyone walk in their garden or run anywhere. At least they have a sense of humour: "Every male must have his hair cut round according to a cap."[162] And there are to be no minced pies. Ever.

The Blue Laws reflects the puritanical stance that lewd customs "include all Sorts of publick Sports, Exercises, and Recreations … as Comedies, Foot-Ball-Play, and Bear-Baitings … and Christmas-Pye is made an Abomination. All games where there is any chance of Hazard of Loss are strictly forbidden, as Tennis, Bowles, and Billiards; not so much as a Game at Stool-Ball for a Tansy [cake], or a Cross and Pyle for the odd Penny at a Reckoning, upon Pain of Damnation."[163]

---

157 Pula, J.S., *Fact vs. Fiction: What do we really know about the Polish presence in early Jamestown?* The Polish Review, 2008, 53:4, p. 487.

158 Mayflower400UK: https://www.mayflower400uk.org/visit/plymouth-england/attractions/the-mayflower-steps/. Accessed 23 September 2023.

159 Bradford, W., *History of Plymouth Plantation 1620–1647.* 2 Vols. Houghton Mifflin Company, Boston, Massachusetts, 1912. Vol. 1. p. 245.

160 Chafetz, H., *Play the Devil. A History of Gambling in the United States from 1492 to 1955.* Clarkson N. Potter, Inc., New York, NY, 1960. p. 13.

161 Ibid, p. 14.

162 Ibid, p. 14.

163 Lewis, T., *English Presbyterian Eloquence.* T. Bickerton, London, 1720. p. 17.

The future governor of Massachusetts John Winthrop arrives in 1630. As a boy growing up in Suffolk, his father records that John "brak his leg at footebal."[164] It may very well have been camping. In 1636/37, Winthrop's sister writes to him about her boy who is settling in New England. She frets about the lack of teachers. It would, she says "greve me in my grave to know that his mynde should be withdrawn from his booke by other sports or imployments, for that weer but the way to make him good att nothinge."[165]

The games colonialists import will influence future homegrown sports, including baseball and football. After the failed Roanoke Colony, another attempt is not made until 1602. The Concord is captained by Bartholomew Gosnold, a man born and raised in Suffolk. Thirty-one travellers accompany him, including his cousin Bartholomew Gilbert, his Norfolk friend John Brereton, Gabriel Archer of south Essex, and James Rosier of Suffolk. The counties of origin of the other passengers and crew are unknown. During the Great Migration of 1620–1642, thousands settle in New England. At the time, Norwich in Norfolk is England's second largest city, Ipswich in Sussex the seventh, Great Yarmouth in Norfolk the eighth, and Cambridge the tenth.[166] Nearly half the settlers are from East Anglia, well over if Essex is included.[167] With over fifty per cent of the early settler population from camping country, it is inconceivable they do not bring the game with them.[168] To what extent does it contribute to the evolution of American football? The two bear many similarities. Did American football stem from a coalescence of football and rugby in the universities of New England, or is there an existing, widely played game, which has descended from camping or other kicking–carrying games

---

164 Ellett, L. R., *John Winthrop, Governor and Magistrate* Unpublished MA thesis, University of Southern California, 1952. p. 43.

165 Sibley, J.L., *Biographical Sketches of Graduates of Harvard University.* 7 Vols. Charles William Sever, Cambridge, Massachusetts. Vol. 1. p. 28.

166 Trudgill, P., *The East Anglican Dialect of English in the World.* Studia Anglica Posnaniensia, 2012, 47:1, p. 451.

167 https://www.themaparchive.com/product/english-immigration-to-america-162042–and-the-congregational-establishment/. Accessed 10 November 2023.

168 New England is filled with East Anglian place names including Cambridge, Newmarket, Norwich, Ipswich, Thetford (birthplace of Thomas Paine), Yarmouth, Hingham (Abraham Lincoln's ancestor Samuel Lincoln emigrated from Hingham in 1637), Haverhill, Wenham, Ely, and Lynn. There is also the Essex village of Dedham, which borders Suffolk. The Suffolk-born captain of The Concord named Cape Cod and Martha's Vineyard.

imported by early colonists? It mirrors the question of modern football in England. One school considers it to have arisen as a blend of the rules of various public schools, notwithstanding that these games descended from folk football. The other school argues that football within working class culture has been widespread for centuries. Judging from the few sources available—principally legal records and literary quotes—this is indisputably true. While the game would never have been codified without public school authority and old boy heft, it was not conducted in a vacuum. A similar argument can be made for New England universities and American football. Camping is a stowaway on the Mayflower. Folk football and its refined brother would have been introduced too, as well as tennis, bowls, bandy and hurling. Different sports would surely blend, the dominant games incorporating the best elements of other games, giving colonial New Englanders a sport of their own.[169]

The first mention of *colonists playing football* is in Boston in 1657: "for as much as sundry complaints are made that several persons have received hurt by boyes and young men playing at foot ball in the streets; these are therefore to Injoyne that none be found at that game in any of the streets, Lanes, or Inclosures of this town, under the pœnalty of twenty shillings for every such offense."[170] There is an amendment three years later: "in the order against footeball playing these wordes bee added inclosures withoutt the owners consent."[171] In 1658, Peter Stuyvesant, last director general of the colony of New Netherland, prohibits Sabbath "ploughing, sowing, mowing, fishing, hunting, and all amusements, as playing at tennis, ballplaying." [172,173] Four years later, he relaxes the restrictions to during divine service only.[174] In 1682, there is mention of boys playing at football in New England,[175] while a plea sees out the century. American freeholders entreat William III to act

169 By a quirk of coincidence, one of the founding fathers of American Football was Walter Camp.

170 *Second Report of the Record Commissioners of the City of Boston*. Rockwell and Churchill, 39 Arch Street, Boston, 1877. p. 141.

171 Ibid, 157.

172 Tennis may be a misinterpretation. In the original Dutch it is balslaen, which means to hit a ball: https://protoball.org/1660c.3. Accessed 15 June 2023.

173 O'Callaghan, E.B. (ed.), *Documents Relative to the Colonial History of the State of New York*. 15 Vols. Weed, Parsons and Company, Albany, NY, 1853. Vol. 12. p. 92.

174 Ibid, Vol. 2. p. 79.

175 J.W., *A letter from New-England*. s.n., London, 1682. p. 8.

"against the pretended Government of Connecticut … The Throne is made ye footstoole & ye Crowne ye football … & theire Ma^{tyes} [Majesties] are made ye patrons of all o^{r} injuryes."[176] The earliest *football reference* in North America relates to Native Americans and is found in William Wood's travelogue, in 1634:

"For their sport activitie they have commonly but three or foure; as football, shooting, running, and fishing: when they play country against country there are rich Goales, all behung with Wampompeage [shells], Mowhackies, Beaver skins, and blacke Otter skinnes … Their Goales be a mile long placed on the sands, which are as even as a board; their ball is no bigger than a hand-ball, which sometimes they mount in the Aire with their naked feete, sometimes it is swayed by the multitude; sometimes also it is two dayes before they get a Goale, then they marke the ground they winne, and beginne there the next day. Before they come to this sport, they paint themselves, even as when they goe to warre … Before they begin their armes be disordered, and hung upon some neighbouring tree, after which they make a long scrowle on the sand, over which they shake loving hands, and with laughing hearts scuffle for victorie[177]… At footeball … if any man be throwne he laughes out his foyle, there is no seeking of revenge, no quarreling, no bloody noses, scratched faces, blacke eyes, broken shinnes, no bruised members, or crushed ribs … but the goale being wonne, the goods on the one side lost; friends they were at the football."[178] Of the Mohawk people, he writes: "Tamahaukes be staves of two foote and a halfe long, and a knob at one end as round and bigge as a footeball."[179]

Half a century later, John Dunton also witnesses "a great Game of Foot-Ball" between two New England towns: "They play'd with their bare feet, which I thought very odd; but it was upon a broad Sandy Shoar … Neither were they so apt to trip up one another's heels and quarrel, as I have seen 'em in England … [it] is the most Innocent of all their sports, but this they only play at in the Summer time."[180]

---

176 O'Callaghan, E.B. (ed.)., *Documents Relative to the Colonial History of the State of New York.* 15 Vols. Weed, Parsons and Company, Albany, 1853. Vol. 3. pp. 853–854.

177 Wood, W., *New England's Prospect. A true, lively, and experimentall description of that part of America, commonly called New England.* John Bellamie, London, 1634. p. 86.

178 Ibid, p. 74.

179 Ibid, pp. 58–59.

180 Dunton, J., *John Dunton's Letters from New-England.* T.R Marvin and Son, Boston, 1867. pp. 285–286.

The Narragansett people of Rhode Island fight with the English against the Pequot people from 1636 to 1638. Forty years later, it is their turn to be massacred or sold into slavery by colonists.[181] In 1643, Puritan minister Roger Williams publishes a book on the languages of native peoples.[182] London-born Williams is a complex figure, banished from the Massachusetts Bay Colony for sedition and heresy. He defends Narragansett rights so staunchly he becomes their most trusted ally, but in the 1650s, while mediating on their behalf, divulges secrets to the colonists. He is opposed to African slavery and the lifelong enslavement of native peoples, but he believes in indentured servitude for ten years for men captured in battle, and profits from it.[183,184]

Williams spends much time with the Narragansett people and writes extensively of their culture and customs. They have a card-like game played with rushes, and a dice game played with painted plum stones. Watched by hundreds or thousands, "they have great meetings of foot-ball playing, onely in Summer, towne against towne, upon some broad sandy shoare, free from stones, or upon some soft heathie plot because of their naked feet, at which they have great stakings, but seldom quarrel."[185] The sublime moment of the passage is what is written next. A single Narragansett word. *Pasuckquakohowaûog*. They meet to football.[186,187] Prescient words appear in the accompanying brief lexicon: *cowàmmaunsh* (I love you), *aquie chechequnnuwásh* (do not rob me), *wúskontawaúnn kemineiucqun* (I fear some will murther mee), and *kunnìshickquock*. They will kill you.

---

181 The virtual annihilation of the Pequot and Narragansett meets the standard for genocide. Murphy, J.D. (ed.)., *American Indian Wars: The Essential Reference Guide*. ABC-CLIO®, New York, NY, 2022. p. xxii.

182 Williams, R., *A Key into the Language of America,* or *An help to the Language of the Natives in that part of America called New England*. Gregory Dexter, London, 1643.

183 Greene, G.W., *A Short History of Rhode Island*. J.A and R.A Reid, Providence, Rhode Island, 1877. p. 32.

184 Rubertone, P.E., *Grave Undertakings: An Archaeology of Roger Williams and the Narragansett Indians*. Smithsonian Institution Scholarly Press, 2001. In: Turgeon, L., *Grave Undertakings: An Archaeology of Roger Williams and the Narragansett Indians. Ethnohistory,* 2004, 51:4, p. 820.

185 Williams, R., *A Key into the Language of America,* or *An help to the Language of the Natives in that part of America called New England*. Gregory Dexter, London, 1643. p. 171.

186 Ibid, p. 171.

187 Narragansett is now an extinct language. A recovery project is based largely on Williams's book.

CHAPTER TEN
1600–1699 III

It is 1635, and Charles I is king. A troubled one. He faces threats from parliament, nonconformists, and Catholics. Lucky for him they loathe one another. Tin-eared Charles tries to soften his public image by re-issuing his father's *Book of Sports*.[1] The manoeuvre backfires spectacularly. The politically articulate Puritans are incensed, and incensed Puritans attack like bees. Another faggot on the fire. Not all clergy lean in. In Essex, eleven reforming parsons actively support Sunday sport, and two openly play.[2] Michael Dalton is a Justice of the Peace (JP) in Essex and Cambridge, counties steeped in camping culture. His *The Countrey Justice* has just been reissued, the go-to manual for JPs. A JP can enter anywhere they suspect illegal games are afoot and arrest and imprison the owners.[3] Games include *Foot ball*, loggets, tennis, quoits, shove groat, bowls, and casting the stone. Dalton assures us it is not a riot if players gather for football, nor if women meet in numbers;[4] neither is injuring another player at football a criminal act, even if they die, as the game is by consent and "for disport & triall of manhood."[5]

In 1638, the future Lord Chancellor of Ireland agrees such deaths are misadventures, not felonies.[6] His years in Ireland have softened him, for he adds that assembling "to drink at an Ale-house", or to play at "Foot-ball, Bucklers, Bear or Bull-baitings, Dancings, Bowles, Cards or Dice … is no Riot, nor prohibited, for these meetings usually are not with any intent to offer or do violence or hurt."[7] Just not on a Sunday, or in the streets. There are ten failed attempts to curb football in London's throughfares in the first third of the century. The 1628 decree complains

---

1 *The Kings Majesties Declaration to His Subjects, Concerning Lawfull Sports to bee Used.* Robert Barker, London, 1633.

2 Egan, M., *Laudians, Puritans and the Laity in Essex*. Unpublished PhD thesis, University College London, 2001, p. 72.

3 Dalton, M., *The Countrey Justice*. John Mori, London, 1635. p. 64.

4 Ibid, p. 219.

5 Ibid, p. 246.

6 Bolton, R., *A Justice of Peace for Ireland*. Benjamin Tooke and John Crooke, Dublin, 1683. p. 58.

7 Ibid p. 158.

of "many hurts … extendinge even to the losses of the lives and limbs of people."[8]

To Michael Dalton, bowling is "at all times in the meaner sort of people by law prohibited", because of its connection to gambling. This is little more than base snobbery. Henry VIII restricts bowling to the wealthy, and Charles is an avid player, as was his father. Charles is not averse to gambling on it, losing £4,000 in a single game.[9] Dalton's manual also covers felonies by statute, including masonic meetings, buggery with a beast, cutting out tongues or putting out eyes, conjuration of an evil spirit, entertaining, rewarding, feeding, or employing an evil spirit, and using sorcery, charms, or enchantments to lame or kill another. He covers the identification of witches in titillating detail. Suspicion should be raised if they vomit needles and nails, the corpse of their victim bleeds on them at touch, they are seen feeding an evil spirit, and, of course, if their dwelling carries the tell-tale smell of evil spirits.

Thomas Randolph has a lighter touch: "Madam, you may in time bring down his legs,

To just the size, now overgrown with playing, Too much at football."[10] He adds, comparing England to Spain, "Foot-ball with us may be with them Baloone, As they at Tilt, so we at Quintaine, runne. And those old Pastimes relish best with me, That have least Art, and most simplicitie."[11,12]

The following year, in a comedy play, Lord Letoy claims, "I and my men can play a match at football, Wrastle a hansome fall, and pitch the barre, And crack the cudgells, and a pate sometimes, … my men can runne at base, and breath our selves at Barly-breake, and dancing"[13] Young women gather in Berkhamsted, Hertfordshire, in 1617, "talking upon football players."[14] Perhaps they knew Elyzabeth Atkins, who

8 Griffiths, P., *Youth and Authority: Formative Experiences in England 1560–1640*. Oxford University Press, 1996. p. 139.

9 One hundred and ninety years' wages for a skilled tradesman.

10 Randolph, T., *The Muse's Looking Glass*. Leonard Lichfield, Cambridge, 1637. p. 70.

11 Ibid, p. 117.

12 Quintain: In this context, a tilting post used for jousting training. It also means a medieval flirting ritual, or a poem with five lines (e.g., a limerick).

13 Brome, R., *The Antipodes*. I. Okes, London, 1638. n.p.

14 Underdown, D., *Revel, Riot, and Rebellion*. Oxford University Press, 1985. p. 75.

fell from a local cherry tree in 1603.[15] Emilia Geddie would have been crestfallen to hear such unholy chatter. The "child prophet and exemplar of godliness" dies in Fife in 1681, aged sixteen.[16] By the age of three, she is chiding the servants of her staunch presbyterian parents for sabbath breaking. "Having one Day taken some View of a Foot-ball Game, she thought it to be vain and idle, and left them. When she returned to the Company, she was asked, 'Why she had retired so quickly, and wept?' She answered, That it was not so much for seeing the Idleness and Wickedness of the Foot-Ball men, as because she had seen a godly and grave Gentlewoman laughing, and taking Pleasure at the Sight."[17] When men and women play stoolball together, it is a chance for censure-free, erotically charged contact. Emilia is twelve when a poem is published, which would have infuriated her:

> Young men and maids,
> Now very brisk,
> At barley-break and
> Stool-ball frisk.[18]

In 1636, the Bishop of Norwich questions his diocese on the measures it is taking to curb profane use of consecrated ground. Any "Playes … Church-ales … dancing, Stoole-ball, Foot-ball"?[19] In 1638, the newly elected bishop, Richard Montagu, poses similar questions. Moving on from fairs, markets, drying of clothes, and dunging of cattle, he adds, "Much less is it to be unhallowed with dancings, morrises, meetings at Easter, drinkings, Whitsun ales, midsummer merriments or the like, stool ball, football, wrestlings, wasters or boys' sports."[20] His call to action is ineffectual, and he dies in office three years later. The efforts of the Puritanical clergy of

15 Cox, J.C., *The Parish Registers of England.* Methuen & Co. Ltd., London, 1910. p. 129.

16 Yeoman, L. A. "Geddie, Emelia [Emilia] (1665–1681), child prophet and exemplar of godliness." *Oxford Dictionary of National Biography.* 23 Sep. 2004; Accessed 15 Feb. 2024. https://www.oxforddnb.com/view/10.1093/ref:odnb/9780198614128.001.0001/odnb-9780198614128–e-55912.

17 Whitefield, G., *Some Choice Sentences and Practices of Emilia Geddie.* T. Lumisden & J. Roberson, Edinburgh, 1741. p. 10.

18 Winstanley, W., *Poor Robin, 1677. An Almanack After a New Fashion.* s.n., London, 1677. n.p.

19 Wren, M., *Articles to be inquired of within the dioces of Norwich in the first visitation of the R. Reverand Father in God, Matthew, Lord Bishop of Norwich.* Richard Badger, London, 1636. n.p.

20 Cressy, D., *Birth, Marriage, and Death Ritual, Religion, and the Life-Cycle in Tudor and Stuart England.* Oxford University Press, 1997. p. 468.

Westmoreland and Cumberland prove equally futile. Both are steadfast footballing counties. In the mid-1630s, Lord William Howard of Naworth, Cumberland, purchases "a footeball for the children" at Christmas; "battell-dores" are also purchased. Elsewhere, Lady Howard gives 5s to a "blinde harper", and a servant is fined 6s 8d for playing at the gambling board game nine holes.[21,22] A further clerical attempt, focussing on Sabbath pursuits, follows in 1656: "All scandalous persons … are to be suspended from the Sacrament of the Lord's Supper." Pastimes include, "masking, wakes … playing at football, stool ball, Wrestling … plays, interludes, fencing."[23]

As the country descends inexorably into war, authorities hear of "a ffoote-ball playe or campe to be holden in Whelpmore."[24] Several hundred are to meet at a Cambridgeshire fen "to playe at foot bale." It is unclear if it is custom, but it is named Anderson's camp after the proposer, who intends to have "the ffirst blowe att the Ball."[25] They turn up with a ball, but rain prevents a decent assembly. Next day, a local constable spots, "John Bryse with a camping ball and he did campe the same two furlongs into a grate parte of the towne and so camped the same backe agayne and so carried it into Whelpmore." Two hundred men, including some from Lakenheath, across the Suffolk border, destroy the drainage dykes. Six are imprisoned. A few years before, there had been Fens riots in Axholme, Lincolnshire. At least one begins under the pretence of camping. The horn blast used to start the game signals the uprising. "Sir Cornelius Vermüden's agent, Mr. Hawthorn, was thrown into the river and kept in with long poles amid cries of Drown him, Break his leggs; and the constables put in the stocks."[26] The troubles go on. In 1642, when fens are drained and houses built upon them, "a great Number of People got together at a Foot-ball playing, and pretending the Houses stood in their way, levelled them."[27]

---

21 Ornsby, G. (ed.)., *Selections from the household books of the Lord William Howard of Naworth castle*. Gilbert and Rivington, St John's Square, London, 1878. Vol. 68. pp. 59, 228, 317, 69.

22 Three and four days' wages for a skilled tradesman respectively. Nine holes is referred to as nine men's Morris in *A Midsummer Night's Dream*.

23 Wilson, J. (ed.)., *The Victoria History of the Counties of England: Cumberland*. 2 Vols. Archibald Constable and Company Limited, London, 1905. Vol. 2. p. 482.

24 Sweeting, W.D. (ed.)., *Fenland Notes and Queries, 1894–10*. 3 Vols. Geo. C. Caster, Peterborough, 1894. Vol. 2. p. 356.

25 Ibid, p. 357.

26 Ibid, p. 357.

27 *Philosophical Transactions*. s.n., London, 1698. Vol 19. p. 345.

By 1641, the walls are closing in on Charles. To placate the Puritan movement, he banishes all Popish Recusants, priests, and Jesuits alike.[28,29] Not all make the deadline. Hugh Green is condemned to death. Three women are hanged first. After rattling off a few words, he is hanged momentarily. A barber, totally unsuited to the job, begins to dismember him, but makes such a hash of it, Green comes to. The barber slices his stomach open, takes out his liver, realises it is not his heart, then plunges his hands back in, desperately searching as Green's guts "tumble out ever'y way." Green, alive after half an hour of fumbling, is finally beheaded. "Found it!" says the barber, or words to that effect, hoisting the heart. The crowd is disinterested. There are frolics to be had. "The ungodly Multitude … from ten o'clock in the Morning, till four in the afternoon … sported themselves at Football with his Head, and put sticks in his Eyes, Ears, Nose, and Mouth."[30]

January 1642, and all Charles's birds have flown. The country spirals into civil war. There is an early swagger to the cavaliers. A satire on Puritan disdain for Shrove Tuesday includes the lines:

> They'r mounted high, contemne the humble play,
> Of Cat, or Football on a Holiday,
> In *Finesbury* fields. No, 'tis their brave intent,
> Wisely t'advise the King, and Parliament.[31]

Elsewhere, "these hypocriticall *Round-heads* (of late so called) … who walke within compasse of their owne circumference … whose minds like footeballs or bubbles of Sope in the Aire, are throwne and tossed too and fro with every winde of Doctrine." [32] Roundheads bite back. The fate of the *Book of Sports* symbolises the purifying of England's soul. In 1643, Parliament orders all copies be sent to London, "to be burned

---

28 *A Petition to the King.* s.n., London, 1641.

29 Russell, C., *The Fall of the British Monarchies 1637–1642.* Oxford University Press, Great Clarendon Street, Oxford, 1991. pp. 265–266.

30 Challoner, R., *Memoirs of Missionary Priests, as well Secular as Regular.* 2 Vols. F. Needham, London, 1741. Vol. 1. pp. 217, 223–225.

31 Cowley, A., *A Satyre Against Separatists* In: *The Foure Ages of England.* s.n., London, 1648. p. 67.

32 Anon., *Sir James Cambels Clarks disaster.* s.n., London, 1642. p. 6.

by the hand of the common Hangman in Cheape-side."[33] The cleansing power of fire.

Puritan firebrand Richard Culmer is one of the most controversial men of the period. His "narrow brain'd" radical zeal and odious nature make him a loathed figure. Around 1640, when he rails against sabbath violations, angry parishioners play sabbath "Crickit" beside his door;[34] and when he refuses to read the *Book of Sports*, he is labelled a hypocrite, with claims he was famous at Cambridge as a football player.[35] The parishioners move on to play in a field. It is only the fourteenth mention of cricket in history, the fourth to mention more than two cricketers. Appointed commissioner in 1643 for "the utter demolishing … of all monuments of superstition" in Canterbury Cathedral, Culmer leads the destruction himself. Unable to exit due to furious demonstrators, he is forced to urinate in the cathedral.[36] In his next position, the parishioners, used to "a common tippler and sabbath-breaker" of a curate, offer to pay Culmer's wages for life, if he will only leave.[37] He is rioted against, pelted with mud, and repeatedly assaulted, once "until he vomited blood."[38] His house is plundered, he is locked out of his own church, and a local defecates on a pew.[39] A mob even try to hang him.[40] In 1657, his son refutes the football claim.[41] Memories are long. An extraordinary rebuttal to the apologia is published later that year. The anonymous author pulls no punches. Culmer's son, "pretending to write a *Martyrologie,* tells a tale of a TURD, wrapping it up in a Legend of lies, forgeries, and other base trumpery, (to say nothing here of his SHITTEN STYLE)."[42] And

---

33 Brayley, E.W., *Londiniana. Or, Reminiscences of the British Metropolis*. 4 Vols. Hurst, Chance, and Company, London, 1829. Vol. 4. p. 204.

34 Culmer, R., *A Parishe Looking-Glasse For Persecutors of Ministers*. Abraham Miller, London, 1657. pp. 4–5.

35 Greaves, R.L., *A Puritan Firebrand: Richard Culmer of Canterbury*. Historical Magazine of the Protestant Episcopal Church, 1981, 50:4, p. 363.

36 Ibid, p. 361.

37 Ibid, p. 363.

38 Ibid, p. 365.

39 Ibid, p. 365.

40 Ibid, p. 365.

41 Culmer, R., *A Parishe Looking-Glasse For Persecutors of Ministers*. Abraham Miller, London, 1657. p. 6.

42 'Philo-katoptrono-klastes.' *Culmers Crown Crackt with His Own Looking-Glass*. s.n., London, 1657. n.p.

referring to Culmer's Cambridge days, "he made a beginning with some proficiency in his laudable, liberal Arts of *Swimming, Thieving, Cuffing, Footbal-playing,* &c. which afterwards he prosecuted."[43]

~

John Barwick is for the king. The future Dean of St Paul's Cathedral writes pro-Royalist pamphlets from Cambridge, communicates by ciphers, and smuggles money from Cambridge to the north. Both Barwick and Oliver Cromwell enjoy football as Cambridge students, though when Barwick breaks the collarbone of an adversary, he is so mortified he never plays again.[44] The rough and boisterous Cromwell was one of "the chief Match-makers and Players at Foot-ball, Cudgels, or any other boystrous sport or game."[45] The passage must be treated circumspectly. The book is a critique, written during the reign of Charles II, whose father had been hung on Cromwell's orders. Sir William Dugdale, who refers to Cromwell as this "grand Impostor", is erroneously believed to add, he "threw himself into a dissolute & disorderly course of life being more famous whilst there for foot-ball, cricket, cudgelling, and wrestling, than for study."[46,47] Similarly, a 1682 farce *The Royalist* has Cromwell knight a man "for breaking his head at a Match at Foot-ball."[48] Charles I enjoyed football when he was still Duke of York, though his passion was tennis. In 1610, when Charles is nine, "John Webb, master of his Majesty's Tennis" is paid £20 for teaching him to play, "and for furnishing him with balls, rackets, and other necessaries within the said year."[49,50] A decade later, Charles loses a wager at tennis with the Duke of Buckingham, and must pay for a banquet and ball.[51] He is still playing

---

43 Ibid, p. 2.

44 Barwick, P., *The Life of John Barwick.* J. Bettenham, London, 1724. pp. 9–10.

45 Heath, J., *Flagellum: Or the Life and Death, Birth and Burial Of Oliver Cromwell.* n.p., 1663. p. 8.

46 Noble, M., *Memoirs of the Protectorate-house of Cromwell.* Peason and Rollason, Birmingham, England, 1784. p. 36. pp. 112–113.

47 The reference perennially given for the quote does not mention "foot-ball, cricket, cudgelling, and wrestling" in any edition. See: Anon., *A Short View of the Late Troubles in England,* by William Dugdale. n.p., London, 1681. It is frequently cited as an early example of cricket.

48 D'Urfey, T., *The Royalist.* n.p., London, 1682. p. 48.

49 The standard wage for a skilled tradesman.

50 Marshall, J., *The Annals of Tennis.* Horace Cox, London, 1878. p. 79.

51 Early Modern Letters Online. http://emlo.bodleian.ox.ac.uk/profile/work/8030693a-679c-47e5-92b9-17bd5e9233de?sort=date-a&rows=50&let_con=tennis&baseurl=/forms/advanced&start=1&type=advanced&numFound=4. Accessed 26 October 2024.

in 1626, the year after his coronation. By then, at least fifteen tennis courts are dotted around London.[52] Tennis sashays down the catwalk: as late as 1643, Charles is sending his groom off for "4 yds of taby, 2 ells and a 1/4 of taffety to be a *tennis-suit*, and 2 pairs of garters and roses with silk buttons, and other necessaries for making up of the said [silk] suit."[53,54] Both sides are in thrall to tennis: it is 1643, the height of the war, yet one of Charles's grooms is granted a pass by Parliament to take the fabrics to Oxford, where Charles is based.[55] Tennis is not all frills and fluff. She can plumb depths. An allegorical poem *On a Tenis-court* opens with the conflict in hand: "Man is a *Teniscourt*, His flesh the *Wall*, The Gamesters *God & Satan*, Th'Hearts the *Ball*."[56]

In 1659, Barwick delivers the funeral sermon for Thomas Morton, Bishop of Durham. The seventh of nineteen children, Morton confuses Puritans with his staunchly Royalist, virulently anti-Catholic beliefs. They play it safe and choose to hate him. Morton hunkers down and plays the long game. Born six years after Elizabeth is crowned, he outlives both Civil Wars and the Protectorate, dying at ninety-five, eight months shy of the Restoration. Barwick recounts an anecdote about Morton's footballing prowess. "Is it true," asks James I, who has a fondness for Morton, "that you struck up the heels of six men so speedily one after another, that the last was down before the first got up again?" "*Three*, Your Majesty," replies Morton, modestly.[57]

For three years, the war blunders on, by skirmish, by siege. No one is left untouched. Charles controls the north, Parliament the south. As Englishmen endlessly slaughter one another, an ironic phrase resurfaces: "All fellowes at Foot-ball."[58] All are equal. It is first heard of in the play *Sir John Old-castle*, in 1600—"Al friends at footebal, fellowes all in field." 'All is fair at football', makes its appearance later, and is just

52 Marshall, J., *The Annals of Tennis*. Horace Cox, London, 1878. pp. 79, 80.

53 Ibid, p. 81.

54 An ell was a unit of length used for cloth. It varied by country. In England it was 45 inches. *Taffety* was taffeta, and *taby* striped taffeta.

55 *Fifth Report of the Royal Commission on Historical Manuscripts*. Eyre & Spottiswoode, London, 1876. Part 1. pp. 2–3.

56 Quarles, F., *Divine Fancies: Digested into Epigrammes, Meditations, and Observations*. M.F. London, 1632. p. 127.

57 Barwick, J., *Hieronikēs*. s.n., London, 1659. pp. 164–165.

58 Anon., *The Character of an Oxford-incendiary*. s.n., London, 1645. p. 5.

as widely used. Within the frantic merry-go-round of rebuttals, one pamphleteer accuses another's posturing as, "To lye like a foot-ball between the Goales, to become the ambition of Competitors."[59] In April 1645, the New Model Army gives Parliament its first cohesive force. Seventy-two days later, they crush the Royalists at Naseby. Cromwell commands the victors, Charles the defeated. What death knell? Tone-deaf Charles is appointed by God.

Both sides pump out propaganda. In October 1645, the Parliamentarian *Weekly Account* carries an edict on what cannot be played in their territory on the Sabbath.[60] Pretty much everything. Hawking and fishing, dice and cards, dancing and plays, football and stoolball, wrestling and fencing. Bowls, of course. Nothing can be sold, and citizens cannot travel without due cause. It should go without saying that it is illegal to marry a Papist or to take advice from a witch, wizard, or fortune teller, but it is said. It also carries a letter from Cromwell, and news of various victories and officers captured. The prohibition does not stop Roundhead soldiers from playing football in Somerset.[61] That Royalists spurn such bans, works in Cromwell's favour when his troops take "Upnor Castle by surprise whilst the soldiers were at bowls."[62] The publication does have an upside: the first mention of football in a newspaper. The second is in a Royalist newsbook, *Mercurius Pragmaticus*, in 1648.[63]

It is not the ideal time to publish a textbook in that Papist tongue, Latin, but Charles Hoole presses ahead. A prudent author would have deleted two sentences: "*Tu pilae palmariae admodum experus es*: Thou art very skilled at the hand-ball," and "*Ego pilae pedalis mediocriter doctus sum*: I am prettie well acquainted at the foot-ball."[64] Richard Busby gets the balance right in his 1647 book of Latin grammar: "*Indoctus pilae*: unskilfull at ball."[65] Now they control Westminster, the Puritans ban the *Book of Common Prayer* and hound ministers

---

59 Lacey, W., *The judgement of a university-man concerning M. William Chillingworth his late pamphlet, in answere to Charity maintained.* English College Press, St Omer, France, 1639. p. 8.

60 *Weekly Account*. 15–22 October 1645. p. 2.

61 Edwards, T., *The Third part of Gangræna*. s.n., London, 1646. p. 250.

62 *Fifth Report of the Royal Commission on Historical Manuscripts*. Eyre & Spottiswoode, London, 1876. Part 1. p. 46.

63 *Mercurius Pragmaticus*. 4–11 April 1648. n.p.

64 Hoole, C., *An easie entrance to the Latine tongue*. William Dugard, London, 1649. p. 335.

65 Busby, R., *A short institution of grammar*. Roger Daniel, Cambridge, 1647. p. 36.

who use it. A church in Blandford, Dorset, is raided. “Zeale had quite eaten up the Braines of some Sectaries in Office; who came on in great fury, and fell aboard the congregation”, but when they try to arrest the minister, “the People made a rescue … and tossed the Brethren about like Foot-balls.”[66] The Devil is also tossed about that year. Found in the guise of a black ram in the cellar of the Bull Inn, St Albans, the landlord yelps in alarm. “A butcher … taken to be the stoutest man … he had broke two armes the last football playing”, grabs the Devil, takes him to his slaughter house and kills him. In this singular act of bravery, rewarded with a gallon of wine, the butcher makes amends “for the black Ram he had lately lost.”[67]

“Scandalous, malignant priests” are singularly castigated. Three stray in south Essex where football is played. The parson of Much Parndon encourages Sabbath “Foot-ball and other like sports.” Pretty lame stuff.[68] The “drunkard, common swearer, and curser” rector of Danbury “doth not only encourage sports and playing on the Sabbathday before his own doore, but hath also … suffered on the Fast-day, Foot-ball playing in his own ground, himselfe being a spectator thereof…”[69] Is that it? The rector of Theydon Garnon shows them how to mutiny. He Catholicises the parish church, spouts the *Book of Sports* from his pulpit, allows the Sabbath to be “much prophaned, by Foot-ball playing and other ungodly practices”, appoints a “drunken, lewd and scandalous” curate, and sides with the “Army of the Cavaleeres and is in actuall War against the Parliament and Kingdome.”[70]

In July 1643, the parson of Henningford, Cambridgeshire, is described as “a common Alehouse-haunter” who, on Sundays, “gave Liberty to the young People for Sports, as namely, Foot-ball-play, and Cudgel-play, and would go and see the same himself, and said ‘Well done’.”[71] In Suffolk, in 1644, the rector of Eyke “hath been with such of his parish as have been at the same tyme camping on the Lord’s day, & shewed no

66 *Mercurius Pragmaticus*. 4–11 April 1648. Issue 2. n.p.

67 Anon., *The Devill seen at St. Albans*. s.n., London, 1648. pp. 4–6.

68 *The First Century of Scandalous, Malignant Priests*. Committee of the House of Commons. George Miller, 1643. London. p. 37.

69 Ibid, p. 36.

70 Ibid, p. 19.

71 *Journals of the House of Lord*s. Vol. 6. p. 152. https://sources-tannerritchie-com.apl.proxy.openathens.net/browser.php?ipid=903178. Accessed 28 December 2023.

dislike thereof."[72] That June, the vicar of Hoxne, in Suffolk, "Suffered vayne sports upon the Lord's dayes and frequent shooting and camping neere his house."[73] Hoxne will camp against Diss on the neutral fields of Stuston Common in 1721.[74] Luckily for Thomas Robinson, Puritanism is crumbling when he is appointed vicar of Ousby, Cumberland, in 1672. The reverend is said, "to accompany the leading men of his parish to the adjoining alehouse, where each man spent a penny, and *only a penny*: that done, he set the younger sort to play at football (of which he was a great promoter) and other rustical diversions."[75]

Clerical outrages are beams in the bulging eyes of repressed Puritans, namely sport, gambling, alcohol, sex, swearing, and preaching. *A succinct traiterlogie* catalogues the sins of those "lazie Abbi-Lubbers … hunted out of their holes": "a pernicious rotten-hearted Popish Ceremony-monger"; "a notorious profaner of the Lords dayes with sports"; "a most wicked Curser and Swearer of most fearfull and bloudy oaths"; and "peevish and perverse malignancie against the Parliament."[76] In fairness, many transgressions will long prove insufferable: "an odious common drunkard, familiarly casting dice for drinking of most cups"; "a curser, swearer and blasphemer, quareller and fighter"; "a wicked incontinent and lustfull Priest, frequently assaulting womens chastity"; "obscene medling and dilating on the secrets of women in the Pulpit, abusively and familiarly comparing wommen to sowes"; "making his neighbours drink drunk under the tables, and being in the night times with their wives, private in their chambers"; and "a lascivious and lustfull Priest, living in adultery with severall women and had divers bastards."[77] John Sheppard, then, is small fry. In 1648, he is "regarded as a subversive … because he allowed drinking and cardplaying in his house, rarely went to church, and spent Sunday afternoons gambling and corrupting youths by

---

72 Holmes, C., *The Suffolk Committees for Scandalous Ministers, 1644–1646*. Suffolk, Records Society, 1970, Vol 3. p. 70.

73 Ibid, p. 75.

74 Dymond, D., *The game of camping in eastern England*. The Local Historian, 2021, 51:1, p. 3.

75 Hutchinson, W., *The history of the county of Cumberland, and some places adjacent, from the earliest accounts to the present time.* 2 Vols. F. Jollie, Carlisle, 1794. Vol. 1. p. 224.

76 Vicars, J., *A Most just Correction and Enlargement of a most lying and scandalous Bill of the Mortality of the Malignant Clergy of London*. s.n., London, 1647. pp. 2–12.

77 Ibid, p. 2–12.

supplying them with 'bowls, balls, or cudgels' … [he] was said to have served both sides."[78]

In 1648, as Royalists rise a second time, they publish a six-pager ending in various threats to Parliamentarians. Warner will have his "leather eares" nailed "to the door post of thine own house", Nol will lose his nose. Challoner is yet to learn "what will become of thee and thy wall eyes." As for Tom Fairfax, "what will become of thee, when thy gowty legs shall be chop't off, with thy head, and armes and the Cavaliers kick thee up and down Westminster as a football."[79] Charles is already in Parliament's hands. He wriggles, he lies, he escapes, he is captured. More lies, fresh deceit, another uprising. Charles beheads himself.

Cromwell's intolerance of Quaker intransigence results in mass imprisonment. One Quaker witnesses a gory diversion in Newgate Prison: "the heads of the men … used to be pickled in order to preserve them, before being stuck up; and amusement in Newgate with the turnkeys and prisoners used to be to play at foot-ball with these pickled heads."[80] A sarcastic letter to the Lord mayor of London, in 1659, suggests that "your Boyes at Foot-ball" could kick all the Quakers out of London in an hour.[81] Like Puritans, Quakers loathe contemporary entertainment: "Do not all sorts of ungodly Meetings abound … Stage-Plays, Beare and Bull-Beatings, Cock-Fights, Footbal and Cudgel-Plays, Race-Running both Horse and Foot, Huntings … Moris-dancers and Mummers … Drunken-Meetings abound with Dice and Cards, filled with Cursing and Hellish Oaths, and the Noise of Fiddlers and Vagabonds roaring like Beasts and Swine."[82] Founder, George Fox, adds, "leapings", wrestling, fencing, stage-plays, tennis, shovelboards, harps, and viols, for they "recreat the vain carnall mind which … lives in the lust of the flesh, and the lusts of the eye."[83]

With Charles dead, Royalists regroup beneath the banner of his son, Charles. In the aftermath of his beheading, a 1649 pamphlet rails

---

78 Underdown, D., *The Problem of Popular Allegiance in the English Civil War.* Transactions of the Royal Historical Society, 1981, Vol. 31, p. 90.

79 M.M., *Out-crie of the Kings at Westminster.* s.n., 1648, pp. 5–6.

80 *Leicester Chronicle.* 4 August 1832. p. 4.

81 Caponi, P., *To the right honourable the lord mayor.* s.n., London, 1659. Single page.

82 Allen, R., *The Cry of Innocent Blood.* s.n., London, 1670. p. 6.

83 Fox, G., *A declaration against all profession and professors that have not the life of what they profess, from the righteous seed of God.* s.n., London, 1653. p. 7.

against senior Parliamentarians. John Cooke, the radical barrister who established the grounds for prosecuting Charles—"the first modern legal argument against tyranny" [84]—is likened to "a company of Boyes in Chancery-lane having recovered a lost Football in the streets, crying out here tis, here tis."[85] In 1638, William Davenant succeeds Ben Jonson as the king's poet. After Naseby, he moves to Paris, and in 1649 resurrects his 1634 tragicomedy: "I will see thy head in a leatherne case first," says a character, "Kickt in a foot-bal match from gole to gole."[86]

Most uprisings are quashed. In 1650, a Parliamentarian newspaper reports, "a great Foot-ball play near Norwich, where the people were very tumultuous and disorderly … marched directly towards Norwich taking horse and armes along the way, and declaring for the King."[87,88] Others fall in but not the numbers expected, and they are routed by Roundheads. A similar event in 1654. Roundheads receive intelligence "of a great meeting neere Warwick, pretending a football match whereunto many did ride and goe all that night, and many cavileeres were ingaged in the same. Whereupon I was forc't to send off a party of horse to disperse them, and accordingly they did."[89] In 1651, "All public meetings on pretence of recreation, as horse-racing, hawking, cock-fighting, and foot-ball playing &c., were prohibited, lest they should afford an opportunity for the gathering of conspirators, the ripening of their counsels and the breaking out of rebellion."[90]

Cornish hurling is also implicated in rebellions. Scottish nobleman Alexander Hamilton is a Royalist, sympathetic to the establishment of Presbyterianism in England. In 1646, as Scottish secretary of state, he negotiates on the subject, but cannot get past Charles I's intransigence. On 28 March 1648, ten months before he flees to Holland to attend the

84 Robertson, G., *The Tyrannicide Brief. The Story of the Man who sent Charles I to the Scaffold.* Vintage, London, 2006. p. 3.

85 Anon., *Reason against treason.* s.n., London, 1649. p. 6.

86 Davenant, W., *Love and Honour.* s.n., London, 1649. n.p.

87 *Several Proceedings in Parliament. 28 November 1650–5 December 1650.* n.p.

88 The incident is near Swaffham, where Dr Botwright's willed field of 1474 was named the Camping Land.

89 Birch, T., *A Collection of the State papers of John Thurloe, Esq.* 7 Vols. Thomas Woodward, and Charles Davis, London, 1742. Vol. 3. p. 212.

90 Green, M.A.E. (ed.), *Calendar of State papers, Domestic Series, 1651.* Longman & Co., London, 1877. p. viii.

court-in-exile of the future king, he sends a letter to the Earl of Lanerick, part of which reads: "The 2 Counties of Devon and Cornewall are on Munday next to meet at a hurling (a sport they have with a ball), though 'tis thought they have an other designe, for they, but espetially theire neighbour countye, Dorsettshire, are very much discontented, and fit to receive the first impression."[91] Their rancour is aimed at the Parliamentarians who control the south of England.

More similes appear. Protestant peacemaker Richard Baxter writes that some think that the Church, "must be won like a game at foot-ball, and therefore scruplest not to toss it in the dirt, and tumultuously to strive with and strike up the heels of all that strive against thee (so that peaceable passengers cannot safely come near you or pass the streets). But when you have the Ball … how uncertain still you are to keep it, and that one spurn can take it from you?"[92] He uses two more in *The Saints' Everlasting Rest.* He is seeking to unite the splintered denominations. The Church is "like at Footbal, in the midst of a crowd of Boyes, tost about in contention from one to another; every one running, and sweating with foolish violence."[93] He adds, shrewdly, "We cast out our doctrine almost as a foot-ball is turned out among boys in the street, in some congregations; few understand it, but everyone censureth it."[94] Football is in his teens, burning with social justice, fighting with the oppressed. Still, he can rub his hands in glee as Baxter hones his skills. In 1685, the simile reaches its apogee when Baxter writes, "Thus Christ is the Football of Cruelty and Heathen Scorn."[95]

A Compleat History of the Lives and Robberies of the most Notorious Highway-men, Foot-pads, Shop-lifts, and Cheats includes the picaresque accomplishments of rapparee Patrick Flemming. "He had true Irish Blood running through all his Veins; for he was stock'd with Impudence and Ignorance to the highest Degree." Aged thirteen, "being a very pretty sort of a Lad", the Countess of Kildare whisks him away from his

---

91 Gardiner, S.R. (ed.), *Hamilton Papers: Being Elections from Original Letters in the Possession of His Grace the Duke of Hamilton and Brandon, Relating to the Years 1638–1650.* Nichols and Sons, London, 1880. p. 171.

92 Baxter, R., *The cure of church-divisions.* s.n., London, 1670. n.p.

93 Baxter, R., *The Saints' Everlasting Rest.* Rob. White, London, 1650. p. 818.

94 Bacon, E. (ed.), *Select Practical Writings of Richard Baxter.* 2 Vols. Durrie and Peck, New Haven, 1835. Vol. 2. p. 84.

95 Baxter, R., *A paraphrase on the New Testament.* s.n., London, 1685. n. p.

parents' "Potatoe-Garden" to be her footboy, "but his Inclination leading him more to mind Tip-cat, Cricket, Trap-ball, Span-Farthing, and Nine-pins … he was, after much Correction, soon turned out of Service."[96] He lands in the service of the Marquis of Antrim, where he utterly humiliates the resident priest.

One night, Patrick finds him asleep on a couch. "Whatever pleasant Dream of the Confession of some pretty Wench had come into his Head, Patrick knew not; but his Label of Mortality [penis] … had broken Prison, and Maypole like, disdain'd its Loftiness should be hid." *Carpe diem.* Patrick "softly tied his legs and hands" then sneaks out. He returns with a calf, directing it to the priest's member, "which he, taking for his Mammy's Teat, greedily seiz'd it and fell to tugging … till he had lugg'd St Domine off the Couch … this Babe of a Cow … finding no Milk to come, sucked and nibbled so hard, that he waked the drowsy priest." His roar brings the maids from the pantry, who flee at the sight of their "Ghostly Father" compromised with a cloven-hoofed beast. "Several young Ladies" then enter but on seeing "the mistaken teat, which, now depriv'd of its Vigor, hung dangling", promptly "scamper and squeek."

When Patrick is turned out again, a stash of £400 tickles his wit.[97] A born highwayman, he robs hundreds of their treasures. He winkles £1000 out of one archbishop and successfully ransoms Lord Baltimore's son for £100, after threatening to "make a Steak Pye of him."[98] He repeatedly slips the noose, once escaping jail by wriggling up a chimney "sooty and smoke-dryed." Yet even he cannot get away with slicing off the nose, lips, and ears of Sir Donagh O'Brien. The souls he murdered hold fast the noose. The book includes a story of a *cutpurse* who mistakes a man's testicles for a moneybag. When the man screams in agony, people flock to him. "Asked If he had lost any Thing; reply'd the poor Man, yes, I have lost a good pair of Bollocks, for which I shall have more a Noise with my Wife, than if I had lost a Hundred Pounds."[99] In 1658, Richard Franck writes: "If two to one is odds at Football and against the Rules and

96 Smith, A., *A Compleat History of the Lives and Robberies of the most Notorious Highway-men, Foot-pads, Shop-lifts, and Cheats.* 2 Vols. Sam. Briscoe, London, 1719. Vol. 2. pp. 49–50.

97 Twenty years' wages for a skilled tradesman.

98 Fifty years' and five years' wages for a skilled tradesman respectively.

99 Smith, A., *A Compleat History of the Lives and Robberies of the most Notorious Highway-men, Foot-pads, Shop-lifts, and Cheats.* 2 Vols. Sam. Briscoe, London, 1719. Vol. 2. pp. 186–187.

Laws of Fair Play…", meaning that one side is unfairly disadvantaged. It becomes a popular proverb,[100] illustrated by an assuredly apocryphal tale. Held up by a notorious Scottish outlaw, Oliver Cromwell and his two servants badly miscalculate. "Three to One was Odds at Foot-ball", they believe. A servant charitably takes a bullet to the head to balance the proverb.[101]

The camp-loving people of East Anglia must have mixed feelings about Cromwell. They strongly support him, and he them, yet he bans football. By 1653, the camping close at Milton in Cromwell's native Cambridgeshire has been annexed by the church rectory.[102] The mention of football in a 1657 sermon in Ipswich, Suffolk, gives an idea of the nature of the sport as it is played in the county: "now one man hath the Ball on his foot, by and by another takes it from him; within the turning of a hand, a third catches it from him, and so it goes on from one to another."[103] The essayist Roger North is a native of Suffolk, and schools in Norfolk. He speaks of the golden days of his childhood: "it was always a custom for the youth of the town, who were men or maid servants, and children, to assemble, after horses baited, either upon the green or … in a close accustomed to be so used, and there all to play till milking time, and supper at night. The men to football, and the maids, with whom we children commonly mixed, being not proof for the turbulence of the other party, to stoolball, and such running games as they knew."[104] North proceeds to Cambridge around 1670. Sharing a chamber with his strict tutor brother, he "did most envy the common scholars for the joy they had at football."[105]

Cornishmen must also resent Cromwell's Puritanical views on ball games. It does not prevent the Lord Protector from attending a Cornish hurling exhibition match at Hyde Park, on May Day 1654. Cromwell

---

100 Franck, R., *Northern Memoirs, Calculated for the Meridian of Scotland*. s.n., London, 1694. p. 67.

101 Smith, A., *A Compleat History of the Lives and Robberies of the most Notorious Highway-men, Foot-pads, Shop-lifts, and Cheats*. 2 Vols. Sam. Briscoe, London, 1719. Vol. 2. p. 300.

102 Malcolmson, R.W., *Popular Recreations in English Society 1700–1850*. Unpublished PhD thesis, University of Warwick, 1970. p. 325.

103 Lawrence, M., *The use and practice of faith*. A. Maxey, London, 1657. pp. 247–248.

104 Jessop, A. (ed.)., *The Lives of the Right Hon. Francis North, Baron Guilford: The Hon. Sir Dudley North; and the Hon. and Rev. Dr. John North. Together with the autobiography of the author*, by Roger North. George Bell and Sons, York Street, Covent Garden, London, 1890. p. 9.

105 Ibid, p. 14.

steers clear of the "hundreds of coaches and gallants in attire, but [with] most shameful powdered hair; men painted and spotted women. Some men played with a silver ball, and some took other recreation."[106] *The Moderate Intelligencer* reports:

"This day there was the hurling of a great Ball, by 50 *Cornish* gentleman on the one side, and 50 on the other: one party played in red caps, and the other in white: there was present His Highnesse the Lord Protector, many of his privy Council, and divers eminent Gentlemen, to whose view was presented great agility of body, and most neat and exquisite wrastling, at every meeting of one with the other, which was ordered with such dexterity, that it was to show more the strength, vigour, and nimbleness of their bodies, then to indanger their persons. The Ball they plaid withall was silver, and design'd for that party which did win the Goal."[107]

Several details emerge: fifty-a-side, distinguished by caps, wrestling, the scoring of a goal. It is clearly an exhibition match: the ball is large and the play tame. The silver ball is interesting, as it usually used in hurling to the country, given as a prize to the winner, or to the local nobleman. That it is used before Cromwell points to the artifice of the display. The 1639 accounts of the bailiff of St Ives in Cornwall list "a silver bole that was brought to Towne 6s. 6d." to be used for hurling.[108] The same issue of the 1654 *Moderate Intelligencer* includes news from France of a "great Eclipse of the Sun, which continued for the space of houres ... there was then seen strange Apparitions in the Ayr ... with sundry other dreadful Signes wonderful to behold: which certainly presageth some mighty *Change* and *Catastraphe*."[109] The following month, Louis XIV is crowned. The Sun King.

~

Quinine comes from the bark of the quina quina tree. In 1630, Jesuits serendipitously discover its use. Cromwell spurns the Papist drug when

106 Knight, C. (ed.)., *London, Volumes 1–2*. Henry. G. Bohn, York Street, Covent Garden, London, 1851. Vol. 1. pp. 212–213.

107 *The Moderate Intelligencer*. 23 February 1654–10 May 1654. Issue 176, p. 1385.

108 Matthews, J.H., *A History of the Parishes of Saint Ives, Lelant, Towednack and Zennor*. Elliot Stock, London, 1892. p. 208.

109 *The Moderate Intelligencer*. 23 February 1654–10 May 1654. Issue 176, pp. 1392–1393.

his malaria flares up in 1658.[110] He dies. His ill-suited son, Richard, becomes Lord Protector, only to resign within eight months. Parliament descends into internecine conflict. On 5 December 1659, London apprentices present a petition to the lord mayor, requesting new elections to Parliament.[111] Colonel John Hewson, one of the fifty-nine signatories of Charles I's death warrant, is ordered to suppress the dissent. Six weeks before, the ex-cobbler is quoted as saying, "Well, i'le march among 'um; the head of a Prentice would make an excellent Foot-ball this cold weather, and I can stitch it up in a leather Case."[112] He marches in to cries of "a Cobbler, a Cobbler." A full day of rioting ensues. Apprentices fling stones, tiles, and turnips at the cavalry detachment, "some they disarmed and kicked … in some places the apprentices would get a football (it being a hard frost) and drive it among the soldiers."[113] Six or seven apprentices are "shot through the head", and "many on both sides dangerously wounded."[114]

Hewson is later said to have been "sent in a rage into London, to kill and still the innocent boyes playing at Football in the streetes."[115] There is no doubting his guilt: "having been the cause of the murder of some boys playing at Foot-ball in the streets, he was found guilty by the Coroners Jury."[116] The event is used to mock Hewson in a satirical play about the Civil War: "It hapn'd one morning that the weather being cold, the young men of the City of *London* went to play at Football in the stréets; Which being related in to the *Councel of Safety* … they sent command immediately to the Gyant *Husonius* … the Christians continued playing at Football, not dreaming that their sport had béen

110 Stalin similarly disapproved of "western" penicillin.

111 Smith, S.R., *Almost Revolutionaries: The London Apprentices during the Civil Wars.* Huntington Quarterly, 1979, 42:4, p. 323.

112 Anon., *A brief account of the meeting, proceedings, and exit of the Committee of Safety.* Thomas Williamson, London, 1659. p. 21.

113 De la Bédoyère, G. (ed.), *The Letters of Samuel Pepys 1656–1703.* Boydell Press, London, pp. 26–27.

114 "Venice: December 1659," in *Calendar of State Papers Relating To English Affairs in the Archives of Venice, Volume 32, 1659–1661*, ed. Allen B Hinds (London: His Majesty's Stationery Office, 1931), 96–104. *British History Online*, accessed February 17, 2024, http://www.british-history.ac.uk/cal-state-papers/venice/vol32/.

115 Anon., *The mystery of the good old cause briefly unfolded.* s.n., London, 1660. p. 15.

116 Anon., *The true characters of the educations, inclinations and several dispostions of all and every one of those bloody and barbarous persons, who sate as judges upon the life of our late dread soveraign King Charls I.* s.n., London, 1661.

offensive … The Gyant … was sorely enraged; wherefore in great fury he laid about … the multitude, killing six."[117]

Public sentiment is damning. Within seven months, the monarchy is restored. They have not done with the exhumed Cromwell yet. A portion of a 1660 pamphlet's interminable title, dubs him, "This Grand Impostor, and Most Audacious Rebel, That Durst Aspire From a Brew-House to the Throne, Washing His Accursed Hands in the Blood of his Royal Soveraign; and Trampling Over the Heads of the Most Loyal Subjects, Making a Foot-ball of a Crown, and Endeavouring Utterly to Extirpate the Royal Progeny, Root and Kinde, Stem and Stock."[118] Within, it adds, "tell him of Magna Charta, he would lay his hand on his sword, and cry Magna Farta."

Charles II has a relaxed attitude to sport. The ban on horse races and theatre is lifted, Sabbath sports are back, and cricket surges in popularity. In May 1666, Robert Paston writes to his wife of their son "verie well engaged in a game att cricquett on Richmond Greene."[119] A 1664 closet drama reads: "She fears no wounds nor dangers … She will play at foot-ball, thresh, and hew woods, as well as her Brother."[120] Ball-related similes are doing the rounds: toss someone like a bag fill of wind (abuse and jeer someone), bound like a ball (to be fickle and inconsistent), and blow up the ball (flatter someone).[121] During the month of March, *The Twelve Moneths* reports that, "The Foot-ball now tryes the legs of the strongest, and merry matches continue good fellowship; but beware of your shins and a broken leg."[122] It is in June 1672 that Lady Barker of Hambleton, Rutland, writes to her husband, "I had a grate dale of compnay [sic] all the 3 halladays, which hath drunke us dry,", adding that a local matron broke her leg playing at ball.[123]

---

117 Flatman, T., *Don Juan Lamberto*. s.n., London, 1661. ch. 18. n.p.

118 Anon., *The English Devil: or, Cromwel and His Monstrous Witch Discover'd at White-Hall*. R. Wood, London, 1660. n.p.

119 *This is Paston*. https://www.thisispaston.co.uk/index.php. Accessed 12 October 2024.

120 Killigrew, T., *Cicilia and Clorinda*. In: *Comedies and Tragedies*. s.n., London, 1664. p. 263. Act 3, Sc 2.

121 Torriano, G., *The Second Alphabet Consisting of Proverbial Phrases*. A. Warren, London, 1662. pp. 128, 227, 128.

122 Stevenson, M., *The Twelve Moneths*. M.S., London, 1661. pp. 12–13.

123 *Fifth Report of the Royal Commission on Historical Manuscripts*. Eyre & Spottiswoode, London, 1876. Part 1. p. 398.

The king is not immune to sport's charms. Like his father, he developed a passion for tennis as a child. She need hardly use her charms. She waves at her cousin football as a liveried servant ushers her into the palace. Football shakes his head, smiles, waves. Charles orders a new court to be built at Whitehall, complete with "two chayres of two foot and a halfe wide in the seat one foostoole two velvet cushions, one velvet Carpett with gold fringe … Curtayne cloathes for the Tennis Court sixty yards of each side in length and six yards of each side in breadth, a corde, and Tarpaulin to goe round the court on the outside and black Bayes [baize] for the ends of the Court."[124] On 3 January 1664, Samuel Pepys visits the new court: "Thence to the Tennis Court … to see how the King's play was extolled without any cause at all, was a loathsome sight … such open flattery is beastly. Afterwards to St. James's Parke … and there spent an hour or two, it being a pleasant day, seeing people play at Pell Mell."[125] Pall-mall is imported from France and is mentioned as early as 1570.[126] It is played in a purpose-built narrow alley about half a mile long, with low side walls. A wooden mallet drives the wooden ball along the alley, and through an upright iron hoop at the end."[127,128] By 1684, "Pelmel" is added to Charles II's "Divertisements." Contemporary prints illustrate a common variation, using three different sticks. While not a predecessor of basketball, there are clear similarities: "We observe a high pole, with a hoop suspended from an arm at its top, and through this the ball was driven."[129] The accompanying print shows the hoop, hanging like a noose. A man swings a crooked stick like a golfer, using only one hand. In the second print a mallet is used, a long, thin-shafted racket in the third.[130]

---

124 Marshall, J., *The Annals of Tennis*. Horace Cox, London, 1878. pp. 86–87.

125 Wheatley, H.B., *The Diary of Samuel Pepys, 1664*. George Bell and Sons, London, 1893. n.p.

126 De Belle-Forest, F., *Des Histoires Tragiques*. 7 Vols. Cesar Farine, Turin, Italy, 1570. Vol. 2. p. 313.

127 Pall-mall emerged from jeu de mail, while croquet was an offshoot of one or the other. The Italian game of *trucco* (troco, trucks) is similar to lawn billiards in England, where it was played well into the twentieth century. *Trucco* descended from either *jeu de mail* or one of the many ground billiard games (some dating back to the 1300s), from which all these games (and snooker and billiards) stem from. The term billiards comes from the French word *billart*: "a short and thick truncheon or cudgell." In: Cotgrave, R., *A dictionaire of the French and English tongues*. Adam Islip, London, 1611. n.p.

128 Brailsford, D., *Sport and Society: Elizabeth to Anne*. Routledge and Kegan Paul, London, 1969. p. 108.

129 Knight, C. (ed.)., *London, Volumes 1–2*. George Lillie Craik. Henry G. Bohn, London, 1851. p. 195.

130 *Cassell's Illustrated History of England*. 9 Vols. Cassell, Petter & Galpin, London. Vol. 3. p. 618.

The king is fond of tennis, often riding to Hampton Court to play, returning the same day.[131] One account has him at the court by five a.m.[132] He is in the habit of weighing himself before and after games, and, "on one occasion it is recorded that he had lost four pounds and a half in his exercise."[133] In 1663, Pepys chats with the keeper of the Pell Mell about the playing surface—powdered cockle shells keep the earth fast.[134] Two years later, Pepys describes "the streete being full of footballs, it being a great frost."[135] Six weeks before the Great Fire of London, he writes: "A wonderful dark sky, and shower of rain this morning, which at Harwich proved so too with a shower of hail as big as walnuts."[136] The Calendar of State Papers adds, "the stones were as big as a football, and some shaped like ships, some like lions, &c."[137] "If footballs are allowed in frosty streets," reasons James Euine, "surely snowballs are allowed inside." With impish impudence he throws snowballs into a Scottish church during divine service.

Export and import duties are re-assessed in 1660. Imported tennis balls incur a tax of £2 per thousand,[138] rackets 8d each.[139] Import duties are also listed for morris bells, caviar, mercury, frankincense, alphabets, tin foil, leopard skins, harp strings, whale fins, tooth drawers, goose quills, copper spangles, and whistles. A contemporary tennis ball is "made of taylors shreds beaten by a hammer & shaped in a wooden mould. Then its hard tyed with packthread. After this they sow white

---

131 "Spelthorne Hundred: Hampton Court Palace, history," in *A History of the County of Middlesex: Volume 2, General; Ashford, East Bedfont With Hatton, Feltham, Hampton With Hampton Wick, Hanworth, Laleham, Littleton*, ed. William Page (London: Victoria County History, 1911), 327–371. *British History Online*, accessed February 17, 2024, http://www.british-history.ac.uk/vch/middx/vol2/pp327–371.

132 *Fifth Report of the Royal Commission on Historical Manuscripts*. Eyre & Spottiswoode, London, 1876. Part 1. p. 168.

133 Cust, E., *Lives of the Warriors of the Civil Wars of France and England*. John Murray, London, 1867. p. 377.

134 Wheatley, H.B., *The Diary of Samuel Pepys, 1663*. George Bell and Sons, London, 1893. n.p.

135 Wheatley, H.B., *The Diary of Samuel Pepys, 1665*. George Bell and Sons, London, 1893. n.p.

136 Ibid, n.p.

137 Green, M.A.E., *Calendar of State Papers, Domestic Series, of the Reign of Charles II. 1665–1666*. Kraus Reprint Limited, Nendeln, Liechtenstein, 1968. p. 554.

138 A month's wages for a skilled tradesman.

139 "Charles II, 1660: A Subsidy granted to the King of Tonnage and Poundage and other summes of Money payable upon Merchandize Exported and Imported.," in *Statutes of the Realm: Volume 5, 1625–80*, ed. John Raithby (s.l: Great Britain Record Commission, 1819), 181–205. *British History Online*, accessed February 17, 2024, http://www.british-history.ac.uk/statutes-realm/vol5/pp181–205.

cotton about it or kersy."[140] Tennis balls are used as rough measurements. This from a recipe for an analgesic: take stone Pitch to the quantitie of a tennis ball, a spoonful of tarre, a peny worth of treacle, the quantitie of a tennis ball of Rossin."[141]

In 1674, Charles Cotton, author of *The Compleat Gamester* and contributor to *The Compleat Angler*, publishes a burlesque of Lucian's *Dialogues*. A satirist himself, Lucian describes how Apollo falls in love with Hyacinthus, then accidentally kills him with a discus. Cotton adds a macabre flourish:

> But playing with the Boy at *Mall*
> (I rue the time, and ever shall)
> I strooke the *Ball,* I know not how,
> (For that is not the play you know)
> A pretty height into the Air,
> When *Zephirus* (who't seems was there)
> And long (as thou thy self hast seen)
> Has jealous of our friendship been,
> Beat down the Ball, without Remorse,
> With such a most confounded force,
> And gave his head so damn'd a thumm,
> As breaking *Pericranium,*
> *Scalpe, Dura,* and eke *Pia Mater,*
> His Brains came poppling out like water.[142]

He adds, "To play at Cat, at Trap, or Ball, Dust-point,[143] Span-counter,[144] Skittle-pins", while satirising Virgil's *Aeneid* he writes, "Puff'd like a

---

140 Cram, D., Forgeng, J.L., Johnston, D. (eds.)., *The Book of Games of Francis Willughby (1635–1672). A Seventeenth-century Treatise on Sports, Games and Pastimes*. Routledge, Abingdon, Oxon, 2016. p. 106.

141 Baird, C., *Games and Gaming in Early Modern Drama. Stakes and Hazards*. Palgrave Macmillan, 2020. p. 53.

142 Cotton, C., *The Genuine Poetical Works of Charles Cotton, Esq.* J. and J. Bonwicke, London, 1741. p. 222.

143 "Our boyes laying their points [laces] in a heape of dust, and throwing at them with a stone, call that play of theirs Dust-Point." In: Cram, D., Forgeng, J.L., Johnston, D. (eds.)., *Francis Willughby's Book of Games*. Routledge, Abingdon, Oxon, 2106. p. 259.

144 Span-counter: A version of marbles.

Foot-ball with Vain-glory."[145] Gods play sport to sport with mortals, little expecting a reverse. In *Hey for Honestie, Down with Knavery*, a youth says of Mars: "Why Mars himself was an arrogant coward to me; I have beat him at foot-ball above twenty times." Jupiter gets worse. "I remember he has many a time sowr'd our drink with his thundring, but we have done him no injury, but once I broke his shins at football in Tuttle."[146] Tuttle Fields in Westminster has been a popular sporting venue since at least 1236, when it hosted "goodly jousts."[147] Henry VIII practises archery there. By 1611 it has a maze—a frequent scene of "private combat";[148] John Locke mentions "wrestling in Lincoln's Inne-field … long-bow and stob-ball, in Tothill Fields", in 1679;[149] and in a 1685 book, St Patrick's "trembling Vessel was kickt about on the Surges like a Foot-ball in *Tuttel-Fields*."[150] It remains a venue into the eighteenth century: the Gentlemen of the Westminster Club and those of the Artillery-Ground play cricket there in 1735.[151]

Some agonise over sport. In 1666, John Bunyan writes of his parson admonishing sabbath sport. Bunyan is consumed with guilt until lunch: "I shook the sermon out of my mind; and to my old custom of sports and gaming I returned." He plays sabbath cat with friends until, "As I was in the midst of a game of cat and having struck it one blow from the hole, just as I was about to strike it the second time, a voice asks, 'Wilt thou leave thy sins and go to heaven or have thy sins and go to hell?' … wherefore leaving my cat upon the ground, I looked up to heaven." He stands agonising over the issue before sense prevails. "I had as good be damned for many sins, as be damned for few … so I returned desperately to my sport."[152] Cat has multiple variations, with many names, though the cat is always a block of wood, conical at each end. The version

---

145 Cotton, C., *The Genuine Poetical Works of Charles Cotton, Esq.* J. and J. Bonwicke, London, 1741. pp. 183, 184, 110.

146 Randolph, T., *Hey for Honestie, Down with Knavery.* London, s.n., 1651. pp. 11, 40.

147 Wheatley, H.B., *London Past and Present.* 3 Vols. John Murray, London, 1891. Vol. 3. p. 386.

148 Ibid, p. 387

149 King, P., *The Life of John Locke.* Henry Colburn, London, 1829. p. 134.

150 Anon., *The Delightful History of the Life & Death of That Renowned & Famous St Patrick, Champion of Ireland.* s.n., London, 1685. p. 99.

151 *General Evening Post.* 19–21 August 1735. p. 3.

152 Sharrock, R. (ed.), *Grace Abounding to the Chief of Sinners*, by John Bunyan. Clarendon Press, Oxford, 1962. pp. 13–14.

Bunyan appears to be playing involves "tipping" the cat into the air with a stick/bat, then pitching it with the bat towards a hole. Sometimes players advance around a number of holes in a circle, hence his comment, "having struck it one blow from the hole."[153] The Earl of Sandwich, a relative and patron of Pepys, witnesses a Cornish hurling to the country match between Penzance and Helston, in 1668. The game draws a crowd of two thousand:

"There was 100 chosen men of each towne, clad all in white (stripped), who mett in the halfe way betweene both townes, when a silver ball, gilt, of about three inch diameter (filled therein with Corke) was throwne up amongst them … the towne that it is brought into gaines the victorie. The hurlers make any play; cuffing one the other on the face, or kicking or wrastling, although they be five or six at once upon one man; or throwinge men downe the cliffs, or downe Tynn pitts … noe gentleman of the country dares come in to rule or part them, for then both sydes will joyne together, and beate them."[154] Four years later, Philip Skippon's account of Cornish hurling is published in Francis Willughby's *Book of Games*. Skippon calls hurling to goals in-hurling, and hurling to the country out-hurling.[155] His in-hurling is a ten-a-side with a leather ball. Like Carew's description out-hurling allows horses, drawing comparison with *knappan*.

In 1688, Pepys watches a satire on Sir Robert Howard, whom, the future James II assures Pepys, plays trapball.[156] In the play the protagonist says he has come to play trap-ball. Howard's character, Sir Positive At-All retorts: "Have you the Confidence to talk of Trap-ball before me … why I was so eminent at it when I was a School-boy, that I was call'd Trap Positive all over the School … I'll dishonour 'em both at Trap-ball. They talk of Trap-ball, ha, ha ha."[157] Later, Sir Positive At-All frenetically reels off a list of his virtuoso skills, including: "Palmestry … Phisick …

153 Ibid, p. 13.

154 Harris, F.R., *The Life of Edward Mountagu, K.G. First Earl of Sandwich (1626–1672)*. 2 Vols. John Murray, London, 1912. Vol. 2. pp. 160–161.

155 Cram, D., Forgeng, J.L., Johnston, D. (eds.)., *The Book of Games of Francis Willughby (1635–1672). A Seventeenth-century Treatise on Sports, Games and Pastimes*. Routledge, Abingdon, Oxon, 2016. p. 155.

156 Wheatley, H.B., *The Diary of Samuel Pepys, 1668*. George Bell and Sons, York Street, Covent Garden, London, 1893. n.p.

157 Shadwell, T., *The Sullen Lovers*. Henry Herringman, London, 1668. Act. III. p. 47.

Logick … Magick… Fight a Duel … Command an Army … Play on the Violin … Hoboy, Sackbut, and double Curtal, speak Hebrew … Welch and Irish … play at Catt, Stool-ball, scotch-hopp and Trapball."[158]

Hopscotch is originally called Scotch hoppers,[159] scotch-hopp, and "Scutch-Hop."[160] The connection to Scotland is erroneous. The etymology is explained in the first edition of Samuel Johnson's *A Dictionary of the English Language*. "Scotch hoppers: A play in which boys hop over lines or scotches in the ground."[161] He gives a definition of "scotch" as "to cut or make shallow incisions." The scoring system for trapball is unknown but a 1660 novel reveals it is a high-scoring game. Competing for the same woman, Lawrence puts a proposition to Sir Toby: "let us play first come to three hits at Ticktack for her, or let us play an hundred and threescore up at Trap-ball."[162]

Unsparing medical textbooks are never far from the printers. A 1672 textbook describes a grisly childbirth gone wrong. When the head is stuck, two midwives pull on it "with so much violence" they separate the neck bones. The author discovers the problem is a gastric hydrocele, so large it must be drained before the dead baby can be delivered. The surgeon who attends considers this nonsense, pulls off the head, and delivers the body piecemeal, "both the Arms, and some of the Ribs, part of the Lungs and the Heart", until he is wet with sweat. The author finally drains the cyst, allowing the rest of the corpse to be removed. Curious as to the quantity of water the cyst held, he refills it through the hole he made. "I poured in, without lying, above five Quarts[163] … it was of the bigness and figure of a very great Foot-ball."[164] Elsewhere, the author describes the uterus of a pregnant woman: "consider the composition of a Foot-bal, imagining the Leather which covers it to be the Womb … and the Bladder blown up with wind, within the Foot-ball, to be this double membrane of the chorion and amnios."[165] A book on horse anatomy includes an insight

---

158 Ibid, p. 74.

159 Anon., *An Introduction to Astrology*. Henry Marsh, London, 1661. p. 25.

160 Griffith, R., *Genuine letters between Henry and Frances*. 6 Vols. s.n., London, 1766. Vol. 3. p. 261.

161 Johnson, S., *A Dictionary of the English Language*. W. Strahan, London, 1755. n.p.

162 Anon., *Don Samuel Crispe*. s.n., London, 1660. Ch. 10. n.p.

163 A quart is approximately one litre.

164 Chamberlain, H. (trans.), *The Diseases of Women with Child, AND in Child-bed*, by Francois Mariceau. John Darby, London, 1672. pp. 234–236.

165 Ibid, pp. 153–154.

into ball-making. Speaking of the chorion, "the Young that is clad with it, lies as loose in the Womb, as a Bladder in a Foot-ball that is not at all tied to the leather."[166]

The "Great Frost" of 1683/84, sees a "blanket fair" on the Thames, so called as most stalls are fashioned with blankets. There is a lottery and music, rope dancing, puppets, coach and horse races, and a printing press. Games comprise football, nine-pins, cudgels, "Sliding in Scates, Chaires, and other devices … sailing Boats, Charriots, and Carrow-Whimbles"[167], and bowling for ladies "of the quality." There are early funfair rides: "a sliding hutch, propelled by a stick" and a whirling chair, "drawn by several men, by a long rope fastened to a stake fixed in the ice." All manner of things are on sale at inflated prices, and "if you have money for to spend, each cunning snap will seem to be your friend." People "sit down by a char-cole fire" and have "a dish of coffee, chocalet, or tea", or eat pancakes, gingerbread, and hot apples. Animals are at the mercy of brutish beasts. A fox is hunted on ice, cocks are thrown at, a bull baited with "poor dogs", that, "with his horns did toss them to and fro", and thousands flock to "the bating of the ugly bear."[168] Football at the fairs is mentioned in poems published in broadsides of the day: "foot-ball play is there so common grown," says one; another, "foot-ball playing there was day by day, Some broke their legs, and some their arms, they say."[169]

Charles Cotton's poem of a perishing match probably refers to 1683. Cotton lives in Beresford Hall in Derbyshire, eight miles from Ashbourne, home of the Royal Shrovetide Football Match, an annual folk football game between two sides of the town. There is no evidence the match was played before the early nineteenth century, but attempts have been made to pin Cotton's poem to Ashbourne. The association is tenuous. Cotton's game is between two towns, December is mentioned, and there are a dozen or so on each side, not the mob involved in folk football. The winter frost is so harsh that the

---

166 Snape, A., *The anatomy of a horse containing an exact and full description of the frame, situation and connexion of all his parts*. M. Flesher, London, 1683. p. 61.

167 Carrow-whimbles were travelling men who made a living at cards and dice.

168 Andrews, W., *Famous Frosts and Frost Fairs in Great Britain*. George Redway, London, 1887. pp. 18–21, 26–36.

169 Mackay, C., *The Thames and its Tributaries*. 2 Vols. R. Bentley, London, 1840. Vol. 2. pp. 377, 383.

players, unable to "run, kick, or trip ye … for they were frozen", give up the game "till the next thaw."[170]

Something chillier is afoot that year. A plot to assassinate the king and his brother. When several conspirators meet in a tavern, they use football as an analogy, in case they are overheard. An informant's testimony of their conversation includes: "if the Foot-ball was laid down, how many we might reasonably expect would come in at first laying of it down from Our end of the Town to play at it? To which it was replyed, it was uncertain, but as many as were there would be concerned; to which it was answered … if we would not in a little time kick the Ball effectually we should be made Slaves [to popery] … upon which *Hunt* replyed, That he could do as much good as any body, for that Foot-ball Players often got broken shins, and he the said *Hunt* could Cure them."[171]

A co-conspirator boasts that he can muster "1000 Men out of the Hamlets, and if occasion were to give satisfaction, he would shew them all a Footbal Match or other Pastime."[172] The Earl of Essex and Lord Russel—the ringleaders behind the attempt to raise "the People of Blackheath, on a pretended Foot-ball match"—are confined to the Tower. "A few days later, it was given out, that the Earl of Essex had cut his own throat … the certainty of this lyes under great suspicion."[173] A ten-year old ditty is republished, containing the lines: "Let all that are Plotters be kick'd like a Ball, And tumbling down, break their Necks in the fall."[174]

A 1669 book lists the sports and recreations of various classes. "The King hath" hunting of otters, foxes and deer, hawking, horse races, "Tennis, Baloon, Biliards, Comedies, Masks &c." While the "Nobility and Gentry" share many of these pastimes, others include fishing, bowling, tumblers, cockfighting, Low-Bells,[175] Bat-fowling, "Catches, Questions, Purposes, Stage-Plays … &c." The "Citizens and peasants have Hand-Ball, Foot-Ball, Skittles, or Nine-pins, Shovel-board, Stow-Ball,

---

170 Cotton, C., *Burlesque; Upon the Great Frost.* In: Cotton, C., *Poems on several occasions.* s.n., London, 1689. p. 96.

171 Sprat, T., *COPIES OF THE INFORMATIONS AND Original PAPERS Relating to the Proof of The Horrid Conspiracy Against the Late KING.* Thomas Newcomb, London, 1685. p. 7.

172 Ibid, p. 58.

173 Kennedy, D., *The Late History of Europe, Being a Narration of All Remarkable Actions and Other Various Affairs.* George Mosman, Edinburgh, 1698. p. 33.

174 H.P., *Wit & Mirth. An Antidote against Melancholy.* J.P., London, 1684. pp. 222–223.

175 Bells used with a hand net and lamp to catch birds at night.

Goffe, Trol Madam [bagatelle] … Quoits, Leaping, Wrestling, Pitching the Bar, and Ringing of Bells, a Recreation used in no other Countrey in the World."[176] "Foot-ball", it adds, is "very *uncivil*, *rude* and *barbarous* within the city." Cricket makes the 1694 edition: "The Natives will endure long and hard Work, they will go in the Evening to Foot-ball, Stool-ball, Cricket, Prison-base, Wrestling, Cudgel-playing, or some such vehement Exercise, for their Recreation."[177] It is notable as one the few seventeenth century references to cricket.

Regal approval softens moods. In 1661, Sir Daniel Fleming of Rydal Hall pays a shoemaker a shilling for a football.[178] Even the king gets involved. In 1681, a twelve-a-side match takes place at Windsor between the "Duke of Albemarle's Men" and "King Charles II's Men."[179] Twelve-a-side wrestling for a wager of 200 gns[180] starts proceedings.[181] The king's men wear red, the duke's blue. Backswording follows, and when the duke wins again, Charles "challenged them at Foot-ball … the Goals stak'd out, and the Ball placed in the middle, the Duke held up an Handkerchief over the Ball, the letting fall of which was the signal to give the start, and the Handkerchief to him that got the first kick", suggesting a purely kicking match. The duke triumphs.

Bowling has been the darling of towns and cities for over a century. London is studded with alleys, which double as entertainment venues. In 1663, the Worshipful Company of the Drapers of London publishes their Garden Orders: Only persons of good quality may "bowl in the ally", no "uncivill" language, no bets above 6d a game, no furtive betting games in the garden's buildings, "no Men, boyes, Children or Servants be suffered to play at Ball, Quoits, or any other Game, or exercise in the Garden." It is free for anyone to take in the gardens, and a maze keeps children occupied. Pattens (wooden overshoes to protect ladies' shoes) are banned on the grass, and the path "after much raine'"[182] Original

176 Chamberlayne, E., *Angliæ Notitia or the Present State of England.* John Martyn, London, 1669. p. 86.

177 Chamberlayne, E., *Angliæ Notitia or the Present State of England.* T. Hodgkin, London, 1694. p. 53.

178 *The Manuscripts of SH Le Fleming, Esq.* Eyre and Spottiswoode, London, 1890. p. 388.

179 *The Loyal Protestant, and True Domestick Intelligence.* 28 June 1681. Issue 33. p. 2.

180 A guinea was a pound and a shilling.

181 Eight and a half years' wages for a skilled tradesman.

182 Johnson, A.H., *The History of the Worshipful Company of Drapers of London.* 5 Vols. Clarendon Press, Oxford, 1922. Vol. 4. pp. 294–295.

alleys are just that, existing laneways suitable for bowling. Inns often take up residency beside them; clearly, there is money to be made.[183]

Bowls waddles to the corner of the field, gives a thumbs up to football and tennis, and off he goes, galloping at high speed across the grass. Deceptive and impressive. Tennis claps delightedly. Bowls looks suitably modest. He knows he has the reach his niece and nephew cannot yet aspire too. He rolls high, he rolls low. "A hundred knyghtes truly tolde, Shall plaie with bowles in alayes colde."[184] The young man he had befuddled all those decades ago had been so impressed with his stories that he included him in more plays than any other sport. "I shall use those stories," the upstart magpie had said. "No royalties, mind, I cannot afford any." Bowls inclines his head, pushes out his lips, looks him squarely in his bloodshot eyes: "Aye, there's the rub."

Sometimes servants go it alone. In 1683, diarist Jacob Bee of Durham, writes: "Seven Bouchers should have play'd at foot ball with seven Glovers … and my man Christo. went without leave to play: and stay'd out all night."[185] The same year Bishop Burnet, in his book *Travels*, reports seeing an elephant "play at ball."[186]A Flemish writer witnesses the same thing in Constantinople in 1694: "he very prettily took up the Ball in his Trunk, and sent it packing therewith, as we do with the Palm of the Hand."[187] In 1663, Charles sends ambassadors overseas to re-establish alliances with European heads of state. Football is played in Moscow when twelve of the English ambassador's company greet the spring with an impromptu game.[188]

Football references appear in Parliament. This from 1675: "He matters the thing of rescue no more than a foot-ball play."[189] And from 1677: "When we contend for money, it puts him in mind of country fellows

---

183 Davies, C., *Bowling Alleys and Playhouses in London, 1560–90.* Early Theatre, 2019, 22.2, p. 45

184 *The Squier of Low Degree*. In: Wharton, T., Price, R. (eds.)., *The History of English Poetry.* 3 Vols. s.n., London, 1840. Vol. 1. p. 179.

185 Bee, J., *Jacob Bee His Booke, Given him the 29th of August 1681.* s.n., Durham. p. 19.

186 In: Butler, S., *Hudibras*. J.G., London, 1663. p. 99.

187 De Busbecq, O.G., *The four epistles of A.G. Busbequius*. s.n., London, 1694. p. 63.

188 Miège, G., *A relation of three embassies from his Majestie Charles II, to the great Duke of Muscovie, the King of Sweden, and the King of Denmark*. s.n., London. p. 142.

189 "Debates in 1675: June 3rd-4th," in *Grey's Debates of the House of Commons: Volume 3*, ed. Anchitell Grey (London: T. Becket and P. A. De Hondt, 1769), pp 239–260. *British History Online*, accessed February 17, 2024, http://www.british-history.ac.uk/greys-debates/vol3/.

going to foot-ball play, or any such country sport. They get up early, though possibly all the sport may end in breaking their shins, and tearing their cloaths."[190] Henry Peacham agrees: "One very well compared worldly Wealth, or Money, unto a Foot-Ball; some few nimble-heeled and headed run quite away with it, when the most are lookers on, and cannot get a Kick at it in all their Lives."[191] Elsewhere he writes of the composition of paintings: "such Winter peece should be graced and beautified with all manner of workes and exercises of winter, as foot ball, felling of wood, sliding upon the yce, [and] batfowling by night."[192]

190 "Debates in 1677: February 19th-20th," in *Grey's Debates of the House of Commons: Volume 4*, ed. Anchitell Grey (London: T. Becket and P. A. De Hondt, 1769), pp. 95–112. *British History Online*, accessed February 17, 2024, http://www.british-history.ac.uk/greys-debates/vol4/.

191 Peacham, H., *The Worth of a Penny*. S. Keble, London, 1686. p. 10.

192 Peacham, H., *The Gentlemans Exercise*. s.n., London, 1612. p. 45.

CHAPTER ELEVEN
1600–1699 IV

Calcio bounces into the seventeenth century. In 1604, a proverb is doing the rounds: *Chi non può dare alla palla, sconce!* Let him who cannot strike the ball, at least offer interference![1] If you are not striking the ball, you are not in the game, and if you are not in the game and stop in the Piazza Santa Croce during *calcio* you are whipped.[2] In 1630, Agostiniano Capradosso uses *calcio* as an allegory of life:

> Ball, comprising airy spirits that form and move it …
> it quietens and keeps silent,
> And between strikes and challenges it stops and pauses:
> Narrow-minded and ignoble world, which flees and deceives,
> And which distributes and grants for equal reward,
> Odes, indignation, blows, humiliation and fury
> to winners and losers.[3]

In 1632, the Venetians entertain the English ambassador with *calcio*, "the football game played in fine liveries."[4] The game flourishes throughout the 1640s, but its light soon flickers and dims, "grown-ups no longer play it, only youths."[5] It retains centre stage at festivals. During the Shrovetide of 1650 an extravagant game plays out, one team in light blue, the other flesh-coloured. They wear white muslin with side pieces, a feather, and silk shoes with crossed lacing all in their colour. "This calcio was hard fought. As a result of the great pique and emulation a great deal of fighting and many disputes ensued."[6] There

1 Magoun, F.P., *Il Gioco del Calcio Fiorentino.* Italica, 1942, 19:1, p. 12.

2 Ibid, p. 12.

3 Von Mallinckrodt, R., Schattner, A., *Sports and Physical Exercise in Early Modern Culture.* Routledge, Abingdon, Oxon, 2016. p. 1.

4 Hinds, A.B. (ed.)., *Calendar of State Papers and Manuscripts Relating to English Affairs, Existing in the Archives and Collections of Venice.* 38 Vols. His Majesty's Stationery Office, London, 1921. Vol. 23. p. 50.

5 Magoun, F.P., *Il Gioco del Calcio Fiorentino.* Italica, 1942, 19:1, p. 14.

6 Ibid, p. 14.

is a revival in the 1670/80s. De' Bardi's book on *calcio*, *Discorso*, is reprinted in 1673, the first time in fifty-eight years, with a fourth edition in 1688. The 1673 version contains thirty-four rules of the game to encourage a wider audience, one element of an orchestrated attempt to resurrect the sport.[7]

In 1670, Yorkshire priest Richard Lassels publishes *The Voyage of Italy*. Of Rome, he writes, "in the sommer evenings they play at ballon, a manly exercise much used in Italy, and farre more gentile than our rude football sport."[8,9] Lassels describes the ritualistic pageantry of seventeenth century calcio: "In Winter their *Giuoco di Calcio* (a play something like our Football, but they play with their hands) [is played] every night from the Epiphany till Lent … this being a thing particular to Florence … the two Factions of the Calcio, the Red and the Green, choose each of them a Prince, some yong Cavalier of a good Purse." The princes choose sides and the teams repair to two palaces, where they establish faux kingdoms.

"[They] receive Embassadors from one another … take prisoners from one another … heare the complaints of their subjects, jeere their enemy Princes in Embassies, and at last resolve to fight … having spunn out thus the time till near Carnavale, or shroftide; the two Princes resolve on a Battle at Calcio, to be fought in the Piazza of Santa Croce, before the Great Duke and Court … the two Princes of the Calcio come to the place … with all the young Noblemen and Gentlemen of the towne, upon the best horses they can finde, with scarfs red, or green, about their Armes … trompets sounding before them, and accompanied with a stately train … Having rancked themselves a pretty distance one from the other … the Ball, or *Ballon* is throwne up in the midst between them, and to it they go with great nimbleness, sleight, and discretion; and sometimes they fall to it indeed, and cuff handsomely: but upon payne of death, no man must resent afterwards out of the lists, whatever happened here … At last, that side which throwes, or strikes the Ballon over the rayles of the other side, winns the day, and runns to the standards, which they carry away all night … the conquering Prince

---

7 Ibid, p. 3.

8 He is probably referring to *pallone*.

9 Lassels, R., *The yoyage of Italy*. s.n., Paris, 1670. p. 151.

entertains them at a *Festino di Ballo* … where all his chief Officers and combatants dance alone with the Ladyes at the Ball, none els being permitted to dance with them that night."[10]

~

Dissenting Protestants are slow to forgive. An article in an 1840 *Stamford Mercury* lambasts Charles as, "one of the most debauched and impious men that ever existed."[11] His subjects "were at liberty everywhere to meet together for frivolous, sensual, and profane purposes … were encouraged in Sunday games and revelry, such as football and races, clerk-ales, and all sorts of merrymaking." In 1672, John Welch recounts a tale of divine retribution against a man who allowed "profanation of the Lords Day at his house … [with] football and other games and pastimes." After several chances to mend his ways, the Minister drops by with a message from God: he is to be cast out of his house and estate. It comes to pass, and the man spends the rest of his days in thrall to guilt.[12]

Sin is rife: "if you step into the *Country*, you will see *Franticks* as well as *Anticks* on this Sacred Day … good God! What *Routs* and *Disorders*, *what Cudgel-playing* and *Wrest-ling*, what *Races* and *Foot-ball Matches* … in their open Fields … [in] every Quarter and Corner of the Nation."[13] In 1681, non-conformist Edward Bury takes aim at the overzealous: "always raving, and tearing in pieces all that come in their way … as men at football they many times make such hast they overrun the Ball, so these men, many times, leave truth behind them."[14] William Ramesey castigates gentlemen who like, "To take Tobacco, Drink all Day long, and Night too, in a Tavern, to discourse of impertinencies, and that tend to no Edification; to Jest, Sing and Roar."[15] He advocates tennis, stop-ball, trapball, ringing, and pitching bars as gentlemanly pursuits but considers "*Hurling, Wrastling, and Foot-ball*, such rude pastimes better becoming the Vulgar, and Labouring Man; the sight of them, however, as a Spectator, is not amiss."[16] Ramesey also mentions two "recreations

---

10 Ibid, pp. 212–215.

11 *Stamford Mercury*. 4 September 1840. p. 2.

12 Welch, J., *Popery Anatomised*. Robert Sanders, Glasgow, 1672. n.p.

13 Bouche, P.P., *The Reformed Gentleman*. s.n., London, 1609. pp. 109–110.

14 Bury, E., *A sovereign antidote against the fear of death*. J.A., London, 1681. p. 125.

15 Ramesey, W., *The Gentlemans Companion*. E. Okes, London, 1672. p. 126.

16 Ibid, pp. 133–134.

which are used abroad … Pilmall, Gauff."[17] Pall mall is originally French, while gauff is a variant spelling of golf.[18] Abroad. Is he referring to Scotland or elsewhere?

References to stow-ball are rare.[19] She is the enigmatic character of English sport. Early references are ambiguous; there are coeval references to stoolball, making it hard to differentiate one from the other. In the c1450s marginalia of John Mirk's *Instructions For Parish Priests*, activities banned from churchyards include "Cotteying [quoits], bollying [bowls], tenessying, hand ball, fott ball, stoil ball."[20] Stoolball or stowball? Stoolball is centred around Sussex, whereas stowball is peculiar to Gloucestershire and its environs. The c1450 manuscript has been reliably assigned to the Bletchley area of Buckinghamshire, only forty miles from the Gloucestershire border.[21] If so, it is the earliest reference to the game, and changes the earliest mention of stoolball to 1567.[22] There is a caveat. The additional text may have been written as much as half a century later. The only other evidence is in a 1967 journal article, which claims the manuscript "contains notes relating them to Herefordshire at the end of the fifteenth century."[23] If true, it is still the earliest known reference to stowball (and, if not, to stoolball). The article provides another clue that stoil ball relates to stowball. Herefordshire borders Gloucestershire.

In 1525, Peter Franklyn is given a 6d fine after he contravenes a court order and lets his sixteen sheep graze in the "Stoballfield."[24]

---

17 Ibid, p. 133.

18 Others include goff, gowf, gowff, goif, and gouf.

19 There are also multiple spellings: stoball, stobball, stowball, and stoeball, all of which may be hyphenated. There is a single reference to stop-ball.

20 Bodleian Library, Oxford: MS Douce 103, *Instructions for Parish Priests*, fifteenth century, fol. 126r.

21 Wakelin, M.F., *The Manuscripts of John Mirk's Festial*. Leeds Studies in English, 1967, Vol 1, p. 105.

22 Clark, A. (ed.), *The Shirburn Ballades, 1585–1616*. Clarendon Press, Oxford, 1907. p. 48; Drant, T., *Horace His arte of Poetrie, pistles, and Satyrs Englished*. Thomas Marshe, London, 1567. n.p.

23 Wakelin, M.F., *The Manuscripts of John Mirk's Festial*. Leeds Studies in English, 1967, Vol 1, p. 105.

24 *Stoolball England*. https://www.stoolball.org.uk/history/story/stoolball-in-sussex-by-russell-goggs. Accessed 24 December 2023; *Stoolball in Sussex*. The Sussex County Magazine, 1928, Vol. 2., p. 326. W.W. Grantham was the official historian of stoolball. He organised a match at Lord's in August 1917, founded the Stoolball Association at Lord's in 1923, and authored *Stoolball Illustrated and How to Play It*, W. Speaight and Sons, London, 1919; its preface ends charmingly: "I was asked to write a pamphlet on the game after the first match at Lord's; but owing to my military duties I had no time till after the Armistice was signed." The 1917 match pitted "2nd London General Hospital (Damaged by Wounds)" against "Ye Anciente Lawyers (Damaged by Age)."

The reference cites the location as the manor of Kirklington, North Yorkshire, "belonging to the Duchy of Lancaster", but it is likely to be Kirtlington, Oxfordshire, as the Duchy possessed this manor but not Kirklington. In 1574, Queen Elizabeth grants Robert Dudley manors in east Gloucestershire. Delighted by her favour, he progresses there "with an extraordinary number of Attendants and multitudes of country people." On a tour of his estate, he "went to Wotton hill, where he played a match at Stoball."[25] The following year, the city of Worcester complains that "all sortes of common people withyn this cytie … play at unlawful games, as bowles, stowleball, and other unlawful devises of plaies … no person … excepte smal chyldren under seaven yeres of age, shall play at any unlawful games in the stretes, as tenys, stowball, catt, and other such like, upon pain of imprisonment."[26] Stoolball *and* stowball are mentioned, demonstrating their individuality. The city is close to the home of stowball: Worcestershire also borders Gloucestershire.

The Dudley anecdote is taken from a 1639 book by John Smyth, who provides another mention. The area of the Cotswolds around Wotton Hill is home to "the inbred delight that both gentry, yeomanry, rascallity, boyes and children, do take in a game called Stoball. The play whereat each child of 12 yeares old, can (I suppose) as well describe, as my selfe: And not a sonne of mine, but at 7 was furnished with his double stoball staves, and a gamster therafter."[27] A local (inbred) game that transcends age and class. *Stave* (archaic for staff) is the term used for a stowball stick. Stoball and stowball. Two near-identical sounding stick and ball games. Similar sounding to stoolball too, but that game is played first with the hand and later with a short paddle bat. In 1755, Samuel Johnson describes stoolball as "A play where balls are driven from stool to stool."[28] Critical detail is revealed in another dictionary three years later: "A sort of play with a ball thrown against a stool."[29] Clearly, the stool is a rudimentary wicket.

---

25 Maclean, J. (ed.)., *The Berkeley Manuscripts*. 3 Vols. John Bellows, Gloucestershire, 1883. Vol. 2. pp. 290–291.

26 Noake, J., *Worcestershire Relics*. Longman & Co., London, 1877. p. 75.

27 Maclean, J. (ed.)., *The Berkeley Manuscripts*. 3 Vols. John Bellows, Gloucestershire, 1883. Vol. 3. p. 10.

28 Johnson, S., *A Dictionary of the English Language*. W. Strahan, London, 1755. n.p.

29 Anon., *A Pocket Dictionary*. J. Newbery, London, 1758. n.p.

John Aubrey provides a rich description of stowball, c1656–1691: "Stobball-play is peculiar to North Wilts, North Gloucestershire, and a little part of Somerset near Bath. They smite a ball, stuffed very hard with quills and covered with soale leather, with a staffe, commonly made of withy [willow], about 3 [feet] and a halfe long. Colerne-downe is the place so famous and so frequented for stobball-playing. The turfe is very fine, and the rock (freestone) is within an inch and a half of the surface, which gives the ball so quick a rebound. A stobball-ball is of about four inches diameter, and as hard as stone. I doe not heare that the game is used anywhere [else] in England ..."[30] The rules are documented by Francis Willughby in his sports book of 1672:

"The ball is either made of a knob of elme or of leather hard wrought up together, the staves they strike with they call Stow Ball staves, which are strong short staffs, a little bigger and longer then those they strike Kit-cats with. They hold the ball in one hand, & throw it up, & then strike it with both hands, putting the hand that held the ball quickly upon the staffe. There are two pins at a convenient distance fastened into the ground; one of them they called the Lay Pin, in the other the Boot Pin. They play 2, 3 or 4 of a side, but seldom more than four."

The ball is struck from the Lay Pin to the Boot Pin. The other side stand opposite and strike the ball back if they can get hit it clean or on the rebound. The team that is in hits the ball to the right of, and then behind the Boot Pin, then to the right of the Lay Pin in a bid to return home. Once done, an in-player has a single strike of the ball from where the opposition stands. The aim is to get as close to the Lay Pin as possible. A single lay is a staff's length. If it is a two-a-side game, the ball must land within three lays; if a three-a-side, within four lays; four-a-side, five lays. The number of strikes required to get around the circuit and within the lays is totted up. Each lay is a stroke, so the closer to the pin the better. The side with the lowest strokes win. Is the Boot Pin a base? Is stowball the earliest bat-base-ball game in history?

It is little wonder Worcestershire-born Willughby has such detailed knowledge of stowball. Notable, too, that the sport is the only one recorded on one of his small notepads, suggesting it is among the earliest

30 Britton J. (ed.), *The natural history of Wiltshire*. J.B. Nichols and Son, London, 1847. p. 117.

written.[31] What is missing from the account is when the staff is used to strike the ball, presumably any time after it is initially struck with both hands. Both Smyth and Aubrey's accounts are in Gloucestershire. Aubrey believes it is not played beyond the county's surrounds, but the stoballfield of 1525 is in Kirtlington, Oxfordshire. Is it any surprise? Kirtlington is only fifteen miles from the Gloucestershire border. A century and a half later, Francis Vernon of Christ Church, Oxford, writes: "Then you see the hills of Bullington rising up on the left mound, with sticks they beat the grass with untamed leaps, the ball beats the grass."[32] In the margin beside it: "Bullington Green. The play of Stow-ball."

A 1666 poem about the Great Plague of London mentions "shittle-cock" and stool-ball, but the author inserts an erratum that, "for stool-ball read stoball."[33] Separate games, then. A 1668 book lists "Tennis, Foot-ball, Stool-ball, Sto-Ball, Pel-mel" as games requiring strength and skill, further proving their distinctness.[34] In 1699, Chamberlayne includes "goffe" and "stow-ball" as pursuits of "Citizens and peasants", so it is unconnected to golf, too.[35] Is it coincidence that "stoole ball" is mentioned in *The Two Noble Kinsmen*?[36] Published in 1634, but believed to have been written two decades before, it is attributed to William Shakespeare and John Fletcher. Is it stool-ball, or do they mean stowball? Stratford-upon-Avon is six miles from the Gloucestershire border.

In 1658, a "humble petition" is sent to "the Colledge and Free Schoole at Westminster", requesting that action be taken against "disorders and entrenchments committed … upon Tuttlefields", which has resulted in "the hindrance of the meeting of the Gentry for their recreation at Bowles, Goffe, and Stowball." Such disturbance includes the dumping of dead horses.[37] A gentrified game contrasts with John Stripe's opinion,

---

31 Cram, D., Forgeng, J.L., Johnston, D. (eds.)., *The Book of Games of Francis Willughby (1635–1672). A Seventeenth-century Treatise on Sports, Games and Pastimes*. Routledge, Abingdon, Oxon, 2016. p. 284.

32 Vernon, F., *Oxonium Poema*. W. Hall, Oxford, 1667. p. 20.

33 Austin, W., *The anatomy of a pestilence*. s.n., London, 1666. p. 8.

34 Wilkins, J., *An Essay Towards a Real Character And a Philosophical Language*. s.n., London, 1668. p. 241.

35 Chamberlayne, E., *Angliæ Notitia or the Present State of England*. John Martyn, London, 1669. p. 47.

36 Anon. *The Two Noble Kinsmen*. Tho. Cotes, London, 1634. ln 2932.

37 *The Athenaeum*. 6 April 1901. p. 434.

in his 1720 version of John Stow's *A Survay of London*. Strype includes stowball as a diversion of the lower classes, along with football, wrestling, bell-ringing, and, intriguingly, cricket.[38] John Locke also mentions "long-bow and stob-ball, in Tothill Fields" near Westminster, in 1679,[39] while in 1701, the London suburb of Islington, then a manor in Middlesex, has a field "commonly called the Stowball-Field."[40] Arguably, stowball catches on in London, played among the gentry before sliding down the social ladder.

The game is mentioned further afield. In the 1673 book *The Present State of Ireland*, the anonymous author writes: "The Common sort meet oftentimes in great numbers … to recreate themselves at a play called Bandy, with Balls and crooked Sticks, much after the manner of our play at Stoe-ball."[41] The terminology is ironic, since bandy is the English stickball game, and far commoner than stowball. Perhaps the author is a native of Gloucester. London is more likely. Thomas Dineley's 1681 description of the Irish adds little: "Gaming and laziness they are much addicted to, their chiefest games are five-cards, all-fours &c. In the meadows att bandy and stoeball &c."[42] Dineley lives twenty miles from Gloucestershire. There is another possible mention, in the Dublin Assembly Rolls of 1612: anyone over thirteen "fownd plaeing at stodball, Coiting, tennes, cudgielles, or any other unlawfull games", will spend a day in Newgate prison.[43] If it is stowball, it is among the earliest mentions. This is in contrast to Dublin dramatist Henry Burnell's 1641 play *Lundgartha*: "I might then 'a' played at stoole-ball with young children."[44]

Further afield, stowball's popularity can be measured by its presence in foreign dictionaries. In 1690, Guy Miège includes "Stow-ball" in a French dictionary as "a sort of ball game."[45] Stowball appears in

---

38 Strype, J., *A Survey of the Cities of London and Westminster*. 2 Vols. s.n., London, 1720. Vol. 1. p. 257.

39 King, P., *The Life of John Locke*. Henry Colburn, London, 1829. p. 134.

40 G.F. (ed.)., *The Compleat Conveyancer*. Richard and Edward Atkins, London, 1701. p. 32.

41 Anon., *The Present State of Ireland*. M.D., London, 1673. p. 153.

42 *Extracts from the Journal of Thomas Dineley Esquire*. The Journal of the Kilkenny and South-East of Ireland Archæological Society, 1856–57, Vol. 1, p. 182.

43 Fletcher, A.J., *Drama and the Performing Arts in Pre-Cromwellian Ireland*. D.S. Brewer, Cambridge, 2001. p. 315.

44 Burnell, H., *Landgartha*. s.n., Dublin, 1641. n.p.

45 Miège, G., *The short French dictionary in two parts*. s.n., London, 1690. n.p.

German, in 1763: "a children's game with a ball and a curved stick"; and in Portuguese in 1782: "[a] type of game that boys play with a ball and a staff."[46,47] Stowball does not make it into Samuel Johnson's *A Dictionary of the English Language*, in 1755, nor any of the many subsequent editions. Trapball does. This, from the first edition, "Trap: A play at which a ball is driven with a stick", and "Trapstick: A stick with which boys drive a wooden ball."[48]

Gloucestershire is manifestly home to stowball. As late as 1837 the town of Stinchcombe (pop. 432) is "famous for the robust game of sto ball."[49] Only three miles from Wotton Hill, Stinchcombe has its own hill. Stowball stands atop, surveying her fiefdom. It is the perfect vantage point; Stinchcombe Hill commands the most extensive prospect in the county. The dipping yellow sun sets the sky alight with orange and pink, vermilion and lilac, and glittering gold. Stowball thinks of the mid-fourteenth century stained-glass panel in Gloucester Cathedral. The player stood in the meadow, readying the raised curved stave with both hands, the ball bounding toward him, all framed in a scarlet disc.[50] She has dwelt among the rolling hills longer than anyone knows. She turns, takes it all in. And then the mist descends.

~

In 1672, nature has its say when a "Horrible and Unheard of Tempest" strikes Bedford: "It threw the Swan Inn Gates off the Hinges into the Street and after it had whirled them there, up and down, as if they had been a Foot-Ball, it brake them to pieces … it carried a great Tree from beyond our River, over our Pauls Steeple, as if it had been a bundle of Feathers."[51] The tables are turned in 1682. A man walking his spaniels comes across a patch of "Cabbages grown to a commendable globosity, the roundness whereof tempted us to a Game at *Foot-ball*; we banded them about sufficiently, and made

---

46 Ludwig, C., Rogler, J.B., *A dictionary: English, German and French*. s.n., Leipzig, 1763. p. 849.

47 Anon., *Diccionario Inglez e Portuguez*. 2 Vols. S. Nourse, London, 1782. Vol. 1. n.p.

48 Johnson, S., *A Dictionary of the English Language*. W. Strahan, London, 1755. n.p.

49 Moule, T., *The English Counties Delineated*. 2 Vols. George Virtue, London, 1837. Vol. 2. p. 20.

50 Clavner, N., *The Great East Window of Gloucester Cathedral and its Heraldic Glass*. Journal of the British Archaeological Association, 2018, 171:1, p. 105, fig. 4C.

51 Mithnal, A., *A True Relation of what hapned at Bedford on Munday last, Aug. 19 instant*. s.n., London, 1672. p. 4.

some of them caper over a Ten-foot wall."[52] He dubs his amusement the "*Olympick* sport of *Kick-Cabbage*."

Puritans be damned. Football has the royal nod and even clergy can play. A syrupy newspaper article describes "A jolly vicar & an honest fellow" who "crossed shins at football upon a Christmas Eve."[53] Both are furious and "were to have boxed it out", but after receiving communion on Christmas Day forgive each other. In 1661, Griffin Lewis publishes a book of satirical character essays, including "A debaucht Courtier", "A Phanatick", and "A Beastly-Drunkard." "A scandalous Minister is a prophane ignorant dunce … they sent him to *Universitie*, where he ate, drank, and slept, plaid a match or two at Foot-ball, stole a Pig."[54] The licentious vicar of Alderminster in Worcestershire fits the description. In 1666, he frequents alehouses "and other places of profane meetings, at wakes,[55] footeball, playings, Bearebaytings."[56] He also cooked the parish books and "most profanely, wickedly and debauchedly quaffed and drunk healthes" in the chalice. In 1679, a Kent cleric follows suit, "a common gamester, given to playing at cards and dice and other unlawfull games for great summes of money."[57] That year, the Lancashire village of Downham hosts an annual 30 December sermon, followed by the distribution of alms to "impotent, lame, blind, decrepid [and] aged" churchgoers. A football match pitting Downham against Newchurch-in-Pendle becomes associated with the occasion. That it kicks off before the sermon is finished proves so intolerable that one year a visiting preacher steps down from the pulpit, proceeds down the aisle, out of the church, and into the fray. He secures the ball and returns inside. Only when he is finished does he march to the church steps and kick the ball back to them. It becomes an annual tradition.[58] A song in *Westminster Drolleries* sums up post-Puritan London:

---

52 Richards, W., *Wallography, or, The Britton describ'd being a pleasant relation of a journey into Wales*. s.n., London, 1773. pp. 47–48.

53 *The Observator, In Dialogue*. 27 March 1684. p. 1.

54 Lewis, G., *Essayes and characters written by L.G.* s.n., London, 1661. pp. 64–65.

55 Annual parish feasts.

56 Barber, M., *Records of the Court of Arches in Lambeth Palace Library*. Ecclesiastical Law Journal, 1993, 3:12, p. 17.

57 Ibid, p. 17.

58 Snape, M.F., *The Church of England in Industrialising Society*. The Boydell Press, Woodbridge, 2003. p. 32.

Thus all our life long we are frolick and gay,
And instead of Court revels, we merrily play
At Trap, at Rules, and at Barly-break run:
At Goff, and at Foot-ball, and when we have done
These innocent sports, we'l laugh and lie down,
And to each pretty Lass
We will give a green Gown.[59]

Fun-seeking Londoners flock to the theatre. In *Sir Barnaby Whigg*, Livia eviscerates the "opinionated fool and cuckold" Sir Walter: "thou wicker-bottle, edg-less knife, thou Ape of generation … Didst thou dare to blast my Virtue, my Integrity, thou laughter of our sex, and foot-ball of thy own? If I were a man, I would cut that Carkass of thine into as small a quantity as thy Wits."[60] In another comedy, *The Folly of Priest-craft*, Cautious, "an old covetous priest", complains of his losses in the stock market: "Ay, but to be kick'd up and down like a Football, that was rude." Bigot, "a zealous priest" points out that "The Poets and Philosophers compare the Life of Man to a Game at Tennis, The World is the Tennis-court, and men are the Balls which the Fates toss up and down with Rackets: But great men, like great Footballs, are kicked up and down with greater violence."[61] Perhaps not: "Why they say the worlde is like a Byas bowle, and it runnes all on the rich mens sides; others say, tis like a Tennis-ball, and fortune keepes such a Racket with it, as it tosses it in to times hazzard, and that devoures all."[62]

Be jolly, Londoners, but not unruly. In 1673, the Lord Mayor directs apprentices to rein in "the throwing of Squibs, Fire-works, Foot-ball Play and the like … in the Streets." As for "Car-men, Dray-men … Tankard-Bearers, Porters, and other Persons laden with Burdens", jostle and bustle away, but the city is weary of uncivil and insolent manners towards "Persons of better Quality … freedom of Passage without the least Disturbance, Affront or Injury" is expected, "as they will answer

59 Ebsworth, J.E., *Westminster Drolleries, Both Parts of 1671, 1672*. R. Roberts, Boston, Lincolnshire, 1875. p. 28.

60 D'Urfey, T., *Sir Barnaby Whigg, or, No Wit like a Woman's*. A.G. and J.P., London, 1681. n.p.

61 Anon., *The Folly of Priest-craft*. s.n., London, 1690. p. 48.

62 Sharpham, E., *Cupids VVhirligig*. E. Allde, London, 1607. n.p.

the contrary at their utmost perils."[63] There are fields where Londoners can play. A "Match at Foot-ball in Moor-Fields" is mentioned in 1698.[64] Wrestling is recorded there in 1672, cricket in 1725, and trapball in 1757.[65,66,67] Other venues include Finsbury Park, Tuttlefields, Artillery Ground, Battersea Park, Hyde Park, Long Fields, and Kennington Common.

~

By 1685, Charles is dead, and James II is king. On the occasion of his birthday in 1686, the "Feast of the Natives and Inhabitants of the Parish of St. Martins in the Fields, will be held in the Tennis Court in Panton Buildings … tickets may be had for the said Feast at Mr. James Pawletts at the Blue Posts in the Haymarket."[68] Two years later, James is dethroned, and William and Mary rule. James briskly tries to regain the crown. Attempts are made to woo the north. In 1690, "Letters from Newcastle gave an account of a great match at football which had been played in Northumberland, and was suspected to have been a pretext for a gathering of the disaffected."[69] Any serious threat is snuffed out in July 1690, when James is defeated at the Battle of the Boyne. Take heed monarchs, England is modernising. Parliament has more power, the Whigs and Tories have formed, and the idea of a United Kingdom is bandied about. For all that, the public still crave prurient witch trials. 1681's *Saducismus Triumphatus* details two Scottish trials of a century earlier. Jannet Clarke was accused of "giving and taking away power from sundry men's Genital-Members", while John Fiene "kissed the Devil's Breech: the Record speaks more broadly."[70,71] John Fienne is complicit in raising winds on King James VI's (VI of Scotland and I of England) passage into Denmark: "Satane delyverit ane catt out of his hand … to

63 Hanson, R., *By the maior.* Andrew Clark, London, 1673. n.p.

64 Dilke, T., *The pretenders, or, The town unmask'd.* s.n., London, 1698. p. 41. Act V.

65 Penn, W., *Quakerism, a new nick-name for old Christianity.* s.n., London, 1672. p. 210.

66 *Stamford Mercury.* 1 April 1725. p. 139.

67 *Kentish Weekly Post.* 27 July 1757. p. 2.

68 *The London Gazette.* 30 September 1686. p. 2.

69 Macaulay, T.B., *The history of England from the accession of James the Second.* Longmans, Green, Reader & Dyer, London, 1877. pp. 170–171.

70 An insinuation he performed fellatio on the Devil.

71 Glanvil, J., *Saducismus Triumphatus.* S. Lownds, London, 1687. p. 470.

"Cast the same in the see hola!"[72] A cat is considered unsuitable for the King's return. More oomph. Satan advises "ane thing lyke to ane fute-ball, quhilk apperit to the said Johnne lyke a wisp, and caist the same in the see."[73] "A thing like a football, which appeared to the said John like a hovering light, and [he] cast the same into the sea." It is the infernal voyage that launches James's fascination with witchcraft.

Football is undeniably popular at Cambridge University. Going forward, it will be the ex-public schoolboys of Cambridge, not Oxford, who meld the various school codes into a coherent whole; arguably, because Cambridge is in East Anglia. In 1609, the Master of Arts at Trinity College, Cambridge, speaks to football's prevalence: "if Law were not costly and tedious … the vulgar sort which are as malicious as Witches, would use Lawes frequently, as foote-ball play, or dauncing about a May-pole."[74] Antiquarian Simonds d'Ewes describes a game soon after he arrives at St John's, Cambridge, c1620, when football is restricted to college fields. After supper, he repairs to "a spacious field at the back of Queens' College called Sheep's green" to play "some hot foot-ball" against rivals Trinity.[75] Trinity do not show, and St John's play a match between themselves. By the end, d'Ewes has a broken shin. When Trinity fail to turn up a few days later, St John's students break the rear gates of Trinity College and use long poles to harry the enemy.

Others pay for their contumacy. In 1618, three of Peterhouse and four of St John's are charged, "for playing football when ordered not to do so and for insulting the proctor … Withers to be whipped by the Dean of Peterhouse in the College hall at dinnertime … Rayement is alleged to have attacked the proctor's man with a sword; to be placed in the stocks in the hall at Peterhouse at dinnertime and to make a speech in the Schools acknowledging his fault."[76] Punishment for a saddler is surprisingly lenient: an hour in the stocks in Trinity parish for playing

---

72 Pitcairn, R., *Criminal Trials in Scotland from 1488–1624*. 3 Vols. William Tait, Edinburgh, 1833. Vol. 1. Pt. 2. p. 211.

73 A thing like a football, which appeared …

74 Wybarne, J., *The New Age of Old Names*. William Barret and Henry Fetherstone, London, 1609. p. 84.

75 Marsden, J.H. (ed.)., *College Life in the Time of James the First as Illustrated by an Unpublished Diary, by Symonds d'Ewes*. John W Parker and Son, London, 1851. pp. 94–95.

76 *Act Book, 7 Nov. 1617–8 Jan. 1622*, GBR/0265/UA/VCCt.I 9. Cambridge University Library https://archivesearch.lib.cam.ac.uk/repositories/2/archival_objects/54895. Accessed May 27, 2023.

football near Queens' College with scholars when prohibited."[77] Other townsmen are flogged for the same offence. Humour is to be found. In the play *A Woman is a Weather-Cocke*,[78] Sir Abraham Ninny says to Count Fredericke, "Indeed there's reason there should be some difference in my Legges, for one cost me twentie pound more than the other … Right hath your Lordship said, twas broke indeed, at footeball in the Universitie."[79]

In July 1620, a number of witnesses provide statements concerning "violence in Castle yard" during football. Seven students from various colleges are implicated.[80] Similar depositions are made in March 1640, when violence erupts during a football match between Cambridge scholars and townspeople at the Castle.[81] Weeks later, four students are up for playing football on the close between King's College and Clare Hall.[82] Other students stand accused of drinking, football playing, and abusing the Bishop of Norwich's chaplain.[83] They are still at it in 1657. Five students "att night in Christ's Greene did plat [sic] at footeball and carried themselves very uncivillie towards him."[84] Cambridge students commit an assortment of misdemeanours: playing cards at The Pheasant Cock, fighting with a butcher on exiting The Dolphin, gaming at The White Swan, keeping fighting cocks.

University courts have jurisdiction over the town for minor offences. In 1617/18, Giles Cree and Faith Maddison are whipped for fornication,[85] widow Tomlinson is entertaining scholars at unreasonable hours with a

---

77 *Act Book, 7 Nov. 1617–8 Jan. 1622*, GBR/0265/UA/VCCt.I 9. Cambridge University Library https://archivesearch.lib.cam.ac.uk/repositories/2/archival_objects/54895. Accessed May 27, 2023.

78 The author Nathan Field (1587–1620) was taught by Richard Mulcaster at St Paul's School. Mulcaster was a trailblazer in sports reform.

79 Field, N., *A Woman is a Weather-Cocke*. William Jaggard, London, 1612. n.p. First performed in 1609.

80 *1619 [Exhibita] coram Dre Scott, Procan:', 1616–1620*, GBR/0265/UA/VCCt.III 24. Cambridge University Library. https://archivesearch.lib.cam.ac.uk/repositories/2/archival_objects/55075. Accessed May 27, 2023.

81 *1639 [Exhibita] coram Dre Cosin: Procan:', 1622–1640*, GBR/0265/UA/VCCt.III 36. Cambridge University Library. https://archivesearch.lib.cam.ac.uk/repositories/2/archival_objects/55088. Accessed May 27, 2023.

82 Ibid.

83 Ibid.

84 Tatham, G.B., *The Puritans in Power*. Cambridge University Press, 1913. p. 145.

85 *Act Book, 7 Nov. 1617–8 Jan. 1622*, GBR/0265/UA/VCCt.I 9. Cambridge University Library. https://archivesearch.lib.cam.ac.uk/repositories/2/archival_objects/54895. Accessed September 06, 2023.

slide-groat board,[86] and a draper is in trouble for setting up "a close-stool privy for children and servants … the stink from which is unbearable."[87] Mary Webster is a trickster. In her position as keeper of the tennis courts at Corpus Christi College, she creates a gap in the college's brick wall, allowing students to sneak back in after hours.[88] John Adamson is more blatant, "bringing shows and booths to Hoggmagogg Hills including Juda Hudson of Cambridge, a suspected bawd … commonly known as Jumping Judy."[89]

James Duport, tutor at Trinity College, Cambridge, from 1635 to 1664, regards football as "a rude, boistrous exercise, & fitter for Clownes than for Schollers."[90] He advises them to "be not wedded to any sport", to "use Tennis sparingly and never immediately after meals", and to play "att bowles, or shooting, or pitching the barre." He discourages "gadding and gossiping from Chamber to Chamber", and chess—"too tedious and time-devouring." Old Oxfordian Sir Thomas Overbury is surgical. Writing on the disposition of a medley of characters, he includes "a mere scholar": "The antiquity of his University is his creed, and the excellency of his college (though but for a match at football) an article of his faith."[91] A Puritan, he goes on, "Is a diseased piece of apocalypse", a Flatterer "the shadow of a fool", and a Dunce "a soul drowned in a lump of flesh."[92,93] Cambridge University minces no words in 1632:

"All Schollers and Students of those severall Colledges which have places to play att footeball within the precincts of theire owne Colledge shall not play att footeball in any other places, but such only as are within the precincts of theire owne severall Colledges. And that such Schollers and Students of other Colledges which have noe private places within the precincts of theire owne Colledges to play in, shall play only in the places hereafter named and noe other viz: The Schollers and Students

86 Ibid.

87 Ibid.

88 Ibid.

89 Ibid.

90 Preston, C.D., Oswald, P.H., *James Duport's Rules for his Tutorial Pupils: A Comparison of two Surviving Manuscripts*. Transactions of the Cambridge Bibliographical Society, 2011, 14:4, p. 354.

91 Morley, H. (ed.), *Character Writings of the Seventeenth Century*. George Routledge and Sons Limited, London, 1891. p. 52.

92 Ibid, pp. 49, 32, 43.

93 Overbury was murdered in the Tower of London, poisoned by his friend's lover.

of Gonvill and Caius Colledge only upon the backside of King's Colledge. etc."[94]

There is context. Charles I and his queen visit Cambridge in March 1631. Queen's College debuts Peter Hausted's new play, *The Rival Friends.* At one point, "Nodle Emptie" (empty head) converses with Anteros, a "humorous mad fellow":

> Ant: I wonder hee did not strike you all this while. Go to, I say no more, I hold him to be the stoutest man of his hands in all this side o'th countrey.
> Nod: Is he so?
> Ant: Why, he is sent for far and neere by the valiant of the Parishes, to play at football: I tell you hee is the onely Hammershin this Shire can boast of; not a Servingman can keep a legge or an arme whole for him, he has a pension from all the Surgeons within the compasse of fortie miles, for breaking of bones.[95]

Hammershin. A man notorious for kicking shins at football. Two other characters are described as "robustious football-players."[96] Later, a man is said to have "never emptyed a buttry pot after a match at football with greater appetite than hee devours this gullery."[97] Students have been specially instructed to keep quiet during the play. With forty-nine scenes and thirty-two characters, the play goes on for hours. No one is impressed, not least "their majesties." It is branded "obscene, profane, absurd, and tedious", and cried down vociferously by students.[98] Ironically, a play put on for the king at Trinity College the following night is a roaring success. The playwright Thomas Randolph analogises football in a cruel way:

> Ballio: I said you had no neck: your chin and shoulders
> Were so good friends, they would ha' nothing part 'um:

94 Clark, J.W., *Football in the Sixteenth and Seventeenth Centuries.* Cambridge Review, 1909, 30, pp. 307–308.

95 Hausted, P., *The Rival Friends. A comœdie, as it was acted before the King and Queen's Majesties.* Aug. Matthewes, London, 1632. n.p. Act 3, Sc 2.

96 Ibid, *Dramatis personae.* n.p.

97 Ibid, n.p. Act 3, Sc 8.

98 Cressy, D., *The Death of a Vice-Chancellor at Cambridge.* In: Feingold, M., *History of Universities.* Oxford University Press, 2012. 26:2. pp. 101–102.

I vow'd your breasts, for colour and proportion,
Were like a writheld pair of o're worn footballs.[99]

The vice-chancellor Henry Butts is blamed for staging Hausted's play. He sinks into melancholia, convinced that "God had deserted him." He commits suicide on Easter Sunday.[100] His rival, who "made his speech without any reflection on his predecessor", takes his place.[101]

In February 1607, Oxford scholars smile smugly when they sidestep a ban by playing football on Bullingdon Green, but they are headed for disaster when an act of tomfoolery gets out of hand and they burn "the fursesses [gorse] … contayninge 3 acres or thereabouts."[102] Universities are determined to maintain the supremacy over students public schools have struggled with.[103] This from Oxford University's Laudian Statutes of 1636: "In like manner, no scholars of any condition (and least of all graduates) are to play foot-ball, within the University or its precinct (and particularly not in the public streets and places of the city) alone by themselves, or in company with the townsmen."[104] They are also banned from spectating and from betting on "ball-play in the private yards and greens of the townsmen."[105] Disregard of the statute is a serious offence. Playing is still sanctioned within the grounds of Trinity College, Cambridge, in 1695: "undergraduates play football on a green to themselves, and the masters play bowls."[106]

In December 1666, Robert Duke of All Souls College, Oxford, is suspended from his degree for a year for playing football—"*lusus pilae*

---

99 Randolph, T., *The jealous lovers: A comedie presented to their gracious Majesties at Cambridge, by the students of Trinitie-Colledge*. s.n., Cambridge, 1632. p. 22.

100 Cressy, D., *The Death of a Vice-Chancellor at Cambridge*. In: Feingold, M., *History of Universities*. Oxford University Press, 2012. 26:2. p. 104.

101 Ibid, p. 104.

102 Clark, A. (ed.), *Life and Times of Anthony Wood, antiquary, of Oxford, 1632–1695, described by Himself*. 5 Vols. Horace Hart, Oxford, 1891. Vol. 4. p. 69.

103 Salter, H.E. (ed.), *Surveys and Tokens*. Clarendon Press, Oxford, 1923. p. 105.

104 Ward, G.R.M (trans.), *Oxford University Statutes. Vol. 1. Containing the Caroline Code or Laudian Statutes, Promulgated A.D. 1636*. William Pickering, London, 1845. p. 161. Ibid, p. 160.

105 Ibid, p. 160.

106 Early Modern Letters Online. http://emlo.bodleian.ox.ac.uk/profile/work/43c8220f-f76d-4b40-afb4-90450c78ae61?sort=date-a&rows=50&let_con=football&baseurl=/forms/advanced&start=2&type=advanced&numFound=3. Accessed 26 October 2024.

pedalis." Two of Exeter College and one of Queen's meet the same fate.[107] Eleven years later, Magdalene College, Cambridge, protests that "divers vitious and disorderly customes have by the petulancy and presumption of some looser schollers been introduced", leading to "manifest corruption and debauchery." It is unclear how sophomores selling cheese to freshers at inflated prices, leads to "ye manifest corruption and debauchery of youth." The need to rein in another wayward custom is clearer: "That no schollers give or receive at any time any treat or collation upon account of ye foot-ball play, on or about Michaelmas Day, further than Colledge beere or ale in ye open hall to quench their thirsts. And particularly, that ye most vile custome of drinking and spending money ... upon ye account of making or not making a speech at y^t^ foot-ball time, be utterly left off and extinguished."[108]

Oxford University's statutes of 1671 ban football within the precincts of the university or in the streets of Oxford, neither can students frequent plays, tumblers, wineshops, or inns.[109] The ban extends to "the absurd and arrogant custom of walking publicly in boots." Undergraduates caught smoking are birched if below eighteen, fined or imprisoned if above. The father of Oxford University's antiquarian Anthony Wood dies on 19 January 1643, the day Royalist hopes are raised by victory at the Battle of Braddock Down, in Cornwall. "A fat and corpulent man ... he was tall and bigge in his yonger days verie strong and active in manly sports and recreations, as football, wrestling, running, etc."[110] Football cannot be quashed at Oxford. As late as 1702, a Magdalen tutor submits a 5s bill to a student's parents for "footballs etc."[111] His parents' household accounts record another payment of 2s for footballs for home use, while his father, "Spent at Bowling Green for ye Season, 10/–."[112]

---

107 Clark, A. (ed.), *The Life and Times of Anthony Wood, Antiquary of Oxford, 1632–1695.* 5 Vols. Clarendon Press, Oxford, 1892. Vol. 2. p. 97.

108 *Fifth Report of the Royal Commission on Historical Manuscripts.* Eyre & Spottiswoode, London, 1876. Part 1. p. 483.

109 Murray, D., *Memories of the Old College of Glasgow.* Jackson, Wylie & Co., 1927. p. 480.

110 Clark, A. (ed.), *Life and Times of Anthony Wood, antiquary, of Oxford, 1632–1695, described by Himself.* 5 Vols. Horace Hart, Oxford, 1891. Vol. 1. p. 78.

111 Hart, A.T., *Country Counting House. The Story of Two Eighteenth-Century Clerical Account Books.* Phoenix House, 1962. p. 18.

112 Ibid, pp. 22, 108.

In 1672, a rallying cry appears in a book of speeches for boys: "We are hale-fellows well met, not onely at Foot-ball, but at every thing else."[113] The same year, the term "football match" appears for only the second time: "I don't mean that when the Nurses back is turned, they skip out of the cradle, and with a huge ashen plant run away to the next fair, Bull-bayting, or Football match; but they do not care for being in the dark."[114] The author, John Eachard, is born in Yoxford, Suffolk, dyed-in-the-wool camping country, and studies at Cambridge University.

~

By 1641, authorities in Kendal, Westmoreland, have their say: "whosoever do play football in the street and break any windows, shall forfeit … the sum of 12d. for every time every party, and 3s. 4d. for every window by the same broken, and to be committed till it be paid."[115] Records show that between 1655–57, constables in Manchester are ordered to arrest those playing "ffooteball … within the streets of the toune."[116] Town criers are employed in Worcester to "cry down" football in 1743 (and snowballs in 1772), and at Louth in 1745 and 1754.[117] There are higher powers. Placating a Mr Roope who is vexed at "the numerous meetings of people at football matches, etc." in Dartmouth, William Trumbull replies from Whitehall, rebuking those who "presumed to play football" rather than "celebrating devoutly the last fast day", and promising action.[118] The outcome is unknown. The game too. It takes place in Devonshire, suggesting hurling. Some love camping, but hate disappointment. In 1673, Matthew Stevenson writes an acerbic poem about a Kirby match that never was:[119,120]

> This morning when we came to see the Camp,
> Some had the Crotchets go,[121] & some the cramp.

---

113 R.S., *Ludus Ludi Literarii.* W.R., London, 1672. p. 73.

114 Eachard, J., *Dr Eachard's Works. Part 3. Mr. Hobbs's State of Nature Considered in a Dialogue Between Philautus and Timothy.* Nath. Brooke, London, 1672. p. 60.

115 Scott, D., *Bygone Cumberland and Westmorland.* William Andrews & Co., London, 1899. p. 199.

116 Malcolmson, R.W., *Popular Recreations in English Society 1700–1850.* Unpublished PhD thesis, University of Warwick, 1970. p. 244.

117 Ibid, p. 245.

118 Hardy, J. W. (ed.), *Calendar of state papers, Domestic series, of the reign of William III.* 6 Vols. Public Record Office, Great Britain, 1913. Vol. 2. pp. 258, 347.

119 Stevenson is buried in Norwich.

120 The Kirby he cites may be Kirby Cane, or Kirby Bedon, both in Norfolk.

121 Camping stick

Where are the pledges of this hot contest?
I doubt in earnest you were but in jest.
Ye talk of Crowns, to heighten your renowns,
And meet like Princes, that contend for Crowns …
…Foxes are best at burroughs, not at Goals.[122]

Suffolk-born Quaker William Bennit sheds no tears: "Instead of being truly humbled under the hand of God, and to mourn in sack-cloathe and Ashes", his fellow East Anglians are, "sporting themselves in Musick and Dancing, in ringing of Bells, Camping and Wrestling."[123] Similarly, in Rickling, north Essex, "the young men do bear the Bell away, From all the Towns about at Foot-ball play."[124] Around this time, the East Anglian legend of Tom Hickathrift makes its appearance. Born in the Isle of Ely, Cambridgeshire, by the age of ten Tom is "six feet high and three in thicknesse." Known for his prodigious strength, he throws the hammer three furlongs, and fights a giant who hangs his victims' heads on a tree. "Thine shall hang higher than any of them all," says the giant. "A turd in your teeth," returns Tom cleverly, before dispatching him. One day, Tom "saw a company at football, and dismounted to see them play for a wager; but he spoiled all their sport, for meeting the foot-ball, he gave it such a kick, that they never found it more; whereupon they began to quarrel with Tom, but some of them got little good by it; for he got a spar [pole] … with which he drove down all opposition before him."[125]

In 1690, a fictional match in Billericay, south Essex, is referred to in another lacklustre homage to Don Quixote. The strength of Sir Billy of Billerecay's father-in-law is touched on: "at a Match of Foot-ball, plaid betwixt that Village and the neighbouring Hamlet, by his alone Manhood and Prowess the Victory was clearly obtain'd of his side."[126] Sir Billy's squire is later advised to steer clear of swords: "Away you

122 Stevenson, M., *Upon a Camp should have been plaid, neer the black house by Kirby for a Crown a piece, and was not.* In: Stevenson, M., *Norfolk Drollery.* s.n., London, 1673. n.p.

123 Bennit, W., *A collection of certain epsitles & testimonies of divine consolation, experience and doctrine.* Andrew Sowle, London, 1685. p. 184.

124 Poor Robin. *Poor Robin's perambulation from Saffron-Walden to London.* T.E., London, 1678. p. 4.

125 Anon., *The History of Thomas Hickathrift.* s.n., London, n.d. p. 18–19.

126 Winstanley, W., *The Essex Champion, or, The famous history of Sir Billy of Billerecay and his squire Ricardo.* s.n., London, 1690. p. 3.

fool … spare your strength to throw a Cudgel at a Pare-Tree, or your Activity in being the best man at a match at Foot-Ball."[127] Doubtless the line between football and camping in Essex is blurred. A 1691 edition of regional dialect describes camp as "to play at Foot-ball … this word, for this exercise, extends over Essex as well as Norfolk and Suffolk."[128] A few pages on, "to kep a Ball is to catch it."[129]

For all the naysayers there is a new modernity, reflected in the papers of the 1690s: "A football being but a little more than half blown in a Valley will grow hard and turgid by such time as you come upon any high hill", demonstrates the inverse law between air pressure and altitude, and a burgeoning interest in science.[130] There are even agony aunts. An apprentice, writing "on behalf of a friend", has an offer of an advantageous marriage. Should he take it or tell her he cannot marry because he is an apprentice? "Fair & gently, Lad," she cautions, "marriage is no foot-ball play … not one marriage in five hundred made before twenty-five, or there abouts, proves happy."[131] A 1697 edition of *The Athenian Mercury* is devoted to a trivia quiz with answers beneath. "Why do we commonly fart in pissing?" asks one. Another: "What is the cause of the Generation of Monsters?" Answer: the feebleness of the feminine virtue, the vice of the womb, the wandering imagination of the woman at the time of conception, and the conjunction of animals of diverse species.[132] Not all progress, then.

Working class football makes the press in 1697, when "Felmongers"[133] win a wager against "the Carr-men"[134] in a two-hour match on "Welford Common", in Berkshire.[135] A pioneering agreement is made. If any player breaks an arm or a leg, "the rest of them should allow him 12d. *per* Week, 'till he was well again." A Carr-man breaks his leg. In 1698, when bakers beat fellmongers on Walworth Common (an early cricket ground

127 Ibid, p. 39.

128 Ray, J., *A Collection of Local Words not Generally Used.* Christopher Wilkinson, London, 1691. Preface, n.p.

129 Ibid, p. 40.

130 *The Athenian Mercury.* 30 May 1693. p. 1.9

131 *The Athenian Mercury.* 19 November 1695. p. 2.

132 *The Athenian Mercury.* 21 May 1697. p. 1.

133 Dealers in hides.

134 Drivers of horse-drawn vehicles.

135 *The Protestant Mercury, Occurrences Foreign and Domestick.* 26 May 1697. p. 2

in Surrey), it ends in a fight, and a baker breaks his leg, "which will badly endanger his life."[136] Directly below, is an advert for the English State Lottery. While this version has been running for four years, the first lottery is in 1567, with a jackpot of £5,000.[137] By the end of the 1700s, a friendly society in Norfolk decides there will be no weekly allowance for those who are infirm through "debauchery, intercourse with lewd women, venereal taint, drunkenness, fighting, wrestling, or football-playing."[138]

On 22 August 1690, James Ogilvie, 1st Earl of Seafield, invites his cousin to play "long *gauff*", a cross-country version of golf. It provides a fascinating glimpse into a rarely reported variation. The game is to play out on the sea braes [hills], near Boyne Castle in Banffshire: "lett me know this night wher I shall waitt on you with a second, or if yee would doe me the honor to come this lenth, because the links ar better." Ogilvie lays a bait to lure him: "we shall see ife ye cannot make better use of a club in this country then ye did at Eden [St Andrews]. This is not that I doubt but ye made good use of your short putting club there.'[139] A 'second' is probably a caddy, a recent development first heard of in 1681/82, when a man collects balls for the future James II.[140] Perhaps caddies, as seconds, have been around much longer; the advantage of an underling foraging for balls must have been evident centuries before.

In 1691, the Gilmours of Craigmillar Castle, near Edinburgh, pay their son's school expenses, including for "a football at fastern's even" (Shrove Tuesday).[141] The same year, Sir John Foulis of Edinburgh buys his son "y[e] football", two weeks before Shrove Tuesday. At other times, he buys his children golf clubs, drums, trumpets, and "chirping birds." Perhaps he bought the golf clubs from Andrew Forrester, an Edinburgh bowyer, who either made or sold balls and clubs. In 1684, Forrester

136 *The Protestant Mercury*. 29 April 1698. p. 2.

137 One thousand three hundred horses, or four thousand three hundred cows.

138 Ruggles, T., *The History of the Poor: Their Rights, Duties and the Laws Respecting Them*. s.n., London, 1797. p. 297.

139 Grant, J.G., *Seafield Correspondence from 1685 to 1708*. The University Press, Edinburgh, 1912. pp. 64–65.

140 *Chambers's Edinburgh Journal*. 22 June 1839.

141 Aucoin, T., *When the Pancake Bell Rings*. Unpublished PhD thesis, University of Bristol, 2019. p. 87.

accuses his apprentice of stealing "twelve dozen of clubs" from him, a round figure the judge does not believe. [142] The following year in Luss, on the banks of Loch Lomond, Sir John Colquhoun "went in [a] coach to a shop, and bought golf-balls."[143] In 1705, Foulis takes his children to see the thirty-year-old elephant in Edinburgh.[144] He treats her to bread and ale. Having traipsed across Europe from show to show, she dies in Dundee the following year.

Death is ever-jealous. Eighteen-year-old Christopher Bundish dies in Suffolk, in 1692, "by falling on a hard causeway while playing football."[145] Sabbath football tragedies are an act of God, not Death: "How many had had their Legs broken; nay, have sunk irrevocably through Ice, in playing at Foot-ball on the *Sacred day*."[146] No one is immune from an infected fracture. In 1702, King William breaks his collarbone when his horse stumbles on a molehill. He dies within the month. He is succeeded by his sister-in-law, Anne. A nursery rhyme does the rounds:

> Queen Anne, Queen Anne, you sit in the sun,
> As fair as a lily, as white as a wand.
> I send you three letters, and pray read one,
> You must read one, if you can't read all,
> So pray, Miss or Master, throw up the ball.[147]

In 1699, a fictional Dutchman and Englishman are comparing notes. "None but the Great Britannia can boast," boasts the Englishman, "their Natives after twelve Hours hard Work, will go in the Evening to Foot-ball, Stool-ball, Cricket, Prison-Base, Wrestling, Cudgel-playing, or

142 *Andrew Forrester against Merstoun and Ker…* Hein Online. https://heinonline.org/HOL/Page?collection=stair&handle=hein.stair/dcsestd0011&id=877&men_tab=srchresults. Accessed 24 February 2024.

143 Laird of Luss against Carden. Hein Online. https://heinonline.org/HOL/Page?collection=stair&handle=hein.stair/dcsestd0004&id=714&men_tab=srchresults. Accessed 24 February 224.

144 Hallen, A.W.C. (ed.), *The Account Book of John Foulis of Ravelston, 1671–1707.* Scottish History Society, 1894. pp. 132, xii, 407. The book provides an intimate portrait of the Foulis household, and of the times.

145 *Report on Manuscripts in Various Collections.* 7 Vols. His Majesty's Stationery Office, London, 1901–1914. Vols. 3–4. p. 311.

146 Anon., *The citizen's companion: or, The trades-man's mirrour.* J.C., London, 1673. p. 87.

147 Halliwell, J.O. (ed.), *The Nursery Rhymes of England.* Frederick Warne and Co., 1886. p. 161.

some such vehement Exercise for their Recreations."[148,149] Riddle me this. Where there is nothing there is something, and where there is something there is nothing. Answer: a football. In 1697, Thomas Brown publishes the satirical verse, *A Prophecy Found in a Football in Spittle Fields by a Weaver.*[150] Football fails to merit a second mention. The decade before, Huguenot weavers, fleeing Louis XIV's dragonnades, settle in Norwich, Cambridge, and Spitalfields. Does *soule* tag along, a sizeable number are from Normandy?[151] Has football gripped Spitalfields before they arrive? Do the Huguenots take up camping in East Anglia? Riddles. Riddles. Brown's final couplet has bite: "Then England, I tell thee, thou art cursedly shamed, 'Tis too late to repent—sin on and be damned." A satirical turn of the century periodical delivers predictions for the following year: "Quoits, Cricket, Nine-Pins, and Trap-Ball, will be very much in Fashion, and more Trades-men will be seen Playing in the Fields than working in their Shops … a Fricasie of *Frogs*, and a *Dandalion* Sallad will be *A-la-mode of Spittle Fields* where the *Hugonots* … feed themselves."[152]

Egregious football play continues to make the news. In 1660, the windows of All Hallows Church in York are "much broken" by servants "playing and strikeing at the football."[153] That year, football, dog tossing, and cock throwing are banned in Bristol. The response is cat tossing and geese throwing.[154] Around 1641, Thomas Wilson becomes minister of Maidstone, and cleans up the town: "before his coming … I have seen Morrice dancing, Cudgel playing, Stool-ball, Crickets, and many other sports openly and publickly on the Lords Day."[155] He has a magic touch.

148 Puckle, J., *England's Way to Wealth and Honour: In a Dialogue between an English-man and a Dutch-man*. Sam Crouch, London, 1699. p. 25.

149 The quote is appropriated from: Chamberlayne, E., *Angliæ Notitia or the Present State of England.* T. Hodgkin, London, 1694. p. 53.

150 Cameron, W.J. (ed.)., *Poems on Affairs of State.* 30 Vols. Yale University press, New Haven, 1971. Vol. 5. pp. 485–487.

151 Kershen, A.J., *Strangers, Aliens and Asians*. Routledge, Abingdon, Oxon, 2011. p. 35.

152 Ward, E., *The Second Volume of the Writings of the Author of the London-Spy.* J. How, London, 1703. p. 324.

153 Griffiths, P., *Youth and Authority: Formative Experiences in England 1560–1640.* Oxford University Press, 1996. p. 139.

154 Ibid, p. 147.

155 Swinnock, G., *The Life and Death of Mr. Tho. Wilson, Minister of Maidstone, In the County of Kent, M.A.* s.n., s.l., 1672. p. 40.

Play resumes the year he dies. That February, Maidstone authorities rail against the many Shrove Tuesday inconveniences caused by those gathered in a "rude and unlawful manner in the streetes and other open places … commonly playeinge at football and cudgells, tossinge of dogs … and throwing of libettes at cocks … in a cruel unchristianlike manner."[156] In 1653, several Maidstone men stand before the quarter sessions for "unlawfully playing at and exercising an unlawful, forbidden game called football." The constables are fined for not taking them into custody.[157] Three years later, a Maidstone apothecary "wilfully and in a violent and boisterous manner … did kick up and down … the High Street … a certain ball of leather, commonly called a football unto the great annoyance and incumbrance … of the good people of the Commonwealth."[158] Times change. Two hundred years later, the local paper reports on a 0-0 ninety-minute football match between Maidstone Grammar Football Club and other pupils from the school.[159]

Thomas Sharrock is released from Lancaster prison in 1679, having been jailed for an assault on Thomas Grantham at football.[160,161] Twenty years later, six constables are in trouble for failing to stop Sabbath football in the Forest of Pendle, in Lancashire. The county sessions report the match as a "notorious riot of above four hundred persons."[162] Fines for street play are common—in 1685, three boys in Manningtree, north Essex, enter the Sessions Roll for playing "at foote ball in the common street", resulting in "breaking the glass and greatly disturbing the inhabitants"[163]—but it is Sabbath football that returns a steady revenue, generally 3s 4d for the poor of the parish, three hours in the stocks if you

156 Griffiths, P., *Youth and Authority: Formative Experiences in England 1560–1640*. Oxford University Press, 1996. p. 147.

157 Russell, J.M., *The History of Maidstone*. William S. Vivish, Maidstone, 1881. p. 281.

158 Parry, L.A., *Some Famous Medical Trials*. BeardBooks, Washington, 2000. p. 225.

159 *South-Eastern Gazette*. 13 December 1859. p. 4.

160 *Release of Thomas Sharrock, imprisoned for assault on Thomas Grantham, lawyer's clerk, at football*. The National Archive: https://discovery.nationalarchives.gov.uk/details/r/20956ee7–3f69–4fe7–8879–2b51353c148d. Accessed 10 September 2023.

161 MacKenzie, R.D., *Kilbarchan: a Parish History*. Alexander Gardner, Paisley, Scotland, 1902. p. 98.

162 Snape, M.F., *The Church of England in Industrialising Society*. The Boydell Press, Woodbridge, 2003. p. 31.

163 *Essex Archives Online*. https://www.essexarchivesonline.co.uk/result_details.aspx?ThisRecordsOffSet=1&id=291184. Accessed 25 October 2023.

cannot pay.[164] In 1683, two yeomen, a husbandman, and a labourer are fined 3s 4d each for the poor of the parish in Sale, Cheshire.[165] It is easy to sympathise. That year, Mayday falls on a Sunday. Of greater note, in Richmond, Yorkshire, in 1668, five from Thorp and five from Whorlton-in Cleveland are charged with "playing football on the Lord's Day in the time of divine service."[166] It is the first recorded *five-a-side* football game in history. The same court charges nine yeomen of Burtersett with the same offence two years later.[167] While Sabbath football is one trespass that is unlikely to change, another trespass is likely to change everything. Across the Channel, "the Court of France amuse themselves with Balls and other Diversions, without having any regard to the misery which reigns everywhere else throughout the whole kingdom."[168]

164 Two days' work for a skilled tradesman.

165 Keble, J., *An assistance to justices of the peace, for the easier performance of their duty*. Rawlins, W. et al., London, 1683. pp. 254–255.

166 Marples, M., *A History of Football*. Secker and Warburg, London, 1954. p. 79.

167 Ibid, p. 79.

168 *Dublin Intelligence*. 3 February 1711. p. 1.

CHAPTER TWELVE
1700–1799 I

An enlightened century dawns. The Industrial Revolution changes England more radically than any other period in history. It is the start of a modern, technology-driven society and the end of the agrarian economy that began five thousand years before. The first decade holds clues. The inventor of cast steel is born, Twinings tea shop and Fortnum and Mason open in London, Benjamin Franklin is born, and the Acts of Union create Great Britain. Football is entering the legal world. In a Scottish court case, in 1709, examples to prove sanity are offered, "besides those common ones of going to kirk [church] and market, such as playing at the foot-ball, going in a boat to shoot marrots [seabirds]."[1]

Football also gets an exotic twist. Foreign translation dictionaries are booming. Football in French is *le balon*, in Portuguese *péla de vénto*, in Spanish *bála de viento*, and in Italian *un pallone*. To play at football in Italy is *giuocare al pallone* and to kick a football in Holland *een voetbal voortschoppen*. A Carnival *calcio* match in Livorno is described in 1702. Two sides try "getting the Goal of each other. The Goal is mark'd out by a Rope stretch'd out round about the Ring, and the Sport is very interesting to the Spectators."[2] Early days, though; Latin dictionaries remain common. Football is *pila pedalis*, a great football *pila pedanica*, to kick a football *pilam pedalem*, and to play at football *pila pedali cetare*.

Football similes thrive. John Dryden translates Chaucer's *The Knight's Tale* in 1700. "He rolleth under foot as dooth a bal" becomes, "One rolls along, a Foot-ball to his Foes; one with a broken Truncheon deals his Blows."[3] In 1702, a play about Sir John Falstaff has a rising habitual: "About two years ago, I got to bed to a Cheesemonger's Wife, and if I was not canted out of bed by her, and kicked like a Football for downright

---

1 *Hamiltons against Pringles*. Hein Online. https://heinonline.org/HOL/Page?collection=stair&handle=hein.stair/sditctses0004&id=775&men_tab=srchresults. Accessed 24 February 2024.

2 De Bruyn, C., *A Voyage to the Levant*. s.n., London, 1702. p. 11.

3 Dryden, J., *Palamon and Arcite*. In: *Fables ancient and modern translated into verse*. 4 Vols. s.n., London, 1700. Vol. 3. p. 71.

frigidity, may I be beaten."[4] In 1704, religion is "made the Foot-ball of Princes to be kick'd about the World as it suits their occasions",[5] while an inquiry into "Naval Miscarriages" three years later reports: "sometimes the Allies have the Advantage of one another by having a sudden Run, as happens in a Game at Football."[6] Ships may do otherwise. In 1718, Sir James Jefferyes makes land at The Hague, "having been 4 days and 3 nights tossed like a football."[7] Some similes are grandiose: "I'l mount the sky, And kick the G—ds like Foot-balls as I fly."[8] *The Tatler* lashes the conceit, comparing the creation of the solar system with a "Game at Football" between the "Inferior Deities". Seven globes are kicked "with a vast Violence … and wander'd in a straight Line, through the infinite spaces", until each is caught by a deity.[9] In 1769, Tobias Smollett satirises English politics in *Adventures of an Atom* published anonymously on April Fool's Day: "He not only kicked, but also cuffed the whole council of twenty-eight, and played at foot-ball with his imperial tiara."[10]

The philanthropist minister Thomas Gouge advises against "sports such as give danger to men, as of old was fighting with beasts, and now Matches at Football, fighting at Cudgels."[11,12] The Church is likely to take a dim view of two *Poor Robin* almanacs. The first, for May 1707, reads:

> The Country Lasses at Pastime make,
> With Stool-ball and at Barley-break;
> And young Men they pass time away,
> At Wrestling and at Foot-ball play."[13]

---

4 Dennis, J., *The Comical Gallant: Or the Amours of Sir John Falstaffe*. A. Baldwin, London, 1702. p. 42.

5 *Review of the Affairs of France*. 29 July 1704. p. 182.

6 *An Inquiry Into the Causes of our Naval Miscarriages*. s.n., London, 1707. p. 30.

7 *Folio 12: Jefferyes to [-]. Acquaint Lord Stanhope of arrival here, having been 4 days...* The National Archives: https://discovery.nationalarchives.gov.uk/details/r/C6720328. Accessed 19 November 2023.

8 Marples, M., *A History of Football*. Secker and Warburg, London, 1954. p. 91.

9 *The Tatler*. 16–19 July 1709. p. 1.

10 Smollett, T., *The Miscellaneous Works of Tobias Smollett, M.D.* 6 Vols. s.n., Edinburgh, 1817. Vol. 4. p. 449.

11 Gouge, T., *The works of the later Reverend and pious Mr. Tho. Gouge*. Tho. Bradyll, London, 1706. p. 222.

12 Gouge's antipathy to football may have grown from exposure to the game: he schooled at Eton, matriculated from Cambridge, was curate at Teddington, and rector at Coulsden. Kingston upon Thames, the site of Shrovetide games since at least the 1790s, lies ten miles from Coulsden, and three from Teddington, which held its own Shrovetide game by the 1840s.

13 Winstanley, W., *Poor Robin, 1707. An Almanack of the Old and New Fashion*. W. Bowyer, London, 1707. n.p.

A little more clerical angst for May 1709:

> Here men at foot-ball they do fall,
> There boys at cat and trap-ball.
> Whilst Tom and Doll aside are slank,
> Tumbling and kissing on a bank.[14]

Matthew Prior is no better:

> While Betty dances on the green;
> And Susan is at stool-ball seen;
> While John for nine-pins does declare;
> And Roger loves to pitch the bar.[15]

Prior returns to his alma mater, Westminster School, in 1695. His friend delivers a poem written by Prior, echoing his years there: "Our candles and the clothes ourselves we bought, Our tops neglected and our balls forgot."[16] In 1709, clergyman Henry Sacheverell is invited to deliver the annual sermon at St Paul's Cathedral, in remembrance of the failed Gunpowder Plot. Far from the expected homily, Sacheverell serves up an incendiary oration, declaiming the government for trying "to overbear and silence our church … in order to break in upon the prerogative of the Crown."[17] The ruling Whigs are incensed. He has said unsaid truths, broken the rules of rule-breaking. Three decades earlier, Matthew Hale wrote: "Or, when I have seen a Match at Foot-ball, one while getting the Ball, and then another kicking up his heels and getting it from him, and then another doing the like by him. These give me a Resemblance of the World, wherein though … there are certain Rules put to the Game, yet they are not always kept; and when they are, yet it is not without a mixture of irremediable Deceit and Violence."[18]

---

14 Winstanley, W., *Poor Robin, 1709. An Almanack of the Old and New Fashion*. W. Bowyer, London, 1709. n.p.

15 Mitford, J., *Alma: or, the Progress of the Mind*. In: *The Poetical Works of Matthew Prior*. 2 Vols. William Pickering, London, 1835. Vol. 2. p. 39.

16 Ibid, p. 206.

17 Kester, R.A., *The Sacheverell Affair: its causes and implications*. Unpublished Honours thesis, University of Richmond, Virginia, 1972. p. 7.

18 Hale, M., *Contemplations Moral and Divine*. s.n., London, 1699. p. 412.

When the sermon is disseminated in a pamphlet, the government acts. Sacheverell is impeached by the House of Commons for authoring "seditious libel".[19] A show trial takes place in Westminster Hall, renovated for the occasion by Christopher Wren. Pilloried from every angle, a supporter comforts Sacheverell: "But *England* must always have a *National Football*; and YOU, at present, are That: And since I have call'd you so, I desire you wou'd not forget, That *Footballs* are chiefly follow'd by Porters, Carmen, and *the very Outcasts of the People*."[20] Sacheverell's trial is seen as an attack on both the Church and on freedom of speech. He becomes a *cause célèbre*, attracting a groundswell of support. On the day of the trial, a mob gathers, who "expressed themselves with the utmost fury."[21] They later riot. The snookered government do what is politically expedient—find him guilty, ban him from preaching for three years, and let him continue his clerical duties. An eye-witness account gives some idea of Sacheverell's feverish speech. The Rev William Bisset is sat opposite him during the sermon: "I was surpriz'd at the Fiery Red that overspread his Face …and the gogling Wildness of his Eyes … he was … transported with a Hellish Fury."[22] Bissett has his own take on football. He will play, "if they'll kick fair, and not basely come behind to trip up my heels."[23]

Henry Hingeston's idea of lusts of the flesh includes heretics, comedies, witchcraft, fornication, murder, dancing, and football-playing.[24] Dancing, football, and other pastimes are "the Devil's Engines, to trappan the Souls of Mortals to their final Destruction."[25] Hingeston homes in on an upcoming football match between Kings-Bridge in Devon, and Dadbrook in Cornwall.[26] "It frequently occasions unnecessary Drinking, and often … Drunkenness … and with great Inhumanity … Broaken Bones, or what not!" His hyperbole snowballs across eleven pages. Football becomes "Vice, Immorality and Profaneness", and players,

---

19 Ibid, p. 10.

20 Inferior Clergyman. *A letter to the Reverend Dr. Sacheverel*. s.n., London, 1711. p. 14.

21 Ibid, p. 13.

22 Bisset, W., *The Modern Fanatick*. 3 Vols. A. Baldwin, London, 1710. Vol. 1. pp. 1–2.

23 Ibid, Vol. 2. p. 81.

24 Hingeston, H., *Mahir Godel*. Sam Farley, Exeter, 1703. p. 57.

25 Ibid, p. 81.

26 Ibid, pp. 33–43.

"Soul-wounded Persons, wallowing in their Blood, or standing on the Brink of the Unsearchable Gulf of Bottomless Perdition."

In 1717, *An Appendix to the Modern Justice* declares that injuring another player at football, backsword, or cudgelling is not a criminal act, "by Reason it is done by consent."[27]

That year, another interminably titled book rails against multiple pastimes; rightly, bear-gardens and cockfights, but masquerades, operas, merry-makings, raree-shows,[28] posture-makers[29] … Rope-dancing,[30] Foot-ball, Wrestling, and Puppet-shows?[31] Of the last four, he believes, "broken Shins, broken Heads, Contusions, Dislocations, unmannerly Grinning, Hoarseness, and offensive Vociferations are the only immediate Effect of these Pastimes." In 1701, a wistful minister theologises, "Where did the Christians in the Apostles Days make and use Matches at Foot-ball, and Wrestling, and appoint Horse-Races, and Hunting for pleasure, and so glory in their own Strength, and abuse the Creatures."[32] As late as 1717, a bill is motioned to prevent "throwing at Cocks and kicking Foot-balls within the Cities of London and Westminster."[33]

Wrestling is among the oldest, if not *the* oldest competitive physical activity in the world.[34] The fifteen-thousand-year-old cave paintings in Lascaux, France, are believed to include depictions of wrestlers. The same four-thousand-year-old tomb that contains the earliest depictions of ball games in the world—the tomb of Baqet III, in the cemetery of Beni Hasan in Egypt—has a wonderful variety of wrestling scenes.[35]

---

27 Jacob, G., *An Appendix to the Modern Justice*. Eliz. Nutt, and R. Gosling, London, 1718. p. 21.

28 Peep shows depicting architectural wonders and landscapes.

29 Posture-makers were in demand in the eighteenth century. Good posture was believed to improve the chances of marriage for both sexes, not least in public displays of dancing. Deportment could be taught, but there was a host of devices to correct bad posture, including tight waistbands, trusses, and "Elastic Breeches Straps" (which could "keep the largest rupture up"). Prophylactic measures for children included leg irons, steel rods strapped to the back, and steel collars to create "a swanlike neck".

30 Rope-dancing was a highly-skilled feat. Performances included dancing round, and vaulting over, ropes; somersaults; tightrope walking; and ziplining from tall buildings with live fireworks attached to the performer's body.

31 Reynell, C., *The danger of masquerades and raree-shows*. W. Boreham, London, 1718. p. 15.

32 Fox, G., *Gospel-Truth demonstrated, in a collection of doctrinal books*. T. Sowle, London, 1706. p. 270.

33 *Stamford Mercury*. 11 April 1717. p. 8.

34 Krist, S., *Wrestling Magic: National Wrestling in Buryatia, Mongolia and Tuva in the Past and Today*. The International Journal of the History of Sport, 2014, 31:4, p. 425.

35 Gardner, E.N, *Athletics of the Ancient World*. Clarendon Press, Oxford, 1930. pp. 6–7.

One wall alone has two hundred and twenty wrestling groups; every conceivable grip and throw is shown. The provenance of Cornish wrestling is unknown, but its origins are likely to be Celtic; Bretons have an equivalent form, *Gouren*.[36] Nottinghamshire-born lawyer Sir Thomas Parkyns publishes a book on Cornish wrestling, in 1727. The title, *The Inn-Play: or Cornish-Hugg Wrestler*, reflects his education at Gray's Inn, Holborn, where he employed a wrestling master.[37] Parkyns advises loose linen drawers, "narrow heel'd Shoes, of a midling height", and a shirt unbuttoned at the neck. His techniques include the Flying Horse, the Back Clamp, the Pinnion, the Gripes, and the Buttock.

Cornish hurling survives into the eighteenth century, as dangerous as ever. In 1714, a collection of satirists, including Pope and Swift, establish the Scriblerus Club. Their first collaboration includes the lines: "It was about this time, he heard to his exceeding content, that the *Harpastus* of the Ancients was yet in use in *Cornwall,* and known there by the name of *Hurling.* He was sensible the common *Foot-ball* was a very imperfect imitation of that exercise; and thought it necessary to send Martin into the West, to be initiated in that truly ancient and manly part of the *Gymnasticks.* The poor boy was so unfortunate as to return with a broken leg."[38] William Borlase describes hurling in 1758. The ball is "a round piece of timber (about three inches diameter) covered with plated silver, sometimes gilt. It has usually a motto in the Cornish tongue alluding to the pastime, as *Guare wheag, yw guare teag*, that is, fair play is good play … this exercise requires force and nimbleness of hand, a quick eye, swiftness of foot, skill in wrestling … address to deceive and evade the enemy, and judgement to deliver the ball into proper hands."[39]

International conflicts dominate the papers, but for most folk the ugly scar of the Civil War remains fresh and ragged. Many who lived through it are still alive. *The Observator* interviews "Countryman" on the establishment of local militias. When his response is in the negative, they suggest he is a coward. Countryman is anything but: "I can venture

36 Jaouen, G., *Transforming Cornish and Devon Wrestling (Britain) and Gouren (Brittany–France) Through Sportification.* The International Journal of the History of Sport, 2014, 31:4, p. 474.

37 Parkyns, T., *The Inn-Play: or Cornish-Hugg Wrestler.* William Ayscouh, Nottingham, 1713.

38 Pope, A., *Memoirs of the Extraordinary Life, Works, and Discoveries of Martin Scriblerus.* George Faulkner, Dublin, 1741. p. 38.

39 Borlase, W., *The Natural History of Cornwall.* W. Jackson, Oxford, 1758. p. 300.

a broken pate at cudgels, or a broken shin at football, but this fighting with Swords & Guns is the Devil; and the Devil may take him that invented it."[40] A contemporary ditty echoes his sentiments:

> To the wars I must alass, though I do not like the Game,
> For I hold him to be an Ass, That will loose his life for Fame …
> Ise would fight with the best of our Parish, And play at Whisters with Mary,
> Cou'd thump the football, yerk the Morrie, And box at Fistycuffs with any,
> But these Guns.[41,42]

A poem entitled *Foot-ball*, published in 1735, uses a winter game as a metaphor for life's mixed fortunes. It is a valuable depiction of a predominantly or exclusively kicking game:

> It's then the swains defy their fellow swains,
> To sport at football on the ample plains…
> The nimble foot-ball scours the fields of air,
> They kick, they push, and pushing loudly cry,
> And their hoarse shouting rends the vaulted sky;
> And now a low and now aloft she's seen,
> Borne up by turns as fortune shifts the scene;
> Thus mounted up she challenges the wind,
> And leaves the Scythian arrow far behind…
> Just so the well-cas'd foot-ball upwards tends,
> Then on a sudden to the ground descends;
> That long the doubtful combat they maintain,
> Till one prevails, for only one can reign.
> The victory got, they all retire,
> Secure from cold, and croud the chearful fire…
> So the swift foot-ball, with a whizzing sound,
> Now mounts in air, now rolls along the ground;

40 *The Observator.* 27–30 December 1704. p. 3.

41 Whist and morris dancing.

42 D'Urfey, T., *Wit & Mirth: Or Pills to Purge Melancholy.* 6 Vols. William Pearson, London, 1707. Vol. 3. pp. 222–223.

Thro' many changes variously she tends,
Till what was nothing in a nothing ends.[43]

Though the short-lived *Tatler* states that, "The Whim of the Football went off upon the breaking of the frost, when that violent exercise naturally ceases", football can adapt to any season.[44] A writer to *Tatler*'s successor, *The Spectator*, watches a game at an August "Country *Wake* which you know is the *Eve-Feast of the Dedication of our Churches*." A player, "Tom Short", plays so well "that most People seemed to agree *it was impossible he should remain a Batchelour till the next Wake*", an indication of the cachet associated with footballing prowess. The writer is soon diverted by the comical sight of a girl "grimacing, writhing, and distorting her body", as her short boyfriend wrestles a "huge, brawny fellow", who rattles him mercilessly. A ring of wrestlers look on, all hoping to win the beaver hat prize. The squire knows it's thirsty work and throws in a hogshead of ale to share. Across the green, cudgel players break "one another's Heads in order to make some impression on their Mistresses Hearts."[45]

According to one writer, injuries are also to be expected in other violent exercises, "tennis, foot-ball playing, leaping, vaulting, running of races"; all foreshorten life as assuredly as the "bewitching herb" tobacco, with which the rich "fill their Brains as full of Soot as the Funnel of a Chimney."[46] George Cheyne disagrees. He advises daily tennis or football to strengthen weak "Arms or Hams."[47] Those with rheumatism should play billiards, tennis, or cricket, while walking is good for the gouty, and ringing bells or working at a pump good exercise for those with "weak Backs or Breasts." Violent exercise? Tennis shrugs her shoulders. That is what comes of toadying to nobility, you are in fashion one century and out the next. Good luck to football. Was it an unconscious bargain? Her cousin chose the impoverished masses, she the mighty few. They are both restless, driven. The seventeenth century was a whirligig of fun but exhausting, even for her. She will sit this one out. It is time to take up

43 Anon., *London Magazine, or, Gentleman's Monthly Intelligencer*. 1735. Vol. 4. p. 151.

44 *Tatler*. 10–13 March 1711. p. 1.

45 *Spectator*. 4 September 1711. p. 1.

46 J.C., *Sin Punished and Vertue Rewarded*. Robert Gifford, London, 1713. p. 13.

47 Cheyne, G., *An Essay of Health and Long Life*. s.n., London, 1724. p. 98.

the offer *jeu de paume* and *soule* extended to her. Luxuriate beneath *le soleil*, concoct unhurriedly. Do they really believe the last century was her apogee? *En plein air* will inspire her.

"Like to a Foot-ball in a Frosty morn."[48] Football *is* the winter game. A sign of cold weather is "when men of the fourscore run at the football."[49] Large numbers, then. Tolerated too: "In winter, youths may as lawfully play football as sit before the fire telling stories."[50] And when the frost comes in 1711, a "crafty glazier" buys a football to entice youths into the streets, who in their fervour break windows, lanterns, "and all the brittle vitreous ware."[51] Two years earlier, a tongue-in-cheek notice in the *Female Tatler* reads: "This is to give notice to all idle 'Prentices, Carmen, and able bodied Footmen, that for the Encouragement of Trade, the Company of Glaziers, during the Season will cause to be distributed every Monday Morning, six dozen of Foot-balls Gratis. Enquire of the Beadle of the said Company."[52] The glaziers are at it again in 1716. John Gay, author of The Beggar's Opera describes football in the capital:

> Here oft' my Course I bend, when lo! from far,
> I spy the Furies of the Foot-ball War:
> The 'Prentice quits his Shop, to join the Crew,
> Encreasing Crouds the flying Game pursue.
> Thus, as you roll the Ball o'er snowy Ground,
> The gath'ring Globe augments with evry Round.
> But whither shall I run? the Throng draws nigh,
> The Ball now Skims the Street, now soars on high.
> The dext'rous Glazier strong returns the bound,
> And jingling sashes on the Pent-house sound.[53]

---

48 Anon., *The Soldiers Resolution*. In: *Westminster-drollery*. s.n., London, 1671. p. 58.

49 Winstanley, W., *Poor Robin, 1706. An Almanack of the Old & New Fashion*. W. Bowyer, London, 1706. p. 45.

50 Hickeringill, E., *Miscellaneous Tracts, Essays, Satyrs, & in Prose and Verse*. Sam. Brisoce, and Benj. Bragge, London, 1707. p. 281.

51 Cooper, A.A., *Characteristicks of Men, Manners, Opinions, Times*. John Darby, London, 1711. p. 15.

52 *The Female Tatler*. 28 November 1709. p. 2.

53 Williams, W.H. (ed.), *Trivia, or The Art of Walking the Streets of London*. Daniel O'Connor, London, 1922. p. 67.

An anthology of poems containing the verse, includes *On a Fart.* It opens:

> I Sing the praises of a Fart,
> That I may doo't by terms of Art,
> I will invoke no deitie,
> But butter'd Pease and Furmetie.[54,55]

Midway through the author writes, "The thunder that does roar so loud, Is but the Farting of a Cloud", and ends with, "What I have said take in good part, If not, I do not care a Fart." It is the age of satire. In 1703, the *London Spy* hurls a fictitious letter from a woman to the man whose "Extasies of Joy, with a Pox to 'em … have struck up such an unextinguishable Fire in my most Pleasureable Appartment, that I fear its past the Power of … the Pick-a-dilly Engineer to stop the flames from Consuming the whole miserable tenement." She pauses. Time to ditch nuance: "So Wishing you may Dye in a Ditch, and Rot like a Dead Horse, that the Boys may make Cat-sticks of your Leg-Bones, and Raisers of your Ribs, to Play at Trap-Ball with in the Bartholomew Holy days. I remain a Miserable Wretch, and your Bitter Enemy until Death."[56] *London Spy* has surplus bile for "Insatiate Lady-mongers … That Libidinous Coxcomb of a Creature … is every Woman's Humble Servant till he becomes her Master … he is blown up with Compliments, as a Foot-Ball is with Wind, and … like the Leathern Bauble, he deserves soundly to be Kick'd."[57]

~

Succession is fickle. Queen Anne's first cousin once removed is heiress presumptive to the British throne. But when she dies two months before Anne, it is her German-born son George who is crowned. Anne's closest relative, her half-brother James, does not get a look-in. There will be no more Catholic monarchs. When George I's reign begins in August 1714, executions are as public and gruesome as ever, and death is ever present. There is *some* good news. Compared with the previous

54 A fourteenth century recipe of wheat boiled in seasoned milk.

55 A Person of Quality., *Westminster-drollery.* s.n., London, 1671. pp. 127–128.

56 Ward, E., *The Second Volume of the Writings of the Author of the London-Spy.* J. How, London, 1703. p. 65.

57 Ward, E., *The London Terræfilius.* s.n., London, 1707. No. 1. pp. 26–27.

half century you can expect to live another two years. To forty-three. If childhood deaths are excluded, it soars to fifty-five. Nothing quite puts a spring in your step as knowing a ninety-year-old or reading of a centenarian. People experience vicarious horror and spirited relief at another's death. They died. I live. It is a century of silent calculations and deals with God.

No surprise newspapers report deaths and life-threatening injuries with brio. On Christmas Day 1719, Samuel Jones breaks his leg when an "abundance of apprentices" play football in St Giles, London.[58] The Boxing Day edition lists the "casualties" of the previous week: drowned eighty-two, executed sixteen, murdered six, self-murdered twenty-six, found dead twenty-nine, fell twenty-three, other accidents forty-four.[59] The same week, a thief steals shoes from Widow Randal's shop; a pair are caught with two brass cannons and five hundred pounds of lead; a man is robbed of 10 gns by footpads (highwaymen on foot) "and used very barbarously";[60] a near-blind woman is killed by a hay cart in Half-Moon Alley; and "a woman that kept the King's Arms Tavern in Drury-Lane … commonly known by the Name of Moll Jolly, was whip't from St Giles's Pound to the New Church in the Strand, for keeping a Bawdy house." Another item reports that, "The Match between the Running Footmen of the Duke of Shandois and the Earl of Essex is deferr'd till New Year's-Day. 'Tis said the Betts amount to above 1500l. [pounds] on each side."[61,62] The *Stamford Mercury* sheds light: "a foot-race" between a footman and a servant from St Giles's Pound to St Albans and back again; forty miles as the crow flies, for a purse of 100 gns.[63] Two years later, two Oxford blacksmiths race naked from Wadham College to New Parks on a wager.[64] Odder still, on 21 July 1715, Oxford antiquarian Thomas Hearne records: "Last Night between 7 and 8 Clock a Fellow, who goes by the

---

58 *Original Weekly Journal*. 26 December 1719. p. 3.

59 Ibid, p. 5.

60 Enough to buy a horse.

61 *Original Weekly Journal*. 26 December 1719. p. 4.

62 Nine hundred and thirty horses.

63 *Stamford Mercury*. 24 December 1719. p. 8.

64 Eleanor Chance, Christina Colvin, Janet Cooper, C J Day, T G Hassall, Mary Jessup and Nesta Selwyn, "Social and Cultural Activities" in *A History of the County of Oxford: Volume 4, the City of Oxford*, ed. Alan Crossley and C R Elrington (London, 1979), pp. 425–441. *British History Online* http://www.british-history.ac.uk/vch/oxon/vol4/pp425–441. Accessed 11 November 2023.

Name, of Cornish Tom, who was lately a Souldier, pretended to fly from Cairfax Tower, but had like to have broke his Neck."[65]

London is a labyrinthine pitch. In the late 1730s, "rushing along Cheapside, or Covent Garden, or by the Maypole in the Strand, came the football players."[66] "Don't play football in London!" cries Samuel Jones from his hospital bed. It falls on deaf ears. The young do not calculate or pray. He is injured. I am not. A youth drops dead playing football in Smithfield, blood streaming from his nose and mouth; another is run over and killed by a coach in Billingsgate; a watchmaker's apprentice meets the same fate in Fleet Street.[67,68,69] Some evade the scythe. In 1722, near the village of Eastlow, "a violent Hurricane" blows down a steeple during Sunday service.[70] The entire congregation is saved as "they happened to be luckily at a Foot-ball Match." Eastlow (East Looe) is in Cornwall, so the parishioners may have been watching hurling.

Such delicious irony is welcomed, humour too. The *London Spy* tells of two drunken sailors who enter the Dark House tavern looking for fun. When they see a hook above the fireplace, they put down their truncheons and hang a "crooked fiddler" by his breeches. The frightened little fiddler "shot that into his Trousers, which made the crooked Vermin stink like a pole-cat." He wriggles and begs, "dripping his Guts upon the Hearth" until his breeches tear, and he falls "into his own sauce." The entire tavern laughs so hard "that if we had seen a Bailiff bogg'd or a Fellow break his neck at football, it could not have been a greater Jest."[71]

In the weekly *British Gazetteer*, a husband in search of his wife consults a doctor of astrology and fortune telling. The doctor goes upstairs and peers through his telescope, returning to report that she is with a lieutenant, "eagerly stuffing her Belly with Sausages." The man explodes, threatening to demolish the telescope and kick a globe around the house like a football if the doctor does not tell him where and when

---

65 Rannie, D.W. (ed.)., *Remarks and Collections of Thomas Hearne*. Clarendon Press, Oxford, 1901. 11 Vols. Vol. 5. p. 79.

66 *The Examiner*. 21 March 1841. p. 5.

67 *The St. James's Journal*. 19 January 1723. p. 4.

68 *The Exchange Evening Post*. 3 March 1721. p. 2.

69 *London Journal*. 12 December 1724. p. 4.

70 *The St. James's Journal*. 1 December 1722. p. 5.

71 Ward, E., (ed.)., *The London Spy*. A. Bettesworth, London, 1718. pp. 43–44.

she will be home. After consulting his charts, the doctor reports that she is near "the Devil's Arse-I'th'Peak in Derbyshire" and will be back in three weeks, "which accordingly happened."[72] Perhaps the lieutenant plays football. In 1721, six Derbyshire men challenge six from any county for six pairs of gloves. That a field is provided by Mr Gee of the *Mitre and Two Brewers* in Highgate, London, seems trivial, yet it is a crucial step in the game's development.[73] Six players, their friends, families, and curious spectators making the trip down from Derbyshire, the same again from the opposing side, plus a London crowd, all buying food and ale. There is money to be had in football.

Perhaps the Derbyshire games are annual. They are certainly crowd-pullers. The Derbyshire men advertise the same terms in 1727, and in 1728 they advertise a six-a-side played by "Twelve Derbyshire Men", beside the Barley Mow, in Islington, London.[74,75] The pub provides "Furmety boiling from Nine in the Morning until Twelve."[76] In Suffolk, in 1726, after Great Harwood had won the previous fixture, "a most obstinate and hard Match at Foot-ball was play'd near Great Harwood in this County, between 7 Men of the Village of Ranse, and the like Number of Great Harwood; which last had challenged the whole Kingdom to match them. The Contest was so great between them, that one of the Harwood's Champions dropp'd down dead on the Spot, whose Brother being engaged on the same Side, would not leave off till the Decision of the Game, which ended in Favour of their Antagonists, the Ranse men."[77]

Matches remain a curiosity to the press. A hook is needed: "A new and extraordinary Entertainment … for our polite Gentry; and what should it be but a Match at Football play'd by six young Women of a Side."[78] It is the first recorded *women's football match* in history. Something critical in the development of football is apparent. All these games with between six and twelve on a side cannot be a coincidence: a smaller, tidier, more

---

72 *Weekly Journal or British Gazetteer*. 16 October 1725. p. 1.

73 *London Journal*. 14 October 1721. p. 7.

74 *Mist's Weekly Journal*. 9 September 1727. p. 3.

75 *Applebee's Original Weekly Journal*. 31 August 1728. p. 4.

76 A fourteenth century recipe of wheat boiled in seasoned milk. In the fair scene in Thomas Hardy's *Mayor of Casterbridge*, raisins and currants are added. A man, dragged by his wife from the lure of the beer tent, gladly accepts a furtive dose of rum in his bowl from the crafty furmety seller.

77 *Ipswich Journal*. 3 December 1726. p. 2.

78 *Ipswich Journal*. 8 October 1726. p. 3.

controlled game has emerged from folk football. A 1721 London game advertised as part of the "ancient Custom of the Derbyshire Wake" must swallow it pride. As much column space is devoted to a five-guinea race between six men on four cows and two bulls, and a boy riding a calf (the cows throw their riders and the calf tumbles).[79,80] Misfortune in Derbyshire in 1716. While playing football, Thomas Baker "set his Foot in a hollow Place, which giving his Body a sudden Shock, he found he had hurt his Left Side under the Short Ribs, at every Step something pricked that Side. In a little Time his Grief spread upwards, and downwards to his Thigh, the Skin being grown dull and almost senseless."[81] From the narrative, it appears to get better, only to return six years later when he catches his foot again. Suffering intense pain, he loses his speech and cannot eat, reduced to sucking food through a quill. He will not live the week out, says the doctor. He hangs on long enough to take a fruitless dip in the celebrated waters of Matlock Bath. Defeated, he tries regular bathing in "an intensely cold Brook" near his home, and is cured.

The century is less than six months old when "a strange and disorderly Uproar" takes place in Dublin. A dispute between the butchers and weavers of the city is to be settled "by a match at Foot-ball", but the butchers "not being willing to hazard their Persons in such Exercise" refuse. The weavers goad them to such a degree that the sides agree to a pitched battle. Armed with "Clubbs, Pikes, Stones, Cleavers, and some Guns, the forty-a-side set to on St Stephen's Green. It is the weaver's day from the get-go. The retreating butchers regroup but another savage assault forces them to their quarter. Six are killed and seventy-two injured, mostly butchers, "some having their Heads broke, others their Arms, Backs, and Leggs in a terrible manner, and 'tis thought many of them will Die of their wounds."[82]

A Match at Football provides a fascinating glimpse of a Dublin game.[83] A six-a-side between Swords and Lusk takes place on Oxmantown

79 *Stamford Mercury*. 11 June 1724. p. 8.

80 A guinea was a pound and a shilling.

81 Short, T., *Discourses on tea, sugar, milk, made-wines, spirits, punch, tobacco, &c*. T. Longman, London, 1750. pp. 325–330.

82 Anon., *A Further and more perticular account of the cruel, desperate, and bloody fight and uproar that happen'd in Ireland on Monday the 6th of May 1700*. s.n., London, 1700. Single page.

83 Concanen, M., *A Match at Foot-Ball*. s.n., Dublin, 1720. pp. 9–40.

Green, a regular footballing venue. It is perfect match weather, and a big crowd expects. Troops of horsemen throng the scene while a man addresses the crowd. The victors will win a ribboned Holland cap, the vanquished a pair of gloves, and both are to share a "cask of humming beer." Swords's team includes Hugh with sinews like a "twanging yew", and Felim who is over sixty. Lusk has Neil and Cabe from the poverty-ridden north, "starv'd on scanty oats … and destitute of coats", and Dick, "few better skilled than him to play the Game, or toss the Football with a surer aim." The crowd is entertained with bagpipes, before one-legged Old Tim sings mournfully of Boyne and Aughram.

Both teams wear white. They are distinguished by a ribbon tied to the back of each cap, Swords blue, Lusk red. The ball is made from three strips of bullock hide fastened with leather thongs and filled with hay, making it "firm and light." The goals comprise a "gate" of pussy willow either side of the green. The ball is cast up, and the game is on. It is thrown, carried, kicked. The opposition stops a player with the ball, others run in and try to extract it. So do his teammates, who lock arms and legs then heave up, each trying to lift an opposing player and free their own, who can then run on unhindered. If the opposition gets the ball, the chance is theirs. The tactic fails, and they all fall in a heap, grappling for the ball. Players are tripped, pushed, tugged. In the confusion, the ball runs clear. A player scoops it up and runs towards the unmanned goal. When the opposition bears down on him, he stops and takes aim, but a Lusk player grabs his arm, winds a leg about him, and sends him down. The Lusk man takes the rolling ball and kicks it towards the other goal. It is quite a kick. A teammate catches it and scores from the spot, despite the distraction of a player leaping to intercept the ball.

The game is rich in detail. There is plenty of contact in stopping a player but no mention of hacking shins. The organised scrummage—believed to have been invented at Winchester in 1825 through a "civilising process" of the folk game—anticipates public schools by over a century. Still, it is the Welsh who can lay claim, having been described in a game of *knappan* in 1587, a quarter of a millennium before Winchester. Standard matches of the day are best of three. In the second game, Paddy kicks the ball, but it is caught by John who returns it "with redoubled force." Dick meets it and knocks it to the floor. It rolls across the green until stopped by Terence:

with gentle Strokes he trolls,
(Th' obedient Ball with short Excursions rolls)
then swiftly runs, and drives it o'er the Plain;
Follow the rest and chace the flying Swain.

Soon, "the sturdy Neal the Football caught, and to his Friends with Strokes repeated brought." The ball passes to and fro until Terence kicks it a short distance, chases it, then kicks it through the goal. One all. The third game, if played, goes unreported. "With *gentle Strokes* he trolls … with *short Excursions rolls* … and to his Friends *with Strokes repeated brought*." In 1720 they are dribbling in Ireland. There is a suggestion of precedence. A c1490 manuscript describes a version of football where they "propel a large ball, not throwing it in the air but rolling it along the ground, and not even striking and turning it with their hands, but using their feet."[84] The author may have never seen football played before; rolling it along the ground may simply mean kicking it along. Either way, Concanen is football nobility. He provides the *first description of an actual football game* in history.

It is surprising the match went ahead at all. The year before, the English are panic-stricken at the possibility of a Spanish invasion to dethrone George I and replace him with Catholic James Stuart, son of James II (who had himself been uncrowned by William and Mary). Convinced—probably correctly—that Irish 'Papists' will support the cause, the government proscribes "all tumultuous and numerous Meetings, and Assemblies, under pretence of Foot-ball, Hurling, Commoning,[85] or other Sports."[86] In 1731, there is a fair in Co. Meath. "There was a lac'd Hat cudgell'd for, a Smock run for by Virgins, a Pair of Brogues danc'd for by old Women, a Match at Foot Ball by married Men and Bachelors, and a Bag of Snuff grin'd for, &c."[87] Another match, in 1746, when farmers take on bachelors, in Parsontown, King's County (renamed Birr, Co. Offaly), afterwards to drink at Sir Laurence Parson's castle, where they toast the king.[88]

---

84 Hanham, A., *Henry VI and his Miracles*. pp. 648–649. https://richardiii.net/wp-content/uploads/2021/08/12-148-Henry-VI-and-his-Miracles.pdf. Accessed 1 November 2023.

85 Winter hurling, similar to shinty.

86 Boyer, A., *The Political State of Great Britain*. 60 Vols. s.n., London, 1719. Vol. 17. p. 398.

87 *Caledonian Mercury*. 21 January 1731. p. 3.

88 Rouse, P., *Sport and Ireland: A History*. Oxford University Press, 2015. p. 43.

In mid-1730s Ireland there is, "A Foot-ball at a place called Aghamore, where the County of Longford challenged the County of Westmeath to meet them, and there determine which had the most able-bodied Men … Women as well as Men thought their Honour concern'd in that Challenge, so as to bring together the greatest Concourse of People … I never observed between hostile Armies … greater Animosities than between these two neighbouring counties."[89] The narrator, the eccentric Captain Dudley Bradstreet, a Tipperary man, is elected Longford's captain. There is more than a touch of aggrandisement. "Men, women, and children cried out for Bradstreet," which, he informs us, "silenced the Envious." He sends an agent to determine Westmeath's tactics and the vices of their star player. Women and brandy. Bradstreet hastens to Blue Pigeon, offering her the "Opportunity of distinguishing" herself to posterity. "Your Part, Madam, is to soften and enervate our Enemy's greatest Hero, by the Charms of your Person and the powerful Insinuation of Brandy, which you may purchase at yonder tent," he adds, with flawless caddishness. The star soon collapses out of sight. When the teams come "within fifty Paces of each other the Ball was left between us." Patrick Harkin and an enemy Hog, "were the first who engaged." Harkin is victorious. "The Enemy seeing the Day lost at Football" start a fight, but are driven "quite out of the Field."[90] Notably, the ball is left in the centre then, and not thrown up.

Bradstreet spends years chasing the glory he craves. After a stint in the army, he leaves a trail of failed businesses, mistresses, bailiffs, creditors, vertiginous tall stories, a dead wife, and any number of children. He repairs to England to try his hand at "Vices, Schemes, and Immoralities." Prostitution and gambling confer modest returns, so he addresses another demand. Gin. The Gin Craze has met with a series of acts to lower consumption. "The selling of Geneva in a less quantity than two Gallons", is prohibited, so the public turn to illegal vendors. Bradstreet comes up with an ingenious scheme. He purchases a wooden carving of a cat and nails it to his house. Word soon gets around. Customers slot tuppence through the cat's mouth and receive a slug of gin through a lead spout that juts out beneath a paw.[91]

---

89 Taylor, G.S. (ed.), *The Life and Uncommon Adventures of Captain Dudley Bradstreet.* John Hamilton Ltd., London, 1929. p. 46.

90 Ibid, pp. 47–51.

91 This is generally considered to be the origin of Old Tom Gin.

Three of Bradstreet's four Irish friends, dandies all, dance at Tyburn; he must sharpen his street smarts to navigate England's social ladder. Up he soars, dazzling Englishmen and fortune alike. With staggering implausibility, he lands a job as a spy and infiltrates the rebel Scottish forces. His crowning triumph—assuming his memoirs are unvarnished—thwarting Bonnie Prince Charlie's invasion of England. He convinces the Young Pretender's council to turn back at Derby by feeding them lies of troops massed on the southern horizon.

Unsurprised at the scant reward—at Liverpool, he "discovered the unaccountable Contempt the English have for the unfortunate Irish"—Bradstreet returns to his old ways. He establishes Bradstreet's State Lottery Office, selling tickets and organising syndicates. It goes the way of his linen and brewery ventures. Bradstreet then takes credit for the celebrated hoax, the Bottle Conjuror. The theatre act features a man who "though six Foot high, and very lusty" will "go into a Quart Bottle before your Face." The conjuror will also "tell all that was past, or was to come in your Life … play to Perfection the Musick of all Kinds of Instruments now in use" on a cane, and summon "the Spirits of any Person that lived on the Earth, since the Beginning of the World."[92] When the conjuror fails to appear on his debut at a heaving Haymarket Theatre, the duped audience gut the building.

Bradstreet writes a play about the hoax, which makes the stage but is closed by magistrates on the fifth night. He returns to Ireland to write his memoirs. The surprising success prompts him to write *Bradstreet's Lives: Being a Genuine History of Several Gentlemen and Ladies, All Living Within these Ten Years Past, Remarkable for their Virtues, or their Vices.* The self-proclaimed adventurer never quite acquires the status he desires, and dies in a village in Ireland at the age of fifty-two.

Football may be popular in Ireland, but hurling flows through the veins. The earliest known advert appears in the *Dublin Flying Post* in 1708: "On St Swithin's Day [15 July], about three in the afternoon, will be a hurling match over the Curragh between thirty men from each side of the Liffey for 30 shillings. A barrel of ale, tobacco, and pipes will be

92 Taylor, G.S. (ed.)., *The Life and Uncommon Adventures of Captain Dudley Bradstreet.* John Hamilton Ltd., London, 1929. p. 212.

given for the hurlers."[93] Crowds can be reckless. In 1732, at a hurling match "near Clenard Bridge, Many Quarrels and Riots ensuing, one Mr. White [a priest] endeavouring to appease the Mob, was himself stoned to death."[94] The following year "an unhappy Accident" occurs at a hurling match in County Kildare: "Two Gentlemen, who sometime before had some Words, met, both arm'd with Pistols, and one of them made a Stroke with his Whip at the other; upon which they fired a case of Pistols at each other, without receiving any damage, but unfortunately at the last Shot, one of the Balls went through the Body of a young Woman who was passing by, of which she instantly died; and also a Man standing near her had some of his Fore-Teeth knocked out, and Part of his Under-Lip taken away."[95] Similarly, in 1755, a lawyer is committed to the Galway County Jail for killing Pierce Clary "at a hurling … by discharging a Fuzee [flintlock] at him loaded with large Shot, which at the same Time wounded several other Persons."[96] He is acquitted two months later.[97] That September, a match between Dublin and Kildare is watched by the Lord Lieutenant the Marquis of Huntington and "a most brilliant appearance of nobility and gentry."[98]

Deaths stack up. In 1777, two Carlow "Gentlemen" organise a match for 50 gns each, "to be hurled for by their own tenantry, which had occasioned a great Number of People to assemble as Spectators." All goes well for two hours, until one side acts "contrary to the Rules of Hurling." The other side "seek Revenge … with their Hurls; two Men were killed on the Spot, and several wounded, amongst the former was the Son of a reputable Gentleman."[99] The following year, Mary Fitzpatrick is killed when she is thrown from her horse "riding to a hurling" in Galway.[100] There is tragedy in 1785. Returning from a hurling match in County Offaly, "not less than thirty, returning to Banagher … in crossing the

93 Rouse, P., *Sport and Ireland: A History*. Oxford University Press, 2015. p. 75.

94 *The Derby Mercury*. 17 August 1732. p. 2.

95 *The Derby Mercury*. 20 September 1733. p. 4.

96 *The Derby Mercury*. 27 June 1755. p. 1.

97 *Sherborne Mercury*. 22 September 1755. p. 1.

98 Biagini, E., Mulhall, D. (eds)., *The Shaping of Modern Ireland: A Centenary Assessment*. Irish Academic Press, Sallins, Kildare, 2016. p. 67.

99 *The Public Advertiser*. 4 October 1777. p. 4.

100 *Saunders's News-Letter*. 22 August 1778. p. 1.

Shannon on a … Boat were all lost, except two Men."[101] In a reversal, a boat at Ferrycarrig, Co. Wexford is to take a full load of passengers across the inlet to a hurling match. A mounted rider attempts to board the ship despite protestations. When thwarted, he tries to swim his horse across instead. Both drown.[102]

In 1786, in Dundrum, Tipperary, one brother kills another with a wayward stroke of a hurl while wrestling for the ball,[103] an accident repeated in 1793.[104] Even small games can be deadly. "During a hurling match between "some country people and three Volunteer light horsemen at Bolaradda, Co. Wexford "a dreadful affray" breaks out. "Aided and assisted by his two brothers, William Gilbert stabs another local to death with a broadsword.[105] Another man is "killed by the stroke of a hurl" at a match in Co. Kilkenny. Fifteen others involved in the quarrel "have absconded."[106] A mere trifle, then, when a man sustains a broken leg at a hurling match at Swords, in 1763, and is taken to the Charitable Infirmary.[107]

Hurling occasions more than death. An advert inserted into *The Dublin Evening Post* by "a haberdasher that provides gentlemen with wives, and ladies with husbands", advances the attributes of a Galway woman "in the forty fifth year of her age": "Graceful in person, good teeth, large soft lips always pouting, breath as sweet as incense, fine eyes and coal black hair, bosom and bottom plump, firm, and white; sings a good song, tender and humane, cheerful in countenance." The lady is happy to marry the gentleman previously advertised as possessing "a fortune … provided he indulges her once every year to partake of the pleasures of a country hurling, and a provincial review."[108] There is wisdom too. In August 1777, "two waiters from a noted Coffee-house" in Dublin hold a hurling match for 5 gns a side. The victor takes his team "to punish his winnings", promising to "never quit the spud while a penny remained."[109]

---

101 *Northampton Mercury*. 24 September 1785. p. 3.

102 *Saunders's News-Letter*. 26 August 1786. p. 2.

103 *Saunders's News-Letter*. 20 May 1786. p. 1.

104 *Saunders's News-Letter*. 9 July 1793. p. 2.

105 *Belfast News-Letter*. 23 October 1781. p. 2.

106 *Saunders's News-Letter*. 10 September 1784. p. 2.

107 *Dublin Courier*. 27 May 1763. p. 1.

108 *Dublin Evening Post*. 6 September 1781. p. 3.

109 *The Freeman's Journal*. 19 August 1777. p. 3.

Other crimes include the 1766 murder of Darby Mullowney "an opulent farmer" from County Kildare with a hurling stick, in what appears to be a robbery.[110] The year before, at a well-patronised hurling match in London "in the Long-Fields behind Bedford House ... The pickpockets made a great Booty; many Gentlemen lost their Watches and Pocket-books."[111] On the same page, a boy drowns, a child is crushed to death by a fire engine cylinder, a woman is murdered, a youth is struck by lightning on Hampstead Heath, a fruitman kills a bricklayer with a punch to the stomach, one man is gored by an Ox, and another dies from a fractured skull after a night of dancing revelry at the *Welch Harp.*

Sport can be talked up. In 1748—after Leinster had won two matches at the same venue the month before)[112]—a hurling match between Leinster and Munster on Crumlin Common, Dublin, which was "to have been the greatest ... that ever was played in this Kingdom", is called off when Munster withdraw.[113] A Michaelmas Crumlin Common game between "Married Men and Bachellors, for 20 Guineas a Side", is advertised eight years later,[114] while in 1757 "there is to be a great Match of Hurling at Irishtown [Dublin], between the Gentlemen of the King's County [Co. Offaly] and the County of Dublin for twenty Guineas a Side."[115] In Dublin, in 1763, the Countess of Northumberland is "entertained with Horse Races" and "a fine Hurling match, which gave her Excellency the highest Satisfaction, there being no Such game as this in any other Part of Europe, which is the most noble and manly Exercise in the World."[116] Leinster against Connaught at Crumlin Common is advertised in 1776 for a purse of fifty pounds: "The Hurlers to be stripped precisely at three o'clock, or the money to be forfeited—Note The Green to be corded around, and none admitted Inside but the two Judges."[117] Transporting players dotted around the provinces to a match requires sound planning, especially when they are playing on neutral ground

110 *The Public Advertiser.* 22 July 1766. p. 4.

111 *The Public Advertiser.* 7 August 1765. p. 2.

112 Blythe, E.P., *The First Decade of the G.A.A. in Dublin.* Dublin Historical Record, 1963, 19:1, p. 16.

113 *The Penny London Post.* 17 June 1748. p. 1.

114 *Pue's Occurences.* 21 September 1756. p. 2.

115 *Pue's Occurences.* 19 July 1757. p. 2.

116 *Newcastle Weekly Courant.* 5 November 1763. p. 1.

117 *Saunders's News-Letter.* 11 September 1776. p. 2.

like Crumlin Common. So when Connaught play Munster, in 1779, "the Lads of Connaught think proper to acquaint those of Munster, that they will be punctual to the Hour."[118] In a match pitting "Munstermen and Leinstermen", in 1780, the Common is corded, the ball thrown up, and three adjudicators "are selected by both Parties to regulate any dispute."[119]

In October 1792, the Countess of Westmoreland takes in a game between Leinster and the combined forces of Connaught and Munster, at Phoenix Park, Dublin. Other nobility and gentry attend. While the pitch is probably cordoned off, some of the "vast concourse of spectators" encroach on the pitch. The game is abandoned without a winner.[120] The incident does hurling no favours. Informal games in the park are barely tolerated as it is. The French Republic was founded only weeks before. What good can possibly come from swarms of Catholics congregating. Yet any attempt to ban the game is futile. When "a surprising multitude of people" turn up for a Sabbath game at the park, they are dispersed, only to reassemble the following week.[121] It cannot last. References to hurling are rare in the 1790s as resolve for a republic quickens, culminating in the 1798 Irish Rebellion. Landlords who patronise games across the island no longer want to be associated with Catholic gatherings, and organised games attended by a wide demographic wither.

In 1784, Dubliners are enraged by the gruesome execution of Mary Fairfield, strangled then thrown on a fire on Stephen's Green for the murder of Mary Funt. Even the governor of Newgate Prison, "his under-keepers", and many in the garrison are disgusted. Soldiers subsequently keep their distance in Phoenix Park, when "a great mob" gathers in the park for a hurling match.[122] A fleeting moment condemns Thomas Wogan Browne. Passing "a party of peasantry" playing football, the magistrate dismounts "and in a moment of good-natured impulse, gave the ball one or two energetic kicks."[123] That it is the Sabbath matters little. It is 1797, and some of the players are United Irishmen, intent on an Irish Republic.

---

118 *Saunders's News-Letter.* 8 October 1779. p. 3.

119 *Saunders's News-Letter.* 26 September 1780. p. 2.

120 Blythe, E.P., *The First Decade of the G.A.A. in Dublin.* Dublin Historical Record, 1963, 19:1, p. 17.

121 Ibid, pp. 16–17.

122 *Saunders's News-Letter.* 25 August 1783. p. 1.

123 Fitzpatrick, J.W., *The Life, Times, and Cotemporaries of Lord Cloncury.* J.M. O'Toole, Dublin, 1855. p. 313.

The bigoted Lord Chancellor removes Wogan Browne as a Justice of the Peace for Dublin and Meath. He is accused of being a United Irishmen colonel, and his yeomanry corps is denounced as seditious.[124] Fellow magistrates unite in his support, and he retreats to Castle Browne. All is quiet until the Irish Rebellion in 1798. Wogan Browne is seized and noosed by Crown soldiers, when a dragoon happens by "with a letter addressed to him by the Lord Lieutenant, on public business."[125] So where do his sympathies lie? He is a Whig politician, after all. When he marries Martha McTier, "an agreeable little woman, though an aristocrat", he nominally becomes a Protestant, but he is raised a Catholic, his brother maintains the faith, his sister is a nun, and he has the legendary Irish Revolutionary Theobald Wolfe Tone around for drinks. The following years are not kind to him. Fourteen years after the rebellion, deeply in debt, he commits suicide. He is fifty-three.

Twenty hurling games are recorded in London between 1733 and 1814. Hyde Park hosts two in 1733: Kildare vs Meath for 100gns, and Wicklow and Wexford vs Meath and "the Queen's County [Co. Laois]."[126] The venue changes to the Artillery Ground from 1747 to 1751, Long Fields from 1764 to 1771, and Kennington Common from 1796 to 1814.[127] The first match at the Artillery Ground follows several interrupted games "in the open Fields." The second is reported to be the last of the season, implying others that go unrecorded. Games are usually twelve-a-side, best of three, but fourteen- and eighteen-a-side games are not uncommon. A 1746 game attracts ten thousand spectators, it will take football fifty years to match the attendance.[128] Many of the games pit Leinster against Munster, others Munster against All Ireland. In a possible exhibition game in 1760, Wales beats Herefordshire in a twenty-five-a-side. A 1771 match report suggests two more matches that season, and three in 1770.[129] After a 1796 game on Kennington Common,

---

124 *Dictionary of Irish Biography.* https://www.dib.ie/biography/browne-thomas-wogan-a1055. Accessed 3 November 2024.

125 Cloncurry, V., *Personal Recollections of the Life and Times, With Extracts from the Correspondence, of Valentine Lord Cloncurry.* J. McGlashan, Dublin, 1849. p. 178.

126 Bergin, J., Kinsella, E., *Hurling matches in London (1733–1818) and New York (1781–2).* Archivium Hibernicum, 2015, 68, p. 159.

127 Ibid, pp. 159, 161, 162.

128 The estimate may be grossly exaggerated.

129 Ibid, pp. 159–162.

the victors are "ornamented with ribbons by their female friends [and] escorted home in procession, with music."[130] Ironically, the year the first hurling match is played in England (Hyde Park, 1733), the first mention is made of cricket in Ireland, when the Earl of Middlesex and his brother Lord John Sackville play in Phoenix Park on 3 October.[131] The event is dignified by "several persons of distinction." Sackville's grandson takes "part in the first recorded century partnership while playing for Kent in 1744."[132]

Two further matches have come to light. In 1722, "28 Irish Men of several provinces" are due to play on Richmond Green. All players "will be provided with Camons and Ball by Mr. Thurmond at the White Hart in Richmond."[133] The next earliest matches are the two in 1733. On the evening of 29 August 1770, "was decided in the Long Fields, Bloomsbury, the great Match of Hurling, 14 Men of a Side, the Province of Munster against the Province of Leinster; which was with great Difficulty determined in Favour of the latter; great Bets were depending."[134] Two unearthed hurling matches of a different kind take place in Devon, in 1773 and 1774, when Cornish hurling is the highlight of Whitchurch Down's annual fêtes; both matches "to begin on Tuesday morning precisely at Ten o'clock."[135]

England and the United States aside, hurling gains little traction overseas. Two matches are played in Paris in the mid-eighteenth century, by "the principal Irishmen then in Paris." The game "was such a novelty, so exciting, so vigorous, and withal so picturesque, that it created a sensation among the Parisians."[136] At length, the novelty reaches the ear of Louis XV who requests a viewing: "Accordingly the ground was selected outside the barriers, and being enclosed with white ropes and pavilioned along the whole line, thither came the whole city of Paris, the king and his court, nobility, gentry, and artisans, all to see this specimen

130 *Hampshire Chronicle*. 25 June 1796. p. 3.

131 Ní Mhurchadha, M., *Two Hundred Men at Tennis: Sport in North Dublin 1600–1760*. Dublin Historical Record, 2008, 61:1, p. 100.

132 Ibid.

133 *Daily Journal*. 17 August 1722. p. 2.

134 *The Public Advertiser*. 29 August 1770. p. 2.

135 *The Western Flying Post*. 14 June 1773. p. 1; *The Western Flying Post*. 11 July 1774. p. 3.

136 *Limerick Reporter*. 19 June 1868. p. 4.

of the peasant games of Ireland. The young men of Leinster and Munster, were selected for the day's sport, the former dressed in green silk jackets, the latter in white."[137]

In 1793: "The Noble Sport of Hurling" is to be played at the "Race Stand" on St Patrick's Day, in Madras [Chennai], India, in all likelihood by Anglo-Irish Protestant soldiers in the British Army.[138,139] Irish Catholics are far likelier to enlist for the Catholic Monarchs of France, Spain, and Austria; as many as half a million by 1792.[140] Eleven years later, Napoleon establishes a battalion of Irish soldiers, *La Légion Irlandaise.* After the 1798 Rebellion, the legion is joined by two hundred of the three hundred United Irishmen sold by Britain to Prussia, where they were impressed into the Prussian army or worked as indentured labour in Silesian salt mines.[141]

The Rightboys are one of several Irish agrarian movements of the eighteenth century. Regarding themselves as redressors of wrongs, from 1785 to 1788 they rise in rebellion—initially in County Cork—against exorbitant smallholder rents, the eviction of tenant farmers, and unjust tithes levied by the Anglican Church of Ireland.[142] When support rapidly spreads across the lower half of Ireland, the Rightboys can muster bands of eight hundred horsemen and seven thousand footmen. Threatening notices and property damage is the usual modus operandi, but landlords and clergy are assaulted, frequently viciously, sometimes fatally. One farmer is buried up to his chin, and his ears and parts of his cheeks cut off and nailed to a water pump.[143] In September 1786, six thousand assemble in Co. Cork "under pretence of a hurling match … each person was to attend with a hurly and a firelock", an effective strategy replicated across the counties. A man assuming the identity of the fictious Captain Right

137 Bergin, J., Kinsella, E., *Hurling matches in London (1733–1818) and New York (1781–2).* Archivium Hibernicum, 2015, 68, p. 139.

138 *Madras Courier.* 14 March 1793. p. 4.

139 Karsten, P., *Irish Soldiers in the British Army, 1792–1922: Suborned or Subordinate?* Journal of Social History, 1983, 17:1, p. 35.

140 Ibid, p. 32.

141 MacGiollabhuí, M.A., *Sons of Exile: The United Irishmen in Transnational Perspective 1791–1827.* Unpublished PhD thesis, University of California, 2019. p. 38.

142 Donnelly, J.S., Donnelly, J.J., *The Rightboy Movement 1785–8.* Studia Hibernica, 1978, 432:17–18. p. 124.

143 Ibid, p. 131.

shows up, riding up and down, while brandishing his sword. He is soon arrested. As he is transported to Clonakilty "a mob of 500 men", try to free him. Several are killed, "and the soldiers were forced to keep up a constant firing all the way."[144]

By 1787, the movement has run its course. The supposed parliamentarian review of grievances leads to suspension of activity; the subsequent interminable wait weakens the movement. Cast as Papist agitation, the movement is never anti-king, it is a parochial movement, panicked by the "crisis of village society."[145] Of those convicted, "none of them ever possess'd more than a cabbage garden." It could have been English workers but was painted otherwise. On New Year's Day 1790, a sardonic passage in *The Times* speaks volumes: "Hurling … was introduced into the British House of Commons, with intent to make it a Royal Game; But being too violent … was smuggled into France by the Jesuits, and nothing but the honour of introducing it remains now with the Bogtrotter who imported it."[146]

~

The Jacobite rebellion is big news. After an English rebel is executed in 1716, his head is kicked through the streets of Liverpool.[147] The same paper mentions that the Aurora Borealis is seen in London, as rare a sight as the total solar eclipse a year earlier—four months before, the Sun King, Louis XIV, who was crowned within weeks of an eclipse, is forever eclipsed. Also, a man "who had been drinking his Morning Draughts a little more Zealously than Ordinary", was heard by passing soldiers to "utter from both ends." Interpreted as an affront to His Majesty's soldiers, he is arrested as "a dangerous Person" and committed to Newgate Prison. "Thus, you see", the paper quips, "a Man may both Whistle Treason and Fart Treason." On that theme, a Scottish book of poems includes a glossary for the English. It describes a *dool*, "the Goal which Gamesters strive to gain first (as at Football)."[148] Directly above is the term for a "heavy-headed dull fellow." A *doofart*. A man may also

144 *Saunders's News-Letter*. 1 September 1786. p. 2.

145 Bric, M.J., *Priests, Parsons and Politics: The Rightboy Protest in County Cork 1785–1788*. Past and Present, 1983, 100:1, pp. 121–123.

146 *The Times*. 1 January 1790. p. 3.

147 *The Original Weekly Journal*. 10 May 1716. pp. 4–5.

148 Ramsay, A., *Poems by Allan Ramsay*. Thomas Ruddiman, Edinburgh, 1728. p. 407.

develop an air-filled cyst in his scrotum. At the start of George I's reign, a medical textbook describes the cyst as being caused by convulsions of the scrotum, which is "stretched like a football … we may perceive a little noise when we strike it."[149] A whistle, a fart, and an agonised yelp. The rest of the chapter *Of the Diseases Subject to the Parts of Generation in Men*; the preceding chapter *Of the Parts of Generation in Men and the Diseases Subject thereto, particularly those of the Penis*; and the subsequent *Of the Organs of Generation in Women*, are stomached by the inured readers of the day. Future generations will be seriously challenged.

John Arbuthnot satirises his social climbing protagonist in his posthumous *The History of John Bull*: "he began to leave off some of his old acquaintance, his roaring and bullying about the streets; he put on a serious air, knit his brows … However, he could not help discovering some remains of his nature, when he happened to meet with a foot-ball, or a match at cricket."[150] To be fair, only seven pages earlier: "If this be your play," he says "that we may not be like a Quaker's dumb meeting, let us begin some diversion; what d'ye think of rouly pouly, or a country dance? What if we should have a match at football?" Elsewhere, football is disdained. It does not help when the game is brought into disrepute. In 1715, Richard Ellis and Jacob Nevill are charged at Westminster Quarter Sessions with assaulting a woman while, "W[i]th many others to the number of near an hundred persons Royetously and Tumultuously gathered together at football wch Ball they kick'd ag[ains]t the kitching Windows of Mrs Askews house in Vine Street and broake them and also at the same tyme by throwing a stick at broak the sash windows one Story high of the said house."[151] Mary Ellis, "spinster" and presumably Richard's relative, is bound over for playing in the match.[152] Ellis becomes the first known women's football player.

The game remains perilous. In Dublin, in 1730, "a Parcel of idle Fellows were assembled, to divert themselves at their usual Games of

149 Clericus, D., Magnetus, J. (eds.)., *Bibliotheca Anatomica*. 3 Vols. John Nutt, London, 1712. Vol. 3. p. 326.

150 Arbuthnot, J., *The History of John Bull*. In: Swift, J., *Miscellanies: The Second Volume*. 2 Vols. Benjamin Motte, London, 1727. Vol. 2. p. 183.

151 Hurl-Eamon, J., *Gender and petty violence in London, 1680–1720*. Ohio State University, 2005. p. 89.

152 Ibid, p. 169.

Foot-ball playing, and throwing of Stones, [when] a Spectator passing cross, was struck with a Stone in the Back of the Head, of which he died in a few minutes."[153] Another paper identifies the man as a young baker and places the match at Oxmantown Green (scene of the Swords-Lusk games).[154] Only passing mention is made that the game was on the Sabbath. The same page reports a rare case of lightning. Shooting down the chimney of a house in Ramsgate, all the windows and parts of the floor and walls are blown out. The occupants are unharmed. Three years later, footballing youths in Co. Galway are not so lucky. When a violent storm erupts, they seek refuge in a house. Four are terrified and step into the chimney. A lightning bolt kills them instantly, takes the leg of another in the room, and singes the rest.[155] If that is not enough for its readership, a reaper in Co. Meath is also struck by lightning, and "had his Scull broke and Brains blown out of his Head, to the great Terror of all the Bystanders." In neighbouring Co. Westmeath, "according to Custom, there was a Match at Foot-ball betwixt two Baronies for the three first Sundays in Harvest. One game turns ugly. Four are killed on the spot and eleven "wounded so desperately that their Lives are despaired of."[156]

In Duns, in the Scottish Borders, football is played annually on *Fastern's E'en* (Shrove Tuesday). It usually ends in a brawl, so in 1724 when players go to the burgher's house for the drum traditionally beat to convene the match, he refuses to hand it over.[157] They play anyway. "You cannot have won," goad the losers afterwards, "the drum didn't sound … Whereupon they fell a fighting and beating and blooding." Coming to their senses, they turn against the common enemy. The burgher. Led by the shoemaker, who probably made the ball, two or three hundred gather round the burgher's house. Stones and threats are hurled through the window, but they eventually disperse, "cursing and swearing."

Casualties pile up in the narrow lanes of London. In a satirical letter, the playwright William D'Avenant has a Parisian character remark, "I would now make a safe retreat, but that me-thinks, I am stopp'd by one

153 *Derby Mercury*. 4 June 1730. p. 1.

154 *Fog's Weekly Journal*. 30 May 1730. n.p.

155 *Ipswich Journal*. 18 August 1733. p. 2.

156 *Kentish Weekly Post*. 3 September 1737. p. 1.

157 *Report on Manuscripts in Various Collections*. 7 Vols. His Majesty's Stationery Office, London, 1901–1914. Vols. 5–6. pp. 43–45.

of your Heroick Games call'd *Foot-Ball*; which I conceive (under your favour) not very conveniently civil in the streets; especially in such irregular and narrow Roads as *Crooked Lane*. Yet it argues your Courage much like your Military pastime of throwing at Cocks."[158] His dart at this affront to the national symbol of France strikes true. The blood sport involves tying a cock to a post and throwing weighted sticks at distance until it dies.[159] Barbarous sports—bull, bear, and duck baiting, throwing at cocks, cock fights, dog fights, cat tossing, and dog tossing—are as popular as ever.

In 1719, a French traveller publishes an encyclopaedia of England, devoting a section to "Sports and Diversions".[160] He lists those common to other European countries—tennis, dancing, plays, billiards, chefs, and tick-tack—and those peculiar to England: "Cockfighting is a Royal Pleasure in *England*. Their Combates between Bulls and Dogs, Bears and Dogs, and sometimes between Bulls and Bears, are not Battels to Death, as those of Cocks: Any Thing that looks like Fighting, is delicious to an *Englishman* ... Wrestling too is one of the Diversions of the *English*, especially in the Northern Counties ... Ringing of Bells is one of their great Delights." He moves on to football. "In Winter Footballs is a useful and charming Exercise: It is a Leather Ball about as big as one's Head, fill'd with Wind: This is kick'd about from one to t'other in the Streets, by him that can get at it, and that is all the Art of it." M. Misson has much to say on other subjects: "The *English* eat a great deal at Dinner; they rest a while, and to it again, till they have quite stuff'd their Paunch ... BLESSED BE HE THAT INVENTED PUDDING ... *To come in Pudding-time*, is as much as to say, to come in the most lucky Moment in the World. Give an *English* Man a *Pudding*, and he shall think it a noble Treat in any Part of the World."[161] And this on disease: "There are four very dangerous Distempers in England that are much less known in other Countries; the Scurvy, Consumption, Rickets, and Hypochondriac Melancholy."[162]

---

158 D'Avenant, W., *The first days entertainment at Rutland-House, by declamations and musick: after the manner of the ancients*. J.M., London, 1656. pp. 62–63.

159 "Forty or fifty paces", according to Maximilien Misson. In: Ozell (trans.)., Misson, H., Misson, M., *Misson's Memoirs and Observations in His Travels Over England. With some account of Scotland and Ireland*. s.n., London, 1719. p. 307.

160 Ibid, pp. 304–307.

161 Ibid, pp. 313–315.

162 Ibid, p. 68.

Other observations include: the English view hairy warts as a sign of good luck; fish "is dearer than any other Belly-timber in London"; whenever a horse dies in Ireland, "they hang up his Hoof to the Ceiling; and this is a very sacred Thing among them"; and "The *English* disposition not being revengeful, there have been few Instances of poisoning", possibly because the previous punishment, "was to be thrown alive into a Cauldron of Boiling Water." M. Misson is not done: "The Punishment of breaking upon the Wheel, tearing of the Flesh with red hot Pincers, and pulling to pieces with four Horses are unknown in *England*." And of the Scottish, "A kind of Scarf of several Colours, carry'd between the Legs, and so over one Shoulder, and sometimes over both, leaving the rest of their Body naked, is their usual Habit."

In 1725, Swiss visitor César-François de Saussure complains of the English, "throwing dead dogs and cats and mud at passers-by on certain festival days. Another amusement which is very inconvenient to passers-by is football. For this game a leather ball filled with air is used, and is kicked about with the feet. In cold weather you sometimes see a score of rascals in the streets kicking at a ball, and they will break panes of glass and smash the windows of coaches, and also knock you down without the slightest compunction; on the contrary, they will roar with laughter."[163] His next observation is worth including, as it was considered a well-patronised and highly competitive sport, was extensively covered in *Bell's Life and the Sporting Chronicle*, and secured more column space than football until the formation of the FA in 1863: "I do not suppose there is a country where bell-ringing is brought to such an art … with six or eight bells of various tones, in an hour's time a good bell-ringer can ring out more than a thousand different peals and chimes …"[164]

The same year, another Swiss man echoes de Saussure's sentiments, grumbling that Englishmen like to kick balls through the streets in an inconvenient and insolent manner and to break house and carriage windows with them.[165] Yet another, Guy Miège, snubs his nose: "Football is

163 Madame Van Muyden., *A Foreign View of England in the Reigns of George I. & George II.* John Murray, Albemarle Street, London, 1902, pp. 294–295.

164 Ibid, p 295.

165 Muralt, B.L., *Lettres sur les Anglais et les Français*. Von Stieger & Cie., Bern, 1897. p. 46.

a rude Diversion for the common sort of People in frosty weather."[166,167] In Chichester, not long after Miège's death, there is "footballing in the streets day after day in frosty weather to the advantage of the glazier."[168] Some who should know better take a simplistic view of football. This from legal scholar Matthew Hale, "I have seen a Match at Foot-ball … one getting the Ball, and then another kicking up his heels and getting it from him, and then another doing the like by him."[169] M. Misson's ill-informed take on football is rejected by historian Thomas Salmon in 1731. In so doing, he reveals precious details: "it is evident he never saw a Foot-ball Match while he was in England: For at this exercise they chuse twelve or fifteen of the most active and boldest young Fellows of a Side, who having adjusted their respective Goals or Stands, the Ball … is thrown down an equal Distance between the two Goals, and each Party endeavour to kick it to the opposite Goal; in which a sufficient Tryal is made of their Speed, their Strength, their Skill in Wrestling, and their management of the Game in general."[170] His description includes fixed sides, goals, throw-offs, a focus on kicking the ball, and a blend of skill, strength, speed, and intelligence.

As D'Avenant's Parisian would advise, steer clear of football in London. In 1731, Susannah Jobbins is shoved in front of a crowd playing football in Kensington, sustaining injuries she dies of a few days later. A man is charged with her murder.[171] Elsewhere in footballing London, the tapster at the George Tavern, Charing Cross, "dropt down dead, in a Fit of an Apoplexy", a footman breaks his leg "in a terrible manner by a Fall amongst the Crowd", a woman has her leg broken when she is thrown down by footballers in Whitechapel, and a butcher breaks his back playing football in Whitechapel.[172,173,174,175]

166 Miège, G., *The new state of England under Their Majesties K. William and Q. Mary*. J.C., London, 1691. p. 40.

167 Ironic, then, that Zurich became the home of FIFA, and Nyon of UEFA.

168 Griffin, E., *England's Revelry: A History of Popular Sports and Pastimes*. Oxford University Press, 2005. p. 107.

169 Hale, M., *Contemplations Moral & Divine*. William Shrowsbury, London, 1699. p. 412.

170 Salmon, T., *Modern History: Or, The Present State of All Nations*. 31 Vols. Geo. Grierson, Dublin, 1731. Vol. 17. p. 156.

171 *Kentish Weekly Post*. 24 February 1731. p. 2.

172 *Daily Post*. 28 November 1728. p. 3.

173 *Kentish Weekly Post*. 25 February 1747. p. 3.

174 *General Evening Post*. 29 December 1739–1 January 1740. p. 3.

175 *Public Advertiser*. 27 January 1555. p. 1.

Not all London matches end in disaster. In 1731, "some Gentlemen from the Other end of the Town" take on "A sett of citizens" for a guinea a head in a field next to Copenhagen House.[176] In 1729, three matches are reported. Nine "Gentlemens Servants" draw with nine tailors in London,[177] and Shoreditch are beaten by Coleman-Street "so shamefully", that "tis thought they will never attempt to challenge them again."[178] Below the item, a man in the belfry of St Katharine's Church has his legs broken by a bell, "and now lies in a miserable condition." The third game sounds like folk football: three hundred tailors "had a Trial of Manhood at Football on Kennington Common."[179] Plenty of other trials end on the common: it is the site of executions for a hundred and twenty-one years, ever since 1678, when Sarah Elston is burned at the stake for killing her husband. The details of her case warrant relating. The couple live in Fishmonger's Alley in Southwark. Sarah is the victim of persistent family violence. In September 1677, her hatter husband, "having beat her very severely, she with a pair of Sizzars gave him a wound on the left part of his breast; whereof, without speaking one word, he died." While she maintains she held out the scissors to protect herself, and he had lunged at her, no mercy is shown. After a few brave words, "the Fire was kindled, and giving one or two lamentable Shrieks, she was deprived both of Voice and Life, and so burnt to Ashes according to the Sentence."[180]

The tailors' 1729 "trial of manhood" is the first known football match on Kennington Common. Five years earlier, cricket is the first recorded sport there. It will become "the most important centre of footballing activity in the London region", until the Oval Cricket Ground is built on the site in 1845.[181] The Oval hosts the first representative football match in the world—England v Scotland, on 5 March 1870; the second official international football match in the world, on 8 March 1873; the first FA Cup Final, in 1872, and nineteen of the next twenty; and will become

176 *The Daily Post Boy*. 8 February 1731. p. 1.

177 *Fog's Weekly Journal*. 15 February 1729. p. 2.

178 *Daily Post Boy*. 1 February 1729. p. 2.

179 *The Evening Post*. 9 January 1729. p. 3.

180 L'strange, Ro., *A Warning for Bad Wives*. s.n., London, 1678. pp. 3, 7.

181 Harvey, A., *Football: The First Hundred Years: The Untold Story*. Routledge, Abingdon, Oxon, 2005. p. 54.

home to the national team until 1889.[182] The Gymnastic Society plays football on Kennington Common in the 1780s, but the tailors anticipate them by over half a century. Previously unheard of, the match has hidden itself away for almost three hundred years.

Football remains a rustic favourite, travelling the country, pressing the flesh. Unlike camping and Cornish hurling, it is played throughout Britain, notwithstanding geographical variations. In 1700, John Gardiner writes to the Rt Hon. John Sanford about a football game in Luppitt, Devon (notwithstanding the possibility of hurling),[183] and in April 1711, the local squire in Little Crosby, Lancashire, teaches some villagers how, "to play at Penny prick with the Foot balle."[184,185] His entry for 14 May 1715 reads, "The Young Folks of this Town had a Merry-Night … the Young weomen treated the Men with a Tandsey [cake] as they had lost to them at a Game of Stoole Balle."[186] In 1711, romance blossoms between James, "a rough Wrestler, and quarrelsome Cudgel Player … a Country Bully", and Betty, "a Publick Dancer at Maypoles, a Romp at Stool-ball … a Country Coquet."[187]

Football may be a winter game, but it is an evergreen holiday fixture. In 1742, Lancastrian doctor Richard Kay records that he "took a Walk to Bury with great Numbers beside to see a Foot Ball Match betwixt Town and Country";[188] while at Hendon, in 1752, there is "a bull-baited, wrestling, cudgelling, foot-ball, and all other country diversions."[189] In 1759, Richard Forster of West Shefford, Berkshire, reports football, wrestling, and cudgelling as the village sports,[190], a particular confirmed

182 The world's first official international game was Scotland v England on 30 November 1872. The goalless draw played out at Hamilton Crescent, a cricket ground in Glasgow. England won the London game 4-2. Wanderers beat Royal Engineers 1-0 in the first FA Cup Final.

183 *Bundle of letters*. The National Archives: https://discovery.nationalarchives.gov.uk/details/r/d424a062–3067–47f3–ba0a-dce061bdd58e. Accessed 1 May 2023.

184 Participants throw iron sticks at a mark, classically pennies perched on wooden sticks.

185 Bagley, J.J. (ed.), *The Great Diurnal of Nicholas Blundell of Little Crosby, Lancashire*. 3 Vols. C. Tinling & Co. Ltd, Liverpool, London and Prescot, 1968. Vol. 1. p. 287.

186 Ibid, Vol. 2. p. 134.

187 *The Spectator*. 22 May 1711. p. 1.

188 Malcolmson, R.W., *Popular Recreations in English Society 1700–1850*. Unpublished PhD thesis, University of Warwick, 1970. pp. 85–86.

189 Goulstone, J., *Football's Secret History*. Soccer & Society, 2018, 19:1, p. 39.

190 Wooders, J., '*With Snail Shells instead of Bells': Music, Morris Dancing, and the 'Middling Sort' of People in Eighteenth-Century Berkshire*. Folk Music Journal, 2015, 10:5, p. 565.

by John Throsby in 1790.[191] Summer and winter combine in June 1772. The worst hailstorm in forty years relinquishes "large lumps of ice … as big as a common football" on Leeds.[192] An obscure poem eulogises a winter's ball game in the town of Tiverton, Devon. It is hard to distinguish if the poem refers to hurling to goals or football, though kicking is infrequent in the former: "Amidst whole Beds of Ice, or Show'rs of Snow, Send forth the Ball … all mark'd with many a Scar … Each kicks and Spurns … But bleeding, shouts, and furious hurls the Ball … His Feet fly up, his Body beats the Ground … Now near the Goal … Tho' this with Force, and that with Art assails … nought avails … and now again engage, And ev'ry Turn redoubles all their rage; Till … their Strength decays, And impotent, they part, with equal Praise."[193] The poem reveals several features: it is a violent game, though skill is employed; kicking and throwing are allowed; goals are used; and it ends in a draw.

Matches are advertised. 1729's Derbyshire Wake match is to be replayed as a twelve-a-side against "Gloucestershire Gentlemen", for 5 gns a head.[194] The same year, "a Gentleman in Essex has given a Holland Smock to be Danced for by Maidens and a Laced Hat to be Wrestled for by young Men on Whitson-monday … also a Holland Smock to be Run for by Maidens; and six pairs of Gloves to be play'd at Foot Ball by six young Men on a Side on Whitson Tuesday."[195] In a ribald aside, the article concludes, "Whether the said Gentleman is to see the said Smocks fit the Winners we cannot determine." The same page reports a suicide, a murder, a smallpox outbreak, a man struck blind by lightning, a child born with hooves, a sleepwalker who fell from her bedroom window in Seven Dials, and the prosecution of several staff of *Mist's Weekly Journal*, a notoriously seditious paper. The apprentice is made "to walk round the four courts in Westminster-Hall, with Paper on his Forehead, denoting his Offence", followed by a month in prison. *Mist's* maid is sent "to the House of Corrections for six Months," for publishing the Paper, "there to be kept to hard Labour, and to be stript down to her Waist, and receive the Correction of the House." Smock races are common at fairs,

---

191 Goulstone, J., *Football's Secret History*. Soccer & Society, 2018, 19:1, p. 39.

192 *Leeds Intelligencer*. 23 June 1772. p. 3.

193 Kiddell, H., *Tiverton: A Poem*. R. Griffiths, London, 1753. pp. 4–5.

194 *Daily Journal*. 13 September 1729. p. 2.

195 *Applebee's Original Weekly Journal*. 14 May 1729. p. 2.

and often salacious. For a 1744 cricket match on Walworth Common, "the gentlemen who play this match have subscribed for a Holland smock of one guinea value, which will be run for by two jolly wenches, one known by the name of The Little Bit of Blue (the handsome Broom girl) at the fag end of Kent Street, and the other, Black Bess, of the Mint. They are to run in drawers only, and there is excellent sport expected."[196]

Complaints are ever near. In 1726, there is friction when street football is played in the Millngate in Manchester,[197] while in 1792, Moravians in Bedford complain about football outside their brethren house.[198] Small fry to what passes at White Conduit Fields near the village of Islington in 1765. During a "grand camping match at football … between several hundred Welchmen and Irishmen", a Welshman calls an opponent Paddy.[199,200,201] Both sides grab "sticks and bludgeons" from the crowd and "a most desperate battle" ensues. Though double in number, "a panic struck the Welch, seeing how resolutely the Irish faced them." They retreat "in great confusion, leaving behind them their hats and wigs." Perhaps hackles are already raised, as the sides have met each Sunday for the last few weeks. The reference to camping in a match between Irish and Welsh is unusual. The same page of *Lloyd's Evening Post* trots out the habitual suicides, murders, house thefts, highwaymen, thwarted duels, and accidental deaths of unattended children.

In 1737, the last of the Tuscan de' Medici rulers dies, ending a dynasty that began in 1434. When Francesco Di Lorena, Duke of Lorraine, is forced to surrender Lorraine to the French in 1735, his honour is upheld when he becomes heir to the Grand Duchy of Tuscany. A decade later, he becomes Holy Roman Emperor, ruling over a thousand-year empire that began with Charlemagne in 800AD and ends in 1806. *Empire* is a misnomer; there are no territories, only political suzerainty over Catholic

196 Malcolmson, R.W., *Popular Recreations in English Society 1700–1850*. Unpublished PhD thesis, University of Warwick, 1970. p. 158.

197 *Examination: William Peploe - disturbance at Manchester Collegiate church and people...* The National Archives: https://discovery.nationalarchives.gov.uk/details/r/fb689fc2–4f6c-4ae5–b3cf-da3588967786. Accessed 5 May 2023.

198 Malcolmson, R.W., *Popular Recreations in English Society 1700–1850*. Unpublished PhD thesis, University of Warwick, 1970. p. 88.

199 *Lloyd's Evening Post*. 22–25 March 1765. p. 7.

200 *Gazetteer and New Daily Advertiser*. 26 March 1765. p. 2.

201 *Lloyd's Evening Post* refers to a "camping match at football", while the *Gazetteer* report calls it football, illustrating the interchangeability of the terms in reports on camping.

monarchs.[202] In 1739, a newspaper reports his visit to Livorno.[203] The English Factory organises a firework display, but it is the French and Dutch who organise a game of *calcio* described by the paper as "a sort of Play at Foot-ball."[204] The game they watch is the liveried kind. That year, Florentine Settimio Alessandro Salvini's 1718 book on the rules of *calcio* is republished.[205,206] In 1766, de' Bardi's *Discorso* is reprinted under the patronage of the English merchants of Livorno.[207] The town is delighted at the thoughtful insertion: "Added to this impression are the chapters and plan of the football of Livorno of the present year." The same page carries other news. Criminals coining guineas are caught red-handed with a thousand freshly minted, and a duel is fought in Covent Garden following an argument over a part in *King Lear*. Both receive slight wounds. And tucked away in the bottom corner is news from York that "the famous Turpin" has been committed to the castle for horse stealing. It is Dick Turpin's last hurrah. The highwayman is hanged three weeks later.

Religion and football do not always butt heads. In 1705, Scottish minister William Chalmers, new to Dunkeld, cannot get "his parishioners to attend service, as it was their custom to play football on Sundays."[208] He succeeds "by joining them occasionally." Football and the Church intertwine little fingers when James King becomes curate of Clitheroe, Lancashire, in 1743. Known as "custodian of the town's football", he kicks it from the church gates on winter Sundays following afternoon service,[209] following the trend set in 1679 by the minister of Downham, five miles away. The minister of nearby Newchurch provides a similar service: "It was his wont on favourable occasions … on passing the portals of the church at the close of service, to dip his hand into the capacious pocket of his great coat, and

---

202 A modern comparison is the European Union.

203 *Kentish Weekly Post*. 14 March 1739. p. 2.

204 English merchants settled in Livorno from the late sixteenth until the late eighteenth century.

205 Von Mallinckrodt, R., *A Cultural History of Sport in the Age of Enlightenment*. Bloomsbury, London, 2022. p. 100.

206 Salvini, S.A., *Instruzione del modo del giuocare il calcio ai giovani nobili fiorentini*. Stamperia Granucale, Florence, 1739.

207 De Bardí, G., *Discorso sul Calcio Fiorentino*. Marco Coltellini, 1766.

208 *Fasti Ecclesiæ Scoticanæ. Synods of Argyll, Perth & Stirling, 4 (1560–1900)*: https://sources-tannerritchie-com.ap1.proxy.openathens.net/browser.php?ipid=796323. Accessed 15 September 2023.

209 Snape, M.F., *The Church of England in Industrialising Society*. The Boydell Press, Woodbridge, 2003. p. 32.

draw from thence a football, and giving it a vigorous kick, would send it spinning into the air, across the churchyard, and over the wall into the adjoining field."[210] Lancashire is an early adopter of football. Two hundred years after the minister of Downham, it will be the driving force behind the introduction of professional players and the establishment of the Football League. Further north, in Cumberland, on Palm Sunday 1782, "Agreeable to the ancient custom (more honoured in the breach than the observance) of a certain parish in this county, an excellent match at foot-ball was played."[211] There is no rebuke for this Sabbath game.

Elsewhere, the Sabbath remains sacred. Men in Colne, Lancashire, are up before the parish court, having played at "ye tyme of Divine sevis."[212] In 1758, a curate complains that in local villages you will "see men of 24, 26, and 30 years of age, playing at foot-ball, throwing a bowl, or pitching a bar."[213] The following year, two men are charged 3s 4d for Sabbath football.[214], Unlike the unpunished Sabbath game where the baker died, six "Felons" are sent to Dublin's Newgate Prison for playing football on Oxmantown Green.[215] "It is hoped," the paper opines, "his Lordship's Vigilance will cause the Sabbath to be more strictly kept."[216] *Fastern's E'en* football is banned in Jedburgh, Roxburghshire, in 1704, as "both old and young near lost their lives thereby."[217] When it presses ahead, in 1706, the butcher's corporation fine those members "guiltie at the rastling at the football."[218] Time softens. A Candelmas Ba' game is recorded in 1796: "On one occasion … the contending parties, after a struggle of two hours in the streets, transferred the contention to the bed of the river Jed, and there fought it out amidst a scene of fearful splash and dabblement, to the infinite amusement of a multitude looking on from the bridge."[219]

---

210 Ibid, p. 32.

211 *Cumberland Pacquet*. 26 March 1782. p. 2.

212 Marples, M., *A History of Football*. Secker and Warburg, London, 1954. p. 79.

213 *Newcastle General Magazine*. May 1758. p. 233.

214 *Westminster Journal*. 26 November 1743. p. 1.

215 *Kentish Weekly Post*. 17 June 1738. p. 2.

216 *Kentish Weekly Post*. p. 2.

217 Magoun, F.P., *Scottish Popular Football, 1424–1815*. The American Historical Review, 1931, 37:1, p. 8.

218 Ibid, p. 8.

219 Thistelton Dyer, T.F., *Popular British Customs Present and Past*. G. Bell and Sons, Limited, London. 1911. p. 57.

At the Northumberland County Court Sessions, in 1706, gaoler George Crey is ordered to keep the "Gaolers house and football … tidy"; a possible reference to an adjoining field.[220] Similarly, in 1709, the Newcastle Corporation is told to "maintain the castle and Football and improve the roads nearby."[221] Church walls continue to be well patronised. In Wells, Somerset, in 1726, a rail is "to be put up from the small west door of the cathedral to the west cloister door, to prevent the playing of ball there against the church wall."[222] In 1733, a town crier is reprimanded for stridently announcing an upcoming football game in the field a preacher is about to address a large congregation: "A Dozen Pair of Gloves to be played for at Foot-ball," he bawls, implying a twelve-a-side.[223] There is another interruption that year. In Chester Cathedral, at 6 a.m. prayers on Christmas Day, a mob runs in and kicks a football down the aisle. Some enter the choir, put out the candles, and pull the reader from the desk. The congregation flees.[224] An angry letter to a newspaper outlines a similar event in 1774: "The *Sabbath* most shamefully broken, by playing at football before the door; hallowing, throwing stones [into the church] … *A subordinate office of justice* like a butcher's dog upon a baited bull, set upon the mob and said it was a pity the riot was not bigger."[225] In 1746, it is football that is interrupted. The Derby Shrove Tuesday game is advertised widely "by some Person or Persons disposed to be the head of Tumults and Disorders." The mayor proclaims a ban to be rigorously enforced "at this unhappy Time of Contagion amongst Horned Cattle."[226] Earlier attempts are made: "In 1731, I saw the Jailor himself, John Greatrex, confined [as] a prisoner for playing at foot-ball, a sport which the Mayor, Isaac Borrow, was determined to suppress. But the man, who had often confined others, could not brook confinement

220 *Gaolers house and football. George Crey to keep them tidy.* The National Archives: https://discovery.nationalarchives.gov.uk/details/r/45378842–5fe5–47d5–9b8d-8d9561125b60. Accessed 6 May 2023.

221 *Newcastle Corporation should maintain the castle and Football and improve the roads...* The National Archives: https://discovery.nationalarchives.gov.uk/details/r/d45bb3eb-dc40–4c82–a7b6–f47e61981cf5. Accessed 6 May 2023.

222 *Calendar of the manuscripts of the Dean and Chapter of Wells. Volume II.* The Hereford Times Limited, 1914. p. 513.

223 *Newcastle Courant.* 15 September 1739. p. 1.

224 *Derby Mercury.* 11 January 1733. p. 2.

225 *General Evening Post.* 31 March–2 April 1774. p. 4.

226 *Derby Mercury.* 20 February 1746 p. 4.

himself." Greatrex swears he will not stay one night. True to his word, "he fled before morning."[227]

In the capital, the *Westminster Journal* is advising servants on the correct way of replying to their master if he asks how well he played at football: "Chuse not to be pressed for an Answer, than to give one that must be either displeasing to the Querist, or insincere in Himself. And if he was only to pay a formal Compliment after the Match was over, without being questioned at all, he would chuse to congratulate him on receiving no Damage, and coming fairly off, or to entertain him with the Recital of any pleasing News; and not to mention his want of Skill or Conduct, when perhaps the Gentleman, for his Part, was alone very well pleased with both."[228]

227 Hutton, W., *The History of Derby*. Nichols, Son, and Bentley, London, 1817. p. 39.

228 *Newcastle Courant*. 31 March 1759. p. 2.

CHAPTER THIRTEEN
1700–1799 II

Cricket stumbles across the seventeenth century, an orphan offshoot no one takes seriously. Yet here he is. His masterly plan bypassed the tedious apprenticeship, the slavish courtesies, the laboured ascent. Ingenious in its simplicity, he had executed it flawlessly. "The plan, you ask?" he says, addressing the air. "Adoption by aristocrats, of course." With a flourish of his hand, he steps back, bends graciously low, straightens. Time to make his presence felt.

In 1705, the *Post Man and The Historical Account* announces a ban on cricket and football on Walworth Common without the consent of the lord of the manor.[1] The same page reports that a thief is sought for a guinea reward, apply at *The Naked Boy and 7 Stars*; a druggist sells tea, coffee, chocolate, and the Jesuit Bark that Cromwell spurned; and a French silversmith makes and sets artificial teeth. Overleaf, two "flushing capers" capture a richly laden French ship; the annual fast day "to implore the blessing of God upon her Majesty's Arms" passes; and a day of celebration takes place in Dorchester with bonfires, bells, illuminations, and fireworks.

There are around fifty references to cricket before the seventeenth century. One is in 1622. A company of parishioners are in trouble "for playing at cricket in the churchyard" of Boxgrove, Sussex. They have already been warned "for three special reasons … secondly for that they use to breake the church-windowes with the ball; and thirdly, for that a little child had like to have her braynes beaten out of her head with a cricket batt."[2] The parishioners playing "Crickit" beside Richard Culmer's door, c1640, is another reference; so too the rarely cited mention in the fictional dialogue between an Englishman and a Dutchman in 1699.[3]

The same 1598 Anglo–Italian dictionary that defines *palloniero* as "a footeball maker", defines both *sgrillare* and *fare frit frit* as "to play cricket-a-

---

1 *The Post Man and The Historical Account*. 3–5 July 1705. p. 2.

2 Hair, P. (ed.), *Before the Bawdy Court*. Paul Elek, London, 1972. p. 100.

3 Puckle, J., *England's Way to Wealth and Honour: In a Dialogue between an English-man and a Dutch-man*. Sam Crouch, London, 1699. p. 25.

wicket, and be merry."[4] Notably, it also defines *tarabara* as "higledi-pigledie, helter-skelter, cricket-a-wicket." Caution is needed. To be as merry as a cricket is a contemporary saying, and the book gives an alternative, onomatopoeic, definition of *sgrillare* as, "to make a noise as a cricket." Cricket-a-wicket's link to the game is dubious. Legal proceedings the same year are more reliable as a first reference to cricket. A fifty-year-old witness recalls how as "a Scholar in the free Schoole of Guldeford, he and several of his fellowes did runne and play there at Crekett and other Plaies And also that the same was used for the Baytinge of Beares in the said Comon."[5] Children enter free schools aged seven and leave at fourteen, putting the possible dates he played cricket from 1555 to 1562, later than the received date of c1550. Nevertheless, Guildford, Surrey, remains the cradle of cricket. Or does it?

What may be the earliest reference to cricket is often disregarded. In 1562, two men in Malden, Essex, are charged with "playing an unlawful game called 'clycett'."[6] What makes Malden so intriguing is that three of the five earliest stoolball games on record—1564, 1583, and 1623—are played there, one within two years of the clycett match. Is clycett cricket? Other than Malden, there is precious little evidence to connect cricket and stoolball. A c1748 book of Lancashire dialect defines *crickit* as "a small stool",[7] a term repeated in several contemporary dictionaries, including as *cracket* in *A Glossary of North Country Words, in Use* in 1825.[8] "Cricket" is defined as a low stool as early as 1685, and is used as such in a translation of Rabelais in 1653.[9,10] Francis Willughby's 1672 account of stoolball mentions only one stool and no bats.[11] A bat is mentioned in 1733 and two stools in 1755.[12,13] By that time, cricket is well established.

---

4 Florio, G. (ed.)., *A VVorlde of Wordes*. Arnold Hatfield, London, 1598. p. 370.

5 *Guild Merchant and Court Leet book*. Exploring Surrey's Past: https://www.exploringsurreyspast.org.uk/collections/getrecord/SHCOL_BR_PART1_3_1_1_7. Accessed 15 September 2023.

6 Benham, W.G., *Essex Borough Arms and the Traditional Arms of Essex and the Arms of Chelmsford Diocese*. Benham and Company, Colchester, 1916. pp. 22–23.

7 Collier, J., *A View of the Lancashire Dialect; by Way of Dialogue*. James Lister, Leeds, c1748. n.p.

8 Brockett, J.T. (ed.)., *A Glossary of North Country Words, in Use*. T. and J. Hodgson, Newcastle Upon Tyne, 1825. p. 47.

9 Meriton, G., *Nomenclature Clericalis*. s.n., London, 1685. p. 299.

10 *The Works of Mr Francis Rabelais*. 2 Vols. s.n., London, 1653. Vol. 2. p. 325.

11 Beharry, S., *The Prehistories of Baseball*. McFarland & Company, Jefferson, North Carolina, 2016. p. 182.

12 Ibid.

13 Block, D., *Baseball Before We Knew It: A Search for the Roots of the Game*. University of Nebraska Press, Lincoln, Nebraska, 2005. p. 112.

A bat and *two* stools are absent from other contemporary descriptions of stoolball, and while cricket is about to blast-off, stoolball's glory days are over by 1720. Are stoolball and clycett synonyms or separate games? Did one branch off from the other? It is unlikely they are unrelated. If clycett *is* cricket, did cricket takes its cue from stoolball and develop its own idiosyncrasies, later to be adopted by stoolball?

That the term "cricket" may derive from *cricce*, the Anglo-Saxon word for staff, is unlikely, as the term cricket has only been in use since the sixteenth century. By the close of the fourteenth century, the Hertfordshire town of Hitchin has a number of pastime-related place names: Pitcher Pightle, Nine Corners, Morris Dell, Reel Place, and Clicketts, Closh, and Cock Closes.[14] Closes are closed fields to play games in; camping closes are an obvious example. If *clicketts* is a ball game, its obscure origins are fourteenth century. It may be a stick and ball game given that a Scottish dialect dictionary defines a "clickett-staff" as a hooked staff.[15] A poem c1533, wrongly attributed to John Skelton, is touted as evidence of a link between the Flemish game of *colven* and cricket.[16] Four of the two and a half thousand lines purportedly rail against Flemish merchants:

> O lorde of ipocrites
> Nowe shut upp your wickettes,
> And clape to your clickettes,
> A farewell, kinge of crekettes![17]

Wickettes, clickettes, creckettes. Cricket. Appealing as this may be, the entire poem is a relentless invective against the Catholic Church; Protestant Flemings go unmentioned. In this context, *clickette* means latch,[18] *wickette* is a small gate, and *clape* means to slam shut.[19] Papist

14 Hine, R.L., *The History of Hitchin*. George Allen & Unwin Ltd., London, 1929. p. 241.

15 Warrack, A. (ed.)., *A Scots Dialect Dictionary*. W. & R. Chambers, Edinburgh, 1911. p. 89.

16 Narayanan, N., *Cricket was imported from Belgium?* https://www.espncricinfo.com/story/cricket-was-imported-from-belgium-614547. Accessed 26 January 2024.

17 Dyce, A., *The Poetical Works of John Skelto*n. 2 Vols. Thomas Rodd, London, 1843. Vol. 2. *The Image of Ipocrysy*. p. 435.

18 Ibid, Note. 43.

19 Both Chaucer (*The Merchant's Tale*) and Tusser (*Five Hundred Points of Good Husbandry*—1573) rhyme cricket and wicket suggestively, in the context of a latch and gate. In *The Magnetick Lady* (1640) Ben Jonson writes, "Had I the keeping of your daughter's clicket, in charge?"

clergy are being told to clear off. And kinge of *creckettes*? The Pope rules over a chirruping army of priests. A play on cricketing terms is improbable. Skelton does write the *The Bowge of Court.* A line of unintentional smut also argues against cricket: "and lytell prety Cate, How ofte he knocked at her klycked-gate."[20] One possibility arises. Does a cricketing wicket represent a small gate? One a stranger must not pass?

If *crekettes* is colloquial for the Flemish stick and ball game *colven*, it makes sense that the word cricket is associated etymologically. *Met de krik ketsen* is Flemish for "chase a ball with a stick", a game played in the Low Countries since the Middle Ages, with *krik* Middle Flemish for stick.[21] *Krik ketsen.* Cricket. A 1647 Dutch–English dictionary, printed in the Netherlands but written by an Englishman, defines *kolven* as "to Bandy a Ball, *or* to play at Bandy."[22] It is not until 1724 that *kolven* is defined as "to play at Gaff [golf] or Cricket".[23] It is found within a *Short guide to the English Language*, written by a Netherlander. It is noteworthy that an early reference to cricket calls it *krickett*; more crucially, it is used to describe the earliest example of cricket played overseas. On 6 May 1676, naval chaplain Henry Teonge records in his diary: "at the least 40 of the English … rod out of the cytty [Aleppo in Syria, then part of the Ottoman Empire] about 4 miles to the Greene Platte, a fine vally by a river syde, to recreate them selves … we had severall pastimes and sports, as duck-hunting, fishing, shooting, hand-ball, krickett, scrofilo."[24,25]

Clicket (as Clicketts Close) is first heard of in Hitchin, Hertfordshire, in the late fourteenth century.[26] Is it a Flemish import? If so, is it a separate game to *kolven* or a colloquialism? Edward III invites Flemish

20 Dyce, A., *The Poetical Works of John Skelton*. 2 Vols. Thomas Rodd, London, 1843. Vol. 1. *The Bowge of Court.* lns 370–371.

21 Luitzen, J., Delhere, P., *Wicket Game: The (Re-) Introduction of Cricket in the Netherlands, 1724–1883.* The International Journal of the History of Sport, 2015, 32:2, p. 185.

22 Hexham, H., *A Copious English and Netherdutch Dictionary.* The Widow of Arnold Leers, Rotterdam, 1675. n.p.

23 Luitzen, J., Delhere, P., *Wicket Game: The (Re-) Introduction of Cricket in the Netherlands, 1724–1883.* The International Journal of the History of Sport, 2015, 32:2, p. 186.

24 Teonge, H., *The Diary of Henry Teonge.* S. and R. Bentley, London, 1825. p. 159.

25 No one has been able to determine the game of scrofilo.

26 Hitchin is said to be the location for the of Council of Clovesho, in 747, during which the Archbishop of Canterbury banned games in the lead up to Ascension Day. In: Wilkins, D. (ed.), *Concilia Magnae Britanniae et Hiberniae.* 4 Vols. R. Gosling, F. Gyles, T. Woodward, C. Davis, London, 1737. Vol. 1. p. 97.

textile workers to England in 1331. Most settle in the second half of the century, many in London, thirty miles south of Hitchin. The spread of any Flemish sport is unknown. When cricket develops three hundred years later, it is the counties south of London—Surrey, Kent, and Sussex—who take the lead, well away from Hertfordshire, but close to where the London Flemish settle. It would make sense that any stickball game the Flemish introduce would spread from London, where the majority settle. Perhaps their game has a small English following, equating to the rarity of the term, and the local game evolves into cricket, in nature and in name.

The next clear reference to *clickets* is in in 1562, when John Porter and his servant play "an unlawful game called 'clycett'."[27] The offence is recorded in the Malden Corporation Book,[28] the Essex town that features those early stoolball games. The county borders London to the west and the early cricketing county of Kent to the south. Malden, however, is a coastal town in the east of the county, well away from future cricketing counties; in fact, it is just south of the arbitrary division of Essex into north and south, demarcating football and camping territory.[29] There is a twist. In 1565, Flemish, Walloon, and Dutch families settle in numbers in Norwich in Norfolk and Colchester in Essex.[30] By 1582, one third of the population of Norwich is made up of migrants.[31] Of the three nations, Colchester hosts more Flemish, though there are plenty of Dutch.[32] Did the Dutch bring *kolven*, and the Flemish clicket? Malden is only twelve miles from Colchester.

There are earlier Flemish migrations. At the time of the Domesday book, in 1086, the greatest density of settlement is along the Northamptonshire–Bedfordshire border.[33] Many settle in Hertfordshire, which also borders Bedfordshire. The overall shape of settlement is

---

27 Bateman, A., *Cricket, Literature, and Culture*. Routledge, Abingdon, Oxon, 2009. p. 17.

28 Ibid, p. 17.

29 Benham, W.G., *Essex Borough arms and the traditional arms of Essex and the arms of Chelmsford diocese*. Bonham and Company, Colchester, 1916. p. 23.

30 Luu, L.B., *Immigrants and the Industries of London, 1500–1700*. Routledge, Abingdon, Oxon, 2016. p. 71.

31 Ibid, p. 73.

32 Ibid, p. 74.

33 Oksanen, E., *Flanders and the Anglo-Norman World, 1066–1216*. Cambridge University Press, 2012. p. 189.

"a lopsided crescent. One end lies in south-western England, at the border of Devon and Somerset,"[34] where Cornish hurling is played. The Flemish are also settled in an area of Wales by Henry I, c1108: "The Flemings were first or second generation immigrants … by uprooting large chunks of the Anglo-Flemish population and by confining them in a far corner of the Welsh marches he ensured that the Flemings were in no position to cause him trouble."[35] That far corner of Wales is Pembrokeshire.[36] The home of *knappan*. The Flemish settle around Haverford West, the largest town in Pembrokeshire. The reason this area of the county is called Little England Beyond Wales is not because of Norman settlers, but because of the Flemings. Flemish is still spoken there at the end of the sixteenth century. *Knappan* is unheard of before the Flemish move in. While the stickball game *kolven* almost certainly influences any existing ball games, the Flemings "frequently clashed with the native Welsh, either under Anglo-Norman command or as independent forces."[37] Neither is *knappan* considered a stickball game. There are also clear differences between the two, not least that *knappan* has mounted players, who alone are allowed to carry "monstrouse cudgells, of iii foote and half longe."[38]

A 1611 English–French dictionary holds an intriguing entry. *Crosse* is described as "a Cricket-staffe; or the crooked staffe wherewith boyes play at cricket."[39] It adds definitions for both *Crosser* and *Crocer*: "To play at Cricket." The three constitute the third mention of cricket in history. It is inarguable that cricket evolves from a stick and ball game—early cricket bats were crooked for one thing—quite when it establishes itself and the name becomes particular to the game appears to be at the beginning of the seventeenth century. It could be decades later. Wicket in the sense of cricket is unheard of before 1646. A 1739 etching designed by engraver Hubert-François Gravelot confirms the bat shape. One boy with a curved stick stands in front of a rudimentary wicket, comprising

34 Ibid, p. 188.

35 Ibid, p. 214.

36 Ibid, p. 213.

37 Ibid, p. 214.

38 Owen, G., *The Description of Pembrokeshire*. Early nineteenth century transcript of the 1603 manuscript. pp. 288–293. Casgliad y Werin Cymru: https://www.peoplescollection.wales/items/9156#?xywh=-588%2C-100%2C2230%2C1999. Accessed 15 May 2023

39 Cotgrave, R. (ed.), *A Dictionarie of the French and English Tongues*. Adam Islip, London, 1611. n.p.

two six-inch stumps, a foot apart, surmounted by a crosspiece.[40] The boy has readied himself to strike the ball, another boy is about to bowl underarm. A wicketkeeper kneels behind the wicket; a second batsman with a curved stick stands beside him. Two other boys stand with their arms out, ready to catch an errant ball. The etching is considered to depict a French game but is almost certainly the earliest depiction of cricket. Gravelot is French, the etching is not. He lives in England from 1732 to 1745 and makes the impression in 1739.[41] It is an early game of cricket in an English pastoral setting. Other contemporary paintings of cricket also depict a curved bat;[42] it is not until the second half of the eighteenth century that it approximates to the modern bat.

Only twenty-nine organised cricket matches are known to have been played between 1610 and 1726. The first two do not make the papers. The full advert for the fourth, in 1700, has not been reprinted since 1896: "These are to inform Gentlemen, or others, who delight in Cricket-playing, That a Match at Cricket, of 10. gentlemen on each side, will be Play'd on Clapham-Common near Fox-Hall, on Easter-Monday next, for 10 l. [pounds] a Head each Game, (five being design'd) and 20 1. the Odd one: And after that Diversion is ended, any Maid may Run for a fine Flanders Lac'd Smock, Value 4 1. they being to start exactly at Three from the Watch-House. There will be likewise an Entertainment Gratis, as soon as the abovementioned Recreations are ended."[43]

Cricket can strut, and does. It has become the main event. Literature contains some early references. In 1701, a lawyer's client "is banded about like a Cricket-ball, till they have beat out all his Estate."[44] The same year, *A Rod for Tunbridge Beaus* pours scorn on this "foppish Crew" who excel at sport and vanity:

---

40 *Children are playing cricket with a bat and ball; others are skipping in the background.* Wellcome Collection: https://wellcomecollection.org/works/cvfu99ax/items. Accessed 8 March 2024.

41 The etching itself was executed by Jacques Bacheley, who produced two similar works, *Le Jeu de la Crosse* (*The Game of Soule*) and *Le Jeu de Quilles* (*The Game of Bowls*).

42 *Cricket on the Artillery Ground, Finsbury*, painted in 1743 by Francis Hayman—an associate of Gravelot's—has the same curved stick and stumpy wicket. In the foreground, a man keeps score with a tally stick. The wicketkeeper is said to be William Hogarth. See also, *The Game of Cricket*, unknown painter: https://wellcomecollection.org/works/mk3qn3kc. Accessed 28 July 2023.

43 *The Post Boy*, 28–30 March. 1700, p. 2.

44 Baker, T., *The Humour of the Age*. s.n., London, 1701. p. 22.

At Nine-pins lies his Excellence,
He out-bowls most that use the Place,
And Tips All-Nine with such a grace …
At Trap-ball too he plays most finely,
And handles Cat-stick so divinely …
It's true he can at Cricket play,
With any living at this day:
And fling a Coit, or toss a Bar,
With any Driver of a Car.[45]

Of far more importance is a 1706 Latin poem. *In Certamen Pilae* contains the first known description of cricket.[46,47] Momentous and unparalleled, it contains more words than all forty-six previous cricket references combined. Rarely read, it deserves its day:

"When spring comes, and the most serene weather smiles forth, and the charm of the green grass encourages fast running over a flat field, a select band of youths, armed with curved bats that an ingenious hand has polished into game-ready form, heads joyfully down into the field. Each has his own talent: this one is more suited to hot-footing it across the ground, and to keeping a close eye out as he goes up and down in every direction in various ways; that one is more skilled at hurling the ball through the air from afar and breaking the headwind; a third is outstripped by no-one else in his skill at launching the ball, with careful balance of his hand, over the flat ground in order to steal a blow by its rapid course.

"The opposing team welcome their arrival with cheerful greetings … soon they are starting arguments and cordial bickering because each wants to impose his own rules on the game. Nestor, whose hoary old age secures the respect of the crowd and the leave to speak, enters into the thickly-packed locals to discharge the role of a fair judge; and although he has long since laid down his rustic tools and enjoyed his old age, he has not forgotten the skill so proposes fair rules and calms down their anger. Then they point out the place where an even surface spreads out flat; on this side and that stumps are erected and driven into the ground directly

45 Anon., *A Rod for Tunbridge Beaus*. s.n., London, 1701. pp. 6–7.

46 Goldwin, W., *Musae Juveniles*. A. Balwyn, London, 1706. pp. 9–12.

47 Lit. *Competition Ball*. In English called *The Cricket Game*.

opposite each other, rising to two points with a small gap separating them once upright; then a white bail is placed on them, the bail on which the doubtful contest rests and which demands defending well: a leather ball hurtles with aggressive force, which if wicked fortune directs it straight, and the device collapses, snatched from its supports, you would lay down your weapons and leave ingloriously.

"The two umpires stand in their appropriate positions, leaning on their bats, which the rules stipulate should be touched with clear contact, or we'll waste the empty effort of running. In another place, where a clear vantage point exists, two loyal-hearted men sit on a small hill, ready to incise the growing score into wood with their penknives. Then the competitors count on their fingers an equal number of people, while standing in a line: a coin flies up into the air as the arbiter, deciding whether the first innings should be played by this team or the other. Once the signal is given, a greased ball thrown with force flies headlong from its trap, and flying over the top of the ground it sweeps its rapid course. The Opposition leans over with bended knee and watches the fast footsteps of the running ball, seeing whether it leaps up, then at once he drives into the certain impact, twisting his arms with swift power, propelling the ringing ball far. It flies through the upper air, rushing with a constant whistle as it cleaves the sky.

"But the clever fielder who is keeping watch of the high heavens prepares his ambush and leaps up to catch the falling ball with palms outstretched—and he throws it back with a triumphant hand. Hereon follows a happy cheer, while anguish falls over those who silently grieve the fate of their unfortunate friend. A huge loss! But, with this one man removed, there's another man at hand … scarcely has the ball made three or four passes, scarcely had it felt three hits from the opposition, when suddenly it was hurled with headlong force and snatched the light bail from its place, thus eluding the threat."[48]

Batters and bowlers and fielders and umpires, and wickets and bails and a leather ball. And rules. They grease the bowl to generate swing,[49]

48 Antigone Journal: https://antigonejournal.com/2022/09/certamen-pilae-cricket/. Accessed 15 September 2023.

49 The forerunner of sucking on sweets. Sweet saliva prolongs conventional swing on an ageing ball: Scobie, J.A., Shelley, W.P., Jackson, R.W., Hughes, S.P., Lock, G.D., *Practical Perspective of Cricket Ball Swing*. Journal of Sports Engineering and Technology, 2020, 234:1, p. 70.

tally the score with notches in sticks, and toss a coin to decide who is in. It is the earliest mention of recording runs by any means in history.

In addition to the twenty-nine known matches from 1610 to 1726, a further nine matches or advertisements are presented. In 1710, "In Lambs Conduit Fields on Tuesday next being the 25th of April, will be play'd a Match at Cricket, and so continue every Tuesday, Thursday and Saturday, at the Duke of Ormond's Head near Lamb's Conduit Fields."[50] There is no record of the outcome, though a book confirms that from 1710, "Matches at Cricket were played for many years on Tuesdays, Thursdays, and Saturdays, at the Duke of Ormond's Head near Lamb's Conduit-fields."[51] While only eleven cricket games prior to the advert are known of, the report suggests a swathe of unknown matches. A novel Sabbath game is reported in an anonymous 1712 broadsheet.[52] A duke and a lord find several boys playing cricket. "When I went to Eaton School I understood this game better than my book," says the lord, implying cricket was played at Eton in the seventeenth century. They choose the two best players, a crown apiece, "and Twelve-pence to a third Boy to knotch the Game down exact." The lord's boy whispers that if he doubles it to ten shillings, he will get both out quickly. The lord agrees and wins the 20 gns bet.

A match is reported in August 1718: "plaid at Farnborough, 15 Miles off, between 12 chosen Gamesters of the City of London, for a Guinea each Man; and the same Number of the Town of Tunbridge; the Londoners were worsted, and a great deal of Money was won and lost in Wagers."[53] It is the first known cricket match played in Hampshire, and the second oldest with a result. A known match is worth mentioning. In May 1719, the *Weekly Journal* reports that: "A Tryal was brought at Guildhall … between two Companies of Cricket Players, the Men of Kent Plaintiffs, and the Men of London, Defendants, for Sixty Pounds played for at Cricket, and after a long Hearing, and near 200l. expended in the Cause, my Lord not understanding the Game, ordered them to play it over again; and they met accordingly on Monday last in

---

50 *The British Mercury*. 24 April 1710. p. 2.

51 Malcolm, J.P., *Anecdotes of the Manners and Customs of London during the Eighteenth Century*. Longman, Hurst, Rees, and Orme, London, 1810. p. 126.

52 Anon., *The Devil and the Peers*. s.n., London, 1712. Single page.

53 *The Weekly Journal*. 23 August 1718. p. 5.

Lamb's-Conduit-Fields, but one of the Players being taken ill, it was deferred till another opportunity."[54,55] London win the rematch.

A fourth game takes place in Smitham Bottom, near Croydon, Surrey, in 1722. It only makes the papers, as it concerns an argument between a player and his long-term partner before the game. He throws himself into the match "being one of the head Gamesters."[56] They make up, and he takes her to London … where she makes off with a dashing captain. In July 1723, Pope Innocent XIII grants Sir Humphry Wildair dispensation "to set up a Bear Garden, and to License Cricket Playing" in Rome, "both of which were prohibited by his Holiness's Predecessors."[57] A month later, Sir Humphry imports "a great Number of batts, and other Utensils for Cricket Playing."[58] The first known game of cricket in Italy follows, during the Papal interregnum of April 1724: during "a late noted Match of Cricket playing … Sir Humphry and Col. Rob. Roy, being Partners, were Jocky'd, and lost the game by Four Strokes only; which has so much inrag'd both … Sir Humphry swears he'll venture no more Rubs at that Game."[59] It is the first known match in continental Europe, and only the third outside England.[60]

In August 1723, "Whereas a Match at Crecket is agreed to be play'd between the Parish of Dartford in Kent, and the Parish of Croydon in the county of Surry, for a Guinea per Man, to be play'd at Dartford Brinth, on Thursday the 15th of August Instant."[61] There are no earlier reports of matches between teams from Kent and Surrey. The seventh match is advertised in London's *Daily Post* on 25 March 1724: "To be play'd on Thursday next in Hyde Park for a considerable Sum of Money by Persons of Quality."[62] The eighth is also in 1724: "The Hon. Sir William Gage, Bart. At West Firle in the County of Sussex, with his servants and 3 Others, are to play at Cricket upon Spittle-Hill, within half a Mile of

54 *The Weekly Journal*. 16 May 1719. p. 142.

55 Ten years' wages for a skilled tradesman.

56 *Applebee's Journal*. 22 September 1722. p. 3.

57 *The Flying Post*. 20 July 1723. p. 1.

58 *The Flying Post*. 15 August 1723. p. 5.

59 *The Flying Post*. 16 April 1724. p. 1.

60 Turkey in 1676, and India in 1721.

61 *The Weekly Journal*. 10 August 1723. p. 4.

62 *Daily Post*. 25 March 1724. p. 2.

the Town of Lewes against the remarkable and famous Club of Bowney, giving the said Club the Liberty of picking three Gamesters within the Liberty of Sussex, to mend their set of Gamesters. It is to be play'd on the 19th Day of May … The Match is for a hundred Guineas."[63] The only two known matches of 1725 are both played by Sir William, an early patron of the sport. There is no Bowney in Sussex. It is probably a misspelling of Bolney, which lies sixteen miles from Firle. Sir William Gage's XI and the Club of Bowney/Bolney are two of the earliest known clubs. Only ten precede them.[64] The final unearthed match, in 1726, advertised as taking place that day, pits "some Gamesters of London and Riverhead in Kent, for a purse of 110 guineas."[65] Other countries struggle with the convoluted rules. In 1728, de Saussure, the Swiss traveller who spoke of the dangers of English football writes: "The English are very fond of a game they call cricket. For this purpose, they go into a large open field, and knock a small ball about with a piece of wood."[66] To be fair, he adds: "I will not attempt to describe this game to you, it is too complicated; but it requires agility and skill."

Cricket news is scarce in the first two decades of the seventeenth century; among them, in a 1704 newspaper, an "Honest Countryman" suggests that the rules of war should follow the rules of "Crecket or Foot-Ball."[67] The 1720s are a little better: an upcoming fair is expected to have cricket and stoolball;[68] a wanted butcher is arrested playing cricket;[69] two footpads "are apprehended playing at Cricket in Moorfields";[70] and the third of the famous Kent–Sussex games of 1728 makes the papers. The "eleven of a side of each county" is played in Kent for 50 gns. Kent score fifty-two, Sussex forty-five.[71] A novelty match makes the 1727 news. Fourteen men play at Cranbrook in Kent. The youngest is

63 *The Evening Post*. 25 April 1724. p. 4.

64 Sir William Gage's XI is erroneously believed to have been established in 1725. The current Bolney Cricket Club claim to have arisen in 1840. The Club of Bowney reference is the only one known to an earlier club.

65 *Parker's Penny Post*. 11 July 1726. p. 3.

66 Madame Van Muyden., *A Foreign View of England in the Reigns of George I. & George II.* John Murray, London, 1902. p. 295.

67 *The Observator*. 19–22 July 1704. p. 1.

68 *Weekly Journal*. 4 June 1720. p. 5.

69 *Newcastle Courant*. 18 May 1723. p. 9.

70 *Stamford Mercury*. 1 April 1725. p. 139.

71 *Ipswich Journal*. 3 August 1728. p. 2.

seventy-two, the oldest eighty-four.[72] It is notable as being one of the first cricket reports to include players' names.[73] The following month, the first known rules of the game are written down as sixteen articles for a match between the 2nd Duke of Richmond and Alan Brodrick.

From the mid-1700s, cricket explodes in popularity. Newspaper references across the next two decades are legion, but several exhumed articles merit inclusion. In July 1727, Edwin Stead's side "very speedily" dismissed "The Duke of Richmond and his club."[74] They meet again at Coxheath, Kent, on Tuesday 2 July 1728, "for a large sum of money"; a rematch of a known game played on Friday 25 June at the same venue.[75] Like Gage, Stead and Richmond are notable patrons of the game. At Hyde Park, on 21 April 1730, the duke is at it again, battling the Duke of Devonshire, the Earl of Albemarle, Lord Cavendish, and a dozen others. They are to have a rematch the following week for 100 gns.[76]

On Tuesday 23 September 1735, "a Cricket Match was plaid on Kennington Common, between the Gentlemen of London and the Gentlemen of the Borough Side of the Water [Surrey], which was won by the former; and on Wednesday next the same Gentlemen are to play in the Artillery Ground, near Moor Fields, the Wickets to be pitch'd by Twelve o'Clock."[77] It is a busy few months. That July, the Prince of Wales and Lord Middlesex play two famous matches for a thousand-pound wager, watched by thousands.[78] When the Prince's team lose the second match by an innings, he stumps off in a huff: "Tis said his Royal Highness lost 500l. besides the 1000l. with the Earl of Middlesex."[79,80] There is worse than losing money: "there was a surprizing Multitude of people present, and a great deal of Mischief was done, some falling from their Horses, others being rode over, &c. and one man was carried off dead."[81] A more notable death the following month, Edwin Stead, aged thirty-five. It is

72 *Derby Mercury*. 15 June 1727. p. 3.

73 A similar match in Gravesend, Kent was advertised in 1737: *Derby Mercury*. 19 May 1737. p. 1.

74 *Derby Mercury*. 11 July 1727. p. 3.

75 *Newcastle Courant*. 29 June 1728. p. 1.

76 *Kentish Weekly Post*. 25 April 1730. p. 3.

77 *Ipswich Journal*. 27 September 1735. p. 3.

78 *Newcastle Courant*. 2 August 1735. p. 2.

79 *Newcastle Courant*. 9 August 1735. p. 1.

80 £1,500 was worth 300 horses or sixty-seven years' wages for a skilled tradesman.

81 *General Evening Post*. 29–31 July 1735. p. 1.

unknown if the prince's team play better in a July 1737 match between William Gage's Sussex and his own side, comprising "the Noblemen and Gentlemen that generally play in Hyde-Park; and will be played in a few Days at Kew-Green or Mouldsey-Hurst."[82] He probably lost: "The Odds are already on the Sussex side." He quickly chases his losses. On 14 July, in another unknown match, he meets the Duke of Marlborough's side in Kew, "for a considerable Sum."[83] He wins.

Some rediscovered matches are droll. Kennington Common is the venue for "a great Match at Cricket … between the Gentlemen of the Hon. Lumber Troop (headed by their Colonel) and the Gentlemen who frequently meet at the Essex-Head … for a very considerable Sum of Money."[84] The Lumber Troop is a gentlemen's club, and their opposition, whose home is a pub on the Strand, is likely to be one too. In 1747, the east Sussex town of Rye hosts a game between the crews of the Swallow and the Royal Oak, twenty-two sailors for a 100 gns a side. Ahead at lunch, and with "liquor being plenty, the Swallow's men, at least the majority of them got very drunk."[85] They lose the game.

The most titillating cricket news for contemporary readers is in a Puritan pamphlet of 1712. Four young men are playing near Maidenhead when "there rose out of the Ground a Man in Black with a Cloven-Foot, which put them in a great Consternation; but as they stood in the Frighted Condition, the Devil flew up in the Air, in a Dark Cloud with Flashes of fire, and in his Room [place] he left a very Beautiful Woman, and Robert Yates and Richard Moors hastily stepping up to her, being Charm'd with her Beauty went to kiss her, but in the Attempt they instantly fell down Dead. The other two, Simon Jackson and George Grantham, seeing this Tragical Sight, ran home to Maiden-Head, where they now lye in a Distracted Condition."[86] A brutal takedown of London's working class is printed in 1720: "The Holidays coming on … whole Shoals … will be flocking thither, to the utter Destruction of Stuff'd Beef, Gammon of Bacon, Cheesecake, Bottle-Ale and Cyder … The Fields will swarm

82 *Newcastle Courant*. 2 July 1737. p. 2.

83 *Newcastle Courant*. 23 July 1737. p. 2.

84 *Weekly Rehearsal*. 18 September 1732. p. 2.

85 *Boston Evening-Post*. 23 November 1747. p. 4.

86 Anon., *The sabbath-breakers*. In: Bateman, A., (eds.)., *Cricket, Literature and Culture*. Routledge, Abingdon, Oxon, 2016. p. 18.

with Butchers Wives, and Oyster-Women, known by wadling Gates, and Gold Chains … with their snotty Offspring, whilst their Spouses and Sweethearts are sweating at Ninepins, some at Cricket, others at Stool-Ball."[87]

Lamb's Conduit Fields is soon eclipsed as a venue by White Conduit Fields, near Islington. After a handful of cricket matches at White Conduit Fields, 1719–c1780, cricket enthusiasts from the Old Artillery Ground in Finsbury begin to play there regularly.[88] Around 1785, the White Conduit Club comes into existence.[89] It is the club's home until May 1787, when the club moves to what is now known as Lord's Old Ground, in Marylebone.[90] Within months, the club disbands. Marylebone Cricket Club rises from the ashes and remains at Lord's Old Ground until 1810, when it moves a half-mile to Lord's Middle Ground, in Regent's Park.[91] In 1814, it moves another half-mile to the present-day Lord's Cricket Ground.

~

North American cricket is bashful. Eighteenth century references are scant; after the first (from what will become the United States), in April 1709, there is a twenty-eight-year gap before the next one, and only twenty-one in all. Several new references have been found. While there are reports of British soldiers and sailors playing cricket in Canada from the mid-1700s, the earliest known reference to Canadians and cricket is a match played near Montréal, in 1785.[92] On 4 September 1783, however, the *Victoria Daily Standard* reports: "Yesterday a gala day for Victoria, and the citizens turned out en masse to witness the review of marines … the scene of the action was the cricket ground at Colwood."[93] The existence of the ground implies that cricket has been played there for some years.

---

87 *Weekly Journal or British Gazetteer*. 4 June 1720. p. 5.

88 Altham, H.S., *A History of Cricket*. Allen & Unwin, London, 1948. p. 53.

89 The exact year is unknown, but the club's first recorded game was on 20 June 1785, beating the Gentlemen of Kent by 304 runs. In: Altham, H.S., *A History of Cricket*. Allen & Unwin, London, 1948. p. 53.

90 The site of the old ground is now Dorset Square, Marylebone.

91 Grace, W.G., *The Classic Guide to Cricket*. Amberley Publishing, Stroud, Gloucestershire, 2014. p. 22.

92 *ESPNCricInfo*. https://www.espncricinfo.com/story/cricket-in-canada-a-historical-review-106282. Accessed 28 December 2023.

93 *Victoria Daily Standard*. 4 September 1783. p. 3.

Another find are adverts for cricket bats and balls aimed at cricket clubs.[94] They appear in 1787 issues of *The Pennsylvania Packet.* An August edition carries a report of an unknown cricket match in New York. It is only the third recorded cricket score in United States history:[95] "Last Monday a match commenced on the Race Ground, by 11 gentlemen of the Cricket Club, against 11 approved good players of the city; for want of daylight it was not finished till late last evening when the notches stood." The club scored eighty-two and one hundred and one, the "approved" players fifty-one and one hundred and one. It adds, "Last night a match for a considerable sum at Cricket, was agreed upon, to be played on 1st of September, by the natives of New York … against those of Great Britain and Ireland, at this time also resident in the city." There is history here. The paper is co-owned by John Dunlap, the first publisher to print copies of the Declaration of Independence in 1776. Further, the month after the cricket report, Congress chooses *The Pennsylvania Packet* to publish the United States Constitution.[96,97] Cricket is convinced he has struck gold in the United States when Benjamin Franklin, one of the Founding Fathers of the country and a signatory of the Declaration of Independence, returns from England with a set of rules.[98]

An advertisement in New York's *Daily Advertiser*, in July 1790, reads: "On Tuesday the 13th inst. will be played a game of cricket, on the old cricket ground behind Delancey's house, between 2 and 3 o'clock. Any gentlemen who wish to partake of the amusement, will please to attend, there being a few wanting to complete the match."[99] A fifth discovery, from Connecticut, in 1791, reads: "The patrons of that manly and athletic exercise … whose nerves are not yet unstrung, from the age of 30 to 60, are invited to appear upon the Cricket Ground, in front of the Court House."[100] It adds, referencing the War of Independence, "it

94 *The Pennsylvania Packet.* 22 May 1787. p. 3.

95 *The Pennsylvania Packet.* 18 August 1787. pp. 2–3.

96 Vile, J.R., *The Declaration of Independence.* ABC-CLIO©, Santa Barbara, California, 2019. p. xlii.

97 Washington, G., *Constitution for the United States of America. The Pennsylvania Packet.* 19 September 1787. pp. 1–4.

98 Ryczek, W.J., *Baseball's First Innings.* McFarland and Company, Jefferson, North Carolina, 2009. p. 101.

99 *The Daily Advertiser.* 13 July 1790. p. 3.

100 *Litchfield Monitor.* 18 May 1791. p. 3.

is presumed the nervous Old Veterans will carry off the prize." Seven years later, in Litchfield, Connecticut, "*Twenty-five* Students, and other young Gentlemen, challenge an equal Number of married Gentlemen, to meet them on the Green on Friday next, at one o'Clock, in a *match* at CRICKET."[101]

In 1794, members of the New York Cricket Club are requested to "attend precisely at ten o'clock this morning, on the usual ground."[102] The club inserts regular notices across the following years, meeting at Battins Tavern or Little's Tavern.[103] The famous gastronome Anthelme Brillât-Savarin, who takes refuge in New York during the stormiest years of the French Revolution, frequents Little's Tavern, where he indulges in turtle soup for breakfast and "welch-rabbit … washed down with ale or cider" for dinner.[104] Finally, in describing the people of New England, William Winterbotham writes in 1795: "The athletic and healthy diversions of cricket, foot ball, quoits, wrestling … foot races, and prison bars, are universally practised."[105]

Cricket holds the honour of being the United States' first international sporting event. On 29 April 1751, American colonists beat eleven "merrie men" from London, all residents of New York.[106] Given the paucity of references, it is noteworthy that history's first bona fide international cricket match was between Canada and the United States, in September 1844. Sporadic games were subsequently played until annual fixtures were established in the 1870s. Canada dominated until 1855, the United States thereafter.[107] Cricket aside, several dozen ball references fleck the annals of eighteenth-century North America. Early examples include a 1704 mention of ball-playing in Connecticut by Madame Knight; a game of base (possibly with a ball) played by "the English and Indians" in 1720; and the 1738 arrest of Joseph and Edward Anderson for grievously

101 *Litchfield Monitor*. 11 April 1798. p. 3.

102 *The Daily Advertiser*. 14 November 1794. p. 4.

103 Battins Tavern was on the corner of Burling Slip and Water Street, Lower Manhattan. Little's Tavern was at 56 Pine Street, a quarter of a mile from Battins.

104 Bayles, W.H., *Old Taverns of New York*. s.n., n.p. p. 377.

105 Winterbotham, W., *An Historical, Geographical, Commercial, and Philosophical View of the United States of America*. 4 Vols. Tiebout and O'Brien, New York, 1796. Vol. 2. p. 17.

106 Blancke. C., *Cricket in America*. Harper's Weekly, 26 September 1891. Vol. 35. p. 725.

107 *Outing*, 1886–1887, Vol. 9, p. 78.

assaulting the watchman who was taking them to the guardhouse for "playing with a bat and ball during the time of divine service."[108,109,110]

Harvard-educated Puritan minister Cotton Mather provides the first colonial football reference of eighteenth-century North America.[111] In 1688, he takes in one of four siblings "of exemplary temper and carriage", who are "arrested by a very stupendous *witchcraft*." The accused, an Irish woman Goody Glover, pleads guilty. Damning evidence found in her home and a self-incriminating detailed testimony condemn her to the Boston gallows.[112,113] In 1702, Mather writes of the girl he safeguarded. When given religious material to read, "she would be cast into hideous convulsions, and be tost about the house like a foot ball. But books of jest being shewn, she could read them well enough … A book which pretends to prove That there are no witches, was easily read by her."[114] Elsewhere, Mather writes of having seen "Many lads playing at their Marbles or Wickets, with one another in the Street."[115] Wicket is the North American version of cricket. Mather's is the earliest known reference, and places the game as early as the mid to late 1670s when he was a youth, at a time when only fifty references to cricket are known of. An American lieutenant records playing "shinny" and "ball" in 1779. Two weeks later, Dr Ebenezer Elmer, a surgeon in the same regiment writes, "Drisly weather in the forenoon, the afternoon of the day more fair—All hands dined at the Colonels to day & after dinner we took a hearty game of Bandy wicket."[116]

In March 1711, Harvard-educated Samuel Sewall makes a metaphorical mention: "At the meeting for the free school at Mr Pemberton's … I said

---

108 *Traveler Observes Ball-Playing in CT.* Protoball. https://protoball.org/1704.1. Accessed 1 March 2024.

109 *Game of Base was "A Peculiar Favorite."* Protoball. https://protoball.org/1720c.4. Accessed 1 March 2024.

110 *Two New Yorkers Get Guard House Sentence for Ballplaying At Time of Religious Rites*. Protoball. https://protoball.org/1738.1. Accessed 1 March 2024.

111 Harvard University was founded in 1636.

112 Glover was found compos mentis by six physicians but appears to have had a delusional disorder.

113 Mather, C., *Magnalia Christi Americana.* 2 Vols. Silus Andrus, Hartford, Connecticut, 1820. Vol. 2. pp. 396–398.

114 Ibid, p. 400.

115 Turner, B., *1726.2 Ballplaying and Boston Common.* Base Ball, 2011, 5:1, pp. 50–54.

116 Cook, F., Journals of the Military Expedition of General John Sullivan. Knapp, Peck, and Thomson, Auburn, New York, 1887. pp. 83, 268.

pleasantly, We are at Foot-ball now; and then he presently Sign[d].”[117] Sewall writes of removing a “Trap-Ball” that was blocking his neighbour’s gutter pipe, on 6 June 1713.[118,119] English-born, Sewall is better known as one of the nine judges in the Salem “Trials of the Witches” of 1692/3.[120] There is a paucity of diary entries covering the trials. He is as concerned that his son “threw a knop of Brass” cutting his daughters forehead, for which he “whipd him pretty smartly.”[121] His impudent grandson, Sam, comes off better. After Sewall admonishes him for playing at wicket on Boston Common, Sam ignores him. “I told him he could not lodge here practising thus. So he lodg’d elsewhere.”[122]

Sewall comes to bitterly regret his Salem judgements. In 1700, he publishes a tract condemning the slave trade in America, the first published in New England. He writes: “It is likewise most lamentable to think, how in taking Negros out of *Africa*, and Selling of them here … men do boldly rend asunder; Men from their Country, Husbands from their Wives, Parents from their Children. How horrible is the Uncleanness, Mortality, if not Murder that the Ships are guilty of … the barbarous Usage of our Friends and Kinsfolk in Africa.”[123]

A 1732 notebook from Boston, Massachusetts, holds an entry on the laws of the city. Offenders may be punished by “stocks imprisonment” or “cage whipping”, with a maximum of “ten stripes” (lashes). Puritan “justice” ensures that butchers, distillers, furriers, and chandlers are fined for cruelty to “brute creatures”, but any “negro” striking a white person is “severely whipp’d.”[124] There is a penalty for selling strong drink “to

---

117 Sewall, S., *Diary of Samuel Sewall 1674–1729.* Massachusetts Historical Society. Boston, 1879. p. 303.

118 Ibid, p. 388.

119 A small ball used in the eponymous game. Trapball evolved into knurr and spell, a hugely popular game in the north of England during the nineteenth century.

120 Harvard graduate Dudley Bradstreet issued warrants for forty-eight suspected witches. When he refused to issue more, he and his wife, Anne, were themselves accused of witchcraft. The revered poet Anne Bradstreet lived in Andover before Anne Bradstreet was born. Confusingly, the poet’s maiden name was Dudley, and the Irish eccentric Dudley Bradstreet is believed to have been the poet’s grandson or great-grandson.

121 Wish, H. (ed.)., *Diary of Samuel Sewall.* Capricorn Books, New York, 1967. p. 74.

122 *Wicket Played on Boston Common at Daybreak.* Protoball. https://protoball.org/1725c.1. Accessed 1 March 2024.

123 Sewall, S., *The Selling of Joseph: A Memorial.* Bartholomew Green and John Allen, Boston, 1700. p. 2. https://digitalcommons.unl.edu/cgi/viewcontent.cgi?article=1026&context=etas. Accessed on 24 February 2023.

124 *Notebook 1731–1763.* American Antiquary Society. Manuscript number: 394581. p. 64.

the Indians", and "Indians to be apprenticed" requires the approval of two justices.[125] Disorderly night walkers are to be taken to "the Whatch", idle persons to House Correction.[126] Breaking windows with "Stones, snow Balls, or foot Balls", carries a 20s fine, stocks imprisonment, or whipping, ditto for swearing profanely.[127,128]

In 1736, a St Andrews Day fair is held in Hanover County, Virginia, with "Prizes for Dancing, Singing, Foot-ball-play … particularly a fine Pair of Silk Stockings for the handsomest Maid."[129] A saddle and fiddle are also up for grabs. In 1739, the *Boston Evening-Post* reports that at Martha's Vineyard, "an Indian Fellow being at Football with others upon that Island, immediately after he had given the Ball a very smart kick, fell down dead."[130] The following year, a writer sees no harm if "a Company of honest young Fellows should once a Fortnight at a proper Season of the Year meet and play a Game at Bandy-wicket, or foot-ball, which are no very sinful exercises."[131] Similarly, in the *New-England Magazine* in October 1758: "Some love the manly Foils, the Foot-Ball some, and some the graceful Dance."[132] In 1783, a writer compares the Pennsylvanian constitution "to a football, which is kicked from goal to goal by two parties or sets of players, with alternate triumph."[133]

There is little on the game of bandy-wicket. Alice Gomme describes it as: "The game of 'Cricket' played with a bandy instead of a bat (Halliwell's *Dictionary*). Toone mentions it as played in Norfolk (*Dict.*), and Moor as played in Suffolk with bricks usually, or, in their absence, with bats in place of bails or stumps (*Suffolk Words*)."[134] Edward Moor who provides the definitive description of camping, mentions it, as being played in Suffolk, and Toone in Norfolk.[135] Whether bandy-wicket, like

125 Ibid, p. 58.

126 Ibid, p. 15.

127 Ibid, p. 58.

128 Ibid, p. 11.

129 *Virginia Gazette*. 26 November 1736. p. 4.

130 *Boston Evening-Post*. 2 April 1739. p. 4.

131 *American Weekly Mercury*. 22 May 1740. p. 1.

132 *The New-England Magazine*. 1 October 1758. 1:2. p. 28.

133 Markoe, P., *The Algerine Spy in Pennsylvania*. Prichard & Hall, Philadelphia, 1787. p. 3.

134 Alice Gomme, *The Traditional Games of England, Scotland and Ireland*. 2 Vols. David Nutt, London, 1894. Vol. 1. p. 17.

135 Moor, E., *Suffolk Words and Phrases*. J. Loder, London, 1823. pp. 64–65.

camping, is an East Anglian game transported to America by early settlers is unknown. It may well be the antecedent of North American wicket. Moor writes: "Snotch A notch. "To cut a snotch in't." Also, I think a knot. At cricket or bandy-wicket, we have so many snotches."[136] Notch was recorded in cricket as early as 1706 and used until at least 1836. It does suggest that bandy-wicket is a blend of an East Anglian stickball game and cricket, which expired as cricket became established.

Native Americans have at least three ball games: *pasuckuakohowog*—"they gather to play ball with the foot"—a cross-country game with large numbers; stick and ball games—early variants of lacrosse; and hand-ball. Kick, stick, hand. In this they mirror their European counterparts, though there is no clear carrying game. Stick variants go by different names: the Choctaw Nation calls theirs *Kobocha*—"stick-ball"; the Mohawk Nation, *Tewaaraton*—Iroquoian for lacrosse; and the Ojibwe Nation, *Baaga'adowe*—"she/he plays lacrosse." The game of the Onondaga Nation is *Dehoñtjihgwa'és*—they bump hips. The homeland of the Onondaga Nation is in eastern North America, spanning what is now the United States and Canada, well away from the hipball playing of Central America; with no playing corridor for transmission, they are unlikely to be related sports.

The Choctaw Nation's homeland embraced central and southern Mississippi, east Louisiana, and western Alabama, far closer to Central America, and their game translates to "stick game." The Mississippian civilisation (c700AD–1540) covered a vast swathe from the Great Lakes to the Gulf of Mexico, incorporating the later states of Mississippi, Kentucky, Alabama, Georgia, Arkansas, Missouri, Illinois, Indiana, and Ohio. Knowledge and culture—agricultural, architectural, ceremonial, iconographic, political, economic, artistic, and recreational—would have been exchanged between Mesoamerican and Mississippian civilisations. Similarly, interchange would take place between the Mississippian civilisation and adjacent territories, including those either side of its northern expanse. Several competing hypotheses have been advanced to support direct Mesoamerican dissemination along defined geographical corridors.[137]

---

136 Ibid, p. 375.

137 Carpenter, M.S., *Mesoamerican-Mississippian interaction across the far Southern Plains by long-range Toyah intermediaries*. Plains Anthropologist, 65:256, pp. 325–356.

Lacrosse's Native American roots are evident as early as 1606/07. Marc Lescarbot's *History of New France* relates how the governor of the colony of L'Acadie, in Quebec, is told a fable about a Native American playing *la crosse* (*jouer à la croce*) against the Devil.[138] The Devil is invisible, only his stick is seen. *Gougou* the man-eating giantess competes in the original story; the Devil is a European conceit. The first European to *describe* Native American football is from Saffron Walden, in the camping half of Essex. In 1610, William Strachey of the Jamestown settlement in Virginia watches men of the Lenape Nation. He prefaces his description: "A kynd of exercise they have often amongst them much like that which boyes call bandy in English, and maye be an auncient game." He goes on: "Likewise they have the exercise of football, in which they only forceably encounter with the foot to carry the ball the one from the other, and spurned [kicked] yt to the goale with a kind of dexterity and swift footman-ship, which is the honour of yt; but they never strike up another's heeles, as we doe, not accompting that praiseworthie to purchase a goale by such an advantage."[139] This is true football, no handling, and played with sportsmanship. Elsewhere, he notes that it is "not unusual to see an Indian whose ears were bored with wide holes, wearing in each ear "a small grene and yellow-couloured live snake … crawling and lapping himself about his neck and oftentimes familiarly."[140]

In 1609, Strachey first sails from England to Virginia on the Sea Venture. Admiral Sir George Somers, from the hurling county of Dorset, commands the ship, and the voyage is led by Virginia's governor-designate Thomas Gates from neighbouring Devon.[141] "A dreadfull Storme and hideous" befalls the ship.[142] When the Sea Venture is about to flounder, they miraculously sight land, and Somers successfully runs it aground. All one hundred and fifty passengers and crew survive. Strachey writes a lengthy letter describing the hurricane to an anonymous "Excellent

138 Lescarbot, M., *Histoire de la Nouvelle-France*. Adrian Perier, Paris, 1617. n.p. Lescarbot is writing of his visit to l'Acadie, in 1606–07, when Jean de Biencourt was governor.

139 Major, R.H., *The Historie of Travaile Into Virginia Britannia*. s.n., London, 1849. pp. 77–78.

140 Sanders, C.R., *William Strachey, The Virginia Colony, and Shakespeare*. The Virginia Magazine of History and Biography, 1949, 57:2, p. 128.

141 Vaughan, A.T., *William Strachey's 'True Reportory' and Shakespeare: A Closer Look at the Evidence*. Shakespeare Quarterly, 2008, 59:3, pp. 255, 270.

142 Clarke, J.S., *Nausragia or Historical Memoirs of Shipwrecks*. I. Gold, London, 1805. p. 142.

Lady", two copies of which are said to have been widely circulated in London.[143] He writes that the storm, "did beate all light from Heaven: which like an hell of darkenesse did turn blacke upon us, so much the more fuller of Horror … for foure-and-twenty houres, the Storme in a restlesse tumult, had blown so exceedingly, as wee could not apprehend in our imaginations any possibility of greater violence; yet did wee still finde it not onely more terrible, but more constant; fury added to fury … the Sea swelled above the Clouds and gave battell unto Heaven … Windes and Seas were as mad as fury and rage could make them…."[144] Strachey is an author, who counts Ben Johnson and John Donne among his wide circle of literary friends.[145] It would be no surprise, and it is strongly conjectured, that Shakespeare read the letter and based The Tempest on it, with its cataclysmic deluge, a run-aground ship, and the miraculous survival of all souls.[146]

Residing in Huron country (now Canada) in 1634, Jesuit missionary Jean de Brébeuf remarks: "Of three games that are popular among these peoples—*la crosse*, dish, and straw—the first two, they say, are wonderful for the health."[147] The sticks are hooked as in *soule a la crosse*, so De Brébeuf christens the game *la crosse*. Not all play the stick and ball game. Without specifying a nation, a 1647 account describes the "Football" of Native Americans in New England: "when they play Countrey against Countrey, there are rich Goals, all behung with *Wampompeage, Mowhacks,* Beaver Skins, and black Otter Skins: Their Goals are a Mile long plac'd on the Sands, which are as even as a Board; their Ball is no bigger than a Hand-ball, which sometimes they mount in the Air with their naked Feet, sometimes it is sway'd by the multitude, sometime also it is two days before they get a Goal, then they mark the Ground they win, and begin there the next day. Before they come to this Sport they paint themselves, even as when they go to War, in policy to

143 Vaughan, A.T., *William Strachey's 'True Reportory' and Shakespeare: A Closer Look at the Evidence*. Shakespeare Quarterly, 2008, 59:3, p. 256.

144 Clarke, J.S., *Nausragia or Historical Memoirs of Shipwrecks*. I. Gold, London, 1805. pp. 142–144.

145 Sanders, C.R., *William Strachey, The Virginia Colony, and Shakespeare*. The Virginia Magazine of History and Biography, 1949, 57:2, pp. 122, 125.

146 Vaughan, A.T., *William Strachey's 'True Repertory' and Shakespeare: A Closer Look at the Evidence*. Shakespeare Quarterly, 2008, 59:3, pp. 245–273.

147 Talbot, F.X., *Saint Among the Hurons: the Life of Jean de Brébeuf.* Harper & Brothers, New York, 1949. p. 69.

prevent future mischief, because no man should know him that mov'd his patience, or accidentally hurt his Person, taking away the occasion of studying revenge. Before they begin, their Arms are put off, and hung upon some neighboring Tree, after which they make a long scrowl on the Sand, over which they shake Hands, and with loving Hearts scuffle for Victory. While the Men Play, the Boys Pipe, and the Women Dance and Sing Trophies of their Husbands Conquests; all being done, a Feast summons their departure."[148]

The French fur trader Nicholas Perrot, welcomed by the Miamis in 1677, describes their game: "A few days later [the Chief] gave the pleasure of Jeu de la Crosse … More than two thousand assembled in a great plain, each with his cross: a big wooden ball like a jeu de paume ball was tossed in the air … there was a great jostling of all the sticks in the air, like arms during a battle. Half … wanted to send the ball northwest the length of the field, the others to the southeast. The contest which lasted for a half hour … these kinds of games are usually followed by broken heads, arms, and legs and people are often killed without any other result."[149]

Perrot adds further detail elsewhere: "Among them is a certain game of cross which has much to do with that of our longue paume. Their custom in playing is to pit nation against nation, and if there is one more numerous than the other, they draw men from it to make it equal … you see them all armed with a *crosse*, that is to say a big baton with a big end at the bottom, laced like a racket; they play with a wooden ball, about the size of a turkey's egg. The goals are scored in the countryside. A side wins by pushing the ball beyond their goal, east-west for one side, north-south for the other. If they are then forced over their own goal, they change goals and start again.

"If the game is drawn, they continue the next day … the games begin after the ice melts and last until seed time … each party has a leader … they gather in the middle of the square, and one of the leaders throws the ball in the air; everyone tries to send it to the side he has to push to; if it falls to the ground, they try to catch with their stick, and if it is sent

---

148 Ogilby, J., Montanus, A., *America: Being the latest, and most accurate description of the New World.* John Ogilby, London, 1671. p. 156.

149 De la Potherie. C., *Histoire de l'Amerique Septentrionale Contenant.* 4 Vols. Jean-Luc Nion, Paris, 1722. Vol. 2. pp. 126–127.

outside the crowd of players, the most alert chase it. You can hear the cries as they hit each other, parrying blows to get to the ball. When the ball is stuck between someone's feet, it's up to him to avoid the blows his adversaries constantly land on his feet; if he's injured, it's his own fault. Some have their legs broken, others their arms; a few have even been killed. It is very common to see them crippled for the rest of their lives … unless you knew, you'd think they were at fighting for real, but whatever injury is sustained they attribute to fate and there is no ill-feeling … the injured try to look as if nothing happened, to signal their courage."[150]

The Native American game is called stickball or *toli* until the French call it lacrosse. It has regional variations, just as stick and ball games do across Britain and Ireland. In 1700, a Jesuit missionary describes a Muskogee game: "The men play in pairs; one of them has a ball in the hand and throws it ahead. Both of them run as fast as they can, throwing a big stick after this ball … the one whose stick is closest to the ball wins play … the one who wins throws the ball next time."[151] A few years later, Baron de la Hontan describes another variation: "the rackets are almost like ours, except for the handle, which is three feet long. The Savages[152] who usually play three or four hundred at a time, plant two stakes five or six hundred paces from each other, then divide into two troops. They throw the ball in the air halfway between the sticks. Then each band tries to push it to their stake. Some run to the ball; others keep to the right and left, to be within running distance of where it will fall … they scrape and bruise their legs very often with their snowshoes trying to reach the ball."[153]

In 1718, the sport of the Potawatomi, Huron, and Outaouais nations of northeast North America is described: "They play a good deal at La Crosse in summer, twenty or more on each side. The bat is a sort of little racket, and the ball with which they play is made of very heavy

150 Perrot, N., *Mémoire sur les moeurs, coustumes et relligion des sauvages de l'Amérique septentrionale.* A. Franck, Leipzig & Paris, 1864. pp. 43–45.

151 Gems, G.R., Borish, L.J., Pfister, G., *Sports in American History: from colonization to globalization.* Human Kinetics, Champaign, Illinois, 2005. p. 10.

152 The use of the word 'savages' is clearly derogatory, and highly offensive to a modern audience.

153 Lahontan, L.A., *Voyages du baron de La Hontan dans l'Amerique septentrionale.* 2 Vols. Charles Delo, Amsterdam, 1706. Vol. 2. p. 113.

wood, somewhat larger than the balls used at tennis. When playing, they are entirely naked, except a breech cloth, and moccasins on their feet; their body is completely painted with all sorts of colors … They set up two poles and commence the game from the centre; one party propels the ball from one side and the others from the opposite, and whichever reaches the goal, wins … They often play village against village; the Poux against the Outaouacs or the Hurons, and lay heavy stakes."[154] In August 1721, a French Jesuit witnesses a game: "The Miamis have two games, the first of which is called *le Jeu de la Crosse*. It is played with a Ball, and sticks curved and ending in a type of Racket. Two Posts are erected, which serve as Boundaries, and which are distant from each other in proportion to the number of Players. For example, if there are eighty, the distance is half a league. The Players are divided into two bands, each of which has its Post, and it is a question of making the Ball go to that of the opposing Party, without it falling to the ground, and without it being touched with the hand; if either happens, that side loses the game, unless the one who made the mistake gets the ball straight to the goal, which is often impossible … these Parties last several days in succession."[155]

The stick appears uniform across these early descriptions. It is the curved stick we see throughout the history of the European game, but with netting attached from the end to part way up the stick. The distance between posts in the Miamis's game depends on numbers. A mile and a half for what appears to be forty-a-side, rather than eighty-a-side. The variable distance rule cannot apply to nation games with large numbers of players. De la Hontan reports up to four hundred players, equating to an unfeasible seven-and-a-half-mile distance between posts, unless it is "to the country". Perrot's two thousand players equates to thirty-seven miles. A smaller game is reported in 1729, when a Jesuit describes the stickball game of those of the Choctaw nation residing in what is now Alabama.[156] Two villages play a twenty-a-side game, "which is like the

154 O'Callaghan, E.B. (ed.), *Documents Relative to the Colonial History of the State of New York*. 15 Vols. Weed, Parsons and Company, Albany, NY, 1858. Vol. 9. p. 887.

155 De Charlevoix, P., *Historie et Description General de la Nouvelle France*. 4 Vols. Rollin fils, Paris, 1744. Vol. 3. p. 319.

156 Stepp, J.R., *Interactions Between the Mississippi Choctaw and European Americans Through the Sport of Toli*. The International Journal of the History of Sport, 2006, 23:2, p. 285.

long racket."[157] While he provides scant detail, his description is notable for being the earliest of a game in the south of North America.

Most descriptions make little mention of the rules concerning the lacrosse stick. In the 1721 game, the stick must be used to catch and throw the ball. If the ball is handled or hits the ground, a penalty is awarded against the offending player, who must hurl the ball beyond the opposition's post. Invariably, the distance is too far for a penalty to be converted. A c1744 game of those of the Choctaw nation in South Carolina is recounted by James Adair:

"Ballplaying is their chief and most favourite game: and is such severe exercise, as to shew it was originally calculated for a hardy and expert race of people, like themselves, and the ancient Spartans. The ball is made of a piece of scraped deer-skin, moistened, and stuffed hard with deer's sinews. The ball-sticks are about two feet long, the lower end somewhat resembling the palm of a hand, and which are worked with deer-skin thongs. Between these, they catch the ball, and throw it a great distance, when not prevented by some of the opposite party, who fly to intercept them. The goal is about five hundred yards in length: at each end of it, they fix two long bending poles into the ground, three yards apart below, but slanting a considerable way outwards. The party that happens to throw the ball over these, counts one; but if it be thrown underneath, it is cast back, and played for as usual.

"The gamesters are equal on each side; and at the beginning of every course of the ball, they throw it up high in the center of the ground, and in a direct line between the two goals. When the crowd of players prevents the one who catched the ball, from throwing it off with a long direction, he commonly sends it to the right course, by an artful sharp twirl. They are so exceedingly expert in this manly exercise, that, between the goals, the ball is mostly flying the different ways, by the force of the playing sticks, without falling to the ground, for they are not allowed to catch it with their hands. It is surprising to see how swiftly they fly, when closely chased by a nimble footed pursuer; when they are intercepted by one of the opposite party, his fear of being cut by the ball sticks, commonly gives them an opportunity of throwing it perhaps a hundred yards; but

157 Swanton, J.R., *Early Account of the Choctaw Indians.* American Anthropological Association, Lancaster, Philadelphia, 1918. p. 68.

the antagonist sometimes runs up behind, and by a sudden stroke dashes down the ball."[158]

Female relatives dance outside the night before the game, "chanting religious notes with their shrill voices" to supplicate the god *Yo He Wah*. "The men fast and wake from sunset, till the ball play is over the next day, which is about one or two o'clock in the afternoon … They turn out to the ball ground, in a long row, painted white, whooping … Each party are desirous to gain the twentieth ball, which they esteem a favourite divine gift."[159]

In May 1755, eighteen-year-old roadworker James Smith is captured in Virginia by three Native Americans. Had he been a soldier he would have been killed but instead is adopted by the Caughnawaga nation, with whom he remains until 1759.[160] In May 1757, he mentions a game similar to *soule a la crosse*: "Many of the young men were now exercising themselves in a game resembling foot ball; though they commonly struck the ball with a crooked stick, made for that purpose."[161] Smith provides richer detail of their more popular game: "they used a wooden ball, about three inches diameter, and the instrument they moved it with was a strong staff about five feet long, with a hoop net on the end of it, large enough to contain the ball … they lay off about half a mile distance in a clear plain, and the opposite parties all attend at the centre, where a disinterested person casts up the ball then the opposite parties all contend for it. If anyone gets it into his net, he runs with it the way he wishes it to go, and they all pursue him. If one of the opposite party overtakes the person with the ball, he gives the staff a stroke which causes the ball to fly out of the net … if the one that gets it can outrun all the opposite party, and can carry it quite out, or over the line at the end, the game is won; but this seldom happens. When any one is running away with the ball, and is like to be overtaken, he commonly throws it, and with this instrument can cast it fifty or sixty yards. Sometimes when the ball is almost at the

158 Holland Braund, K.E. (ed.)., *The History of the American Indians*, by James Adair. The University of Alabama Press, Tuscaloosa, Alabama, 2005. pp. 392–393.

159 Ibid, p. 394.

160 Whitlock, H.L., *Skins: White Masculinity in James Smith's Remarkable Occurrences in the Early National Period*. Unpublished MA thesis, University of Wyoming, Laramie, Wyoming, 2014. pp. 6–7.

161 Smith, J., *An Account of the Remarkable Occurrences in the Life and Travels of Col. James Smith*. John Bradford, Lexington, Kentucky, 1799. p. 44.

one end, matters will take a sudden turn, and the opposite party may quickly carry it out at the other end. Often times they will work a long while back and forward before they can get the ball over the line, or win the game."[162]

In 1763, the Native American ball game *baggataway* is described for the first time when a game takes place between the Ojibwe and Saäkies nations at Mackinac Island, in what was then *Mishi-Anishinaabaki*, later the state of Michigan. The game is a ruse to occupy the British fort. They play beside it and invite the garrison to watch. They deliberately throw the ball over the palisades, then rush inside, kill seventy soldiers, and successfully take the stockade. The account is told by fur trader Alexander Henry, who missed the game, but is afterwards taken prisoner. He lives with the Odawa Tribe for a year. "Baggatiway," he writes, "called by the Canadians *le jeu de la crosse*, is played with a bat and ball. The bat is about four feet in length, curved, and terminating in a sort of racket. Two posts are planted in the ground a considerable distance from each other, as a mile or more. Each party has its post, and the game consists in throwing the ball up to the post of the adversary. The ball, at the beginning, is placed in the middle of the course and each party endeavours as well to throw the ball out of the direction of its own post as into that of the adversary's.[163] The game of *baggataway* … is necessarily attended with much violence and noise … the ball … if it cannot be thrown to the goal desired, is struck in any direction by which it can be diverted from that designed by the adversary."[164]

The Choctaw Nation is clearly passionate about lacrosse. A third game, played in Louisiana, is described in 1759 by a captain in the French Marines: "The Chactaws are very active and merry; they have a play at ball, at which they are very expert; they invite the inhabitants of the neighbouring villages to it … in their best ornaments, they pass the whole day in singing and dancing; they even dance all the night … they agree upon a mark or aim about sixty yards off, and distinguished by two great poles, between which the ball is to pass. They generally count sixteen until the game is up. They are forty on each side, and everyone

162 Ibid, p. 44.

163 Henry, A., *Alexander Henry's Travels and Adventures in the Years 1760–1776*. The Lakeside Press, Chicago, 1921. p. 78.

164 Ibid, p. 86.

has a battledoor [bat] in his hand, about two feet and a half long, made very nearly in the form of ours, of walnut or chestnut, and covered with roe-skins.

"An old man stands in the middle … and throws up into the air a ball of roe-skins, rolled about each other. The players then run and endeavour to strike the ball with their battledoors; it is a pleasure to see them run naked, painted with various colours, having a tyger's tail fastened behind, and feathers on their heads and arms … they push and throw each other down; he that has been expert enough to get the ball, sends it to his party; those of the opposite party run at him … and send it back to their side; and thus they dispute it … with such an ardour, that they sometimes dislocate their shoulders … some old men, who assist at the play, become mediators."[165] Here is a contained game with a small playing area, smaller sides, and more goals scored. There are also referees. When the game has ended, a women's game ensues: "The battledoor they make use of, differs from that of the men, in being bent; they are all very active, and run against each other with extreme swiftness, pushing each other like the men, they having the same dress, except on those parts which modesty teaches them to cover."

The Choctaw are also recorded playing in Florida in 1775:

"Their play at ball is either with a small ball of deer skin or a large one of woollen rags; the first is thrown with battledores, the second with the hand only; this is a trial of skill between village and village; after having appointed the day and field for meeting, they assemble at the time and place, fix two poles across each other at about an hundred and fifty feet apart, they then attempt to throw the ball through the lower part of them, and the opposite party trying to prevent it, throw it back among themselves, which the first again try to prevent; thus they attempt to beat it about from one to the other with amazing violence, and not seldom broken limbs or dislocated joints are the consequence; their being almost naked, painted and ornamented with feathers, has a good effect on the eye of the bystander during this violent diversion; a number is agreed on for the score, and the party who first gets this number wins. The women play among themselves (after the men have done) disputing with as much

165 Forster, J.H. (trans.)., *Travels Through that part of North America formerly called Louisiana. By Mr. Bossu, Captain in the French Marines*. T. Davies, London, 1771. pp. 304–305.

eagerness as the men; the stakes or betts are generally high. There is no difference in the other game with the large ball, only the men and women play promiscuously, and they use no battledores."[166]

Colonel Marinus Willett is born in the town of Jamaica, later absorbed into New York. He dies in the city ninety years later, but not before taking a lead role as a New York Patriot leader in the American Revolution and serving as mayor of the city in 1807/08. On 29 May 1790, he witnesses a "superb ball play" by the Tallapoosa nation, in future Alabama. The initial account could be a description of contemporary folk football: "070 [seventy] players on a side. The men, women, and children from the neighbouring towns, were assembled …all the paths leading to the place were filled with people, some on foot, and some on horseback … The play, which is conducted with as much order & decorum as the nature of the business will admit of. The play is brought on by one town sending a challenge to another, which on being accepted the time and place is fixed on."

The night before there are ceremonies and dancing, and on the morning of the game, "the players paint and decorate themselves in the same manner they do when they are going to war." The two sides approach from opposite directions with choreographed timing. When they are half a mile apart, they begin yelling and chanting and continue this when they meet, while dancing around one another. Willett includes a potentially critical line, as the account reverts to what could be a British or Irish game: "each player places himself opposite to his antagonist." In an unusual variation, each player has two rackets, all of which are laid down at the centre of the pitch. Other similarities follow. Two poles are erected at either end—one hundred and fifty feet from the centre—through which the ball must travel to score a point. The ball is thrown up from the centre, and each player endeavours to catch the ball with their two rackets and get it between the poles positioned nearest to their town. Twelve to twenty points are needed for victory, presumably decided on before the game. "The whole of the present exhibition was grand, & well conducted … Among other things the great attention of the women who attend with bottles & gourds filled with drink, watching every opportunity to supply the players … ought

166 Romans, B., *A Concise History of East and West Florida*. 2 Vols. s.n., New York, 1775. Vol. 1. p. 79.

not to be omitted … the day was fair, and I returned home, much pleased by the amusement."[167]

In 1791, the Quaker William Bartram publishes his American travelogue. He clearly admires Native Americans: "The males of the Cherokees, Muscogulges, Siminoles, Chicasaws, Chactaws, and confederate tribes of the Creeks, are tall, erect, and moderately robust; their limbs well shaped, so as generally to form a perfect human figure; their features regular, and countenance open, dignified and placid; yet the forehead and brow so formed, as to strike you instantly with heroism and bravery."[168] Bartram gives an account of *kobocha*, played in what is now Alabama. It differs little from the *baggataway* played a thousand miles away:

"The ball play is esteemed the most noble and manly exercise. This game is exhibited in an extensive level plain, usually contiguous to the town: the inhabitants of one town play against another, in consequence of a challenge, when the youth of both sexes are often engaged, and sometimes stake their whole substance. Here they perform amazing feats of strength and agility. The game principally consists in taking and carrying off the ball from the opposite party, after being hurled into the air, midway between two high pillars, which are the goals, and the party who bears off the ball to their pillar wins the game; each person having a racquet or hurl, which is an implement of a very curious construction, somewhat resembling a ladle or little hoop-net, with a handle near three feet in length, the hoop and handle of wood, and the netting of thongs of raw hide, or tendons of an animal. The foot-ball is likewise a favourite, manly diversion with them."[169]

The Mississippian civilisation (c700AD–1540) covered a vast corridor of America from the Great Lakes to what would become Mississippi. Any contact with the ball-playing Mesoamericans would have had an impact on the development of their ball games. The glaring differences between hipball and the precursors to lacrosse imply a

---

167 *Marinus Willett's Journal of Expedition to the Creek Indians*. Original MS. pp. 57–64. Miami Libraries Digital Collection: https://digitalcollections.library.miami.edu/digital/collection/kis0001/id/2412. Accessed 12 June 2023.

168 Bartram, W., *Travels Through North & South Carolina, Georgia, East and West Florida*. James and Johnson, Philadelphia, 1791. p. 481.

169 Ibid, pp. 506–507.

southward spread. Tolerance toward Native Americans is woeful, though a letter to the *Massachusetts Spy* in 1795 exposes a narrow seam: "It is a subject of real regret, with men of enlightened minds and pure independence of character to see the native Americans the dupes and footballs of foreigners."[170] The final eighteenth century account provides most detail. Samuel Woodruff attends a match between the Seneca and Mohawk Nations, in the summer of 1797. Woodruff has more than a passing knowledge of sport:

"The place … was a broad and beautiful green, of perhaps one hundred acres, perfectly level, and smooth as a carpet … the Senecas had collected in a sort of irregular encampment—men, women, and children—to the number of more than a thousand. On the other side the Mohawks were actively assembling in yet greater numbers. The stakes deposited by each party were laid upon the ground in heaps, consisting of rifles, hatchets, swords, belts, knives, blankets, wampum, watches, beads, broaches, furs … [worth] upward of a thousand dollars a side.[171]

"… The combatants numbered about six hundred upon a side … their persons were naked with the exception of a single garment … descending nearly to the knee. The area of the play-ground was designated by two pair of 'byes', placed at about thirty rods distant from each other,[172] and the goals of each pair about thirty feet apart. The combatants ranged themselves in parallel lines on each side of the area, facing inward, and leaving a space between them of about ten rods in breadth.[173] Their bats were three feet six inches in length, curved at the lower end somewhat in the form of a ladle, the broad part for striking the ball being formed of net-work, woven of thongs of untanned deer-skin, strained to the tension of tight elasticity. The ball, large as a middling-sized apple, was also composed of elastic materials.

"On one side of the area, near the centre of the line, and in a conspicuous place, were seated a body of elderly sachems, of each nation, with knives and tally-sticks, to score the game. The rules governing the game were somewhat intricate. None of the players were allowed

170 *Thomas's Massachusetts Spy*. 4 March 1795. p. 1.

171 £225. Five years' wages for a skilled tradesman in England.

172 One hundred and sixty-five yards.

173 Fifty-five yards.

to touch the ball with hand or foot, until driven beyond the 'byes' or land-marks. It was then thrown back by hand toward or into the centre of the area, when the game proceeded as before. Their mode of counting the game was peculiar, the tallies-men … [were] left to the exercise of a certain degree of discretionary power. Each passage of the ball between the goals, at the end of the play-ground, counted one, so long as the contest was nearly equal; but, for the purpose of protracting the game, whenever one party became considerably in advance of the other, the tally-chiefs were allowed to check or curtail their count in proportion to the excess. For instance, if the leading party had run up a regular count to thirty, while their opponents had numbered but fifteen, the tallies-men, at their discretion, and by consent of each other, though unknown to the players, would credit the winning party with only two notches for three passages of the ball—varying from time to time, according to the state of the game. The object of this course was to protract the game, and to increase the amusement, while despondency upon either side was prevented, and the chance of ultimate victory increased. Frequently, by this discretionary mode of counting, the game was continued three or four days.

"The game on this occasion was commenced by about sixty players on a side, who advanced from their respective lines with bats in their hands, into the centre of the play-ground. Of this number about twenty were stationed at the end land-marks, to guard the passage of the ball. The players who were to begin, were apparently mingled promiscuously together. All things being thus ready, a beautiful maiden, richly dressed in the native costume of her people, wearing a red tiara plumed with eagles' feathers, and glittering with bracelets and other ornaments of silver, came bounding like a gazelle into the area, with the ball, which she placed upon the ground in the centre … The match was begun by two of the opposing players, who advanced to the ball, and with their united bats raised it from the ground to such an elevation as gave a chance for a fair stroke; when, quick as lightning, it was sped through the air almost with the swiftness of a bullet. Much depends upon the first stroke, and great skill is exerted to obtain it.

"… so great were the exertions of the players, that each set was relieved by fresh hands every fifteen or twenty minutes; thus alternating, and allowing every player of the whole number to perform his part, until the game was finished … The contest was continued three days … the Senecas were proclaimed the victors, sweeping the stakes, to the great mortification of the proud-spirited Mohawks."[174]

The use of tally-sticks is intriguing. They are first mentioned in William Goldwin's 1706 *In Certamen Pilae*, ninety-one years before. But who gave the idea to whom? It is as likely to have been a Native American invention as an English one. The mention of byes in the absence of point-scoring implies a reference to the extent of the pitch either side of the goal. These may have been marked out with moveable posts or fixed landmarks.

~

In 1794, Savannah, Georgia, bans Sabbath football, bear-baiting, hunting, fishing, plays, music "for the sake of merriment … nor any other sports or pastimes whatsoever."[175] Four years later, football is appropriated lamely for a book by American author James Butler. His Mercutio is a swashbuckling adventurer, not the quicksilver friend of Romeo killed in a street fight. When Romeo realises Mercutio is dead, Shakespeare has him declare, with characteristic self-regarding whininess, "O, I am fortune's fool!" With uninformed sacrilege, the title is *Fortune's Football: or, The Adventures of Mercutio*.[176] The book fails to mention football again.

On 8 September 1636, Harvard becomes the first college in the American colonies. Harvard's first football reference is in a sermon by Thomas Shepard, the college's Puritan minister, delivered sometime between 1643 and his death in 1649. The sport allows both carrying and kicking, "and herein Satan now appears with the ball at his foot, and seems to threaten in time to carry all before him, and to kick and carry God's precious Sabbaths out of the world with him."[177] The original charter of 1646 omits any games, ordering only that students eschew,

174 Stone, W.L., *Life of Joseph Brant*. 2 Vols. J. Munsell, Albany, NY, 1865. Vol. 2. pp. 446–449.

175 *The Georgia Gazette*. 1 May 1794. p. 6.

176 Butler, J., *Fortune's Football: or, The Adventures of Mercutio*. John Wyeth, Harrisburgh, Pennsylvania, 1798.

177 Shepard, T., *Theses sabbaticae. Or, The doctrine of the Sabbath*. John Rothwell, London, 1649, p. 49; Morison, S, E., *Harvard College in the Seventeenth Century*. Harvard University Press, Massachusetts, 1936. Part I. p. 117.

"bitter scoffing, frothy wanton words and offensive gestures", and avoid "such men as lead an ungirt and dissolute life."[178] *The Lawes and Orders of Harvard Colledge* of 1655 mentions dice and cards but no ball games: "and in any case that be convicted of Drunkenesse, Fighting, Rayling, Swearing, Cursing, filthy Speaking, Profanesse, Revelling, playing at Cards or Dice, or such like, for the first offence, if it bee private, hee shall bee privately admonished by the President or his Tutor."[179]

The earliest mention of *sport* dates from c1672. Thomas Shepard's son sends his own to Harvard with an educative letter: "I would not have you neglect seasons of recreation a little before and after meals ... or (if it be in fitt season) recreate your Self a little, and so to your work afresh; let your recreation be such as may stir the Body chiefly, yet not violent, and whether such or sedentary."[180] The *playing of ball sports* at Harvard is mentioned on 30 March 1729: "The Batchelors Play Batt & Ball mightily now adays which Stirs our bloud greatly."[181] The game is unmentioned, probably trapball. Wicket is possible, cricket too, as it is banned in Salem in 1762: "no Person shall use the Exercise of playing or Kicking of Foot-ball, or the Exercise of Bat-and-Ball, or Cricket ... within the Body of this Town, under a penalty of One Shilling and Six Pence."[182] Snowball fights in public places are also prohibited.

The first mention of *football* at Harvard is in 1734–35, when College Customs state that, "Freshmen are to find [furnish] the rest of the Scholars with bats, balls, and foot balls."[183] The rule in relation to

---

178 Goodchild, L.F., Wechsler, H.S., *The History of Higher Education.* Simon and Schuster, New York, 1997. p. 125.

179 *Harvard University. Corporation. Laws and statutes of Harvard, 1655–1890.* Colonial North America at Harvard Library. *The Lawes and orders of Harvard Colledge 1655.* UAI 15.800 Box 2, Volume 1, Sequence 22 (p. 13). Harvard University Archives. Accessed 18 February 2024.

180 *A Letter from the Revd Mr Thos Shephard to his Son att His Admission into the College.* Publications of The Colonial Society of Massachusetts. Volume 14: Transactions, 1911–1913. Published by the Society, Boston, Massachusetts, 1913. pp. 193–194.

181 Shipton, C.K., *New England Life in the Eighteenth Century: Representative Biographies from Sibley's Harvard Graduates.* Harvard University Press, Massachusetts, 1995. p. 287.

182 *Sextant: The Journal of Salem State University,* 24:1, Spring 2018, p. 8.

183 Hall, B, H., *A Collection of College Word and Customs.* John Bartlett, Cambridge, Massachusetts, 1856. p. 215. "Find" had been altered to "furnish" by 1781. See: Lewis, H.R., *Excellence Without a Soul: Does Liberal Education Have a Future.* Public Affairs, New York, 2007. p. 224.

football is never revoked. It adds that freshmen cannot talk "saucily" to a senior, laugh in his face, or address him with a hat on. Neither can they "mingo" against the College wall, or enter a Fellows "cus john".[184] An article is added to Harvard's statutes, c1776: "No scholar shall play foot-ball or any other game in the College yard, or throw anything across the yard."[185] Yale University does not mention ball games until 1765, when the college statutes ban playing football or handball within the university precinct, on pain of a fine of up to sixpence and making good damages.[186]

Writing of his time as a Harvard schoolboy in 1794, Sidney Willard, son of the Harvard president, relates that before the annual sophomore–freshman football game came into being, there was an annual wrestling contest between the two: "Wrestling, was at an after period, I cannot say in what year, superseded by football; a grovelling and inglorious game in comparison."[187,188] There were other sports: "We wrestled and ran, played at quoits, at cricket, and various games of bat and ball, whose names perhaps are obsolete, and leaped and jumped in rivalry."[189] In his father's schooldays, the Buttery sold gingerbread, pastries, bats, and balls.[190] In 1796, Elias Mann records taking part in the annual wrestling on the first Monday of the academic year: "I had poor success in the ring this evening flung only one."[191] On 5 September, he "played at ball some."[192] He records playing ball again, in May 1798.[193]

---

184 Mingo: urinate. Cus john: cousin john, toilet

185 Quincy, J., *The History of Harvard University*. John Owen, Cambridge, Massachusetts, 1840. p. 540.

186 Deming, C., *Yale Yesterdays*. Yale University Press, New Haven, 1915. p. 192.

187 Willard, S., *Memories of Youth and Manhood.* 2 Vols. John Bartlett, Cambridge, Massachusetts, 1855. Vol. 1. pp. 260–261.

188 An epitaph inscribed in 1860—after the faculty ban the sophomore-freshman game—declares it was sixty years old in 1860, giving the birthdate of Harvard football as 1800. In: Blanchard, J, A., *The H Book of Harvard Athletics*. The Harvard Varsity Club, Massachusetts, 1923. p. 313.

189 Willard, S., *Memories of Youth and Manhood.* 2 Vols. John Bartlett, Cambridge, Massachusetts, 1855. Vol. 1. p. 316.

190 Ibid, p. 31.

191 Elias Mann, 1788–1807. *Diary of Elias Mann, 1796–1800*. Colonial North America at Harvard Library. Harvard University Archives. HUD 800.5, Sequence 3. Accessed 18 February 2024.

192 Ibid, Sequence 4.

193 Ibid, Sequence 8.

His diary is peppered with diversions: boating, fishing, backgammon, cards, scrumping pears, chestnut hunting, theatre, taverns, "charming" girls. He is a member of the Hasty Pudding Club,[194] the Coffee Club, and the Phi Beta Kappa Society. The most shocking news of his undergraduate years is the death of George Washington.[195] The announcement takes nine days to reach Harvard.

194 Still extant, the club was founded in 1795. Until 1800, two members "brought the pot of [hasty] pudding between them from Mrs Frosts.": Price, L., *The Thirteenth Catalogue & A History of the Hasty Pudding Club.* The Riverside Press, Cambridge, Massachusetts, 1907. p. 2.

195 Puritanical sanctimony had little reach: Washington was an inveterate card player, losing or winning up to £9.00 a night (£800 in 2024); Benjamin Franklin was one of the few printers in the colonies to manufacture playing cards; and when Jefferson was supposed to be drafting the Declaration of Independence, he was betting small on games of backgammon, lotto, and cross and pyle. He lost 3s to Mrs Jefferson at cards.

CHAPTER FOURTEEN
1700–1799 III

In May 1728, the *London Journal* publicises a new edition of the poem *The Bastard* by satirist Richard Savage. It is dedicated "with all due Reverence to Mrs. BRET, once *Countess* of MACCLESFIELD."[1] Savage is raised in distressed circumstances, but at the age of seventeen discovers he is the illegitimate child of Anne Brett, the ex-wife of the Earl of Macclesfield. She rejects his overtures and treats him with cruelty whenever he makes contact. At thirty, and now a poet, Savage kills a man in a coffee-house brawl, and there is a well-publicised trial. When his death sentence is pardoned by Queen Caroline, his poetry becomes popular, and he writes the autobiographical *The Bastard*, with its stinging dedication.[2]

Below Savage's notice, a book of moral poems for children is advertised. Included are *The Folly of Drunkenness*, *Upon a Boy's being whipp'd at School*, *Upon waking out of a frightful Dream*, and *On playing at Foot-ball.*[3] The football poem contains the lines:

> What crowds pursue the tumbling ball,
> To hasten on its course,
> With eager eyes they watch it fall,
> and loudly to their partners call,
> to shew their utmost force. …
>
> the rising ball before them flies,
> and swiftly bounds along.
> But e'er he gains their distant goal,
> he slackens in his race;

1 Savage, R., *The Bastard*. S. Powell, Dublin, 1728. n.p.

2 Samuel Johnson declares that Savage was legitimate, and that his mother claimed adultery to engineer a divorce. In: Tracy, C. (ed.)., *Life of Savage*. Samuel Johnson. Clarendon Press, Oxford, 1972. p. 4.

3 *London Journal*. 28 May 1728. p. 3.

then numbers soon his aim controul,
and back the flying globe they roll,
while shouting fills the place.[4]

That same May, the *Stamford Mercury* leads with London's weekly Bill of Mortality. Of a total of four hundred and fifty-six deaths, one hundred and seventy are under two years of age, and fifty per cent under five. The death rate is alarming, one in every one thousand four hundred citizens.[5] At least readers will be happy that five were over ninety years old. Some of the more outlandish deaths include: "Evil 2 … Horshoehead 1 … Mortification 3 … Purples 1… Rising of the Lights 1 … Teeth 30 … Thrush 1 … Water in the head 1"[6]

The British winter of 1739/40 is bitterly cold. The most ferocious since daily records began in 1722, it will remain the coldest winter ever. Passengers die as watermen ferry them across the Thames, post boys as they ride on horseback. Trees split; others are killed to the roots. Rivers and lakes in the north are encrusted with thick slabs of ice, twenty-two inches in Carlisle. Football and sliding are played on the Tyne, and there is horse racing on the Tees.[7,8] Twenty play football all day on the Derwent, probably the ones described a century later as playing on frozen river, "without any apprehension of danger", when it was precariously thin.[9,10] The ice storm advances south. The Thames freezes for seven weeks. There is football and skittles on the river, and the Men of Eton play the Men of Windsor at football for 10 gns.[11,12] In Ireland, "a great frost rotted almost all the potatoes … in half an hour", while the ice on the River Corrib in Galway is so thick hundreds

4 Watts, I., Foxton, T, *Moral Songs Composed for the Use of Children*. n.p., London, 1728. p. 28.

5 To give perspective, deaths in London in 2019 (pre-COVID) totalled nine hundred and sixty-two a week; approximately double the number of deaths in 1728. London's population in 2019 was nine million. England's entire population in 1728 was ten million.

6 *Stamford Mercury*. 9 May 1728. p. 1.

7 *Kentish Weekly Post*. 10 January 1739. p. 3.

8 *Derby Mercury*. 24 January 1739. p. 1.

9 *Derbyshire Courier*. 20 February 1841. p. 3.

10 *Derby Mercury*. 26 January 1776. p. 4.

11 *Kentish Weekly Post*. 10 January 1739. p. 3.

12 *Kentish Weekly Post*. 23 January 1740. p. 4.

play football on it.[13] The following winter, football is played on the glittering Liffey.[14]

George II dies in 1760, the last monarch born abroad, the only one to lead a British army into battle, the longest lived to date, and the last to be buried in Westminster Abbey. Football barely flinches. From humble origins, he gathers speed under the next George. He has secret ambitions others would think absurd. Why rule a country when you can rule the world. Match reports up the detail. Many are twelve-a-side. One in Co. Dublin, pitting the villages of Santry and Clonshaugh against Malahide, lasts three hours—"with equal strength, agility, and spirit"—until darkness prevails.[15] "Agility" suggests a developing skillset. Some years later, Bag take on Liffey at a Dublin fête for a dozen pairs of gloves and a barrel of ale.[16] Other prizes include a silk handkerchief for the "best female dancer … and to the old woman who dances the best jig, one pound of tobacco." A "grand Match at football" at "Marybone Fields", London, pitches north against south Wales for fifty pounds "upon which many betts are depending."[17] The rebranding of gambling.

Knappan's violence can engulf the Welsh countryside, but his taciturnity makes even Cornish hurling ostentatious. His sons are the celts of Wales, gracious and reclusive in their sporting habits, reserved in a manner the English and the Irish could never be. Folk football has a foothold there. For how long can never be known beyond the Welsh soul. Football will honour the secret. It is first mentioned in 1593, as *pêl droed* (football), in a poem by William Middleton.[18] In the mid-sixteenth century, the sports of students at Friar's School in Bangor, north Wales, are restricted to archery and "running-at-base" (presumably prisoner's base).[19] Ruthin Grammar School, in north Wales, similarly bans ball games in 1589: "the walls … and glass windows of the school, shall not be damaged or defaced by the scholars by playing at ball or any like

13 Dutton, H., *A Statistical and Agricultural Survey of the County of Galway*. R. Graisberry, Dublin, 1824. pp. 312–313.

14 Blythe, E.P., *The First Decade of the G.A.A. in Dublin*. Dublin Historical Record, 1963, 19:1, p. 17.

15 *Dublin Courier*. 4 April 1763. p. 1.

16 *Dublin Evening Post*. 12 October 1782. p. 3.

17 *Morning Chronicle*. 6 June 1772. p. 2.

18 Lile, E., *Rural Sports in Wales, c1750–c1900: Continuity and Change*. Unpublished PhD thesis, University of Glamorgan, 2006. p. 35.

19 Ibid, p. 160.

Diversions."[20] In 1629, the vicar of Chirk, in Denbighshire, mentions football's popularity, including on Sabbath days, while in 1656 1d is recorded in the accounts of Chirk Castle as payment for balls.[21,22] They are likely to be footballs or tennis balls; this is north Wales, where *knappan* is not played. An eighteenth-century game on the island of Anglesey is recorded:

"As a youth, my whole object was to excel in the two chief games of that time—football and tennis. Scores of us assembled near Llandrygan on a Sunday morning ... and near the churchyard entrance, about the hour of service, down with the ball and away with it, everyone with his kick, taking it backwards and forwards, until sunset found the players sometimes on the Malltraeth Sands, sometimes on the Gader Point, from which it would be kicked into the sea in the direction of Gogarth [the Great Orme] Head or Bardsey Isle. Numbers of players would be left here and there on the road, some having limbs broken in the struggle, others severely injured, and some carried on biers to be buried in the churchyard nearest to where they had been mortally wounded."

The deaths are surely an embellishment. Annual games are held there from 1737 to 1749.[23] An Easter twelve-a-side in in Anglesey, in 1734, attracts four thousand spectators. It ends 1-0 after three to four hours. This more contained affair has its share of violence, but the sides part, "as good friends as they came, after they had spent half an hour together in cherishing their spirits with a cup of ale ... having finished Easter Holydays innocently and merrily."[24] The "sour spirit" of the local Methodist movement should look away in 1779. The people of Anglesey "delighted in nothing except sport and carnal pleasures", the men playing football "all in their pants and shirts ... the women in scores contended and yelled at the top of their voices; in their excitement and wild rage."[25] That year, a Methodist in Anglesey laments that, "Before the recent Methodist revival broke ... the common people ... had no more knowledge than the

20 Ibid, p. 160.

21 Ibid, p. 35.

22 Myddelton Family. *Chirk Castle Accounts, A.D. 1605–1666*. Gibbs & Bamforth Ltd., St Albans, 1908. p. 58.

23 Lile, E., *Rural Sports in Wales, c1750–c1900: Continuity and Change*. Unpublished PhD thesis, University of Glamorgan, 2006. p. 36. Ibid, p. 54.

24 Ibid, p. 36.

25 Ibid, pp. 81–82.

wild creatures of the Mountains; they delighted in … playing with dice and cards, dancing and singing with the harp, playing football, tennis, mock trials and hostages … the lads and young men, by the hundreds, kicking the Football."[26] Even so, the church has always held a line. In 1726, when John Lewis asserts that "Tennis-playing is an Innocent and Inoffensive Diversion", he is still prosecuted for Sabbath "tennisball and fivesball" in the churchyard of Llanvapley, in Monmouthsire.[27]

By the second quarter of the eighteenth century some ministers are encouraging ball games in south Wales, though it is unclear if they are *knappan* or football. Thomas Davies plays with his parishioners in Ystradyfodwg, in Glamorganshire, another minister officiates at important ball games.[28] Crimson mounts in football's cheeks, embarrassed he has overtaken *knappan* in a way Cornwall, Ireland, and East Anglia would not suffer, invading from the north, eclipsing the Romans. In 1780, a sports day is held in Mynydd Pysgodlyn, in south Wales.[29] Sack races, donkey races, and bandy, yes, but him? Mynydd Pysgodlyn. Site of an eighteen hundred-year-old barrow. Little wonder the victors of the twelve-a-side are bribed with a bottle of gin a man. When bandy is first played in Wales is unclear, but it is unlikely to be much different to the rest of the isles, where stickball games are first heard of c1000AD. In Pembrokeshire, that most *knappan* of counties, it goes by the Welsh *chware bando*: bandy play.[30] The name was shortened to bando and adopted by the Welsh. Despite claims to the contrary, there is no evidence that it was materially different to bandy.

Cricket adopts a different stance to football. He springs shamelessly into Wales, looking for an angle. As early as 1693, Thomas D'Urfey writes of "Rice ap Shinken … A young, whimsical Welsh Fop", who plays cricket. The verse is twenty-seven years earlier than the generally accepted date of 1719, and a rare addition to the sixteenth century canon:

---

26 Ibid, p. 108.

27 Barber, M., *Records of the Court of Arches in Lambeth Palace Library*. Ecclesiastical Law Journal, 1 January 1993, p. 17.

28 Ibid, p. 109.

29 Ibid, p. 27.

30 Waddington, H.M., *Games and Athletics in Bygone Wales*. Transactions of the Honourable Society of Cymmrodorion, 1953, p. 95.

Hur [He] was the prettiest Fellows, *trum*, *trum*, &c.
At Bandy once and Cricket, *trum*, &c.
At Hunting-Chace, or High-foot Race,
Gadsplut [God's blood] how hur could Prick it: trum, &c.[31]

Admired by Charles II, D'Urfey is from the hurling county of Devon. He provides another cricket reference the year before: "the Cricketty Minute, a Minute when they say a Woman can deny a Man nothing; besides, I love cricket hugely."[32] The better part of the eighteenth century passes before the next reference to cricket in Wales. In 1770, the Welsh word for the insect—cricced—is adopted for the game.[33] The third mention is in a 1771 letter to a London newspaper, from a man in Swansea, taking aim at local Sabbath pursuits: "football, wrestling, cricket, fighting, jumping and an enormous use of oaths is made their exercise and the pastors of these places generally take too little pains for restraining this vice of profaining the Lord's day."[34] The second mention is of far greater importance, the first mention of a cricket match in Wales—. The full text has never left the archives. On 12 July 1783, Richard Jones writes to John Philipps, from Carmarthenshire, in southwest Wales:

"Dr Philipps—I have frequently heard you talk of cricket as a favouri't game and that you would willingly make one of a sett at any time. The following gentlemen are prepared upon to enter into my list and are willing to meet any sett which you can produce. There is a very good place on the little common between me and Court Henry. We may fix the tent near and dine in it. Batts, balls, &c, shall be provided by me. If you accept the challenge it should be soon as the ground and weather are favourable. The dress, if you approve it, may be a swan-skin jacket with sleeves edged with coloured ribband, which will not stand each

31 D'Urfey, T., *The Richmond Heiress*. s.n., London, 1693. n.p.

32 D'Urfey, T., *The Marriage-Hater Match'd*. s.n., London, 1692. p. 24.

33 Harris, J. (ed.), *The Red Dragon: The National Magazine of Wales*, Vol 11, 1887, p. 269; Walters, J., *An English-Welsh Dictionary*. s.n., London, 1794. The dictionary was first printed in twelve parts (each of ninety-six pages) between 1770 and 1783 (ending in "*Rampied*") by the Cowbridge Press, in Wales. No copies are known to exist. Cricket would have been in the first or second parts, published in 1770. The earliest definite mention is in the complete 1794 version, which was a collation of existing parts.

34 Hignall, A., Harragan, B., *Whites on Green: A History of Cricket at St Helen's, Swansea*. Association of Cricket Statisticians and Historians, s.l., 2018. p. 6. The reference is given as the *General Evening Post*, April 1771. I was unable to locate the article in any of the April editions.

person above 2s 6d or 3s 6d at the utmost, and be of use afterwards. If you should not be able to make up a sett we may meet and toss up for choice of partners, as I am sure there will be number sufficient to make up a double wickett. With my best compliments to Mrs Philipps and Mrs Jones, believe me Dear Philipps. Yours Sincerely Rd Jones. PS Have you heard how Mrs Lloyd of Llanwili is [?]"[35]

The date and location is provided in an issue of the *Hereford Journal*: "Court-Henry Down, near Cross Inn, in the county of Carmarthen, between the Gentlemen of the East side of the Cothy and those of the West; to play eleven of a side.[36] A fifty guinea-a-side prize does little to endear cricket to the Welsh. Nevertheless, within a year—possibly two—Swansea, Glamorganshire, has its own cricket club: "according to last Year's Resolutions, the sixth day of May next was fixed upon for the first Meeting this Season … to meet at the Bathing House early … Wickets, as usual, to be pitched at 11 o'clock."[37] Cricket fails to take off in Wales. And Scotland. And Ireland. Is he too patently English? There *is* one corner of Wales that develops a soft spot. Is it coincidence that both Court Henry Down and Swansea are in southwest Wales? Unlikely. The home of knappan is tough enough, confident enough to overlook his Englishness. Cricket repays the debt, points to the horizon. Craning, Glamorganshire can just about see itself as the only first-class Welsh county cricket team. Otherwise, cricket is pooh-poohed. Perhaps he needed a lesson in humility. The future is oval. Is it any wonder a carrying game, cast from *knappan*'s forge, will captivate the entire nation, or that Wales's original rugby club, Neath, is in Glamorganshire. The most successful Welsh rugby teams will come from the southwest, and the southwest shall become the heart of Welsh rugby, and will provide the lion's share of red dragons for that most stirring of things. The Wales national rugby union team.

Cricket smiles ruefully. He that never climbed, never fell. He lowers his standard, turns east, crosses the border. When he reads the milestone, his face crumples with satisfaction. Gloucestershire!

~

35 *Letter: Richard Jones, Pantglas to John George Phillips, esq, Cwmgwilly.* Archives Hub. https://archiveshub.jisc.ac.uk/search/archives/e3371cd9–6d04–33f9–971a-9e7014c24063?component=a01c8638–b57e-3b01-bf47–0a21fd9d5cf5&terms=cricket. Accessed 24 February 2024.

36 *Hereford Journal*. 31 July 1783. p. 2.

37 *Hereford Journal*. 5 May 1785. p. 2.

Camping is born stubborn, and the years do not blunt his recklessness. Or his temper. Brittonic, Angle, and Viking blood pump through him. Composure is for other sports. There is ice in his grey eyes as he surveys the North Sea. He will never concede his stronghold. His ball play is awesome, and he has fast hands and a great reach. And when he is battle-mad …

Throughout the eighteenth century he is the undisputed king of East Anglia. The editor of a 1710 edition of Thomas Tusser's *Five Hundred Points of Good Husbandry* adds: "Camping is Foot-ball playing, at which they are very dextrous in Norfolk; and so many people running up and down a piece of ground, without doubt evens and soddens it … the trampling of so many People drives also the mole away."[38]

Camping is enough of a nuisance for Norwich to declare that, "Whereas complaint … of a great disorder committed by Apprentices and Others in the Castle Dykes and other places in this Citty under pretence of camping and throwing at cocks I am hereby to order that if any further disorders be committed by the meeting of 3 or more upon the like pretence … they will be prosecuted for a Ryott."[39] In 1720, the rector at Landbeach, Cambridgeshire, pays 2s 6d "by custom on Shrove Tuesday for the Football men."[40] More camping matches are recorded at Landbeach, in 1727.[41] In 1715, the publican of the Galliot Hoy[42] in Holbrook, Suffolk, regularly organises "Camps, runnings, wrastlings and other diversions as Cards, Nine Pins, etc", an enterprise the local magistrate rails against for its "encouragement of lewdness and debauchery."[43]

Matches are advertised in local papers. As early as 1723, a game in Rickinghall, Suffolk, is publicised.[44] Linking a match to better patronised

38 Hillman, D. (ed.)., *Tusser Redivivus. Five Hundred Points of Good Husbandry*. J. Morphew, London, 1710. p. 15.

39 Griffin, E., *England's Revelry: A History of Popular Sports and Pastimes*. Oxford University Press, 2005. pp. 99–100.

40 Clay, W.K., *A History of the Parish of Landbeach in the county of Cambridge*. Deighton, Bell & Co., London, 1861. p. 60.

41 Ibid, p. 60.

42 A small single-masted vessel resembling a Dutch galliot used to convey passengers and goods short distances.

43 Dymond, D., *The game of camping in eastern England*. The Local Historian, 2021, 51:1, pp. 3–4.

44 Dymond, D., *A Lost Social Institution: The Camping Close*. Rural History, 1990, 1:2, p. 190.

sports guarantees larger crowds. In 1728, in the village of Chelmondiston, Suffolk, a camping match for ten pairs of gloves follows a horse race, while a 1741 match at Harford Bridges, Norfolk, is sandwiched between archery and ten-pins.[45,46] Holiday ball games are frequent, representing an uninterrupted lineage to the less structured games of the Middle Ages. A two-day Whitsun fête at Layer-de-la Haye, north Essex, has a horse show, an ass-race, and a football match.[47] In 1735, Cambridgeshire take up Norfolk's challenge of a twelve-a-side foot-ball match for 200 gns, best of three. Norfolk has done this before, winning 200 gns at Lambeth, in 1709. The size of the pitch will be 201 by 210 yds, and is to be "rop'd or hurdled in."[48,49] The proprietor of the Artillery Ground in London offers his services then backs out "unless they would play in Frosty weather." Two appointees decide on an alternative venue, which, they have ruled, must be within ten miles of London, presumably to attract a crowd. They settle on Putney Heath, "where the Turf being very short, firm, and level, will be very convenient to play the Foot Ball Match upon."[50] Thirty-nine years later, a hundred and fifty thousand spectators gather at the Artillery Ground to see the first balloon ascent in England, the Prince of Wales among them. "The Daredevil Aeronaut", Vincenzo Lunardi, controls the balloon horizontally by flapping a pair of wings, and vertically by rowing with oars. He has three companions: a cat, a dog, and a caged pigeon. And a bottle of wine. Journalists play on lunatic and Lunardi. The pigeon escapes and the air-sick cat necessitates an unplanned pit stop in South Mimms, but Lunardi and his dog land safely, bottle-empty, twenty miles away. When he asks farmhands for assistance they refuse "one who came in the Devil's house", until a young woman intervenes.[51]

By the mid-eighteenth century, excessive violence deters burgeoning sponsorship at camping matches. Money and sport are bedfellows. It was ever so. Gambling, food tents, drinking booths, prizes. A threat to their

45 *Ipswich Journal*. 14 September 1728. p. 4.

46 Dymond, D., *The game of camping in eastern England*. The Local Historian, 2021, 51:1, p. 7.

47 Brown, A.F.J., *Essex at Work, 1700–1815*. The Tindall Press, Chelmsford, Essex, 1969. p. 72.

48 *London Daily Post*. 20 October 1735. p. 2.

49 Approximately twice the size of a modern football pitch.

50 *London Daily Post*. 24 October 1735. p. 4.

51 Lunardi, V., *An Account of the First Aërial Voyage in England*. John Bell, London, 1784. pp. 27–28, 31–32, 35, 37.

alliance? That cannot be. Rules are implemented. In Langton Green in 1730, anyone who kicks an opponent who has been thrown to the ground is fined 2s 6d.[52] In Ditchingham, Norfolk, in 1741, a ten-a-side inter-county game is called off when the Suffolk players fail to show. They are challenged again, adding that "if any Person strikes another when down, he is not entitled to a Hat" if his side win.[53] It casually mentions the presence of judges, as if it is the norm. In Eye, Suffolk, in 1752, engaging in combat is strictly one-on-one, while in Boxford, Suffolk, such combats only allow for one strike at an opponent.[54,55] Geographical variability of rules appears minor and does not change the essence of the game. Numbers are limited by the size of the camping close. Ten-a-sides are standard, but twelve-a-sides are not unusual. Cross-country games enable much greater numbers, though substantially fewer are reported. Games in camping closes are brief, punishing affairs and generally last thirty minutes; cross-country games can last for hours. Scoring is by goals, notches, or byes.

Mixed nomenclature is demonstrated in May 1736. An inter-county "game of camp or foot-ball" with a 5s prize to each winning player, is advertised to take place on Homersfield Heath, Suffolk. Norfolk wear red, Suffolk white. The game is unique for requiring players to carry "a piece" in each hand, presumably an object to prevent handling of the ball. A football style of camping, then, suited to a close.[56,57] The next month a "camp or match of foot-ball" is to take place at the Three Horse Shoes in Ashby, Norfolk. The pub hosts a match of "Foot-ball" in 1737, "to camp at 5 o'clock … A glass of good wine, with a glass of good beer, and a hearty welcome" is offered to the players.[58] In 1740, a match at Harleston, Norfolk, with a prize of a crown each for the winning side, is jointly sponsored by the publicans of the Three Tuns and the White Horse. There is further incentive. The first player

52 Dymond, D., *The game of camping in eastern England.* The Local Historian, 2021, 51:1. p. 9.

53 *Ipswich Journal.* 10 October 1771. p. 4.

54 Dymond, D., *The game of camping in eastern England.* The Local Historian, 2021, 51:1. p. 9.

55 *Ipswich Journal.* 8 September 1750. p. 4.

56 David Dymond details evidence that the terms were used interchangeably: Dymond, D., *A Lost Social Institution: The Camping Close.* In *Rural History*, 1990, 1:2, pp. 165–192.

57 Dymond, D., *The game of camping in eastern England.* The Local Historian, 2021, 51:1, pp. 2, 4.

58 Ibid, pp. 2, 4.

to score gets half a crown. Landlords have a preternatural sense for good business.[59]

Prizes draw star players. "TEN HATS are to be Campt for by Ten Men of a Side" near the Lantern-Green tavern in Eye, Suffolk, in 1741, one of four advertised that year.[60] "TEN HATS to be CAMP'D for" in Ditchingham, Norfolk, is sponsored by the Bath House Inn. The ball for "the best of half an Hour" ten-a-side will be "thrown off at three."[61] A third match is "to be Camp'd for Free, at Brundwell White Horse, near Blofield, on the 10th of May, Ten Hats with Silver Buttons and hoops: To hand up at One o'clock and play between Two and Three."[62] An hour-long ten-a-side. To "hand up" and "thrown off" are probably Norfolk dialect for throwing the ball up. In August, "to be camped for Gratis" two camping matches on the same day at New Buckenham, Norfolk.[63] Judges officiate the thirty minute ten-a-side games. The first ball is "thrown off" at two, for a prize of ten crowns or ten pairs of buckskin gloves, the second at five for ten laced hats. The prize at Harford Bridges that year is a "Gold Button and Loop" for each winner.[64]

On Whit Monday 1748, "TEN pair of GLOVES, given Gratis, will be Camp'd for at the Ostrich" at Bonebridge, Suffolk.[65] Two consecutive half-hour games in Boxford, Suffolk, are well-advertised in 1750. The prizes are ten silver-laced hats the first day, ten hats with silver loops and buttons the next. The prizes are donated by two local pubs, confident they will draw plenty of thirsty spectators. It is all quite lavish. The playing area is roped off, a stopwatch is used to time the game and a French horn to call time, and there is a spectators' gallery with 6d seats.[66,67] Half a guinea to each winner is "to be camp'd for" by twenty men in Eye, Suffolk, in 1752, while a 10-a-side at Cranley Green in Eye is announced in the *Ipswich Journal* in 1754: "made by

59 Ibid, p. 4.

60 *Ipswich Journal*. 29 August 1741. p. 3.

61 *Ipswich Journal*. 29 October 1771. p. 4.

62 Glyde, J., *The Norfolk Garland*. Jarrold and Sons, London, 1872. p. 165.

63 *Norwich Gazette*. 15–22 August 1741. p. 3.

64 Dymond, D., *The game of camping in eastern England*. The Local Historian, 2021, 51:1, p. 4.

65 *Ipswich Journal*. 21 May 1748. p. 3.

66 6d per seat, or half a shilling. A skilled tradesman earned two and a half shillings a day.

67 *Ipswich Journal*. 8 September 1750. p. 4.

the gentlemen of Suffolk … booths erected for refreshments etc." [68,69] The sponsoring publican assures all gentlemen, "a hearty welcome from their humble servant."[70] In 1755, the *Ipswich Journal* carries a notice: "This to acquaint all lovers of that manly exercise of Foot-Ball playing, that there will be Ten Hats play'd for on Bury Race-Ground [Suffolk] by Ten Men on a side … to meet at John Place's Booth at the sign of the Three Pigeons … to play the best of three-quarters of an Hour: The ball to be thrown off at Six o'clock."[71]

In 1769, a football match between Essex and Suffolk is to take place at Thorpe-le-Soken, north Essex.[72] The shortness of the game—"the best in half an hour"—suggests camping. No less than twenty men to play for ten gold-laced hats, a common prize. The page carries an advert for a jeweller who has moved to the Sign of the Golden Cup and wants, "a Journeyman Tallow-Chandler … Likewise, at Michalemas next, a Man that understands making Malt for Home Consumption." In 1774, Jacob Bryant attempts to connect the entire canon of folklore and mythology to the Book of Genesis. He links camping to "Amonian temples" otherwise known as "Campi": "the exhibition of those manly sports in vogue among country people is called Camping: and the inclosures for that purpose, where they wrestle and contend, are called Camping closes."[73]

The victory of Wickham Market, Suffolk, over Parham, Suffolk, is reported in 1784. Suffolk antiquarian David Davy remembers camping in the late 1700s, "as the favourite amusement of the labouring youth of Suffolk … [who played] two or three times a week … during the summer evenings … real battles with much activity, agility and strength."[74,75] In the version he saw, the ball was not thrown up but left at the centre for the teams to race to. There is prohibition of bowling, football, or gaming at alehouses in the Essex village of Theydon Garnon, south Essex,

---

68 Dymond, D., *The game of camping in eastern England.* The Local Historian, 2021, 51:1, p. 4.

69 Malcolmson, R.W., *Popular Recreations in English Society 1700–1850.* Unpublished PhD thesis, University of Warwick, 1970. pp. 86, 91.

70 Dymond, D., *The game of camping in eastern England.* The Local Historian, 2021, 51:1, p. 4.

71 *Ipswich Journal.* 17 May 1775. p. 3.

72 *Ipswich Journal.* 30 September 1769. p. 3.

73 Bryant, J., *A New System, Or, An Analysis of Ancient Mythology.* s.n., London, 1774. p. 53.

74 *Ipswich Journal.* 10 July 1784. p. 2.

75 Dymond, D., *A Lost Social Institution: The Camping Close.* In: *Rural History*, 1990, 1:2, p. 183.

in 1757.[76] Two years later, when magistrates in Suffolk ban the Upper Street Fair, publicans are barred from offering gloves or saddles for football matches and donkey races.[77]

Camping enjoys its share of patronage. In 1730, Sir Robert Walpole—eight years into his two-decade service as the first and longest-serving prime minister—organises camping matches for his friends at Houghton Hall, Norfolk, close to where he is born.[78] The 5th Earl of Rochford is also fond of the game, attending matches near his estate in Easton, Suffolk.[79] William Windham often organises camping matches near his seat at Felbrigg Hall, Norfolk, where he was raised.[80] It speaks of the robustness of the game when Windham records that camping "combined all athletic excellences, a successful combatant requiring to be a good boxer, runner, and wrestler."[81] His diaries record him in a coach en route to a ball at Blickling Hall, Norfolk: "[I] suffered myself to think on idle things, camping, &.," [82] He regularly refers to attending matches, including camps at St Omer and Sheringham, both in Norfolk.[83]

Windham attends the Norfolk Sessions in 1787, as he believes resolutions against camping are to be made. He is known to love "the sports of the people… [and] vigorously defended these diversions in Parliament against all attempts to suppress them."[84,85] Both he and Walpole attended Eton, an early adopter of ball games. Windham organises a game at Fellbrigg Hall in October 1789, instructing his man: "You will go to Somers of Southrepps, I think, a publican with one arm, and tell him to prepare some men for a camp. Inform yourself from him the best way of making an equal & good match … two men to prepare

---

76 *Essex Archives Online*. https://www.essexarchivesonline.co.uk/ViewCatalogue.aspx?ID=21340. Accessed 27 December 2023.

77 *Ipswich Journal*. 13 June 1759. p. 3.

78 Dutt, W.A., *Highways and Byways in East Anglia*. MacMillan and Co., Ltd., London, 1901. p. 153.

79 Forby, R., *The Vocabulary of East Anglia*. 2 Vols. J.B. Nichols and Son, London, 1830. Vol. 1. p. 51.

80 Dutt, W.A., *Highways and Byways in East Anglia*. MacMillan and Co., London, 1901. p. 153.

81 Ketton-Cremer, R.W., *Camping—A Forgotten Norfolk, Game*. Norfolk and Norwich Archaeology Society, 1931. p. 90.

82 Baring, C.A. (ed.), *The Diaries of the Right Hon William Windham, 1784–1810*. Longmans, Green, and Co. 1866. p. 91. Windham was present at the first balloon ascent.

83 Ibid, pp. 157, 257.

84 Ibid, p. 121.

85 Ketton-Cremer, R.W., *Camping—A Forgotten Norfolk Game*. Norfolk and Norwich Archaeology Society, 1931. p. 90.

each a side … the hour of meeting 2, and of beginning precisely three … he [Somers] shall have the privilege of selling ale, and erecting a booth … & he, and any other, that may be chosen, must find the ropes between them." The match is advertised locally: "A PRIZE will be given to be camped for in FELLBRIGG PARK: the Prize to the Winners to be a HAT of the real value of Ten Shillings as cost at the shop;—and to the Losers, A PAIR of STOCKINGS each, of the real value of Two Shillings & Sixpence."[86]

In his book on East Anglian vocabulary, Robert Forby includes: "Camping-land, *s.* a piece of ground set aside for the exercise of *camping.* Land was given for this purpose with all due formalities." He adds: "Camping-ball, *s.* a ball particularly adapted to the sport of *camping.* It is to be feared that the same name is sometimes most abusively misapplied to the common light foot-ball."[87] Elsewhere, a rector who dies in 1785, "was a fighting man. He also took part in 'the camping': the camping ground was to the west of the church. Camping is not football. The ball was about the size of a cricket-ball, and was driven through a narrow goal."[88] In other words, camping used purpose-made balls. The use of "driven" suggests that the ball was kicked rather than thrown or carried through the narrow goal. There may have been two sorts of ball: an inflated one suitable for kicking in camping closes and a hard one for "to the country", where balls were more commonly carried and thrown across the long distances involved.

The most notorious camping match of the era is said to have been played in 1830 but probably took place in the late 1700s.[89] It has an apocryphal peal. "I have heard old persons speak of a celebrated camping, Norfolk against Suffolk, on Diss Common, with 300 on each side. Before the ball was thrown up, the Norfolk men inquired, tauntingly, of the Suffolk men, if they had brought their coffins! The Suffolk men, after fourteen hours, were the victors. Nine deaths were the result of the contest within a fortnight. These were called "fighting camps", for much boxing was practised in them."[90]

---

86 Ibid, pp. 90–91.

87 Forby, R., *The Vocabulary of East Anglia.* 2 Vols. J.B. Nichols and Son, London, 1830. Vol. 1. p. 53.

88 *Notes and Queries*, 1892, 8:2, pp. 137–138.

89 Dutt, W.A., *The Last Camping Match.* The Badminton Magazine, 1899, 9:48, p. 91.

90 Diss Common is in Norfolk, near the Suffolk border.

What is unknown is how commonplace kickabouts are. The camping land in East Bilney, Norfolk, is used after evening service on Sundays, while in the late 1700s camping is described "as the favourite amusement of the labouring youth of Suffolk … [who played] two or three times a week … during the summer evenings."[91] Arguably, camping is played extensively in groups large and small, by children, youths, and men, in villages, towns, fields, and streets throughout East Anglia, just as football is elsewhere. And played in the early fourteenth century and surely long before.

~

Lincolnshire-born Amos Appleyard is raised by strict Methodist parents and becomes a champion of the religion. One expects a model boy, but during his schooldays in the late 1750s, "being of a very lively disposition, he became one of the foremost at foot-ball, cards, and other vain and sinful pursuits."[92] In 1768, a Lincolnshire paper reports:

"We hear from Donington, that on Saturday last a Paper was fixed upon the Market Cross, with notice for a Foot Ball match to be played on the Monday following … and that the inhabitants of Horbling, Billingborough, and Quadring, would assist the Parish of Donington in any case of the Fen Riots. But notice of this being sent to the Gentlemen of the country, they, together with their friends and servants, proceeded to Donington, in order to preserve the peace, and defend their property; by which prudent step the Rioters were prevented from making their appearance."[93]

Calmer waters in Wroxham, Norfolk, five days later: "the great Camping Match between the towns of Blofield and Worstead, for a considerable sum of money is decided in Favour of Blofield. There was smart fighting and it lasted about 33 minutes. The concourse of people were supposed to be about 10,000."[94,95] Camping is at its apogee. Still, it is not all about camping in East Anglia. Three attempts are made to curb trapball in Norwich in 1785. It is testament to trapball's popularity that it

91 Dymond, D., *A Lost Social Institution: The Camping Close*. In: *Rural History*, 1990, 1:2, p. 183.

92 Chapman, B., *Memoir of Mr. Amos Appleyard*. Methodist Magazine, 1815, 38, p. 401.

93 *Stamford Mercury*. 23 June 1768. p. 3.

94 *Public Advertiser*. 28 June 1768. p. 4.

95 It is likely that attendances for all ball sports were consistently inflated, though not necessarily wildly so.

is the only game singled out, when "other games" are also embargoed.[96] Not so good when it appears in a murder case in 1729. The man was seen playing trapball a few weeks before he is killed.[97] Trapball is making the ads. In 1768, Robert Rutty reports the relocation of the Coffee-House, Stoke Newington, to new premises that have a "large field for cricket and trap-ball, besides a private ground for Dutch pins."[98] Two years later, George Lambert of the Adam and Eve tavern, beside St Pancras Church advertises, "this season for the Mineral Waters … the house and garden are genteel and rural, and [a] trap-ball ground in the adjoining field … coffee, tea, and hot loaves every day, and cows kept for having new milk, cream, and syllabubs, neat wines, cyder."[99] There is even a rhyme: "All those that love trap-ball to Lambert's repair [,] Leave the smoak of the town and take the fresh air."

Trapball is a survivor. You wouldn't see him if he walked straight past you. Collar up, head down, lost in the crowd. His provenance stretches back to the fourteenth century and forwards to the late twentieth century. He evolves into knurr and spell, a popular game in the north of England. A walnut-sized ball (the knurr) is launched into the air using a wooden trap with a release mechanism. The player uses his bat (the spell) to thwack the knurr and send it as far as possible. Incentivised by generous cash prizes, a good player can catapult it two hundred yards. A common variation is a requirement to land the ball between two lines: "if it falls withoutside of either, he gives up his bat and is out." Ditto if the knurr is caught, or if it hits the trap when thrown back, or falls within a bat's length of the trap.[100]

Throughout the seventeenth and eighteenth centuries, trapball games are regularly advertised and draw large crowds. Not everyone is enamoured. In Kendal, a 1657 order states that anyone above twelve who plays, "in the streets at a game commonly called Kattstick and Bulluett [trapball] shall forfeit and incur the penalty of 12d. for every offence …

96 *Norfolk Chronicle*: 16 July 1785. p. 1; 27 May 1786. p. 2; 18 August 1787. p. 3,

97 *Cobbett's Complete Collection of State Trials*, 1726–1743. p. 534. https://sources-tannerritchie-com.ap1.proxy.openathens.net/browser.php?ipid=1284225. Accessed 31 December 2023.

98 Harris, B., *Gambling in Britain in the Long Eighteenth Century*. Cambridge University Press, 2022. p. 85.

99 *Gazetteer and New Daily Advertiser*. 13 July 1770. p. 2.

100 Block, D., *Baseball Before We Knew It: A Search for the Roots of the Game*. University of Nebraska Press, Lincoln, Nebraska, 2005. pp. 84, 124.

and where they have no goods to be imprisoned two hours."[101] There is more to Suffolk than camping; an 1825 book reports an annual tradition in Bury St Edmonds: "On Shrove Tuesday, Easter Monday, and the Whitsuntide festivals, twelve old women side off for a game of trap-and-ball, which is kept up with the greatest spirit and vigour until sunset. One old lady, named Gill, upwards of sixty years of age has been celebrated as the "mistress of the sport" for a number of years past … the merry combatants dexterously hurl the giddy ball to and fro."[102]

Trapball lets slip his guard, smiling affectionately at his offspring while reminiscing on his own long stretch in the sun, the rudimentary levers and triggers, the future James II's gossipy talk with Pepys,[103] that game on ice in 1814,[104] the one played in wheelbarrows,[105] another pitting Bell's Life against Dispatch at the Half Moon, Dulwich,[106] chimneysweeps in Hyde Park,[107] the dedicated clubs and greens and grounds,[108,109,110] crossing to the United States.[111] He savours his four favourites last. That mention in the first edition of Samuel Johnson's dictionary; the Kent-Surrey five-a-side "Grand Match of Trap-ball" for 200 gns, at the Porcupine Inn, Mottingham, Kent, reported with eccentric fortuity in London's *Porcupine* newspaper;[112] the 1773 *Juvenile Sports and Pastimes* appearance, cheek by jowl with *Observations on Cricket, a Dissertation on Marbles*, and the earliest mention of hockey in history.[113] Hockey and trapball merit a woodcut. His depicts five men in tricornes enjoying a game.[114] His best-loved treasure is abstract. The rhapsody of

101 Scott, D., *Bygone Cumberland and Westmorland.* William Andrews & Co., London, 1899. p. 199.

102 Hone. W., *The Every-day Book.* A. Applegath, London, 1825. p. 430.

103 Wheatley, H.B., *The Diary of Samuel Pepys, 1668.* George Bell and Sons, London, 1893. n.p.

104 *Windsor and Eton Express.* 7 March 1914. p. 6.

105 *Middlesex Journal.* 22–24 July 1773. p. 3.

106 *Bell's Life and Sporting Chronicle.* 30 September 1849. p. 8.

107 Public Advertiser. 14 June 1792. p. 6.

108 *Kentish Weekly Post.* 22 May 1798. p. 3; *Chester Chronicle.* 25 May 1798. p. 1.

109 *Bath Journal.* 21 May 1798. p. 3; *Morning Chronicle.* 1 April 1801. p. 4; *Kentish Gazette.* 11 June 1802. p. 4.

110 *Cobbett's Complete Collection of State Trials*, 1794. p. 679. https://sources-tannerritchie-com.apl.proxy.openathens.net/browser.php?ipid=1298708. Accessed 31 December 2023.

111 *Norfolk and Portsmouth Herald.* 11 February 1820. p. 3.

112 *Porcupine.* 31 July 1801. p. 4.

113 Master Michel Angelo. *Juvenile Sports and Pastimes.* T. Carnan, London, 1773.

114 Block, D., *Baseball Before We Knew It: A Search for the Roots of the Game.* University of Nebraska Press, Lincoln, Nebraska, 2005. p. 179.

his youth. The glorious anarchy of playing on Sundays, turning soil in the farmer's field.

Trapball's smile dissolves. The poor lad. "Some boys in Cold Bath Fields, being at play at Trap-Ball, the Boy who was striking at the Ball accidentally hit another with the Stick at the Corner of his Eye, which instantly fell out of his Head on the Ground."[115] Trapball inhales sharply, pinches the bridge of his nose. "A young Lady had her Eye struck out by a Ball, as she was passing through Moorfields, near some Men who were playing at Trap Ball."[116] Cut to the quick, he plays uneasily with his heavy knuckles. "playing … at trap-ball near the river Thames, the son of Mrs. Knight, running too hastily, and missing his stroke, fell into the river, and was drowned."[117] Trapball stares blankly ahead, as guilt storms about his solitude. The player whose calf was torn off by a bystander's mastiff, the servant killed on the spot when his horse rears, struck on the ear by an errant ball.[118,119] After a prolonged fit of the despair he is prey to, he is gripped by a surge of nostalgia. Ah! But all those fêtes and fairs. A thousand delirious children pulling at their parents' sleeves, eager to get to the game, serious and united in their pursuit of fun. A clack and a thwack. Trapball turns back to the game as the knurr fizzes past his ear.

From the 1740s, cricket spreads across England. Publicans who have historically sponsored football and camping sense the inevitable.[120] In 1751, an All-England eleven play old Etonians at cricket at Newmarket, Suffolk, resplendent in silk jacket and velvet caps: "During the cricket matches, there were above 6000 people to see a great Match at Foot-ball; and that for the Diversion of the Populace, there was Cocking, Smock-Racing, Camping or Foot-ball, Wrestling, and Cudgelling."[121,122] Not for long. Cricket is debonair and dandy. And ruthless. Siphoning the oxygen, appraising a granule of arsenic. The horrors of those orphan years have disfigured his conscience. Camping is blindsided by the unsporting rules

115 *Sherborne Mercury*. 1 June 1752. p. 2.

116 *Kentish Weekly Post*. 27 July 1757. p. 2.

117 *London Evening Post*. 7–9 June 1763. p. 1.

118 *London Evening Post*. 11–13 June 1767. p. 1.

119 *London Evening Post*. 7–9 May 1765. p. 1.

120 Brown, A.F.J., *Essex at Work, 1700–1815*. The Tindall Press, Chelmsford, Essex, 1969. p. 72.

121 *Derby Mercury*. 5 July 1751. p. 2.

122 The absence of a comma further supports the notion of the interchangeability of the terms camping and football.

of modern engagement. A cricket match is advertised at "the Camping-land" in Stowmarket, Suffolk, in 1773, for eleven pairs of gloves; in September, a more formal match is advertised between Ipswich Corporation and Needham for 11 gns.[123,124] Stumps will be pitched on the camping close of Needham Market. In August 1785, cricketers use the camping closes of both Needham and Stowmarket.[125] The King's Head at Bradwell-on-Sea had been promoting "football as usual"; but in 1787, when Bradwell-on-Sea and Tillingham play Dengie Hundred, north Essex, at football for "eleven pair of valuable gloves, and eleven half crowns", a cricket match follows for the same prizes.[126,127,128] A return camping game is played two years later, but stumps are here to stay, and have little need of an opening act.[129]

In 1791, the *Ipswich Journal* advertises "a Match of Foot Ball … for Ten Gold laced hats, value One Guinea each, gratis, by any Twenty able men."[130] The venue is Thorp-le-Soken, north Essex, site of the original burden of proof case almost four hundred years earlier. "Gentle" cricket has ferocious camping in a chokehold. Above the advert is the annual meeting of the Holton Cricket club and a challenge by "The Cricketers of the Newton Club" to any other in Suffolk; below the advert, a cricket match in Debenham for "Eleven Pair of Gloves." In 1783, of camping: "this active game of our ancestors is still much in fashion" in *some* parts of Suffolk.[131] Still, you cannot take the camp out of campers. A cricket match in Suffolk between farmer's servants ends in a fatal stabbing in 1786.[132] Poignantly, on 20 July 1775, in Little Shelford, Cambridgeshire, "Will Jennings … began to open ye ground for a buriall vault in ye Camping close … and finished the same in four days."[133] A mausoleum.

123 *Ipswich Journal.* 10 April 1773. p. 3.

124 *Ipswich Journal.* 11 September 1773. p. 3.

125 *Ipswich Journal.* 13 August 1785. p. 3

126 Brown, A.F.J., *Essex at Work, 1700–1815.* The Tindall Press, Chelmsford, Essex, 1969. p. 72.

127 *Chelmsford Chronicle.* 22 June 1787. p. 1.

128 Shires were subdivided into hundreds for administrative and judicial purposes.

129 Malcolmson, R.W., *Popular Recreations in English Society 1700–1850.* Unpublished PhD thesis, University of Warwick, 1970. p. 87.

130 *Ipswich Journal.* 17 September 1791. p. 2.

131 Cullum, J., *The History and Antiquities of Hawsted, in the County of Suffolk,* J. Nichols, London, 1784. p. 113.

132 *Ipswich Journal.* 19 August 1786. p. 4.

133 Wale, J.H., *My Grandfather's Pocket-book.* Chapman and Hall Limited, London, 1883. p. 176.

Ghosts do not deter children. In 1787, the field keeper is sent to stop boys playing in what is left of the camping close, bequeathed to the owner's son two years later.[134,135]

What becomes of camping closes? Do they suffer the humiliation of becoming the village greens cricket is so famed for? Camping scratches his stubble and reflects. Cast aside like old shoes, yes. Nine parts dead, for sure. But the memory of an old child is long, and this grizzled warrior knows the lore of every field and close. He has centuries of tales behind him, and he is not quite done yet. And at the end? A mausoleum. It cannot be otherwise.

Residents of Steeple Bumpstead, north Essex, are accused of illegally entering a field to play sport, in 1759.[136] They plea that there "hath been a certain antient and laudable custom … that all the inhabitants have the liberty and privilege of exercising and playing … upon the said close."[137] The verdict finds for the defendants. A similar case in Great Tey, north Essex, also ends in success when the defendants argue that football has been played there for seventy years (1658).[138] The farmer had ploughed the field, which had also been used for a November the fifth bonfire.[139] It is the opposite in White Roding, south Essex, in 1724, when their right to play football on Grass Croft is revoked.[140]

~

By the late 1770s, ten-a-side football matches make the press: in Nottinghamshire, South Muskham beat North Muskham after four hours,[141] while the villages of Anlaby and Hessle do battle in the East Riding of Yorkshire.[142] Anlaby can only field nine but still win the "first two allies out of three" to claim the 20 gns. Allies are synonymous with goals.

---

134 Ibid, p. 257.

135 Ibid, p. 303.

136 A village with a camping ground.

137 Blackstone, H., *Reports of Cases Argued and Determined in the Courts of Common Pleas and Exchequer Chamber*. Richard Pheney, London, 1837. p. 393.

138 Malcolmson, R.W., *Popular Recreations in English Society 1700–1850*. Unpublished PhD thesis, University of Warwick, 1970, pp. 322–323.

139 Brailsford, D., *A Taste for Diversions: Sport in Georgian England*. The Lutterworth Press, Cambridge, 1999. p. 41.

140 *Essex Archives Online*. https://www.essexarchivesonline.co.uk/result_details.aspx?ThisRecordsOffSet=186&id=15177. Accessed 10 August 2023.

141 *Stamford Mercury*. 21 October 1796. p. 3.

142 *Leeds Intelligencer*. 26 May 1778. p. 3.

A later newspaper tells the story of a man who catches a hare through a hole in a hedge sealed with his hat, "an old football player would call this completely stopping the alley mouth."[143] The Anlaby paper also reports on a man working in a grovelling pit—an open mine for the extraction of gravel. The timber gives way, and he is buried sixty-six feet underground. His workmates dig desperately. After thirty-two hours, with all hope lost, they find him alive "without experiencing the smallest injury." Other organised matches are reported in parts of Devon, Rochdale in Lancashire, and Hitchin in Hertfordshire.[144] In 1772, when Hitchin play Gosford, the ball ends up in the priory pond. Gosford retrieve the ball, forcing it along Angel Street, across the Market place, and into the "Artichoke beer-house" before it is "goaled in the porch of St Mary's Church."[145]

In 1792, a sailing match on the River Orwell is followed by "a foot ball match" in a field adjoining Ipswich's Strand, "which was conducted with much agility and great good humour."[146,147] Two years later, in Norfolk, "as some young people are playing at football, at Hockham, near Thetford, one of them, the son of Mr Horax, blacksmith, was so much exhausted by his exertions in the game, that he fell down, and expired immediately."[148] Elsewhere on the page, William Windham donates 19s 6d to the prisoners in the city gaol, which they spend on beef and beer.[149] Ironically, the same sessions imprison a pair for a fortnight for stealing a leg of pork. And in a case of nominative determinism, Miss Pricks has £30 of thread lace stolen from her shop in Tombland.[150] Overleaf, a twenty-one-year-old Yorkshire woman secretly marries her lover. "Meeting with a number of obstacles from her relations", her husband decides to go to sea. She argues that if he joins a regiment instead, she will dress as a man and accompany him. They are enlisted together, she as a drummer. They see action in several battles, and she is injured three

143 *York Herald*. 23 January 1808. p. 2.

144 Malcolmson, R.W., *Popular Recreations in English Society 1700–1850*. Unpublished PhD thesis, University of Warwick, 1970. p. 86.

145 Hine, R.L., *The History of Hitchin*. George Allen & Unwin Ltd., London, 1929. p. 244.

146 Dymond, D., *A Lost Social Institution: The Camping Close*. In: *Rural History*, 1990, 1:2, p. 190.

147 *Ipswich Journal*. 7 July 1792. p. 2.

148 *Norfolk Chronicle*. 25 January 1784. p. 3.

149 Eight days' wages for a skilled tradesman.

150 Three horses.

times, once severely in the breast. She even escapes when taken prisoner. The surgeon who attends to her wound agrees to conceal her sex, and it is only when her husband is killed that she reveals it. Assuredly, she fought "where thundering Cannons did roar, Their bullets like Footballs flying from the Shoar."[151] Irrespective. She is a woman. There is no medal.

Satire and football are boon companions. Thomas Holcroft views the stage as the "optimal arena for social reform because of its large size [and] heterogeneous audience."[152] A political radical, his plays surgically lampoon the aristocracy. His most subversive, *Knave or Not?*, questions if there is justice for those who lack "the varnish of gold and hypocrisy." "Fools and knaves are the two grand classes," says the protagonist in the opening scene, "honest men are too insignificant, and too few, to form a class … Such is the world: and shall I, like a driveller, make myself its football? No, it shall be mine! And I will spurn it before me with the contempt it deserves."[153]

Knave or Not? is staged within a year of the 1794 Treason Trials. In 1792, English radicalism is revitalised by the French Revolution and the publication of the *Rights of Man* by Norfolk-born Founding Father Thomas Paine.[154] The government glances nervously across the Channel. Swift action is needed. Tact too: public support is crucial. Reform societies are infiltrated, arrests made, and the guilty transported, but the circulation of the *Rights of Man* balloons.[155] Slippers off, boots on. Reformers are branded seditionaries and thirty-eight arrested for treason, Holcroft and Paine among them.[156] All tried are acquitted on a technicality. The government fumes, but there is a serendipitous outcome. The defendants have overwhelming public support. The liberation of these unshrinking men is all the victory the people need. Boots off. Secretary of War, William Windham, is still pulling at a camping boot when he calls them "acquitted Felons." It draws a tart reply from Holcroft, branding him

151 Anon., *The Midship-Man's Garland.* s.n., London, c1694. p. 3.

152 Carlson, J.A., *Knave or Not?* In: O'Shaughnessy, D. (ed.)., *The Censorship of Eighteenth-Century Theatre*. Cambridge University Press, 2023. pp. 133, 139.

153 Holcroft, T., *Knave or Not?* s.n., London, 1798. p. 2.

154 McDonald, L.E., *A New Definition of Treason: The 1794 Treason Trials.* Unpublished Ba (Hons) thesis, University of Georgia, 2009. p. 10.

155 Ibid, p. 23.

156 Brown, P.A., *The French Revolution in English History.* Routledge, Abingdon, Oxon, 2014. p. 120.

a petulant child with the stark mad spleen of a cynic.[157] Who wins out in the end, the boy kicked out of Eton for fighting or the son of travelling pedlars?

In 1778, a Dickensian advert in the *Manchester Mercury*:

> A MATCH at FOOT-BALL
> Between ASHTON LEVER, Esq;
> And the TOWNSHIPS of
> Middleton, Blakely, Prestwich
> AGAINST
> CAPTAIN AYTOUN
> (of the ROYAL MANCHESTER VOLUNTEERS)
> And the TOWNSHIPS of
> Rochdale, Royton, Oldham
> For 100 GUINEAS.
> To begin at Twelve o'clock, on *Wednesday* the 11th of *February* 1778.
> To Dine at the BOAR" S-HEAD, in MIDDLETON
> Dinner on the Table at Two o'clock[158]

The advert is supplemented with handbills "delivered plentifully." After the match, forty men get drunk and join the army.[159] In 1773, Ashton Lever opens a museum in Leicester Square. His "Holophusicon" is a treasure trove of natural history and ethnography, amounting to twenty-seven thousand "curious subjects."[160] London has never seen the like. Belemnites and barnacles, horns and tusks, hummingbirds and vultures. There are cases of butterflies and beetles, and scorpions and spiders, and a cornucopia of animals: leopard, lynx, and tiger, crocodile, sea lion, and dolphin, armadillo, porcupine, and anteater, hippopotamus, and rhinoceros, elephants and bears, orangutangs and baboons, and "the dog-faced monster." A penguin is a singular sight, "as near a resemblance

157 Holcroft, T., *A Letter to the Right Honourable William Windham, on the intemperance and dangerous tendency of his public conduct*. s.n., London, 1795. pp. 6, 9.

158 *Manchester Mercury*. 3 February 1778. p. 4.

159 *Derby Mercury*. 13 February 1778. p. 2.

160 Baird, I., Ionescu, C. (eds.), *Eighteenth-Century Thing Theory in a Global Context: From Consumerism to Celebrity Culture*. Routledge, Abingdon, Oxon, 2016. pp. 78–80.

to a fish as a bird." There are antiquities from Rome and Persia, and a miscellany of eggs and pipes, instruments and idols, slippers and suits of armour.[161] All on view for half a crown. Though a wealthy man—he had inherited the family seat of Alkrington Hall—Lever's obsession with collecting leads to bankruptcy. In 1786, he disposes of his beloved collection in a one guinea lottery. Valued at fifty-three thousand pounds, Lever claws back eight thousand four hundred pounds.[162] He commits suicide two years later.

The first overseas player is mentioned in 1766. Mr Bug, a London broker, recalls a match he watched as a boy, a six-a-side between Romford and Brentwood for "a laced hat and feather, and a considerable sum of money"; best of three.[163] "The gole being fixed, and two Inns [ins][164] out of three being to determine who were the conquerors", up goes the ball at the halfway mark. Will Longlegs of Brentwood catches it and off he goes, until "Hal Reynard, a Dutchman, gave him such a rap on his knuckles with his sharp toed shoe" that Romford get the ball and score first. Will is so anxious to score he shins his own teammates and "almost lamed them." Charles scores instead, 1-1. Will and Charles then "elbow'd, scratched, and bit their antagonists so severely" that Will gets the winner.

A Shrove Tuesday football match plays out between the married and bachelor men of Walton, Yorkshire, in 1773. After an hour's play "and many falls and broken shins", it remains goalless. One of the wives runs on to the pitch, pursues the ball, "and determined the victory."[165] An adjacent column tells the story of a wife who goes to a masquerade ball at the Pantheon in London, against her husband's wishes. He shadows her, masked himself. She falls for the mysterious stranger, who leads her to an empty room "where he began to paint his passion in the strongest terms." A carriage takes them to a secluded area, where they remove their masks. The thunderstruck wife dissolves into tears, but a separation swiftly follows. Sixteen years later, "an extraordinary match of foot-ball

---

161 Anon., *The London Guide*. s.n., London, 1782. pp. 182–188.

162 £5.8M and £922,000 in 2024.

163 *Gazetteer and New Daily Advertiser*. 3 September 1766. p. 1.

164 Getting the ball *in* the goal.

165 *Leeds Intelligencer*. 2 March 1773. p. 3.

took place at Dunstable downs.[166] A young gentleman took the hill for 200 guineas against eleven of the best foot-ball players in the country, which was decided in his favour, after a contest of four hours and a half."[167,168] Directly above, an Eton scholar delivers a lethal punch to a Windsor tailor during a boxing bout. Elsewhere, all ships of the Second Fleet, transporting convicts to Australia, must be at Portsmouth within twelve days, and workmen lifting flagstones in a house discover the skeletons of seven children.

In 1789, Westmorland play Cumberland at football on Kennington Common, sixty years after the shadowy tailors. The counties also compete at wrestling. The sports fall under the umbrella of the Gymnastic Society, a joint venture by the "gentlemen of Westmorland and Cumberland … for the practice and cultivation of their favourite sports 'wrestling' and 'foot-ball.'" The exact date of formation is unclear, but in 1849, on the occasion of the formation of the Surrey Foot-ball Club, William Denison, chair of The Surrey Cricket Club, states that the Gymnastic Society had existed for several years prior to 1789, implying the mid-1780s.[169] The club, Denison continues, consisted of "most of the leading noblemen and gentlemen, who being natives of the two northern counties … had taken up their residence in London." They met fortnightly at the bowling green beside the Belvedere Tavern in Pentonville, where "they carried on the wrestling, whilst all their foot-ball playing was held on Kennington-common … matches were played accordingly on the common every year, sometimes for small, and at other times for large sums."[170] The last large purse was in 1789: "Twenty-two gentlemen of Westmoreland were backed against twenty-two gentlemen of Cumberland for one thousand guineas. After a severe contest gentlemen of the former proved victorious."[171] Denison's father played for Westmorland that day, authenticating his account. "About this time," he went on, "some of the leading members of the society retired from London, and the 'blood' and activity of the club … in a short time ceased to exist."

166 Bedfordshire.

167 Three years' wages for a skilled tradesman, twenty horses, or forty-two cows.

168 *Bury and Norwich Post*. 20 May 1789. p. 2.

169 *Bell's Life in London and the Sporting Chronicle*. 7 October 1849. p. 6.

170 *The Sunday Times*. 7 October 1849. p. 5.

171 Twenty-three years' wages for a skilled tradesman.

Shortly afterward, Denison explains, subscriptions were collected for prizes, "to be wrestled for, and for football playing on Good Friday, by all young men who were natives of Westmorland and Cumberland. Their contests had always been held on Kennington-common till within the last twenty years." The wrestling moves on to several locations, "but foot-ball playing had eventually ceased, because the grounds to which the former had been taken were not sufficiently capacious."[172] In April 1790, the first of the new Kennington Common Good Friday contests is reported: "A large party of gentlemen from Cumberland and Westmorland assembled on Kennington Common, for the purpose of playing at foot-ball and wrestling, (being diversions they excel all England in); but on account of the wind being so very high, not much dexterity was displayed at the former, for there was not one game won."[173] The knockout wrestling between thirty-two contestants is more enthralling: "we never witnessed greater powers of agility than were there displayed … the belt (the palm of victory) fell to a Westmorland man."

On Good Friday 1792, a combined county team are to take on "All England" at wrestling and football at White Conduit Fields, with a football and gold-inscribed belt as prizes.[174] Only two more football matches on Kennington Common appear to have made the papers. The first is when Cumberland beat Westmorland on Easter Monday 1796.[175] Directly below, bell-ringing receives twice the ink when the Sherwood Society perform the intricate treble bob royal for four hours, at St Mary's Church, Nottingham. In 1818, a journalist writes that football, leaping, and wrestling are "the usual public diversions" in Cumberland and Westmorland. He recalls a well-attended football match in London "about twenty years ago", a ten-a-side between both counties for 20 gns. Both sides wear kits: "The combatants appeared in an appropriate dress prepared for the occasion … the game was played with great spirit by both parties who discovered an agility that surprised and astonished the

172 The wrestling moved to private grounds beside a Kentish Town pub, then to the Eyre Arms, St John's Wood, proceeding to Highbury Barn Tavern, and eventually Copenhagen Fields (ironically, a venue with extensive grounds), where it was still practiced at the time of the article. Football ceased at Kennington Common "within the last twenty years" of 1849.

173 *General Evening Post*. 3–6 April 1790. p. 3.

174 *Cumberland's Pacquet*. 3 April 1792. p. 3.

175 *Sporting Magazine*. May 1796. p 105.

honest cockneys", who, nevertheless, consider it "low and vulgar."[176] Defending the game, the journalist asks who would be more dependable if France invaded, "the North country lads, or the *chicken-hearted* cockneys." Despite its short tenure, the Gymnastic Society has a claim to being the world's first football club, notwithstanding that the *ffootballe pleyers* at the Brewers Guild c1421–1423 may have constituted a club. The Surrey Foot-ball Club will be the first to produce its own football rules.

The English should be worried about the French. Napoleon may be exiled in St Helena, but Waterloo is only three years ago, and the Bourbon restoration looks nothing as stable as it turns out to be. The combative Bretons remain passionate about *soule*. In 1794, author Jacques Cambry writes: "Men have sometimes been seen following the ball into the sea, and drowning in search of it. As a child, I saw a man break his leg, jumping into a cellar to grab it."[177] *Soule* is recorded in the village of Mareil-sur-Loir in 1703 (fifty miles south of Normandy). It hosts annual Shrovetide games from 1718–1750, with incomplete manuscripts recording games until 1786.[178] The goals were three miles either side of the town, one a barn, the other a farm. Uniquely, the ball was disc-shaped, not round. One side was inscribed with "Long live the Sire, the Marquis of Clermont", the other carried his coat of arms.[179]

Bans continue, as they have done for centuries. In 1761, the town of Brée-au-Maine—twenty miles south of Normandy—forbids, "anyone to throw leather balls on the day of the king nor any other day; likewise bans any crowding … to compete in the ball game on any pretext, upon pain of a fee of fifty livres against each violator."[180] The Count of Olliamson bans it in the Normandy town of Condé-Sur-Noireau, in 1770, and the Parliament of Normandy follows suit, in 1776, slapping a hefty fine of three hundred *livres* on offenders.[181] Brittany waits until 1779,

176 *Lancaster Gazette*. 31 October 1818. p. 4.

177 Camby, J., *Voyage dans le Finistère*. 3 Vols. Fils Ainé, Brest, 1835. Vol. 1. p. 62.

178 Loudcher., J-F., *Of the game of Folk-football in France (16th to 19th century)*. p. 6. https://www.researchgate.net/publication/289999487_Of_the_game_of_Folk-football_in_France_16th_to_19th_century_The_impossible_sportivisation_of_a_traditional_physical_practice#fullTextFileContent. Accessed 11 March 2024.

179 Ibid, p. 6.

180 Ibid, p. 6.

181 Ibid, p. 3.

its legislation justified by the death of forty players in the pond of Pont-L'Abbé.[182]

Burgeoning interest in football means nothing to the law if a fine can be issued. The 1793 Manchester Police Act bans various activities in the city's thoroughfares: the dumping of dung, muck, offal, blood, and carrion; building bonfires; setting off squibs, serpents, rockets, and other fireworks; and "playing at the game called Foot Ball", with a maximum penalty of 20s.[183,184] Bath imposes similar legislation against football, throwing rubbish into rivers before "scavengers" have come to collect it, "watchmen, beadles, and constables, for neglect of duty, and on publicans for harbouring them in their hours of duty", using a horn or trumpet for announcing news, and walking unmuzzled mastiffs or bulldogs.[185] A prescient article in a 1753 *Dublin Journal* comments: "The many riots and robberies in and near this city, are attributed to the enclosure of the fields and gardens round this town, where all degrees of people formerly had the liberty of walking for business, ease of safety, to and fro, and where they used to wrestle, play at hurling, pitching of quoits, football and other healthy amusements, which have been tolerated in all wise governments in the known world."[186] It will be another seventy years before such sympathies coalesce in England.

Sometimes the public use football to advance their own justice. In 1740, during the food riots, "a Mach of Futtball was Cried down at Ketring of five Hundred Men of a side, but the Desighn was to Pull Down Ladey Betey Jesmains Mills."[187] Fifteen miles away, a 1765 *Northampton Mercury* announces a match: "This is to give notice to all Gentlemen Gamesters and Well-Wishers to the Cause now in Hand, That there will be a Foot-Ball play in the fields of Haddon, Cambridgeshire, on Thursday the 1st day of August, for a Prize of considerable value; and another good Prize to be play'd for on Friday the 2d. All Gentlemen Players …

182 Ibid, p. 3.

183 *Manchester Mercury*. 1 January 1793. p. 1.

184 A week's wages for a skilled tradesman.

185 *Bath Chronicle and Weekly Gazette*. 27 June 1793. p. 2.

186 Ní Mhurchadha, M., *Two Hundred Men at Tennis: Sport in North Dublin 1600–1760*. Dublin Historical Record, 2008, 61:1, p. 98.

187 Malcolmson, R.W., *Popular Recreations in English Society 1700–1850*. Unpublished PhD thesis, University of Warwick, 1970. p. 89.

will be joyfully received, and kindly entertained, etc."[188] A week later, the crimson-faced paper reports: "We hear from West-Haddon, in this County, that on Thursday and Friday last a great Number of People being assembled there, in order to play a Foot-Ball Match, soon after meeting formed themselves into a tumultuous Mob, and pulled up and burnt the Fences designed for the enclosure of that field, and did other considerable damage."[189] The crowd is dispersed by a detachment of dragoons.

The people of the Fens are rioting against drainage and enclosure. Between 1750 and 1830, six million acres of common land is taken into private ownership.[190] On 1 July 1767, two hundred men from Brothertoft, in Lincolnshire, "threw up a foot-ball in the fen, and played for about two hours, when a troop of dragoons, some gentlemen from Boston and four constables, having seized four or five of the rioters, committed them to Spalding gaol." Two weeks later, "another ball was thrown up and no one opposed them; and on the 16th, five men were sent by Sir C. Frederick to guard Brothertoft. On the 29th, another ball was thrown up without opposition."[191] The following year, football is played on the Holland Fens again, while in 1769, six men are convicted of entering the Fens under the guise of playing football and pulling down half a mile of fencing erected to divide the land into parish lots.[192,193] An old Lincolnshire saying about rooks sums up the troubles: "When th' craws plaays foot-ball it's a sign o' bad weather."[194,195]

The collective endeavours mirror the 1638 Whelpmore protest when two hundred men, gathering under the pretext of a camping match, destroy the drainage dykes.[196] There is a similar incident in 1699 when corporate attempts to drain the Fens are hampered by "the Ruyne and

---

188 Ibid, pp. 90–91.

189 *Stamford Mercury*. 15 August 1765. p. 1.

190 Collins, T., *How Football Began*. Routledge, Abingdon, Oxon, 2019. p. 13.

191 Gutch, E., Peacock, M., *Examples of Printed Folk-lore Concerning Lincolnshire*. David Nutt, London, 1908. p. 258.

192 Malcolmson, R.W., *Popular Recreations in English Society 1700–1850*. University Press, Cambridge, 1973, p. 40.

193 *Cambridge Chronicle and Journal*. 26 May 1770. p. 4.

194 Gutch, E., Peacock, M., *Examples of Printed Folk-lore Concerning Lincolnshire*. David Nutt, London, 1908. p. 42.

195 In essence, when rooks are restless and circle one another expect stormy weather.

196 Sweeting, W.D. (ed.)., *Fenland Notes and Queries, 1894–10*. 3 Vols. Geo. C. Caster, Peterborough, 1894. Vol. 2. p. 356.

Destruction lately committed by divers desperate and malitious Persons … under Colour and pretence of Foot Ball Playing … the Captain or Chief of the Mobb in the late Ryat in Deeping Fenns by Whittlesea was to be at the said Foot Ball Play, and that they would pull down the mills and Cutt the Banks as had already been done in Deeping Fens."[197] Further unrest in June is suppressed by force. Football and the Fens are never far apart. When the Scottish Conspiracy is uncovered in 1794, Robert Watt and David Downie are hung, drawn, and quartered. At their trial, the prosecution declares that treason "may be disguised under any other pretence whatsoever, as of reformation of abuses, casting down inclosures … and wrestling, football playing, cock fighting."[198]

When four youths are fined in Lincoln for playing football, it makes the *Stamford Mercury*, "as a caution to others."[199] The issue feasts on juicy titbits: a woman in Yorkshire remarries having "remained a disconsolate widow almost five weeks"; a ninety-three-year-old woman dies, leaving two sisters aged ninety and ninety-six; a woman has triplets; two fifteen-year-olds are to be married; a highwayman is executed; a riding master is killed by a horse kick; a man finds a fifty-pound note in a library copy of the Old Testament;[200] disliking his lottery ticket number, a man swaps it only for the original to scoop a prize of ten thousand pounds;[201] "a poor unhappy girl … much intoxicated" is pushed into the street and her head "crushed to pieces" by a wagon; a ten-year-old dies of rabies; "a great number of children" are killed by a herbal remedy for worms; and a footpad strikes again.

In Leicester, stocking makers meet at the Turk's Head intent on a football game in the marketplace. As the ball goes up, two are seized and thrown in jail. The mounted Royal Regiment of Blues later parade through the streets to drive the point home.[202] It could be worse. When football players gather in Hyde Park, in 1771, seventeen are press-ganged

197 Malcolmson, R.W., *Popular Recreations in English Society 1700–1850*. Unpublished PhD thesis, University of Warwick, 1970. p. 90.

198 *Trial of David Downie*. Hein Online. https://heinonline.org/HOL/Page?handle=hein.trials/acqm0001&id=1&collection=stair&index=. Accessed 24 February 2024.

199 *Stamford Mercury*. 26 March 1790. p. 3.

200 Four horses. Eleven month's wages for a skilled tradesman.

201 Three hundred years' wages for a skilled tradesman.

202 *Derby Mercury*. 18 June 1779. p. 4.

into His Majesty's Forces.[203] Sixty ice skaters in Southwark meet the same fate.[204] The winter is deadly. The same paper reports the discovery of two girls frozen to death, two miles apart in London; a soldier in Aberdeen similarly submits.[205]

Football and the military collide again, in 1799. The *Kentish Gazette* is "sorry to learn that His Majesty is indisposed with a cold in his head." No such sympathy is extended to, "a melancholy accident on Hampton Court Green … Quarter Master Colston, of the Light Horse, was kicking a foot-ball, he tripped up and falling with his breast on a lump of ice, was killed dead on the spot. It is remarkable, that the regiment to which he belonged had been repeatedly sent for (but never came) to quell a riot at Kingston, occasioned by kicking [a] foot ball in the town, to the annoyance of the inhabitants, contrary to the express order of the Magistrates, who had issued hand bills to prevent so odious a practice."[206] Reporting a week after the Kingston Shrovetide game, it goes on: "it is to be hoped that another year the Magistrates will be assisted by the military, in preventing a practice which puts a stop to all trade, obliges the inhabitants to barricade their windows, [and] makes travelling through the town dangerous. The mob plead CUSTOM." The Kingston Shrovetide football game is first recorded in the 1790s but is clearly older.

On the same page, a goose, a gander, a cock, and three pullets are stolen from a farmyard (reward 5 gns): "It is supposed the thieves were alarmed, as they left behind them three asses which are now in custody." Also, a windmill for sale, and barrels of herrings. Various cure-alls jostle for custom. Dr Anderson's Scots Pills are "extremely useful … in Bilious and Dropsical complaints, Indigestion, after hard drinking … Rheumatism, Gravel, and all Obstructions. Worms cannot breed in the Bodies of those who frequently take this Medicine." It is also good for scurvy, and women "at a certain advanced Time of Life." But will it outsell Dr James's Analeptic Pills, Dr Smyth's Restorative Drops, Cundell's Improved Balsam of Honey, or Whitehead's Essence of Mustard?

---

203 *Caledonian Mercury*. 16 January 1771. p. 2.

204 Ibid, p. 2.

205 Ibid, p. 2.

206 *Kentish Gazette*. 12 February 1799. p. 1.

CHAPTER FIFTEEN
1700–1799 IV

The winter of 1775/76 is merciless. January records non-stop sub-zero temperatures, allowing cricket and football, and a sheep to be "roasted whole", on the frozen Stanswell Pool, near Coventry.[1] There is another great freeze. One that will not thaw. The American colonies are left to their own devices until French and American forces clash in 1754. A war ensues that lasts until 1763. The Americans are heavily outnumbered, but when the British come to their assistance, the tables turn. France cedes all its North American territory to the British, including Canada. The war is expensive, and George III wants the colonies to pay. He levies a series of punitive taxes. American rancour soars. Without representation in Parliament, they feel cheated. A bitter war unfolds. By 1778, British recruits are badly needed. Press-gangs are everywhere. Persuasion also works. In Somersetshire, "where the Spit it constantly going, and the Cyder continually flowing", the army promise an immediate payment of six golden guineas for three years in the military. "From the time of enlisting they may feast upon Beef and Figgy Pudding, and an Ox will be roasted whole … for every twenty gentlemen … a band of music is also provided, with foot-ball, wrestling, cudgel-playing, &c."[2] The war drags on, though the colonies declare independence within months of that cruel winter's end.

France gets its revenge, sending troops and heavily financing the colonies. It proves decisive. It is a glorious victory for the French. One to savour. But the victory proves pyrrhic. When the dust settles, Louis XVI is crippled with debt. By 1788, he owes the government 4.5 billion *livres*. And *he* cannot tax America. When the calendar turns, there is no going back. He is allowed to remain on the throne for three years until his repeated attempts to betray the constitution are exposed. As the Comte de Provence says of Louis's weakness and indecision, "imagine oiled

1 *Derby Mercury*. 2 February 1776. p. 4.

2 *Leeds Intelligencer*. 17 February 1778. p. 2.

billiard balls that you might try in vain to keep together."[3] Three weeks before his execution, a princess is beheaded by an angry mob. Her head is put on a pike and her heart on a sabre, and they are raised to Marie Antoinette's window in the Temple keep. The next day, seven-year-old heir, Louis Charles, is distracted in the Temple garden, "either at quoits, or football, or running, or other games of exercise."[4] The following day he plays ball, battledore, and shuttlecock.

Parliament take note. Europe's citizens are stirring. The industrial revolution shunts workers from the countryside to cities on an unprecedented scale. The cities are ill-equipped for wholesale resettlement and need rapidly outgrows infrastructure. Football is a long-delayed afterthought; the critical issues of housing, sanitation, and hospitals must first be addressed. There is nowhere to play football except in the streets, and no other time than Sundays. Workers, removed from closely knit agrarian communities where they possessed at least some degree of autonomy, feel disconnected and powerless. With Tostolvian naivety, Friedrich Engels laments rural culture: "They did not need to overwork; they did no more than they chose to do, and yet earned what they needed … and they could take part besides in the recreations and games of their neighbours, and all these games—bowling, cricket, football, etc. … their children grew up in the fresh county air and, if they could help their parents at work, it was only occasionally; while of eight or twelve hours work for them there was no question."[5] From frosty fields to smoggy streets. Manacled to progress. It is a vertiginous learning curve. There is hope. An increasingly literate working class is finding its voice, and the swelling middle class is only a few generations from tilling the earth.

Richard Gough has an eye for the absurd. "It was no light thing to be shoved across the water in a hog trough and carried over a river on a fellow's back," he writes, recounting his travels in the northwest of England. He is particularly struck by a Greenland whaler at the mouth of the Mersey, firing guns to signal she had fish (at which the church bells

---

3 Webster, N.H., *Louis XVI and Marie Antoinette During the Revolution*. Constable and Company Ltd, London, 1937. p. 121.

4 Wormeley, K.P. (trans.)., *The Life and Letters of Élisabeth de France*. Hardy, Pratt & Company, Boston, 1902. pp. 127–128.

5 Kelley, F (trans.)., *The Condition of the Working Class in England in 1844*, by Friedrich Engels. John W. Lovell Company, New York, 1887. pp. 4–5.

struck up), and laments the extinction of "Lancashire witches", or he may not have returned alone. He turns to reminiscing of his days in Enfield, of his "fossilising", playing bowls on the common, star-gazing, or taking tea.[6] In his 1780 travelogue of Ireland, Arthur Young describes hurling as, "a sort of cricket … instead of throwing the ball … the aim is to pass it through a bent stick, the ends stuck in the ground."[7] He describes, a "very ancient" country custom amongst the poor, "to fix upon some young woman that ought… to be married; they also agree upon a young fellow as a proper husband … on the sunday following *she is to be horsed*, that is carried on men's backs. She must then provide whisky and cyder as a treat … as soon as she is *horsed*, the hurling begins … the young fellow … if he comes off conqueror, he is certainly married to the girl, but if another is victorious … she is the prize of the victor … the common expression is, that *such a girl was goal'd*."[8] Directly before the passage, he mentions that a love of dancing is "among the poor people, almost universal … dancing masters … travel from cabin to cabin … it is an absolute system of education."

Young excessively praises Irish virtues but reveals an English penchant for lazy bigotry by calling hurling "the cricket of savages" and condemning the Irish as "lazy to an excess at work … hard drinkers and quarrelsome; great liars, but civil, submissive, and obedient."[9] Perhaps he can be forgiven. He is shrewd enough to describe them as "warm friends and revengeful enemies … their love of society is as remarkable as their curiosity is insatiable … strokes in their character are evidently to be ascribed to the extreme oppression under which they live. If they are as great thieves and liars as they are reported, it is certainly owing to this cause." Coquebert de Montbret arrives in Ireland within months of the Storming of the Bastille. While establishing the first French consulate

6 Early Modern Letters Online. http://emlo.bodleian.ox.ac.uk/profile/work/0ced2470-051e-4f69-89c2-440023ffebc8?sort=date-a&rows=50&dat_to_year=1799&let_con=bowls&dat_from_year=1500&baseurl=/forms/advanced&start=6&type=advanced&numFound=7. Accessed 26 October 2024.

7 Young, A., *A Tour in Ireland: with General Observations on the Present State of that Kingdom. Made in the Years 1776, 1777, and 1778, and Brought Down to the End of 1779.* 2 Vols. James Williams, Dublin, 1780. Vol. 2. p. 251.

8 Ibid, p. 250.

9 Pinkerton, J., *A General Collection of the Best and Most Interesting Voyages and Travels in all Parts of the World.* 17 Vols. Longman, Hurst, Rees and Orme, London, 1809. Vol. 3. pp. 872–873.

in Ireland, his travels allow him to come into close contact with people in the remotest parts of the country.[10] "In August hurling begins to be played," he says of a match in Galway in 1791.

"Each team is divided into three divisions … the third, called the "whip" … The ball is made of cow's hair, very compact and covered with leather. The spectators are on the ground, the majority of them dancing … the sides are distinguished by the colour of their caps. It is terrifying to see the way they rush against each other to force the ball to pass under the goal. The game only exists in Munster and Connaught. In Leinster they have football. In Ulster the Presbyterians are scandalised by the playing of games on Sunday."[11]

A French aristocrat taken to a Sabbath game reflects hurling's importance to national identity. De Montbret's declaration that the season starts in August indicates a winter sport. Of the four provinces of Ireland, football has gained ascendancy in overwhelmingly Catholic Leinster. His assertion that hurling has vanished from Leinster is erroneous; football is charming its way into the national fabric by degrees. Hurling is unruffled. She is the flame bathed in absolute darkness, the water of the ninth wave. She is the choice of gods. She strikes the hurley against her palm, then descends the shoulder of the heathery hill, towards the cloven meadows.

Prior to leather casing, the matted, twisted, or woven cow hair of hurling balls was encased with intricately-plaited horsehair.[12] Given de Montbret's comments, it is no surprise that the majority of such recovered balls are from Munster and Connaught. Other hurling balls (*sliotar/slitter*) are made of wood, cork, or thread, with coverings of gutta-percha or waxen thread. The oldest ball found dates c1157–1227, the earliest ball in modern European history.[13] A similar ball found nearby, c1663–1683, demonstrated "a continuity of tradition within nearby parishes spanning almost 500 years."[14] In 1698, during

---

10 Kennedy, S., *Coquebert de Montbret in Search of Hidden Ireland.* The Journal of the Royal Society of Antiquaries of Ireland, 1952, Vol. 82, pp. 62–63.

11 Chinnéide, N.P., *Coquebert de Montbret's Impressions of Galway City and County in the Year 1791.* Journal of the Galway Archaeological and Historical Society, 1952, Vol. 25, p. 11.

12 Doyle, C., *Hair Hurling Balls: Review, Research, and Scientific Investigations.* Folk Life: Journal of Ethnological Studies, 2016, Vol. 54, p. 3.

13 Ibid, p. 3.

14 Ibid, p. 17.

his travels in Ireland, John Dunton writes that "when their cows are casting their haire, they pull it of [sic] their backs and with their hands work it into large balls which will grow verie hard. This ball they use at the hurleings, which they strike with a stick call'd commaan about three foote and a half long in the handle. At the lower end it is crooked and about three inches broad."[15]

Country sport is accepted. Even hurling is upwardly mobile, with matches recorded between the gentlemen of Kilkenny, Tipperary, and the Queen's County.[16] In April 1763, "a great Match at Football" makes the headlines of the *Dublin Courier*: "Played at Clonshough, the Lodge of James Maffy Dawson, Esq; between 12 Lads of Sanntry and Clonshough, against the same number from Mallahide. The Game afforded the highest Entertainment to the lovers of Rural Diversions, being disputed for upwards of three hours."[17] A decade later, Tipperary beat Galway in front of a crowd of ten thousand for a 1000 gns, a stupendous sum, equivalent to thirty year's wages for a skilled tradesman.[18] Tipperary is hurling country. In 1775, the Barony of Lower Ormond are to take on the rest of Tipperary on Ballingarry Green for fifty pounds a side.[19] In 1792, the county lays down a challenge to "their pretended patron the Major, and their antagonists the Garrison, to a hurling match … as a national sport, Ireland ought to excell, and we answer for her victory."[20] The challenge has context. Captained by Charles Lennox, the Garrison of Dublin had beaten an all-Ireland side, captained by Robert Hobart[21] at cricket. It is a spectacle. "Two handsome marquees were pitched, one in Mr. Hobart's shrubbery, for the reception of a brilliant circle of ladies of distinction … the second for the accommodation of the cricket players, on the other side of the Ha Ha."[22] The purse is a lavish 500 gns a side, and the Countess of Westmoreland loses 10 gns. The match

15 Carpenter. A. (ed.)., *Teague Land, Or, A Merry Ramble to the Wild Irish.* John Dunton. Four Courts Press, Dublin, 2003. p. 91.

16 Prim, J.G.A., *Olden Popular Pastimes in Kilkenny.* Transactions of the Kilkenny Archaeological Society, 1853, 2:2, p. 332.

17 *Dublin Courier.* 4 April 1763. p. 1.

18 *Saunders's News-Letter.* 15 October 1773. p. 1.

19 *Hibernian Journal.* 9 August 1775. p. 3.

20 *Dublin Evening Post.* 14 August 1792. p. 3.

21 The Australian city is named after him.

22 *Cricket, A Weekly Record of the Game.* 25 September 1884. The Association of Cricket Statisticians and Historians. https://archive.acscricket.com/cricket/1884/480/#zoom=z. Accessed 1 November 2024.

takes less than a day. It is a drubbing. Ireland lose by an innings and one hundred and five runs. While the ignominy is profound, it is unclear if the gauntlet is seized.

A few months later, "Colonel Lenox proposes to establish a prize of 100 gns annually for superiority in hurling … in the Phoenix Park … the contending parties are to consist of at least twenty-four on each side."[23] Lennox is born in a barn, and dies in a barn. In between, he duels with the Duke of York, is present at Waterloo, becomes Governor-General of British North America, and contracts rabies from his pet fox.[24,25] An all-round athlete, he arranges a cricket match for quartered troops days before Waterloo, is a founding member of the Marylebone Cricket Club, a guarantor for the establishment of Lord's Old Ground, and plays forty-six first-class games.[26,27] The cricket match of 1792 is the first known in Ireland. It may deserve another laurel. The first recognised international cricket match was between Canada and the United States in September 1844. If Lennox fields an exclusively English side and Hobart an exclusively Irish one, the game becomes the earliest known cricket international, eclipsing the other by half a century. It is fanciful. 'All Ireland' field Hobart, Wesby, Box, Morris, Hickson, King, Emerson, Saunderson, Simpson, Cooke, and Poyle.[28] All except Poyle can be Irish surnames, though Saunderson and Wesby are listed as military captains. It is likely they belong to the garrison, though they could be Protestant Irish.[29] The Garrison of Dublin is highly unlikely to have Catholic Irishmen on the team sheet, and none of the names are clearly Irish. Even if Lennox's side included

23 *The Evening Mail*. 16 November 1792. p. 2.

24 *Dictionary of Canadian Biography*. http://www.biographi.ca/en/bio/lennox_charles_richmond_5E.html. Accessed 6 December 2023; Pycroft, J., *The Cricket Field*. Longman, Brown, Green, and Longmans, 1854. p. 85.

25 Lennox and the Duke of York were reconciled the following year at the match between England and the Hambledon Club at Lord's Old Ground.

26 Altham, H.S., Swanton, E.W., *A History of Cricket*. George Allen & Unwin Ltd., London, 1947. pp. 54–55.

27 *Cricket Archive*. https://cricketarchive.com/Archive/Players/30/30969/30969.html. Accessed 26 November 2023.

28 *Cricket, A Weekly Record of the Game*. 25 September 1884. The Association of Cricket Statisticians and Historians. https://archive.acscricket.com/cricket/1884/480/#zoom=z. Accessed 1 November 2024.

29 *Irish Surnames*. https://www.johngrenham.com/surnames/. Accessed 1 November 2024.

Scottish and Welsh soldiers, the tie would still be an international: Ireland versus Great Britain. But Poyle, Poyle.

John Magee becomes proprietor of the *Dublin Evening Post* in 1779. Ten years later, Frances Higgins, owner of the *Freeman's Journal*, sues him for libel. Higgins is an intriguing figure. Born in a cellar, "the barefooted redhaired urchin" becomes a shoe-black and pot boy. Gaining the position of scrivener, he uses his new skills to forge documents testifying to his extensive landed property. His duplicity secures a union with an eligible daughter who thinks him "extremely ugly" and "slightly deformed." His skills yet to be honed, he ends up in prison in Cutpurse Row. Soon released, he continues to ruin lives remorselessly. A merchant is severely injured, a husband "goes insane", a woman "dies miserably." With the ready wit of a charming psychopath, he slithers up the social ladder, insinuating his way into the confidences of the proprietor of the *Freeman's Journal*, before double-crossing him in a loan deal and acquiring his paper.[30]

It is not altogether surprising that Magee fires a fusillade of riotous barbs his way, accusing him of bribery, corruption, and "keeping a gambling hell and brothel at 42 Crane Lane." Higgins's skin is thick. Both hurl mud from their ink-stained parapets, lampooning each other endlessly. Both boast street smarts, but Magee is "popular with the crowd, and always got an acclamation from the mob."[31] The future 1st Earl of Clonmel becomes embroiled in Magee's defamations, and becomes a powerful co-litigant. Clonmel, known for his prodigious food and alcohol consumption, has earned the soubriquet Copper-Faced Jack. Higgins's smarts are tenebrous, unprincipled. Judges and barristers. Magee walks into court a guilty man. His inability to make the increasingly unjust bail imposed results in lengthy incarcerations.

Unbowed but almost certainly mentally ill, Magee purchases a plot of land next to the magnificent gardens of Clonmel's opulent villa in Dunleary, and slips an advert in his paper. There is to be a boat race "for a complete train of nets", and a football prize: "the boy that plays his game most active and clever shall be enrobed in triumph glorious, with

---

30 Lysaght, M., *The Sham Squire*. Dublin Historical Record, 1972, 25:2, pp. 64–71.

31 Greene, J.C., *The Trials of Richard Daly and John Magee*. Eighteenth-Century Ireland, 2009, Vol 24, p. 137.

an excellent frieze great coat." There is cudgel playing for a silver-laced hat; prior to each bout "every stout combatant must shake hands and kiss." In a magnificent dig at Clonmel, he adds: "A learned Pig, a Pig of knowledge, a DUNLEARY PIG, to be coursed over the ground, only by the boys who sailed, kicked the ball, or cudgelled—the pig's tail nicely soaped and shaved."[32] Magee signs off his advert: "Magee of the Arms of Ireland, Late of Fiat Dungeon, Cell No. 4, in the New Bastile."[33] All under the guise of a Lammas Day celebration in honour of the future George IV. The "Grand Olympic Pig Hunt" is attended by thousands who are plied with bottomless whisky and porter. Magee arrives by boat in a ridiculous plumed hat. He mounts a horse and gallops through the fields, as the concourse cry "Mad Magee". Dogs dance in barrister attire, bewigged asses dressed in scarlet cloaks are raced by jockeys, and soaped piglets are released. With a prize for securing one, the drunken crowd grows unruly, and when the piglets escape through the hedge into Clonmel's estate, hundreds follow, terrifying the earl, who believes a rebellion is at hand.[34]

Clonmel's paranoia is shared. Ball sports played in the cities of Ireland are deemed one step from rebellion, and met with steel. No where is this more prudent than Dublin. In 1754, police break up a group that has the temerity to play football on Baggot Street.[35] Four years later, "a great number of young fellows assembled at a match of football in Oxmantown Green." The Sabbath game ends when soldiers, "took up eight of the ablest and sent them on board for tenders."[36] No one is press-ganged the following Easter Sunday, when a fight breaks out at a football match at Finglas, northwest of Dublin. One paper reports that several people are dangerously hurt, two others that a player's skull is fractured and part of his nose cut off.[37] In 1766, "a great match at football was played at Miltown to the great scandal of

32 *Dublin Evening Post*. 1 August 1789. p. 3.

33 Madden, R.R., *The History of Irish Periodical Literature*. 2 Vols. T.C Newby, London, 1867. Vol. 2. p. 326.

34 Greene, J.C., *The Trials of Richard Daly and John Magee*. Eighteenth-Century Ireland. 2009, Vol 24, pp. 149–151.

35 Rouse, P., *Sport and Ireland: A History*. Oxford University Press, 2015. p. 56.

36 Ní Mhurchadha, M., *Two Hundred Men at Tennis Sport in North Dublin 1600–1760*. Dublin Historical Record, 2008, 61:1, p. 99.

37 Ibid, p. 99.

religion and this Metropolis" while in 1774, the 55th Regiment is called to disperse a riotous mob in Drumcondra "who weekly assemble there to play at Foot Ball." [38,39]

Another paper reports, "several disorderly people ... breaking down the fence and trampling the grass", when they play football in Dublin.[40] A month later, it bemoans the Sunday gatherings in Merrion Square Fields in Dublin of "between 3 and 400 riotous and disorderly Persons ... to fight, play Football, &c. whereby some Lives have been lost, and many persons maimed and wounded; the laws openly violated."[41] On a February Sabbath in 1799, "a foot-ball match is played at the foot of the mountain called Three Rocks [Co. Dublin] ... between a party of Mountaineers, and the neighbours of the adjacent valley, when a desperate quarrel ensued, in which much bloodshed and battery was the consequence."[42] That summer, Sabbath football is played in Phoenix Park, despite the high sheriff living a stone's throw away.[43] Sheriffs beware, this is the era of revolutions. Two weeks later he acts: "a prodigious concourse of people were assembled to play at a hurling match. The sheriff came upon them by surprize, took from them a number of hurls, and dispersed this riotous mob ... [this] wicked set of persons ... an evil example to the lower order of working people."[44] The following year, players gather to play at Mount Eccles, Dublin. The owner of the field hires several constables to stop them. When they are met with "abusive language and throwing of stones", one constable discharges his blunderbuss, and a baker's apprentice is mortally wounded. Had he been in his day job, the law might justify the constable's actions, but this volatile nation needs placating, and he is sent to Dublin's Newgate prison.[45]

In 1785, "Multitudes of vagabonds and profligate people" meet every Sunday, "in the suburbs or outskirts of Dublin" for "foot-ball, wrestling,

---

38 Rouse, P., *Sport and Ireland: A History*. Oxford University Press, 2015. p. 55.

39 *Hibernian Journal*. 20 April 1774. p. 4.

40 *Saunders's News-Letter*. 18 April 1773. p. 1.

41 *Saunders's News-Letter*. 20 May 1774. p. 1.

42 Ibid, 11 February 1789. p. 2.

43 *Dublin Evening Post*. 20 July 1779. p. 3.

44 *Saunders's News-Letter*. 4 August 1779. p. 1.

45 *Saunders's News-Letter*. 10 April 1780. p. 1.

quarrelling and fighting."[46] Two years later, two thousand gather in Merrion Square, "for the Purpose of fighting, playing at Games, and other unlawful Pastimes, to the great Profanation of the lord's Day and terror of the peaceable Inhabitants of this City."[47,48] When the Alderman asks that they disperse, he is pelted with stones, "whereby the Lives of three of the Police Watchmen are deemed to be in imminent Danger from the Wounds which they received." There is a one-hundred-pound reward for the man who injured the Aldermen, ten pounds for each watchman. Not until 1796 are large assemblies banned, including football, potato picking, and reaping corn; to the authorities, subterfuges to foment revolution. Panic grips Parliament. Ireland has sympathisers in America and France. In 1798, Ireland rises in an audacious thrust for independence. But the Irish Sea is no Atlantic, and sympathisers only sympathise. England has no logistical conundrums, needs no Parliamentary whip. Anticipated for years, the rebellion is crushed within months.

Football is not all gloom. Headlined "A Country Dance and Football", a 1782 Dublin paper advertises Bag against Liffy "for one Dozen pairs of gloves, and one barrel of ale." A pound of tobacco goes "to the old woman who dances the best jig", and Colonel Talbot is to give "the best Female Dancer, a Silk Handkerchief."[49] That Boxing Day, the paper reports that a certain colonel will only attend "garran-racing, women-racing, foot-ball, cudgel-playing &c." at Rathcoffy, Kildare, after "his late unhappy reception at Crow-Street house in Dublin."[50,51] Perhaps the dig is aimed at Talbot, who had ordered in ten barrels of whisky for the Bag-Liffey game. In 1786, an acerbic journalist takes aim at an unnamed well-to-do Roscommon man, describing him as "rather of a rustic education, frequenting hurling-greens, foot-ball matches, intermixing with the populace at fairs and patrons, drinking to excess spiritous liquors … he is a man of dissipated character and abandoned habits."[52] Dissipation aside, football is climbing stealthily up Dublin's

46 *Saunders's News-Letter*. 10 June 1785. p. 1.

47 *Saunders's News-Letter*. 15 May 1787. p. 3.

48 The 14 May edition (p. 5.) clarified the games as wrestling and football.

49 *Dublin Evening Post*. 12 October 1782. p. 3.

50 *Dublin Evening Post*. 26 December 1782. p. 3.

51 A garran is a horse.

52 *Saunders's News-Letter*. 10 February 1786. p. 1.

social ladder. It may still be snubbed by the wealthier students, but it is played every evening at Trinity College.[53]

~

The world's first football-related venue, the Foot Ball Inn in Kendal, Cumbria, has been trading since at least 1758.[54] Its name is reputedly coined after a football "was won and retained as a trophy in a fierce contest" against a neighbouring town. "For many generations it hung suspended in the kitchen until the house was rebuilt."[55] Eccentric bibliophile Anthony Askew is born in the building facing the inn in 1722. His passionate ambition is to own every printed edition of the Greek classics, and his collection became known as the *Bibliotheca Askeviana*. His house in London, is "crammed full of classical books, curious MSS., and rare editions; the passages were full, and even the garrets overflowed, yet the book appetite of Dr Askew was not satisfied."[56] Slaked enough for him to lay his books aside and sire twelve children. In the 1780s, the warden of the newly-built Kendal Prison regularly allows the three or four prisoners it holds out to play football, "but when it was time to leave he used to say, 'Noo lads, you mun follow me, or if ye don't, I'll lock ye out.'"[57] In 1789, a prisoner he escorts to London gives him the slip. Bow Street run a notice: "ESCAPED. From the Swan Tap-room, in Lad Lane … convicted … and ordered for transportation … 50 years of age … lusty made … full face … and a pair of handcuffs fastened to her wrists."[58] She is spotted selling apples years later but never apprehended.

Football emulates cricket. In 1789, a fête is held in Brighton for the Duke of York's birthday, organised by the Prince of Wales. The day begins with the sailing of two Dieppe packets for a silver cup. Cricket follows, "in which the Duke of York and many gentlemen of rank and fashion" take part. The duke also engages in the next game,

---

53 Marples, M., *A History of Football*. Secker and Warburg, London, 1954. p. 88.

54 According to Sybil Rosenfeld, "A previous theatre connected with the Football Inn, Marketplace, had been opened by Thomas Ashburner in 1758." In: Rosenfeld, S.M., *The Georgian Theatre of Richmond, Yorkshire and Its Circuit*. The Society for Theatre Research, London, 1984. p. 103.

55 Curwen, J.F., *Kirkbie-Kendall: fragments collected relating to its ancient streets and yards; church and castle; houses and inns*. T. Wilson, Kendal, 1900. p. 304.

56 Ibid, p. 309.

57 Ibid, p. 338.

58 Ibid, p. 338.

an eleven-a-side football match.[59] Football can hardly contain himself. A member of the royal family playing is a pivotal moment. The fête returns in 1790. An eleven-a-side football match for 5 gns accompanies an eleven-a-side women's stoolball match and a jingling game—a man dressed in bells avoids blindfolded seekers.[60] Directly below the report is a story of an overweight man married to a beautiful woman. Unable to sire a child, he receives advice from his wag of a friend that hot lobsters give "a manly tone to the constitution." Off he trots to eat lobsters at a restaurant some miles away, repeated excursions driven by ardour. After nine months, he is overjoyed when his wife gives birth to a boy. Proud of his stirring virility and desirous of more children, he continues to patronise the restaurant. Within the year, his wife has twin girls. Only when he returns home early one evening, does he find her in bed with the wag's friend.

By the time the aristocracy turn to football, it is old hat for the country's spiritual head. When John Moore becomes Archbishop of Canterbury in 1783, a childhood friend who knew him when he was a butcher's son itemises his sporting prowess: "he was superior to his comrades in agility of body; at cricket, foot-ball, fives, &c. he was excellent; but his grand sort lay in the *hop*, *step*, and *jump*."[61] Old news too for the King of Denmark, for in 1772 he "makes himself very easy, and diverts himself at football, and with driving along the ice on sledges."[62] Two winters before, it is so cold it is possible to walk two and a half miles across the glassy sea from Helsingør in Denmark to Helsinborg in Sweden.

In the wake of the duke's fête, others crop up, many held by employers for their workmen. A Twelfth Day festival is held near Salisbury for three hundred workers "and other poor persons of the neighbourhood." Bread and strong ale are provided. There are prizes for wrestling, running, and single stick, but the star attraction is football. With ten thousand spectators, it is the highest attendance at a football match to date.[63,64] When Doddington play Chatton, in Northumberland, on

---

59 *St James's Chronicle or The British Evening Post*. 20–22 August 1789. p. 1.

60 *Chester Chronicle*. 3 September 1790. p. 3.

61 *Kentish Gazette*. 16 April 1783. p. 4.

62 *Newscastle Courant*. 7 March 1772. p. 2.

63 *Kentish Gazette*. 31 January 1797. p. 4.

64 Equivalent to fifty-seven thousand in 2024.

Easter Monday 1767, "a good many tents were erected, a vast number of the principal people in the county attended, and the ground where they play'd was corded quite around. The players' agility and dexterity were inimitable, and each one met his partner with such ferocity at the ball, that a deal of blood was drawn, and the game played with such severity" the crowd winces at the knocks and falls.[65] After ending 2-2, the judges propose a decider. Doddington refuse, and "the ball is given to the Chatton heroes, who came off the field in triumph, with flying colours, music playing &c." In Lincolnshire, in May 1791, Billingboro best Osbournby in a six-hour "match at foot-ball". The winners "wore favours of blue ribband, as a mark of distinction."[66] Shrove Tuesday games remain popular. In the late eighteenth century, a Shrove Tuesday fixture still takes place in Messingham, Lincolnshire.[67] Another, in Bletchley, Buckinghamshire, plays out on the village green.[68]

In 1774, an anonymous poem is published in a book of selected works.[69] *Pila Pedalis* ("Football") is a Neo-Latin mock-epic poem, a genre that emerged in the late seventeenth century. Much of it is dull bombast, but there are some gems:

"A quick sideways sliding ball … he finds the field open and flies away … and now the war is raging, now with their whole bodies, foot pressed against foot … bodies are strewn about … he eludes the outer circle and misses the next one. By the way he advances … he reaches the goal … At the threshold of the camp fierce battles arise … heel against heel, breast against breast, and hearts are restless … they run together; they fall equals, they rise; rush … let him gladly wage war with his enemies. And do not delay, fortune favours the brave: There is the flying ball. He leaps violently at it, conjures hands, and through the plains of the field he rushes on with impunity. The camp is laid bare, and the conqueror stands at the top of the threshold."[70]

~

65 *Newcastle Chronicle*. 2 May 1767. p. 2.

66 *Stamford Mercury*. 6 May 1791. p. 3.

67 Malcolmson, R.W., *Popular Recreations in English Society 1700–1850*. Unpublished PhD thesis, University of Warwick, 1970. p. 47.

68 Goulstone, J., *Football's Secret History*. Soccer & Society, 2018, 19:1, p. 38.

69 Popham, E. (ed.), *Selecta poemata Anglorum latina*. 3 Vols. Fletcher & Hodson, London, 1774. Vol. 2. pp. 82–84.

70 Camp refers to a Greco-Roman battle camp, not the game.

Speaking of his childhood in the 1720s, a Scottish Border's man recollects his rigid Presbyterian father's proscription of dancing in his house, or allowing his sons to drink "that effeminate drug" tea, though he endured it when the pastor visited.[71] "Field sports were eagerly followed by both masters and servants … [before] the obnoxious game laws were not generally enforced to restrain the peasantry from this hardy amusement … Many a time have I seen my grave worthy father toss down the foot-ball, or the kittycat, to us and the serving lads."[72] The annual Scone game between married men and bachelors is described in John Sinclair's *The Statistical Account of Scotland, 1791–99.*[73] Thrown up from the market cross, whoever gets the ball can run with it until caught, at which point he passes it, or it is wrested from him. No one is allowed to kick it. Married men must put the ball into a *dool* (small hole) on the moor three times; the bachelors must dip it three times in a deep part of the river. The winners keep the ball, if drawn it is cut into equal pieces. "All is fair at the ball of Scone", as the saying goes.[74] Sinclair claims far-fetched origins from "the days of chivalry": an Italian is said to have challenged all the local parishes to a ball game.[75] Scone alone accepts. The townsmen win and establish an annual match. Every working man had to turn out and play for their local parish or face a fine. "This custom," Sinclair says, "being attended with certain inconveniences," had been abolished a few years before. Elsewhere, a *dool* is described as the "den" or goal in a game; while a *dool-tree* is "a tree which marks the goal in playing ball", or "a tree or post on which evil-doers were hanged."[76]

Fastern's E'en football is still played in Hawick, in the Scottish Borders, around 1760. Those west of the River Slitrig oppose those east of it. The game maintained "a species of war or fighting that had been carried on, time out of mind … This feud, in which boys below sixteen years of age were the chief combatants, was fostered by their seniors … this warlike propensity was fiercest for two or three weeks before and

71 *The Scottish Journal*, September 1847–February 1848, 1:29.

72 *The Scottish Journal*. p. 30.

73 Sinclair, J., *The Statistical Account of Scotland, 1791–99.* William Creech, Edinburgh, 1796. Vol. 18. pp. 88–89.

74 Hazlitt, W.C., *Faiths and Folklore*. 2 Vols. Reeves and Turner, London, 1905. Vol. 1. p. 244.

75 Ibid, p. 89.

76 Warrack, A. (ed.)., *A Scots Dialect Dictionary.* W. & R. Chambers, Edinburgh, 1911. p. 139.

after playing on Fastern's-eve, and for the same length of time previous to and after the 4th of July annually."[77] Violence ends in tragedy after a 1771 *Fastern's E'en* football match in Aberdeenshire, when a pub brawl ends in the fatal stabbing of a man by a wheel-wright.[78] On Ash Wednesday 1786, a women's football game takes place at Lennel in the Scottish Borders. As usual, it pairs married against singles. In an article entitled, "Petticoats Run Mad; or, The World Turned Topsy-Turvey", the Berwick Museum writes: "The ancient game of football, which seems to be neglected by men of the present age, is likely to be handed down to posterity by women … the jolly wives and buxom lasses" play with "uncommon keenness", fully attired in "Caps, handkerchiefs, petticoats, and every other article of female attire … darkness prevented victory being declared on either side; but we are told the parties mean to retake the field on Easter Monday." Afterwards, "Our heroines … retired to the ale-house."[79] Similarly, it is reported that in 1795, at Inveresk, in East Lothian, an annual Shrovetide match between married and unmarried women is invariably won by the former.[80]

Scottish women and sport is nothing new. In August 1738, "two married Women, of this City, stept out to Burntsfield [sic] Links, to a concerted Match at Golf, followed by their Husbands carrying the Clubs. Curiosity led thither a great Crowd, who were charmed with seeing the half-naked Viragoes tilt the balls so manfully, and their Dexterity in holeing. Considerable wages were laid."[81] Caddies are new on the scene. The first known collected balls for the future James II in Edinburgh in 1681/82: "I remember … in my youth to have often conversed with an old man, named Andrew Dickson, a golf club-maker, who said that, when a boy, he used to carry the duke's golf clubs, and to run before him and announce where the balls fell."[82] The term itself is not applied to golf until the nineteenth century. In 1842, a visiting German declares: "his

---

77 Wilson, R., *A Sketch of the History of Hawick*. Robert Armstrong, Hawick, 1825. pp. 161–162.

78 *Aberdeen Press and Journal*. 21 March 1763. p. 4.

79 McBrearty, R., *Scottish Football Origins*. https://scottishfootballorigins.org/2021/04/21/standing-free-the-ancient-story-of-womens-football-in-scotland-part-one/. Accessed 1 October 2023.

80 Sinclair, J., *The Statistical Account of Scotland, 1791–99*. William Creech, Edinburgh, 1795. Vol. 16. p. 19.

81 *Pennsylvania Gazette*. 24 August 1738. p. 2.

82 *Chambers's Edinburgh Journal*. 22 June 1839.

explanations were so crammed with expressions peculiar to Scotland … 'tee', 'holing', 'caddy', 'putters'."[83]

John Sinclair's meticulous book references football elsewhere. This from a 1793 entry on Perthshire: "on holidays, all the males of a district young and old, met to play at football but oftener at shinty."[84] A footnote adds: "Shinty is a game played with sticks, crooked at the end, and balls of wood." From the same year, of Duffus, a village in the north of Scotland, "true blue Presbyterians never took possession of our common people here: and they still celebrate … Christmas Day, &c. by assembling in large companies to play at foot-ball, and to dance and make merry."[85] The perception that shinty is thriving is at odds with the words of Alexander Stewart of Moulin, Perthshire, that year. "It is remarkable that those gymnastic exercises, which constituted the chief pastime of the Highlanders 40 or 50 years ago, have almost totally disappeared. At every fair or meeting of the country people, there were contests at racing, wrestling, putting the stone, &c.; and on holidays, all the males of a district, young and old, met to play at football, but oftener at shinty. These games are now only practised by schoolboys."[86] Similarly, in 1799, a Scottish judge laments the general lack of exercise, which brings "vigour and fortitude to the mind." "Formerly," he goes on, "in every village, and all over the country, cudgel-playing, wrestling, foot-ball, shooting with the bow, &c. were the favourite diversions of the people."[87]

Does the failed "Forty-five Rebellion" kill off the passion for sublimated battles? It certainly leads to the destruction and widespread contempt of Gaelic culture.[88] It takes half a century of rehabilitation for it to return, albeit in the form of anodyne Highland Societies. Nevertheless, English primacy cannot expunge centuries of Scottish tradition, nor molest the games of rural parishes. In 1799, Sinclair writes of Monquhitter, Aberdeenshire: "So it was with our fathers. They frequently met to exert

83 Kohl, J.G., *Travels in Scotland*. Bruce and Wyld, London, 1844. p. 110.

84 Sinclair, J., *The Statistical Account of Scotland, 1791–99.* William Creech, Edinburgh, 1793. Vol. 5. p. 72.

85 Ibid, Vol. 8. p. 399.

86 MacGregor, R., *Pastimes and Players*. Chatto and Windus, London, 1881. pp. 73–74.

87 Monboddo, J.B., *Ancient Metaphysics*. 5 Vols. J. Balfour and co., Edinburgh, 1779. Vol. 1. pp. 36–37.

88 Jarvie, G., *Sport, Parish Life, and the Emigré*. Journal of Sport History, 1998, 25:3, p. 384.

their strength in wrestling, in casting the hammer, and in throwing the stone; their agility at football; and their dexterity at coits and penny-stone. The midsummer-even fire … and the hallow-even fire, another relict of druidism, was kindled … Various magic ceremonies were then celebrated to counteract the influence of witches and demons."[89]

John Skinner's 1738 *The Monymusk Christmas Ba'ing* describes a Christmas Day game near Aberdeen. The introduction to an 1809 anthology of Skinner's work states: "at that period, and from time immemorial, it had been the practice in most of the country parishes in Aberdeenshire, for parties of young men to assemble, about the Christmas season, to try their strength and agility at the athletic exercise of *foot-ball.* The contest generally took place in the kirk-yard of the parish."[90] Aberdeen is one hundred and fifty miles from Kelso, so football is not only played in the Scottish Borders; there is longstanding popularity farther afield. Skinner's slapstick poem, written in dialect, starts in Monymusk's kirkyard. The ball is thumped around as players run through bogs and streams, rampaging, barging, grabbing, flinging, and flailing. In each stanza, a fresh character gets the ball, only to be thwarted by a bigger or craftier opponent. Local dignitaries are sucked in and upended, embodying the saturnalian reversal of carnival days. The ball is kicked, thrown, and carried:

> And a' the tricks of fit and hand,
> That ever was in being;
> Sometimes the ba' a yirdlins ran,[91]
> Sometimes in air was fleeing.

The stranger "in Highland claise" is carrying the ball when he bears, "the ba' thro' a his faes."[92] And when a tanner gets the ball, "He ran wi' neither fear nor wit, as fu' a winds a bladder."[93] The hapless tanner comes

---

89 Sinclair, J., *The Statistical Account of Scotland, 1791–99.* William Creech, Edinburgh, 1799. Vol. 21. p. 145.

90 Skinner, J., *Amusements of Leisure Hours: Or Poetical Pieces, Chiefly in the Scottish Dialect.* John Moir, Edinburgh, 1809. pp. 41–55.

91 "Sometimes the ball ran along the ground."

92 "The ball through all his foes."

93 "As full of wind as a bladder."

a cropper, "and tann'd his ain bum-lether." Eventually, a shout goes up: "the ba' spel's won, and we the ba' ha'e hail'd."[94] No timid game this: lost teeth, flattened noses, flayed arms, battered bodies, and bloody shins. Anything is used to wrest the ball, knees, elbows, shoulders, chins. All's fair at football.

In 1760, an anonymous Scottish book mentions a number of sports played by the protagonist. While at Aberdeen University he was "sorry proficient in learning; being readier at cat and dog, cappy-hole, riding the hurly hacket, playing at kyles and dams, spang-bodle, wrestling and foot-ball, (and such other sports as we use in our country) than at my book; by which I provoked my master to that degree, that my buttocks often felt the weight of his severity."[95,96] Robert MacGregor designates cat and dog as a precursor to cricket.[97] It is the game John Bunyan is playing when he wrestles with his conscience.

Jamieson in his 1722 *Scottish Dictionary, and Supplement* says: "This is a game for three players at least, who are furnished with clubs. They cut out two holes, each about a foot in diameter and seven inches in depth, and twenty-six feet apart; one man guards each hole with his club; these clubs are called Dogs. A piece of wood, about four inches long and one inch in diameter, called a Cat, is pitched, by a third person, from one hole toward the player at the other, who is to prevent the cat from getting into the hole. If it pitches in the hole, the party who threw it takes his turn with the club. If the cat be struck, the club-bearers change places, and each change of place counts one to the score, like club-ball."[98] Jamieson is clearly describing runs. Swapping the catstick for a ball would be problematic if it had to land in the holes but not if the holes were exchanged for two wickets. Indeed, before 1702, a large hole was "dug between the stumps, into which the wicket-keeper, in running out

94 "The football match is won, and we have hailed the ball."

95 Anon., *The Scot's Rogue; or the life and actions of Donald MacDonald, a highland Scot*, s.n., s.l., 1799. p. 8.

96 Cappy-hole: a game of marbles with a bowl-shaped hole cut out of the earth; hurly hacket: sliding down a steep hill in a trough or on a sledge; kyles or kayles: an early version of skittles; dams: Scottish dialect for draughts. Spang-bodle is unknown outside of *The Scot's Rogue*. In Scottish dialect, spang can mean to pitch, toss, or flip, while a bodle was a Scottish tuppenny bit. Spang-bodle, then, is probably a coin tossing game. Spangie-wangie and langie-spangie are marble games.

97 MacGregor, R., *Pastimes and Players*. Chatto and Windus, London, 1881. p. 9.

98 Brand, J., *The Cricket Field: or The History and the Science of the Game of Cricket*. Longman, Brown, Greenman and Longmans, London, 1854. p. 10.

or stumping a batsman, had to place the ball."[99] In those days, wickets had two stumps, two feet apart.

~

South of the border, Shrove Tuesday football thrives in Cumberland. The county's Bromfield Free School has a custom "time out of mind" of playing the game as part of an elaborate tradition. The master is barred, while the pupils barricade the school and protect it with elder popguns. If they hold out for three days, they are allowed privileges, including a football match where the ball is thrown down in the churchyard. The winners are the first to get the ball to their captain's house, two or three miles away, "every inch of which ground was keenly disputed. All the honour accruing to the conqueror at foot-ball, was that of possessing the ball." It is indicative of football's popularity in Cumberland that, "details of these matches were the general topic of conversation among the villagers; and were dwelt on, with hardly less satisfaction than their ancestors enjoyed in relating their feats in the border wars."[100] The football game even has its own song:

> At Scales, great Tom Barwise gat the ba' in his hand,
> And t'wives all ran out, and shouted, and bann'd:
> Tom Cowan pulch'd, and flang him 'mang t'whins,
> And he bledder'd, od-white te', tou's broken my shins.[101,102]

Down the road in Workington, a 1777 Easter Tuesday game is reported on, Upper Town beating Lower Town after two hours.[103] Similar reports make the press in 1792 and 1796; in fact, the game is reported annually until at least 1863.[104,105] The 1796 "annual foot-ball prize was strongly disputed; but Victory at length declared in favour of the champions of Priest-gate; the ball having been kicked into the river, and carried, by the

---

99 Selkirk, G.H., *Guide to the Cricket Ground.* Macmillan and Co., London and Cambridge, 1867. p. 8.

100 Hutchinson, W., *The history of the county of Cumberland, and some places adjacent, from the earliest accounts to the present time.* 2 Vols. F. Jollie, Carlisle, 1794. Vol. 2. pp. 322–323.

101 Ibid, p. 323.

102 "Tom Cowan pushed/polished [?] and flung him among the bushes, And he bellowed, old white thee [?], you've broken my shins."

103 *Cumberland Pacquet.* 8 April 1777. p. 3.

104 Ibid. 24 April 1792. p. 3.

105 *Carlisle Journal.* 14 April 1863. p. 3.

stream, below the goal."[106] The same day's paper reports on the execution at Tyburn of highwayman Spence Broughton. Cut from the gallows, his corpse is gibbeted in Sheffield for an unprecedented thirty-six years. The macabre always draws a crowd. The first day's display attracts forty thousand visitors.[107]

Such customary football games are symbolic of greater things. In 1733, inhabitants of the parish of Sebergham, near Carlisle, Cumberland, "considered the Sabbath … a day of recreation … generally spent in tumultuous meetings at ale-houses, or in the rude diversions of foot-ball."[108] Two years later, it is said of a twenty-one-year-old Carlisle man that, "there was scarce a man in the county, who durst contend with him at the ordinary rural diversions, of running, leaping, wrestling, and playing at football."[109] A Shrove Tuesday 1762 match is described in Alnwick, in the neighbouring county of Northumberland. Crowds "congregated before the castle gates; and at 2 o'clock, forth came the tall and stately porter dressed in the Percy livery, blue and yellow, plentifully decorated with silver lace, and gave the ball its first kick, sending it bounding out of the barbican of the castle into Bailiffgate; and then the young and vigorous kicked it through the principal streets of the town, and afterwards into the Pasture, which has been used from time immemorial."[110] In 1866, George Tate writes: "A similar custom was almost universal in the north of England … at Wooler the game was between the married and unmarried; after kicking it through the town, one party endeavoured to kick it to the hopper of Earl Mill, and the other over a tree … in the days of yore, the contest sometimes continued for three days."[111]

In 1791, an observer of the Derby Shrovetide games quips, "I have seen this coarse sport carried to the barbarous heights of an election contest; nay, I have known a foot-ball hero chaired through the streets like a successful member, although his utmost elevation of character was no

---

106 *Cumberland Pacquet*. 5 April 1796. p. 2.

107 Equivalent to two hundred and forty thousand in 2024.

108 Hutchinson, W., *The history of the county of Cumberland, and some places adjacent, from the earliest accounts to the present time.* 2 Vols. F. Jollie, Carlisle, 1794. Vol. 2. p. 417.

109 Ibid, Vol. 1. p. 551.

110 Tate, G., *The History of the Borough, Castle, and Barony of Alnwick*. 2 Vols. Henry Hunter Blair, Alnwick, 1866. Vol. 1. p. 435.

111 Ibid, p. 435.

more than a butcher's apprentice. Black eyes, bruised arms, and broken shins are equally the mark of victory and defeat ... the very infant learns to *kick*, and then to walk."[112] Sadder news from Derby in 1796. John Snape drowns in the Derwent while attempting to cross with the ball.[113] A week later, the *Derby Mercury* carries an address from the jurors to the mayor and Justices of the Peace at the Eagle and Child Inn. "the Custom of playing at Foot Ball on Shrove Tuesdays; a custom, which whilst it has no better recommendation than its Antiquity, for its further continuance, is disgraceful to Humanity and civilization; subversive of good order, and Government, and destructive of the Morals, Properties, and very lives of our Inhabitants." The mayor agrees. In all caps. "the custom of playing at FOOT BALL in this Borough on Shrove Tuesdays—We have unanimously resolved THAT SUCH CUSTOM SHALL FROM HENCEFORTH BE DISCONTINUED."[114] The following year, local magistrates rail against the upcoming Shrove Tuesday game but are powerless to stop it.[115] A battle lost. They have football in their sights.

Football tragedies whet readers appetites. On Easter Monday 1771, a man in Lichfield, Staffordshire, breaks his leg, while a Northumbrian has a stroke and dies.[116,117] In Weston, Northamptonshire, while Thomas Woddams "was kicking a Foot-Ball, he fell down and broke his leg in a terrible manner." Elsewhere, a Scottish youth kills a friend in a pub argument after a *Fastern's E'en* game; and William Waterfall is charged with the death of George Twigge, "in a Quarrel at Foot-Ball, in Ashford-in-the-Water, Derbyshire."[118,119,120,121] In 1792, a football match in Timolin, Co Kildare, is followed by heavy drinking. "The demon of discord, whiskey, soon introduced a battle, in which all were engaged, and almost all suffered." One man is felled "by the stroke of a bottle

112 Hutton, W., *The History of Derby*. Nichols, Son, and Bentley, London, 1817. p. 184.

113 *Derby Mercury*. 11 February 1796. p. 4.

114 *Derby Mercury*. 18 February 1796. p. 4.

115 *Derby Mercury*. 23 February 1797. p. 1.

116 *Aris's Birmingham Gazette*. 8 April 1771. p. 3.

117 *Newcastle Courant*. 22 March 1794. p. 4.

118 *Northampton Mercury*. 8 January 1770. p. 3.

119 *Aberdeen Press and Journal*. 21 March 1763. p. 4.

120 *Derby Mercury*. 12 May 1775. p. 3.

121 Two Waterfall brothers were instrumental in the early development of football, seventeen miles away in Sheffield.

from the wife of a person whom he had just knocked down; and the woman's feelings for her husband, being stimulated by liquor, she cut the head of his opponent to pieces, and immediately received from one of the combatants a casual blow that fractured her own. There is little prospect of her recovery. Two men in prison in Ashby are likewise despaired of, and a multitude of others are dangerously wounded."[122] Tucked away in a corner of the page is a short death notice for Sir Joshua Reynolds, England's leading portraitist. Midway up is an article on Joseph Priestley, among other things, the chemist who discovered oxygen. As a philosopher and theologian, he holds unorthodox views that are considered seditious. He condones the American and French revolutions and, as a Dissenter, advocates the separation of church and state. The press incites the public into such a frenzy that a three-day riot breaks out in Birmingham, and Priestley's house is razed.

More violence is reported. In 1771, an eighty-guinea Yorkshire derby between the Gentlemen of Sharlston and the Gentlemen of Crofton becomes increasingly ill-tempered after Sharlston break the deadlock on the two-hour mark. Two players met "at the ball with such violence, that one of them had his leg broke, and the other his shoulder dislocated."[123] When outraged teammates wade in, an eight-year-old boy is trampled underfoot and dies. Other boys are luckier. When a Chester steeple collapses in 1770, boys at football in the churchyard escape with bruises, and when a boy breaks his leg near a chapel, the sympathetic paper gently reproves it happening on a Sunday afternoon.[124,125] Jeremiah Lowther also gets off lightly when he breaks his leg playing football and makes a full recovery. He is eighty years old.[126] Four years before, another Jeremiah Lowther is not so lucky. A purveyor of toasting forks, he dies overnight on a frozen street.[127] There are other Jeremiah Lowthers. One steals poultry;[128] another loses his infant daughter after her clothes

122 *Sheffield Public Advertiser*. 2 March 1792. p. 3.

123 *Kentish Gazette*. 26 October 1771 p. 3.

124 *Chester Courant*. 29 May 1770. p. 3.

125 *Cumberland Pacquet*. 13 March 1777. p. 3.

126 *Gazetteer and New Daily Advertiser*. 19 January 1768. p. 2.

127 *Aris's Birmingham Gazette*. 21 November 1763. p. 3.

128 *Leeds Intelligencer*. 7 July 1838. p. 5.

catch fire;[129] and a third is a chimney sweep in court for not sending his children to school.[130]

Sport has become entrenched in public schools. In 1741, the Earl of Chesterfield writes to his son at Westminster School: "Dear Boy … if you have a right ambition, you will desire to excel all boys of your own age at cricket or trap-ball."[131] The poet William Cowper, who left Westminster School in 1749, wrote how he excelled at cricket and football as a child.[132] It is the same year rugby acquires its first playing field.[133] By 1794, Charterhouse School has its own song, which includes the lines, "I challenge all the men alive to say they e'er were gladder, Than boys all striving who should kick most wind out of the bladder."[134] That year, future politician Coningsby Waldo Sibthorp writes home from Westminster School: "We play at Football in the Cloisters the general consequence are broke heads and shins."[135] Charterhouse and Westminster School play cricket in London that year, the first recorded between public schools, but when Eton cricketers sneak down to play Westminster on Hounslow Heath two years later, they are rumbled and flogged by their headmaster.[136] The Eton Field Game, a version of football exclusive to the school, is codified in 1847, though its roots lay further back. In 1775, the *Hibercadian Journal* mentions football played in the fields, as does the *London Courier*, in 1801.[137,138]

Thomas Gray's 1742 poem *Ode on a Distant Prospect of Eton College* includes the lines:

> Say, Father Thames, for thou hast seen
> Full many a sprightly race

129 *Hull Advertiser*. 21 February 1840. p. 6.

130 *Selby Times*. 25 May 1883. p. 4.

131 Stanhope, P.D., *Earl of Chesterfield's Letters to His Son*. 3 Vols. E. Duyckink et al., New York, 1813. Vol. 1. p. 147.

132 Marples, M., *A History of Football*. Secker and Warburg, London, 1954. p. 89.

133 Ibid, p. 89.

134 Tod, A.H., *Charterhouse*. George Bell and Sons, London, 1900. p. 154. Sung to the tune of the Irish reel *Ally Croker*, which was written by Wexford man Larry Grogan c1725.

135 *From Coningsby Waldo Sibthorp*. The National Archives: https://discovery.nationalarchives.gov.uk/browse/r/h/04118b09–30d3–4da8–8c4d-f52dc750c3d4. Accessed 5 May 2023.

136 Ford, J., *Cricket: A Social History, 1700–1835*. David and Charles, Exeter, 1972. p. 20.

137 *an Journal*. 25 January 1775. p. 1.

138 *London Courier*. 14 August 1801. p. 3.

Disporting on thy margent green
The paths of pleasure trace;
Who foremost now delight to cleave
With pliant arm thy glassy wave?
The captive linnet which enthrall?
What idle progeny succeed
to chase the rolling circle's speed,
or urge the flying ball? [139]

In the poem, an Old Etonian gazes at the innocent pupils and reflects on the grim realities they will face as adults. Gray attended Eton from 1725 to 1734. A kicking game is implied by "chase the rolling circle's speed", a handling one by "urge the flying ball", and "delight to cleave with pliant arm thy glassy wave." "Many a sprightly race, disporting [enjoying] on thy margent green" is evidence the game was played on the fields. Gray is likely to be describing an antecedent to both, rather than an early example of one or the other. There is another possibility. Gray is describing cricket. *Nugae Etonensis* (Etonian Nonsense), a manuscript written by a scholar in 1765/66, includes a list of games, one of which is "goals".[140] It is unclear if it is a synonym for football, though "football fields" are mentioned elsewhere in the manuscript.[141] In 1776, a more comprehensive list of games in vogue at Eton is provided by William Dutton when he writes home to his father:

"Cricket, Fives, Shirking Walls, Scrambling Walls, Bally Cally, Battledores, Peg-top, Peg in the ring, Goals, Hopscotch, Headimy, Conquering Lobs, Hoops, Marbles, Trap ball, Steal baggage, Puss in the corner, Cat Gallows, Kites, Cloyster and Flyer Gigs, Tops, Humming Tops, Hunt the hare, Hunt the dark lanthorn, Chuck, Sinks, Starecaps, Hustlecap, Football, Slides in School, Leaping poles, Slide down the sides of the stairs from Cloysters to College Kitchen."[142,143]

---

139 Rolfe, W.J. (ed.)., *Select Poems of Thomas Gray*. Harper and Brothers Publishers, New York, 1895. p. 51. lns 21–30.

140 Lyte, H.C.M., *A History of Eton College 1440–1884*. MacMillan and Co., London, 1889. p. 304.

141 Ibid, p. 305.

142 Lyte, H.C.M., *A History of Eton College (1440–1910)*. Macmillan and Co., London, 1911. pp. 318–319.

143 Many of these are to be found in the definite book of children's games, Alice Gomme's *The Traditional Games of England, Scotland and Ireland*. 2 Vols. David Nutt, London, 1894.

A number are peculiar to Eton; sliding downstairs and headimy are exclusive by virtue of the school's architecture. Cricket is listed first. If Dutton wrote them as they sprang to mind, football is almost an afterthought. "Goals" is up there again, providing further evidence it refers to field football. "Football" is not included in the list of 1765/66.[144,145] The wall game is only invented in 1766, so it is probably "football", well down the list, as it is yet to catch on. Horace Walpole attends Eton from 1727 to 1734, where he is good friends with Thomas Gray. Son of Robert Walpole, Horace penned the *Castle of Otranto, A Gothic Story.* Written in 1764, over fifty years before Mary Shelley's *Frankenstein; or, The Modern Prometheus*, it is regarded as the world's first gothic novel. One of the first gothic plays *The Castle Spectre* includes the lines: "Lord Hildebrand, who was condemned for treason some sixty years ago, may be seen in the Great Hall, regularly at midnight, playing at foot-ball with his own head!"[146]

A final clue to early football at Eton lies in a comment made by Horace Walpole. He refuses to attend Lunardi's hot air balloon ascent, considering the venture ludicrous. When he finally sees an ascending balloon, he is reputed to have said it resembled an Eton football.[147] Two years earlier, he said of balloons: "I hope these new mechanic meteors will prove only playthings for the learned and the idle, and not be converted into new engines of destruction to the human race ... The wicked wit of man always studies to apply the results of talents to enslaving, destroying or cheating his fellow creatures. Could we reach the moon, we should think of reducing it to a province of some European kingdom."[148]

144 Lyte, H.C.M., *A History of Eton College 1440–1884*. MacMillan and Co. London, 1889. p. 305.

145 Headimy is written, possibly correctly, as heading, and hustlecap as hurtlecap.

146 Lewis, M.G., *The Castle Spectre*. s.n., London, 1798. p. 23.

147 Wasey, S., *Annals of the King's College of Our Lady of Eton beside Windsor*. Methuen, London, 1898. p. 163.

148 Robins, J., *Up in the Air: Balloonomania and Scientific Performance*. Eighteenth-Century Studies, 2015, 48:4. Special Issue: Performance. p. 524.

CHAPTER SIXTEEN
1700–1799 V

The stick game cannot be dislodged in Ireland, though it loses popularity in England as football takes off. It falters in Scotland, excepting the Highlands, where it rules supreme. Further south, a predominantly carrying game is played, increasingly so as the border gets closer. Quite why the stick game loses out is unclear. On record, it is the oldest of the three. A stick is needed, though, and ball contact with hands and feet is largely prohibited, limiting the development of skills. Then again, kicking–carrying games require a ball; bandy and shinty can be played with a rounded piece of wood, or even a stone. Perhaps folk football is so ingrained in the collective unconscious of the working classes its kicking and carrying descendants triumph organically. The stick and ball game does have one thing in its favour, one that will ensure a thriving longevity: it can be played on ice. Exactly when and where it was first played on ice is unknown. Fitzstephen's c1180 chapter on twelfth century London has more to say about ice games than ball games:

"When the great fenne or moore (which washeth the walles of the citie on the north side) is frozen, many young people play upon the yce some stryding as wide as they may; some doe slide swiftly: others make themselves seates of ice, as great as milstones: one sits downe, many hand in hand do drawe him, and one slipping on a sudden, all fall together: some tye bones to their féete and under their heeles and shoving themselves by a little piked staffe doe slide as swiftly as a birde flyeth in the aire, or an arrow out of a crosse-bow."[1]

Skates and trekking poles. We are indebted to Fitzstephen for this passage, far more so than the ambiguous Shrovetide game, for it is the first mention of skates in history. As for the stick and ball game on ice, the Netherlands has a legitimate claim. Like Robert de Boron, the Flemish poet Jacob van Maerlant wrote his own thirteenth century version of Nennius's ninth century story.[2] Like Boron, the boy is

1 Stow, J., *A Survay of London*. John Wolfe, London, 1598. p. 480.

2 Nijs, G., Nijs. S., *750 Years 'Mit ener Coluen.'* Golfika—The Magazine of the European Association of Golf Historians & Collectors, 2011, Issue 7, p. 30.

Merlin, and he plays "*mit ener colven*": with a club. In 1387, sports associated with gambling are banned in Brielle, Holland, though *kolven* is permitted beyond the city walls.[3] A mid-thirteenth century Flemish manuscript on the history of science and philosophy contains a marginal of four men with curved sticks. Two are fighting over a ball on the ground, another is at ease, and the fourth has swung his stick above his shoulder.[4] The land game also appears as *het kolven* in a Dutch woodcut from 1497.

The first ice version is depicted in Brueghel the Elder's *The Hunters in the Snow* in 1565. A man with a curved stick is about to hit a ball; two other men with sticks have their backs to him but are peering round. Two other men stand on the lake, each with a curved stick and a ball. Elsewhere, a man pulls a sledge with a seated woman. Others are playing curling, skating hand in hand, or chasing one another. Representations of stickball on ice are found in multiple paintings from the Dutch Golden Age,[5] including *Winter Landscape with Ice Skaters* (c1608), by Hendrick Avercamp; *Amusements on the Frozen Moat* (1618), *Skaters and Kolf Players on a Frozen River* (1628), and *Winter Landscape with a Farmhouse, Skaters and Kolf Players on a Frozen Stream* (1628), by Esaias van de Velde; *Skaters and Kolf Players on the Ice Near Kampen* (1640), by Barent Avercamp; and *Winter in Holland: Skating Scene* (1645), *A Frozen River near a Village, with Golfers and Skaters* (c1648), and *A Frozen River by a Town at Evening* (c1665), by Aert van der Neer. The Netherlands are unquestionably the first nation to make stickball games on ice popular.

In 1669, an Englishman describes Dutch skates as, "a certain sort of Shooes call'd Skates, which have a long, shining, narrow, crooked iron that stands out before … they fly like birds in the air."[6] There are several other mentions of skating in English books over the next forty years; none mention a stick and ball game on ice. An English–Dutch dictionary of 1708 sees fit to translate skates as *schaatsen*, and in 1685 there are

---

3 Ibid, p. 32.

4 Bibioltheek Brugge: MS 251, *Speculum Doctrinale*, c1250, fol. 149r.

5 Hardy, S., Holman, A.C., *Hockey: A Global History*. University of Illinois Press, 2018. pp. 27–28.

6 Aglionby, W., *The Present State of the United Provinces of the Low Countries*. John Starkey, London, 1669. p. 217.

import duties on, "Skates of Wood for sliding, shod, the dozen: 1s. 3d."[7,8] Duties also apply to panther and tiger skins, mineral water, pickled cucumbers, balls for children, "racket hoops" and "cornu unicornu"—unicorn horns.[9] That skates are still imported in 1796 demonstrates their popularity.

Hurling aside, the first known record of a stickball game is by Bata, c1000. We must then turn to Iceland. At least a dozen sagas contain ball games. The earliest stickball game is in *Egils Saga*, c1225–c1250. Land-based stickball games are also referenced in *Göngu-Hrólfs saga* and *Þorsteins saga Vikingssonar* (both fifteen century). Six games are played on ice, three of them stick and ball games. *Grettis Saga*, c1400,[10] and the sixteenth century *Víglundar saga* are played on fjords.[11] The stickball game in *Gisla Saga Súrssonar*, c1410, is probably played beside Seftjörn pond, as the ice is referred to as *svellinu*—ice formed on land, rather than *ís*—ice formed on water.[12] Three fjord-based ball games are mentioned without sticks: *Gull óris saga* (fourteenth century),[13] *Harðar saga og Hólmverja* c1400,[14] and *Þórðar* [Thordur] *saga hreðu* (late fourteenth century).[15,16] Why *sagas* are repeatedly ignored as a source of ball games on ice is mystifying. The *Grettis Saga*, c1400, is the earliest bat, ball, and ice game in history.[17] These games are sporting mythology, excavated treasures as precious as the scintillating expanse they glide across.

---

7 Sewel, W., *A Large Dictionary of English and Dutch, in Two Parts*. De weduwe van Steven Swart, de Beurs, Amsterdam, 1708. p. 534.

8 *An Additional Book of Rates of Goods and Merchandizes, &c.* Signed by Spencer Compton, Speaker of the Honourable House of Commons. J. Baskett, London, 1725. p. 168.

9 In 1690, unicorn horns are described as not from a "Creature like to a Horse, but come from a Fish, and therefore a Sea-Unicorn; they are brought from the Straits Davids, near the North-Passage." In: Berlu, J.J., *The Treasury of Drugs Unlock'd*. s.n., London, 1690. p. 29. They were probably narwhal tusks.

10 Gunnell, T., *The Relationship between Icelandic 'Knattleikur' and Early Irish Hurling*. Folklore of Ireland Society, 2010, 80, p. 59.

11 Ibid, p. 64.

12 Ibid, p. 58.

13 Ibid, p. 64.

14 Ibid, p. 63.

15 Þ, pronounced 'th' as in *thick*, is an Old English character. ð is also pronounced 'th'.

16 Ibid, p. 62.

17 Most sagas recount events later than *Egil's Saga*, generally c930–c1030. In: Thurber, B.A., *The Viking Ball Game*. Scandinavian Studies, 2015, 87:2, p. 168.

The next reference to a *stickball game on ice* is in Scotland during the winter of 1607/08: "A vehement frost continued from Martimease till the 20th of Februar. The sea freized so ferre as it ebbed, and sindrie went in to shippes upon yce, and played at the chamiare a myle within the sea marke."[18] *Chamiare* is another name for shinty (cf. shammie and caman).[19] It is probably a contraction of *car-sham-ye!* (left hand-shame-you!) the cry when an opponent unfairly strikes the ball with the club in their left hand.[20] The earliest newspaper reference to a stickball game on ice is not until 1803, when two boys playing shinty near Glasgow fall through the ice and die.[21]

The first successful English colony in the New World is established in Jamestown in 1607. But it is neither the Scottish nor the English who introduce the stick game; evidence points to the Netherlands, who have had their own stick and ball game since at least the mid-thirteenth century. When Dutch migrants arrive in 1617, their first foothold is Fort Orange, New Netherland, now Albany, New York. The location provides the earliest mention of a colonial stickball game in American history.[22] In mid-December 1650, a group of men go to De Vrouw Maria inn in Bowewijck near Fort Orange, having played *kolf* for brandy. The eponymous dame who serves them is accused of withholding the brandy. The two winners complain, a fight ensues, and Gysbert the tavernkeeper is hit with a *kolven* stick then cut with a knife.[23]

Given the season, they may be playing *kolf* on ice, but definitive proof of a game must wait until March 1657. Gysbert Van Loon and others in Fort Orange stand accused of playing "*kolven op het ijs*"—*kolven* on the

18 Thomson, T., *History of the Kirk of Scotland by Mr David Calderwoord.* 8 Vols. The Edinburgh Printing Company, 1845. Vol. 6. p. 688.

19 Over the years, the Scottish stick game has gone by multiple names: *cammanach, cummock, cammock, camac, cammon, camman, caman, chamiare, camie, shammie, shimmie, schinnie, schynnie, shinnie, shinny, shinye, shinty, shenty, shinnock*, and *club.* It is *iomain camanachd* or *cluich-bhall* in Scottish Gaelic. It was *heytie* and *hummie* in the Lothian region of the Lowlands, while a variation, *knotty*, was played in the Caithness area.

20 Jamieson, J., *Supplement to the Etymological Dictionary of the Scottish Language.* 2 Vols. W. & C. Tait, Edinburgh, 1825. Vol. 2. p. 181.

21 *True Briton.* 9 February 1803. p. 4.

22 The first reference to a stick and ball game in America is by Marc Lescarbot, when he records a Native American game he saw in 1606/07.

23 Baart, J.M., *Material Culture in Seventeenth-Century Dutch Colonial Manuscripts.* New World Dutch Studies. Dutch Arts and Culture in Colonial America, 1609–1776. Albany Institute of History and Art, 1987. p. 43.

ice—on a prayer day.[24,25] At the same sitting, Claes Ripsen and others are fined "for tippling after bell-ring", while in September, Hendrick Andriessen is up for "standing in the middle of the street at ten o'clock at night with a drawn cutlass in his hand."[26] In December 1659, Fort Orange magistrates issue an edict: "having heard divers complaints from the burghers of this place against the practice of playing golf [*kolven* in the original] along the streets, which causes great damage to the windows of houses, and also exposes people to the danger of being injured … [we] hereby forbid all persons to play golf [*kolven*] in the streets, under the penalty of Fl. 25 for each person."[27]

The first mention of a game on ice in eighteenth century America is football. In 1737, a boy "playing at Foot-Ball upon the Ice" near Boston almost drowns when "he happen'd to fall into an AirHole."[28] Five yards on, he bumps up against thick ice, which somehow breaks. Nothing is heard of the stick game on ice until 1783. A freshwater pond The Collect, lost in the advancement of New York City, is the site of winter games: "The ground between the Collect and Broadway rose gradually from its margin to the height of one hundred feet; and nothing can exceed, in brilliancy and animation, the prospect it presented on a fine winter-day, when the icy surface was alive with skaters, darting … or bearing down in a body in pursuit of the ball driven before them by their hurlies; while the hillside was covered with spectators, rising as in an amphitheatre."[29] Twelve years later, John Stevens exhibits a steam-powered boat on the Collect.[30] He goes on to invent the first steam-powered ferry, is the first to advocate for railroads, and builds the first steam locomotive in the United States.[31]

---

24 Browning, R., *A History of Golf The Royal and Ancient Game*. E.P. Dutton & Company, Inc., New York, 1955. p. 113.

25 O'Callaghan, E.B., *Calendar of Historical Manuscripts in the Office of the Secretary of State, Albany, N.Y.* Weed, Parsons and Company, 1864. p. 314.

26 Ibid, p. 316.

27 Browning, R., *A History of Golf The Royal and Ancient Game*. E.P. Dutton & Company, Inc., New York, 1955. pp. 113–114; Van Laer, A.J.F., *Minutes of the Court of Fort Orange and Beverwijck*. 2 Vols. University of the State of New York, Albany, 1923. Vol. 1. p. 235.

28 *The Boston Gazette*. 7 February 1737. p. 3.

29 Duer, W.A., *New-York as it Was, During the Latter Part of the Last Century*. Stanford and Swords, New York, 1849. p. 13.

30 Curry, D., *New-York: A Historical Sketch of the Rise and Progress of the Metropolitan City of America*. Carlton & Phillips, New York, 1853. p. 180.

31 Stevens, J., *Documents tending to prove the superior advantages of rail-ways and steam-carriages over canal navigation*. T. and J. Swords, New York, 1812.

On 2 January 1786, John Rhea Smith, a freshman at Princeton University writes: "disappointed studying ... by the lads who came in to make a ball to play with on the ice."[32] A year on—ten years prior to becoming the second president of the United States—John Adams advocates the insertion of, "running, wrestling, riding, swimming, skating, fencing, and dancing" into school curricula to "fortify the bodies and invigorate the minds of youth."[33] In the late 1780s, future naval officer Stephen Decatur takes to the frozen Schuylkill, in Philadelphia. When the river "invited the boys to skim over it on the swift skates, no one excelled him in hurly, prisoner's base, and the other games of the season."[34] Hurly and hurlies. The 1783 game on The Collect also mentions hurlies. An Irish influence? It seems so. Nenagh, Co. Tipperary, is famous as the site of the earliest known game of *hurling* on ice. This from an account on January 5, during the savage winter of 1739/40: "The Shannon is frozen over, and a hurling match has taken place on it; and Mr. Parker had a sheep roast whole on the ice, with which he regaled the company who had assembled to witness the hurling match."[35] There is no mention of novelty, suggesting previous games. Soon after, twenty miles away, "North Tipperary gentleman roasted whole sheep on the top of nineteen inches of Shannon ice near Portumna "at the eating of which they had great mirth, and drank many loyal toasts"; afterwards "a match of hurling" was played between two gentlemen's teams."[36]

Ice hockey is not the only sport at Princeton in 1786: "handball and cricket were in vogue, and shinny and its derivatives, hawkey and hurley, continued in sporadic popularity."[37] It is unclear which of these ball games were prohibited in May 1761, when the college, "been sensible of the Damages done to the President's House by the Students playing at

32 Woodward, R.L., *Journal at Nassau: The Diary of John Rhea Smith. The Princeton University Library Chronicle*. The Princeton University Library, 1985, 46:3, p. 272.

33 Adams, C.F., *The Works of John Adams, Second President of the United States*. Charles C. Little and James Brown, Boston, 1851. p. 555.

34 Mackenzie, A.S., *Life of Stephen Decatur, a Commodore in the Navy of the United States*. Charles C. Little and James Brown, Boston, 1846. p. 13.

35 O'Rourke, J., *The History of the Great Irish Famine of 1847, with Notices of Earlier Irish Famines*. James Duffy and Co., Ltd., 1902. p. 15.

36 Dickson, D., *Arctic Ireland: the Extraordinary Story of the Great Frost and Famine of 1740–41*. White Row Press, Belfast, 1997. p. 14.

37 Savage, H.J., *American College Athletics*. Bulletin Number Twenty-Three, The Carnegie Foundation for the Advancement of Teaching, New York, 1929. p. 16.

Ball against it, do hereby strictly forbid all … students … playing at Ball against the President's House under the Penalty of Five Shillings."[38] With mention of stickball games in New York, New Jersey, and Pennsylvania, they are flourishing far from New England—the home of kicking–carrying games. Across the states, field and ice varieties, and Dutch, Irish, Scottish, and English versions are referenced, and the English version is termed "hawkey", as it is in Sussex.

Ice hockey belongs to Canada. A nucleotide in its national identity. The birthplace of Canadian ice hockey is robustly disputed. One claim stems from King's College, Windsor, Nova Scotia, founded by royal assent in 1789.[39] Reverend William Cochran is born in Co. Tyrone and educated at Trinity College Dublin. He becomes Principal of the Academy (the grammar school within the university), and President of King's College in 1790, a position he retains for four decades.[40] A Greek and Latin professor, he is "a man of singularly mild and amiable manner",[41] who wins "the respect and love of the young men under his care, by whom he was regarded more in the light of a kind parent than of a stern professor."[42] Cochran is said to have taught his pupils hurling but to use the ball on the ground rather than pick it up with the bat, and that at some point this took to the ice. One book, talking of light relief at the college during the early nineteenth century says: "Hockey (or shinny) and all kinds of skating could be enjoyed on the ponds and flooded marshes in winter, and snowshoe tramps and tobogganing were fairly common."[43] While the implication is that it relates to the first two decades of the century, no year is given; neither does the anecdote mention Cochran.[44]

---

38 Collins, V.L., *Princeton*. Oxford Univeristy Press, New York, NY, 1914. p. 207.

39 The university relocated to Halifax after a fire devastated the buildings in 1920.

40 Hind, H.Y., *The University of King's College, Windsor, Nova Scotia, 1790–1890*. The Church Review Company, New York, 1890. p. 24.

41 C. P. Wright, 'COCHRAN, WILLIAM,' in *Dictionary of Canadian Biography*, Vol. 6, University of Toronto/Université Laval, 2003. http://www.biographi.ca/en/bio/cochran_william_6F.html. Accessed 13 April 2023.

42 Vroom, F.W., *King's College: A Chronicle, 1789–1939, Collections and Recollections*. The Imperial Publishing Company Limited, Halifax, Nova Scotia, 1941. pp. 54–55.

43 Ibid, p. 59.

44 Cochran makes no mention of hurling in his brief memoirs, though there is no reason why he should have: he died in 1833, well before ice hockey was established. Thomas, M.H. (eds.)., *The Memoirs of William Cochrane, Sometime Professor in Columbia College, New York, and in King's College, Windsor, Nova Scotia*. New-York Historical Society Quarterly, 1954, 38:1, pp. 55–83.

Thomas Chandler Haliburton (b1796) attends the school, matriculating in 1815. He is the author of the internationally acclaimed Sam Slick novels. In one book, Slick imagines how another character might reminisce on his school days: "and you boys let out racin', yelpin, hollerin, and whoopin like mad with pleasure, and the playground, and the game at base in the fields, or hurly on the long pond on the ice, or campin' out at night."[45] Is "base in the fields" baseball or prisoner's base, the tag game?

An anonymous letter to the Windsor Mail in 1876 provides more tangible evidence of ball sports on ice. Writing of his time at the school from 1816 to 1818: "The Devil's Punch Bowl and Long Pond, back of the College, were favourite resorts, and we used to skate in winter, on moonlight nights, on the ponds. I recollect John Cunard ... having his front teeth knocked out with a hurley by Pete Delancey of Annapolis."[46] Hurlies again. King's College's claim rests on whether Haliburton's passage is "evidently autobiographical",[47] if Cochran taught hurling or not, and if Anonymous's memory is solid. Halifax-Dartmouth, Nova Scotia, also has a claim to be the home of ice hockey. The Halifax Arcadian Magazine publishes a poem in 1827;

> Now at ricket with hurlies some dozens of boys
> Chase the ball o'er the ice, with a deafening noise.
> Now some play at curling, and some with great ease
> Cut circles or figures whichever you please
> On their skates, or else letter—the true lover's knot,
> And a dozen such things which I've really forgot.[48]

Ricket was another stick and ball game played on land and ice. Its name may stem from the childhood condition caused by prolonged vitamin D deficiency, which causes bandy legs. The term is first recorded in 1634, when out of ten thousand nine hundred deaths in the City of London,

---

45 Haliburton, T.C., *Sam Slick in England*; Or, *The Attaché*. George Routledge & Co., London, 1858, p. 335.

46 Gidén, C., Houda, P., Martel, J-P., *On the Origin of Hockey*. Hockey Origin Publishing, Stockholm and Chambly, 2014. p. 3.

47 Chittick, V.L.O., *Thomas Chandler Halliburton, "Sam Slick" A Study in Provincial Toryism*. Columbia University Press, New York, 1924. p. 25.

48 Hardy, S., Holman, A.C., *Hockey: A Global History*. University of Illinois Press, 2018. pp. 29–30.

fourteen were attributed to rickets.[49] Whatever the origin of the name, there is glorious harmony. Ricket, wicket, cricket, clicket.

What defines the birthplace of ice hockey in Canada needs sensible reflection. Is it where the first known recorded stick and ball game is played—the reductive arena King's and other would-bes slug it out—the home of the first ice hockey club, where the first fixed rules were drawn up, or the venue of the first organised competitive fixture? Or has Canada evolved beyond its colonial prism? Is the home of ice hockey the epicentre of *Duwarken*, the stick and ball game played on ice by the Mi'kmaq First Nation's people in Mi'kma'ki, now part of Nova Scotia?[50] Surviving sticks have been carbon dated to 1633–1666.[51]

~

In 1755, Samuel Johnson defines the word bandy as: "(From *bander*, Fr [French].) A club turned round at bottom for striking at ball play."[52] Johnson believes that all other uses of the word stem from this: "TO BANDY [probably from *bandy*, the instrument with which they strike balls at play, which being crooked, is named from the term *bander un arc*, to string or bend a bow.]". He gives several examples of the verb: "To beat to and fro, or one from another … To exchange: to give and take reciprocally … To agitate: to toss about … To contend, as at some game, in which each strives to drive the ball his own way." Johnson provides literary examples for each of the verb's definitions. The earliest known use is in Shakespeare's *The Taming of the Shrew*, c1589–1592. At the end of the play, Katharine [Kate] says: "To bandy word for word and frown for frown: But now I see our lances are but straws." Her suitor Petruchio replies: "Why, there's a wench!—Come on, and kiss me, Kate."[53] Shakespeare peppers his plays with metaphorical references but not the game itself. The first known is in a 1578 English translation of a Spanish book that tells of the Spanish Conquistadors' encounters with the Aztecs:

---

49 O'Riordan, J.L.H., Bijvoet, O.L.M., *Rickets before the discovery of Vitamin D.* BoneKEy Reports, 2014, 3:478.

50 Bennet, P.W., *Reimagining the Creation: Popular Mythology, the Mi'kmaq, and the Origin of Canadian Hockey.* In: Ellison, J., Anderson, J. (eds.), *Hockey: Challenging Canada's Game – Au-delà du sport national.* University of Ottawa Press, 2018. p. 50.

51 Ibid, p. 51.

52 Johnson, J., *A Dictionary of the English Language.* W. Strahan, London, 1755. n.p.

53 Irving, H., *The Complete Works of William Shakespeare.* P.F. Collier and Son Company, New York, 1901. Act V, Sc 2, p. 343.

"Sometimes *Mutezuma* went to the Tennis Courte. Their ball is called *Villamaliztli*, and is made of the gumme which commeth from a trée called *Vlli*. This trée groweth in a hote Countrey. The gumme being kneded togither, and so made roūd, is as blacke as pitch, and somewhat heavie, and very harde for the hande, but yet good and light to rebound, and better than our windballes. They play not at chases, but at bādie [bandy], or at check, that is, if the ball touch the wall, it loseth."[54]

So bandy as a term for the stickball game is adopted no later than the 1570s, and the verb follows soon after. The next mention of the game is in 1610. William Strachey of the Jamestown settlement in Virginia watches men of the Lenape Nation play, "A kynd of exercise they have often amongst them much like that which boyes call bandy in English, and maye be an auncient game."[55]

In the winter of 1813/14, there is bandy on ice on the Fens—the fifteen hundred square miles of marshland that spans Leicestershire, Cambridgeshire, and Norfolk.[56] The swampy, peat-rich, low-lying wetlands has always been at the mercy of capricious sea levels, and there is little means of livelihood for locals, who subsist on reed cutting, fishing, and fowling. Following an unprecedented high tide in 1625, wealthy "adventurers" sense an opportunity to convert the Fens into arable farming and are granted the rights to drain it.[57] Ironically, they choose a Dutchman to engineer the project. The colossal venture is only partially successful, so too other attempts over the next two centuries.

A constant irritant is the impoverished locals who, fearing loss of their traditional livelihoods, are decidedly antagonistic. The interlopers describe them as an "almost barbarous, sort of lazy and beggarly people";[58] elsewhere as, "rude, uncivill, and envious to all others whom they call Upland-men [and] who stalking on high upon stilts, apply

54 Nicholas, T. (trans.)., *The Pleasant Historie of the Conquest of the VVeast India, now called new Spayne,* by Francisco López de Gómara, 1552. Henry Bynneman, London, 1578. p. 179.

55 Major, R.H., *The Historie of Travaile Into Virginia Britannia*. s.n., London, 1849. pp. 77–78.

56 Pre-drainage, the Fens extended to Huntingdonshire, Northamptonshire, Suffolk, Sussex, Essex, and Kent.

57 Wheeler, W.H., *A History of the Fens of South Lincolnshire*. J.M. Newcomb, Boston, England, 1897. p. 31.

58 Cole, C.N. (ed.)., *The History of Imbanking and Drayning of Divers Fenns and Marshes*, by William Dugdale. W.W. Bowyer & J. Nichols, 1772. p. 171.

their minds to grasing, fishing and fowling."[59] Men assemble to destroy drainage works under the guise of playing camping or football matches. An ironic consequence of the projects is that the regular sharp frosts cause the residual vast expanse to freeze over. It "affords the best skating ground in this country, and has long been celebrated for the matches which have taken place here."[60,61] It becomes the national home of speed skating and bandy on ice.

Skating contests have probably been around for millennia. In 1555, the Archbishop of Uppsala in Sweden publishes an exhaustive account of his travels through Scandinavia. In the far north, he sees men with "a plain polished Iron, or plain Deers or Sheeps bones; namely the shank-bones that are naturally slippery … a foot in length, fastened to the bottome of their feet. In which kind also there are found men every where striving for pleasure and price: the Goal they set is over the congealed Lakes, as smooth as Glasse, for eight or twelve *Italian* miles from both ends, or somewhat lesse. The prize is Silver Spoons, Brasse Vessels, Swords, New Garments and young Horses" The deer shanks have an edge over the iron skates, for they can be "be•meared with Hog's-grease, because so they cannot be hindered or stopt by the co•d drops of water, that in the most vehement cold weather will rise up as it were through the pores of the Ice."[62]

A long-held belief is that the first recorded speed skating contest was at Wisbech, Cambridgeshire, on 20 and 21 January 1763, between the celebrated local "Hare of Thorney" and a Danish sailor.[63] The Dane won both two-mile races before a crowd of two thousand spectators, for a wager of 70 gns.[64] Two others contested a long-distance race, either as a curtain-raiser or an after-match; John Lamb navigated the fifteen-mile course in forty-six minutes.[65] However, on January 6, 1763,

59 Darby, H.C., *The Draining of the Fens*. Cambridge University Press, 1956. p. 23.

60 Wheeler, W.H., *A History of the Fens of South Lincolnshire*. J.M. Newcomb, Boston, England, 1897. p. 311.

61 In 1890, the River Whitham froze over for six weeks, enabling the seven-mile journey from Lincoln to Boston navigable by skating. Ibid, Appendix V. p. 11.

62 Olaus, M., *A Compendious History of the Goths, Svvedes, & Vandals, and other northern nations*. J. Streater, London, 1658. p. 29.

63 *Museum of Cambridge*. https://www.museumofcambridge.org.uk/2021/09/the-history-of-fen-skating/. Accessed 4 January 2024.

64 Twenty-three and a half years' wages for a skilled tradesman.

65 *Capturing Cambridge*. https://capturingcambridge.org/wp-content/uploads/2020/07/Fenland-Skating.pdf. Accessed 4 January 2024.

"a sweepstakes skaiting match" was held along the River Isis in Oxfordshire, a two-mile contest from Iffley to Sanford. An apprentice to the cook at Corpus Christi College, "won the two first heats very hollow."[66]

The bitterly cold January is notable for skating. On 23 January, "a gentleman of Lincoln's-Inn undertook a Wager, to pick up one Hundred Stones upon the Serpentine River in Hyde-Park, which were placed in a direct Line one yard distant from each other."[67] Allowed ninety minutes, he completes the trial in fifty-two. Three years earlier, Joseph Merlin, the man who had invented roller skates, in 1743, shows them off at a masquerade ball, skating among the guests while playing a violin: "not having provided the means of retarding his velocity or commanding its direction, he impelled himself into a mirror of more than 500*l* value, dashed it to atoms, broke his instrument to pieces, and wounded himself severely."[68,69]

Ice skaters are apt to drown. "An agreeable singer and a good Mimick … unhappily drowned" in St James Park, in January 1740;[70] others survive a similar event in 1742. Two years later, a man drowns in the moat of the Bishop of London's palace. More deaths across the subsequent decades, one following a fractured skull. Some escape with broken arms or legs, most with hypothermia. The Duke of Cumberland, third son of George II, skates with titled insouciance in St James Park throughout the 1740s. The future James II is equally nonchalant. On 15 December 1662, Samuel Pepys records: "To the Duke and followed him into the park where, though the ice was broken and dangerous, yet he would go slide on his scates, which I did not like, but he slides very well."[71] A fortnight earlier Pepys wrote: "and then over the parke (where I first in my life, it being a great frost, did see people sliding with their skeates, which is a very pretty art)."[72] Things move swiftly on ice; by 1772, the first book on figure skating is published.[73]

---

66 *The Fortnight's Register*. January 1–15, 1763. Number 12. p. 95.

67 *The Fortnight's Register*. January 16–29, 1763. Number 11. p. 102.

68 Heathcote J.M., Tebbutt, C.G., *The Badminton Library of Sports and Pastimes: Skating*. Longmans, Green. and Co., London, 1892. p. 11.

69 Twenty-two years' wages for a skilled tradesman.

70 *Ipswich Journal*. 12 January 1740. p. 2.

71 Wheatley, H.B. (ed.)., *The Diary of Samuel Pepys M.A. F.R.S.* George Bell & Sons, London, 1893. n.p.

72 Ibid, n.p.

73 Jones, R., *A Treatise on Skaiting; founded on certain Principles deduced from many Years Experience*. Printed for the Author, London, 1772.

When bandy on ice began on the Fens is uncertain. The first recorded games are in the winter of 1813/14, while the first reported is c1827, when the famous Bury Fen players of Bluntisham-cum-Earith defeat Willingham for a leg of mutton.[74] The bandy is usually followed by a "randy" where "good healths were drunk, defeat and hard luck forgotten, and fresh matches arranged."[75] Sides are captained, and goalkeepers deployed. A ball (the "cat" or "kit") is usually used, sometimes a "bung of cork or wood did service, sometimes a cricket ball, more recently an indiarubber ball was used."[76] The lower branches of pollard willow-trees grow curved, the perfect shape for bandies, whose handles are often bound to prevent hands slipping.[77,78]

The earliest mention of field hockey is in Richard Johnson's 1773 *Juvenile Sports and Pastimes*, which contains *New Improvements on the Game of Hockey*.[79,80] A woodcut accompanies the text. Five boys are playing with curved hockey sticks. At either end is a small arch, "a very long piece of briar, each end being stuck in the ground." The game "was undoubtedly first taken from the Irish." True enough if you are going back centuries. The stick must be easy to grasp, the thicker the "crooked" end the better. Strangely, the ball is referred to both as a hockey and a kockey, four times apiece. There is no other record of the use of kockey, suggesting typos.[81] Hockey here refers to both the game and the bung. It "must be made of the finest cork bung you can find", which is shaved round. The clustered players fight for the "kockey" thrown up in the centre. One goal decides a game, which can last two to three hours. "The use of the crook part is to disengage the Hockey from your antagonists … by a sudden jerk." Unlike modern field hockey, opponents will try to prevent a disengagement by "beating their hockey sticks against his."

---

74 Heathcote J.M., Tebbutt, C.G. *The Badminton Library of Sports and Pastimes: Skating.* Longmans, Green. and Co, London, 1892. p. 431.

75 Ibid, p. 432.

76 Ibid, p. 433.

77 Ibid, p. 433.

78 Goodman, N., Goodman, A. *Handbook of Fen-Skating.* Sampson, Low, Marston, Searle, and Rivington, London, 1882. p. 30.

79 Master Michel Angelo. *Juvenile Sports and Pastimes.* T. Carnan, London, 1773. pp. 92–96.

80 Both *Juvenile Sports and Pastimes* and *Juvenile Trials for Robbing Orchards, Telling Fibs, and Other Misdemeanours* are advertised in *The Little Female Orators.* T. Carnan, London, 1778. p. 108.

81 The chapter contains no misspellings.

Knocking another down, or tripping up their heels is foul play, and handling the ball is illegal.

One theory of the sport's name is that balls were originally made from the cork stoppers (bungs) used to seal casks of ale. Hock, ale, and porter were all popular beers in the eighteenth century, so the assumption is that it comes from bungs specifically used to stop casks of hock. No more than that is known. But there is more. The derivation of "hock" itself is believed to derive from Hocktide, the second Monday and Tuesday after Easter. Both are festival days, especially Tuesday, which is called Hock Day. This appears not to have always been the case. In 1467, the Monday is referred to as Hokday and Tuesday as Hoktewesday.[82] The holiday has been around a while. An edict in Normandy c1175 decrees that, "All cowherds … from Hocedei to August must drink milk on Sunday mornings."[83] On "Ochedai" 1242, Henry III crosses the English Channel to wage war on France, and in 1252 the village of Esseburne is "burned miserably" on "Hokke-Day".[84] Now called Ashbourne, the Derbyshire village's Shrovetide folk football game is the most famous in England. Finally, a 1409 decree prohibits the Hocktide tradition of "hokkyng": couples married in the preceding year are "kidnapped", and held prisoner until they provide money to buy footballs.[85] The term Hocktide likely stems from the Middle High German *hoghgezit* meaning "festival" or "highest joy", just as *hochzeit* means wedding in High German (literally "high time").[86]

At harvest time, the last-cut grain is brought back in the Hock Cart, otherwise known as a *Horkey* Cart, signifying that the wain is piled high. Villagers cheer and sing as the cart approaches, bedecked with ribbons and the horses fully trapped.[87] In East Anglia, the horse is "decorated with flags, streamers, and garlands, and attended by a

82 Redstone, V.B., *Social Condition of England during the Wars of The Roses*. Transactions of the Royal Historical Society, 1902, Vol. 16, p. 195.

83 Kuhn, S.M., (ed.), *Middle English Dictionary*. The University of Michigan Press. Part H.4. p. 831.

84 Bickerdyke, J., *The Curiosities of Ale & Beer*. Swan Sonnenschein & Co., London, 1889. p. 241.

85 '*Memorials: 1409*,' in *Memorials of London and London Life in the 13th, 14th and 15th Centuries*, ed. H T Riley (London: Longmans, Green, 1868), 570–576. *British History Online*, accessed February 23, 2024, http://www.british-history.ac.uk/no-series/memorials-london-life/pp570-576.

86 Brand, J., *Observations on Popular Antiquities*. 1777. Chatto & Windus, London, 1900. p. 101.

87 Bickerdyke, J., *The Curiosities of Ale & Beer*. Swan Sonnenschein & Co., London, 1889. pp. 254–255.

troop of masquers in grotesque disguises."[88] "The harvest swains and wenches bound, For joy to see the Hock-cart crowned," goes a 1648 poem.[89] The day ends with a harvest feast, with beer donated by the local squire. In some counties, the beer is presented in gigantic bottles, capable of holding dozens of pints. In Suffolk, the harvest-home feast is called the *Horkey*. Beer is brewed especially for the occasion. A local poem *The Horkey: A Provincial Ballad* c1790 reveals the name given to the beer:

> And Farmer Cheerum went, good man,
> And broach'd the *Horkey beer*,
> And *sich a mort* of folks began,
> To eat up our good cheer.[90]

That *horkey* is local dialect is confirmed in the opening stanza:

> What gossips prattled in the sun,
> Who talk'd him fairly down,
> Up, Memory! tell; 'tis Suffolk fun,
> And lingo of their own.

Each regional word is italicised and *Horkey beer* is no different. The Harvest beer to celebrate the Hock Cart in Suffolk is called *horkey*. In Hexton, Hertfordshire, in 1728, the hockey cart brings in the last corn harvested, and hockey cake is distributed to revellers.[91] Is the stick and ball game named in honour of harvest time? Are the shaved cork bungs used in the game named after the beer? *Horkey* bungs. Hockey bungs. Is *horkey* beer the original hock beer? At the time, hock was a well-known white wine from Hockheim, in Germany. The 1482 accounts of St Michael's Church in Bishop's Stortford, Hertfordshire, record an "Item payed in exsepences at diverse tymyse w^{t} beryng [brewing] of

---

88 Wright, J., *The English Dialect Dictionary*. 6 Vols. Henry Frowde, London, 1902. Vol. 3. p. 190.

89 *The Hock-Cart*. In: Pollard, A (ed.), *The Hesperides & Noble Numbers*, by Robert Herrick. Lawrence & Bullen, Ltd., London, 1898. p. 125.

90 *Robert Bloomfield: The Works*. Routledge, Warne, and Routledge, London, 1864. p. 168.

91 Salmon, N., *A New Survey of England*. J. Roberts, Warwick-Lane, London, 1728. Parts 1–5. p. 415.

ye hokkyng ale."[92] Two years later, transactions are recorded for the purchase of bushels of malt and wheat, and payment for the brewing of hock ale.[93] The 1486–87 accounts include nine bushels of "malte to the hoke-ale", four bushels of "whete to the hoke-ale", payment "for brewing of the hokyng ale", and "Profit from the "Hokkyng Ale, 15s."[94,95] The money is incoming, so it is likely to be brewed on behalf of the church and sold at church ales—fundraising fêtes with beer. Similarly, the sixteenth century accounts of the parish of Wing in Buckinghamshire record regular receipts for "May ale". In 1557, alongside May ale, is an entry for money "Receavyd of the hock ale."[96] There is a similar entry in 1582.

Hock ale is intrinsic to Hocktide. Almost certainly, the name used by breweries follows on. Hocktide ale is unlikely to differ from standard ale, but future hock ale as sold in breweries will. When the name is first applied to a specific type of ale is unknown. In 1677, old Hock still refers to wine, as it does in 1715.[97,98] In June 1685, St Michael's accounts record: "pd to Mr Meade for a bottle of Hock when Mr. Ward pretcht", and in 1699, the character of a drunken "sot" requests a quart of hock.[99,100] Two pints is unlikely to be wine. Hard proof only arrives in the eighteenth century. In 1742, Parson's Old Hock beer is sold at the Three Tuns in Fishamble Street, Dublin.[101] The same year, Handel's *Messiah* has its world premiere at the Great Music Hall on Fishamble Street. The hock is brewed at Parson's Red Lion Brewery, in East Smithfield, London.

Two years later, the *Newcastle Courant* reports that, "the French King's illness was occasion'd by his Drinking too freely of his favourite Liquor,

---

92 Glasscock, J.L., *The Records of St Michael's Parish Church, Bishop's Stortford.* Elliot Stock, London, 1882. p. 25.

93 Ibid, pp. 25–26.

94 Blair, L., *English church ales as seen in English churchwardens' accounts.* Edward Brothers, Inc., Ann Arbor, Michigan, 1940. p. 38.

95 A month's wages for a skilled tradesman.

96 *Archaeologia.* Society of Antiquaries of London, 1855, Vol. 36, p. 221.

97 D'Urfey, T., *Madam Fickle.* James Magnes and Rich. Bentley, London, 1677. p. 4.

98 Johnson, C., *The Country Lasses.* J. Tonson, London, 1715.

99 Glasscock, J.L., *The Records of St Michael's Parish Church, Bishop's Stortford.* Elliot Stock, London, 1882. p. 81.

100 Jacob, G., *The Country Gentleman's Vade Mecum.* John Harris, London, 1699. p. 27.

101 *Dublin News Letter.* 4 January 1742. p. 3.

Alderman Parson's Old Hock."[102] The terms overlap. In 1774, James Boswell writes: "I was in prodigious spirits, and drank beer copiously to allay the thirst of last night's drinking. We had a deal of merriment; and I drank old hock, which cooled my fever and really sobered me."[103] In the same book, he uses "old Hock" to refer to wine. By 1788, it merits an entry in a dictionary of colloquialisms: "Hockey: Drunk with strong stale beer, called old hock."[104] A Cumberland definition of hock is: "old hock: sour ale sold at a cheap rate for harvesters … It was esteemed superior for slockenin [quenching] than the higher priced article."[105]

The 1784 history of Hawsted in Suffolk defines hockey as, "the merrymaking of the reapers after harvest."[106] So, the feasting *is* called *horkey* and hockey. It follows that the beer may also be called hockey beer. Hockey bungs. Hockey. West Sussex's stick and ball game is *hawkey*, presumably after its local harvest festival. A 1902 dictionary of dialect presents regional variations on a theme: *horkey* in East Anglia, *hawkie* in Cumberland and Suffolk, *horky* in Hertfordshire, and *hooky* in Ireland. In Hertfordshire it is also called hockey, and there is a hockey load and a hockey cake. The first entry for hockey in the 1902 dictionary reads, "A harvest-home or supper; the last load in harvest."[107] Examples of the use of hockey include: "Ess': the feast is also called hockey in Essex, a county fringing London." London has no harvest feast, but it calls bandy hockey too. So does Worcestershire. Hock-tide was also known as *Hockney*-day in Berkshire and Gloucestershire.

An 1825 edition of a Scottish dictionary describes shinty as, "an inferior species of golf, generally played at by young people … in London this game is called hackie, Add; or perhaps more properly Hockey."[108] *Hackie* does not appear in the 1808 or 1818 editions. Of course, to hack is to kick wildly or roughly, but kicking of the ball or bung is not allowed in hockey. It does not necessarily mean that hockey

102 *Newcastle Courant*. 18 August 1744. p. 2.

103 Wimsatt Jr., W.K., Pottle, F.A. (eds.)., *Boswell, For the Defence 1769–1774*. McGraw-Hill Book Company Inc., New York, 1959. p. 232.

104 Grose, F., *A Classical Dictionary of the Vulgar Tongue*. S. Hooper, London, 1788. n.p.

105 Wright, J., *The English Dialect Dictionary*. 6 Vols. Henry Frowde, London, 1902. Vol. 3. p. 189.

106 Cullum, J., *The History and Antiquities of Hawsted*. J. Nichols, London, 1784. p. 171.

107 Wright, J., *The English Dialect Dictionary*. 6 Vols. Henry Frowde, London, 1902. Vol. 3. p. 190.

108 Jamieson, J., *An Etymological Dictionary of the Scottish Language*. W. & C. Tait, Edinburgh. 1825. n. p.

was adopted as the name for bandy c1825; an 1828 "improved" version of Samuel Johnson's dictionary only mentions hockey ("or hawkey") in relation to harvesttime.[109] When the game is played at Eton in 1832, it is called hockey. So, is a harvest stick and ball game widely played, or is it a tradition limited to East Anglia, Sussex, and Essex? Is it a descendant of a stickball version of camping? Either way, it appears to be the root of the sport's name.

~

John Rhea Smith's Princeton journal also mentions battledore, shuttle [cock], hoop, quoits, skating, snowball fights, fencing, long jump, prison baste (base), and sleigh races along Nassau Street.[110] More importantly, on 22 March 1786: "A fine day, play baste ball in the campus but am beaten for I miss both catching and striking the Ball."[111] It is the earliest known mention of baseball in *American* history. An English children's poem entitled *Base-Ball* is invariably cited as the world's first reference:

> The *Ball* once struck off,
> Away flies the *Boy,*
> To the next destin'd Post.
> And then Home with Joy.[112]

An accompanying woodcut shows three boys, each at a post. One appears to be throwing a ball at the second boy, who is wearing the same glove the players in the rhymes about stoolball and fives are wearing. There is a marginal possibility it is a bat, not a glove. The third boy has his hand firmly on his post. There are also illustrated poems for fives, tip cat, trapball, stoolball, and cricket. But is it the earliest mention of baseball? The poem is found in *A Pretty Little Pocket-Book*, first published in 1744. This is the year cited as the earliest mention of baseball. The earliest extant copy is the tenth edition, from 1760. The title page details the contents. Below that it says, "Tenth edition", and beneath that: "To which is added a little song-

---

109 Johnson, S., *Johnson's English Dictionary improved by Todd and abridged by Chalmers*. Charles Ewer and T. Harrington Carter, Boston, Massachusetts. 1826. p. 469.

110 Woodward, R.L. *Journal at Nassau: The Diary of John Rhea Smith. The Princeton University Library Chronicle*. The Princeton University Library, 1985, 46:3, pp. 269–291 & 47:1, pp. 48–70.

111 Ibid, 46:3 p. 286.

112 Newbery, J., *A Little Pretty Pocket-Book*. s.n., London, 1760. p. 41.

book." It is within this new section that "Base-ball" is to be found. An advert for a 1757 edition also mentions the songbook; adverts for the first edition do not.[113,114] While this dates the book's baseball reference to 1757, it is possible that baseball is included in editions from 1745 to 1756.[115] What can be said for certain, is that John Newbery's book is recognised as the first dedicated to the pleasure of children and not solely for their edification. Newbery is regarded as the Father of Children's Literature and the prestigious Newbery Medal is named in his honour.

Lady Mary Hervey is a keen letter writer. Possessed of a shrewd mind, a beauty in her day, she is praised by Pope and Voltaire. Pope is witheringly caustic about her husband, as much thwarted love as gallant reaction to the lord's bisexual liaisons. Lady Hervey maintains correspondence with the Rev Edmund Morris from 1742 to 1768. In a letter dated 14 November 1748, she mentions a visit to the family of Frederick, Prince of Wales: "the Prince's family is an example of innocent and cheerful amusements ... now, in winter, in a large room, they divert themselves at base-ball, a play all who are, or have been, schoolboys, are well acquainted with."[116] It is remarkable that this is the first known mention of baseball in the world, for the second, ten months later, has Frederick playing: "On Tuesday last his Royal Highness the Prince of Wales, and Lord Middlesex, played at Bass-Ball, at Walton, in Surry; and notwithstanding the Weather was extreme bad, they continued playing several Hours."[117]

In 1735, the two had played a cricket match for a thousand-pound wager, watched by thousands.[118,119] Eighteen months after the baseball match, Frederick is dead, thought at the time to have been a delayed consequence of a blow to the head from a cricket ball. One paper

113 *Manchester Mercury*. 20 September 1757. p. 3.

114 Even then, there is confusion over when the first edition actually came out, "it might have been published a year or two before or even in 1745 or later." In: Roscoe, S., *John Newbery and His Successors, 1740–1814: A bibliography*. Five Owls Press Ltd., Wormley, Hertfordshire, 1973. p. 392.

115 The oldest known advert is in the *Daily Gazetteer*, on 19 May 1744. It is headed, "This Day Is Published." Adverts from later in the year are similarly headed, e.g., in the *General Advertiser*, on 1 September 1744; and even in 1745: *Aris's Birmingham Gazette* 10 June 1745 (the second edition was advertised in 1747).

116 *Letters of Mary Lepel, Lady Hervey*. John Murray, London, 1821. p. 139.

117 *Whitehall Evening Post*. 19 September 1749. p. 3.

118 *Newcastle Courant*. 2 August 1735. p. 2.

119 Forty-five years' wages for a skilled tradesman.

writes of the injury: "'tis thought was the Occasion of his Death, having a Bag, near six Inches long, down his Side, full of Corruption."[120] Other cricket tragedies are reported. In 1730, a soldier is struck by a ball from a game on Tower-Hill. He draws his sword and cuts a player across the face. When pursued, he stabs another in the shoulder. Overpowered, he ends up in the Tower on a court martial.[121] London passers-by are in peril. In 1731, Mr Legat, "a considerable dealer in Brandy and Rum", passing by Moorfields, is hit on the nose by a ball "which set him a Bleeding more or less till the Day of his Death."[122] Similarly, in 1770, "an eminent tailor from Fetter Lane" is killed by a cricket ball on Richmond Green, so too a Shoe Lane cabinet maker, in Hoxton the following year.[123]

In 1735, a mounted spectator lies moribund after he falls, "and two horses trampled over him."[124] The following year, a two-a-side single-wicket match pits "the two famous Richmond Men, who have beat all they have play'd" against George Oldner and Mr Wakeland. One of the Richmond men tries to parry a ball, and slices it into his face. He "broke his Nose, hurt his Eye, and brusi'd his Face in a most sad manner, and lost a great Quantity of Blood." Some "*Human Brutes*" who bet on the opposition insist he carry on or lose the match. After his nose is reset and his face bandaged, "his Nose fell a-bleeding a fresh, in such a violent manner, that he was forced to throw up his bat."[125] A rematch is begrudgingly granted. A single-wicket match on Kennington Common, in 1737, bears similarities. It is the only single-wicket game known that year, and only the eighteenth on record. The Mitcham man is "beaten by a considerable Number of Notches, occasion'd by his receiving in his first Hands so smart a Blow by the Ball that he was knock'd down, and lay stupid for a considerable Time."[126]

---

120 Block, D., *Pastime Lost. The Humble, Original, and Now Completely Forgotten Game of English Baseball*. University of Nebraska Press, Lincoln, 2019. p. 26.

121 *Kentish Weekly Post*. 17 June 1730. p. 2.

122 *Stamford Mercury*. 15 July 1731. p. 19.

123 Harris, B., *Gambling in Britain in the Long Eighteenth Century*. Cambridge University Press, 2022. pp. 84–85.

124 *Derby Mercury*. 7 August 1735. p. 2.

125 *Kentish Weekly Post*. 30 June 1736. pp. 2–3.

126 *Old Whig*. 18 August 1737. p. 3.

There is crowd disturbance during the Kent versus Surrey and London game at Kennington Common in 1737. A woman is thrown and breaks her leg.[127] A royal whip-round collects 20 gns for medical bills.[128] The man who "had his Nose beat flat to his Face by a blow from the Ball" is in need of a family Bible. Worse follows. During the melee, mechanic John Smith is hit on the head with a stone. He makes it home but dies from his injury.[129] Days earlier, two batsmen in Petersfield, Sussex, collide so violently they knock each other over. "They both got up again, but one of them drop't down dead as he was running to his Wicket."[130] Remarkably, John Small, the greatest batsman of the eighteenth century, is born two months before, only five miles away.

Early in the 1755 novel *The Card*, the narrator says, "the Younger part of the Family, perceiving Papa not inclined to *enlarge* upon the Matter, retired to an interrupted Party at *Base-Ball* (an *infant* Game, which as it advances in its Teens, improves into *Fives*, and in its State of Manhood, is called *Tennis*)."[131] A diary entry that year by William Bray of Surrey reads: "After Dinner Went to Miss Seale's to play at Base Ball, with her, the 3 Miss Whiteheads, Miss Billinghurst, Miss Molly Flutter, Mr. Chandler, Mr. Ford, H. Parsons & Jolly. Drank tea and stayed till 8."[132] A mixed gender game, played by young adults. The 1755 reference relegates *The Little Pretty Pocket-Book* into fourth place. The first American mention—John Rhea Smith's 1786 *baste ball*—is the world's seventh, following two 1768 references. The first, is an entry in an English dictionary: "Baseball: A rural game in which the person striking the ball must run to his *base* or goal." Another world first: baseball is unhyphenated.[133] The second is provided by English author Cassandra Cooke in her 1779 novel *Battleridge*. Set at the end of Cromwell's reign, a man reminisces on his clerkship twenty years before: "'Ah!' says he, 'no more cricket, no more base-ball, they are sending me to Geneva.'"[134,135]

127 *Kentish Weekly Post*. 18 June 1737. p. 1.

128 Seven months' wages for a skilled tradesman.

129 Waghorn, H.T., *Cricket Scores, Notes &c. from 1730–1733*. William Blackwood and Sons, London and Edinburgh, 1899. p. 19.

130 *Kentish Weekly Post*. 15 June 1737. p. 1.

131 Kidgell, J., *The Card*. 2 Vols. J. Newbery, London, 1755. Vol. 1. p. 9.

132 Block, D., *The Story of William Bray's Diary*. Base Ball, 2007, 1:2, p. 8.

133 *A General Dictionary of the English Language*. J. and R. Fuller, London, 1768. n.p.

134 Cooke, C., *Battleridge*. 2 Vols. G. Cawthorn, British Library, London, 1799. Vol. 1. p. 2.

135 Baseball being played c1638 is anachronistic.

The 1768 dictionary also defines *base*: "A rural play, called also Baseball." An abridged quote from Shakespeare's c1610 play *Cymbeline* follows. The full quote reads: "He, with two stripling-lads more like to run, The country base than to commit such slaughter."[136] The implication that base and baseball are the same sport is erroneous. In a book on *Cymbeline*, Samuel Johnson describes, "The country-base ... A rustic game called *prison-bars*, vulgarly *prison-base*." Why base is base goes unsaid.[137] The second American reference to baseball is a 1791 prohibition of "any game of wicket, cricket, baseball, batball, football, cats, fives or any other game played with ball" within eighty yards of the new meeting house in Pittsfield, Massachusetts.[138] The last two references of the eighteenth century appear in 1796. Both are in German. It is the year Catherine the Great, the Prussian-born Empress of Russia, dies, as does John Snape in the Derby Shrove Tuesday game. It is the year Adams beats Jefferson to replace Washington, and the Irish poet Colm de Bhailís is born, departing in 1906 aged 109, his final years made comfortable by the intercession of New York-born Éamon de Valera, an Irish Volunteer in the Easter Rising of 1916, misguided President of the Republic, his country divided on his watch, and another batter of time, dying in 1975, aged 92.

The first German reference is in a literary newspaper, dated Saturday 10 September 1796.[139] A list of ball games includes: *deutsche Ballspiel*, *Geyerspiel*, *Schnurball*, *Fangball, Federball*, and *der englishe Baseball und Cricket*. The second is astounding. In a German instructional book of sport, one section is entitled *Ball mit Freystäten (oder das englische Base-ball)—Balls with Sanctuaries [bases] (or English base-ball)*. A seven-page description follows.[140] It is succeeded by a short description of *deutsch-englische Ballspiel* and, in turn, by *Thorball, or English Cricket*. It is the first baseball reference to mention a bat. The author, J. C. F. Gutsmuths writes:

---

136 *A General Dictionary of the English Language*. J. and R. Fuller, London, 1768. n.p.

137 Johnson, S., Stevens, G., *Annotations and the Various Commentators Upon Cymbeline*. n.p., London, 1687. pp. 70–71.

138 Thorn, J., *1791.1 The Pittsfield 'Baseball' Bylaw: What it Means*. Base Ball, 2011, 5:1, p. 46.

139 *Allgemeine Literatur-Zeitung vom Jahre 1796*. 3:122. p. 1038.

140 GutsMuths, J.C.F., *Spiele zur Uebung und Erholung des Körpers und Geistes fur die jugend ihre erzieher und alle freunde unschuldiger jugendfreunden*: Games to Exercise and Relax the Body and Mind for the Youth, Their Educators and all Friends of the Innocent Joys of One's Youth. Bookshop of the Educational Institution, Schnepfenthal, Germany, 1796. pp. 78–84.

"... it is mostly equivalent to the German ball game ... One plays the game with two teams, of which one is serving the ball, the other batting (as with ours) ... the bat is lighter, a little under two feet in length, four inches wide at its widest point, and about one inch thick ... For this reason, one can only make short, light hits. The pitcher stands five to six steps from the batter and lobs the ball to him in an arc. The line of the curve ... constitutes the home plate. From here the ball is hit, as in the German ball game. Instead of a limited fielding area, one finds on the field as many bases, marked with handkerchief-covered stakes, as there are members of each team ... the home plate is counted as a base as well. They ... are arranged ten to fifteen feet apart in a variable pattern.

"The batter has three attempts to hit the ball while at the home plate. Even if he touches the ball so lightly that one can hear only a slight crackling, or if he pushes the ball through even light contact out of the home plate area, of if he has struck three times without hitting the ball, then he must begin to run ... through all of the bases until he comes back to the home plate ... The at-bat can be lost by the batting team in three ways: by having the ball caught, by 'burning', or by having a runner touched by the ball."

Gutsmuths details the three outs. If the ball is caught, the catcher must shout "In! In!" and his team races to the home plate. As the catcher runs, he must throw the ball backwards. A player is burned when he forgets to touch the base he arrives at. The fielding player closest to the base receives the ball, shouts "In! In!", and throws the ball to the base, while shouting "Burned!" A complex alternate burn is also provided. The third out is when the ball touches the runner in any way outside the home plate or base. If two players end up on the same base, a fielder may throw the ball at either of them. Alternatively, if the ball is returned to the home plate and the batter is closer to the base he is leaving from than the one he is running to, he can be hit or touched, and the "at-bat" is lost. The new batting team must get to the home plate before the outgoing batters can touch any of them with the ball, otherwise they are out again.[141] David Block, who discovered Gutsmuths's work, and championed it as the first account of baseball in history, reattributed it as a description of

141 Block, D., *Baseball Before We Knew It: A Search for the Roots of the Game*. University of Nebraska Press, Lincoln, Nebraska, 2005. Pp. 275–278.

rounders.[142] It makes sense; there is no evidence that English baseball is played with a bat. The problem is, the first reference to rounders is not for another thirty-five years.[143] Block suggests that the several references to "bat and ball" in the interim, refer to the as yet unnamed game.

Whether it is rounders or baseball, it says much about the evolution of games that there are as many differences as similarities with its modern counterpart. A suitable comparison is the set of rules developed by the fledgling FA in 1863, and the game played today. Baseball, then, is an English children's game, played by young adults, perhaps in irony, or with the rosy nostalgia of remembered childhood, much as youths return to swings. Baseball is in its infancy, reared in a pastoral nursery, a starry-eyed game of innocence. Will it always be so?

~

Football is on the brink of the nineteenth century. He plucks a daisy, absentmindedly pulls at its petals. Russet leaves escape the clump of birch trees. Wither or thrive. How to up his popularity? He needs an angle. A revamp. Distance himself further from folk football, for one; no longer his fun-loving, drunken alter-ego, more the embarrassing, purple-nosed uncle that always turns up on festival days. Football props himself on his elbows. He needs to make tough decisions, to be surgical. And ruthless. Remove the violence that has been a staple for centuries, the cornerstone that has thrilled generations? Surely not. And yet. He rolls onto his back and runs his hands through the tall grass. Too long, he thinks, envisioning a football gliding across a bowling green. That too. What else? Stickball games are experiencing a resurgence, riding on the coat-tails of cricket. What have they got that he needs? He peers into the slate grey sky. It comes to him slowly, trundling from the back of his mind. His head begins to swim. Why had he not listened? Artless impetuosity and stubbornness … and callow desires. Figures follow thought. Mulcaster in 1581, Willughby in 1672. Rules! He needs rules. Football feels a sharp stab of disappointment. He inhales sharply, draws his hands into fists. Centuries wasted.

---

142 Block, D., *1796.1 German Book Describes Das englische Base-ball: But Was it Baseball or Rounders?* Base Ball, 2011, 5:1, pp. 50–54.

143 Clarke, W., *The Boy's Own Book*. Vizetelly, Branston and Co., London, Fourth edition, 1829. p. 20. It does not appear in the third edition of 1828.

He lays for a while, stony faced. Well, it ends here, he thinks at last. No cross, no crown. Perhaps he can acquire something they need. He sucks on his upper lip, adopts a thoughtful expression. A flurry of ideas criss-crosses his mind, driven by hope and conviction. It is there, he knows it, there but just out of reach. At last he sees it, hidden like a pearl in a hailstorm. The passion of the people. Gift them undying fascination, and they will gift their devotion. It would confer an almost insurmountable edge. Football smiles to himself. There is one more thing. Something they lack that he possesses, something they cannot seize, that escapes their hands like a fistful of fog. He had known from the start, known when he threw the stick away, a crutch he no longer needed, when he unclasped his hands and let the ball drop, investing his feet with the future. In his deepest being, he knew. Beauty. He has beauty. He points a wagging finger at the clouds. The loveliest under the sky. The smile breaks free, and he laughs aloud, giddy as he rolls over and over the sloping expanse.

Credits

Cover and interior design:	Anja Elsen
Layout:	DiTech Publishing Services, www.ditechpubs.com
Cover photo:	© AdobeStock
Author photo photographer:	Nicholas Hubicki
Managing editor:	Elizabeth Evans
Copy editor:	Sarah Tomblin, www.sarahtomblinediting.com